The Chinese Communists

Inside the capital the streets and thoroughfares
Were unobstructed and reached out far and wide.
The outer gates and inner portals of city wards
Were to be counted by the thousands.
On the public grounds there were nine markets;
Their merchandise was grouped and displayed
In sorts, each differing from the others,
Along the busy lanes sprawling in between.
The people there could hardly pause for a long look;
Carriages could not find space to turn around.
The meddling crowd filled the inner city, flooded the outskirts,
And flowed into the hundreds of suburban shops.
The red dust arose from all four directions,
Merging with the smoke and the clouds.

—PAN KU (A.D. 30–92)
The Western Capital

内則街衢洞達閭閻且千九市開場貨

別隧分人不得顧車不得旋闠城溢郭

旁流百廛紅塵四合雲烟相連

　　班固西都賦

THE CHINESE COMMUNISTS
Sketches and Autobiographies of the Old Guard

Book I: Red Dust
Book II: Autobiographical Profiles and Biographical Sketches

HELEN FOSTER SNOW
[NYM WALES]
Introduction to Book I by
Robert Carver North

Greenwood Publishing Company   *Westport, Connecticut*

Library of Congress Cataloging in Publication Data

Snow, Helen (Foster) 1907–
  The Chinese Communists.

  Book 1 is a reprint of the 1952 ed. entitled
Red dust.
  Bibliography: p.
  1. Communists, Chinese. 2. China--Biography.
I. Snow, Helen (Foster) 1907–   Red dust. 1972.
II. Title.
DS778.A1S499   335.43'4 [B]   77-104236
ISBN 0-8371-6321-8

Library of Congress Catalog Card Number: 77-104236
ISBN: 0-8371-6321-8

Book I first published in 1952 by Stanford University Press; first
reprint edition published in 1972 by Greenwood Publishing Company
Book II first published in 1972 by Greenwood Publishing Company

Greenwood Publishing Company
A Division of Greenwood Press, Inc.
51 Riverside Avenue, Westport, Connecticut 06880

Printed in the United States of America

For Soong Ching-ling

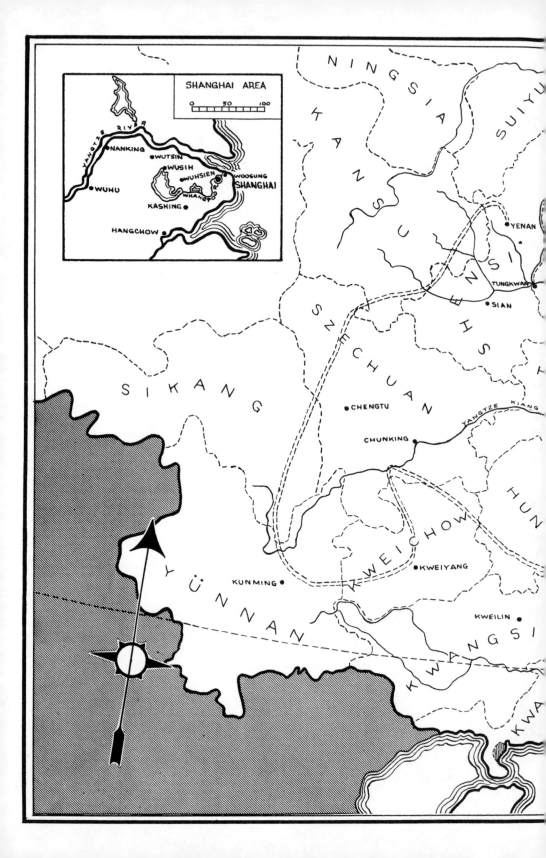

SHANGHAI AREA

0   50   100

YANGTZE RIVER

NANKING
WUTSIN
WUSIH
WUHSIEN
WHANGPOO R.
WOOSUNG
SHANGHAI
WUHU
KASHING

HANGCHOW

NINGSIA

SUIYU

KANSU

SHENSI

YENAN

TUNGKWAN

SIAN

SZECHUAN

SIKANG

CHENGTU

YANGTZE KIANG

CHUNKING

HUN

KWEICHOW

YÜNNAN

KUNMING

KWEIYANG

KWEILIN

KWANGSI

KWA

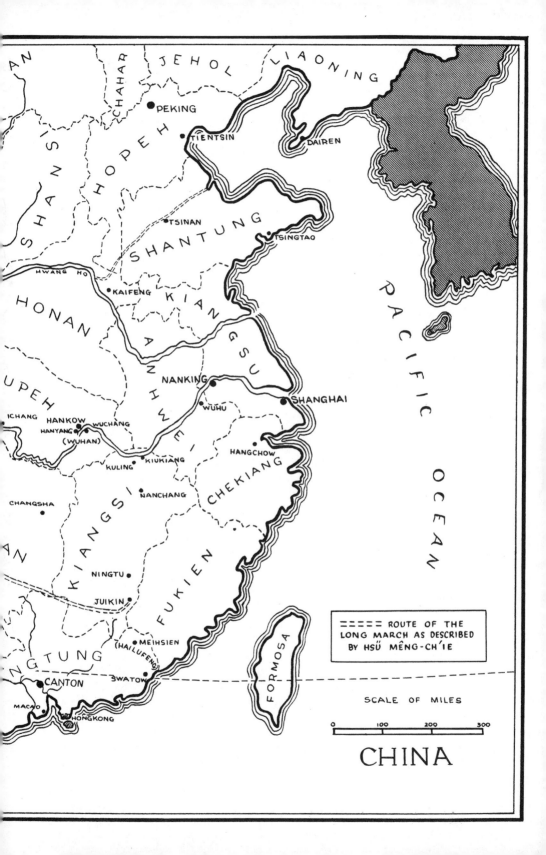

Contents

ix

List of Illustrations

Preface to the Enlarged Edition

In the 1930s my then husband, Edgar Snow, and I were vaguely of the opinion that we were having the grand experience of our generation, and we made the most of it.

In the spring of 1937 I left Edgar writing *Red Star Over China* in our haunted house at 13 K'uei Chia Ch'ang and took the train from Peking to Sian. I was on my way to Yenan to explore the Soviet Republic of China at any cost, as he had the year before, and to interview the individuals he had missed. The last Chinese emperor, Pu Yi, was still alive and this heir to the Manchu dynasty had ruled China from Peking as recently as 1910. Yet in 1949, twelve years after the Snow expeditions, Mao Tse-tung was enthroned in the Forbidden City of Emperors and reviewing his populace from T'ienanmen. We had a premonition then that this might be the course of Chinese history, though Japan was poised to strike at any moment. It did attack near Peking on July 7, 1937, and most of the coastal part of China was occupied by the end of 1938.

In Peking we were directly in the path of the Japanese advance, and no American wanted "to lose China" to Japan. I knew that China was mortally ill of senility and degeneration and so paralyzed with internal conflict that nothing could save this ancient nation from Japan but the "New Youth," as they had called themselves since 1917. But there was no armed leadership of this New Youth except the Red armies of Mao Tse-tung in the far interior, with a central government in Yenan. In Peking, the student aristocracy were being arrested for demanding armed resistance to the Japanese threat. Since the first Japanese attack in 1932, the students had been at war with Chiang Kai-shek. To oppose Chiang was dangerous. Those who did might be called Communists. They might even be arrested as such without evidence, though they were known to be non-Communists.

David Yui sponsored my trip to Yenan, and he was on the same train with me, as delegate to the Communist conference scheduled there in May, though we pretended not to know each other. He had been the secret brains of the student movement, from which the rest of the country took its instructions, and, when we were safely in Yenan, he told me proudly that he was the No. two Communist either in Peking or North China (I cannot now remember which). I had assumed he was a Communist but did not know his numerical importance.

On the train with me, along with David, was the son of President Wang of Tungpei University. Wang, Jr., planned to be my interpreter and to write news stories on his own.

After we arrived in Sian, I found a recently enacted military order forbidding any journalist to go to the Red areas, and especially anyone by the name of Snow—no name was more disliked in Sian or Nanking by that time. I escaped from the surveillance of four of my regular six bodyguards by climbing out of a window at night during martial law and arrived in Yün-yang in a car owned by General Yang Hu-ch'eng (who had been a partner in the kidnapping of Chiang Kai-shek in December 1936, five months earlier).

I had come to the cradle of Chinese civilization—the northwest of China. Yenan was a tiny city with a Sung dynasty gate and a capable premedieval crenellated wall around it, as well as a river to serve as a moat. Set like a jewel in a crown of hills bristling with ancient and modern battlements, Yenan had a character all its own. The citadel itself was part of the Yenan mystique. Through the pass, Mongol and Tartar horsemen had galloped to conquer the civilized Chinese. Yenan had not replaced Pao-an as the capital of the Chinese Soviet Republic until the end of 1936, after Edgar Snow had left in the fall, nor had the Second Front and Fourth Front Red Armies completed their separate Long March.

My Yenan experience was one of pure primitive communism, I suppose. No one received anything but food and barely enough clothing for protection in sun and cold, except that Mao Tse-tung had a cigarette allowance. It was not a money economy. It was a labor exchange economy.

There was almost no machinery in Yenan and no sound of a machine age, except the clanking of rifles slung over shoulders. There was no auto exhaust, no chemicals, none of the effluvia of affluence. The essence of the Yenan mystique was purity. The whole profile was one of purity, with no nonessentials.

The Yenan mystique was plain living and high thinking almost in the New England way, but spiced with danger. It was as happy as a Boy Scout camp. The only unhappy persons I knew were foreigners—the German, Li Teh; the American, Agnes Smedley; and the Korean, Kim San (Chiang Ming). For individuals who had survived so much danger, the fact of being alive was enough to make them happy, with a sense of special achievement.

The cultural shock of Yenan was not light. I was suddenly confronted by a

Helen Foster Snow with girl Communist leader, Yenan, 1937

top elite of China, nearly all in their twenties (some of whom like Lin Piao and Hsiao K'eh were already legendary figures), all of them remarkably attractive and charismatic. As Edgar Snow had done the year before, I sat hour after hour writing down information and life stories of these exceptional persons, thereby establishing a special relationship with them. This was the first time they had told their life stories to anyone, probably. Telling these to a foreigner required soul-searching and introspection, which probably none of them had taken time before to do.

Looking back on the Snow expeditions to Red China, one sees even more significance now than we did then. Edgar had been received as an ambassador from outer space. I was welcomed as "the wife of the American newspaperman." It was important when the non-Communist youth of America took the initiative in establishing a contact with the blockaded Communists of China.

Mao Tse-tung was the first to realize this significance. But had Edgar Snow not made a favorable impression on him, not one of them would have opened up to either one of us. Mao Tse-tung set the pattern; others followed it. It was not proper etiquette before 1936-1937 among the Communists to tell their autobiographies for publication—nor did it become etiquette later on. In 1971 Chou En-lai told journalist James Reston: "none of us kept a diary and none of us want to write our memoirs."

The underlying reason why the Communists told us life stories was that we had both faced real danger in running the blockade. If a non-Communist foreigner had the enterprise and courage to break through this news blockade, special cooperation was called for. Almost everyone of the top personnel paid me a call of welcome, except Lin Piao. I called on him, and I imagine he was aware of the difference. It was an advantage to me that I had taken so much trouble and risk getting out of Sian, defying a military order. This established me in my own right, to some extent.

From this distance, one can see what happened: Edgar was likeable enough and intelligent enough to establish a Snow-Mao entente in 1936, which lasted up to the 1970s. It was diplomatic under the circumstances all those years—an American line of communication to Mao Tse-tung. He made friends with Mao Tse-tung, and also with others. In 1971, Chou En-lai told Reston that he had no old friends in the United States except the journalist Edgar Snow.

I wrote down about thirty-four autobiographies during the summer of 1937, twenty-four of which were published in *Red Dust* (1952) and three in *Women in Modern China* (1967). Those of Miss Liu Chien-hsien, Chang Wen-ping, Lily Wu, and the schooldays of Ting Ling have been added to the enlarged edition. I was told brief accounts also by Ch'en Chia-kang, Ch'eng Fang-wu, and Tsai Ch'ien of Taiwan. I put the story told me by General Chu Teh in *Inside Red China*, with a few other brief accounts. I ended up with a personal history of a revolution told by its participants.

Getting these life stories was a job of difficult, painstaking research. It was done by asking dozens of questions. I had to draw the information out, and it was most exhausting. Few of the people had ever been interviewed before by anyone. They were not quite sure what I wanted, and it was not considered modest to volunteer any personal information of any kind. Hsiao K'e was so worried that he had not been modest enough that he made a special visit to apologize to me.

When I left Yenan for Sian, I carried "My Yenan Notebooks" around my waist in a kind of life-belt I had sewed up. I never trusted my bodyguard with them nor anyone else all during my trip, until I arrived in Shanghai from Peking. I was worried every minute about losing the notebooks. Most of all I was afraid I could not get them through Sian without their being confiscated. I was under extraterritoriality but I had gone against a military order. (Without extraterritoriality I would never have been able to get to Yenan in the first place, nor would anyone have helped me. Without the help of some friends in Sian I could not have made my trip. They were entirely unsympathetic to my trip but they helped out of human kindness and the freemasonry that existed between all foreigners in China in time of trouble.)

I have never been so frightened as at the Central army post of Tungkuan on my return to Peking. Without explanation I was dragged off the military troop train with my luggage by sinister-looking gendarmes, who had held up the train searching for me. I imagined the fascist Blue Shirts were taking revenge. I knew well how they hated both me and my husband for defying them in Sian. But I was not put under military arrest. I was being held on orders from Sian because my husband and a friend had arrived in search of me a few hours after I had left. Back to Sian I went with my Yenan notebooks under my coat. The train I had been on at Tungkuan was bombed by the Japanese, so providence was at work.

I next had to carry my notebooks through Tsingtao, a former German colony, where I parted with Edgar who next went to Shanghai to cover the war. Then I had to go through Tientsin under the Japanese, then to Peking under the Japanese—then out of Peking again and to Tientsin again and on to Shanghai by boat. At every check point, the Chinese were searched, but foreigners were not touched by the Japanese.

I had tried to keep my trip to Yenan secret—but it was known to certain people. I arrived in Shanghai on November 21, 1937. At the Medhurst Apartments, my husband was busy writing in one room and I in another. We had surplus energy only to smile triumphantly at each other from time to time like a couple of canaries who had swallowed a couple of cats.

I have long looked forward to a new edition of *Red Dust*. Much has happened in Mao's China since its publication a score of years ago, which makes its appearance in expanded form something of an important event. Some of the original material, which was left out, has now been added and appears in Book II. The result is a larger and more substantial work. It naturally pleases me to see it launched again in this enlarged edition, especially at this moment in history when China has become so crucially important in world affairs and when a knowledge of the past is essential to the understanding of this most complicated of Communist movements.

I want to express my real appreciation to Herbert C. Cohen, vice president of Greenwood Publishing Company, for making this enlarged edition possible, and to the editors, Beverly H. Miller and Jeannette Lindsay. Let me also thank the printers, as well as Mrs. Miller, for patient deciphering of an old manuscript.

Madison, Connecticut
September 1971

Preface to the
First Edition

The twenty-four autobiographies collected here were told to me through an interpreter during a stay of five months in the Communist regions of China in 1937. My husband, Edgar Snow, was at that time preparing his book *Red Star Over China* and I was a research student of social and political changes in the country. Both of us found it necessary to make the journey to Yenan, the then Communist capital, in Shensi Province, in order to secure historical material on the Chinese Communist movement.

The necessity for such a direct approach—for the materials of recent history the same as for contemporary happenings—is apparent when one considers that biographies and memoirs are still little known in Chinese literature, that letters rarely are available or even in existence for purposes of research, and that, journalism in China being almost in its infancy, newspapers do not provide reliable information, aside from their being heavily censored. For my studies, personal interviews offered the best materials. Thus there came about the autobiographies assembled in this book. The subjects were persuaded to give me verbal narratives of their life stories, and, taken together, these represent an inner history of the civil war in China, from the viewpoints of a variety of personalities on the Communist side.

Upon arriving at Yenan I discovered that the Communist officials had lost nearly all their records during the Long March, in 1935. I was, during those months, the only person there who was comprehensively gathering historical information. Hsü Mêng-ch'iu, the Communist historian whose own narrative is included here, was frustrated in his efforts to compile party history, owing to the preoccupation of other officials with affairs of the moment. My position as a foreigner and a guest gave me, then, an advantage over the official keeper of the records in that the individuals with whom I sought interviews felt bound by courtesy to spend some time with me—even the busiest ones.

Though traditional courtesy was a convenience without which these narratives could not have been secured, I encountered another side of it which presented an obstacle difficult to surmount. The idea of autobiography seemed entirely new to these persons, and it seemed to them a violation of etiquette to individualize their personal histories and exploits. I had to ask hundreds of questions to pry out the stories that the subjects could tell me, if they would. In time, they did yield to questioning, and their narratives were interpreted to me as the stories came forth.

From subject to interpreter to me, these personal histories have, I think, retained their import. No statements have been knowingly altered to diverge from the meaning intended from the speaker. I have endeavored to carry over the conversational manner of my subjects, at some sacrifice of felicity of style, and have departed from literal translation only to approximate the same expressions as they would have been put in English. Where clarification was needed, I have supplied footnotes.

Some of these autobiographies unfold like stories. Some few tend toward a terse summary of events. Not everyone, of course, is gifted with the ability to recount his life interestingly. But as I read over these autobiographies again, it seems to me that revelations of individual character as well as aspects of national viewpoint come through all of them rather pointedly. They do, for me, and I believe that they will for readers who approach them today.

To provide an interpretation of the historical and political setting in which the lives of these individual "Communists of the Chinese Revolution" have unfolded, Robert Carver North has written an Introduction under that title, going back to the founding of the Chinese Communist party in 1921 and bringing forward into the present the story of the party, its activities, and its best-known members. Some documentary notes for the Introduction seemed necessary, as well as a few explanatory notes for the autobiographies themselves; these will be found at the back of the book. Mr. North has also provided the lists of "Influential Chinese Communists" and suggested books for further reading, included in the Appendix [not included in reprint edition].

I should like, however, for the reader to think of the autobiographies as standing quite alone. Even the word *autobiographies* should be suspended, perhaps; for that word has formal implications, and these are spoken narratives as told to me, and are lacking in formal organization.

Yet, this material which I collected in Yenan has unique significance for any reader wanting to relate these lives to the broad aspects of Chinese history in the twentieth century. It is for him that the supplementary parts of the book have been prepared. They will serve him by providing career outlines of persons already well known and others whose names are unfamiliar but whose weight in Communist affairs in China is noteworthy, and by bringing attention to useful books which have appeared in recent years—from varied and often opposed points of view—on the course of events in the country. I am grateful to Mr. North for this contribution to the book and its potential readers.

I should like to express here my appreciation to the editorial staff of Stanford University Press for their helpfulness during my illness of the past year. It was Shau Wing Chan, professor of Chinese at Stanford University, who provided the translation of the old poem "Western Capital" which contained the phrase that suggested the title of the book. I wish also to thank Marie Rodell for her helpfulness with the manuscript.

Most of the photographs were taken by me. For others I am grateful to Lewis Gannett, who gave me several historical pictures he brought back from a trip to China in the 'twenties; to Edgar Snow; and to the Chinese who generously gave me their treasured personal mementoes of the Long March in photograph and sketch—to K'ang K'ê-ching, Wang Chêng, Liao Ch'êng-chih, and Lo Ping-hui.

Madison, Connecticut
November 10, 1951

Book I

RED DUST

The ancient city of Yenan, former Chinese Communist capital in Shensi Province, 1937—since demolished in the war with Japan and the Chinese civil war.

Introduction

ROBERT CARVER NORTH

COMMUNISTS OF THE CHINESE REVOLUTION

DURING the latter part of July 1921 thirteen men met in a girls' private school on Puhalu Street in the French Concession of Shanghai. This was during the summer vacation, and the school was empty; so the men made their homes there, settling on the top floor of the building. They were Communists from different parts of China who had met to strengthen their party structure.

On instructions from a go-between, the school watchman served meals for the unexpected visitors while they consulted with one another. This conference, the First Congress of the Chinese Communist party, lasted four days and dealt with party rules and foremost tasks, with questions of organization, and with the political situation in China. The final endorsement of party statutes, however, was delayed until the last day of the conference when, unluckily, the proceedings were cut short.

"On this day," one of the participants wrote a decade and a half later, "after supper, when the delegates gathered together at eight o'clock in the evening in Li Han-tsin's [Li Han-chün] apartment, and the chairman announced the continuation of the work of the Congress, a suspicious person in a

long coat appeared in a neighboring room. Li Han-tsin went along to find out who was the unknown. This person replied that he was seeking for the chairman of the Association of Social Organizations, Wan, by name, and then said he was mistaken and speedily left. It is true that the Association of Social Organizations was three houses away from Li Han-tsin's apartment, but everybody knew that it had no chairman, and least of all one named Wan. The appearance of the person seemed suspicious to us, and so we quickly gathered together our documents and disappeared. Only Li Han-tsin and Chen Chun-bo [Ch'en Kung-po] stayed behind, and it was a fact that before ten minutes had passed after our departure, nine spies and policemen turned up at Li Han-tsin's apartment to institute a search. Apart from legal Marxist literature, they found nothing there, and were therefore unable to arrest anybody."[1]

Unable to find any other safe place for continuing deliberations, the delegates retreated to a lake near Tsiasin, some hundred miles from Shanghai, where they hired a boat, bought food and wine, and carried through the work of the Congress under the

3

guise of having a quiet and respectable outing.

At that time there were not a hundred real Bolsheviks in China; today the Kungch'antang, or Chinese Communist party, boasts a membership of more than five million, and the country it controls is perhaps the most formidable Red stronghold outside the Soviet Union. In our morning papers we read of Communist leaders in China and of their successes, and we ask ourselves who these people are and what they are up to. Are they creatures of Moscow, puppets dancing on the end of Russian strings? Or are they Chinese patriots who see Chinese salvation in a voluntary and calculated alliance with the Soviet Union? Above all, will they place the interests of China above a doctrinaire loyalty to Moscow, or will they hew the Cominform line to the point of consciously betraying their own people?

These are questions which no Westerner —and perhaps no Communist—is yet in a position to answer objectively. For the time being we can only piece together the various odd-shaped bits of knowledge we have and guess what belongs in the empty spaces. With this incomplete and probably distorted picture before us, we can make conjectures and hope that further research and new, on-the-scene developments will fill in a few of the more important vacant spots within the puzzle.

In the past we have suffered from the fact that we knew almost nothing about the Chinese Communists themselves. For years our information was limited to gleanings from scattered and largely inaccurate Chinese and treaty-port newspaper accounts of so-called "bandit" activities in the mountains of Kiangsi and Hunan. Confusion reached the point where it was widely assumed that reports about Chu-Mao (Chu Tê and Mao Tsê-tung working in concert) referred to one man.

The first intimate interviews with Chinese Communist leaders reached American readers with the books of Edgar Snow and Nym Wales. These were readable, circumstantial reports of what the authors saw and heard during personal experiences in areas controlled by the Chinese Communists, and it was a long time before we had further information to supplement the biographical data so presented. This was valuable material, some of it among the best that was then obtainable, but it was only one segment of an intricate Chinese Communist story.

Today we have vast quantities of documentary material not widely available in the days when Edgar Snow and Nym Wales were tramping around Yenan. These include Comintern plans for capturing leadership of the indigenous revolution in China and a long series of Moscow-written directives that dictated nearly every twist and turn of the Chinese Communist party for at least a decade.

Such documentation is extremely valuable, scotching once and for all the myth once prevalent, that Chinese Communists were not really Communists, but merely Jeffersonian democrats of a Chinese stripe, or simple agrarian reformers. Yet material of this sort does not tell the whole story, either. From it the scholar can extract a historical sketch of the Chinese Communist movement and the general outlines of Communist political strategies and tactics in Asia, but there is painfully little concerning the human elements which must surely have been a critically important factor in the growth of Chinese communism.

In this present book Nym Wales gives us many of these hitherto missing human elements in the form of autobiographical sketches presented as they were told to her more than a decade ago. Here are the life-stories, self-told, of outstanding leaders like Tung Pi-wu and Lin Piao and of others less well known, perhaps, but vitally important to a chain of events that is already almost legendary. What these Communist leaders tell us about themselves could easily stand alone as short sagas of birth and growth and human struggle, and a hundred years from now they may be told that way. But today these same stories have a more pressing, if less universal significance, that cannot be ignored here or in China or Moscow, or in any other corner of this uneasy earth. For there is a struggle over the world for the minds of men, and in this conflict the Communists have won in China a victory with implications that strike far beyond the borders of their country into the lives of human beings here and everywhere.

It is now clear that the uninvited guests who connived together in the girls' school in Shanghai that day in July 1921 were not like any revolutionists that China had known before. Among these men were Tung Pi-wu and Mao Tsê-tung, and they were part of a new, world-wide movement dedicated to the overthrow of nearly all existing orders and the building of a soviet world. In China they stood in the very midst of a vast, human upheaval. The country's population was growing by tens of millions every decade, while the resources of the earth remained insufficient to support the rapidly increasing number of people. There were shocking extremes of poverty and wealth. There was famine. There was agrarian discontent. Most of these problems had been developing for a hundred years or more. Most of them had reached the point of utmost urgency. Most of them appeared nearly insoluble.

To men like Tung Pi-wu and Mao Tsê-tung this human upheaval was more than a matter of theory, for they themselves were already a part of it. Tung Pi-wu was a veteran of Sun Yat-sen's revolutionary movement and had spent time in prison long before the first Bolshevik agent arrived in China. Mao, born of peasant stock, had seen famine on the countryside, and as a small boy had observed what happens when starving peasants riot. In 1911 he had served in the revolutionary army against Imperial forces and in subsequent years had engrossed himself with revolutionary activity.

Later, as these men accepted communism, they extended their horizons to the point

Chairman of the soviet republic in Kiangsi Province, 1931—Mao Tsê-tung, age 38.

where the revolution in China appeared to them as part of a larger, world-wide struggle. Their special task, therefore, was to study the nature of this Chinese upheaval and to develop means for turning it into world-Communist channels. The consequence was that they found themselves increasingly compelled to look beyond Chinese borders both for inspiration and for visions of the larger Bolshevik future.

These men, together with Chinese intellectuals generally, had been deeply impressed by developments in Russia. Vicariously, the new soviet literature was enabling them to experience what they considered to be the only really successful revolution of their time. Beyond that, they had become interested in communism as a method for spreading technology over vast, economically underdeveloped areas like China. For the Bolshevik system seemed to many of them a logical step beyond the inventive and technological genius of a capitalism which tended to keep industry concentrated in its own well-developed areas to the apparent disadvantage of areas like most of Asia.

In Moscow, meanwhile, it had become evident that the postwar revolutionary wave was subsiding from Europe, and in July and August of 1920 the Second Congress of the Communist International, turning toward the Middle and Far East, worked out a plan for bringing revolutionary forces of China and other economically backward areas into a highly integrated and disciplined offensive against world capitalism.

Karl Marx had seen an inevitable struggle in capitalist countries between the industrial lord and the industrial wage slave. During early stages of the conflict, he said, labor is weak, but industry, in seeking to increase production, strengthens the working class and gives it coherence. Meanwhile, as capitalism tends to overconcentrate its power, a series of crises results, and dissolution sets in among the controlling classes. Labor then starts a revolt which can end only with the destruction of lord and slave and the emergence of a classless society in which, he said, there will be no need for force.

Elaborating on this concept, the Second Congress of the Communist International developed a strategy for harnessing Asian revolutions and bringing them to bear against the forces of world capitalism. Yet there were, in this plan, two mutually contradictory concepts which plagued Red leaders through early phases of Chinese Communist history and which were not satisfactorily resolved until the rise of Mao Tsê-tung to leadership.

At the Second Congress M. N. Roy, an Indian delegate who has since left the Communist movement, emphasized the idea that Western capitalism draws its chief strength from colonial possessions and dependencies. Without this control of raw materials and markets, he said, the capitalist powers of the world could not maintain their existence even for a short time. "Super-profit gained in the colonies," he said, "is the mainstay

of modern capitalism, and so long as the latter is not deprived of this source of super-profit, it will not be easy for the European working class to overthrow the capitalist order."[2]

Lenin accepted this principle, maintaining that it was implicit in his own earlier writings, but he disagreed with the heavy emphasis which Roy seemed to place on indigenous class conflict in Asia.[3] Roy, he said, went too far in declaring that the destiny of the West would depend exclusively upon the degree of development and the strength of peasant and working-class revolution in Asian countries.[4] On the contrary, it was necessary for all Communist parties to enlarge their influence by rendering assistance to existing "nationalist-bourgeois-democratic liberation" movements in economically backward areas where, he said, working-class revolutions had not matured sufficiently to be effective.[5] In the end, the Second Congress tried to resolve the contradiction between class conflict and the concept of co-operation with "nationalist-bourgeois-democratic" revolutions by advocating both: *While extending support to middle class nationalists that were truly revolutionary, Communist leaders were expected to make every effort to arouse and organize the working masses and to penetrate and gain leadership over the existing revolutionary movement.*[6]

The handful of Chinese Communists who held their First Congress in a boat late in July 1921 had already been in touch with Moscow for at least twelve months. In the spring of the previous year the Third International had dispatched two agents to China, where they aided in the preliminary organization of the party; and a Comintern agent, a Hollander called Maring, was present at the Shanghai Congress. During the next six years Russian and Chinese Communists undertook a triple policy in China, carried out on three levels.

Between 1922 and 1924 the Soviet Union sent a number of envoys, notably Adolph

Joffe and later Leo Karakhan, to negotiate with the Peking government. But Joffe, before leaving the Far East, conferred also with Dr. Sun Yat-sen, who was dedicated to overthrowing the Peking government; and Karakhan, who enjoyed the rank of ambassador in Peking, where he made strong protestations of Soviet friendship and good will, acted concurrently as an undercover agent for the Third International. In line with these later, subversive duties, Karakhan aided Dr. Sun Yat-sen's Kuomintang and plotted with it for the overthrow of the Peking government to which he was accredited. And finally, while supporting the Kuomintang, the Third International was urging Chinese Communists to join that party in order to capture it eventually, or to oust it from leadership of the revolution.

Uncertain where its own interests lay, the Peking government wavered in its attitude toward Soviet overtures, but Dr. Sun was ready for Bolshevik help. His followers had been painfully disillusioned by Western treatment of China at Versailles, and even the results of the Washington Conference of 1921–22 were something less than many Chinese had hoped for. China was seething with indigenous revolt against the old order, but neither Great Britain nor the United States was showing any inclination to aid Dr. Sun.

Both in Moscow and in China, on the other hand, certain Bolshevik leaders saw potentialities in the Kuomintang which, while lacking the organization and discipline demanded in a Communist party, had, nevertheless, a larger following than communism. A Chinese Communist delegate to the Fourth Congress of the Communist International in 1922 put it this way: "If we do not join this party (the Kuomintang), we shall remain isolated and we shall preach a communism which consists of a great and noble ideal, but one which the masses do not follow. The masses certainly would follow the bourgeois party, and this party would use the masses for its purpose. If we join the

Commandant of Whampoa Military Academy—Chiang Kai-shek in Canton, 1924.

party, we shall be able to show the masses that we too are for a revolutionary democracy, but that for us revolutionary democracy is only a means to an end. Furthermore, we shall be able to point out that although we are for this distant goal, we nevertheless do not forget the daily needs of the masses. We shall be able to gather the masses around us and split the Kuomintang party."[7]

For nearly three years Sun Yat-sen's Kuomintang and the Chinese Communists marched together in the so-called Great Revolution of 1925–27. Dr. Sun's government had been weak and almost fatally dependent upon the good will of militarists like Ch'ên Ch'iung-ming, who often dominated its policies. Now a Comintern agent, Michael Borodin, reorganized the Kuomintang after Communist patterns and established the Whampoa Military Academy where Chiang Kai-shek was commandant, where Chou Ên-lai served as a political instructor, and where well-known Kuomintang generals of the

Wang Ching-wei (fourth from the left, bareheaded) addresses a Canton gathering, 1925. Sixth from the left (with military cap and cape) is Chiang Kai-shek. Next (bareheaded, with mustache) is Michael Borodin, Comintern adviser to the early Kuomintang and founder of Whampoa Military Academy. Last is Lin Tsu-han, comrade of Sun Yat-sen, associated with Sun in forming the Kuomintang, and long-time official in the Chinese Communist party.

future, as well as Communists like Lin Piao, received their training. Early in 1926 Comintern agents and Chinese Communists helped in the launching of Chiang Kai-shek's Northern Expedition against North China's militarists. Members of both parties faced foreign rifles and machine guns in the Shanghai shootings of May 30, 1925 (the May Thirtieth Incident) and the Shameen Massacre less than a month later.

But Communist attempts to befriend the Peking government, support the Kuomintang, and stir peasant revolt—all at the same time—led to the nearly disastrous consequences which have been so carefully documented by Harold R. Isaacs in his account of Comintern activities during the mid-'twenties.[8] In 1927 Soviet Russian relations with the tottering Peking government collapsed. Concurrently, Bolshevik agitation among labor and peasantry antagonized middle-class leaders before Communist forces were strong enough to defend their position. On March 20, 1926, Chiang Kai-shek effected a coup that weakened the Bolshevik position, but Communist leaders soon regained their influence. By April 1927 they and the Kuomintang Left were dominating

the Nationalist government, then situated in Wuhan. Right Wing leaders under Chiang Kai-shek broke with both the Communists individually and with the Wuhan government, and established a new regime in Nanking. Three months later, the Kuomintang Left Wing also repudiated its Bolshevik alliance. Within the course of a few months Russian representatives were officially expelled from Nationalist China and the Chinese Communist Party was nearly annihilated.

Throughout the period of Communist-Kuomintang co-operation and for at least three years thereafter, Moscow sought through lengthy directives and on-the-spot agents to dictate every twist and turn of the Chinese Communist line. And when, time after time, these Moscow-made policies came close to wrecking the Chinese Communist movement, it was nearly always a Chinese leader, rather than a Russian, who accepted responsibility.

On advice from Moscow the Chinese Communists called a Special Conference, August 7, 1927, which "welcomed the energetic intervention of the Comintern" that was enabling them to expose the mistakes of the previous party leadership and thus save the movement in China.[9] The Special Conference condemned Ch'ên Tu-hsiu and T'an P'ing-shan for restraining the peasantry and for committing other errors of "right opportunism" and censured the leadership for "retreating temporarily in order to retain the alliance with the Kuomintang." But at the same time, in harmony with a policy initiated by Stalin, the Special Conference decided against a Communist withdrawal from the Left Wing of the Kuomintang.[10]

Supporting a Moscow resolution urging Communists to "take all measures necessary to arouse the lower strata of the Left Kuomintang against the upper,"[11] Chinese leaders promised struggle against militarists, imperialists, and feudalists with the "really revolutionary" members of the Kuomintang and with the masses of the Kuomintang.[12] But when it became evident that the possibility of carrying out this tactic had passed, the Comintern did not hesitate to censure the Special Conference on the charge that it "had raised false hopes for the emergence of a left revolutionary Kuomintang and had actually called for action under such a banner."[13]

The mood of the new leadership was for action to replace the caution which Ch'ên Tu-hsiu had displayed. Six days prior to the opening of the Special Conference, a Communist uprising "under the banner of the Kuomintang Left" had taken place at Nanchang, when Red elements under Ho Lung, Chu Tê, and Yeh T'ing, supported by armed miners from Hanyehp'ing, carried out a successful mutiny within the "Ironsides," reputedly the best army corps in Kuomintang service, and thus brought into Communist ranks a reported total of nearly twenty thousand men.[14] Flushed with victory, Ho Lung, Chu Tê, and Yeh T'ing began a "drive to the sea" that resulted in a temporary occupation of Swatow. But soon the revolutionary army, "because of the superiority of reactionary militarists and its own wrong tactics,"[15] was in full retreat. Re-

Chu Tê, commander in chief of the Red Army, 1936. From a pencil sketch by an artist of the Fourth Front Army, made at the end of the Long March.

Ho Lung, commander of the Second Front Red Army, sketched in the autumn of 1936 when his forces from the Hunan-Hupeh soviet joined the central Red armies.

sponsibility for this failure was pinned—not on Stalin or his agents or even on the Special Conference—but on T'an P'ing-shan, who was denounced and expelled for his "Kuomintang Left illusions."

During the years that immediately followed, Stalin and his Russian advisers, abandoning their attempts at co-operation with middle-class revolutionists, emphasized class conflict. But, in doing this, they threw their weight behind waning labor unrest rather than behind swelling peasant revolt, and all but ignored Mao Tsê-tung who has since become a symbol for agrarian revolution in China. "If we allot ten points to the accomplishments of the democratic revolution," Mao wrote in 1927, "then the achievements of the urban dwellers and the military units rate only three points, while the remaining seven should go to the peasants in their rural revolution."[16] But Stalin and his advisers, obsessed with ideas of urban insurrection and a proletarian "solution" of the agrarian problem, continued to think of the peasant movement as auxiliary, rather than the central force. During the autumn of 1927 the Chinese Communist hierarchy, dominated by two Stalinist representatives, dismissed Mao from the Politburo and from the Party Front Committee.

Shortly after the Special Conference, Communist leaders had sent Mao to Hunan, his native province, for the purpose of organizing what later was known as the Autumn Crop Uprising. Within a little more than a month, he and his associates succeeded in organizing a revolt of peasants, Hanyang miners, and dissident troops of the Kuomintang. During succeeding weeks Mao's small army fought its way southward through Hunan. But discipline was poor, the troops lacked tactical training, and at one point Mao himself was captured and nearly executed. He made his escape, however, and led what remained of his troops to Chingkangshan, a mountain stronghold on the Hunan-Kiangsi border, where he was joined by Chu Tê.

The Bolshevik hierarchy now charged that the Autumn Crop Uprising had not been sanctioned and that "from the angle of the cities"[17] the movement had been doomed to failure, but Mao made no effort to revise his estimate of the peasant's role in the Chinese revolution. In the meantime, a number of peasant soviets had been organized in various rural areas, and in subsequent years many more were established throughout central China.

During this growth of peasant soviets the Chinese Communist movement underwent a complete transformation from primarily working class to primarily peasant membership. In 1926 Communist sources classed 66 percent of the Chinese Communist party as workers, 22 percent as intellectuals, and 5 percent as peasants.[18] By 1930 the membership was overwhelmingly peasant, while no more than 8 percent could be considered working class.[19] Yet the Russians continued to hold Mao's rural "rifle movement" subsidiary to the Shanghai underground leadership of men like Ch'ü Ch'iu-po and Li Li-san.

A Stalinist protégé named Heinz Neumann supervised Li Li-san in the engineering of the first Chinese Communist attempt at urban insurrection. Although he had studied in France and had accumulated considerable experience as a labor organizer, Li Li-san was only twenty-seven years old at the time, and Neumann was near the same age. Both were bold and adventurous; both were ambitious. In December 1927 they attempted a coup in Canton and organized a short-lived revolutionary Commune. Their planning, however, had been hasty and inadequate, and the attempt failed at a cost of some six thousand Chinese lives. Despite this nearly disastrous defeat, Stalin, as well as various Communist leaders in China, continued to be intrigued by the possibilities of urban insurrection in the course of a new revolutionary upsurge which, he believed, was imminent.

During the latter months of 1928 the

Sixth Congress of the Third International, reaffirming the Lenin and Roy theses for revolution in economically backward countries, laid out for China a program of armed insurrection essentially similar to the one which had failed in Canton. This was described as the "sole path to the completion of bourgeois democratic revolution"[20] and to the overthrow of the Kuomintang.

After addressing a long series of preparatory directives to the Central Committee of the Chinese Communist party, the Comintern in October 1929 dispatched a letter ordering Chinese Reds to consolidate and expand guerrilla warfare, develop political strikes, change various non-Communist rebellions against Chiang Kai-shek into a class war, and transform peasant struggles into urban insurrections.[21]

During the summer of 1930 Li Li-san tried to carry out this policy at Changsha and other urban centers, but the attempts failed, whereupon the Communist International dispatched Ch'ü Ch'iu-po and Chou Ên-lai, who were in Moscow at the time, to China for the convening of the Third Plenum of the Chinese Communist party in Lushan. The Report of the Third Plenum, drafted by Ch'ü Ch'iu-po and Chou Ên-lai, while rebuking Li Li-san for having "overestimated the tempo" and for having committed tactical mistakes, stated that the general line was still "in complete harmony with the Comintern."[22] But within a few weeks the Comintern, on the basis of further Chinese Communist defeats, ordered a complete change of policy, the withdrawal of Li Li-san from active policy-making, and the substitution of a new party leadership.

A Comintern agent, Pavel Aleksandrovich Mif, supported by a group of recently returned Chinese graduates from Sun Yat-sen University in Moscow, oversaw the dismissal of Li Li-san. Weeks later, Li Li-san, answering for his failure before the Oriental Department of the Comintern in Moscow, admitted a long series of errors: he had thought that he could mobilize the working

Hammer-and-sickle flag of the "First Regiment of the First Division of the Chinese Workers' and Peasants' Red Army" carried by followers of Mao Tsê-tung. This first Red Army flag was adopted when the Chinese Communist party began its sponsorship of independent soviet movements, after the Hunan insurrection of 1928. The hammer-and-sickle ensign was discontinued in 1937.

class "simply by raising the slogan of military insurrection"; he had attempted an insurrectionary policy without proper political preparation; he had taught that the revolutionary situation was spread evenly throughout China and that a revolutionary government could not be set up until he had occupied large industrial and administrative cities; he had overestimated the upsurge of the world revolutionary movement; he had maintained that the victory of the bourgeois democratic revolution would go directly over into a socialist revolution.[23]

Having confessed his own political sins to the investigating commission, Li Li-san criticized various of his Chinese comrades and added that Chinese Communists were often prejudiced against the Russians, being unwilling to trust them, and that Russian Bolsheviks, likewise, were inclined to be sus-

Assembled chairmen of the "Chinese Soviet Republic" at their Second Congress, January 22, 1934, at Juikin, Kiangsi Province. Included are: Mao Tsê-tung (front row, fourth from right), Chu Tê (front row, third from left), and Lin Tsu-han (back row, fifth from right).

picious of those committed to "practical work" in China.[24]

Li Li-san's words disturbed the investigating commission and especially its chairman, Manuilsky. The Chinese Politburo, he said, had sent Li Li-san to Moscow "upon the request of Moscow," whereupon the atmosphere of the Russian capital had "dealt Li-san a heavy blow," and he had confessed his own mistakes. But these admissions had come too easily, Manuilsky said, as though Li Li-san thought that his case would not be further questioned if he "held his fist clenched." This was a mistaken idea. "The most dangerous thing," Manuilsky warned, "is for one to agree with our decisions externally and to follow one's own line in practice."[25]

Manuilsky, noting that Li Li-san had accused Russian Communists of guarding their own interests at the expense of the Chinese revolution, charged the Chinese leader with seeing only the situation within his own country and ignoring the "interwoven and complicated" international environment. Under these circumstances, confession was

not enough, for China represented the model from which all infantile colonial Communist parties must learn, and therefore, in order "to lance the boil which must be lanced," Manuilsky urged Li Li-san to "expose the whole clique situation" among his Chinese comrades, handing in all material and information "honestly and openly." And finally in regard to the punishment of Li Li-san, Manuilsky said, "We want him to attend the Bolshevik school here in order for him to understand the substance of his errors."[26]

It was fourteen years before Li Li-san returned to China.

From January 1931 until January 1935 nominal leadership of the Chinese Communist party—at least partly on Russian advice—rested in the hands of a group centering on Wang Ming (Ch'ên Shao-yü). Born of a well-to-do farmer family, Wang Ming had studied in Japan and at the University of Shanghai before entering Sun Yat-sen University in Moscow during 1925. Two years later he reappeared in China as interpreter for Pavel Mif, at that time vice-president of Sun Yat-sen University, but he

returned to Moscow shortly thereafter. Only twenty-four years old, he re-entered China in 1930 and, under Mif's supervision, led the attack on Li Li-san. Closely associated with him were two other returned students, Chang Wên-t'ien, who had studied at the University of California as well as in Moscow, and Wang Chia-hsiang.

Just prior to the fall of Li Li-san, Chiang Kai-shek began the first of his major "bandit suppression campaigns" against the Chinese Communists. These attacks did not succeed in their avowed purpose — to exterminate the Chinese Communist forces — but did finally dislodge them in the autumn of 1934, thus setting in motion the Long March.

This same period (1931–35) brought about a critical transition in the development of the Chinese Communist party, a period during which the peasant composition of the Red movement achieved recognition and during which Mao Tsê-tung gradually rose to power. Shortly after Li Li-san's trial in Moscow, Manuilsky laid down three objectives for the current stage of the Chinese revolution: the Red Army must be con-

verted into a regular workers' and peasants' Red Army with a sound territorial base; the economic and political struggles of the working class and peasantry in nonsoviet territories must be developed through trade-unions, peasant committees, and propaganda work in various militarist armies; and a central soviet government must be formed in China in order to carry out a program of anti-imperialist and agrarian revolt.[27]

During November 1931, two months after the Japanese action in Manchuria, the First All-China Congress of Soviets, meeting in Juikin, established a Chinese Soviet Republic with Mao Tsê-tung as chairman and Chang Kuo-t'ao and Hsiang Ying as vice-chairmen. This Congress approved a government constitution, passed agrarian and labor laws, and elected a government Central Committee under Mao's chairmanship. Early the following year, moreover, the new government declared war on Japan and sent out a call for all classes and political groups in China to join in resisting Japanese aggression.

For another year the Central Committee

of the Chinese Communist party maintained its headquarters in Shanghai, while Mao and his followers, according to some accounts still relatively unimportant in the party hierarchy,[28] devoted themselves to affairs of the Juikin Republic, to the building of the Red Army, and to resisting a series of Nationalist attacks initiated by Chiang Kai-shek. During the autumn of 1932, Wang Ming, Chang Wên-t'ien, Po Ku (Ch'in Pang-hsien), Shên Tsê-min, and other Central Committeemen, under Kuomintang pressure, moved to Juikin. Shortly thereafter, Wang Ming was relieved as secretary-general and was recalled to the Soviet Union, where he served from 1932 until 1938 as Chinese Communist representative in Moscow. Po Ku now took over as secretary-general.

Throughout the existence of the Juikin Republic, Communist areas were subject to continual attacks from the Nationalists. At the Second Congress of Chinese Soviets, in January 1934, Mao Tsê-tung demanded an aggressive program to save the soviet republic and to enlarge it in the face of Chiang Kai-shek's most recent offensive. But at the Fifth Plenum of the Chinese Communist Central Committee, Po Ku attacked Mao for his "countryside policy" and "banditry doctrine," and, according to Chang Kuo-t'ao, used this opportunity to reduce Mao's power by making him Minister of Education.[29]

By the autumn of 1934 it became clear that the Chinese Communists could not hold their ground against Chiang's intensified offensives, and plans were therefore laid for a complete evacuation. Sometime in late October or in November, according to Chang Kuo-t'ao, Chinese Communist leaders received a radiogram from Moscow advising them to pull out, and on November 10 the Long March began.

Fighting their way through four enemy lines of machine-gun nests and concrete emplacements, the Communist columns first drove through to the frontiers of Kweichow. At Tsunyi, Mao attacked the policies of Po Ku and the "returned students," maintaining that Red guerrilla tactics had been ineffective against the Kuomintang and charging the leadership with failing to co-operate with an anti-Kuomintang revolt in Fukien during the previous year. Although not present at the meeting, Chang Kuo-t'ao, communicating by telegraph, made the additional charge that soviets were entirely unsuitable to conditions in China.[30] The conference supported Mao's attack, but refused to condemn the principle of soviets for China. In consequence of these deliberations, Mao achieved power, while Chang Kuo-t'ao appeared increasingly in the role of an oppositionist.

After leaving Tsunyi, the Communists were able to take the initiative in attacking Nationalist forces which were still seeking the annihilation of the Reds. In the course of numerous engagements, Red troops succeeded in capturing badly needed uniforms, ammunition, and pack animals from Nationalist units. A Chinese Communist writer of the time put it this way: "We must say that our men don't very much like fighting the local generals, but rather prefer to fight against the Nanking [Nationalist] generals, for after we have demolished one of the Nanking generals we usually obtain a large quantity of foodstuffs, uniforms, and ammunition. The local generals are considerably poorer."[31] These were tactics which Chinese Communist troops were to use with much greater effectiveness while driving Chiang Kai-shek from the Chinese mainland fifteen years later.

In June 1935, the main column of the Long March under Mao made a junction in Szechuan Province with troops of Chang Kuo-t'ao and Hsü Hsiang-ch'ien, who had set up a base in this area a short time previously. After proceeding to Mao-erh-kai, the two groups held a joint meeting where differences between Mao and Chang broke into open debate. Chang contended that Communist forces should proceed westward into Sinkiang in order to establish contact with the Soviet Union, but Mao, on the

Capitulation of a Chinese city, with little resistance offered—a photograph taken by a Red Army participant in the occupation of Chihsien, Shansi Province, in March 1936.

other hand, insisted on moving toward Shensi with the hope that, by so doing, they could settle as close as possible to the troops of Kao Kang.[32]

At this point, according to Chang, contact was momentarily re-established with Moscow, whereupon Comintern authorities made several attempts at mediation. In the end, partly as the result of circumstantial pressures, both leaders proceeded to Shensi, where a new disagreement arose between them.

During the period from the termination of the Long March through the summer of 1937, Bolshevik leaders tried once more to combine Communist-Kuomintang co-operation with the stirring-up of class conflicts,

this time with notable success. While Chiang Kai-shek's Nationalist forces had been trying to exterminate the Communists, Japan had begun a series of encroachments on Chinese territory, beginning with the Japanese occupation of Manchuria in 1931 and leading up to the Marco Polo Bridge incident on July 7, 1937. These aggressions caused an upsurge of Chinese nationalism on which the Communists now sought to capitalize.

Russian and Chinese Communists alike had recognized the Japanese invasion of Manchuria as dangerous, not only to China, but also the Soviet Union. As early as April 1932 Chinese Communists had "called upon the masses of the Chinese people to join . . .

On the Long March—troops of the Twenty-Fifth Red Army crossing the Wei River, Kansu Province, in August 1935.

in the fight against Japanese imperialism," and in January 1933 a Comintern publication carried a similar appeal signed by Mao, Chang Kuo-t'ao, Chu Tê, and others.[33] On August 1, 1935, the Mao-erh-kai Conference issued a proclamation urging all classes to fight against Japan and making a special appeal to Chiang Kai-shek, promising to co-operate with the Kuomintang if Chiang would cease fighting "his own people."[34] In Moscow a day later Georgi Dimitrov told the Seventh Congress of the Communist International: ". . . We therefore approve the initiative taken by our courageous brother Party of China in the creation of a most extensive anti-imperialist united front against Japanese imperialism and its Chinese agents, jointly with all those organized forces existing on the territory of China who are ready to wage a real struggle for the salvation of their country and their people."[35] On August 5, Wang Ming told the same Congress: "In my opinion and in the opinion of the entire Central Committee of the Communist Party of China, the latter, together with the Soviet Government of China, should issue a joint appeal to the whole nation, to all parties, groups, troops, mass organizations, and all prominent political and social persons, to organize together with us an all-China united people's government of national defense."[36]

These and subsequent Communist proposals for a united front against Japan proved particularly effective in neutralizing Nationalist anti-Communist campaigns in northwestern China. There, by the latter part of 1936, the army of Chang Hsüeh-liang, assigned to "bandit suppression," was unwilling to fight Communists in the very face of Japanese aggressions. Consequently, Chang Hsüeh-liang "arrested" Chiang Kai-shek while the latter was in Sian planning his Sixth Bandit Suppression Campaign. Whether or not the Chinese Communists played any part in the Sian kidnaping has never been established precisely, but after Chiang had been released, Kuomintang-Communist negotiations moved ahead.

In February 1937, Chinese Communist leaders offered specifically to call off their policy of armed uprisings against the Nationalist government, to abandon the soviet in favor of a regional government of the Republic of China on the basis of universal suffrage, to change the Red Army into a National Revolutionary Army under the central government, to put an end to the policy of expropriating landlord holdings, and to execute persistently the common program of the anti-Japanese united front. In return, the Communists demanded that Nationalist leaders agree to the suspension of civil wars, the recognition of basic freedoms and release of all political prisoners, the amelioration of living conditions throughout the country, the convocation of a congress of various political parties and groups, and the prosecution of a war of resistance against Japan.[37]

In August of 1937 Nym Wales, visiting Communist regions, saw her bodyguard "fingering his new Kuomintang cap in gingerly fashion, rubbing the bourgeois blue-and-white enamel symbol,"[38] and in September the Chinese Communist Central Committee issued a manifesto stating that an agreement with the Kuomintang had been reached and proposing a set of "general objectives for the common struggle of the entire people."[39]

But like the Communist-Kuomintang alliance of the early 'twenties, this new relationship proved to be an uneasy one. On the one hand, Chiang Kai-shek made every effort during the Japanese War to strengthen his personal control over Kuomintang and Central government machinery without concern for democratic method or traditional party procedures.[40] On the other hand, the

Communists, while vociferously advertising their adherence to the Three People's Principles of Sun Yat-sen and the sincerity of United Front proposals, emphasized in their own councils that their actions were strategic moves for meeting requirements of the "current stage" and did not nullify their belief in class warfare nor their adherence to Bolshevik doctrine. The Politburo warned Communist membership against both an ultra-leftist opposition to united front tactics and—equally serious—"the rightest opportunist" tendency toward too close an association with the Kuomintang.[41]

It was a disagreement over the precise nature of this Kuomintang-Communist alliance that led to a final break between Chang Kuo-t'ao and Mao Tsê-tung who, despite disagreements with Moscow, remained a disciplined Communist. Mao considered the united front in terms of strategy and tactics, while Chang maintained that Communists, through a genuine alliance, could lead non-Communist elements in a progressive direction. As a result of this conflict, the Chinese Communist party expelled Chang Kuo-t'ao on the basis that he had betrayed communism and the cause of the united anti-Japa-

Red cadets — students at the Military and Political Academy in Yenan—in exercises on August 1, 1937, commemorating the founding of the Red Army.

nese front, and Moscow confirmed the action.[42]

Throughout the Japanese war, Mao's prosecution of this strategic united front policy came increasingly to represent a successful resolution of the old conflict between Lenin's principle of co-operation with nationalistic forces in Asia and Roy's insistence on class conflict. For the Chinese Communist leaders, while championing the cause of the peasant, made what use they could of the Kuomintang alliance. Supporting Chiang so long as Chiang was useful, they trained peasant armies to turn against him when the proper moment came. From the years of the Japanese war the Communists emerged, not only with tough troops expert in guerrilla warfare, but also with military and political cadres of young leaders who supported and in some cases overshadowed the veterans of earlier years. Chiang and the Kuomintang were less successful.

After 1938 Communist-Kuomintang relations deteriorated into a series of charges and countercharges. Communist military forces were expanding beyond the zones assigned to them by the Nationalist government; the Kuomintang was suppressing Communist organizations in Nationalist territory. There were a number of armed skirmishes culminating in the "New Fourth Army Incident" of January 1941, during which Communist and Kuomintang forces engaged in heavy, open fighting. Neither side showed any inclination toward genuine compromise. Shortly after Pearl Harbor, Mao initiated the Chêng Fêng or "ideological remolding movement" to tighten party discipline and indoctrinate members with Bolshevik historical background and theory. Chiang Kai-shek, retaliating Communist aggressiveness, strengthened his party hierarchy and his secret police.

Foreign observers disagreed in their estimates of Chiang. Some considered him a worthy military ally and a great political leader. Others, like General Stilwell, accused him of "milking" the United States and insisted he had no intention either of instituting a democratic regime or of co-operating with the Communists. Few were then in a position to state precisely what the Communists intended, or whether anyone could safely co-operate with them.

Diplomatic circles did not abandon the hope for a unified China. In 1944 General Hurley, sent by President Roosevelt to Chungking, reported a seeming willingness on the part of the Kuomintang and the Communists to co-operate. Stalin, furthermore, assured Hurley some months later that the Soviet Union had no intention of recognizing any government in China except the Nationalist government with Chiang Kai-shek as its leader. But Chiang and Mao, meanwhile, seemed more interested in preserving their respective parties than in driving out the Japanese.

Necessarily, the United States assumed increasing responsibility for prosecuting the war against Japan, but amphibious drives across the Central and South Pacific had already taken a shocking toll in American lives. Estimates of the human cost of an assault on Japan were frightening. By the end of 1944 both soldiers and civilians were demanding to know why the Soviet Union had not accepted a share of the war in Asia.

It was from these circumstances and from Allied relationships with the Soviet Union in other theaters that the Yalta Agreement emerged. Through this document, the United States and Great Britain paid a heavy price for Russian aid in a war which—although few outside Japan knew it—was all but won. For the two Western powers, without consulting China, recognized a Soviet Russian claim to nearly all imperialist concessions on Chinese soil which Czarist Russia had lost to Japan through the Treaty of Portsmouth in 1905. Great Britain and the United States also agreed, without consulting China, that the status quo in Outer Mongolia, that is, the Communist-dominated "Mongolian People's Republic," should be preserved.

Young commanders and political commissars — when this photograph was taken, in 1937, the Red Army had become the "Eighth Route Army" in the united front against the Japanese invasion. Left to right: Kuan Shan-yin, commissar, Second Front Army; Kan Shih-ch'i, vice-chairman, political department, Second Front Army; Wang Chêng, commissar, Sixth Army; Nieh Jung-chên, commissar, First Army Corps; Hsiao K'ê, commander, Second Front Army; Cheng Tzǔ-hua, commissar, Fifteenth Army Corps; Ch'en Po-chun, commander, Sixth Army; Yang Shan-kun, chairman, political department, First Front Army.

Essential aspects of this agreement served as a framework for the Sino-Soviet Treaty of Friendship and Alliance, August 14, 1945. In this later document, however, the Soviet Union agreed to give the National government of China both moral and material support and offered formal assurances that the Soviet Union would not interfere with China's affairs.

Under these circumstances, the Treaty of Friendship and Alliance was, for the time being, well received in Nationalist China and in the United States. It looked to many observers as though the Soviet Union had turned its back on the Chinese Communists, and there were speculations that both Russian and Chinese Communists had reconciled themselves to the government of Chiang Kai-shek. In retrospect, it is clear that these observers did not understand the fundamental Communist tactic of co-operation combined with opposition. Within a few months Nationalist and Chinese Communist troops were engaged in a full-scale civil war.

With the formal surrender of the Japanese on September 2, 1945, Mao Tsê-tung's peasant armies began racing Nationalist troops for control of areas which had been occupied by the Japanese. At that time Nationalists held an estimated five-to-one advantage in troops and rifles and a virtual monopoly of heavy equipment, transport and air strength. Mao Tsê-tung's guerrillas, on the other hand, enjoyed a geographical advantage in being closer to many of the Japanese areas, including Manchuria.

In an effort to help the Nationalists reoccupy Japanese-held territory, the United States transported three Nationalist armies by air to East and North China and over 400,000 troops by water. United States Marines, moreover, were moved into North China to hold key railroads and coal mines for the Nationalists. With this and other American assistance Chiang Kai-shek's troops were able to accept the capitulation of a great majority of the 1,200,000 Japanese troops in China proper. But the Nationalists did badly in Manchuria.

In discussions leading up to the Sino-Soviet Treaty, Stalin had assured the Nationalist Chinese that Soviet forces would begin to withdraw from Manchuria within three weeks after the Japanese surrender and that the evacuation would be completed in three months. But when Russian troops began pulling out, Nationalist forces, with extended lines of communication and limited rolling stock, were unable to take over areas being evacuated in time to prevent poised Chinese Communist troops from moving in. The Nationalist government found itself in the embarrassing position of having to ask the Russians to postpone their departure.

When the Russians did withdraw, they stripped the area of Japanese-built industrial equipment, but left behind for Chinese Communist forces sizable caches of Japanese rifles and a well-trained Communist army of local Chinese and former Japanese puppet troops. At the risk of stretching their already overextended lines, the Nationalists tried to reoccupy Manchuria by force.

In the meantime, President Truman, late in 1945, had dispatched the Marshall mission to bring peace to China under conditions that would permit a stable government and progress along democratic lines and to assist the Nationalist government in establishing its authority over widest possible areas of China. The first object was not realizable. The greatest obstacle to peace, General Marshall reported, was the complete, overwhelming suspicion with which the Chinese Communist party and the Kuomintang regarded one another. On the one hand, Marshall criticized irreconcilable groups within the Kuomintang, interested only in preserving their own feudal control of China; on the other, he condemned "dyed-in-the-wool" Communists who quite readily used abuse, lies, and any other drastic measures, even to wrecking the economy of China, in order to achieve their ends. The only solution, he said, lay in assumption of leadership by liberals in the government and in the minority parties. These men were without influence or support, however, and entirely unable to act.

The second objective of the Marshall mission, to help the Nationalists extend their authority, seemed easier to realize, since by early 1947 Chiang's government had reached a peak of military successes and territorial expansion. But Chinese Communist generals soon brought superior forces to bear at points of greatest Nationalist extension—just as they had done during the "bandit suppression campaigns" in the days of the Juikin Republic—destroying isolated bodies of troops, cutting communications and seizing arms. By the end of 1947 they were supplementing Russian-donated Japanese rifles with American weapons captured from American-trained and American-equipped Nationalist armies.

Nationalist troops now rapidly lost the will to fight, and in October 1948 Nationalist defenders of Mukden defected to the Communists, taking with them both weapons and other equipment. Thereafter, Communist victories followed one after another: Tientsin fell on January 15, 1949; Peking surrendered later that month without a fight; in April the Communists crossed the Yangtze; Shanghai fell in May, and on October 15, Canton, Nationalist capital for the previous six months, capitulated without resistance. Chiang Kai-shek had already moved his headquarters to Formosa.

In the meantime, Mao Tsê-tung on September 21, 1949, had proclaimed the establishment of the People's Republic of China. With the founding of this new government, the Chinese Communists achieved a position unparalleled in the Communist world. As *de facto* rulers of China, they controlled an area more than seven times larger than all the Soviet satellites put together and a population nearly two and a half times that of the USSR itself. The Chinese Communist party, with a membership—still largely peasant—of over three million (over five million in 1951) was second in size only to that of the Soviet Union, and its generals commanded a victorious army of a reported five million regulars. This army, moreover, had driven from the mainland a government with recognized Great Power standing, and Communist leaders consequently claimed an equivalent status, with accompanying prerequisites, for their Chinese People's Republic.

This People's Republic or "new democracy" is a special kind of Communist state. Superficially, it represents an economy undertaken partly by the state, partly by private concerns, and partly by co-operatives. But for Communists it is only one stage in a planned and inevitable advance toward Stalinist socialism and communism and eventual integration into a world-wide soviet body. As such, it is at once a Bolshevik tactic for separating capitalist countries from access to raw materials and markets of an economically backward area, a temporary and calculated alliance with non-Communist elements, and a broad program for social, political, and economic change in areas where reforms are long overdue.

What Mao Tsê-tung calls a united front between communism and the Three People's Principles of Sun Yat-sen can be expected to survive during the new democratic stage of Chinese Communist development. Then, after the test of war and the test of land reform are passed, according to Mao, the only remaining test—the test of socialism, of carrying out socialist reform throughout the nation—will be passed easily.[43] The new democracy thus constitutes a transitional stage from precapitalism to Bolshevik socialism and communism.

The socialism which Mao and his followers anticipate should not be confused with social democracy. On the contrary, Chinese Communist theoreticians have made clear that the people's democracy and Bolshevik socialism are separate from and antagonistic to the principles of social democracy. "Our party," wrote Ch'ên Po-ta, "is founded after the traditions of Bolshevism and Leninism without the traditions of social democracy. . . . This Bolshevism was forged through long struggle against social democracy, which betrayed Marxism and which advocated social reform, opposed social revolution, and co-operated with imperialism and is entirely in contradiction to social democracy." Bolshevism has been victorious, according to Ch'ên Po-ta, because it is a correct science and represents the aspirations of mankind.[44]

With the victory of the Chinese Communists, Bolshevik leaders see China playing a critically important role throughout the Far East. "The path taken by the Chinese people in defeating imperialism and in founding the People's Republic of China,"

Mao Tsê-tung and Chu Tê, 1937

Liu Shao-ch'i has said, "is the path that must be taken by the peoples of the various colonial and semi-colonial countries in their fight for national independence and people's democracy."[45] The Cominform supported this view in an editorial dated January 27, 1950. Quoting Liu Shao-ch'i, the Cominform cited India (suffering from a sham independence!), Burma, Malaya, Indonesia, Viet-Nam, the Philippines, and South Korea, laying down the same broad outlines for their future—armed struggle for national independence and the setting up of a Communist-led people's democracy.[46]

So today, Tung Pi-wu and Mao Tsê-tung, party founders who connived in the girls' school on Pubalu Street and plotted in a rowboat on a lake near Tsiasin—these two men and the others appearing in this book are not only taking part in the new Chinese People's Republic, but are looking beyond the borders of China toward a Communist Asia and, eventually, a soviet world. Much of Asia is now grinding through one of those changes in historical cycle, one of those stupendous, nearly uncontrollable upheavals that sometimes bury the mighty and raise the lowly to high places.

At this point in history it is impossible to forecast what the outcome of this upheaval may be, but its current aspects suggest that neither the United States nor any other power on earth can stop it. So far Russian and Chinese Communists have been extraordinarily successful in channeling it for their own devious purposes. The problem for Americans is to discover for themselves what the causes of this upheaval are and to develop new, constructive, and effective ways for dealing with it.

One of our chief problems is to decide why millions of Chinese have turned—or have been driven—to communism, and it is here that the autobiographies in this book are of the deepest interest. In these narratives we have raw materials, such as a psychologist might use, to help decide what makes a Bolshevik.

Until now, such material has been lacking. The Chinese have traditionally shunned emphasis on the individual—especially the intimate particulars of a life—and it is doubtful that a foreigner, or perhaps anyone else, will ever again be in a position to draw out such stories as these from Chinese Communists. For a long time after Nym Wales collected this material it seemed too localized and probably too ephemeral for publication. Since then, the Chinese Communists have achieved power, and we have come to recognize the totalitarian character of their thought and action. The springs of that character in some twenty-four of these persons, some of them active leaders in China today, are accessible here. Among the family relationships, the early experiences, the loves and psychological quirks, the hopes and fears and hates, we can find the biases that disposed the person toward the discipline of Communist dogma. Some of the distortions of Western attitudes that seem to us so grotesque—the "imperialist" phobias and the ambivalences concerning Christianity, for example—can be seen here in their development in particular individuals and thus we can begin to understand them and take them into account.

The stories are biased, of course, and always from the Communist point of view. Yet out of all the prejudice and political distortion come not only some absorbing yarns, but also a number of fundamental truths, unwittingly revealed, and more human data about the Chinese revolution of our time than is likely to appear again for years to come.

—R. C. N.

Hoover Institute and Library
on War, Revolution, and Peace
Stanford, California
October 15, 1951

PART ONE

Teachers and Students

Liao Ch'êng-chih

SECOND-GENERATION
REVOLUTIONARY

Liao Ch'êng-chih, center, as purchasing agent for the Red Army, in Hongkong, 1938. In the foreground is his sister, Cynthia Liao, for many years one of the secretaries to Mme Sun Yat-sen.

MISS WALES:

ONE first night at the theater in Yenan, I was attending a performance of a play about Spain called "The Spy." I was much impressed by the haughty realism with which a young man with a sharp, aristocratic profile took the part of one of Franco's Falangist officers grilling a Republican spy.

"Who is he?" I whispered. "He must be a professional."

"Oh no," I was informed, "that's Liao Ch'êng-chih, the son of Liao Chung-k'ai and Ho Hsiang-ning. He's expert at everything and professional at nothing. He translates from Japanese, German, French, Russian, and English, and writes articles and plays in Chinese. He can write Chinese characters faster than anybody else in Yenan and does stenographic notes of important conferences."

I was also told that he had the best sense of humor in the region, which was not lacking in wits and humorists. Moreover, he had a talent for painting in both Chinese and Western styles. He had inherited it from his mother, Ho Hsiang-ning, a noted revolutionary who had been known as a painter in her youth. He did water colors, etchings, woodcuts, and cartoons. As if this were not enough, he was admired for his singing and had taught a large number of soldiers the ":Hornpipe Jig," a song and dance he had learned from American sailors.

He was also in 1937 chief of the Press Relations Bureau and editor of the official magazine

Chieh Fang. He used the name "Ho Lu-hua," and refused to have his photograph taken, as he intended to work secretly in the Kuomintang areas.

I first met Liao Ch'êng-chih in 1937, in a very dirty room in Yenan. He was recovering from a serious attack of dysentery, and was much emaciated. I met him again about a year later in Hongkong, and did not recognize him —he had become so plump as to be called "Fatty" Liao. He now had a wife and children. This pleased his mother, who was anxious that the line of her husband (Liao Chung-k'ai, who at the time of his assassination had been second only to Sun Yat-sen in the Kuomintang) should not end without posterity.

25

It was only after much persuasion that Liao Ch'êng-chih told me his story. He was one of the most Americanized Chinese I have ever met, though he had never been in the United States. He spoke in jerky, fast Americanese, punctuated by slang and "God only knows." This manner of speech he apparently had picked up from his father, who was born in San Francisco. Liao Ch'êng-chih was full of wisecracks and was quick and nervous in all his movements.

In 1938 Liao was openly put in charge of the Eighth Route Army headquarters in Hongkong, where he became acquainted with many foreigners. At the time of the attack on the New Fourth Army in 1941, he was arrested on orders of Chiang Kai-shek. In prison he became so ill with tuberculosis that his life was despaired of by his mother and by his sister, Cynthia Liao Lee, who had been for many years an assistant to Madame Sun Yat-sen. In 1946 he was released.

In 1949 Liao became head of the All-China Democratic Youth Federation. He also became vice-director of the Commission of Overseas Chinese Affairs, his mother, Ho Hsiang-ning, being director. In addition he was a member of the Central Committee of the Communist party.

LIAO CH'ÊNG-CHIH:

MY father, Liao Chung-k'ai, was born in San Francisco, where my grandfather was an interpreter in an American bank. We are a Cantonese family, our ancestral home being in Huichow, Kwangtung. My father came to China for the first time at seventeen and, like most Chinese-Americans, hardly knew anything of the language then. After that he traveled most of the time. Because of my father's revolutionary activities, the family hardly ever stayed in one place longer than six years. It seemed to me that he was never at home with the family and was always either just escaping arrest or hiding in exile.

When Father was nineteen he married Miss Ho Hsiang-ning, the daughter of a rich Hongkong family of tea merchants. It was an arranged marriage, but the two became acquainted before the ceremony and liked each other, and their life together proved to be very happy. As my grandfather had died, leaving no money, just before Father left America, my father was too poor to continue in school. Mother provided the finances for the family, and the two went to Japan, where he attended Central University while she studied Chinese painting at the Women's Art College. She is a very good artist.

My mother is a remarkable woman. Although she was born in a rich compradore family, she soon became a revolutionary in her own right. Living in the imperialist atmosphere of Hongkong, she hated the British, especially after the events of 1925–27, although she always said Japan would be China's chief enemy.

Exiles in Japan

I was born in Tokyo in 1908 and spent the first eleven years of my life in Japan. Father was twenty-three when he arrived in Tokyo, and he there became one of the earliest members of Sun Yat-sen's revolutionary party, the T'ung Mêng Hui. He was in charge of the North China work of the T'ung Mêng Hui and traveled constantly between China and Japan, with Tientsin as his secret headquarters. With Yüan Shih-k'ai in control of China, Father could never stay there long because of the danger of arrest.

When I was several months old we went back to China for six months but had to escape and return to Japan. I went to a Catholic school in Tokyo, where I was the only Chinese boy among thirty Japanese. My grandfather had been a good Christian, but my father was not. There was very little of the Christian spirit in this school, and I learned to hate the Japanese Catholic teacher, who looked down on me as an inferior being. Whenever I could not answer questions in class he would say, "As a little Chinese pig, of course you don't know anything." Then when I was offended and stubbornly refused to try to answer questions, he would announce loudly, "I'm not surprised to find a Chinese acting like a pig. No Japanese would act this way." I often had to fight with the Japanese pupils to keep up my dignity, but the majority were not unkind to me. I had several good school friends and one special pal who once beat up another boy for insulting me.

I learned both Chinese and Japanese, and studied French five years. Mother spoke no English, but was a good Japanese student. Father sometimes taught English to me when he returned to Japan in the summers.

When I was a child, I knew that my father's profession was "patriotic work," but I did not know the nature of it, except that it was dangerous and that my mother was constantly worried about his safety. Many of his friends were executed.

I met all the leading T'ung Mêng Hui revolutionaries in Japan. Most of those that I knew are now dead. I talked to Sun Yat-sen many times. Father was his closest friend. Sun Yat-sen was a big husky man with whiskers and seemed to be a very earnest revolutionary. None of the others impressed me much except Chu Chih-hsin, who I think was the only other truly revolutionary character in the old T'ung Mêng Hui. He was killed in battle at Canton in 1924. Wang Ching-wei seemed to me to be only a mouth full of words.

I was always fond of drawing, like my mother. I remember that one day one of Father's Japanese friends came to see us and asked me to draw something for him. We knew that he was connected with the secret service and I had been told to be careful, but I decided to give him an eyeful. I drew a cartoon showing France and China together beating up Japan. His face turned red and he was furious.

Just after the World War all the exiled revolutionaries in Japan went back to China, hoping to be able to work there again. I went with my father, but my mother and my sister stayed in Japan. Mother had only two children, and my sister was five years older than I. They left Japan later, just before the earthquake of 1923. My sister had gone to a girls' school in Tokyo and later on became very political-minded. She married a revolutionary who was imprisoned. He was just released last month.

Most of the exiles went to Shanghai, where they published a new magazine called *Construction*. It was at this time that my father became interested in Marxism, like several others of the T'ung Mêng Hui, such as Tung Pi-wu. Up to this time, Father had wanted a democracy for China exactly as in America. Like Sun Yat-sen's, his political program was not very well developed. He had translated many American books into Chinese, including one that had considerable influence called *Politics for All People* —in Chinese, *Chüan Min Chêng Chih*. He had formerly been a bitter enemy of Liang Ch'i-ch'ao's ideas on a reformist monarchy. Now he wrote many articles introducing Marxist ideas into Chinese thought.

Sun Yat-sen's group was entirely financed by overseas Chinese. He did not get money from Canton, even. It was the American and Javanese Chinese who gave him the strongest support.

I couldn't go to school in Shanghai because there was no Cantonese school there and I didn't know the Shanghai or northern dialects. Father taught me English two hours a day, and his friends taught me mathematics. After fifteen or sixteen months there, I went to Canton and attended Christian College. I stayed there during the next six years.

Before leaving Japan, I had wanted to be in the navy. In Japan all the boys wanted to join the navy. I hoped to help build up

China's rotten navy someday. In college, however, I was chiefly interested in Western history. I got bad marks in algebra and physics but for some reason did very well in trigonometry and geometry. The one thing that fascinated me in Western history was the Industrial Revolution in England and the whole process of development of scientific industry. I used to ask myself why the steam engine never developed in China, why we must persist with our wasteful, backward handicraft work.

Christianity and Canton

Canton Christian College was one of the most conservative schools in all China. We had to listen to the idiotic preaching of the missionaries for two hours every day and during the whole of Sunday morning, together with two hours a week of Bible lessons. Most of the students hated this compulsory religionizing, and it had the opposite effect from that desired by the preachers. Practically the only students who really liked Christianity were the girls.

I was a very bad boy in school and made a lot of trouble for the authorities. A small group of us decided to change the trend of the college. The student government and the majority of the student body were under the Y.M.C.A. But we Kuomintang students had all the school workmen on our side. The college was on an island one mile from the city of Canton and had its own independent water and electric supply, as well as its own agricultural workers. There were altogether five hundred workmen connected with the college, including the cooks and farmers, and all were organized. There were eight hundred in the student body, and our Kuomintang members numbered only forty or fifty. The teachers hated us. After the May Thirtieth Incident in 1925 we chased away the only British teacher and all the American teachers soon left, too. It seems that only the most backward American missionaries come to China. Apparently, those Christians with progressive social and po-

litical ideas never arrive. The faculty dinned into the students their ideas that students must never participate in politics and that China must never try to fight any nation because it is too weak—and certainly must not fight the Christian nations from which the missionaries come. They talked incessantly about peace and internationalism, while China was under the heel of imperialism and bravely struggling to rise against injustice.

The Shakee Massacre, 1925

In protest against the May Thirtieth Incident in Shanghai, when British police fired upon a demonstration, the Canton workers went on strike and a big demonstration occurred spontaneously in Canton. Twenty or thirty thousand people participated. All the students in my college joined, and even the meekest and most backward demanded the removal of the British teacher.

On June 23 a second demonstration was organized in Canton to support the Shanghai movement. The demonstration started at one o'clock in the afternoon. The Hongkong strikers marched at the head of the column, the Canton peasants came second, the Boy Scouts made up the third unit, followed by the middle school and college students, and the Whampoa Academy cadets brought up the rear. Altogether a hundred thousand were marching on the streets of Canton. The atmosphere was full of excitement and the spirit was thrilling.

The students of Canton Christian College marched with the other schools just in front of the Whampoa cadets. Just as our students were passing by the Shameen Bridge in the Shakee district, which leads to the foreign concession at Shameen, we heard three shots fired by the British there, followed by the rattle of machine guns. It was the first time I was ever under fire. One of the bullets went through my cap. Being only seventeen, I was much upset. We were all taken by surprise. The first thing I saw when I looked around was a young boy-student torn open by a bullet. When doctors examined the body later on, they decided it was a dumdum bullet, because it had splattered as it came out. This made all of us furious, and there were other cases too.

I ran away as fast as I could to escape behind a building. Some of the students and cadets had sense enough to fall flat on their faces, but the younger boys and girls ran about in wild confusion and it was they who received most of the bullets. The British and French were behind sandbag barricades only thirty feet from the street along which the demonstration marched. The firing continued for twenty minutes, and we later received the report that one hundred eight were killed.[1] God knows how many were wounded. Half of those were Whampoa cadets. All the others were students. Perhaps the British meant to fire on the armed cadets, but because the students were just in front of them, they were in the line of fire as the machine guns swept the street. The students had been shouting anti-British slogans as we passed Shameen, and we thought this had made the foreign soldiers angry. Girls were killed and wounded as well as boys, and even some Boy Scouts were caught in the long-range machine-gun fire.

The real reason for the incident was that the British wanted to warn the Cantonese by terrorism not to have any anti-imperialist activity in the future. The Chinese did not fire first. Only a few of the Whampoa cadets returned the fire, individually and spontaneously. They immediately received an order to retreat, so they withdrew as soon as possible. Each cadet had only five bullets and had been told not to permit any conflict to arise.

Suddenly rain began to fall heavily, and the streets were flooded with red blood when the Red Cross arrived at the scene to take care of the wounded and the dead.

It was interesting that the demonstrators from Canton Christian College, the most reactionary and pro-British school, should also have been fired on by the imperialists. A few teachers had marched with us and one of them was killed. One Chinese student from America was killed, I remember. My sister, who also attended the college, was in the demonstration with me; the student she was in love with and later married, named Li, was wounded.

The Whampoa cadets were very angry—especially that the defenseless students had been fired on. Chiang Kai-shek, president of Whampoa, was not in the demonstration. Most of the cadets who took part have been killed by now, I guess, as they were largely leftist in sympathy. Chêng Kên, who is now with the Red Army, was in the Shakee massacre, I think.

Anti-British feeling rose to fever pitch. A general strike was declared and a boycott of British goods was put into effect. When the great Hongkong strike became effective, Hongkong was nothing but a dead island of rock.

I went back to school and organized a strike. After two or three weeks, however, the reactionary students of the college lost their patriotic fervor. Some even blamed the affair on the fact that we dared to have a demonstration! That showed Christian impotence. However, the American staff of the college were indignant against the massacre.

Assassination of Liao Chung-k'ai

My father was assassinated on August 20, 1925. I was living with him and Mother in Canton at that time. Mother had gone with him to the Kuomintang headquarters. They arrived at nine o'clock in the morning, and just as the two of them were walking up the stairs, father was shot. He had two bodyguards, but two or three men tried to kill him. One of Father's bodyguards was seriously wounded, but the other shot the assassin. The rest of the attackers ran away. The assassin lived for two days in the hospital, and confessed that Hu I-shêng, brother of Hu Han-min,[2] had ordered him to kill my father. Martial law was declared and the scandal caused the fall of Hu Han-min.

Mother was not hurt during the assassination. Always courageous, she was very cool and not nervous afterward. She was the second woman to join the T'ung Mêng Hui, the first being Madame Ch'iu Chin who was executed by the Manchus in Chekiang in 1907. Only a few women joined the T'ung Mêng Hui, and both my parents were among the founders of the Kuomintang, Father being the chief figure in the work of reorganization. He was the delegate who talked in Japan with Adolf Joffe—the Soviet Russian special envoy—about co-operation between Sun Yat-sen's party and the Soviet Union, and became the leader of the Left Wing of the Kuomintang.

The T'ung Mêng Hui was reorganized into the Chung-hua Kê-ming Tang and finally into the Kuomintang in 1924. The Sun-Joffe manifesto, which laid the basis for the Soviet-Kuomintang Entente, was issued on January 26, 1923. After that, Father was ordered by Sun Yat-sen to make arrangements with Joffe in Japan, and returned to Canton in March 1923 to report on these.

Father was Sun's right-hand man, or, rather, "left"-hand, and had his complete confidence. After studying Marxism from Japanese translations in 1919, Father had moved more and more to the left, and was wholeheartedly in favor of radicalizing the revolution and co-operating with Soviet Russia. His opinion had great influence on Sun Yat-sen. After the downfall of Sun's field marshal government at Canton—when Ch'ên Ch'iung-ming's revolt forced him to flee from Canton in 1922—Sun Yat-sen saw clearly that in order to complete the national revolution it was necessary to have international support, a broad mass basis, and a mass party. He realized at last that militarist methods could never be successful. In December 1922, he talked with Joffe in Shanghai, and after my father's discussions with Joffe in Japan, it was decided to reorganize the old party into the new Kuomintang along the lines of the Russian Communist party. My father and Sun Yat-sen took the initiative in this reorganization, supported by the younger rank and file, and the party developed rapidly. Wang Ching-wei was at first opposed to the reorganization. Chiang Kai-shek was silent. Hu Han-min, of the Right Wing, was openly antagonistic. Father was assassinated by the Rightist clique because he represented the Leftist leadership of the Kuomintang after Sun Yat-sen's death on March 12, 1925.

My father's political position was further to the left than Sun Yat-sen's. Sun's third book, *National Democracy*, criticized Marxism in a nonsensical way, but my father never did. He sympathized with the new Communist party from the beginning and talked of Lenin constantly. Sun Yat-sen never reached the point where he wanted to follow in Lenin's footsteps. Father was loyal to the Kuomintang, but saw clearly that a true democracy must lead to socialism in the end. I think I can say that he had become a real socialist by the time he died. He was firmly convinced that co-operation with the Communist party and with Soviet Russia was basic to the realization of the national-bourgeois-democratic revolution. Mao Tsê-tung, Chou Ên-lai, Lin Po-ch'ü, and other Communists were his close friends, and Chêng Kên was his student. I remember when I first met Chêng Kên.[3] He looked very handsome in his uniform when he came to call on us, and was then a female impersonator in school dramatics at Whampoa Academy because of his good looks.

At the time of his assassination, Father was the dominant leader of the Kuomintang. He was chairman of the Military Council, party representative for all the armies and military academies, head of the Workers' and Peasants' Department of the Kuomintang, and minister of finance in the National government organized in Canton on June 1,

1925. He therefore held all the key positions—the offices in control of the labor and peasant policies, of the soldiers, and of the finances. He worked valiantly to squeeze out every dollar of possible support for the revolution.

After Sun Yat-sen's death, Father was the only strong leader who resolutely insisted upon maintaining the bloc between the Communists and the Kuomintang, and because of this he made many enemies. Wang Ching-wei came next on the left, being chairman of the National government. Hu Han-min and his Right Wing were out of power because of Father's dominant control, and they hated the bloc with the Communists. Hu Han-min had a position in the Foreign Office, but no control over affairs at all. He apparently thought Father's assassination would break the power of the Leftists. Hu had been put out of power after Sun's death and was anxious to stage a comeback. He and his brother, Hu I-shêng, made connections with the British compradores and received financial support from the Hongkong and Shanghai Bank. They had already begun working secretly among the Kwangtung troops.

At that time Chiang Kai-shek was president of Whampoa Academy and commander of two divisions but was not very influential. He was considered leftist, not middle, and was popular because it was thought he was pro-Communist, though he kept silent and never talked politics. Some thought Chiang had a hand in my father's death, but that was not true. He was entirely dependent upon Father for his money and arms, and this would have been suicide.

The Kuomintang armed forces were divided into: the Kwangtung troops under Hsü Ch'ung-chih, who were the most reactionary; the Yünnan troops under Chu P'ei-tê, consisting of four to six divisions which had become revolutionary in 1917; and the Hunan troops under T'an Yen-k'ai, who were more or less useless.

It was a period of crisis, a struggle for leadership between the Left and the Right. But the Leftists still kept control, more or less, until 1927.

Father was only forty-eight when he was killed. He was a very, very short man, but strong and healthy. He was a man of action, and not of a peaceable nature, and he strongly opposed religion as an opiate of the people. He saw the necessity of force and struggle to overthrow the old society. Though he was a Confucian scholar, like most of his friends, the only classics he ever quoted were obscure bits that sanctioned revolt. He was very brave, honest, and incorruptible. I always admired him immensely. When he was assassinated, I pledged myself to carry out his life's work to the best of my ability.

After my father's assassination, the Right tried to create a mutiny, but before they could prepare this, they were disarmed. However, the Kuomintang Left still took no decisive action against them. They kept their underground forces and encircled Chiang Kai-shek.

Chang Ching-kiang and the Chekiang bankers were already beginning secretly to buy over Chiang Kai-shek, as is always the way in China to win generals to the counterrevolution. The financial condition of the Canton government was difficult and military men were uncertain of the future. Most of the revenues seemed to come from taxes, especially on gambling and opium, and the second source of support was from overseas Chinese in the South Seas and America, who had not yet withdrawn support from the Kuomintang. After the March Twentieth Incident in 1926, Chiang Kai-shek won the support of the Rightists, and this affair indicated to these elements that he might be relied upon for counterrevolutionary purposes in the future. On that date Chiang took the occasion to dismiss all Left elements from the army and Whampoa Academy. Wang Ching-wei was dismissed and Chiang Kai-shek remained the chief figure. After my father's death, Wang and Chiang had been jockeying for position, Chiang being on the right of Wang. At that time Chiang dared not join with Hu Han-min's Rightists, however, but as soon as he occupied Nanchang, he openly co-operated with them. The Left took no action against Chiang after March 20 because they still trusted him as a military figure, though he was suspected politically. It was thought he would not dare betray, because of his need for arms and support from the Left, which controlled these vital supplies. Also, the Northern Expedition, which began on July 1, 1926, was in preparation, and it was considered unwise to permit any split among the revolutionary forces.

Just after my father's assassination, I organized a strike of all the workmen at Canton Christian College, and at the same time my sister's future husband led a supporting student movement. We demanded better wages for the workers, the abolition of compulsory Sunday services, and lifting of the ban on cigarette smoking. The strike was the first the workmen had ever tried, and it was victorious. They were surprised and delighted. The teachers tried to force Li and me to leave school, but they dared not expel me because of my father's influential position in Canton.

This college was a truly colonial school for the sons and daughters of the compradore-bourgeoisie, and did its work well. Most of the students were ignorant of political affairs and had little common sense. I disliked intensely the type of young compradore that I found there. These students, true to their compradore origin rising out of dependence upon the foreign imperialists, attacked our revolutionary students, saying that the struggle against imperialism was nonsense. The reaction grew stronger and stronger, so we organized a second strike in 1927 to try to break it. Then April 15 came.[4]

Our strike had the support of progressive forces outside, so we were able to take a strong stand. The school closed down and most of the pickets and strikers had to go into Canton city. The school authorities asked the police to come to the school and guided them in their attempt to make arrests. Three of the worker leaders were executed. Such is Christianity in China! Fortunately, the leftist students escaped before the secret-service agents made their search. About twenty of these were Communists. I was only a Kuomintang Leftist, but sympathetic with the Communists. After a while the school reopened.

At Waseda University in Japan

During the arrests, I left the school and went to Japan, where I entered Waseda University. I didn't do much studying there, but instead organized a "League for the Investigation of Social Science."

In 1927 there were about four thousand Chinese students in all Japan. They had a general student association with headquarters in Tokyo. The leftist students also had a separate organization, including both Chinese and Japanese. This leftist society numbered three hundred Chinese and two hundred Japanese members in Tokyo, of whom there were six or eight at Waseda. Most of the Chinese members of this group were those who spoke Japanese well. It was necessary to spend a year or so studying Japanese, because no classes were held in Chinese.

I stayed in Japan ten months, then was kicked out after the Tsinan Incident on May 3, 1928. We had organized an anti-Japanese demonstration in Tokyo, and the police ordered us to leave the country. Some were arrested and tortured, and about forty of us ran away.

Organizing Chinese Seamen in Europe

I went to Shanghai and started anti-Japanese underground work there for a short time. Then I went to Germany and around Europe, where I carried on political activi-

A *shao kuei* (little devil) —one of the boy-soldiers serving with the Red Army as nurses and orderlies. Ink and wash drawing by Liao Ch'êng-chih, 1937, under his revolutionary pseudonym Ho Lu-hua.

ties among Chinese seamen in Hamburg, Rotterdam, Antwerp, and Marseilles.

These seamen all worked on foreign boats and were very anti-imperialist and nationalistic. The Chinese were segregated from the other sailors, so as to make strikes impossible. The Americans usually bribe the Chinese not to join the strikes of the American sailors. Even the Chinese mess-boys, however, were patriotic, because most of them are literate and in their varied travels to all ports they see the unfairness and oppression levied on Chinese in foreign countries.

There were about thirty thousand Chinese seamen in Europe then, but no important action was possible because they were so circumscribed and suppressed in every way. There was no possibility of doing anything except in co-operation with the foreign seamen. All the Chinese saw this clearly. Holland was the best place for action, as most of the Chinese seamen congregated there. In America our seamen could not even go ashore, but in Europe this was permitted. In Rotterdam, when the Chinese sailors are jobless, the Dutch government refuses to give up their passports. The foreman gives the sailor a job, say for three voyages, and the most he can earn is six pounds, which the foreman holds for him. If the sailor has no trouble whatever with the foreman, he can stay in the seamen's dormitories in Holland. If the foreman wishes, he can put the sailor out of the dormitories and then the sailor is jobless and homeless and without money to live. In general, I found that Chinese seamen were treated like indentured slaves.

While I was in Europe I organized several hundred seamen, all by careful secret activity. None of the seamen ever joined the Kuomintang except a few headmen, but most were sympathetic with the Communists. In Berlin I appeared in public as a student. In Rotterdam I was a teacher giving English lessons to the seamen. I led two strikes there and was arrested as a Communist. I was in prison two weeks. The treatment and the food were so good that I didn't want to come out! In one big room the prison had thrown together stowaways, opium smugglers, and other elements of all nationalities. All these people were good to me and gave me cigarettes and matches. Upon my release, I was deported from Holland. We organized many strikes, here and there, some of which were successful, others not. The usual procedure of the ship's authorities during such strikes was to block the docks, break windows and pretend that the sailors had done it as grounds for arrest, and send for the police. The Chinese were always beaten up, but Belgium was the place where they received the cruelest treatment of all. Chinese are liable to a penalty of from one to six months in prison for even participating in a strike.

Once in Hamburg I led a Chinese strike on

a British ship. The British broke the glass windows and called the German police, swearing that our Chinese seamen had done this. Some German agitators had helped us and had been brutally kicked off the ship. I told this to the police and demanded that our German friends be returned to us before negotiating with the authorities. All the Germans were pleased at this.

In Hamburg, Antwerp, and Rotterdam we had Chinese strikes in which the foreign sailors stood as pickets for us and joined our meetings to show solidarity. They saw that unless the wages of the Chinese were raised, their own could never be kept up but could be cut any time by the threat of employing Chinese seamen.

Finally I was arrested in Hamburg and was deported. Then I went to the Soviet Union for a while, and back to Shanghai.

Arrest in Shanghai

I arrived in Shanghai just after the Shanghai fighting in 1932 and was immediately betrayed by a former comrade and arrested by British-controlled police in the International Settlement. I had been detained at the Bureau of Public Safety for two weeks when I decided to fool the police by saying I would betray the whereabouts of another comrade in exchange for my own liberty. I led the police to my mother's house, as she happened to be in Shanghai then. Luckily she was at home. When she found that I was a prisoner, she raised heaven and earth and secured my release.

Several of us had been arrested at that time (including Chêng Kên, an old friend of Canton days, who was sent to Nanking on the same train with me and was also released) and one of my best comrades was sent to Nanking and executed.

As soon as I was free I went to the Oyü-wan[5] soviet and from there I set out with Hsü Hsiang-ch'ien for Szechuan. After the Long March I came to Yenan.

Tung Pi-wu

COMMUNIST SCHOLAR

MISS WALES:

TUNG PI-WU is a veteran of three revolutions. In 1911 he became a member of the T'ung Mêng Hui—Sun Yat-sen's party which was the forerunner of the Kuomintang. He was prominent in the revolution of 1925–27 within the Kuomintang. And since then he has participated actively in the Communist-led revolutionary movement.

When I met Tung Pi-wu in 1937, he was chairman pro tem of the Shensi-Kansu-Ninghsia government, and was in charge of installing the new machinery of universal suffrage which took the place of the former soviets. I last saw him in 1945, in San Francisco, when he was a member of the Chinese delegation at the United Nations Conference. Meantime he had been elected a member of the National People's Political Council at Hankow in 1938, and had been for many years a member of the Political Bu-reau of the Communist party and one of the chief liaison figures between the Communists and the Kuomintang.

When the North China Liberated Area was formed in 1948, he became chairman in Peking. In 1949 he was elected vice-premier of the State Administration Council in Peking; in 1950 he was elected vice-chairman of the People's Relief Administration of China, of which Madame Sun Yat-sen became chairman.

Tung Pi-wu is a grizzled veteran of remarkable physical strength and vitality, and has a cheerful, outgoing personality. He wears an old-fashioned mandarin mustache, and speaks in halting English when required. The life-story that he told me is chiefly about his native region, Wuhan—that cluster of cities composed of Hankow and Hanyang on the north bank of the Yangtze River and Wuchang opposite them on the south.

TUNG PI-WU:

IT seems to me that I have lived through many ages in the life of China. Under the Manchu dynasty I wrote the "Eight-Legged Essay" for the imperial examinations in archaic *wen li* characters. Now I write my Chinese in Latinized characters. Every day of my life has been spent in revolutionary work since the Chinese Revolution broke out on October 10, 1911, in Wuchang.

Although the place where I was born in 1886, Huangan *hsien*,[1] Hupeh, was not very far from Wuhan, it was very backward, and only a few persons ever went to school. Nevertheless, I was determined to have a modern education and went to Wuchang, where I passed my examinations well and entered middle school.

At fifteen I became a hsiu-ts'ai scholar under the dynasty. My father was also a scholar, and worked as tutor in a rich family. My uncle and a brother were likewise teachers in the city. I never did any work as a boy, since my family owned no land. There were thirty of us living together in one big house, and all the earning members of this large family worked at the liberal professions. My immediate family consisted of one brother, two sisters, and my parents.

When I arrived in Wuchang I lived at the dormitory of a well-known club called the "Society for Increasing Knowledge Day by Day." This was the original revolutionary center of Hupeh Province, the province which led the 1911 Revolution. The society had been organized by Liu Chia-jên, a Hupeh native who died in prison in 1909 or 1910, having been arrested about 1906 or 1907. Liu was a devout Christian and some of the other members were also Christians. The society was small but had a great influence, especially through the personality of Liu Chia-jên. It had a reading club which disseminated information widely.

At that time I was sympathetic to the idea of revolution but did not want to devote much of my time to it. My aim was to support my family in the approved tradition and to raise their standard of living. Some of my friends organized a new secret group, but I had no desire to join it. However, I was a good student and always read all the new magazines and newspapers I could get my hands on, though such printed matter had to be bought secretly. I received a good deal of influence from the *Hsin-Min Pao* ["New People's Magazine"] edited by Liang Ch'i-ch'ao. Later this was edited by members of the T'ung Mêng Hui, including Hu Han-min, Wang Ching-wei, and Chang T'ai-yen.

The educational system was then divided into a junior middle-school course of five years and a senior middle-school course of three years. After I had finished junior middle school, my family had no money for me to continue, but the principal liked me and set me to correcting student essays so that I could earn my way. This work was difficult because the principal always looked over the essays after I had corrected them and held me responsible for every mistake. After only a few months in senior middle school I got a job teaching in a middle school at Huangchoufu. I was then about twenty-three.

I had taught at my new job only two weeks when the Revolution broke out at Wuchang on October 10, 1911. I rushed to join the uprising as quickly as possible and three days later arrived in Wuchang ready for work. From that day on I have been constantly engaged in revolution as a profession.

The Wuchang Incident

At Wuchang I found out what had happened. The Chinese soldiers of the Manchu garrison there had been permeated by revolutionary ideas, and part of one division of doubtful loyalty had been sent to Szechuan with T'ang Huang, a high Manchu official, to investigate the railway trouble in Szechuan caused by the Manchus' desire to "nationalize" the railroad there. This uprising was the signal for rebellion. The rest of the division in Wuchang raised the standard of revolt and attacked the viceroy's yamen on the night of October 10, only to find that the viceroy and the garrison commander had already fled to Shanghai. During the night they occupied the whole city of Wuchang. This uprising was spontaneous and had no leadership at first. It had been caused prematurely by the fact that on the afternoon of October 9 a bomb had exploded in one of the secret storehouses of the T'ung Mêng Hui in the Russian Concession in Hankow. The Russian police found revolutionary documents, seals, flags, badges, and plans in the storehouse and reported the whole thing to Jui Chêng, the viceroy at Wuchang. The viceroy promptly ordered that the city gates be closed and raided the T'ung Mêng Hui headquarters in Wuchang. He found a list of the officers and soldiers belonging to the T'ung Mêng Hui. Thus the garrison had to revolt immediately to forestall suppression. Since the revolutionaries then in Wuchang had had no military experience, they decided to ask Li Yüan-hung, a colonel in the Manchu army, to be temporary commander. When they went to his house for this purpose, Li Yüan-hung was terrified and hid under his wife's bed, expecting to be killed as an Imperial officer. One of his heels was sticking out from under the bed, however, and he was pulled out. He agreed to become commander, brought over his brigade, and co-operated with General Huang Hsing[2] in forming the revolutionary military government in Wuchang after Huang arrived on October 20 to assume the supreme command.

The Manchu officials in Wuhan were so surprised and demoralized by the uprising that on October 12 the revolutionaries were able to take both Hankow and Hanyang, including the arsenal.

I was given a post in the supply department of the Wuchang revolutionary army, chief of which was Chang Yi-wu. The people helped our army very much, bringing food and water, especially during the battles at San-tao-ch'iao and such places.

We fought several weeks against the Manchu troops stationed on the north bank of the Yangtze River, just opposite Wuchang on the south bank. Our forces altogether consisted of only seven thousand troops, made up of part of the one division and one brigade. Against us the Imperial Army had much greater forces. At first the revolutionaries won the engagements, but later the Manchus increased their troops by twenty-four thousand well-equipped men and we were defeated. On October 30 the Imperial forces under Fêng Kuo-chang and Tuan Ch'i-jui recaptured Hankow after two days' fighting and burned almost half the city, excluding the foreign concessions. On November 27 the enemy also captured Hanyang, though General Huang Hsing, a great fighter, defended it during two weeks of battle with three thousand men against twenty thousand. But we still held Wuchang in spite of our difficult position. The Manchus then sent a warship which launched an attack from the river bank and this attack was what finally defeated us.

After the fall of Hanyang, Huang Hsing went to Shanghai. Under his leadership Nanking was captured by revolutionary troops. When he left, command of the remaining troops in Wuchang was given to Chang Yi-wu, my former chief. Chang Yi-wu was the real soul of the uprising in Wuchang. He was later killed by Yüan Shih-k'ai after the "Second Revolution" in Kwangsi in 1913, which was organized to overthrow Yüan.

In the meantime, I had begun work in the financial department of the military government in Wuchang.

The Wuchang revolutionary movement had been organized by three groups: the Literary Society led by Chang Yi-wu, the T'ung Mêng Hui, and a third revolutionary group led by Sun Wu. While I was in the financial department of the government at Wuchang, I joined the T'ung Mêng Hui, at the end of 1911. The T'ung Mêng Hui had a council and an executive committee in Hupeh. The chairman was Su Yin—he was once mayor of Nanking. I was elected one of the twenty members of the council.

After the Wuchang uprising on October 10, the revolutionary movement spread fast. When General Huang Hsing arrived in Shanghai, following his defeat at Hanyang, he took command of the expedition against Nanking and succeeded in capturing this important position on December 3. The Imperial troops in several places mutinied and joined the revolt, the provinces refused to send remittances to the Throne, and even high officials of the dynasty showed tendencies toward joining the rebellion. After the fall of Nanking an armistice was arranged and negotiations were begun with the Imperial delegation which had arrived in Shanghai for this purpose. The revolutionary leaders had no co-ordinated plan. General Huang Hsing and Colonel Li Yüan-hung were struggling for control, and Sun Yat-sen was still en route from America. On December 21 Sun Yat-sen finally arrived in Hongkong and proceeded to Nanking. He was elected president of the provisional republic on December 29, taking office on January 1 [1912], while Huang Hsing was made Minister of War. In order to win over all the Chinese in the north without delay, Sun volunteered to give up the presidency to Yüan Shih-k'ai—who was in command of most of the Imperial armies—if he would agree to join the Republic. Yüan agreed. Sun resigned, although he distrusted Yüan Shih-k'ai, and on February 15 Yüan was elected provisional president in his place, changing the capital of the republic to Peking.

The revolutionaries paid dearly for their bargain with Yüan Shih-k'ai. In 1913 he declared war on Sun Yat-sen and, with loans from the foreign powers, defeated him. On December 11, 1915, Ts'ai Ao—a good revolutionary, with whom Chu Tê worked—declared his province, Yünnan, independent of Yüan Shih-k'ai's regime. Kweichow, Kwangsi, and Kwangtung followed, and by the spring of 1916 revolt had broken out everywhere. On March 22 Yüan Shih-K'ai was forced to abdicate. Before his death on June 6, he recommended Li Yüan-hung, former vice-president, as president of the republic. Li assumed this office. Sun Yat-sen had gone to Japan during those years to reorganize his activities.

In the meantime, I had been doing political work in Hupeh Province. I was made head of the Salt Tax Bureau in Ichang for a while, but I did not want to become an official. I felt that I needed more knowledge to prepare myself for the future. When Li Yüan-hung betrayed[3] to Yüan Shih-k'ai, the members of the T'ung Mêng Hui opposed him. We organized a small uprising in Hupeh but this failed when Yüan sent troops to Hupeh. The members of the T'ung Mêng Hui had to flee for their lives, and I and a comrade went to Japan in 1913 to join Sun Yat-sen. In 1913 Sun had reorganized the T'ung Mêng Hui into the Chung-hua Kê-ming Tang [Chinese Revolutionary party]. *Kê-ming* is an old word which first appeared in the *Yi Ching*, in the old classics. Literally, it means "change fate." It was formerly a very rare word, and it was first given the true meaning of "revolution" by Sun Yat-sen. This Chung-hua Kê-ming party was reorganized into the Kuomintang in 1924.

Sun Yat-sen's Military Alliances

I joined the new Chung-hua Kê-ming Tang in Tokyo, and worked there with Sun Yat-sen, Liao Chung-k'ai, Chü Chên, and others, meanwhile studying at the Japanese Law College. In 1915 Japan presented the Twenty-one Demands to Yüan Shih-k'ai, and we Chinese students in Japan strongly opposed this. I was ordered back to China to do secret work among the military forces, as it was always Sun Yat-sen's policy to influence the troops. When I arrived in Wuhan, I found my situation very dangerous and had to flee to my home village for safety. Even so, I was arrested there in 1915 and was imprisoned for half a year. After Yüan Shih-k'ai's power was broken, in 1916, I returned to Tokyo to continue my college course in law.

When the Russian Revolution broke out in 1917 I was greatly influenced by it. I read the news in the papers with keen interest, and new ideas began to ferment in my head.

Upon graduating from the Japanese Law College, I returned to China again to do secret military work. My job was to influence the troops of Ts'ai Chi-ming stationed at Lich'uanhsien on the Hupeh-Szechuan border. This army had joined the revolution in 1911, but its fighting power was not very good because many of the men were bandits. I worked with these troops and had considerable success. (Later about three thousand of them defended Sun Yat-sen's Canton government when it was formed.)

Ts'ai Chi-ming's army had little money, so in 1918 I went out to try to collect funds for it. Ten days after I left, Ts'ai decided to unite with another so-called "revolutionary" army under T'an K'ai-min. Ts'ai was killed by some of T'an's men, also partly bandit, and I went to Shanghai to report these happenings to Sun Yat-sen. At that time peace negotiations were in progress between the Northern government and the South, so I had a little time to study. I read all the Marxist literature I could find and studied the problems of the Versailles Conference with interest. Some of this I had to read in English, which I had studied in middle school. (I later continued my English study in the U.S.S.R.)

At this time the magazines *New Youth* and

Renaissance were taking China by storm, and soon the May Fourth Movement[4] began, in 1919. I did not participate in this movement. Sun Yat-sen was influenced by it, but inactive.

After the May Fourth Movement, I wondered about new tactics and methods of revolutionary work, and discussed these problems with my friends. A Chinese student named Li Han-ching had just returned from Japan, where he had read many Marxist books. He told me about these, and that was how I had become so much interested in Marxism. From my own experience, I decided that secret work among the troops was useless and that it was necessary to lay the foundation for a people's movement. We had always worked with the military leaders, who usually betrayed because they had no revolutionary understanding. We never worked with the common soldiers nor even with the common bandits. Our policy was opportunistic and without foundation. The whole 1911 Revolution had been more or less a militarist maneuver, in spite of the good support from the rank and file of the soldiers. I decided that the revolution had to have a real mass base, and wanted to start a newspaper or school for this purpose.

I went to Wuhan and helped organize the Wuhan Middle School, together with seven other teachers, all without money. We used two rooms in an old building belonging to the educational department of the government. Our school opened in 1920, and we were the first school to teach *pai hua*.[5] I taught both *wên yen* and *pai hua* to our students, and had hopes that the *pai hua* would create a new consciousness among the people. I used no textbooks, but chose current problems for essays. The students gladly used *pai hua* in their work.

At that time teachers such as we not only received no salary but also had to find money to support the schools, so I also taught in a girls' school to earn these needed funds. We had one hundred twenty pupils when the school opened. Later we expanded by adding one new class every term.

Founding the Chinese Communist Party

Until this time there had been only a few Marxist societies in China. Then, in 1920, Li Han-ching—the returned student from Japan who had been my tutor in Marxism— planned to help organize a Communist party in Shanghai and came to Wuhan to talk with me. I decided to join and took the responsibility for organizing the foundation of the Hupeh branch of the party which was formed in September 1921.

The central Chinese Communist party had been founded in May 1921, when Ch'ên Tu-hsiu arrived in Shanghai for this purpose, together with Li Ta-chao. I was not present at this meeting but I joined the First Conference[6] held in Shanghai in July 1921. Each province that was represented sent two delegates, and the returned students from Japan sent one delegate—Chou Fu-hai,[7] who later betrayed and joined the Kuomintang. Hupeh Province sent Ch'ên T'an-ch'iu and myself. Hunan sent Ho Tsao-hên—later killed while serving with the Red Army at the same time as Ch'ü Ch'iu-po, about 1935 —and Mao Tsê-tung. Peking sent Chang Kuo-t'ao and Liu Jên-ching, now a Trotskyist. Shanghai sent Li Han-ching, who was executed in Hankow in 1927, and Li Ta, now a liberal who became a professor in Pingta University. Kwangtung sent Ch'ên Kung-po, who later betrayed and became Minister of Industries in the Nanking government, and Pao Hui-shêng, who also became an official of the Kuomintang—in the Department of Home Affairs. Shantung sent Têng Ên-ming and Wang Ching-wei— both executed later. Two delegates from the Comintern also attended this conference. One was from Holland—we called him Malin[8] in Chinese. The other was a Russian whose name I have forgotten.

It was originally intended that Ch'ên Tu-hsiu should be chairman of this conference but he happened to be in Canton at that time, so Chang Kuo-t'ao took his place. All the historical data of this first conference have been lost. We decided upon an anti-imperialist, antimilitarist manifesto, but we haven't a single copy of this first document of the party. I remember that one of the points of debate was whether or not officials and technical workers could be members. Some opposed this. The resolution passed was for a "closed door" policy, to keep membership secret and "pure." We also decided that the party members could not join any other parties, such as that of Sun Yat-sen. Our main work was to be that of expanding the party. I remember that the Central Committee elected at the conference included Ch'ên Tu-hsiu, Li Ta-chao, Chang Kuo-t'ao, Li Han-ching, and others.

Several of these party "fathers" besides myself were old T'ung Mêng Hui members, such as Ch'ên Tu-hsiu, Tai Chi-t'ao, and Sun Hsüan-lo.

The Wuhan Middle School was the Communist center of Hupeh Province then. The party branch had been founded by five of us, and soon ten of my most progressive pupils organized a Socialist Youth branch. Three of the five founders later left the party. One became a liberal, one is now in Nanking, and one is a lawyer in Hankow. Only Ch'ên T'an-ch'iu and I kept the faith. I don't know what has become of Ch'ên, but I think he is still alive.

Wuhan soon became an important Communist stronghold. It was planned to open a school for foreign language as a center of propaganda, and a Russian Communist named Mamayev and his wife came to Wuhan to teach, but the project could not be realized so they returned to Shanghai.

In the summer of 1921 Ch'ên Tu-hsiu himself came to Wuhan and made a speech in Wen Hua University, a Christian school. He happened to meet one of the workmen connected with the university, whom he influenced to join the Hupeh [Communist] party and through him made a contact with

some workers in a cotton factory. Thus the party spread to industry.

At that time in Wuhan there was a group of radical young people, Utopian and semi-anarchist in their ideology, who were interested in the New Village Movement. This centered in Chung Hua College, and the group had organized the Li Chün Book Company. Their leader was a brilliant young man named Yün Tai-ying, who had great influence over the students and was one of the best youth leaders China ever had. These "New Villagers" did not believe in Marxism, but they soon began discussing it and many joined the Communists. Yün Tai-ying joined the party in Szechuan later on and was executed in 1932.

At our first congress in Hupeh, the party had thirty delegates. We sent the students out into the villages to organize unions and do propaganda, and their work had much influence during the Pinhan railway strike in 1923.

My next work was to go to Szechuan to revive some of my old tactics of winning over the military forces to revolution. At that time certain troops in Szechuan had an anti-militarist tendency, so I went there to develop this movement. I spent a year in this work, and then the party ordered me to return to Hupeh. Also, the Wuhan Middle School was badly in need of funds and I had to return to collect money for it somehow.

On my return I was delighted to find how well the party work had progressed, both in the schools and in the factories. At that time the Communist labor movement centered in the Pinhan railway workers and we had a labor secretariat in Changhsintien.

My father, who was teaching in Wuchang, became ill and I had to take him home, where he soon died. When I returned to Wuhan the Pinhan railway strike of 1923 broke out, Chang Kuo-t'ao being in charge of this.

I was still able to remain in Wuchang, because I was known only as a Kuomintang member and not as a Communist. Even my family had no idea I was a Communist until the period of the Great Revolution of 1925–27, when my wife came to Wuhan and found out. She was an old-fashioned wife, to whom my family had married me in 1910. I have had only one child, who died.

Wuhan, 1925–27

In the spring of 1925 I was again delegated to do secret work among the troops. One of my friends in the Kuomintang wanted me to go to Szechuan with him for this purpose. We spent February in Szechuan, then went to Liaoning, in Manchuria, in March, and back to Chahar, Changchiakou, and Peking. I was in Peking when the May Thirtieth Incident broke out in Shanghai, and received a letter from the Party ordering me to go to Wuhan. This was during the "United Front" period of the Kuomintang and Communist parties, and I was put in charge of this liaison work in Hupeh because of my good Kuomintang connections. The Kuomintang was still a secret party in Wuhan and the terror was strong. After a while, I went to Shanghai to discuss the United Front work with Ch'ên Tu-hsiu and then proceeded to Canton.

The Kuomintang had then issued the call for its Second National Congress to be held in Canton and had sent me a telegram to join the congress as a delegate from Hupeh. This congress was held in January 1926. Since Liao Chung-k'ai had been murdered and Hu Han-min was in exile abroad, the congress was dominated by Wang Ching-wei, T. V. Soong, Tai Chi-t'ao, T'an P'ing-shan, Lin Po-ch'ü, Ch'ên Kung-p'o, and Kan Nai-kuang—the latter five all having been Communists. At this conference Chiang Kai-shek was elected to the Central Executive Committee—the first time he received recognition by the Kuomintang.

This conference was under the influence of the Leftists entirely, and its resolutions were excellent. Our important resolutions were to strengthen the United Front, to expand the antimilitarist and anti-imperialist movement and the alliance between all the oppressed nations, and to strengthen the peasant movement.

Several Rightists were expelled from the Kuomintang, and the Kuomintang Leftists expressed the hope that many Communists would be elected to the Central Executive Committee in order to consolidate the United Front. The Communist party, however, did not want to come out so openly in control of the Kuomintang and permitted only a few Communists to be elected to the Central Executive Committee. These were: T'an P'ing-shan, who was later expelled from the C.P.[9] after the Nanchang Uprising[10] in 1927 and became the leader of the Third party; Lin Po-ch'ü; Yün Tai-ying, the youth leader; Yü Hsü-tê, who afterward left the C.P. and became a professor at Yenching University; and Wu Yü-chang, now in Moscow. Mao Tsê-tung and I were elected to the Alternate Central Executive Committee.

After the Congress I went to Wuhan in 1926 to organize a progressive newspaper of neutral policy called *Tsa Kuang* ["Light of Hupeh and Hunan"]. After four months in Wuhan I went to Changsha to do some important United Front work. My mission was to win over T'ang Shêng-chih and his army to the United Front. I was sent by the Kuomintang as its delegate, together with Pai Ch'ung-hsi and Ch'ên Ming-shu. We were successful, and T'ang Shêng-chih—then in control of Hunan Province—and his army immediately became the vanguard of the Great Revolution.

I had arrived in Changsha in March and in April received a telegram from the Kuomintang to attend a conference at Canton in my capacity as a member of the Alternate Central Executive Committee. After this conference I went to Wuhan and worked again on the newspaper *Tsa Kuang*, also continuing my secret military work aiming to sabotage the rear of the enemy.

On July 9, 1926, the Northern Expedition against the northern war lords began, and the armies swept victoriously across southern China.

T'ang Shêng-chih occupied Changsha, and Chiang Kai-shek, commander in chief of the expedition, also arrived there. I went to Changsha to talk with Chiang about various military problems. As is his habit, he merely listened and grunted occasionally.

When I returned to Wuhan, *Tsa Kuang* had been suppressed, and I had to hide in the foreign concession, as Wu P'ei-fu had occupied the city.

At that time my work was to carry out sabotage and destruction against enemy troops. I organized the destruction of the bridge at Ting-ssü-ch'iao so our army could get a good strategic position for occupying the city. Our troops occupied Hankow in August, and my work was then moved to the Kuomintang provincial headquarters. Wuchang was still in Wu P'ei-fu's hands, however. Before we occupied Wuchang, Chiang Kai-shek came to Hankow for a few days and then went to Nanchang to fight Sun Ch'uan-fang.

As soon as Hankow was taken the labor movement in the Wuhan cities expanded very rapidly, and also the peasant movement elsewhere. And when Wuchang fell, we built up the Kuomintang and reorganized the defeated troops of Wu P'ei-fu into the revolutionary armies. At that time Chiang Kai-shek wanted to organize a new Kuomintang provincial committee in Hupeh and I was asked to be a member. I hesitated— and because of my attitude Chiang Kai-shek knew I was a Communist. When Chiang-Kai-shek left Wuhan, the government decided to move from Canton to Wuhan in November.

At that time T'ang Shêng-chih and Ch'ên Ming-shu were in Wuhan and were very leftist in sympathy, as was Chang Fa-k'uei. Chiang Kai-shek became frightened by the rising mass movement and was afraid the Communist party would seize sovereignty at Wuhan, so he wanted to change the seat of the new government to Nanchang—his own stronghold. When Chiang arrived at Chochow, in Kiangsi, the Kuomintang sent me as delegate to ask him to come to Wuhan, where a Kuomintang conference would be held. Chiang didn't agree to having this conference in Wuhan, but in the end decided to come. When the conference opened, Chiang made a speech. The Hupeh provincial Kuomintang sent him a banner. Chiang went around and investigated conditions in both Wuchang and Hankow and what he saw made him very sad, so he went away. He was unhappy about the great mass movement that was developing under leftist influence. However, when the British Concession in Hankow was returned to the Wuhan government, Chiang could not refuse to recognize Wuhan's authority, but he bided his time for a counterstroke from central China.

On his return to Kiangsi from Wuhan, Chiang Kai-shek ordered the execution of many Communists in Kian because of their work in March [1927].

In April [1927] Chiang Kai-shek occupied Nanking, while his other military wing, led by Ho Ying-ch'in, went from Chekiang to Shanghai, which was occupied in March.

By the time Chiang had occupied Nanking, the labor and peasant movement in Hunan and Hupeh was very militant, and also the labor movement in Shanghai. Several gunboats prepared to attack Nanking and the Japanese sent emissaries to talk with Chiang, so he betrayed the revolution and created the new pro-imperialist Nanking government.

During these months, I was in Wuhan. The C.P. decided to participate in the Wuhan government, and I was made a member of the Hupeh provincial government—as head of the Peasants' and Workers' Bureau.

Then the split began. The financial condition of Wuhan was very bad because of the blockade by Nanking and the imperialists. Also the Wuhan government's armies had to fight the Tungpei army.

On May 21 the reaction began in earnest, when Hsia Tou-yin, Hsü K'ê-hsiang (in Hunan), and Yang Shên began killing the revolutionaries. Hsia Tou-yin's army was near Wuhan. The Wuhan government sent troops to fight him and destroyed his forces.

Then the revolutionary army returned from its victory over the Tungpei troops, and in May 1927, the "Peasants' and Workers' Delegates Congress of the Pacific" opened in Wuhan. These delegates represented two million farmers in the peasant unions and about four hundred thousand[11] workers in the trade-unions of China.

The workers, shop clerks, and apprentices of Wuhan all wanted wage increases, showing their new power. These demands caused a great crisis, and, because of this and the blockade, the Wuhan Kuomintang began to fear the situation. Fêng Yü-hsiang was showing signs of betraying also.

The final split between the Kuomintang and the Communist party occurred on July 15. The demands of the workers, the pressure of the peasants for land, the bad economic condition of the government, and the general high tide of revolution had caused many Kuomintang members to shift to the Right.

When the terror began I had to hide. I kept connection with only one other comrade. Both Nanking and Wuhan sent special orders for my arrest. I did not join the Nanchang Uprising, but was elected a member of the Revolutionary Committee formed afterward, nevertheless. On August 7, the party gave up Ch'ên Tu-hsiu's "Right Opportunism" and a new era began.

Nanking and Wuhan soon decided to join forces. However, T'ang Shêng-chih hoped to keep control of Wuhan, so Chiang Kai-shek sent an army to attack him, led by Ch'ên Ch'êng. In the meantime, the Com-munist party organized the "Autumn Crop" uprisings in Hunan and Hupeh.

During the fight between Chiang Kai-shek and T'ang Shêng-chih, revolt arose in Huangan, my native *hsien*, and the local magistrate was killed.

After Pai Ch'ung-hsi and Li Tsung-jên occupied Wuhan, many Communists were killed. I have no idea how many—several thousand, at least. I was hiding in the Japanese Concession, and so was Li Han-ching. Li Tsung-jên sent one brigade to surround this Concession to make arrests and captured Li Han-ching, who was executed that night. I was able to escape to the French Concession. There I disguised myself as a sailor and escaped to Shanghai and thence to Japan. When I arrived in Japan, I learned that a laborer in the house in which I had hidden in Hankow had been arrested and executed! It was a very narrow escape.

I lived in Kyoto, Japan, for eight months. Then the party sent me to the U.S.S.R. I arrived in September 1928 and attended classes at Lenin University. I finished my college course in 1931 and returned to China in 1932.

I stayed in Shanghai forty days and then went to the Soviet districts—via Swatow overland to Kiangsi. In Juikin I was political director of the Red Academy. Later I organized the party school, of which I was principal. After the Second Soviet Congress in 1934, I was elected member of the executive committee of the Soviet government and judge of the supreme court. Later on I became chairman of the Workers' and Peasants' Inspection Committee.

During the Long March I was commissioner of public health. The Long March was not bad. I was never sick but couldn't sleep well at night. When we reached north Shensi, I was made principal of the party school at Waiyapao and later had the same position in the party school at Paoan.

Hsü T'ê-li

PATRIARCH

Bearded teacher in uniform: Hsü T'ê-li joined the Communist party at fifty, became commissioner of education in Chinese soviet districts, and at sixty, when this picture was taken, had arrived in Yenan after making the Long March with Red troops.

MISS WALES:

Hsü T'ê-LI is the patriarch of the Communists and in 1949 his seventy-third birthday was officially observed all over the new capital in Peking. His longevity is remarkable in China where the average life expectancy is twenty-seven years.

I found that the Confucian respect for age still existed among the Communists. They took a reverent attitude toward the "four grand old men," Tung Pi-wu, Hsü T'ê-li, Lin Tsu-han, and Hsieh Chüeh-tsai, all of whom are still active at this writing. Hsü T'êh-li was elected to the fifty-eight-member Government Council in 1949, while Lin Tsu-han, born in 1882, became its secretary-general.

Hsü T'ê-li told me that his father was an illiterate "half-coolie" who had married him to a slave girl. The zeal for education was born in the son, however, for he has studied and taught for most of his life, living at times in Japan, France, and Russia, and finally becoming an expert on the Latinized Chinese for which he was crusading diligently at the time

I talked with him. He was then commissioner of education in Yenan.

Hsü was the most beloved person among all the Communists, probably because he was so warmhearted, open, and affectionate. He usually walked along the street hugging with one arm the shoulder of someone and gesticulating animatedly with the other. He had an unusual face and bright, intelligent eyes. Whatever is the secret of growing old gracefully, he had it to perfection.

HSÜ T'Ê-LI:

I WAS born in 1876 near Changsha, in Hunan, of a family with only four children—myself, my older brother, my sister, and my younger brother. My father was half-farmer, half-coolie, and was illiterate. With fifty dollars that he had saved he bought a piece of land and began farming.

I studied Chinese in an old-fashioned

44

classical school from the age of nine until I was fifteen. At sixteen I became a teacher in a classical school. The fee I charged was only one dollar a year, my food being supplied from home. I taught in this manner until I was twenty-nine, then I entered Hunan Normal School in Changsha. After graduating I became a teacher of mathematics in a girls' higher primary and middle school.

Then, at thirty-two, I went to Shanghai and studied at the Kiangsu Educational Council. I also studied Japanese and went to Japan to investigate educational systems in Japan for a Changsha school. After staying only a month and a half, I returned to Changsha, and taught eight years more—I was principal and taught in a girls' middle school, and also taught in a normal school where Mao Tsê-tung was one of my students.

I was forty-three in 1919 when I went to France with the "Work and Study"[1] students. There I had a job as a metal worker and studied a year at Lyons, afterward studying three years at the University of Paris. I taught mathematics to Chinese students to earn my way, preparing them for college. This and savings from my teaching at Changsha and from my work at Lyons enabled me to go to the university. I studied French, but with difficulty, learning only two words a day at first. Finally I went to Germany for six months and in 1923 returned to China, where I established two normal schools at Changsha.

At the time of K'ang Yu-wei, I sympathized with the Reform Movement. Later I began to read Sun Yat-sen's articles in the *Min Pao* and changed my opinion, sympathizing with revolution. I joined the T'ung Mêng Hui in Changsha in 1911, becoming a progressive after my visit to Shanghai and Japan. Upon my return to Changsha in 1923, I became active in the Kuomintang and participated in the 1925–27 revolution. I joined the Communist party after the counterrevolution in 1927 and went to Moscow,

where I studied for two years at Sun Yat-sen University.

In 1930 I returned to China and went to the soviet districts. There I became assistant commissioner of education under Ch'ü Ch'iu-po. When he was killed by the Kuomintang in 1935, I became commissioner. I was fifty-nine during the Long March but my health is good—except for one missing tooth. I was married to a slave girl in my home, and we had four children, one son dying. I do not know where my wife is now. My daughter was arrested in Shanghai for putting up a revolutionary poster. I have not seen any of my family since 1927.

I cut off the end of my finger during the dynasty and wrote a manifesto in blood against the nationalization of railways! At fifty I wanted to join the Communist party—I had been on that side during the 1925–27 period but I was afraid the party would not accept me because I was already too old. I was in Changsha in 1927 and, since I was already committed to Communist ideas, I had to live in hiding. One day the party secretary met me, said he knew my history well, and asked if I wanted to join. I was very much pleased and said that I would if the party had any use for an old man like me.

I first read Marx in Kautsky's version while in Europe and didn't like it, though I did not know then that Kautsky was a reformist. I did not have much use for parliaments or the parliaments of nations. I had been a member of the Hunan provincial parliament in the early days of the republic and knew how much corruption could exist. I did not believe in Marxism until 1925, when I read Stalin's *Problems of Leninism*. This influenced me decisively. I have written many textbooks for use in the schools, and some of them are still being used by the Kuomintang, though I have outgrown those old ideas. I have written many articles on education, revolution, mass culture, and Latinized Chinese. My job has been as commissioner of education.

Hsieh Chüeh-tsai

MINISTER OF THE INTERIOR

Under arrest as a Communist, Hsieh Chüeh-tsai was released because he looked more like an old scholar. As a propagandist, he filled both roles.

MISS WALES:

HSIEH CHÜEH-TSAI had been a classical scholar under the dynasty and in 1949 he was made Minister of the Interior in the new Peking government. He is one of the fifteen members of the Law Commission and also a member of the State Administration Council. He was middle-aged before joining the Communist party.

When I met Hsieh, in 1937, he was secretary of the Communist government, as he had been since 1933. In 1948 he became chief of the Judicial Department of the North China government under Tung Pi-wu.

Like the other three patriarchs, Hsieh was in excellent health and spirits. They had all made the Long March together and seemed to have enjoyed it.

HSIEH CHÜEH-TSAI:

I WAS born in 1881 in Ninghsiang, Hunan, of a family of small landowners holding forty *mu*. I studied the classics during my boyhood and was a *hsiu-ts'ai* scholar under the dynasty.

Toward the end of the dynasty I quarreled with the local gentry, who had formed into a party against reform. Agitation for modernization was being led by Ho Hsü-nung—who became judge of the supreme court in the Kiangsi soviets and later was killed, by Chiang Mêng-chou—who also later became a Communist and was killed by the Kuomin-tang, and by Wang Lin-po—he was a revolutionary in 1927 but I have heard nothing of him since then. All of these men were my friends.

In 1924 I joined the Kuomintang. When the Northern Expedition reached Hunan in 1926, I worked in Changsha in the Kuomintang office in that city. I was a member of the executive committee of the provincial Kuomintang, edited the Hunan *Min Pao*—the Kuomintang organ, and was counsel to the Special Court.

I was in the Left-Wing Kuomintang and

46

had secretly joined the Communist party in 1925, so I left Changsha during the Hsü K'ê-hsiang massacre of liberals and Communists on May 11, 1927. T'ang Shêng-chih then became chairman of Hunan. At that time Mao Tsê-tung was secretary of the local Communist party, and T'ang Shêng-chih asked the Wuhan government for permission to arrest Mao. Communists in Wuhan warned Mao to leave and he went to Kiangsi. In December I went to Hankow, and from there to Shanghai. That winter I traveled to Mukden for the Communist party, doing secret work, and returned to Shanghai in 1929.

In 1931 I left Shanghai and proceeded to the Hunan-Hupeh area, Ho Lung's district in western Hunan, where there was a provincial soviet. There I edited the workers' and peasants' newspaper and worked in the party school, where peasant and worker students were trained in party history, tradition, organization, etc. Ho Lung's army and the soviet district were surrounded by the enemy in 1932, so we evacuated and headed for Hung Lake, where we were again surrounded. I was arrested by enemy troops but they then lacked a definite policy for dealing with us, and I was released because

I "did not look in the least like a Communist but like an old scholar." I went to Shanghai and worked in the party trade-union secretariat, but when the secretary, Lo Tung-hsien, was arrested, the organization was destroyed. I then went in 1933 to Kiangsi where I became secretary of the Central government.

I walked during the Long March with no serious trouble, arriving in Shansi in 1935 in good health. I am married and have a son and daughter, but I have not seen them or had any direct contact with them since May 1927. My family property in Ninghsiang was seized by the Kuomintang. My son is a peasant. My daughter is a teacher. I have an older brother and a younger brother but have lost contact with them.

Before I joined the soviets I used to think that the struggle for liberation would be very difficult. Now after my experience with the Red Army and the soviets, I know it will not be so very hard—especially now that the people are being organized on an anti-Japanese basis. I have written many articles on revolutionary theory and politics, on popular mobilization, and on Soviet Russia. I am at present secretary of the government, as I have been for many years past.

Wu Liang-p'ing

PROPAGANDA CHIEF

MISS WALES:

THE history of Wu Liang-p'ing is a particularly interesting one, since he is a native of Fenghua, a little village in the hinterland near Ningpo, in Chekiang Province south of Shanghai. This region has been the breeding ground for Chiang Kai-shek's most devoted followers, and you do not expect to find any Communists among its natives. Chiang Kai-shek was born and brought up in Fenghua, and Wu Liang-p'ing was affianced against his will to one of Chiang's relatives. Both men came from merchant families of the same status, attended the same school, and went to Shanghai. Wu, however, learned to read English at an early age and took a liking to Lincoln, whereas Chiang Kai-shek, who did not read foreign books in his youth, took Tsêng Kuo-fan, who broke the T'aip'ing Rebellion, as a model for his life.

Though Wu Liang-p'ing is a propagandist by profession, he has also compiled and translated books on socialism, including a trans-

lation of Engels' *Anti-Dühring*. At fifteen he became propaganda chief of Great China University, and when only twenty-seven was chief of the Propaganda Department of the Communist government in Yenan. It was his job to provide material for the press, and especially for foreigners, for he spoke excellent English, besides other languages.

Wu had been one of those youthful prodigies with prodigious memories, such as China often produces. With his horn-rimmed glasses and highly intellectual face, he looked the part. He had little sense of humor, and he loved Marxist dialectics. He tried to read every known book in Russian and English bearing on the subjects he was interested in. When I asked a question, he did not answer offhand, but came back next day with a long, responsible, well-reasoned lecture. What he told me includes a first-hand account of the May Thirtieth Incident.

WU LIANG-P'ING:

I WAS born in 1910 in the same town as Chiang Kai-shek—Fenghua, Chekiang, a shore town where commerce was much more developed than elsewhere in the region. My great-grandfather and my grandfather had operated a grocery shop, selling sugar, flour, food, and utensils, but my father became principal of a normal school. The shop had been started with small capital, and my grandfather had learned to read and write by himself. He saw from his own experience that it is unfortunate not to be educated, and determined that his son should go to school. My father, therefore, was placed as a boy under the tutelage of an old scholar, and afterward graduated from Chekiang Provincial Normal College. He was for a time principal of the Normal School in

Ningpo, but when it closed for lack of funds, he became principal of the Fenghua Normal School. My father then decided to try his luck in the commercial field. He went to Shanghai and entered a stockbrokerage business, but he was not a good businessman and he lost money. He had to abandon this effort and retired, living at home until his death in 1935. Because it was known that I was a Communist, no one would give my father a post as government official, although he was a Fenghua native and had good connections with the government personnel.

My mother was a country woman, illiterate but a good mother. She had eight children—four daughters and four sons. All the girls died, but the younger boys are now in school. My great-grandfather was still alive when I was born. He loved and treasured me greatly because I was the first great-grandson and the first son in my father's family. My mother also had an excessive regard for me, and at meals on every festival day she set aside the most delicious part of the food for me. Though I have been away a long time, she still does this, hoping I will return to her.

We were a peculiar family in that we lived well but had no real property and father was always losing money. My family originated in the old gentry and was well known and respected in Fenghua, though never having landed estates. In my time, it was a petty-bourgeois family, based on commercial capital, but our economic condition changed for the worse until we were only rootless intelligentsia. As a boy, however, I grew up under good conditions, entering primary school at five. I had an unusual memory and always ranked first in examinations. I remember that I did not like school when I first went there, being so young, but my grandfather insisted on my going as young as possible and an aunt, who studied at the same school, took care of me. I was neither naughty nor obedient as a child. My father was severe and beat me at times if I did not come up to his approval, but my mother was gentle. I feared my father, but my mother loved me so much that she spoiled me and made me selfish.

By the time I was eight, I was always the leader of my group because I was an oldest son. When I was nine, my father took me alone to Ningpo, where he was principal of the Normal School. Mother did not come, and for six months my father and I were together. He took me along with him wherever he went, to shops, to government offices, and to dinners. I liked to wander around alone, however, buying candy, playing ball, and seeing old plays on the street corners. Several times I was gone a whole day, and my father called out many men to help search for me.

I now discovered that my father wanted to take a pretty concubine. Just as he was about to do this, I hurried to Fenghua on the steamer to tell my mother. She rushed to Ningpo and threatened to kill herself, so Father dared not carry out his plan.

After this, Father left Ningpo for Fenghua and I entered the Ching Ch'i Higher Primary School there, the same school that Chiang Kai-shek attended. He was entirely unknown then, and when he became famous later, the townspeople could hardly place him in memory. The Chiang family is unknown in the region, but he is also related to the Sun family, which is one of the good families and of gentry-merchant background.

In school days I liked to read the old Chinese romances—the *San Kuo*, *Chih Yen I*, *Hung-lou Mêng*, *Shui Hu Chuan*, and all such. I read all the time, and I also soon liked stories of great people in the West. My favorites were Napoleon, Washington, Lincoln, and Nelson. As I read, my young brain was always wanting China to have such great men—so rich and powerful. I liked them better than the old Chinese heroes, and I never had any old Chinese hero in my mind to emulate. I studied the Classics some, but I hated Confucius and Confucianism and all it stood for. My father was modern and never quoted Confucius to me. Yet I thrived on the "older brother" theory of Confucius. My young brothers respected me and were as obedient as servants just because I was the oldest son. We did not fight much. The rule of precedence was fixed.

I knew already about Sun Yat-sen and the Kuomintang, but I had no particular interest in Sun, for he seemed outdated. I liked modern things and European culture. Of course, I knew nothing then of any Russians. Most of the students merely wanted to be modern. In our school there was a new European-type building and it was so much better than the Chinese architecture that we all wanted to live in houses of the same kind. I first studied English at the age of nine. Father wanted me to be a successful businessman, and for this English was important, because of our compradore economic system.

My happiest days were on trips to the mountains. But I was always happy at home, too. Our home was very pleasant and had no conflict, even after the concubine incident. My mother was so kind that she made the house a refuge of comfort.

I was supposed to be the best student in the school, and the local gentry were anxious for their daughters to be connected with such a promising business future! One landlord —incidentally, he is connected with Chiang Kai-shek's family—arranged with my father for a marriage for me. I was only eleven and knew nothing about it until it was fixed. I had no way of objecting, anyway.

The May Fourth Movement, 1919

The May Fourth Movement broke out in 1919 when I was in primary school. It affected even us young pupils. We had a demonstration and talked to people on the streets. I remember being impressed by some students who had come from Ningpo and held a meeting and put on patriotic plays. I wanted to be patriotic. I knew China was a weak nation and I wanted her to be made strong. I knew the slogans of the May Fourth Movement: "Oppose the Twenty-one Demands of the Japanese! Down with the Three Traitors—Ts'ao, Lo, and Chang! Down with the Anfu Clique!" But I did not understand what imperialism meant.

I had seen foreigners and received a bad impression of them because their attitude was arrogant. I contrasted their wealth with the poverty and backwardness of the Chinese and felt bitter. I never liked foreigners, even though I liked their books and national heroes.

My father wanted me to join the Christian church, as he had learned that this was useful to anyone engaged in foreign trade— but I refused even to go to the Y.M.C.A., though Father bought me a ticket. Once a Christian missionary came and read verses from the Bible. I did not understand it and thought it was all nonsense. There were Christian schools in Ningpo and they gave religious plays, but I could not like even these. Ningpo is the cradle of compradores and Shanghai servants, and it is a tradition to look for a job with the foreigners. Yet, for some reason, I did not like this attitude and felt that it was servile, no matter how well paid. I made no distinction then between any kinds of foreigners. I never had seen any Japanese, and knew nothing about them except that they were foreigners who were making demands on China.

After May Fourth, I began to read popular essays on the political situation in China in *New Youth* and other student magazines. On May Fourth, in Fenghua only students participated, but my father was liberal toward the movement. Nobody was arrested. The local militia and the troops were near our school, and I thought that if we had to fight against the foreigners we would win because of having such a large population.

I finished this school at thirteen, and Father took me to Shanghai with him. I was sorry to leave Fenghua, which is a beautiful place. Again, Mother did not go with us. She was a Chinese woman of the old type who considered it not good to go to big cities or to insist on following the husband.

Shanghai surprised me, even though I was already accustomed to Ningpo, which is a big city, and was not quite a clodhopper. The noise bewildered me. I felt there was something wrong because all the big modern buildings were owned by foreigners, not Chinese. Why?

Father chose the best middle school for me—Nanyang—and I passed my exams. I now systematically read the newspapers and modern magazines, and even began to write short articles. I felt that I wanted to be a literary writer and I loved to read foreign fiction, even though I hated the foreigners in China and their injustice. I liked this fiction much better than Chinese and was surprised at the quality of the writing. I remember how absorbed I was by Tolstoy, Dickens, de Maupassant, Dumas, Shakespeare, the Lambs, and Turgenev. *The Three Musketeers* was a favorite, also *Camille*. I cried and cried when I read the scene of Armand at the grave of Camille in the rain. The story reminded me of *Hunglou Mêng*, as both heroines have tuberculosis and sad love affairs. I like de Maupassant very much because his characters are cunning rogues, and Chinese always love this kind of thing.

I read Ch'ên Tu-hsiu's and Hu Shih's works, and various social theories. Finally I read Kautsky's *The Class Struggle*, translated by Wên Te-ying, and was stimulated to learning socialist ideas. When I finished middle school, in 1923, the *New Youth* era was already over. We read *Chüeh Wu* ["Waking Up"], edited by Shao Li-tze when he was a Communist—he later became governor of Shensi. I also read *Hsiang Tao* ["Guide"], an organ of the Communists, but I had no definite opinions then.

From 1920 to 1923 there was no student movement in China. We had no student union and no activity. I learned chiefly geography, history, physics, biology, and mathematics. I also wrote some short stories which were published in magazines and some articles on student life for *Chüeh Wu*.

I was much impressed by my study of American history, especially the period of the freeing of the slaves. I read *Uncle Tom's Cabin* with intense interest. I always liked Lincoln. I also liked to read of the American colonial war against Great Britain and thought China, too, was a colony under the British boot. I was much impressed by Western science. At first I wanted to be a great author, but now I wanted to be an engineer, as I longed to know the technology of industry.

I had many friends and amused myself in this period, being not very diligent. I always sat on the last row in class so I could read books instead of listening, for I was ahead of the class usually and passed exams easily by a little cramming. I would drink coffee and stay awake the night before, cramming. After school I often went to the Lungwha Pagoda for an excursion. I now began to distinguish among foreigners. I received a good impression of America because of its good attitude in the Washington Conference but I hated the Japanese after May Fourth, and I questioned the British.

The Founding of "Great China University"

I decided to go to Amoy University in Fukien, and passed my entrance examinations. This university was founded by T'an Ka-k'i, the rubber magnate from Singapore, and had more money and better professors and equipment than most. I had also applied to Shanghai College but changed my mind because of the Christianity there. I could not face hearing prayers and blessings said all the time. I was never interested in any religion. My father's family had none and my mother's were all Buddhists.

At Amoy there were coeds. Also, my English teacher was a girl who had been in America. In middle school there were no girls and I was very shy. On the first day, I had not yet bought a book and the teacher asked me to sit beside a girl to read with her, there being two students to each desk. I was so startled that I ran across the room and pushed over two boy students to make room for three. Another woman who had been in America taught music. She was pleasant, but I did not like her because she wore such fine clothes and was too bourgeois.

During this year I paid much attention to the natural sciences and also received good marks in chemistry, mathematics, and the like.

At the end of the year there was a student strike against the president because some good teachers had been fired. The Amoy district people fought against outsiders, but we demanded the return of the teachers and, when the president refused, sent a telegram to T'an Ka-k'i in Singapore demanding the removal of the president.

T'an replied: "I give full responsibility to the president. He can settle matters as he likes." Nothing could be done peaceably. We called a strike, which most of the students joined. We had pickets, and the strike lasted a week. It was a democratic move against the tyranny of the president. It was settled by putting summer vacation forward and dispersing the whole student body to their homes. No compromise was reached.

We now drew up a plan to organize the "Great China University" in Shanghai. Five or six professors agreed to teach, and a student committee was started which got the signatures of two hundred students who would attend. Money was paid in advance to this committee, which sent delegates to Shanghai to rent furniture and private houses. I was one of the students who were active in this plan.

We collected only several thousand dollars, but in the autumn of 1924 the Great China University opened in Shanghai near Ferry Road. I became editor of the weekly magazine of the school and was also propaganda chief of the student union.

We started the school in a factory district and the students organized night schools for the workers, thus getting into close contact with them, especially the textile workers. This area had a concentration of many Japanese-owned mills. I received a deep impression of the exploitation of the workers when I compared their misery with the big estates of the Japanese. There was a Japanese school on the same street, and the students were driven up in motorcars with chauffeurs, but the children of the workers lived lower than animals for they were not so clean.

Shanghai, 1925: the May Thirtieth Incident

The initial episode that caused the May Thirtieth Incident took place in our district. During 1925 a general depression existed in China's textile industry. The Japanese owners wanted to lengthen working hours and reduce wages, and the workers objected.

The Japanese foremen were always beating the workers for little or no reason. Every day there was news of such beatings. I remember that one small girl was beaten so seriously as to endanger her life.

In March the workers in the Mill Number Seven of the Nei Wai Mien [Nagai Wata Kaisha] Company demanded better conditions of the Japanese owners but were rebuffed and went on strike. The police wanted to drive all workers out of the cotton mill, and those who lived outside were trying to rush in to present their demands. The police closed the gate to the compound and the trouble began. The Japanese fired a pistol, and one of the strike leaders, Ku Cheng-hung, was killed and several seriously wounded. The workers dispersed and the factory was cleared out. Because of the depression the owners were not anxious to reopen, and the strike lasted about a month. The strike soon spread to other Japanese factories and the strike movement had not been stopped at the time of the May Thirtieth Incident, though some strikers had resumed work.

This factory where Ku Cheng-hung was killed was very near our university. We became much exercised about the trouble. At first the Japanese and the police tried to keep the whole episode a secret, so we students felt called upon to go out and tell the citizens the whole story. The student union sent delegates to all other universities, asking the students to do propaganda work and collect money for the strikers. It was voted to have a sympathy campaign on May 30.

I was propaganda chairman of my school and led a propaganda corps along Jessfield Road while others went elsewhere. Groups from different universities went to Nanking Road and other main thoroughfares to do street publicity. The crowds gathered more and more around our speakers—the police wanted to drive them away but couldn't.

Near the Louza Police Station on Nanking Road—the main street of Shanghai—the British and Sikh police saw a crowd gathering around one of our student speakers, and the British officer in charge ordered the police to open fire. Seven students and one or two workers were killed. Several tens were wounded. The firing continued several seconds into a crowd of one or two thousand, until it dispersed. The students had given no provocation and there had been no demonstration, only a speech, but it was near the big Wing On Department Store, the most crowded corner in the city.

The news spread instantly and all the Shanghai students were deeply upset. The federated "Shanghai General Student Union" called an emergency meeting and voted to go on strike. The municipal council mobilized all its police and its armed volunteer corps.

I was appointed delegate to go to the Chinese Chamber of Commerce to ask them to protest the incident to the municipal council, but they were afraid and said it was not their business. They said that they sympathized, but they took no action. On the one hand, the students united with the labor unions; on the other, they wanted support from the owning class. We did not get support from the big merchants, but the little merchants sympathized—they had a merchants' union of small shops. The three big organizations now joined and formed the "United Committee of Labor, Students, and Merchants," composed of the Shanghai General Labor Union, the Student Union, and the Merchants' Union.

The workers were much stirred by the May Thirtieth Incident and more and more went on strike until over three hundred thousand were out. Almost all Japanese mills and many Chinese mills were on strike. The movement spread all over China, partly because of student propaganda everywhere. This became the greatest anti-imperialist movement China had ever seen.

I was one of the members of the executive committee of the Shanghai Student Union, which was dominated by the Left, with no Right opposition. The whole student body was unified. The Student Union, which had great authority, began a big propaganda drive. Over a million dollars to help the strikers was collected from students in many parts of the country and even from overseas Chinese. Money came pouring in. Even merchants gave. One mass meeting that we held at the West Gate was attended by a hundred thousand persons.

But the backbone of May Thirtieth was the working class. Some of their strikes lasted two or three months, until August, and many lasted one month. The second influence was the petty-bourgeois students who did effective propaganda in every city in China and even out in the country. The small merchants sympathized and even went on strike for several days. The Shanghai Chamber of Commerce never joined the committee and was afraid of the mass movement, though we did everything to urge them. At this time the Fengtien Tungpei Army from Manchuria was garrisoning Shanghai, and the soldiers were impressed.

At first all organizations were open and legal, and right after May 30 mass meetings were openly called. But gradually the authorities hindered them. Then, at the beginning of September, Sun Ch'uan-fang attacked Shanghai. After this the authorities began to repress the Student Union, and the Labor Union was closed down. Gradually students went back to school and strikers back to work. The foreign powers had to appoint a committee to investigate, though the incident was never settled. After a year or two, however, compensation was given to the families of those killed.

The main slogan of May Thirtieth was: "Down with British Imperialism!" Others were: "Cancel the Unequal Treaties!" "Drive Away the Military Forces of the Imperialist Powers in China!" "Get Back Control of the Customs!" "Oppose Extraterritoriality!" All were anti-imperialist slogans and it was a united front movement. But the big bourgeoisie did not participate, only the middle and lower middle classes and the students and workers. The May Thirtieth Movement directly affected over a million people in Shanghai, including the three hundred thousand striking workers and their families. We had 120 schools in the Student Union, numbering about thirty thousand students. Many Communist party and Kuomintang members participated and helped to spread the movement.

The May Thirtieth Incident was the beginning of the Great Revolution of 1925–27, though we did not suspect what we were starting, down there on Ferry Road.

At this time, Yang Hsi-min and Liu Chên-huan were liquidated in Canton by the Whampoa cadets, and a big demonstration was held in the city. As it passed Shameen, the foreigners fired killing many and wounding others.[1] This was followed by the Hong-kong strike, and the revolution was on in full force.

I worked in the Shanghai Student Union office from June to September, 1925. I was the delegate from Great China University, as each school elected its representative. The Shanghai University led the movement. Of the original Executive Committee, only two of us remain active, myself and one in the Red Academy. One went to Moscow later, and others were killed in 1927. Some who joined the Kuomintang dropped out of all activity. After May 30, many students joined the Communist Youth as I did, though my family did not know about it then.

After this I had little contact with my family and supported myself by working in various ways. During 1924–25 I had a big conflict with my family over the marriage question, and we fought back and forth a whole year. They were eager for me to marry Chiang Kai-shek's relative, but I refused. I had known the girl in Ningpo and she also wrote to me every day, saying how much she cared for me. I did not have any real reason for not wanting to marry this particular girl except that I refused to permit my family to govern this part of my life and wanted free choice. Though my family loved me dearly, they began to threaten me and that made me stubborn. They also objected to my work in the Student Union. Finally, I ran away to Russia at the end of October and did not write to them till I had reached there safely.

At Sun Yat-sen University, Moscow

After May Thirtieth, the Sun Yat-sen University was established in Moscow and the Russians welcomed nationalist students. But, as for me, I joined the Communist party when I left China. During 1925 I had read a good deal on Marxism and the U.S.S.R. and my contact with the workers in the nearby factories caused me to sympathize with their cause and to want to spend the rest of my life fighting for them. I remember that a book called *A New Viewpoint on Society* by some Russian influenced my mind greatly, and I decided China had no other way out.

I was a member of the first class at Sun Yat-sen University in 1925. There were one hundred eighty students, including a few workers. Thirty were from Shanghai but I was the only one from my university. It was not necessary to be a Communist member—some were only Kuomintang and all of us went as Kuomintang members. I had joined the Kuomintang in 1925.

I arrived in Moscow at the age of eighteen and studied there four years. I first worked as a translator, and organized an "English group" of eleven students, of whom most were killed or later betrayed. I studied Russian in a group of five, and we had a pretty Russian girl teacher. Karl Radek lectured to us on China's problems. At nineteen, I taught a class in world economy. When I left, the university had three hundred students.

I was favorably impressed with the Soviet system as soon as I arrived at Vladivostok. I saw that the working people were not despised as in China and that they had good jobs, time to rest, vacations, and freedom, and that they were happy no matter what material conditions existed. What impressed me most was the hopefulness toward tomorrow: everyone had a future and worked toward it. In China nobody could be sure of tomorrow. I also liked the friendly attitude of equality toward the Chinese. In Shanghai, foreigners despise Chinese, but in Russia all kinds were made welcome, whether or not they were Communists. I had read many old Russian novels, and I compared the ignorance and darkness of the conditions described in them with the conditions in the modern farms and other collectives of the peasants. I saw that the peasants had found a way to raise their standard of living by collectivism.

During 1925–27 we eagerly and constantly discussed the China situation and the world situation. We traveled all over Russia and the comradely spirit everywhere was warm and made us very happy. In 1927 there was a political split in the university, and the Kuomintang students went back to China. Many of these students betrayed later because they feared to die for their beliefs and wanted to keep alive under the Kuomintang. Some of them even became Fascists, using their Marxist training to destroy the working class. There were fifty or sixty Chinese girls in the university. Of these, some became passive, some betrayed, some worked in the Communist party, and some were killed. One girl I liked was executed in 1932 by the Kuomintang. I was in love with a Russian girl but I did not marry her as I could not bring her back to China with me, and so I have never married.

In 1929 I spent several months in Berlin and also traveled in France, Belgium, and England. Then in the winter I returned to Shanghai. As soon as the ship passed east of Suez I noticed the change in attitude of foreigners toward the Chinese. In their own country people are more democratic, but when you enter the imperialist zone the contrast is very sharp and marked. In Singapore, especially, I noticed how arrogant the British were. They seemed always worse than the Americans.

I went home secretly to Fenghua for two days. Mother did not recognize me as I was now wearing glasses. The marriage contract had been broken in 1926, so we only made jokes about it now. This was the last time I saw my mother. She does not know now if I am still alive, as I have not been able to write to her.

I worked a year and a half in the underground in Shanghai and compiled and translated three books. I compiled a history of socialism, compiled and translated a book on historical materialism, and translated and published [Engels'] Anti-Dühring.

Imprisonment at Shanghai

One day on the street I accidentally met a former schoolmate from Moscow who was then a member of the Central Committee of the Kuomintang. He recognized me and asked what my business was and I told him I had none. He reported to the police and my room was raided. They found some Marxist books and took them as proof of my being a Communist. I was arrested and put on trial, but they had no proof. My younger brother was then living with me and he was arrested too, but I proved that he had nothing to do with me or my work and he was released. My father came to Shanghai instantly to help, and my family and friends had enough influence to prevent me from being executed. I was sentenced to two years in prison.

When I was arrested, Pat Givens[2] talked to me and asked about the Communist party. He tried to get information from me and said that if I would give the names of other persons and of organizations I would be released. Otherwise, he threatened, I would be turned over to the Chinese and probably would be executed. A man named Robertson also tried to influence me to betray. These two men we call "man hunters," for they hate the Communists and love to arrest them. The young people of Shanghai hate Pat Givens very much and all know about him. Because of one such man we hated the British a thousand times more.

I was a prisoner in the Ward Road Jail in the International Settlement. I was told that this municipal prison is the biggest in the world, with nine thousand prisoners, Sing Sing in America having fewer. Before 1931 Communists were tried in the foreign settlement and afterward were extradited to Chinese authority. Sometimes there were sixty to a hundred political prisoners in this jail. They were kicked and beaten by the foreigners. This also happened to me. There are now [1937] probably at least ten thousand political prisoners in China.

I was put in a "black cell" for one month and was not permitted to come out for even an hour. The reason was this: Once when the British jailer came, I said: "We are all prisoners and beg you to allow us to work." He took this word "we" as an excuse to think I had been organizing political prisoners, so I was put in the "black cell" and isolated from all other prisoners. Those who worked had more freedom and better food, but the Communist suspects were not permitted to be associated with the other prisoners for fear they might influence them. If we tried to talk together, we were beaten, but we could get news from the outside. I was always hungry and thinking of food, as I did not have enough to eat. This was my experience of imperialism. However, when prisoners are turned over to the Chinese authorities, they are likely to be executed. Once the Chinese government demanded that I should be turned over to them but luckily this was not done.

One cell had either three prisoners or only one—never two—to prevent trouble. The three were permitted to talk on any subject so long as the warden did not know. Every day I walked around and around in my cell, eight feet square, for exercise. Some prisoners were in irons. I was not permitted either to write or read, except the Bible. If one pencil was found, the prisoner was beaten with stripes and fined. I read the New Testament twice and to my pleasant surprise found it was based on a concept of Christian socialism. The foreigners were more afraid of books than the Chinese, for in a Chinese prison you can get books to read—but you are likely to be shot at any time. Friends could visit a prisoner only once in three months. Three times a week we could walk outside for a few minutes. If the foreign warden liked a prisoner, he could let him out more often for good behavior. I hated foreigners and they did not like me. We privately called the wardens "Senior Big Nose" and "Junior Big Nose." Prisoners were punished by being deprived of food or exercise, or by being put in irons.

I counted the days and estimated how many were past and how many were ahead. Just before I was released in 1932, I was very hungry all the time because rations had been reduced one-third because of the Shanghai War between the Japanese and Tsai T'ing-k'ai. Our regular food was this: rice and water in a tin for breakfast, rice and a vegetable and salt at noon, rice and soya bean or a sliver of beef, pork, or fish at night. But the meat was so small you could not see it—only taste, and if distinguishable it was usually nothing but skin.

The first day of my freedom, the sensation was so great that I could not sleep or stand still. I rested a whole month, just enjoying the feeling of not being a prisoner.

In 1932 I went to the Kiangsi soviet region by a secret route, first doing political work in the Red Academy. Then I became people's commissioner of economics of the Central government at Juikin.

After about two years, we started the Long March. During the march I worked in the political department of the Red Army and also specifically in that of the First and Third Army Corps. It was not so difficult. I both rode and walked, but I got stomach trouble. Yet, my health was actually helped by the Long March. When I reached north Shensi with Mao Tsê-tung, I was made responsible for the propaganda department.

Hsü Mêng-ch'iu

HISTORIAN OF THE LONG MARCH

At thirty-six Hsü Mêng-ch'iu recalled: "I decided that being a teacher was of little use, for only the rich could afford to hire me and I would not be able to help the poor."

MISS WALES:

WHEN I met Hsü Mêng-ch'iu in Yenan, he was chief of the Rear Political Department. In addition he was official historian for the Communist districts.

Though Hsü was thin and with his heavy, horn-rimmed glasses looked like the most typical Chinese scholar imaginable, he had military ambitions. He told me that he had wanted to graduate from Whampoa Academy and become a military commander. Any remaining hopes he may have had for a military career

had been ended by the loss of both legs, which had been amputated after exposure to extreme cold toward the end of the Long March.

Hsü has one of the most Chinese minds I have ever encountered—that is, he seemed to tell everything backward. The denouements always came at the first of the chapter, so to speak; but this habit disappeared when he came to tell the story of the Long March, and his spoken narrative became quite direct and, I think, very interesting.

HSÜ MÊNG-CH'IU:

MY family belonged to the old aristocracy of scholars and landholders. My grandfather was a landlord but had no education. My father was a scholar and the oldest son. I was born in Hsü *hsien*, Anhwei Province, in 1901, the third of four sons. I had two sisters.

From the point of view of the old Chinese morality, my father was a good man. He was kind to all and no one had a bad word to

say about him. Because of his natural generosity, when the property was divided he gave it all to his younger brothers. My grandfather had three hundred *mu* of land, and father gave each of his three brothers one hundred *mu*, saying he had been well educated and could earn his living as a teacher. After teaching a while, he became a merchant. However, he was so honest and goodhearted that his business failed, and

57

by the time I was ten years old my family had become poor. My uncles and relatives were now comparatively rich. They treated my father's family as despised poor relations.

Searching for a Free Education

I received no education in early childhood, but my oldest brother was educated and was active in the 1911 Revolution. In the summer of 1911 I entered a school taught by my brother, but after I had been there three months the Revolution broke out and the school stopped. Then in 1912 my native village established a school and I was able to attend it. In 1913 this school was closed and my studies were again interrupted. In 1914 I began at a private school taught by one of my uncles. There were thirty students, all relatives, and my younger brother also went there. Every day we walked the two *li* and had lunch in school. The fee for us both was twenty dollars a year. No charity was considered—our rich relatives demanded payment. We studied the old Classics. My parents determined to send me to school with the object that I should go into business. However, I progressed so fast that Father changed his mind and hoped that I would be a teacher.

After three years of schooling, however, I found my ideas beginning to change. My oldest brother worked outside and sent newspapers home, and in that way we learned of what was going on. My uncle treated me well, but I thought he was a hypocrite and false because if I had not paid on time, I would have had to stop studying. This uncle was very rich but he never helped my family. Both my third and fourth uncles were rich, but my second uncle had died early and his family had become poor, so we had good relations with them, but not with the other two. Thus early I saw how property makes friends only in its own class. I felt myself one of the poor and was sympathetic with them, and I decided that being a teacher was of little use, for only the rich

could afford to hire me and I would not be able to help the poor.

In 1919 my two brothers and my third uncle's son started a school and invited me to teach there. For a year I worked very hard but I was not satisfied, and decided to quit. I received no salary—only food and a place to sleep. The pupils paid four dollars a year, two dollars a term, and the school was intended to help poor students. However, the other three teachers had bad habits and were often absent from class, so that I had to teach most of the lessons. These teachers were romantic and drank wine and played mah-jongg and "bamboo court," but my own habits were regular, quiet, and serious.

There were two other reasons why I wanted to leave. The important one was that I wanted to learn the new knowledge, and on the outside now were schools supported by the government free for poor students. The other reason was that in 1920 my family ordered me to marry a girl who was old-fashioned and ignorant and I was determined not to have that kind of wife. In the spring of 1920 I borrowed twenty dollars from my younger brother and went to Peking, where my oldest brother lived. However, I found I could not go to school: money was required—even though tuition was free—and I had none. After three months my oldest brother gave me money to return home. I was miserable at home, particularly because in Peking I had seen many new things and found that material conditions in the cities were much better than in the interior.

I now heard of a school in Hsienchün, Anhwei, for training in the culture of silkworms. I entered there and studied hard, though the natural science they taught was not much good. I became the student leader, as my manner was apparently such as to command a following, though I did not know this before. I disliked the principal and the teachers, so I opposed them and led an uprising. Several teachers were driven away, but the staff controlled the boarding fees of the students, so we failed and the oppression of the school authorities was heavier than before. The co-operation of the student body was not strong, and ten students were dismissed, myself being one of them. The reason for the strike was this: the school had about one hundred forty students supported free by the government as apprentices—some rich, some poor—but the majority had some relation with government officials or they could not have secured the post. The school authorities and teachers had been appointed by the Northern militarists and their knowledge and character were bad. We students hoped to drive them away and to get progressive and technically trained teachers in their places.

The government ordered that the student leaders be arrested because they had beaten the chief of police, and that the *hsienchang*[1] and the chief of police be reprimanded because they had tried but failed to stop the uprising. We ten students escaped to Wuhu, a big commercial port of Anhwei. There we went to learn English and mathematics in a Christian missionary church, paying two dollars a month. The missionary wanted us to join the church but we did not want to enter any religion.

At the end of the year, at "New Year," my family sent a letter telling me to return. I complied, yet I had nothing to do at home. Until the summer of 1921 I had hoped to enter a normal school but my scholastic background was not up to standard, especially in natural science, and I had no diploma. I therefore was obliged to join a commercial school in Chen Yang Kuan, in Anhwei, hoping not to do commercial work but to learn English and mathematics. Here also I was student leader. We did not like the incompetent and dishonest principal and had a strike to try to drive him away, but some of the students betrayed to the principal, so at the end we failed, and three other students and I were dismissed. This principal kept for himself the government money provided

for the school, which was why the students hated him. It is only the students who can check up on such corruption, and we felt it our duty to expose it.

I returned home for another time, but in 1922 I ventured away again, this time joining with some old schoolmates to enter an agricultural school in Wuhu, where tuition was free. I enjoyed this student body—many of these four hundred students were poor so I organized twenty students in a troop which had much influence over the students and was very forceful. We did not join the Student Union but nevertheless we led all the student activities. We began a struggle against the corrupt school authorities and opposed the highest class because they worked with the authorities. The character of this administration was bad, as it was in most of the schools at that time.

A "New Village" Experiment

We organized a reading society of the twenty students in order to study social problems together and to draw up a plan for the reconstruction of the village life of China. We wanted to experiment in the Hsin Ch'eng [New Village] Movement, and our ideas were of Utopian socialism like Fourierism or Owenism. We bought all kinds of socialist books. I have forgotten most of them, but one was *The Study of Ancient Communism in Chinese Society*, published by the Commercial Press. It was not correct but we read it with interest.

We raised two hundred dollars and bought a small, uncultivated hill in Anhwei at the end of the year, and one person went there to live. This was in the winter of 1922. At this time, I did not live in the dormitory. A schoolmate and I rented a house outside for privacy and we began reading the new Communist magazines *Hsiang Tao*, *New Youth*, and the *Leader*. By 1923 my ideas had changed because of these new magazines and I wanted to organize a "Society of Marxism," but some of the members of the reading society opposed it because they still wanted to build the new society according to the Utopian "New Village" idea. We were all boys, no girls. Until this time I had had no correct idea of revolution. May Fourth had no influence on me or on my brother. I now had a deeper consciousness and began to choose good books to read. Finally in the spring of 1923 we had an uprising in the school and our group fought physically with another group. About ten students were dismissed, including myself, for I was the leader.

During the summer vacation we heard the news that Shanghai University would be founded by the progressives, including Yu Yu-jên as president, Têng Chung-hsia as dean, and Ch'ü Ch'iü-po, Ts'ai Ho-shên, and a social scientist, Shih Tsêng-t'ung. All except the president were Communists. My schoolmates and I eagerly went to Shanghai. When we arrived, we rented two rooms where we eight poor students lived together and cooked our meals. In a short time, I joined the C.Y. [Communist Youth] and one month later the C.P. [Communist Party]. A branch was organized in Shanghai University and I worked in it. This was in 1923.

At this time the Kuomintang was beginning to reorganize in Shanghai. Many leaders came, such as Liao Chung-k'ai, Hu Han-min and Tai Chi-t'ao. We students joined the Kuomintang, as it was becoming progressive under the new organization, and worked openly. In the winter, Whampoa Military Academy invited good students in Shanghai to join, but I missed this opportunity. A letter came from my family saying that my father was dangerously ill, and I had to return home. Seven of my friends went to Whampoa: Wang I-ch'ang, now with the Kuomintang Fifty-third Army; Ts'ao Yüan, killed in Wuchang in 1926 during the war; P'êng Kan-ch'ên, who worked in the Kiangsi soviets and was killed in 1934; and others. All remained Communists except Wang I-ch'ang.

After remaining at home briefly, I planned to enter Paoting Military Academy, and went to see my oldest brother in Changchiak'ou—he was an official there in the Salt Gabelle—hoping to be introduced to the school. Again I was disappointed, as the school stopped receiving students because it was divided into two groups in internal politics. The militarists had two factions— the "Chih Hsi," led by Wu P'ei-fu and Ts'ao K'un, and the "Wan Hsi," or Anhwei clique, led by Tuan Ch'i-jui.

I now had to return home again, and I persuaded by brother and many friends to help me establish a school, for which I borrowed fifty dollars. But it was difficult to secure money and the district authorities opposed the idea of the school. They had control of public funds for education, and if a new school were started the authorities would not be able to get government money for the old schools. I had planned a free school, where students bought only their books. This school lasted barely a year, as money was impossible to get.

During this year I organized a "C.Y." of ten persons and also a "Kuomintang" of eighty persons.

In 1925 I again left home for Shanghai where many of my schoolmates were attending Shanghai University. I stayed two months and was then appointed by the party to go to Anking, capital of Anhwei, where I began to organize the two parties. The May Thirtieth Incident now occurred. In Anking I organized a "C.Y." of twenty students, many of whom were later sacrificed. One named Wu and one named Yang were executed by the Kuomintang in 1928. Another, Li Chi-shên, now working in the Kuomintang, betrayed.

In July I left Anking for Shanghai and worked in the headquarters of the labor association one month. Then in August I went to Canton, planning to enter Whampoa.

The Political Department, 1925–27

Arriving at Canton, however, I was disappointed that the party would not permit me to enter Whampoa and, instead, ordered me to do political work in the 1st Division of the First Army, the only army directly under Chiang Kai-shek. Ho Ying-ch'in commanded the 1st Division. I was chief of the political department of the 1st Division, in charge of propaganda. At that time we students imagined Chiang was progressive, for he had not shown his colors. I was in the Eastern Expedition fighting Ch'ên Ch'iung-ming. At the end of 1925 I was transferred to the 14th Division under Fung I-p'ei—later killed—at Meihsien in Kwangtung. Then [in 1926] the March Twentieth Incident occurred. Chiang Kai-shek arrested all the Communists he could get hold of in Canton—I don't know how many, but probably three or four hundred at least. I was arrested but was released in a few days. This was the beginning of the split that finally was breached in 1927. As an excuse for the March Twentieth Incident, Chiang Kai-shek told a lie, saying, "Some military man is intending to start an uprising planned by the Communists." This was not true. Chiang Kai-shek hoped by these arrests to decrease the rising power of the Communists by teaching them a lesson.

The Kuomintang and the Communist Party had united on a common program, and we joined the Kuomintang to influence it in a more progressive direction. There was always friction between the political elements, however. In 1925 a Rightist Kuomintang group organized a "Society for the Doctrines of Sun Yat-sen" for the purpose of struggling against the Communists. Many of these later became real Fascists. One was Hu Tsung-nan from Hunan, now head of the Fascists under Chiang Kai-shek. Another was Fêng T'i, a Whampoa cadet, now military attaché in Germany. Still another who became a Fascist was Ch'ên Kuang-ch'ing, who held a high post under Ho Ying-ch'in in Peking and was chief of the political department in Sian, where he was arrested during the Sian Incident of December 12, 1936. However, he was patriotic and later had some sympathy for Chang Hsüeh-liang[2] and Yang Hu-ch'êng.

The Sun Yat-senists quarreled constantly with the Communists and Leftists, and invented any kind of lie against them to decrease their progressive influence over the rank and file. It was the Sun Yat-senists who influenced Chiang Kai-shek to act on March 20. Chiang became the leader of the group at this time, along with Tai Chi-t'ao and others. Originally, Liao Chung-k'ai, the leader of the Kuomintang Left Wing after Sun Yat-sen's death, had made himself head of this group with the object of decreasing the quarrel between the Right and Left. Then Liao was murdered by the Rightists to destroy his power and influence.[3]

I continued to work in the 14th Division in Mei *hsien*, where I was the only Communist, but I could not work well—someone knew my party connection—and I wanted to ask leave to go to Canton. There were two other Communists, one working in the 3rd Division and the other in the First Army. We three talked with Ho Ying-ch'in but he refused to give us leave to go to Canton, and his troops marched off to Fukien. Ultimately, however, Ho Ying-ch'in gave permission to me and to the member in the 3rd Division, and we left for Canton. I stayed a short time, went to Shanghai with about ten others and from there went on to Wuhan.

In Wuhan I was ordered to work in the 12th Division political department as secretary to Chang Fa-k'uei, who was at that time very progressive. This was the best army of the Kuomintang, the "Old Ironsides," and here the general political work was very good. The fighting power was high, the organization was strict, and the officers were good.

In the winter of 1926, the army marched to fight in Kiangsi against Sun Ch'uan-fang, returning to Wuchang after defeating him. In the spring of 1927, we fought in Honan against Chang Hsüeh-liang. Ho Lung was with us then, a commander under Chang Fa-k'uei. We captured Kaifeng, stayed several days, and then returned to Wuhan. By this time the political situation had already changed. Chiang Kai-shek had gone to Nanking and revolted against the Wuhan government, and there were two rival governments and an interparty struggle.

At Wuchang I was sick and had to go to the hospital. Chang Fa-k'uei's Fourth Army went on to Nanchang without me, and on August 1, 1927, the Nanchang Uprising occurred among our troops. I missed participating in this as I was still ill in the hospital. The Ironsides Army had four divisions, the 10th, the 12th, the 24th, and the 25th, almost equally good. Yeh T'ing was commander of the 24th and joined the uprising. Ho Lung's troops were excellent because of much political work among them done by Communists. He was not then with Chang Fa-k'uei.

In April, Communists and Leftists were killed in Canton, Shanghai, and Kwangsi, and several of my close friends were executed in Canton. However, the killings did not extend to Honan, where I went trying to recover from my fever.

Student in Russia, 1927–30

As soon as I was well enough to travel, the party sent me to the U.S.S.R. to study. I set out in September 1927. I went first to the Eastern University, which in 1928 was changed to the "Labor University of Chinese Communism." Eastern University had three hundred students of eighty different nationalities, including Japanese, Turks, Persians, Mongols, and some from Sinkiang. The largest contingent was eighty Chinese. We could not talk to each other until after we learned Russian as a common language. The curriculum was chiefly an intensive study of Marxism and Leninism, and the students were much interested in these subjects. There was also a branch of Eastern University that taught military work. Two hundred Chinese students were enrolled there.

Labor University was only for Chinese Communist party members, and we had four hundred students, many being workers as well as students. Before 1927 this had been called Sun Yat-sen University and half the students were Kuomintang and half Communists. When the split occurred in 1927, the Kuomintang members were sent back to China, leaving only Communists, and the name was changed. At this time, Chiang Ching-kuo, the son of Chiang Kai-shek, was still there, also Fêng Yü-hsiang's son, and Shao Li-tze's son, who later betrayed the party and finally went to Italy where he died. I knew Chiang Ching-kuo. He was a Communist party member and wrote a manifesto against his father.

Secret Return to China, 1930

I stayed in the U.S.S.R. until August 1930. Then I returned to China, secretly and in disguise, across the dangerous border line. I was leader of a group of five other returning students, three girls and two boys, but we tried to pretend not to know one another while traveling. We left the train and started to walk along a lane before reaching the border but the guards discovered us and took us to the station.

At the border was a small railway station where few strangers ever came and police surveillance was strict, everyone being suspected of coming from the U.S.S.R. As Chang Hsüeh-liang's police were certain we came from there and we had no baggage, we admitted it but denied we were students. We said we were merchants returning because business was not good, and I claimed one girl as my sister-in-law and another as a friend's wife. Just then I heard a worker at the station speaking my native Anhwei dialect and I made friends with him. The police decided to believe our story and we were not held.

Police boarded the train with us, however, and talked with me, giving me tea and asking many questions about Russia. I read the newspapers on the train and studied the map of Harbin to know about what was happening so I could pretend to be a native of Liaoning. I also talked with a student and a teacher on the train, but I was afraid they were spies. However, on my arrival at Harbin, nobody followed me when I took a ricksha.

I had pretended to be stopping in Harbin but instead I changed trains to Dairen and there I had to register at a hotel under police requirement. I said I lived in Harbin and was taking the girls to Shanghai to school.

I was too nervous to be very collected. Next morning as I slept in bed, with one of my friends sitting up dressed on the bed to get some sleep, a stranger entered my room. He asked:

"How many are sleeping in this room?"

"Two," I answered. Then I was awake enough to see that the stranger was not a traveler looking for a spare bed, as he was very clean and wore foreign clothes. I therefore changed my story because I did not want him to think that I was an acquaintance of my companion.

"Actually there is only one person for this room, myself," I informed the stranger.

He then demanded to know why I changed from saying that two had rented the room.

"Because I wanted to occupy the whole bed as I am very tired and need sleep," I answered. "This man on the foot of the bed is a stranger to me. I have two girls with me but I don't know this person."

"What is your business?" he next asked.

"I teach in my brother's home in Harbin and the two girls with me are his daughters whom I am taking to school in Shanghai," I answered, giving him a street address in Harbin that we had decided upon.

"What subject?" he wanted to know.

"Chinese," I answered.

"What is your brother's profession?"

"He is opening uncultivated land in Manchuria," I replied.

When we left to go to the steamer, this stranger came along too. I had no luggage but a little box which was in fact empty except for a cup, a handkerchief, and a newspaper. On the steamer, I put this box with some other baggage on deck, and the stranger asked: "Where is your luggage?"

"There!" I said, pointing to the whole pile.

I now discovered that he was a Japanese spy, speaking perfect Chinese. When the boat left, he went away.

At this time in Manchuria, Chang Hsüeh-liang was on the whole very liberal, though many Communists doing local work had been arrested. Some were arrested and imprisoned a short while, but if they left Manchuria it did not matter.

Entering the Blockaded Kiangsi Soviets

Arriving safely in Shanghai, I stayed a month; then the party ordered me to go to Kiangsi to work. I went to Hongkong and from there to Swatow in Kwangtung. Near by was a small soviet district with an armed force. We took a little steamer from Swatow, then a bus, and then we walked—always at night. It took three days to reach the district, and, as our credentials were known, the partisans received us. We had scarcely arrived when, before dawn, the enemy came to capture our party by surprise; we ran away and hid in a rock cave. They failed to trace us and went away, and we returned. Next morning they came again, and again we escaped. Then the armed partisans arrived and fought them.

The enemy was in a good position to command our site on an opposite mountain. I decided to escape by going around behind the mountain, though this was dangerous, too, and two girls and another boy agreed on this plan. One of the girls was Ch'ên Hui-ch'ing, the wife of Têng Fa, and the boy was later killed in Kiangsi. We four found safety, but our two other comrades who had refused to go to the rear were shot by the enemy.

I stayed in this place only a few days, then left with one comrade and a few partisans to guard us. We walked at night, hiding by day. When we arrived five *li* from P'u-ning, a village under our influence but not a soviet district, the peasants reported that the enemy was sending thirty soldiers to collect agricultural products, and that they planned to defend themselves with ten guns and also wanted to capture the enemy's thirty guns. During the fighting, the enemy was defeated but they ran away with their guns so the peasants did not capture them. Now another enemy squad of twenty was sent out. This time the peasants retreated. We had to escape to a mountain and the soldiers followed and fired on us.

We climbed three mountains one after another under pursuit and I became very much exhausted because I had heart trouble. I had had this since I was young as a result of tuberculosis, but in the army my tuberculosis was cured. At night the enemy stopped following and I took a rest. There were now several hundred persons with us. All of them went back to their village when the enemy stopped pursuing them, but many of their cattle had been taken by the soldiers.

This same night, however, I had to go on with my friend. We were disguised as merchants and were on our way to the Tungkiang soviet first, then to Fukien and on to Kiangsi. For five days we had no sleep except briefly in an orchard or on a mountain.

On the Fukien-Kwangtung border, we entered a bandit district. The bandits were very kind to us. I slept in the room with the leader, and he became friendly and liked me. He taught me the secret passwords to give if I should be captured by bandits in this district. A week later we arrived at the Fukien soviet district where Têng Fa was the leader.

Intervening between the Fukien and Kiangsi soviet regions was an enemy district which was very dangerous. Ten party workers wanted to go to Kiangsi, however, so the Fukien soviet sent eighty Red soldiers with us as a guard. Hsü Tê-li and Tso Chuan were with me.

We had two fights in crossing the enemy territory and the journey took three days.

We walked a hundred *li* the first day and also the second day, and one hundred forty *li* the third day. The third day was extremely dangerous. We were delayed by a deep river where there was no boat, and the *min t'uan*[4] were firing at us from all directions. Just then a peasant came up and saw the Red Army uniforms so he asked where we were going. "To the soviet district in Kiangsi," he was informed. He then smiled and said, "That is very far off." He guided us to a lower part of the river where it was shallower and through the mountains by a long roundabout way, but we escaped in safety.

On the fourth day we arrived at the border and visited Chu Tê and Mao Tsê-tung at Hsiao P'u. I had left Shanghai in October 1930. It was now January 1931 when I met Mao and Chu.

I was now put to work. At this time the Military Committee was being organized for the Red Army and I was made secretary. In 1931 we had three blockades against us by the Kuomintang but all were broken. Then at the end of the year we began to organize the headquarters of the political department and I was chief of propaganda in this department and also chief secretary of the Military Committee. At the end of 1933, I changed my work and taught political science at the Red University.

In February 1934 I again changed to be political commissar of the Red Military Academy. Then in July 1934, in preparation for the Long March, I was changed to the political department of the First Army Corps, commanded by Lin Piao, with Nieh Jung-chên as political commissar. This was the vanguard of the Long March.

The Long March

Preparations for making the Long March were kept secret except from the highest authorities. The first public indication of the idea was in an article by Lo Fu in the newspaper *Red China* on October 1, telling of the emergency. Only one week was given for mobilizing to leave, though from one hundred twenty to one hundred thirty thousand started on the Long March. Personnel were withdrawn from the front and gathered in the rear, and all were given guns. Meetings were held and food supplies organized.

The people knew the Red Army was mobilizing to move somewhere but they did not know where. They were never afraid of the defeat of the Red Army. They considered it invincible. However, the soviet areas were completely blockaded by the enemy and surrounded by blockhouses, so it appeared a plan to destroy the enemy's rear and release the blockade—for no salt, even, was available. Many Kiangsi soldiers took money from their families to buy salt and tobacco and other things from districts outside the blockade. During the mobilization week, the spirit was good, not passive, and nobody deserted secretly. The original plan was to break through the blockade by surprise and go to west Hunan to join with Ho Lung's Second Front Army. We left Juikin, Kiangsi, on October 15, 1934, nearly the whole Red Army moving out of Kiangsi.

The "Night March" lasted over a week. We marched secretly and only at night because of air bombing and reconnaissance and also because we were afraid news of our maneuver would get to the enemy.

The second week, our troops began to fight the Kwangtung Army and scattered it easily. We now marched four hours and rested four hours, alternately, both day and night. The "Fast March" lasted three days and we did ten *li* an hour, resting only for meals. This left the enemy behind. After this we rested two days, upon arriving at the Hunan-Kiangsi border in November.

For a week we marched along the Wu Ling Mountains on the Hunan-Kwangtung border, climbing at night. This was very dangerous, with fighting every day. Hunan troops attacked on one side and Kwangtung troops on the other.

Upon reaching south Hunan the Red Army occupied six cities. The Hunan armies were scattered and could not gather, so it was easy for us to take the cities. Then the Hunan armies concentrated and Chiang Kai-shek sent several divisions to pursue us. Kwangsi troops also attacked us—Pai Ch'ung-hsi's from Kweilin. Surrounded on all sides, we had to abandon the plan of meeting the Second Front Army and decided to break through the Kwangsi and Hunan lines at Taochu, Hunan, with Chiang Kai-shek's troops pursuing relentlessly. Our position was highly dangerous and we again marched night and day to escape, the road ahead being constantly cut off by the enemy. For five days our troops battled all the time to break through.

At the Hsiangchiang River, we crossed by a pontoon floating bridge but the bridge was destroyed by the enemy and one division, the 34th, was left behind and turned back to south Hunan. During this time, many groups of the Red Army were cut off from the main force, but all were able to join up later on except the 34th Division. The 34th became partisans in south Hunan.

Our fast march again left the enemy behind and we arrived in Kweichow, in the mountains where there are many Miao tribesmen. When we appeared, they all ran away and we used their houses to cook food in, leaving Kuomintang money and propaganda letters for them when we evacuated. They were won over by this and came back to their homes. Never once did the Miaos fight the Red Army either in Kwangsi or Kweichow. They hated Li Tsung-jên bitterly and when we told them we were fighting Li, they agreed to let us pass freely. On the Kwangsi border a small group of Miaos sent a delegate to the Red Army for good will and wanted to join, but none joined at any time. The Red Army sent them guns and a red banner, which they used independently.

The Kwangsi political authorities played a trick at this time. On the Kwangsi-Kweichow border they hired rascals to pretend to be poor people and Red partisans, and paid them to set fire to houses secretly and then blame the Red Army, for the purpose of rousing the people against us. Meantime all the local people of the district had been forced to leave, so scarcely any remained in their villages. At first the Red Army was amazed and saw no reason for the burning of houses on the way, then they arrested some men discovered in an empty house and the men confessed. The Red Army never burned any houses on the Long March.

Leaving the Kwangsi-Kweichow border, we went to central Kweichow and fought the troops of Wang Chia-lieh, chairman of Kweichow Province. These were easily demolished, as their fighting power was low.

Chiang Kai-shek's troops were following along behind from Hunan to Kweichow, and the Red Army's slogan was: "On to Capture Kweiyang"—the capital of Kweichow. But we used this only as a trick to divert his troops, and when he switched off and marched northwest, Chiang's troops continued on directly west and occupied Kweiyang.

Then we passed the Wukiang River and captured small towns like T'ungchih, Chenyi, and Meit'an. The Red Army stayed in Chenyi a week. Local students there organized the "Friends of the Red Army," and the people organized a "revolutionary committee."

We now—January 1935—intended to cross the Yangtze River into Szechuan to join the Fourth Front Army under Hsü Hsiang-ch'ien,[5] but the enemy had done so much defense work on the other side and the river was so wide and dangerous to cross that we returned to Kweichow and another plan was changed. If we had met Ho Lung as originally intended, I don't know whether we would have stayed in Hunan then or gone on to the Northwest.

When we marched out of Kweichow previously, General Wang Chia-lieh's army had occupied Chenyi and T'ungchih, and Wang himself was in Chenyi. The Red Army now destroyed eight of Wang's regiments and occupied Chenyi. A few of his men joined our army, but most of them smoked opium and we did not want them.

The very next morning after we occupied Chenyi, Chiang Kai-shek's army attacked fiercely with three divisions under Wu Ch'i-wei, a clever commander who is now head of the Fourth Kuomintang Army. We drove them back and destroyed one of the divisions.

Chiang Kai-shek's Kuomintang armies followed all along the Long March, under first one commander and then another, including Wan Yao-huang, Wu Ch'i-wei, and Hsüeh Yüeh—now chairman of Kweichow —who was Chiang's highest-ranking general then. It was difficult for these pursuers, however—partly because they were so much afraid of the Red Army and partly, also, because we constantly changed our direction and tactics to confuse them and to waste their energy in roundabout ways. They never knew from one day to another where we were going, nor did they ever guess our final destination in the northwest. Chiang Kai-shek believed he could annihilate us now because we were isolated from our base in the soviets, and he tried every way to destroy us. His officers never did manipulate the direction of the March to their own purposes and could not have done so had they tried. They merely took advantage of being present in a province to occupy part of it, as they did at Kweiyang. Chiang Kai-shek naturally wanted to take the city, but it fell into his lap. His main idea was to annihilate the Red Army, and he simply chased us through one province after another, taking what advantage he could of the provincial war lords. We weakened the power of these war lords as we passed, both by propaganda and actual fighting. Every effort was made to cut us off and bottle us up. For the Central government troops the Long March was more difficult than for the Red Army because the people hated them and gave them no help, and their morale was not good.

In Kweichow we confiscated the property of the landlords and distributed the goods to the people, whom we also organized. Here four thousand new volunteers joined us. The educational level in Kweichow is low and the people are superstitious. They said the Red Army troops had three wonderful magic instruments—one to put on their legs so they could walk very fast, another for hearing sounds from far distances, and a third for crossing rivers without boats. They believed the Red Army always won victories; in fact, our own soldiers convinced them of this, because it is true that we have strong rules never to fight unless victory is certain, and always to maneuver out of a bad position.

The second time we returned to Kweichow, Chiang Kai-shek guessed that we would go east to join Ho Lung, so he concentrated his armies there and in north Szechuan on the banks of the Yangtze. We now carried out a fast surprise maneuver and marched to Yünnan, but made a preliminary feint southward pretending to attack Kweiyang. Chiang was so alarmed at this trick that he himself flew by plane to defend Kweiyang. On this maneuver toward Kweiyang, the Red troops marched so fast that Chiang's soldiers could not follow. We came within fifty li of Kweiyang. The city looked to be in a precarious position. Chiang was in a quandary. If he left, his troops would be demoralized. If he stayed, his life was in danger. He decided to go to a temple on top of a hill, where he prepared an airfield so he could fly off whenever we took the city. We passed around and marched north.

Chiang Kai-shek now believed that we would march on Kwangsi. The Kwangsi militarists were alarmed, thinking we would go to a small soviet district in west Kwangsi to reorganize our forces and supplies. When we went northwest to Yünnan, they were all much surprised.

The strategists of all these maneuvers on the Red Military Council were chiefly Mao Tsê-tung, Chu Tê, Chou Ên-lai, Wang Chia-hsiang, and Liu Po-ch'êng. At the beginning of the Long March, "Li Teh,"[6] the German, was in charge, but so many mistakes were made that Mao Tsê-tung himself took charge after Chenyi.

The Story of a Straggler

I kept a diary during the Long March, and one day a straggler from the Third Army Corps told me this story, which I wrote down. His name was Wang, and he was a native of Kiangsi, but I don't know his first name.

In January 1935, when we reached the border of Szechuan and Kweichow and were having a difficult time, being completely surrounded by enemies, this man Wang was left behind. He walked half a day before meeting four other stragglers. They discussed how to find the army, he taking leadership of the group. At sundown they found two houses. The five of them were hungry. The other four wanted to cook food in one of the houses, but the leader said, "No, the min t'uan will come." They were insistent, however, and before they had finished cooking there appeared about fifteen min t'uan who seized their five rifles, but Wang also had a pistol which they did not see.

The five were ordered outside and expected to be shot immediately. One min t'uan officer stood near the door. As the captives passed out, Wang shot him with the pistol and all five of them ran away fast. Many of the min t'uan set out after Wang and shot at him, but they missed and he killed several of his pursuers. When he arrived in some very tall grass and woods, he was too tired to go on, and so hid himself. The min t'uan surrounded him and searched, but they were foolish and shouted in the woods, so when he heard their voices in one direction he would run in another and they could not find him. In the evening they went away. He built a fire in the grass and went on. Soon he found a lamplit house and thought that maybe the owner would be kind. He knocked, but there was no answer. Then he knocked a long time, for he knew someone was there, refusing to open the door. He spoke through the door, saying he was a traveler and meant no harm. The owner finally opened the door and demanded to know who he was and what he wanted. Wang had taken off his Red Army uniform, and he answered:

"I am a native of Chenyi. I was captured by the Red Army and forced to do transportation for them. Now I have escaped and I am going home."

But the man knew it was not the Chenyi dialect that he spoke, so the soldier had to do much explaining before he could prove that he knew Chenyi. He had been there a little while on the march and was able to convince the man. It was the time of the old-year festival, and the family gave him good food. The husband, wife, mother, and son lived in the house. The old mother was very kind but she did not believe he was a Chenyi man. Before long she said to him:

"I hope you will tell the truth and not a lie. We are poor people and the Red Army helps the poor. If you tell the truth perhaps we can help you to find the Red Army again. I have only one son, so I cannot want to do you any harm. I, myself, like the Red Army."

Next day the son of the family went with him to find the Red Army, pretending to be a relative. When they arrived where the Red Army had been, however, it had marched on.

Many *min t'uan* were near here and were angry because their leader had been killed. The leader's son, who had succeeded him, swore revenge. The *min t'uan* now discovered the stranger and wanted to kill him on suspicion of being a Red soldier. But the common people took a hand and said there was a question whether or not he was a Red, and there was no proof. Another good old woman said to the *min t'uan* leader:

"You have no proof he is a Red Army man, and even if he is, your father was not killed by him. So release him!"

Because this old woman was so insistent, Wang was only beaten and released.

He now had to part with the son of the kind family and go his own way alone. On the mountain he met two bandits. He still had the pistol and twenty dollars. He gave them the twenty dollars but they also wanted his clothes. "No," he insisted. "It is too cold. I want to keep my clothes."

Then one bandit indicated that he would kill him with a knife, but Wang shot him with the pistol and the other bandit escaped.

Next day Wang arrived at a small town and found five other stragglers there. The four originally with him had been recaptured by the *min t'uan*. Since there were no enemy forces here, he organized the group to propagandize the town, and told about the Red Army and its principles. The people gave them food and help. They stayed only two days. Then he led the group to try to find the Red Army.

Arriving at one village, they saw a young man crying because another man was trying to drive him out of the house into the snow and cold outside. They could tell from his dialect that he was a Kiangsi man, and he said: "I have only this thin clothing and I will surely die if you drive me out."

They knew he was a Kiangsi Red soldier, and he admitted it and told them: "I was with the Red Army before and deserted secretly and sold my gun for twenty dollars. I met some robbers who took my twenty dollars and nearly all my clothes. Now I am sick. I have stayed in this house only one day, and the owner is driving me away to die."

They asked if he intended to return to the Red Army or what else he would do, and he answered: "I'm afraid to go back because I sold my gun and that is a crime."

"No matter," the others said. "Come back with us and we can guarantee for you."

They all went away together, after paying the man in the house some money.

A few days later this group arrived at Red Army quarters and the leader received much praise for his courage and ingenuity. Wang is now working in the Fifteenth Army Corps under Hsü Hai-tung.

Crossing the Yangtze

In Yünnan, since the provincial military forces were weak and the army was divided into many parts, Kunming [Yünnanfu], the capital, was not garrisoned. The Red Army marched so rapidly that it came within sixty *li* of the city before the defense was aware, causing great consternation.

When the Red Army was in Yünnan, Governor Lung Yün and Chiang Kai-shek discovered our plan to cross the Yangtze on the Yünnan side. On the Szechuan side, north, Liu Wên-hui's troops were on guard, very unreliable and weak, and also there were weak troops on the south side. Lung Yün was, therefore, alarmed and ordered all the boats on the upper river to be burned so that the Red Army could not pass.

The Red Army was divided into three parts: the left wing was the First Army Corps, led by Lin Piao; the right wing was the Third Army Corps, led by P'êng Tê-huai; and the middle column was led by the Military Council with Mao Tsê-tung as chairman. One brigade of Red Academy cadets was in the middle. The left and right moved slower than the middle, which was smaller and also had the best brigade—the Red Academy cadets, led by Liu Po-ch'eng. Halfway to the Yangtze River, a messenger from the *hsien* magistrate was captured carrying an order to burn all boats. He was treated well and was won over, and agreed to lead the middle column to the river bank. Only one boat was left there by now, and this could carry only ten persons at a time. It took thirty to forty minutes for the boat to cross over and back. On the north side of the river was a small tax office with twenty guards. When the first Red soldiers crossed over it was night, and the people in the building were smoking opium and playing mahjongg. The soldiers knocked, and the tax collectors asked who they were. They an-swered that they were Kuomintang troops and were invited in for tea and cigarettes— they had taken the red star off their caps. Later on, the guards were disarmed, but they were not alarmed, because they had already made friends. No harm was done to them.

The Yangtze here is two *li* wide. It took eight days and nights for the troops to cross, even though later on four other boats were discovered. The middle column crossed first, led by Liu Po-ch'eng's Red cadets, and the left and right wings came later. Lo Ping-hui's 9th Division had been cut off. They had to cross at another place.

We had originally tried to cross the Yangtze in January, and now it was just after May 1, our Labor Day. We had no time for a celebration. We just sang songs and shouted slogans along the way and made a few speeches. Sometimes we celebrated holidays on the Long March if conditions were not too dangerous. We always sang on the way, and many new songs were made up on the March. I made up the "Tsunyi Song," about the capture of that town, and P'êng Chia-lun wrote one about the "River of Golden Sand."[7] Another song was about the endless maneuvers in Kweichow to break through the encirclement.

We crossed the great rivers in May—the Yangtze, the "River of Golden Sand," and the Tatu Ho.

Chiang Kai-shek's troops were in Kunming and could not follow our fast march quickly enough to prevent the crossing. They reached the bank of the Yangtze just as the last of our troops were about to cross, and were defeated. Lung Yün's troops also pursued us and were defeated. The Red Army burned the boats so the enemy could not cross—they turned back to Yünnan and Kweichow and Szechuan, where they again took up the pursuit. We next met Chiang Kai-shek's troops under Hsüeh Yüeh near Chengtu.

Near the River of Golden Sand is the mountainous country of "Independent Lolo-land."[8] The Red Army sent friendly letters to treat with the Lolos and told them of our definite policy to give self-determination to the tribes of China and to preserve them. Ultimately, our negotiations were successful. In the future the Lolos will all support our party and policy, but for a while it seemed touch and go before we could establish good relations with them.

Lololand and the Tatu River, May 1935

We crossed the River of Golden Sand on May 15, 1935. The Red Army was marching northward between this river and the Tatu River in a very dangerous position. The distance between the two great rivers is about six hundred *li*. Behind, the River of Golden Sand was held by the Central Government army. Ahead, the Tatu was defended by Szechuan provincial troops. East and west were high and wild mountains with many wild and unfriendly tribesmen, the *I Min*, or Lolos. We could march only at night because of the airplanes in the sky. The road was narrow between the high mountains.

We marched several nights. Then, at a distance of two hundred *li* from the Tatu River, we could not continue because of an ambush of many *I Min*. We turned aside, and on May 22 reached Miening Hsien, a boundary town of the Lolo district. Here many Lolos were imprisoned by the military lords of Szechuan, either for nonpayment of taxes or because of invading the *hsien*. The penalty was death. The Red Army set free these two hundred prisoners, among whom were some who could speak Chinese. They were grateful to us and wanted to help guide us through the Lolo district. Except for their help in diplomatic relations with the tribes, we would have had serious trouble. The prisoners went ahead to negotiate as we marched through. But in this district were many tribal feuds and two distinct classes, the society being based on slavery. One group would be friendly to us, but their enemies unfriendly. Each group was controlled by a lord owning many slaves. The Lolos

have a primitively simple life and live in houses made of wood, sleeping on the ground with no bed. Their clothing is a woolen blanket and full trousers, and they wear no hats. Agricultural production is very backward, though they have cattle and horses and many sheep. Their livelihood comes from hunting and capturing animals. The slaves captured from near-by Chinese districts were forced to do all the manual work.

Only a few Chinese had ever crossed these areas before—traveling merchants only—and they had to give big "squeeze" to the tribal chiefs.

When the Red Army arrived at Mien Ning, the *hsien* magistrate, the militarists, and the merchants—seven hundred altogether, with their wives—had all run away to the Lolo districts. All were captured by the Lolos, and the magistrate was killed. They feared us more than their enemies, the Lolos. Many of the rich landlords were released, but the Lolos took off all their clothes except their trousers—even their shoes. We met them in this condition on the way.

The Red Army then marched from Mien Ning and reached the town of Ta Ch'ao on the border between the Chinese and the Lolo district. The people of the town had run away, and the Lolos had heard the news and were planning to come down to capture them and take all their goods. The people begged the Red Army to defend them against the Lolos. We had no alternative, and we defeated the Lolos.

Next morning the Red Army began to march from Ta Ch'ao and climbed the mountain. Here was the heart of the Lolo district, all hidden in the wilderness. One squad of vanguards went ahead and one company of engineers, who build bridges and trenches, went behind them. The Lolos captured this company and blocked the way. The squad was cut off from the main body. We then hardly knew what to do, and had no way to negotiate. However, he found one Lolo chief and sent him good wines and

These Lolo tribesmen joined the Red Army during the progress of the Long March across Szechuan Province and became students of Marxism at the Communist Party School in Yenan, where they posed for this photograph in 1937.

money, and Liu Po-ch'êng tried to negotiate peacefully with him. The chief wanted to do this in the tribal way and to pledge blood brotherhood, so he ordered his servant to bring a live chicken and poured out the blood on a board. Then he and Liu Po-ch'eng each drank of it as a pledge, as they bowed to the sky to propitiate the tribal gods. The Red Army sent red banners and many guns and horses to the Lolos, and ultimately they led us through the district. The Lolos use old-style methods of ambush warfare but they have guns and move with amazing speed.

These Lolos were first-class confiscators, and we were not too much amused to find someone who could do this much better than ourselves. The whole body of troops was mobilized to hand over gifts to the Lolos to buy our way through, but the tribesmen were never satisfied and took more and more. They looked in the pockets of our soldiers and even pulled off their clothing very rudely. In fact they took away everything portable that the Red Army had to spare. But we had no way to save our lives but to grin and forbear. At all costs, we wanted to be friendly with them, and we had to be extremely careful. They had many taboos, and we had to learn what these were and observe them. We never entered their houses. One of their taboos was that nobody should ever move the iron vessels in which they cook.

It took only two days to cross Lololand,

but we did not breathe easily until we were out of there. Thousands and thousands of Lolos were mobilized along the way.

As we passed the Lolo region, we came upon many Szechuan provincial soldiers. When they saw our soldiers they shouted: "What army are you?"

The 1st Division of the First Army Corps, leading the way, replied: "We are the Central Army." When they got near, they disarmed the Szechuan soldiers and found a good deal of rice provided for their troops. We took part of it and gave part to the local people.

This place was near the Tatu River. The people said that four hundred Szechuan soldiers were defending the river and that the commander of the Szechuan army had ordered the people of the whole area twenty *li* wide on each side of the Tatu River to remove all food and burn the houses. The plan was not fully completed, however, when we came up. Close to the river was a small village named Anshunch'ang. Our army planned to cross here. This was where, in the T'aip'ing Rebellion, the T'aip'ing general, Shih Ta-k'ai, was captured and deprived of power. The Szechuan commander stayed here, but most of his soldiers were on the opposite bank. He had planned to return across by boat.

Before dawn, the Red Army came by surprise and surrounded and disarmed this small unit of soldiers and captured their boat, but the commander escaped. The water here is terrifyingly swift and roars so that it can be heard from a distance. You cannot hear a word if you speak on the bank. The Red Army had only the one boat, which required sixteen boatmen—and the boatmen had to be natives, since nobody else could navigate the treacherous river. After a time, we found sixteen local men and they took seventeen of our soldiers over in the boat.

Meantime we had concentrated our best machine gunners to cover the other side of the river, about one hundred meters across, which was defended by enemy troops. There was a stone cliff on the opposite side and it was difficult to land the boat, though our men were covering the landing with a constant barrage. The seventeen men had one hundred hand grenades which they threw into the enemy trenches. Thus they broke the defense, and the front line gave way a little. Our men now occupied the defense work and drove about two hundred of the enemy farther away. Only one of the seventeen was killed and one wounded. These men had all volunteered when the soldiers were told: "This is a critical time. If we cannot pass, we will be disorganized."

The 1st Division crossed over by this one boat and another which we discovered on the other side. Since it took two days for the one division to cross, the main Red Army went around to another place.

The main body of troops marched along the bank of the Tatu River to reach the Luting Ch'iao bridge, surrounded by the enemy and fighting constantly for three days before they got there. They climbed a mountain to reach the bridge, which is over a high gorge. When they arrived, they found that the bridge consisted of twelve swaying iron chains, where wooden boards had been stretched across, but all the boards had been taken off by the enemy.

It was very dangerous and required great physical strength and stability to cross by these chains, but it had to be done and quickly because the 1st Division was alone on the other side of the river and might be annihilated by the enemy at any moment. On one side of the river was a small street and houses and on the other, close to the bank, was a town where the enemy had good defense trenches.

Twenty volunteers were asked for and more responded. The opposite side was covered with machine-gun fire, and under enemy fire the twenty men crossed over on the chains, carrying only pistols and big swords. Not one was killed on the chains, but the enemy set fire to the houses on the other side to prevent the men from landing because of the flames and intense heat. Nevertheless, all twenty went into the burning buildings and got the boards, which they put on the chains so the army could cross. The enemy had been driven away by the machine-gunning and the volunteers' pistols. Only three of the twenty were killed.

The division which crossed first at Luting Ch'iao was commanded by Liu Chin-kwei; the political commissar was Huang Ssŭ. Liu Po-ch'êng also crossed leading this division, He now commands the Fourth Front Army.

After crossing the Tatu, our two divided forces met on the other side of the river and marched to Yaan [formerly Yachow] a few hundred li from Chengtu. The Red Army marched east and pretended to want to occupy Chengtu, but changed its direction northward because of having news that it could meet the Fourth Front Red Army under Hsü Hsiang-ch'ien. We always had radio connections with all units and also telephones. Every division had a radio, and used telephones the whole time. Our "veteran wires" from the Long March can be seen here in Yenan, still in good use.

In Tibet and the "Grasslands"

Marching north, the Red Army captured two cities, T'iench'üa and Lushan, then continued on to the snow-covered mountains several thousand feet high, the Chia Chin Shan or Hsüeh Shan. There was no fighting here, and no houses and no people. The weather underwent rapid changes dan-

Red troops crossing at Luting Ch'iao Bridge. This scene and the two following are from contemporary ink and brush sketches by Communist artists.

gerous to health. After a fair morning, there might be snow in the evening. As it was summer, our people had no heavy clothes at all and were unprepared. Before we climbed the mountain, many people told us of the danger of the thin atmosphere up where it was difficult to breathe. They also advised that when too tired, never sit down but stand, or you may never rise again. And they said not to drink the snow water or it might induce death, it was so cold. We found much of this to be true, and many Red soldiers died in crossing the Snowy Mountains.

In Mokung *hsien* we met the Fourth Front Army, then marched north to the land of the *Fan Min*, who are Tibetans. Here the tribes gave us much trouble, firing on our men from ambush and escaping quickly. They carried away all food, making the problem of supply acute. Tibetan leaders also betrayed us to the Szechuan militarists. At first the Red Army wrote letters and left them in the houses, asking for food and leaving money to pay for it. Then we discovered that the money was being stolen by passers-by. Finally, some Tibetans changed their hostility and we organized a revolutionary committee among them and exchanged tea for food. We had confiscated the tea from rich Tibetan landlords. The worst problem was food. You cannot eat much wheat or it harms your stomach. I knew two men who died from eating green wheat. In the beginning, some food remained in the houses

even though the people all ran away, but it was only wheat and beans. We had to take green wheat from the fields and cook it, which was very unpleasant.

After marching through Maoerhkai near Sungp'an[9] where General Hu Tsung-nan was stationed, we prepared to go to Kansu but did not know the direction as we had no map. We had to find Tibetan guides among the mountain people. As they did not speak Chinese, we also had to find interpreters on the border of the Tibetan district. Some of these were sympathetic and wanted to join the Red Army.

We now prepared to cross the dreaded "Grasslands." As the Tibetans told us that no food would be available, each person carried twenty *chin*,[10] enough for fifteen days. All we had to take, however, was green wheat [*ch'ing lo mai*], though it was different from that we had previously had.

The swampy Grasslands [*Ts'ao Ti*] were deep quicksand, soft mud and grass, and deep pools. Many soldiers fell in and were drowned—also many horses. It was here that we had our greatest losses of the Long March. There were no rocks or trees. The hills were dripping wet. Scarcely any dry spots existed where one could sleep. The weather was also very unpleasant, rain every night making sleep impossible. The grass was too wet to burn, to cook food, or to dry clothing. Each person had carried wood for

Soldiers in the "Grass-
lands" carrying their
fifteen days' supply of
grain for food.

a fire, but after two days, all this was used up and no fires could be made. Nobody lives in the Ts'ao Ti—no human being could.

The Red Army command estimated that it would take fifteen days to cross the Grass-lands, but on the sixth day a new road was discovered, leading down to a village and some houses. Here we found food and were very happy. The route was changed to the eastward to Paichow, where we encountered Hu Tsung-nan's army and fought his 49th Division, destroying two regiments. His soldiers marched a little way into the Grass-lands but gave it up.

The Fourth Front Red Army marched into the western part of the Grasslands, but in the middle there was so much water that they could not pass and had to go back and around northward. Later the Fourth Front Army went south to Sikang and we went on north.

We now marched to the Szechuan-Kansu border, in September, and at Latzŭk'ou we fought a Kansu army commanded by Lu Ta-ch'ang. Here we marched along a river with high cliffs on either side, and on both banks were fortresses defended by the enemy. These cliffs were straight up and impossible to climb in some places. Then our method was to throw up a rope with a stone at the end and fix it around a tree, each man clambering up this way. One of our companies climbed up in this way and defeated the enemy at the top. In Kansu there were not many Kuomintang elements, so the fighting there was only small frays. When Hu Tsung-nan was defeated in the Sungp'an by the Red Army, Chiang Kai-shek ordered him to follow us, but Hu refused and said: "I have now only half my army left. If I follow, the whole body will be destroyed, so I will not do it."

The first time the Red Army ever had any cavalry was when we captured a hundred horses in a fight with the 6th Cavalry Division of the Central government and destroyed one regiment. This was at Huat'ing in Kansu, near P'ingliang. After this fight, the Red Army marched on to north Shensi, pursued by three cavalry elements—those of Ma Hung-k'uei, Ma Hung-p'ing, and Chiang Kai-shek. Because of the speed of the cavalry, many Red troops in the rear were cut off and captured.

North Shensi, October 20, 1935

After five days, we arrived at Wuch'ichên on the north Shensi border, where we stayed. Here we saw the Red Flag and knew we were not far from the soviet region which Liù Tzŭ-tan had organized in north Shensi long before. The men said: "Now we are at home again after this Long March."

The soldiers also said: "We can't go empty-handed to our comrades. We must take some horses to them." So they fought the cavalry and captured dozens of horses, forcing the rest of the cavalry to retreat.

We had left Kiangsi on October 15, 1934. We arrived at Wuch'ichên on October 20, 1935, just a year later.

The march now continued on to Paoan in north Shensi, and part of the troops went south to Kanchuan. There the soldiers continued southward to meet Hsü Hai-tung's army coming up from Oyüwan. The government personnel went north to Waiyapao and passed Yungp'ing on the way. Here, on September 18, Hsü Hai-tung had arrived, and photographs were taken to celebrate.

After joining Hsü Hai-tung, the Red Armies now began fighting the Tungpei troops of Chang Hsüeh-liang. Chang's 1st Division was destroyed and much equipment was captured, such as food, clothes, stockings, shoes, guns, and bullets. This victory made all the troops happy and all north Shensi was excited. A regimental commander, Kao Fu-yüan, was captured, and negotiations for a united front began about November 11 or 12, 1935.

In June 1936 we changed the soviet capital from Waiyapao to Paoan and in January 1937 to Yenan. The reason we changed the capital was that Wang Yi-cheh of Chang Hsüeh-liang's army was secretly discussing stopping the civil war and knew that in two months Nanking would order his troops to make an advance. The Nanking officer on the Tungpei general staff ordered an attack on Waiyapao, so we were advised to move to Paoan. The Tungpei troops then held Yenan but gave us this town later. The Red

Making friends with tribesmen encountered on the Long March.

Army had surrounded Yenan from the winter of 1935 to the spring of 1936. Chang Hsüeh-liang was then in Nanking.

Our last fight with Tungpei troops was when Kao was captured, the division commander being killed. Before this, Hsü Hai-tung had also fought Tungpei troops in Kanchuan.

We lost nearly all of our official documents in the Grasslands and in crossing rivers. Many carriers were drowned, being hampered by the dispatch cases. We also burned many documents that could not be conveniently carried. Now we have scarcely any historical records.

We brought sewing machines from Kiangsi; every regiment had one or two; and many of these precious machines arrived safely in north Shensi. We also started out from Kiangsi with a printing plant and the arsenal machinery, but most of these pieces were lost or destroyed. Each group had its own transport corps. About five or six thousand persons were required to carry the machinery of the Military Committee and the Central government.

I had changed from the First Army Corps to become chief of propaganda of the Third Army Corps when we arrived in Kansu, in September 1935. This had originally been P'êng Tê-huai's command, but at this time P'êng Hsüeh-fêng was the commander.

Then, when we had arrived in north Shensi and just begun to fight, I lost both my legs because of cold weather—after they had carried me six thousand miles! I always wanted to do military work, but I have always done political work, and now I always will. I am at present chief of the Rear Political Department.

Wang Shou-tao

POLITICAL COMMISSAR

MISS WALES:

WANG SHOU-TAO is typical of the men in the political departments of the Communist armies who keep civilian control over the soldiers and enforce the Party line. He is also typical of the Liuyang Hunanese: all it took for the young student of eighteen to begin organizing peasant associations in his native district was an article in a Canton newspaper, as he tells in the following narrative. This was in 1923 and was one of the earliest instances of class organization in Hunan. Later he became chairman of the Hunan provincial soviet and worked in the government of the Hunan-Hupeh-Kiangsi Border District, a soviet region of one million population.

After the Long March, Wang was chairman of the political department of the Fifteenth Army Corps under Hsü Hai-tung. He continued in this post in the Eighth Route Army during the war with Japan. In 1949 he was a reserve member of the Central Committee of the Communist party.

WANG SHOU-TAO:

I WAS born in Liuyang, Hunan, in 1907, of a poor peasant family.

When I was nine, I entered a free primary school where students had to furnish only their clothes, books, and food. I was diligent and the teachers liked me. Once I asked a teacher to draw a picture for me but when it was finished a landlord's son asked for it and the teacher gave it to him instead. I fought with the student and the teacher punished me for that. I was embittered by that unfair experience and I did not forget it. From then on I was imbued with a hatred of landlords.

I had to earn my own money to pay for food, and to get money I cut wood. The only wooded places were owned by landlords and I had to steal from them. My brother often went on these escapades with me. One day we were caught and my brother was imprisoned by the landlord. I felt depressed and hopeless, and thought life offered no way for the poor.

When I was twelve, my family moved a distance of a hundred *li* and went to live with an uncle, my mother's brother. I was apprenticed to the master of a firecracker shop but half a year later, with the help of my uncle, I began to study in an old-style Chinese school. The teacher was a landlord named Li, a relative of my uncle. I worked and studied over a year. Then, helped by Li, I went to a higher primary school. There I was influenced by the May Fourth Movement and organized the poor students in the school into a brotherhood to oppose the Twenty-one Demands. With several friends, I began a movement in the village to start a night school and to oppose the old Chinese teaching methods and ideas. I also organized a dramatics club to present plays.

My father, fearing that when I grew up the family would be too poor to get a wife for me, had engaged me when very young. I was now fourteen and my father wanted me to marry. I refused. I had acted in a play as the girl victim of an arranged marriage and felt strongly on the subject.

At seventeen, I entered the Changsha Shu Yüeh middle school, supported by Li and some family friends. Because my family was very poor and I had not enough money to eat with the other students in the school, I ate outside in street stalls and borrowed money from other students. Sometimes I was ashamed to borrow and sometimes I could not, so I was often hungry. I got along by eating only two meals a day. One night, feeling extremely hungry, I went to the school restaurant to sneak some food and was discovered by the manager. I felt both humiliated and indignant. I wrote an essay in my notebook called, "On the Way to Huang Tan Lin." This was a graveyard with beautiful trees where I often played. The essay described and contrasted the rich and the poor students and pointed out the idleness of the rich and the diligence of the poor, who received no reward. I asked: What can we do to change such an unfair world? The teacher found this in my notebook. He was a liberal and decided to help me through the next term. Next year I concluded I could learn nothing of practical use in the middle school and entered the government agricultural school, which was also a free school. Here the tuition fee was very low, eight dollars a year, and I was supported by the middle-school teacher who sponsored me.

A year and a half later, the Changsha student movement began against the Japanese who had killed a Chinese wharf worker in Changsha. I joined the Communist Youth in the school and took part in the agitation. I wrote a manifesto attacking the school administration and authorities, and was expelled.

I returned to Liuyang and there began to read the magazine *New Youth*. An article appeared describing the peasant associations in Canton and this inspired me to organize peasant groups and political discussion groups in my own rural community. By this time I understood the nature of the class struggle and I explained it to the peasants. The landlords objected, and the provincial government ordered my arrest. I ran away to Canton and on the way stopped in Shanghai. I used a counterfeit silver dollar in Shanghai, unknowingly, and was arrested by the British police. I was innocent, but the police were rough to me and fined me five dollars of my small funds, all borrowed from friends. This introduction to foreign

concessions filled me with hatred of imperialism.

In Canton I entered the school for peasants organized by Mao Tsê-tung. P'êng Pai[1] was also a teacher there. Here I joined the Communist party in 1925 and received further instruction, learning the fundamental principles of the land revolution. I returned to Hunan, and in Changsha I joined the Kuomintang, being also a member of the Communist party branch in the city.

In 1926 I went to southern Hunan and began work among the peasants in Chiyang. Then because of the Hsü K'ê-hsiang massacre[2] in 1927, I had to escape from Chiyang to Tunghu in south Hunan, where I stayed with a peasant family nearly five months. Here I read the *Communist Manifesto* and *Essentials of Capital*. In the winter of 1927 I returned to my native town, Liuyang, and helped the peasant uprising there. I found the peasants opposed to taxes and the slaughter of progressives, and I organized them into a Liuyang *hsien* committee, of which I was secretary. The peasants made three attempts to capture Liuyang, the *hsien* city, and began to confiscate the property of landlords and gentry. The first time, I had one pistol and twenty men with me. The hatred of the peasants for the landlords was so intense that when they went to the house and found the landlord gone, they burned his house.

Small partisan districts were organized throughout the *hsien*. In 1928 I was appointed secretary to the special committee of the Hunan-Hupeh-Kiangsi border district. The collective system of cultivation was experimented with in Liuyang and P'ingk'iang, but nobody knew how to begin the land revolution, having had no experience. Later on we received instructions from the party, after the Sixth Congress [of the Comintern]. The collectivization experiment had no good result. We attempted to consolidate all farms and share work among the peasants, dividing crops at harvest. The peasants did not respond well to this. Their demand was for land of their own which each family could cultivate for itself. The party recognized this and altered its policy. At present, collectivization is not necessary. The division of land then began, and development was accelerated. In 1929 the "Soviet Government of the Hunan-Hupeh-Kiangsi Border District" was established, and I was a member of the committee, being then twenty-two years old.

In 1930 when P'êng Tê-huai captured Changsha, I was secretary of the activities committee. Later I became chairman of the Hunan provincial soviet. Li Li-san was nominal chairman but he never arrived. When I was appointed by the Central Committee to conduct secret work, my wife and I went to Changsha to work among the textile factories. During the destruction of the provincial committee, my wife was arrested and executed by Ho Ch'ien. I escaped to Shanghai, where I worked in the party until 1932, when I entered the Hunan-Kiangsi soviet and began work as party secretary.

The mass struggle in this area was very enthusiastic. In the district of Ch'aling [about eighty miles southeast of Changsha], the villages had been occupied by Ho Ch'ien's troops for two years, but still the peasants outside remained sovietized. When the *hsien* police went out to collect taxes, the peasants beat them and drove them away. The landlords, too, could not collect rents.

In 1933 Hsiao K'ê became commander of the Sixth Red Army, and in 1934 I went to the Second All-Soviet Congress as delegate. On the Long March to the north, I worked in the political department of the Military Committee. Then, during the Eastern Expedition to Shansi, I was transferred to be chairman of the political department of the Fifteenth Army Corps.

The political commissar is all-powerful in the policies of the army, and the political department is under his direction to carry out his plans. The department also carries out work in the enemy armies.

PART TWO

Recruits from Industry

Ts'ai Shu-fan

HANYEHP'ING MINER

MISS WALES:

IN spite of having a poker face, Ts'ai Shu-fan is like most of the provincials from Hunan and Hupeh in being frank, outspoken, critical, and hot-tempered. His figure is slight and wiry. In 1931 he was badly wounded by shrapnel; then in 1933, while fighting against the Nineteenth Route Army in Fukien, he received a bullet wound which led to the amputation of one arm—as he tells in his story. He gets on well with foreigners, and foreigners seem to like him. I found that most of the working-class Communists I encountered were, like Ts'ai Shu-fan, not antiforeign; antiforeignness was rather a characteristic of the middle-class elements.

Ts'ai's story shows some of the early stirrings of the labor movement in China among miners, railway workers, and seamen. Hanyehp'ing, near Wuhan, was the center of the iron industry of China, and its Miners' Union was one of the four main labor unions of the country—the others being the General Railway Workers' Union, the Seamen's Union, and the Canton General Labor Union. It is worthy of note that the closing of the Hanyehp'ing mines in 1925 provided about one hundred thousand jobless workingmen, already educated by Li Li-san, for the revolutionary armies. The first units of the Red Army under Yeh T'ing were largely filled by men from the Hanyehp'ing mines, while those of Mao Tsê-tung came mainly from the Tayeh mines.

In 1937, when I was in Yenan, Ts'ai Shu-fan was Commissioner of the Interior and also Commissioner of Judicial Affairs. Afterward he went to the "Chin-Ch'a-Chi Liberated Area" (the Communist-held border areas of Shansi, Hopei, and Chahar—"Chin," "Ch'a," and "Chi" being the ancient names for those provinces) as chairman of the political department. There he was in the government headed by General Nieh Jung-chên. He continued in political work under Nieh and in 1947 was stationed at Kalgan in Chahar.

TS'AI SHU-FAN:

I COME from the Chinese working class. My family were Hupeh miners. My father and an uncle worked in the Hanyang, Anyang, and Tayeh mines and also in mines and arsenals in other places. My grandfather had been a poor peasant.

I was born in Hanyang *hsien*, Hupeh, in 1908, and three days afterward the family moved to Anyuan, a district in P'inghsiang *hsien*, where my father and my uncle worked in the Anyang mines. I studied in school only two years, then entered the mine at fifteen to begin three years' apprenticeship. Until that time I had done no special work, my father being able to support his family well enough, though it consisted of eight persons, including my mother and my two younger brothers and three younger sisters.

I earned three dollars a month as a laborer, working from six in the morning until six at night. This was in the Hanyehp'ing mines, where I did manual work on the motors, pumps, and trams. Most of the workmen were young—the majority from fourteen or fifteen to twenty-three years of age. Some had a very hard life and could not even earn three dollars. If the men made mistakes their wage was forfeited. The average wage was six or seven dollars a month.

At that time Hanyehp'ing was owned partly by private capital, Sun Hsien-huai being the biggest stockholder, and partly by the government. It was later owned by the Japanese. It is the largest iron mine in China.

There were thirteen thousand workers in the Anyang section alone. In the entire Hanyeh-p'ing mines, of which the Anyang mine was part, there were over one hundred thousand miners—the others being the mine at Hanyang and the mine and iron foundry at Tayeh.

Li Li-san and the Miners' Strike, 1922

In 1921 Mao Tsê-tung came to Hanyeh-p'ing and organized a workers' club. This was the beginning of labor organization in the mine. He stayed a very short time and only talked about the general political idea of struggle. In 1922 Li Li-san, who was then known as Li Lung-tzŭ, came and began to organize a "Supplementary School for Workmen." At first the school had only about ten persons. Later, about ninety joined. I entered the school as soon as it opened in 1922. We had no books—only mimeographed sheets. These told of the workers' struggle against the owners in order to gain increased wages. Through these mimeographed sheets the miners learned to read and write. There were only two teachers—Li Li-san and Ts'ai Ch'ên-chün. Both were Communists though Ts'ai later betrayed. The school soon expanded and from it developed a large "Anyang Workers' Club" which demanded wage increases from the owners. In the beginning the club had only a few hundred members but after our first strike was victorious every worker joined.

Our strike in 1922 was the first in the history of the mine. The workers had no idea of such a method before this time, and were surprised and happy to discover the use of the strike. Only the young boys joined in strike, the old men being more conservative. All the young men were radical and stood as pickets to keep the old men away from the mine. In the very beginning only a few hundred joined the strike; later, more and more were mobilized. We made up a propaganda team which went to the workers in their dormitories and talked with them, asking each one to join with us. Luckily, we persuaded the men in charge of pulling the whistle to go on strike, and as no siren ordered the men to work, nobody went! We also sent delegates to the management and said: "If you don't receive our demands, we will strike for a long time and destroy the mine. You know that if the pumps are stopped for even one day, the mine will be flooded." They granted all our demands and the strike lasted only three days. Li Li-san led this strike, together with Ts'ai Ch'ên-chün. There were several other worker-leaders, all Communists. These included Chu Hsiao-lien, who was arrested after the Great Revolution and betrayed, but was executed anyway; Chu Chin-t'ang, who is still working in the party—I saw him in Shanghai in 1930; and Li Tê-pin—I don't know what happened to him. I myself helped organize the propaganda team for the strike.

After the strike, wages were increased and Sunday rest was instituted. We also got some funds for accidents and sickness. In the mines at this time were six or seven German inspectors who were in the habit of beating the workmen with sticks and dismissing us for the slightest offense. After the strike they never dared beat a workman. Before the first World War there had been forty Germans in the mine, and the workers hated them very much because of their privileged position. Of course, we hated the Chinese engineers as well.

This strike in 1922 was not the first strike for Chinese labor. But it was a very important beginning of the Chinese labor movement because it was victorious. All the miners were jubilant after the strike and began to organize many night schools, supplementary schools, and reading centers. We also began to build a workmen's union headquarters. Anyang was then called the "Moscow of China."

Our original workmen's club was called the "Anyang Mine Workers' Club" until about 1924. During the Pinhan railway strike in February 1923, in which many railway workers were killed, we at Hanyehp'ing went on a general strike in sympathy. All the one hundred thousand miners joined, and we changed the club to a union and founded the headquarters of the Hanyehp'ing Workers' Union, representing the three mines of Tayeh, Anyang, and Hanyang.

After this there were many civil wars in Hunan and the financing of the mine became difficult. The workers could not get regular wages, so they always sabotaged and made many demands on the owners. Then the son of Sun Hsien-huai brought two regiments— about two thousand soldiers—to the mine and began discussions with the workers. The head of our union was Lo Ch'ên, a Communist. He was a student, not a miner, but he represented the workers, and the management treated him well. He had much faith in the capitalists, even though he was a Communist, but finally the discussions failed and none of our demands were granted. The whole labor movement of Anyang soon failed.

The soldiers took up a position near the mine, the union was closed down, and the schools were closed. The leaders of the movement ran away, and none of the active workers could stay, either. About ten were arrested and fifty ran away to Changsha. I had to escape, too—I had joined the Socialist Youth in 1923. At that time we were accused as "radicals," not as "Communists" like the workers at present. The soldiers did not beat us because we all ran away before they could catch us.

Before the troops had been called out, we had had police in the mine. These three hundred police were useless, however, as there were too few of them in spite of the fact that they were armed. Moreover, the police sympathized with the strikers because we were able to get wage increases, though they did not join our first strike and, in fact, never went on strike. The soldiers had no sympathy for the movement; they were mercenaries and merely took orders.

Li Li-san stayed at Hanyehp'ing about three years, leaving for Shanghai about 1924. He had a great influence among the workers. He was a student but a good labor leader and an unusually convincing agitator, influencing nearly everyone who heard him speak.

Labor in China was never conservative. Right from the beginning it took to radical leadership. In my district, the Socialist Youth became the Communist Youth about the end of 1923. We had no Communist party there at all until the end of 1923. The Communist Youth then had only four hundred members—all young laborers from sixteen to twenty-three years of age. At the end of 1923 some Communist Youths, together with older men, organized the Kungchangtang, which then had only a hundred members in all. At its highest period at the mine, in 1925, the Kungchantang had about three hundred members, and the Communist Youth about five hundred.

We had no real "Yellow"[1] trade-unions at all. The owners did not know any method of opposing the union except by violence. At one time, the management, staff, and engineers organized a club to oppose our workmen's club, but the two clubs co-operated instead of fighting each other. Their group once had a strike; we supported them and so had good relations with them. They could get only six hundred members, and these were engineers and staff people; they had no workmen. The purpose of this group was to bargain for salary increases, but the owners were not afraid of them because the mines could go on producing without the staff, provided that the workmen carried on. The group had to appeal to us to support them in their strike, and we did so, but even then they did not get the salary increases.

The mine then was very prosperous and produced monthly about half a million tons of many different kinds of ore. The Germans got one thousand to two thousand dollars a month as salaries, and this angered the workers. The Germans all left in 1923—

why, I don't know; they were not driven away by the workers.

Miners Arming for Revolution

After I arrived in Changsha the party wanted me to return to Anyang, so I went back and re-established the union for a while. Of the ten persons arrested, only one was executed, but we planned a demonstration against this. However, the situation looked too serious for action then and the other nine were released. When the authorities ordered the arrest of my family, I had to escape again, together with some other workers. My father was a poor worker, but he was old and conservative. He tried to prevent me from joining the Communist Youth but later became sympathetic and joined the union himself. This was the last time I saw him. For ten years I have heard nothing from my family nor have I written any letters to them.

I never went back to Anyang but I later heard that in 1925 the labor movement there failed completely, the mine was closed down, and the workers all driven away. All three mines of Hanyehp'ing were closed. I suppose this was because of want of capital, for later the mines were sold to the Japanese. They were never opened after 1925 except for a small part employing only a few hundred miners.

Of the one hundred thousand miners of Hanyehp'ing who were thrown out of work, many joined the Red Army when P'êng Tê-huai occupied Changsha in 1930, passing Anyang on the way. Before that, a number had joined the Great Revolution in 1925 and were killed. At one time nearly all the soldiers in Yeh T'ing's division of the Kuomintang Fourth Army were Hanyehp'ing miners, and a great many were killed in the attack on Wuchang. It was the Hanyehp'ing miners under Yeh T'ing who led the Nanchang Uprising in 1927. If the mine had not been closed down, there would not have been this free proletariat for revolutionary action and perhaps no Red Army movement

then. Most of these workers have been killed but there are at present in Lin Piao's First Army Corps many who were originally under Yeh T'ing. These workers are concentrated in the famous 1st Division led by Chêng Kên, which has never been defeated by the enemy armies. But, because of many changes, I am afraid that of the original Hanyehp'ing workers not many are left now.

Ch'ên Tu-hsiu Disarms the Workers, 1927

I went to Changsha again and then to Nanchang, where I was to do Communist Youth work at the arsenal. In 1926 I was imprisoned by the provincial army of Huang Pin-jên but released after a few days because they had no proof against me. Soon the Kuomintang army arrived in Nanchang and many workers joined. However, I stayed behind to work for the party. I changed from the Communist Youth to the Kung-ch'antang in 1927, being then nineteen years old.

After this I went to Wuhan, where I continued to do party work in the industrial district of Ch'aok'ou. When I heard the news of the 1927 split with the Kuomintang, I carried our guns away, and buried them in the ground. I was arrested in June by T'ang Shêng-chih, together with three women and five other men, but the guns were never discovered. There they are in the ground now, I suppose, after ten years—ten rifles and six pistols. We were soon set free, however, as no evidence was produced against us. At Ch'aok'ou there were only six factories, one silk, two cotton, two flour, and a chemical factory owned by the Japanese. We had only ten rifles for all the members of our workers' union!

Chiang Kai-shek had begun killing the workers in April [1927] in Shanghai. When the Wuhan workers heard of this killing of their fellow workers in Shanghai, they immediately called a strike. I was present at the big meeting of over a hundred thousand, which lasted from six in the morning to five in the afternoon. Our slogan was "Strike Down Chiang Kai-shek!"

In the beginning only four or five worker-leaders were killed in Hankow. The Communists who had done open work all fled to Nanchang or Moscow. Before April, many of the factory workers in China were well armed. Afterward they were disarmed by the Kuomintang. In Wuhan, for instance, the workers had over one thousand rifles, but Ch'ên Tu-hsiu (head of the Kungch'antang) himself ordered them to give these up to the Kuomintang. Not one of the workers wanted to surrender his gun, and all were perplexed and angry. Many were arrested as soon as they gave up their arms. About May or June the killing began. It was not until *after* the workers gave up their arms that the executions started. The killing of workers and Communists began about the same time in all four places—Wuchang, Hankow, Hanyang, and the small P'inghan station of Ch'angan. Every day there were ten or twenty or thirty executions. Hundreds were killed. Some of our comrades were taken out and shot after meetings. The workers planned a great strike against this, but failed. They wanted to resist the Kuomintang counterrevolution but couldn't do anything. These killings were done by T'ang Shêng-chih's army, of which Ho Ch'ien was an officer.

Many women were killed at this time. In the cotton factories most of the workers were women and girl-children. These women and girls were active and brave. It was fifteen *li* from Ch'aok'ou to Hankow, but they walked to meetings with their bound feet, anyway. I found that always in the struggle and strike movements the women were more positive than the men, especially in organizing propaganda teams and in gathering for meetings. The women always take leadership of this special work. They are often as strong as men and, because they get lower wages and are more oppressed, they become very revolutionary. Their active leadership in the revolution has been very important.

After the split, capitalists in Wuhan recruited women and children instead of strong men for their factories, because they could pay them lower wages and prevent revolutionary action more easily. These capitalists at the same time dismissed all the active women and took new girls, fresh and ignorant from the villages.

You ask what broke the labor movement in China? At that time the labor movement was dominated by Ch'ên Tu-hsiu, who made the error of Right opportunism. He didn't believe in the power of the workers' unions. We then had many guns but Ch'ên wanted to give them up to the Kuomintang and did so. This was a great mistake. He also opposed the struggle for economic gains, because he said that wage increases would give the workers a good life and their revolutionary emotion would be decreased! So it was decided that the slogans were "too high."[2] The Kungch'antang was afraid of breaking the United Front with the Kuomintang.

In general, the workers did not understand the nature of the revolution. They knew that it meant to strike down the Northern militarists and imperialism, to realize the eight-hour day and higher wages and a more progressive life, to win the right to organize and the right to print our own magazines and newspapers, and to get civil liberties. But for them it was mainly an economic struggle. Even I did not then understand the nature of the revolution clearly. When Chiang Kai-shek began killing the workers, we all thought he had simply "betrayed." We didn't know why, or who supported him—whether it was the imperialists or the banks. Some workers thought he had joined with foreign imperialism and that the British concession in Hankow was given back as payment for betrayal.

Though Chiang Kai-shek accused the workers of organizing the Kungch'antang to seize the power for labor, this was a lie and an excuse only. When the revolutionary work had developed up to the 1927 period, the workers demanded better wages and the peasants demanded land, so the national bourgeoisie became frightened and betrayed the revolution. But, in fact, the workers' economic demands and the peasants' demand for land and for the overthrow of feudalism and imperialism are part of the bourgeois-democratic revolution.

However, the workers realized the extent of their great power and knew that they were feared by the bourgeoisie. They thought the *real* cause of the betrayal was the capitalists' fear of the workers, so they didn't want to give up their guns, but the Kungch'antang headquarters gave the order to surrender them and they had to do so without objecting. When Hsia Tou-yin's army came, in July, the workers planned to fight him but they did not realize this plan.

At that time the workmen were fully conscious that they were the important power of the Kuomintang revolution and that the proletariat was its leadership. The Wuhan workers had great confidence in their strength and thought they could fight Hsia's army, and so didn't want to surrender their guns. These workers had had considerable military training at Nanfu under Han Ying. About two thousand had trained there for three months. Han Ying was the leader of the workers wanting to fight Hsia, but at the meeting the Ch'ên Tu-hsiu line prevailed and the fight did not take place. The workers had already begun to march but when they got the order to stop, they returned. Han Ying was a Hupeh man; he later joined the Red Army and stayed in Kiangsi after the long march.

The workers were not afraid but glad to join the Kungch'antang at that time. There were several hundred party members in Ch'aok'ou, but I don't know how many in the whole district.

Labor Delegate in Moscow and Shanghai

I left for Moscow in August. When I arrived I entered Eastern University and studied Chinese and natural sciences. I had finished one six-month term when I joined the Sixth Congress of the Comintern in 1928. Then I transferred to the Labor University of Chinese Communism, which originally had been called Sun Yat-sen University. Here I studied six months also. Hsü Mêng-ch'iu was there at the same time. After that I studied at Lenin College for nine months. During this period at Lenin College the Chinese Eastern Railway Incident occurred. Many of Chang Hsüeh-liang's soldiers had been captured by the Soviets, and I was ordered to work with them. After that I returned to Lenin College and completed my course.

I was one of twenty Chinese delegates to the Fifth International Labor Congress at Moscow, after which I left for China in 1930. I had no trouble on my way back.

In Shanghai I worked in the headquarters of the All-China Labor Federation for two months and then applied to go to Kiangsi. I went to Hongkong, then to Swatow, and then began walking to the soviet districts. This was difficult for me because the road was mountainous and I had never in my life traveled on foot. I had always worked in close quarters in factories. Sometimes we passed bandit districts, but the bandits were good to us and gave us food and guards for escort. It was one month from the time I had left Hongkong when I arrived in the Fukien soviet area. When we arrived on the border, Lo Ping-hui came to welcome us. We stayed in the Fukien soviet two months, then were sent to the Kiangsi central soviet with a guard.

Political Director for Lo Ping-hui

In the Kiangsi soviet district I had a post in the General Labor Union at first. Then I joined Lo Ping-hui's Twelfth Army as political director. After several battles this army was reorganized under the 1st Division of the First Army Corps but was still commanded by Lo Ping-hui. I participated in defeating the "Second Surrounding Campaign" of the Kuomintang, during which I was wounded by a bomb.

The first time I was, wounded was in May 1931, at Kwangch'ang. The army of Chu Tê and Mao Tsê-tung had retreated and I was in the rear when the planes came to bomb, but I had to continue my work and could not hide. I received nine shrapnel wounds but walked for one *li* afterward in a daze, not knowing what had happened. The nurses treated my wounds with iodine, but I did not recover until the Third Campaign began. There was no hospital, and I was carried on a stretcher by the nurses most of the time. However, I was able to participate in the Third Campaign and to attend the First Soviet Congress on February 7, 1931.

I was wounded again, in July 1933, in the fighting against Ts'ai T'ing-chieh at Lien-ch'êng and P'êngk'ou in Fukien, while I was political director of the Seventh Army Corps. I was then with the 19th Division under Chou Chien-p'ing. Ts'ai's forces were at P'êngk'ou and we were at Lien-ch'êng. Our troops could not advance, so Chou and I together led some of the troops to P'êngk'ou for an attack. I had been looking through a telescope held in both hands. Just as I was about to put it down and had moved my left hand a little, a rifle bullet zipped through my left arm. It was not a bad wound, but the hospital and medical staff were not good. Perhaps it was not necessary for me to have lost my arm, but there was urgent need for me to hurry and get busy with my work, so Han Ying, who was then chairman of the Military Council, advised me to have it cut off. This was at the time of the organization of the new Ninth Army Corps under Lo Ping-hui, and I was needed as political director.

The Long March began in October 1934. In Kweichow I changed my work to become political director of the Military Council. When we arrived in north Shensi I was made Commissioner of the Interior and of Judicial Affairs.

The Long March was not difficult for me. It was about the same as other army life except that we never got any rest. I had no particular adventures except one at the beginning of the march, when the headquarters of our corps was attacked suddenly and Lo Ping-hui and I had to get away quickly on horses. When our men began resisting, we turned back.

Last year when the Red Army crossed the Yellow River, the Military Committee ordered me to collect partisans into an army. I organized the Thirtieth Army under Yen Hung-yen. Later I went back to Paoan and had to rest several months, as I was sick. Then I came to Yenan.

Wang Chêng

RAILROAD WORKER

MISS WALES:

GENERAL WANG CHÊNG is modest, quiet, and matter-of-fact. His prominent teeth are usually exposed in a broad smile, and he is exceptionally friendly. In 1937, when he was twenty-eight years old, he was political adviser to Hsiao K'ê, who was the same age. The pair had already made a great deal of history. A few days after I interviewed Wang, he rejoined the troops to fight the Japanese. He soon was made commander of the 359th Brigade of the 120th Division of the Eighth Route Army, which became one of the famous units. He was considered completely reliable, politically and militarily.

After three years at the front, the brigade was called back to guard the blockaded Yenan region, and Wang Chêng was given the job of initiating a system of agricultural production by the army for its own use. His ten thousand soldiers produced their own food in the Nanniwan Valley. In 1949 Wang was Director of Telegraphic Administration of the Chinese People's Revolutionary Military Committee and was appointed the only Vice-Minister of Posts and Telegraphs. He was also a reserve member of the Central Committee of the Communist Party.

Wang Chêng's story shows how progressive workmen organized the peasant movement after 1927 and gives an insight into the inner nature of the labor movement. In the P'ing-kiang-Liuyang area in eastern Hunan province occurred the oldest continuous peasant struggle in the country. It began under the Kuomintang, and kept a soviet of ten thousand functioning until the summer of 1937, two years after the troops had left on the Long March to the north.

WANG CHÊNG:

I LEFT home when I was twelve years old to try to get a job in Changsha. My father was a tenant farmer of Pohsiang village in Liuyang *hsien*, Hunan, where I was born in 1909. He was so poor that he could not possibly support his ten children. I was the oldest of five brothers and five sisters, so I left home as soon as I was capable of earning a living.

Changsha Labor in Revolt, 1925–27

My first job was as a servant in the army. After three months of this, I went to the stationmaster's office at the Canton-Hankow Railway and secured work as a servant. That was in 1922. When I was thirteen or fourteen I was promoted to the job of switching rails at seven dollars a month. Soon afterward I became an oil feeder, and examined, repaired, and oiled the locomo-

tives. For this I received fifteen dollars. Next I was made locomotive fireman, at seventeen dollars and fifty cents a month.

In 1924 I joined the new Railway Workers' Union. Just after the May Thirtieth Incident in Shanghai, in 1925, we declared a strike. This was led by a student named Kuo Liang, who had formerly worked on the railway. He was a Communist, though most of the workers did not know this then. The strike was partly political, echoing the May Thirtieth Movement, and partly economic. Before this time we had had a twelve-hour day, and a six-hour shift at night, with no Sunday wage. Our strike resulted in securing the eight-hour day and a Sunday wage of one dollar twenty cents monthly. I had been a picket for the union during the strike. When it was successful we were all surprised. Every worker felt happy to discover the new power of organized labor. I immediately became keenly interested in the labor movement. All the railway workers participated in this strike, and in fact the strike movement had spread throughout China. We experienced no suppression—nobody was wounded or arrested—because the railway was at that time under the control of the then-revolutionary Kuomintang, with its liberal labor policy. I joined the Kuomintang in 1925, and when only sixteen was elected a member of the executive committee of the Changsha branch of the General Labor Union. The seventeen members of this committee represented three thousand workers. Though I was uneducated, I was very active in the labor movement and was enthusiastic.

When the Northern Expedition began, July 9, 1926, all the workers eagerly supported the armies. Our economic condition was much improved, we had our union, and we felt that in working for the Kuomintang we were working for ourselves. During 1925–27 the railway workers organized many new night schools for themselves and their children.

Even before Changsha was occupied by the Kuomintang armies in the summer of 1926, the Railway Workers' Union was the center of the revolutionary movement. We did propaganda work throughout the city and often had demonstrations in the streets. At that time Chao Hêng-t'i, the governor of Hunan, dared not arrest anybody because the revolutionary tide was high and he feared it. On the contrary, he surrendered to our side on almost every point. When Changsha was occupied, the workers were tremendously happy. We ourselves took charge of the railway and of all communications to support the army—protecting munitions shipments and food supplies, and handling all transportation work. This was all spontaneous volunteer work, rising out of our new consciousness.

Our workers' movement was not only antifeudal, but also consciously anti-impe-

In his narrative, Wang Chêng omitted mention of the incident commemorated in this photograph. The Sixth Red Army crossed the territory of the aboriginal Miaotzŭ tribes during the Long March. As political commissar, Wang negotiated a peace treaty with the Miaotzŭ to permit passage through the region without hostilities. Wang (first from the left, in black overcoat) is shown here with the Miao group with whom he negotiated his treaty, in Kweichow Province, February 1936.

rialist. The Canton-Hankow Railway was a British capital investment, though nominally the property of the Chinese government. In the head office there was a British engineer whom we called Fan Ehr-pi in Chinese. The locomotive engineers had orders never to sound the whistle when passing near his house, so as not to disturb his sleep! We all hated this foreign imperialist, and I was one of a hundred pickets who ordered him to leave the office, which he did without ceremony.

During 1925–26 the Communists had little influence, but after the Northern Expedition this influence increased rapidly. By the end of 1926 *all* the Changsha workers supported the Communists, because of their new class consciousness. We saw that it was the political party of the working class merely by observation of the objective situation. I often wonder why America has thirty million workers and only about sixty thousand Communist party members. I suppose the American workers will see their way clear when the situation approaches. In China we had no Communist tradition to guide the workers in 1927 except a few ideas from the Pinhan railway strike of 1923—and also we had no tradition of real bourgeois reform or social democracy. The hard facts of our lives taught us to depend upon our own power.

After 1923 the ideas of the Communist party spread through the unions, especially along the railways. Our understanding of them was very simple at first. We thought only to improve our livelihood. We had no idea of seizing power from the ruling class. We thought the workers' unions introduced by the Communists were only to gain a bargaining advantage for us.

By 1927 the Chinese workers were fully class-conscious, however. Our chief slogan was anti-imperialism, especially against the British and the Japanese. The first demands of the working-class movement were for improvement of livelihood, increased wages, abolition of child labor, and opportunities for education for the workers and their children. We demanded these concessions in the name of strengthening labor for the fight against imperialism. We understand that the revolutionary duty of labor was to seize power from the imperialists and win control of our railways and factories and modern cities—and not to attempt to take the power from the native bourgeoisie. We felt that we could co-operate with the peasants, the intellectuals, and the national bourgeoisie in the anti-imperialist front. Then came our blood bath.

The Hsü K'ê-hsiang Massacre

I joined the Communist Youth in January 1927 and during that year was one of the leaders of the "Training Class for Labor Leaders" in Changsha, though I had had only three years of primary school as a child and could barely read and write. This class was held for four months under the name of the Kuomintang but it was really directed by the Communist party. Part of the education was military training. This was in preparation for arming the Changsha workers. We had received some arms during the capture of Changsha.

On May 21, 1927, Hsü K'ê-hsiang, a Kuomintang general under T'ang Shêng-chih, turned openly reactionary and sounded the bugle call for the counterrevolution in Hunan.

At that time the Communist party was under the direction of Ch'ên Tu-hsiu's "Right Opportunism." Ch'ên had been criticizing the radicalism of the Hunan workers. The Communist party then not only neglected building up an armed force but actually did not want to arm itself, preferring to be a tail for the bourgeoisie. Therefore, the masses were defenseless when Hsü K'ê-hsiang and others turned the armed forces of the reaction against them.

Even before May 21, all the members of the local organ of the Communist party knew that Hsü K'ê-hsiang had turned reactionary, but they did not lead the workers to defend themselves against him. Instead, they wavered and ordered the workers to be vigilant but not to fight. That was why we could not prevent the May Twenty-first Incident in Changsha, even though we had a thousand workers all armed with guns.

The only warning which the party organ gave the workers was this: "Chiang Kai-shek will buy over some reactionary elements in the workers' union to ruin the labor movement." This warning was received after the split between the Left and Chiang Kai-shek. Actually, this estimate was not correct. The Communists paid attention only to the situation *within* the ranks of labor, and not to the arming of the true reaction. This was a mistake, for Chiang Kai-shek was then co-operating with Hsü K'ê hsiang.

In Changsha, at eleven o'clock on the night of May 21, Hsü K'ê-hsiang's troops attacked the armed pickets, of whom I was one. We were totally unprepared. Only three hundred of our one thousand armed pickets were on duty. Receiving no orders from above, we fought spontaneously without directions.

At the same time, Hsü's army clashed with the other workers. There was serious fighting at the labor union headquarters on Tung Mêng Han Street, and also at the Peasants' Union at Shao Wu Mên. The Peasants' Union had one thousand armed pickets, too, but only two or three hundred guns. Consequently, most of the killing was done there. Shao Wu Mên was covered with blood.

Hsü K'ê-hsiang had only one *t'uan* [regiment] of two thousand soldiers, but he used machine guns, while we had none. The fighting lasted only three hours. Over a thousand peasants and workers were killed, but no students. That night many others were arrested, People within the city were also killed.

I was wounded in the knee during this fighting, but hobbled as fast as I could to the railway station, carrying my gun. I was the only one to carry the news to the station. As soon as I arrived, the railway men prepared to fight, though they had only ten guns.

Hsü K'ê-hsiang's troops soon came to the station and we fought, but since we were taken by surprise and had no command, no plan, and practically no guns, our defeat was certain. We hid our ten guns, however, before giving up the station.

Hsü K'ê-hsiang was able to capture many guns from the workers, and a great majority of the arrested leaders of the organizations of workers, peasants, and students were later executed.

After May 21 there was no more fighting in Changsha. The revolution went underground.

More than ten of my personal friends were killed that night. My wife was later either killed or executed. I have never learned what happened to her. Her name was Ti Shou-han and we had been married only two weeks. She worked in a textile factory. It was a love match. My family had married me to a girl when I was a child of six or seven, but as she had just died in 1927, I was able to marry the girl I was in love with.

I pulled the bullet out of my knee that night. The next day my friends sent me to the hospital, though I wanted not to go but to continue the struggle.

I didn't run away from Changsha. None of the members of the executive committee of our union ran away except the chairman. I went back to the railway office and got a job as locomotive inspector and fireman.

After May 21, the reaction spread all over the province and several tens of thousands were killed in Hunan and Hupeh, where the suppression was worse than elsewhere.

The Changsha Workers' Last Stand

During the next few weeks our work was very secret. We distributed handbills among the workers and did underground propaganda. Then when Mao Tsê-tung organized the "Autumn Harvest" uprisings in Hunan in the fall and fought with his new Peasants' and Workers' Army, we tore up the railway tracks to prevent troop trains from going out to suppress him.

By November the Changsha workers were ready for a new attempt and wanted to try to seize power from the ruling class. We had a thousand organized workers but only twenty-five guns, of which I had one. My Communist friends and I lived at the North Gate of Changsha, and it was here that the movement began. We called a general strike, cut the telegraph and telephone service and all communications, and began the attack. The workers first beat up one reactionary inspector, who died from this. Then we attacked a tax office outside the city, which collected the rice tax, and killed the chief. All the workers in the electric plant joined and spoiled the machines in the plant. The workers in the flour and textile factories and the longshoremen also joined, as well as a part of the near-by peasants. We dispersed the police easily enough.

All this occurred outside the city near the North Gate, however, and the workers at the other three gates and inside the city did not support us, though they had been ordered by the party to do so. When we marched back through the North Gate and found that the rest of the workers were not taking action, the leader ordered a retreat. We hid our guns and dispersed, with neither victory nor failure. None of us was killed, and only a few had been arrested.

We received no support from the other workers because so many Changsha leaders had been killed on May 21 that we could not organize effectively. At the same time the peasants in Changsha, Liuyang, and Liling *hsiens* near by were threatened by the reaction and could not come to our aid. In the villages outside Changsha there was much agitation for the Autumn Crop movement, but since it was not under the pure direction of the party, it failed. We therefore had no mass basis. Our November action was a final gesture of retreat, in desperation and self-defense.

The Changsha newspaper said that the "agitator-bandits" of November were all railway workers; but we denied this, and many clerks and other petty-bourgeois elements supported our denial. At that time our railway workers' union was still strong, and the ruling class was alarmed by the November action, and was anxious to prevent the development of the labor movement, which was inflaming revolutionary feeling in Changsha.

At that time over half of the one thousand Changsha railway men were Communists. We were firmly organized, but the other unions were not, although the workers in the flour and textile mills and in the electric plant were also mostly either Communist Youth or Communist party members. All the Communists were very young. No-

body over thirty ever joined. Although after May 21 all organization was illegal, the workers knew they had to protect their unions, and their political morale was very high. We were never afraid to fight in Changsha. All the workers over fourteen or fifteen and under thirty had been trained as armed pickets. Forty percent of the railway workers were fully trained.

After May 21 the Communist party in Changsha had been secretly but continuously active, and the ruling class paid much attention to us. They put paid spies in our ranks, through whom the police discovered the organs of the C.P., the C.Y., and the railway union. When their information was complete, the police swooped down in April 1928 and arrested nearly everybody, seizing one of the factories during the raid. Two railway police, named Yi Jung-sheng and Yi Ting-ao, had joined the C.P. These two worked very hard in the party and we trusted them. However, they surrendered to the police and gave them every detail of our organization, so that we were completely betrayed. One hundred leaders were arrested.

Luckily for me, I was in Yochow when this raid occurred. I was then C.Y. delegate on the executive committee and also worked closely with the C.P. Had I been arrested, I would have been executed immediately. A boy in the telegraph office who was a C.Y. member telegraphed us the news in Yochow so that we would be on guard. Some were able to escape to Wuhan and other places.

The reason I happened to be in Yochow was this: In February, Kuo Liang had been arrested in Yochow. He was the young Communist student who had led our big successful strike in 1925, and we all loved him very much. Since the Yochow police knew he was an important leader, they sent him to Changsha immediately by a special train with only one locomotive and one coach. As soon as the railway workers learned of this, they tried to rescue him by breaking the tracks and stopping the locomotive, but this action came too late. The train had already passed over. Three days later he was secretly beheaded—in Changsha the revolutionaries were always beheaded. When we learned of this, the workers were all angry and unhappy. They sounded all the sirens and whistles in the city to commemorate his death. The railway workers went on strike for three hours. The police dared not arrest anybody then because of the tense feeling. Instead, they waited until April. I had gone to Yochow with several others to investigate the conditions there after Kuo Liang's arrest.

The summer of 1928 was the most vicious period of the Hunan ruling class, I think.

Days of Wandering

Together with seven or eight others I escaped to Hankow. I could get no connection with the local C.P. and was unemployed and starving, so I joined the White Army under Li Tsung-jên—the Kwangsi army which had occupied Hupeh. After I had been in the army a month, I found my connection with the party and left to get a job at the Tayeh Iron Foundry as a coolie for seven dollars a month.

One of the inspectors at the foundry became suspicious of me, as I was active in the labor union. Consequently, I had to escape after only one month.

Near Tayeh there was partisan fighting, and when I left the foundry I expected to join the Chu-Mao-P'êng main column of the Red Army. However, on my arrival in Hankow city I happened to read a C.P. document which the police published in the newspaper after a raid in order to warn people [against the Communist plans]. This document said that all party members who had lost their connection with the C.P. must work in the armies. I therefore rejoined Li Tsung-jên's troops. This was at the end of 1928. Chiang Kai-shek and Li Tsung-jên had been fighting. When Li was defeated, his army moved to western Hupeh and the border of Szechuan. I retreated with them. With me in the army were three others who also had

lost their connection with the C.P. We four secretly organized our own branch of the C.P. in the army. If Li had known, we would surely have been executed. In other units of the army, many suspected Communists were executed every day. When we arrived at Chienli *hsien*, these three young students were too weak to walk any farther. I knew there was partisan fighting near this *hsien*. I led ten of the soldiers to join the partisans, together with the three students. We all took our guns, of course.

We saw handbills and slogans of the secret party organization, and thus knew there was one near by. My men hid in the long reeds of the river bank, while I went out to find a peasant to talk with. This peasant helped me to find the Red Vanguards.

After leaving Changsha I always lied and said I was a peasant. To admit that you were a Changsha worker was to invite execution in those days. In Changsha my name had been Wang Chen-lin and all my friends had called me "Hsiao Wang" ["Little Wang"], because I was so young. I was only nineteen. In the army I changed my name to Wang Chên-t'ing.

When I met the Red Vanguards, they wouldn't believe my true story, as I had no credentials from the party or proofs of my past record. They wanted to pay me twenty dollars for my gun and let me go my way. I was so persistent, however, that they told me to try to join Ho Lung and Tuan Tê-ch'ang—Tuan was a famous partisan leader from 1928 until 1933, when he was killed in battle. These two were then leading partisans near by in western Hunan and Hupeh.

We were anxious to join Ho Lung and Tuan Tê-ch'ang, but since the Vanguards in Chienli refused to give us any recommendations, we hesitated. Then I saw in a newspaper that partisan fighting had broken out in my native *hsien*, Liuyang. I decided to go there where I was known. I had contracted typhoid fever in the meantime from the bad food and water, and was sick three months in Hankow. I found many friends among the railway workers in the Wuchang railway station. They gave me money for medicine and hid me safely, as they knew of my good record in Changsha.

Partisans in Liuyang

In the early autumn of 1929 I went to Liuyang. I found that there was no fighting in Liuyang, but in near-by P'ingkiang *hsien*. I therefore decided to organize the people.

My family were distressed that I could not help them financially. I had sent no money home during 1928 and 1929, though I always had done this previously. My family were in terrible poverty, just as were all other families in the village. My father had gone to Changsha to do short-labor as a coolie, and could not earn enough to send home either. My mother had to sell my young brother to a *t'uhao*[1] family as a slave in the fields, receiving three hundred dollars for him. In 1930 this brother ran away from his master and joined the 16th Division of the Red Army, but was soon killed. My father also joined the 16th Division in the same year, and was killed in our native *hsien* in 1932. This was at the time K'ung Ho-shêng, a Red commander, surrendered to the Kuomintang and betrayed.

Of course, nobody in my village knew I was a Communist, though my uncle knew I had been active in the railway union in Changsha. He sympathized with my ideas, fortunately. None of the local *t'uhao* had any idea of what I had actually been doing. As soon as I arrived, however, I went out into the villages and organized secret Red Peasants' and Workers' unions and local branches of the C.P. In the winter of 1929 the C.P. was well organized in the villages near by, and in the north suburb of Liuyang *hsien* city I organized a very good peasants' union.

One day a peasant told me that a local landlord in Hsia-chia-san had four guns in his house. The C.P. branch decided to send him a letter demanding that he surrender these guns to us. It was signed in the name of the Communist Party! We went to his home that very night and took the four guns. He "gave" us five thousand dollars at the same time, but we did not confiscate anything else and did no harm to the landlord himself. At that time the C.P. had the slogan of confiscating the landlords' property, but we hadn't begun to realize it then. Our political program for the moment was merely to arm ourselves—the confiscation of land would come later. We had several thousand peasants armed with agricultural implements but only our four guns.

At the time of the old-style Chinese New Year, when debts and taxes had to be paid, the C.P. branch led the peasants to oppose the collection of taxes, always unbearably oppressive. At the same time the tailors and carpenters got only one dollar for ten days' work. The workers' union demanded one dollar for five days' labor, and the peasants and workers united for action. The workers' union had four or five thousand members and the C.P. had several hundred. That New Year the *t'uhao* and the other landlords dared not collect any taxes, and the workers' wages were increased thirty percent. It was the happiest New Year the people had ever had! The party expanded rapidly, and out of these original economic demands new political consciousness arose.

At that time P'êng Tê-huai was active in Hunan. His work had been phenomenally successful. By the beginning of 1930 the countryside was full of revolutionary agitation. In all the near-by *hsien* C.P. branches were established and interconnections made. We still had only four guns—but our political influence was enormous. I was secretary of the Communist party of the district.

In the spring of 1930 we organized our own armed Red Vanguards of twenty or thirty partisans in this way: Four thousand peasants and workers attacked the estate of a big landlord in the north suburb of Liuyang city. His name was Po Shêng-chên. This landlord had about two hundred *min t'uan* organized, with one hundred twenty guns. We brandished our four guns at the head of the big column when we went to the attack. The landlord imagined that we were well armed, and so didn't put up much resistance. We defeated the *min t'uan* and captured many of them, together with twenty precious guns. None of the *min t'uan* were killed and only one of our peasants died. I had led the C.P. work of the uprising, and the open leader was Hsü Hung, a paper worker.

In the spring all peasants are very poor and hungry because the crops have not been planted, and so they are in desperate need. Part of our reason for attacking Po Shêng-chên's estate was to get salt and grain to distribute to the people—as well as guns for the partisans—as he had many rich granaries. Everyone jubilantly carried a sackful of food home to his starving children after our foray on this landlord.

Our Red Vanguards then increased to fifty or sixty. The captain was Chang Chêng-k'un—he is now with the army as commander of the 18th Division of the Sixth Red Army.

By this time Ho Ch'ien was the Hunan Kuomintang leader and had started a big anti-Communist campaign. Partisan warfare broke out in several different districts. When Ho Ch'ien came to suppress my troops of Red Vanguards, all fifty or sixty dispersed to different places and hid in the homes of the peasants in units of two or three. The army couldn't find us.

Most of us hid on the high mountain, Shihkaofeng, on the two peaks called Shang-p'ingling and Liuyentung. This mountain is between Liuyang and P'ingkiang *hsien*. During the summer of 1930 we used this place as a base from which to make sallies against the enemy, and got a good long rest between our small battles with the White troops.

In July 1930 P'êng Tê-huai occupied Changsha and our unit was renamed the "First Detachment of Partisans." We increased to one hundred men and captured sixty guns from the Whites. Many workers and peasants from other districts joined us, and we attacked my native *hsien* city, Liuyang, with four thousand men. I was promoted to become political commissar of the whole four thousand, which was named the "Sixth Army of Red Vanguards." The captain was my close friend, Chao Ju-ch'ing, a worker like myself. This was during the "Li Li-san period"[2] when the party wanted to capture the big cities.

Because P'êng's troops were busy attacking Changsha and couldn't help us, we were too weak to occupy Liuyang. We lost five hundred partisans and captured only six guns. When our attack was defeated by the White Army, the Red Vanguards made a general retreat. Together with ten others, I hid on Chaohsiling Mountain. There was no food on this peak, and we found only one big pear to divide among the ten of us. The C.P. had ordered all the fighters to return to their homes, because Ho Ch'ien had two thousand regular troops in Liuyang and further attack would have been useless.

After a short while, the Red Vanguards reconcentrated on the side of a mountain called Taowushan and took over a monastery of several hundred monks. This monastery was rich and owned a good deal of land, and the monks were extremely feudal-minded. At first we meant only to live with the monks in a friendly spirit, but the abbot sent word to the landlords near by to send *min t'uan* to attack us, and the monks refused to give us food, feeding it to their pigs and cows and horses instead. This caused our men to hate them, and we took measures to suppress the worst among them. After some of the high priests were killed, we had no more trouble and lived among them peaceably and well fed.

In August news came of P'êng's successful capture of Changsha on July 27. In great excitement we made a quick march to Changsha, only two days away, and entered the city while P'êng was still there.

The C.P. ordered all the peasants and workers to go to Changsha to help the Red Army. Over ten thousand arrived. I shall never forget the happy smiles on the faces of all these poor people when they saw Changsha flying the Red Flag. They thought Heaven had come at last. In their enthusiasm, the peasants confiscated commodities from some of the reactionary shopkeepers. This was not a good method—it was Li Li-san's line to confiscate the property of some of the merchants.

The Partisans Become Regulars

When P'êng Tê-huai gave up Changsha after only ten days' occupation, a part of my Red Vanguards stayed in a near-by village to fight partisan warfare. We had one hundred men, all armed with good guns. During those few days some of the partisans acted a little like bandits. They confiscated pretty clothes to wear—for the first time in their lives—and took money from the rich people. This was natural, considering their oppression. However, we expelled all the elements with bandit tendencies, and organized a "Soldiers' Committee" to teach the men revolutionary theory. The political commissars got busy and taught the men Marxism, and told them of the experiences of Mao Tsê-tung, Chu Tê, and P'êng Tê-huai in keeping discipline and revolutionary law and order. Only forty of my hundred Vanguards were party members.

Under the Li Li-san line, P'êng was ordered to attack Changsha again. Our men were still carrying on partisan attacks near the city, of course. Chu Tê, Mao Tsê-tung, and Huang Kung-liu arrived in Hunan, but P'êng was unable to reoccupy Changsha. All these Red Army commanders then went to Kiangsi.

All during this time, the three students who were in Li Tsung-jên's army with me had carried on. All three were wounded in the second attack on Changsha, however, and stayed behind. I never saw them again. Chang Chêng-k'un was also badly wounded.

Hsü Hung, the worker, remained in command of forty guns. Later, at the beginning of the Long March, he disappeared. I think he was killed.

Until this time the partisans had been operating only in the rear of the Red Army. Now Chu and Mao ordered most of the partisans to be reorganized into the regular Red Army.

At that time the Communist party's initiative and direction were very strong, and troops could be moved here and there by direct command.

I led my troops to eastern Hunan, where there were many other partisan units. These were all reorganized into the "Independent First Division" under command of Liu Po-ch'êng, with T'ang Shih-chên as political commissar. I was political commissar of a regiment which was commanded by T'an Chia-ssŭ, who had participated in the Nanchang Uprising. This was in the winter of 1930.

Our "Independent First Division" stayed in the bordering districts of Hunan and Kiangsi, where Mao and Chu had stayed a long time before. Sometimes we climbed to Chingkanshan, which was near by, and sometimes marched to central and south Hunan.

In the spring of 1931 we were still following Li Li-san's policy of attacking the big cities. But this was "adventurism," and we were never able to occupy any big cities. At that time Mao and Chu were in central Kiangsi. The first anti-Red campaign was beginning.

We fought with the White troops every day. My troops lived in great poverty. We had ragged clothes and not enough food to eat. We always attacked at night to ensure success. Once we moved into south Hunan to co-operate with the Red Army in Kwangsi Province. Then Li T'ien-chü became the division commander.

During the whole of 1931 we fought all over Hunan, organizing partisan units in different villages as we passed. In the winter we took an estimate and found that we hadn't lost any guns and had captured many. Our Hunanese troops fought very bravely. We were usually victorious, because we refused to engage the enemy when we knew they were strong. I fought in so many battles that I can't remember how many.

The Mobile Eighth Army

When the "Central Soviet Government" was established in Juikin in November 1931, I was one of the Hunan delegates to the congress. After the meeting I returned to the army on the Hunan-Kiangsi border. T'an Shih-chên, a middle-school student, died, and I was made political commissar of the Independent First Division in the beginning of 1932. When the Chu-Mao army attacked Kanchow, our division was reorganized into the Eighth Red Army under P'êng Tê-huai. The commander of the Eighth Red Army was still Li T'ien-chü, and I was political commissar.

In August of 1932 we captured many machine guns and munitions from the Kuomintang. In Fenyi, Kiangsi, our troops wanted to occupy a blockhouse where the Whites were garrisoned. I led nine men to climb the mountain to lead the attack. All nine were killed. I was badly wounded in the arm and side, and fell down the mountainside. This saved my life, as our troops soon surrounded the bottom. This was a hard battle. The enemy sent four regiments to reinforce the garrison, and we retreated, having lost about three hundred killed and wounded. But we lost no guns and captured fifty or sixty rifles from the enemy. Since the Red soldiers have orders to carry all guns back from the front at the risk of their lives, we seldom lose any.

After gathering the bodies of our dead and wounded, the peasants always come to help burn the dead and take the wounded to their homes to nurse them, so we received good care. At that time, however, we had no medicine and no food even for the wounded. The peasants merely washed the wounds with boiling water and put on rough bandages. We had no radio then, either, and communications with the Central Soviet Government were difficult.

I was soon sent to a hospital in the soviet districts to rest and recover for three months. Li T'ien-chü was wounded two weeks after I was. He was killed in 1936 on the Kiangsi-Kwangtung border.

Once while I was still convalescent, one Red regiment went out to fight the same White regiment that had defeated us so badly at Fenyi and captured their regimental commander, Chang Ch'ao. All the Reds wanted to kill him, but I opposed this idea when I heard of it. I said to the men, "We have no medicine and no money. We will release him if he will send these things to us." The Whites agreed to this proposal and sent us twenty thousand dollars in money and ten thousand dollars' worth of medicine, all paid for out of the commander's own pocket. We knew he was a very rich man. He had been a friend of P'êng Tê-huai before the split. We sent him back to his men safe and sound. Once, though I didn't want him to do it, this White commander insisted on carrying my stretcher because he was grateful to me for saving his life.

In the autumn of 1932 Hsiao K'ê came to take over command of the Red Army.[3] Ts'ai Fei-wên was in general command of the whole district and had taken over my duties during my illness. When I was well enough to work, in the winter of 1932, I was made political commissar of the 22nd Division of the Eighth Army, because this division was weak and needed special attention to strengthen it. Our army fought in many different localities. The soldiers and political workers all had confidence in Hsiao K'ê and Ts'ai Fei-wên, since these two had been sent to us from the Central Soviet Government.

On the Border with Hsiao K'ê

In the autumn of 1933 the Kuomintang started a big campaign—with foreign help, airplanes, artillery, and blockhouses for blockade. We reorganized our forces and reduced the whole army to the 17th Division, strengthening it into a solid-iron unit. At that time Hsü Hung was on the Hunan-Hupeh border with the 18th Division, commanded by Yen T'u-kê. They came to join with us, the united forces being stationed on the Hunan-Hupeh border. Hsiao K'ê was made commander and I was made chairman of the political department of this 17th Division.

In the winter of 1933 I was elected delegate to attend the Second Soviet Congress in Juikin. In the spring of 1934 I returned to the army, where the 17th Division was still garrisoning the Hunan-Hupeh border and the 18th Division protected the Hunan-Hupeh soviet district. On this return journey I had a narrow escape at the Kan River in Kiangsi. The river was lined with White blockhouses, and strangers were shot on sight. I was carrying many official documents and translations of Leninism to my troops, also a radio. I crossed at night safely, however.

On my return I was given Ts'ai's position as political commissar of the 17th Division, while he was transferred. At that time, Jên Pi-shih was in charge of all political work for the whole district.

In 1934 the 17th and 18th Divisions were merged and the number of soldiers was reduced. The Whites thought us a small force and paid no attention to us. Then we attacked them by surprise, after organizing the masses in all the soviet districts to resist. The Whites had only one division, the 16th. We annihilated one whole regiment and captured the division commander.

During the spring, summer, and autumn of 1934, when the "Fifth Campaign" of the Whites was in progress, we fought hard battles every day. We could not live in big houses, because of air bombing, but had to hide in caves or the forest. The planes killed many of the people but few Red soldiers. We always won all engagements, because we

attacked only at night. Though he was young, Hsiao K'ê was very brave and always at the front, and his military tactics were good, as he had learned them from Chu Tê. Even during our most serious difficulties, our Red troops kept their high morale. Under Jên Pi-shih we stood firm on all orders from the Central Soviet government. Class consciousness strengthened among the troops and the direction of the leadership was exactly right. We carried on with banners flying.

Finally, the Whites seized the soviet districts by moving in slowly from different directions. This soviet was only fifty or sixty *li* in diameter, but we fought the blockade for six months. Our army had been born and nurtured in this area. It was much loved by the people, who supported us with food and money, enabling us to hold out a long time. Every single young man in the area helped the Red Army—carrying guns, food, letters, and information. The old men and women sent their sons to fight in the army, and the soviet women made bullets for us. During our worst period, the people had to take care of many wounded from the front every day.

In order to preserve our fighting forces, we decided that we had to leave our soviet districts and march away. In August 1934 we started our "long march."

Retreat from the South, 1934

I was sorrowful to have to give up the soviets. I had had to give up my work in Changsha, give up my work in the army, and give up my home. None of these things had mattered much, but now I deeply regretted leaving our hard-won soviets, defended at such great sacrifice. Victory seemed far in the future.

In our soviet we had given the people the land of the landlords, we had given them political freedom, and they had learned self-government. We had emancipated women and guaranteed free education for all. Now the Red Army had to leave the soviet to the mercy of the counterrevolution. Before our departure, we did not tell the people—we had to keep this maneuver secret—but they knew we should soon have to leave because of enemy pressure. Even now many partisans are still fighting there, however.

Only ten women left with us on the Long March, but several hundred *hsiao kuei*[4] came along. My new wife remained behind. She was arrested in 1935, and is still in prison in Nanchang. We had no children. Of course, she didn't want to stay behind, but I was political commissar of the army and if my wife had gone on the Long March, all the other wives would have insisted upon going, and that would have caused great trouble. I had to give her up to set an example of sacrifice for other comrades. My wife was a farmer's daughter who became a Communist Youth nurse.

When the Red Army left, the Whites killed every revolutionary they could catch. Many escaped, however, and still remain there. T'an Yüeh-pao, chairman of the soviet, is still leading partisans in Kiangsi, we hear from letters. Several Red Army men have received letters saying their families are still safe in Kiangsi. There were few illiterates in Kiangsi, and the soldiers even receive letters from their wives.

I was with Hsiao K'ê all during the Long March as his political commissar. Jên Pi-Shih was our representative from the Central Soviet government.

We had started our first stage of the Long March three months before the central Red armies, who did not leave the central soviets until October 1934. We were able to join Ho Lung successfully, after defeating the White blockade in eastern Kweichow. In 1935 we continued our way to the north to-

gether with Ho Lung's troops. In October 1936 we met with all the other Red armies in Kansu.

I was wounded twice at the beginning of the Long March in 1935, first in a battle in Ho Lung's native *hsien* and later in Lung-shan, also in Hunan.

You ask how the working-class elements regard the new United Front with the bourgeoisie. At first the working classes didn't understand the new line clearly, but after the party explained it fully, they all agreed with it. At present the interests of the peasants and workers and other classes coincide on the anti-Japanese front. All the people of China want the United Front, and Nanking dares not fight us again, or the people will rise and overthrow the government. The Chinese bourgeoisie is a wavering class. In 1927 they turned reactionary, but now that they are becoming more progressive, it is possible to co-operate with them. Even in 1927, though that was the worst period, not all the bourgeoisie turned reactionary. In 1931, after September 18, we decided not to seize the power from the Kuomintang but to try to co-operate to fight Japan.

Especially must the party now win over the petty bourgeoisie. Our party represents the interests of the workers, peasants, and petty bourgeoisie, although it must stand basically on the proletarian interests. The petty-bourgeoisie class cannot take any action itself—some elements in it turn to the bourgeoisie and some to the working class—but now because of the menace of fascism they are turning to us. Fascism is the most reactionary tendency possible in a colonial country like China, because it is pro-imperialist.

Têng Fêng

CHIEF OF THE SECRET POLICE

MISS WALES:

ONE of the obscurest phases of the agrarian movement in China occurred after the Kuomintang took power and tried to bring back the landlords. Têng Fêng, who had been the chairman of the Hunan-Hupeh-Kiangsi border government from 1934 to 1936—as well as chief of the Pao Wei Chü, a police force similar to the Russians' Gay-Pay-Oo—shed some light on this topic in the account he gave me of what happened in this region after the Communist armies left on the Long March.

This border region, containing Liuyang and P'ingkiang, lies not far from the Yangtze River, and at one time had a population of around one million, but during the period it was under Têng Fêng's control it contained only about ten thousand, nearly all women and children; the men either had been killed or had gone on the Long March with Hsiao K'ê's army. Here in Liuyang at the village of Linho, in the Yü (or Yi) district, was the oldest surviving soviet in China, the earlier ones in Hailufeng and Ch'alin having been destroyed. The organization of this agrarian movement had been begun near the city of Liuyang as early as 1923. It was also in Liuyang and P'ingkiang that Mao Tsê-tung held his first Autumn Crop uprisings in 1927. It is important to note that this region, like Hailufeng, contains independent-minded tribespeople among its population, which is therefore known in other parts of China as very *li hai*, or high-spirited. Here, too, the status of women is higher than elsewhere, as in Hailufeng.

Têng Fêng was a hard-bitten old campaigner, whose face showed marks of hardship, responsibility, and character, but I found him friendly and animated. During the interview he gesticulated with much energy as he described various incidents.

TÊNG FÊNG:

I AM a watch repairer by profession and worked at my job until 1927, when I joined the revolution. Since then I have been active in the longest-surviving soviet of any in China. This is in Liuyang *hsien* in Hunan province. In 1928 the soviet was started there in the village of Linho, in Yü district, now called Yenshih. The founders are all dead now but two: Huang Shou-tao, who is still there, and Chang Ch'i-lung, who is here in Yenan. The others were Huang Kung-liu—a high army commander who was killed, Liu Hsien-shun, Liu Hsü-fa, Liu Ta-yung, and Chang Yüan-kao. The Kungliu School in the central districts in Kiangsi was named for Huang Kung-liu, as were a pavilion and several monuments. I knew him. He was a scholar, a soldier, and a very handsome man and popular leader.

P'ingkiang and Liuyang *hsien* had uprisings at the same time, though there is a high mountain border between the two. The leaders in P'ingkiang were Lo La-ch'uan and Tu Chên-kuan. Tu is now the Communist party secretary there, though only thirty—he was once a Kuomintang man but changed and joined the Communist party. Lo La-ch'uan was the original leader there from 1925 to 1930, the year he was killed. I was with Lo in 1928 at Ku Chia T'ung when three hundred of his men were killed by machine guns in one day and he had a narrow escape. The organizers in both *hsien* that I have mentioned were all young students under thirty, not farmers. Liuyang, with a population then of eight hundred thousand, and P'ingkiang, with six hundred thousand, are the two richest and biggest *hsien* in Hunan, having many workers, especially in papermaking and mining. They are the *hsien* neighboring Changsha. Wan Tsai is also large. Even the villages there are larger than Yenan.

They had only one gun to start with in Linho village. They acquired the gun by having one of their men join the *min t'uan* and desert with it. I was in Liuyang then. We got ten other guns from P'ingkiang, where the people had captured a great many in the uprising. None of us in Liuyang knew how to use a gun except by trying, until Huang Kung-liu organized the partisans which he led to join P'êng Tê-huai after the uprising. We used these ten guns to fight the *min t'uan*, as the people did not trust them any more, and the soviet developed day by day.

Once, in 1928, just after starting the soviet, the leader Chang Ch'i-lung was captured by the enemy army. People told the partisans, who went out and took him back. Another time, being chased by the enemy, he climbed the border mountain which we call Fushoushan. It was winter, with a heavy snow, and as Chang was wearing shoes with an iron nail on the bottom his steps could easily be traced. He turned the shoes around and climbed up the mountain, but the enemy thought he had come down and could not find him. He had no food on this mountain for seven days except roots of the *shu* plant. Fushoushan was a convenient place for hiding. Without this mountain the partisans could not have operated so well. It was three hundred *li* long and at the widest place was about ninety *li* from bottom to top and down to the bottom on the other side. Chang later became secretary and then chairman of the soviet of Liuyang *hsien*, not far from Changsha.

The partisan movement first expanded in this way: Farmers would assemble and decide which *t'uhao* landlord they wanted taken care of. They would then elect one of their number as a representative, contribute money for his expenses, and send him to the soviet to ask the armed partisans to come. These farmers, who identified their leaders by false names, would lead the partisans to the landlord's house, explaining that they must pretend not to be involved. They would help catch the landlord, bind him with ropes, and carry him away to the soviet court for trial, but afterward they would pretend before the reactionaries of their village that they had been forced to do this. The people often bought gunpowder and other necessary things to give to the partisans. At first the partisans used primitive guns but now all have good guns captured from the Kuomintang—all kinds, but usually "38" rifles from America and Japan. But the partisans had to make their own bullets.

In 1930 I was with the partisans when we started from P'ingkiang with P'êng Tê-huai to capture Changsha, the capital of the province. We occupied it several days and took many guns. P'ingkiang was the strategic base from which to capture Changsha, though we went in a curve to effect the victory. We then turned back to Liuyang *hsien* and to the Wênchiashih district near my home. Starting from there on July 27, 1930, three generals— Chu Tê, P'êng Tê-huai, and Huang Kung-liu—together attacked Changsha a second time, staying about twenty days and establishing a soviet. At that time, these three and Mao Tsê-tung were the only noted leaders and the Third Army Corps was the main force. Then the enemy surrounded Changsha and those in the city had a hard time. A Red leader named Hu Piao led the *Chung Tui Pu*, a main column, to attack the enemy outside Changsha and free our people penned in the city.

At the time of the Changsha attack, twenty-four district soviets were established in Liuyang, each with officers and administration. Some of these continued until 1932. P'ingkiang also started soviets. After the return from Changsha, P'ingkiang was the center of the Hunan soviet region, and the whole *hsien* was sovietized. The first month after Changsha, P'ingkiang city was made the central soviet capital of Hunan, and we established a Lenin School, a Red Academy, a library, and a recreation center. Then the capital was changed to Ch'ang Hsü Kai in P'ingkiang *hsien*, where the First Delegates' Congress of Hunan Province was held and a permanent government was elected, in September 1930. Formerly the administration had been temporary. The chairman elected was Yang Yu-lin, a Communist—I don't know where he is now—and the vice-chairman was P'êng Tê-huai.

Pao Wei Chü Chief

In 1931 the Central Soviet Government in Kiangsi sent Lin Shui-shên to be secretary of the party of the provincial soviet, and we changed the name to the "Hunan-Hupeh-Kiangsi Border Government." Both the chairman, Wang Hsien-teh, and the vice-chairman later became reactionary. In 1933 Tu Chên-kuan became chairman instead of Wang, and Chang Ch'i-lung became vice-chairman and also Minister of Justice.

By 1931 the population under this border government was many hundred thousand. The Second Congress was held at Hsiushui *hsien* in the T'aichang district of Kiangsi, in the winter of 1931. The Third Congress was held at Wantsai *hsien* in Hsiaoyüan district in Kiangsi, in October 1933; Ho Chên-wu was chairman. I was chairman from 1934 to April 1936, and the chairman in 1937 was Hu Chin-t'ao, a poor farmer, then only twenty-seven.

After the Third Congress, the enemy surrounded and blockaded the whole region of the border government. In February 1934, we changed the capital to Huangchint'ung in Hunan, which was central to the three provinces. At this time there were about a thousand government officials in the whole border government and in the party and the labor unions. The best period of this region was from 1930 to 1931. The worst was in 1934, because of the Kuomintang oppression then.

In April 1934, under enemy pressure, we had to move the central soviet capital to a mountain in Kiangsi called Lungmei Shan. The mountain is in the middle of four *hsien* and is a safe retreat—there are four ways to escape from it. This central soviet had an area of three hundred *li*, and other soviet districts existed elsewhere. The four *hsien*, all in Kiangsi, were Hsiushui, Fênghsien, Yifêng, and T'ungku.

I was then Minister of External Affairs, handling all work in "White" areas. The enemy was bearing down upon us during the twenty days that we were moving to the mountain. All the officials, including the women, moved. We were bottled up there for two months, surrounded by enemy troops. Then the government returned to the town of Huang-Chin-T'ung, and there I became chief of the Pao Wei Chü [secret police], as this post had become essential to our safety. This town has remained the capital and I am still chief of the Pao Wei Chü.

The central government at Juikin sent Ch'ên Shou-ch'ang as party secretary. He proved to be a good man, and under his leadership the soviet progressed rapidly.

I had a narrow escape in August of 1934. I was on a mission in enemy territory and at San Tou in T'ungku *hsien*, Kiangsi, I was trailed. Sixteen people were searching for me. I jumped from a high place into some water and remained hidden among the reeds with only my mouth on the surface to breathe. I had several secret things on my person which would have caused my execution if they had been found, but I placed some of these and the seals of the Pao Wei Chü under the mud at my feet. For a long time I could see only two possibilities— either to commit suicide by strangling in the water to save myself from torture, or to try to run away and hope to be shot and killed. I saw no way to escape. The searchers were all around me, poking into the water and looking everywhere. They were completely amazed, for they had seen me just before I jumped off. There was a high reward, so they would not give up easily.

I stayed in the water, under constant scrutiny, from five in the morning until eight at night. The guards still kept watch all around near by, but I hid in the grass for eight days, eating nothing but grass. Then I escaped at night and went to a mountain where I slept. My stomach made me feel very ill and I was starving. In the morning I saw a woman in her doorway calling a little boy to eat but saying, "We have no salt." Then I knew that she was poor and would help me. She asked who I was and I told her I was a Red soldier in need of protection. She asked me in and gave me food. I ate three bowlfuls but this made my stomach worse. She guarded the house and then guided me ten *li* to a place where I could find my way to the soviet district. I had no money at all to give her and she did not want any.

At this time the Red armies were leaving on the Long March, and we decided to make the soviet stronger and more consolidated.

In my district the Red Army was under Hu Ch'u-t'ao. It was the 16th Independent Division, a regular army division originally part of the Sixth Army under Hsiao K'ê. Before the Long March we had three armed divisions: the Sixteenth, the North River Division of partisans and the Third Division of partisans. Altogether there were about thirty thousand men, including armed partisans. Now only two thousand of the 16th Division are left. All others have been killed in the fighting.

The Kuomintang built blockhouses around the area in August 1935, but in 1936, when Nanking and Kwangtung were having trouble, the people destroyed nearly all of them. There were nine hundred blockhouses around Liuyang alone, but now only twenty are left. The people, mainly women, carried wood into them and burned them.

When our army wants to occupy a place or to attack a blockhouse, the women are spies for us and advise how to approach in the particular situation. Once at Hsienchang Chu in P'ingkiang the army wanted to attack a blockhouse which had a small outpost near by. There was no way to get near enough, so a woman volunteered to go in carrying vegetables and shoes to sell. Having seen that the small post was defended and the blockhouse was empty, she advised our army to burn the empty blockhouse and to smoke out the enemy in the post. This was done successfully.

In a Blockaded Soviet

There are many incidents I could tell you of life there [in Hunan] now to show how the peasants spontaneously manage their affairs. In general, in the partisan districts the *lao pai hsing*[1] send clothes, shoes, utensils, umbrellas, and other things to the government and to our soldiers, to help.

The partisans operate at night. If they want to take a rest, they can knock at any farmer's door and stay in his home no matter how great the risk he takes. The farmers never report to the Kuomintang, though they would be killed by the Kuomintang if it were known that they were sheltering our people. We have certain signals. If our soldiers knock at night, the farmers open quickly. If anyone else knocks, they keep him out. Sometimes in the soviet areas we have no food on the mountain and the people in the near-by partisan areas have to supply it to us.

Sometimes we have complicated problems such as this: In December 1936 a farmer in P'ingkiang *hsien* loaned his land out to his sons and wanted them to pay rent. They objected and he ran away. Then the sons went to the soviet authorities and asked them to arrest their father as a landlord. The sons insisted and under the laws it was justified, so they led the authorities to catch their own father.

In Kukang, Liuyang, the Kuomintang called a mass meeting to spread propaganda on "suppressing bandits," and about a thousand people came, but they just sat at the side to see what would happen and nobody went to the meeting place. The *lao pai hsing* themselves had distributed pamphlets to the people telling them what was happening and asking them to show this passive resistance. The Kuomintang found that everybody that showed up was a "bandit"!

Once I had this experience: I was walking through the P'ingkiang countryside at night and I missed the road. I knocked at a farmer's door but he would not open. After awhile I said that I was of the soviets. Still he did not open. He became angry that I knocked so persistently, but I explained politely that I really was from the soviet district and needed help. Finally he was convinced and opened the door, saying he was sure that no Kuomintang soldier or person would ever be so polite—only a Communist would. I asked to be directed to the road and promised a dollar. A woman led me two *li* but refused to take the money. When I asked why, she said: "You work so hard at night just for the benefit of us farmers. We do this little thing to help you now, and our sons and grandsons will be benefited by it later ten times over."

During a battle at Hsiangtung in Liuyang, in April 1937, seven of our people were wounded, including a company commander and a squad leader. They lived secretly in a farmer's house and the people found medicine and cared for them and afterward took them back to the army. The people were ordered to report every month to the Kuomintang troops any information of our soldiers but, of course, they paid no attention to this order.

In T'afu district in Liuyang a traitor named Mao Ya-fêng used the name of the soviet and collected a considerable amount of money from the people. One day an old man of that district met the vice-minister of finance of our government and asked him about Mao and so found out that Mao was stealing money. The old man asked for an order to arrest Mao and it was given to him. Three days later when Mao came to his house to drink wine, the old man and two others bound Mao and threw him into a river. This was in January 1937. In such ways the people protected themselves.

In the Lungmen district of P'ingkiang there was a man who had once served in our soviet organization but had become a traitor and was helping the enemy to catch our soldiers and the soviet people. One day a farmer was on the mountain digging roots with an iron spade and saw this traitor. He played a trick on the traitor by talking awhile and then got near and killed him with the spade so that he could not betray any more to death. This was in March 1937.

When the Kuomintang occupies a place they organize a Nung Min Sao, or "Peasant Guard." Once our army caught one of these guards and talked to him. He went back and organized fifteen of the guards and they came with their guns to join us. The Kuomintang did not trust the peasants to be organized there again.

Once a farmer was put in prison for four months for helping our partisans. The day after he returned home, one of my men went to see him and wanted to give him two dollars. He refused to take it and said that the house and land were given to him by the soviet and that it was his own government. He helped us just as before.

The Liuyang-P'ingkiang area was the foundation of the whole soviet territory and the central soviets were based on it. In these districts, no matter how hard the Kuomintang tries to alienate the people from us, they have no success. We have always been able to maintain either secret or open organizations.

In the Wutang district of P'ingkiang *hsien*, Kiangsi, where the soviet was occupied by the Kuomintang army, for two years none of our soviet people went near the place even to do propaganda, but the people wanted us to return and re-establish the soviet. One night two of my Pao Wei Chü men went to a house to stay and found two young men writing on pieces of paper. The two young men were much frightened, thinking our men were Kuomintang people, and hid the papers under a desk. My men asked to see what they had written but they refused and tore it up. My men took the papers and later pieced them together. On them had been written over and over: "Support the Communist party!" and "Welcome the Communist party to re-establish a soviet here!" My men then went back and invited those men to work in the soviet government, which they did.

At present there is not much work in the soviet district except in partisan areas, and our people have to work there to earn a living, with the protection of the *lao pai hsing*. The Minister of Labor, a worker, took a job at Chup'ing in P'ingkiang in a farmer's house, and many other farmers warned him to leave and tried to get him away but he paid no attention, saying, "Never mind, I can work here for a while." But he was in a reactionary place, as the others had warned him, and the farmer killed him and collected a high reward.

In the early spring of 1937 the people in P'uchi district in Liuyang met and prayed before their old idols for the Red Army to come back. They said: "It is only necessary for the Red Army to pass by here and the price of rice will fall two dollars a *tan²* and our life will be better." (The landlords want a high price but the farmers who pay rent want it low because the rent is paid from the harvest, not in money but in kind. The landlords collect the harvest and won't sell until spring, when the price is high. At harvest time the price is low and the farmer has food to eat, but in spring the poor people cannot afford to buy rice. The landlords have plenty but the price is too high. That is why the farmers want a low price in the spring.) When the partisans came to this area, the reactionaries tried hard to oppose them, but the *lao pai hsing* were delighted. The farmers took their big measures for holding grain and put them up in the trees so that the partisans could hide in them without being seen in the daytime. Then at night they led the

partisans out to the places where they wanted them to arrest bad *t'uhao* and confiscate their goods.

The people of this region still have many guns, though the Kuomintang has taken away all they could find or buy. We have a small arsenal to make weapons and can make light machine guns, rifles, pistols, grenades, and trench mortars—also a heavy gun that can fire an eight-*chin* shell. We have seventy-two workers employed there. All those making bullets are women and children, and the work is all handcraft work. The men do the metal work and repair guns. The mountain near by has metals, gold included.

In many places far from the soviets, even a hundred *li*, the *lao pai hsing* have organized themselves spontaneously into partisan groups. They go to catch the landlords and bring them all the way to our government for trial. One of the best of these partisan groups is in Chênwu district in Liuyang and is named for Ho Chen-wu, the leader who was killed here. A Communist party group also was organized here.

I remember one incident in this same Chênwu district which shows how the farmers arm themselves. In the spring of 1935 three farmers were working in a field when they saw a Kuomintang official being carried in a sedan chair and carrying two rifles and one Mauser. The farmers secretly killed him to get the three guns.

The Women Take Over

It is mainly women and children who are left in the soviet areas and the neighboring partisan region. The women do the farm work and support their children, and as the boys grow up they join the self-defense work, while women do espionage for us. The women are more determined than the men that the government and the land system shall not revert to the old ways, for they have their freedom now.

Every day the population is being destroyed by the Kuomintang armies in our regions in the south. For example, at San

Chia T'ung in the P'ingkiang soviet, once our best place, there is not now a single house standing nor a single man left. All have been killed or have had to run away, but they did not submit.

I remember many incidents concerning women. In 1936 the Kuomintang occupied Kaop'ing in Liuyang *hsien*, where land had been distributed under our administration, and the landlords returned and went to the farmers, demanding their rent. At one place, a landlord found no men, only women managing the farm. One woman ordered her boy to cook food for the landlord and asked him to wait, saying that she would go away to get money to pay him. What she did was to rush to the mountain near by and get three women to volunteer. They went back together and tied a rope around the landlord and strangled him.

Another typical story about women is this one from Wantsai, Kiangsi, in the Chentung district. A girl named Yang Shu-yin had been married against her will. The soviet government granted her a legal separation. She then married a worker whom she liked. When the Kuomintang returned, her former husband demanded that she come back and she had no way to escape from him. Two years later the partisans came and her first husband ran away saying, "The bandits are here." But she played some stratagem and refused to go with him, waiting till she could go with the partisans and join her real husband.

In the winter of 1936, in Tenghsi, Liuyang, the daughter of a rich farmer fell in love with a poor farmer. Her father locked her up in his blockhouse—there the rich farmers have their own blockhouses for protection. She told the poor farmer to join the Red Army and lead it to attack the blockhouse and take her away. At first we were afraid that the girl and her friend had been sent by the reactionaries as a trick and did not trust them. However, the friend led the partisans to attack. Signals were arranged, and when the girl in the blockhouse signaled, this was the time for the partisans

to attack. They took the blockhouse, but the girl was wounded and they left her there so that she could have medical care. The partisans never were able to come back, and the two could not marry. The poor farmer is now a company commander and has not married.

At Tsahsichih in Liuyang, after a battle with the Kuomintang in January 1937, our wounded were taken by the people to their own homes and were nursed there. An old woman of sixty took a soldier to her hut on the mountain and got rice for him by going begging. When she was asked why she went to so much trouble to support another person, she answered: "I don't want our government abolished. If it is changed I must pay land rent. I provide rice for this soldier temporarily, but, if he fights, perhaps I can own land a long time in the future."

Before 1930 we held thirty-four sovietized *hsien* but afterward the Red Army did not occupy *hsien* cities and occupied border districts only. This soviet area was smaller than the central soviet in Kiangsi. We held the *hsien* capitals in 1930 in the following places, the rest being border districts: P'ingkiang and Liuyang, in Hunan; Wantsai, T'ungku, Hsiushui, Fênghsin, and Ch'ingan, in Kiangsi; Wulin, Ch'ungyang, P'uch'i, T'ungshan, Yanghsin, Och'êng, and Tayeh —where the Hanyehp'ing mines are—all in Hupeh.

From 1930 to 1935 the area was a narrow strip eight or nine hundred *li* long. At present [September 1937] the soviet district is still five hundred *li* long but it is a very thin line along the mountain, and we have a population of 10,000. These districts are not well connected, and some places are isolated, but we can still pass at night from one to another and send messages.

Our condition is now this: The Kuomintang armies still attack our regions, though we are demanding a stop to the civil war, so we resist in self-protection. The *lao pai hsing* have organized themselves into the

Tzǔ Wei Chün, or "Army for Self-Defense."

There are two main soviet districts. The first is about three hundred *li* on the borders of three *hsien*—P'ingkiang in Hunan, and Hsiushui and T'ungku in Kiangsi. The second is about a hundred *li* in Hunan, where the capital, Huangchint'ung, is located. This oldest soviet has never been conquered by the enemy. Here the peasants have been organized since 1925, and here P'êng Têhuai set up the soviet in 1930. P'êng had his first uprising at P'ingkiang in 1928 with one regiment.

P'ingkiang and Liuyang are the seat of the most serious struggle, and the *lao pai hsing* there can fight and organize spontaneously without any party leadership. When women see spies or Kuomintang soldiers, they often kill them or capture them and bring them to our government for handling. However, we hold fifteen *hsien*, with a population of ten thousand, though P'ingkiang and Liuyang are the most important. We do not have the *hsien* cities, but we reorganized and renamed these fifteen *hsien* [districts].

In addition to the soviet areas I have described there are the partisan districts of constant fighting—about thirty *hsien*. The people in these places are anxious for our army to come back. However, we cannot expand in the soviet districts and we have to recruit from the partisan areas. Last year over two thousand joined and already over a thousand have joined this year. They come to us spontaneously in small groups of thirty or forty men together, the largest being a group of one hundred twenty men. In January and February of 1937 many came over in groups.

Many *pao chia*³ leaders influenced the people to join our army. The leaders are appointed by the Kuomintang officials to be responsible for the *pao chia*. It is an important sign when they come over to us. Many women in the White districts send their husbands, sons, or relatives to join us. The women bring them to our districts and ask them to work hard when they say farewell.

Most of our men are young, under twenty. The army has a minimum age of sixteen for joining, but in Liuyang, boys of twelve are always crying because they cannot be admitted.

Each *hsien* has about fifteen partisans; and all the *hsien* together total several hundred. Each *hsien* has one *pan* [squad] of ten Pao Wei Chü men, under my command, for self-defense.

We have given all our organizations new names, such as the "Anti-Japanese Army" and the "Farmers' Anti-Japanese Union." This is in accordance with the new United Front policy. We have not yet changed the soviet in Hunan but will do so now by popular elections. We have primary schools but we don't teach Latinization. We have a new movement for "Common Education," teaching singing, sports, handcrafts, reading, writing, and so on.

Under the new policy, landlords write letters to our government asking permission to return. If a landlord was kind in the past and not a *t'uhao*, the people do not object and we permit him to return, but most of them are afraid to come back, though only a few were killed in the past—most of them ran away. They are afraid of the peasants now, and their attitude has changed, and they are not much different from small holders. All the people are politically conscious now and want our armies to come back and to keep the new land system. They are entirely changed from what they were before they were sovietized. The only reason why the soviet was not destroyed by the enemy is that the people have protected it with their entire ability and have voluntarily fed and clothed the government personnel. Every person is vigilant, and we receive immediate warning of enemy approaches and plans.

The largest remaining soviet region in the south in 1937 is the Fukien-Chekiang-Kiangsi border soviet under Han Ying and Ch'ên Yi. Next is Oyüwan, formerly under Hsü Hsiang-ch'ien. My own soviet is not so large. It is on the Hunan-Hupeh-Kiangsi border, centering in the Yü district, Hunan.

PART THREE

*Soldiers from
the Ranks*

Lo Ping-hui

FOE OF LANDLORDS

General Lo Ping-hui with his bodyguards and orderlies—Miaotzŭ tribesmen—photographed in Kansu Province, 1936.

MISS WALES:

READING this autobiographical account gives one the feeling of being in touch with the rank and file of Chinese soldiers. Though Lo Ping-hui had risen to the rank of general by the time I met him, he remained a common soldier in spirit. He was full of humor, and I think he spoke quite sincerely when he said that he had always enjoyed campaigning and living a hard and dangerous life. He was jovial, of enormous girth, and—except for General Fêng Yü-hsiang—the largest and most powerfully built Chinese I had ever seen. I suspect that there is a stalwart mountain tribesman of Yünnan in his ancestry to account for his size and animation and the unusual quality of his eyes.

Lo Ping-hui is in line of descent from the days of T'ang Chi-yao and Chu P'ei-tê—military figures of the early days of the Revolution. Lo himself says that T'ang Chi-yao was "an old feudal militarist war lord, not at all revolutionary." Chu P'ei-tê was one of Sun Yat-sen's generals. In Lo's narrative can be traced a soldier's development from simply a profes-sional soldier under T'ang to a fighter for the revolutionary forces of the early Kuomintang under Chu and gradually to a supporter and member of the Chinese Red Army. He took part in the capture of Canton for Sun Yat-sen, fought against Chu Tê and then changed his mind and joined him, and subsequently commanded the rear guard on the Long March.

General Lo continued in the high command during the war with Japan. It was reported in 1947 that he was ill with heart disease. This was not surprising, considering the strain he had undergone in active soldiering since the age of sixteen.

I also met Ho Ch'ang-kung, political adviser to Lo Ping-hui and his mentor in all things. He was one of those who studied Marxism in France with Chou Ên-lai after the first World War. On his return he helped to form the "Chinese Returned Laborers' Association" in Shanghai, in 1919. When I met him, he was one of the directors of K'ang Ta University. Though I could not get him to tell his story, I

113

did succeed in taking his photograph. He was particularly helpful to Lo Ping-hui in handling the difficult problem of rear-guard morale during the Long March.

LO PING-HUI:

MY family home is in Yi-liang *hsien*, Yünnan, where I was born in 1899. My father belonged to the middle peasant class but later became poor because of bad economic conditions. In my home were my parents, my brother and I, and my wife and child.

When I was very young I helped with the work on the farm. My life was hard and bitter under our harsh landlord, and I ran away to join the army when I was twelve. I walked for two days, then turned off the main road to hide in a peasant's house and rest. My family had sent some men to bring me back. This group had searched for five days when I accidentally met them on their way back, after they had given up hope. I was obliged to return home, and after that my family had a very bad feeling toward me. Finally they divided the house and gave me a wife so that I could live apart from them. Though I was only twelve when I became an independent householder, I was grown-up at that age. My parents thought that I was always anxious to run away and that a wife would tie me down. I didn't like this marriage but didn't know how to escape it. The family liked the new arrangement because I had embarrassed them by fighting against the landlord and insulting and cursing him. Although I was the eldest son, I was a "bad boy," while on the contrary my younger brother was a "good boy." He was a kind of ally of the landlord against me and I hated him for his obedient, kowtowing attitude as if he were a worm. In that part of Yünnan we did not count by *mu* of land but by the quantity of the crops. We had a good harvest, and my share of our crop was seven thousand *chin*. This was enough for me and my wife.

My relations with my family and with the landlord were never good. I was always anxious to leave. At sixteen I ran away again and joined the army in Yünnanfu. At that time the army held a high position in society in Yünnan, taking the place of the old scholar-officials. When the old scholastic examination system was abolished, a new military examination was instituted. It was very strict and required perfect health, eyesight, and the like. My personal reason for wanting to join the army, however, was mostly in order to have freedom to revenge myself upon the landlords. I got this idea from seeing two soldiers (who had returned to my *hsien*) beating up a landlord with impunity.

Three years after I ran away I heard that all my family's property had been confiscated by the landlord because they were accused of "stealing" from him. I have never heard a word about any of my family since then. Recently I wrote a letter to inquire about them but I have received no reply as yet. Lo Ping-hui is not my real name but a "fighting name" which I took when I left Canton to join the Northern Campaign.

The "Model Soldier" of Yünnanfu

I joined the artillery—we had only six cannon—in the Yünnanfu garrison, T'ang Chi-yao being garrison commander. This was in 1915.

I never went to school. When I joined the artillery I learned a little, and later I received my education in the Red Army. Though communications were bad and the people in my *hsien* were ignorant of outside affairs, I knew about the 1911 Revolution when it happened and of the formation of the new modern army. It was my ambition to be a soldier in this new army.

After two years of common soldiering I became a sergeant. Next I was put in charge of the company commissariat. I was promoted from the ranks because I learned my studies well and enthusiastically. In the garrison I was nicknamed "the Model Soldier." Every day we had lectures on military training. I passed all examinations well and had no bad personal habits, and so made a good impression on the higher officers. After a while I became a member of T'ang Chi-yao's staff and went with him to Hongkong in 1920 when he was defeated by other militarists. I lived there in T'ang's house for eight months. T'ang Chi-yao was an old feudal militarist war lord, not at all revolutionary. He considered me honest and reliable, and trusted me very much, and so made me his purchasing agent. Much money passed through my hands and I could have made a good deal of "squeeze" but somehow I didn't care about money. My regular salary was forty dollars a month and I considered that enough. My life with T'ang was luxurious but I didn't like it. I was revolted by an easy life and have always enjoyed hard soldiering.

T'ang Chi-yao had been governor-general of four or five provinces. He had a fortune of ten to twenty millions at least. He opened his main account in the Sino-French bank in Yünnan and Shanghai, and when this concern went bankrupt, T'ang fainted! This bankruptcy cost him ten million dollars. Later he lost another portion of his fortune in a Japanese bank.

Because I didn't like either the life or the society of Hongkong, I left T'ang and returned to Yünnanfu. Hongkong had made a deep impression on me. I saw what imperialism meant to China and I realized the extent of the corruption in the Chinese ruling class when I saw the way the militarists went to the treaty ports and wasted the tens of millions they had squeezed from the hard-working people. I had seen French imperialism in operation in Yünnan and I understood the meaning of it still better when I passed through French Indochina on the way to Hongkong. On the Yünnan border, if you take one piece of silver or one needle into Indochina the French fine you, but coming in the other way they themselves bring in anything they like free of duty. I remember seeing a typical incident when I went through customs in Indochina. A Chinese had bought a water pipe for four dollars and the customs demanded a tax of six dollars. He threw the pipe into the sea and refused to pay. For this he was boxed on the ear by the customs officer and was fined twelve dollars.

The First Northern Campaign

When I arrived in Yünnan I was arrested because of my connection with T'ang Chi-yao but after a week two officers got me released. Seeing that the old feudal forces still dominated in Yünnan, I went to Kweichow for a while. Then I heard that Sun Yat-sen's group were in Kwangsi. I went there and joined Chu P'ei-tê's army as a staff officer.

I hadn't read any of Sun Yat-sen's books, but I had heard all about him in Hongkong in 1920, and I was especially impressed with his ideas of destroying the reactionary militarists and fighting against imperialism. As soon as I heard about him, I wanted to go to Canton to join him but could not make connections with any of his group at that time.

Sun Yat-sen's group were then planning the first Northern Campaign in Kwangsi. In 1922 Chu P'ei-tê's army attacked Kwangtung and occupied it, and continued on to the attack of Kiangsi. When we arrived in Wan-an *hsien* (the home of the wife of Chu Tê), we learned that Ch'ên Ch'iung-ming (Sun's general in Canton) had revolted and that Sun was surrounded. Chu P'ei-tê had to return to save Sun in Canton, and he sent me to another army, the Kwangtung provincial forces under Li Fu-lin and Hsu T'ung-chih, in order to control those troops—Chu suspected they had some connection with Ch'ên's revolt. I was commissioned as an intelligence officer of Chu P'ei-tê to observe operations.

These Kwangtung provincial forces were defeated, and they withdrew into Fukien.

We had no telegraph or radio then, and I traveled night and day for 190 *li* in order to tell Chu P'ei-tê of the defeat—this act of mine saved him from being surrounded by the enemy. After I made my report, Chu retreated because one flank was exposed. The enemy had already attacked his rear. We retreated from Hunan to Kwangsi. When I was sick on the road, Chu P'ei-tê gave me his own horse to ride, and he always invited me for tea and meals with him. He had a good deal of respect for me, and after my recovery he gave me a captain's commission. Chu was a good commander, compared with others of that time. He was a believer in moderation, did not want bad relations with anybody, and tried not to displease people. But he was not a good revolutionary.

From Kwangsi we again launched an attack on the renegade Ch'ên in Kwangtung, and succeeded in capturing the province. Chu P'ei-tê's troops became Sun Yat-sen's special bodyguard. Chu then had only one weak brigade of two thousand men, two other brigades having revolted. Incidentally, this bodyguard brigade was recently [about 1936] sent to the Northwest under Wang Chün to fight the Red Army. When Wang Chün was reported killed in an airplane accident a short time ago in Kansu, Chiang Kai-shek issued an order to arrest him thinking he had joined the Red Army.

I was made commander of the arsenal guards in Canton. With my company as a nucleus I organized two more companies to guard the arsenal. Soon the Northern war lord, Fan Pên-jên, a follower of Wu P'ei-fu, attacked Canton. Because the forces in Canton were weak, I was made acting battalion commander and was sent to the front of the attack with my companies from the arsenal. I was wounded in this battle but did not go to the rear to recover. After a while the enemy put up the white flag and wanted to surrender to us. I ordered my troops to cease fighting, took another man with me, and went to their camp to negotiate the surrender. While I was in the enemy camp, they received an order not to surrender but to retreat. They took me along with them as hostage, afterward putting me into prison in Kanchow, Kiangsi, for nine months. This was in 1923.

At first the enemy battalion commander wanted to shoot me, but others objected. It was decided merely to imprison me for the time being. As I had two wounds in bad condition, one in the neck and one in the hand, it was difficult for me even to think of escaping. When I had been in prison about nine months, a number of our Kwantung troops who had betrayed to the North were stationed in Kanchow. The Kwangtung commander, named Yang, knew me and when he heard I was in prison there, he secured my release because he admired me for my bravery in battle.

We used to think we had big battles in the time of the Northern Campaign, but they were nothing compared to the fighting between the Kuomintang and the Red Army. Those were militarist wars, and the soldiers didn't know what they were fighting for. Even so, all the one hundred thirty men in my own company had been killed except twenty. But this was unusual. I was noted for leading my company to attack. I have always had friendly, intimate relations with the men under me, and I am careful to make all my ideas clear and to give just reward and punishment; therefore I have always kept good order and discipline among my troops.

In the days of the Northern Campaign there were many mutinies among the Northern soldiers, but not among the Southern. These mutinies were partly based on provincialism and partly on the antagonism between soldiers and officers. In Kanchow, Northern soldiers mutinied against their officers who were Southern, killing many Kwangtung division commanders. A second uprising that occurred there involved about one thousand troops. The main reason for the mutinies was that the soldiers hated the Southern officers—most of them were from Yünnan and Kwangtung — because they were corrupt and squeezed the money meant for the soldiers' food and clothing. After some fighting, the mutinies were put down.

I escaped from Kanchow by changing my name and disguising myself as a peasant. The day I arrived in Canton I had no money even to buy my supper when night arrived. I went out to find my old general, Chu P'ei-tê, but was unable to locate him that afternoon. Next morning I met some Kwangtung officers for whom I had done favors in other days and asked them to take me to see Chu P'ei-tê. They refused, despising me because of my poor clothes—they being all dressed like fine gentlemen indeed. Finally a policeman told me where Chu P'ei-tê was staying. I went to the house but was not permitted to enter. When the sentry tried to shut the door in my face, I said to him authoritatively:

"I have a special message for General Chu. He sent me to Kiangsi on a mission and if I cannot see him now, I must write this to him. You will be held responsible for any delay."

The sentry decided to take me to a guest room and give me paper on which to write a message. Just then a motorcar drove up, bringing the commander of the Kweichow troops for an appointment with Chu P'ei-tê. The sentry tried to drive me out of the compound but when Chu came down the steps to greet the Kweichow commander, he saw me and was very much surprised and very cordial. "We all thought you were dead!" he exclaimed. Needless to say, the sentry became very polite to me after that.

After Chu P'ei-tê finished with his appointment, he talked with me and told me to find a hotel and let him know the address. I said that this was impossible, as I had no luggage and could not register without luggage or money. Chu gave me one hundred dollars and told me to go to a hotel. I had

stayed in the hotel for several days when one night I heard fighting in the streets. I didn't know the reason for this but I heard that Chiang Kai-shek was driving out Hsü Ch'ung-chih, a local militarist. I was hesitant to go outside on the street because I was a stranger. As soon as the fighting began, the Cantonese people said to each other, "Why should we be controlled by these strangers?" and became very hostile to outsiders. Next morning I went to Chu's headquarters to stay, as it was not safe for me in the hotel. Investigation was very strict, and I had no guaranty.

While I was talking with Chu, a report was received that Liao Chung-k'ai had been assassinated. This was in 1925. Chu appointed me as staff officer in his headquarters.

Then a war broke out between Kwangtung and General Shun K'o-wu, of Szechuan. After fighting in this war, I returned to Canton. The Northern Expedition began and I was appointed commander of a battalion.

I fought in the Northern Expedition from Kwangtung to Hunan and from there to Nanchang, Kiangsi, through many serious battles. I was wounded twice, and of my battalion of four hundred only eighty remained when we reached Nanchang.

We left Nanchang to attack Nanking. At a conference there, my troops were ordered back to Kiangsi as part of Chu P'ei-tê's forces. This was the time of the split between Wuhan and Nanking.

We were stationed in Nanchang when the uprising occurred there on August 1, 1927. My men were disarmed by Yeh T'ing, Ho Lung, and Chu Tê. All of Chu P'ei-tê's troops were disarmed then. After the uprising I met Chu Tê. He asked me to join with the Communists but I refused, as I was not clear on the political situation then.

I had been acquainted with Chu Tê before the uprising, when he was pacification commissioner of Nanchang under Chu P'ei-tê, and we had had several meals together.

Formerly Chu Tê had been a brigade commander in Yünnanfu and I recognized him on sight but he did not know me in the Yünnan days. Although he was a native of Szechuan, Chu Tê was even then famous throughout the Yünnan army for his bravery and his ability to command troops, and was already known for his special tactics. In the war against Yüan Shih-k'ai's forces in Szechuan, Chu Tê's crack brigade became famous for its fighting ability. Later he was commander of the Yünnan Gendarmes but had to leave Yünnan because he was not liked by the Governor. He went to Shanghai and afterward to Germany, where he became a Communist. At the time of the Nanchang Uprising I did not have any Communist personal friends, but I had heard of the Red leaders—Chou Ên-lai, Mao Tsê-tung, Ho Lung, and Ch'ên Tu-hsiu. I knew Kuo Mo-jo, having met him in two memorial meetings.

I stayed on in Nanchang for a while until Chu P'ei-tê came and appointed me battalion commander of his remaining troops, ordering me to go to Foochow to do "bandit suppression." In Foochow I won a victory over the Red forces and then marched into Kiangsi to the Kian, Yunghsing, Ningkang, and Tai-ho regions. I fought against Chu Tê himself during this time. I then believed in the *San Min Chu I* [Three People's Principles] and did not know about the Kuomintang reaction against it. I was on the outside of the political movement and did not know much about the internal struggles and the dark side of the Kuomintang.

In this locality I had the support of the people because, though I fought against the Communists, I opposed the landlords and punished them according to the original Kuomintang program. I also enforced strict discipline over my troops, and when two other officers came to my district and raped and robbed, I had them executed. The battalion commanders of these two sent to me to ask for their return, but they were already dead. Because of this action of mine, many high officers signed a petition to Chu P'ei-tê asking him to punish me. Then they tricked me. One day I had an appointment to visit a friend on a small steamer at Changhsu. As soon as I stepped aboard, the boat moved off. I knew something was wrong. I was taken to Nanchang and the officers again petitioned Chu P'ei-tê to punish me. In the meantime, to tell the people what had happened, I wrote manifestos to be distributed throughout the *hsien* in which I had been stationed in Kiangsi. My troops had already been reorganized and dispersed, and only the civilians remained, but the *hsien* magistrates petitioned to save me.

While I was in Nanchang many students and townspeople from my old *hsien* sent money to support me, but I refused it. Some old reactionaries, even, came to see me and were so disgusted with the actions of the Kuomintang troops that they said that the revolutionary period had been better and that China still needed another revolution. Everyone saw that the Kuomintang had turned into an organ for mere personal gain and self-interest.

In Nanchang I went to see Chu P'ei-tê. I told him, "I don't want anything from you at all, neither a job nor money. I want only to exchange greetings as old friends. I intend to return to my village."

Chu said to me: "You have done nothing wrong, but too many men are against you. I will arrange something for you, anyway."

Chu P'ei-tê gave me a letter of introduction. I went to Shanghai, then to Canton where I met Ch'ên Ming-shu. I stayed with Ch'ên until he was hurt during a fire in his hotel in Hongkong. Then I went back to Shanghai and Kiangsi.

By this time the reaction of the Kuomintang against the revolution was clear to me. I returned to live with my family in Kaoan for a time and there I had trouble with the local gentry. The *hsien* magistrate at Kaoan had formerly been a Kuomintang political director under me during the Northern Expedition. I went to call on him in a friendly way, but when this new-made magistrate saw that I had no army and no money he openly despised me. I left his house feeling very angry.

Then I wanted to start a sulphur business there, but one of the local gentry had a monopoly on the sulphur trade and threatened me. This made me angry and I beat the man thoroughly. I had not much money, but over ten years had saved about two thousand dollars. This I had already invested in Kaoan. It was all lost when the gentry forced me to leave. They destroyed my office and threatened to kill me. I had to return to Nanchang. After that I hated the gentry and wished I had force in my hands to destroy them.

In the meantime, many of my old officers and soldiers came to me for help and I had twenty or thirty people staying with me. We were all angry at the change in the Kuomintang, which had joined forces with the corrupt gentry instead of opposing them. This was part of the cause of my conflict with the gentry of Kaoan.

Anti-Red Campaigner in Kiangsi

When I returned to Nanchang, I met some old officer-friends like Wang Chün, but I didn't want to join the army because many of my old friends had received high promotions and I would have been their subordinate and would have lost face. Soon, however, a conference was held to organize a "Peace Preservation Corps." I was given command of this in Kian, Kiangsi, to fight against the Red Army.

As soon as I arrived in Kian I began reorganizing the garrison force there. This *Ching Wei Tui*, or "Peace Preservation Corps"—which is the same as the *min t'uan* —had originally had one thousand men. I cut the force down to five hundred because a big force was only a waste of money. The gentry were very much opposed to the change because I left out most of the representatives of their class. They said to me: "This reorganization may be all right while

you are in command, but what if a new commander turns out bad?" These *min t'uan* in China are organized on a basis of loyalty to certain gentry and their discipline depends on their loyalty.

At this time the Communist areas were very close to Kian, and every day some of my soldiers deserted to them. I knew that the local poor people supported the Reds and I soon realized that the Communist slogans on the walls could not be washed off with gunfire. I could see that the high taxation and the oppressive rule of the gentry forced people to join the Communists, and my mind became much clearer about the cause of the antagonism between the people and the Kuomintang-gentry combination.

While fighting the Red troops, I captured many soldiers. These Red soldiers said to me: "We are sentenced to death under the Kuomintang regime anyway. We cannot keep alive. It was to solve the problem of livelihood that we joined the Red Army."

I was sympathetic with what they said, because I knew it was all true. The peasants had no way to live except by fighting together in the Red Army.

Because I was sympathetic with these Reds, I released several hundred that I captured at different times. The gentry were infuriated at this, and groups of them followed my troops to check up on me. Whenever I captured some "bandits," the gentry promptly published the news and tried to force me to pass the death sentence, but I paid no attention to them.

When they protested to me, I said: "In Kian *hsien* there are three hundred thousand peasants and only twenty thousand of you gentry. You say that all except you are bandits. If I kill all of these three hundred thousand, how will you be able to live on their labor as you now do? These Reds are just peasants trying to solve the problem of living."

And when they talked about "the people" opposing the Reds, I asked: "If 'the people' are menaced by the Reds, why do they all want to join with the Reds instead of the Kuomintang? Surely nobody joins with his enemy. If you gentry would solve the livelihood problem of the peasants, nobody would join the Reds."

In Nanchang I had met a student from Peking National University. He wrote to me in Kian and explained the character of Chinese society as semifeudal. He told me of the example of Tsêng Kuo-fan, who organized the *min t'uan* in the Ch'ing Dynasty and destroyed the people's movement. This student, whose name was Chao Hsin-wu, wrote several letters to me. I wondered what he wanted to do with me. Then he came in person to see me. When Chao visited Kian, I didn't want to see him at first, but finally I did. We talked about the international situation, then about the militarist conflict in Kiangsi, and then about the reaction of the Kuomintang. Gradually Chao began talking about the relative forces of the Communist party and the Kuomintang—which was stronger? I said, "Of course the Kuomintang is stronger. It controls more area, it controls the finances, and it has a huge army. The Communist party is not even in power."

But Chao said, "No, that is not true, because the majority of the Chinese people are poor, not rich. The Communist party represents the poor and stands for the liberation of the people and the solution of the problem of their livelihood, while the Kuomintang is only an armchair supported by the poor. Once the poor decide to throw down this armchair, the Kuomintang can do nothing but sit in the mud. It is like building a wall. The Kuomintang is the decoration on the top, but the people are the base. If the people at the bottom don't want to support the top, the upper layer will collapse, won't it?"

On the third afternoon of our conversations, Chao said to me, "I came here at the risk of my life. You can get a great deal of money for me if you like."

"I never betray a friend, or I could have been rich long ago," I replied. "I guess you are a Communist party member—aren't you?"

Chao turned pale and said, "Yes, it's a question of life or death. What will you do about me?"

"Of course I must do my duty and kill you," I said, joking with him.

Then we discussed the Communist theory and general policies.

Chao told me that the Communist party had investigated my past and that the provincial committee of Kiangsi had ordered him to come to see me to establish personal relations.

"I thought the Communists hated me worse than anybody else," I said. "I have fought against them so long and have won many victories over them."

But Chao replied that the Communist party knew my history well, and admired my bravery, honesty, and straightforwardness. He told me that another of their members would call on me soon.

Chao remained several days more; then a member of the Kiangsi Communist committee came to see me and continued the discussions. He asked my opinion of the Kuomintang, the Communist party, imperialism, and all such matters. Later the Party gave me a list of questions to answer. I was introduced to the Party by Chao, Liu, and Ts'ai Shên-hsi (later commander of the Fourth Red Army). All three of these were later killed. The student Chao was captured by the Kian troops not long after the Kian uprising and was executed. Ts'ai was killed in battle in the Hunan Anhwei district. I don't know exactly how Liu was killed.

I have always kept a picture of Chao. He was very brilliant, also tall and good-looking. He was only twenty-eight when he was executed.

The Kian Uprising of Min T'uan, 1929

I began to do Communist party work in Kian, in my capacity as commander of the Peace Preservation Corps. The comrades told me to keep "gray" in color, to be clever, and not to talk openly or show that I was "red." Because Kian was under my command, the party·organization developed quickly, but the party workers became careless and put documents under tables, beneath beds, around the ceiling, and everywhere. I became a party member in July 1929.

One afternoon a brigade commander of regular Kuomintang troops stationed in Kian called a conference with the *hsien* magistrate. This was secret, with locked doors. I was one of those present. In the conference this commander said, "The Communists in Kian are very active and we must clear them all out." He then disclosed the plan to investigate every single room in the city, including all the Peace Preservation Corps quarters. We were all sworn not to reveal anything of what had been said.

The conference finished at eight o'clock in the evening, and two *t'uan*—two or three thousand men—were already moving out to guard every house during the search. I was extremely worried and could not find the party secretary until ten o'clock. The "clearing out" was to begin at midnight, so the secretary rushed away to prepare for the search.

During the conference, the brigade commander had said: "We should arrest ten innocent people, rather than let a single Communist escape." That night one thousand people were arrested and put in the local temple for detention. Then the order was given that those guaranteed by the gentry not to be Communist members could be released.

A comrade came to me and said: "Only two of our comrades have been caught, but they know you and if they make confessions it will be very dangerous."

I managed to get their release.

Of the one thousand arrested only one hundred got guaranties. The others were imprisoned a long time. Many must have been killed later, after my uprising. I don't know what happened to them. No guaranty was acceptable except one from the gentry —naturally, the poor people could not easily get this.

About this time the *min t'uan* of several *hsien* near by, including Kian, Chishui, T'aiho, Yunghsin, and Anfu, agitated for a united garrison force and wanted me as commander because I was a well-known fighter. I sent my old officers and also some Communists to these *hsien* to work among the *min t'uan* and win their confidence.

Once when I sent a force of three battalions to fight the Red Army, some gentry who knew the local topography were leading the troops. Some of these gentry led the troops away from the line which I had directed, in order to have protection to reach their homes—it was a Red partisan area and they dared not return home individually. I found this out, and it was a good chance to get rid of such reactionaries, so I had them executed "for having connections with the bandits." Other gentry then raised a cry that I was "suppressing the gentry, not the bandits," and the local landlords petitioned the brigade commander against me, saying that I had connections with the Reds. I went to the commander and said: "How can a man who has fought faithfully for the Kuomintang ten years have connections with Red bandits? These people who have sent you the petition are undoubtedly trying to get rid of me so that they can dare to send Communist party members into the city for an uprising. Why else do they want to get rid of the *min t'uan* commander? Don't be cheated by their lies!"

This accusation scared the gentry, who promptly stopped making trouble for me.

I had the confidence of the local people because of my past military record. The rumor among the gentry about my connections with the Communists developed because a party organization had been discovered and some information about my activities had been unearthed at that time. Some of the gentry didn't believe this rumor about me, but asked that I pay special attention to my lower officers.

It was possible at that time to concentrate all the important gentry in one big meeting and clean them up with one stroke, and to disarm all other troops, concentrate the Red troops near by, and capture the city of Kian without much trouble. This was my plan, but the Party disagreed with it and called it a "military plot," and I gave it up.

Then my connection with the Communist party was discovered by my wife. I had a falling-out with her but was able to send her back to her own family without further trouble. But, once again, a local Party organ was discovered and my connection became more and more apparent. It was necessary for me to act.

I led my *min t'uan* to Chihhsia, a place outside the city, and stayed there, fearing that there would be a coup against me and that I would be bottled up within the city walls if I stayed inside. The brigade commander and the gentry wrote to me saying, "You must come inside the city. We guarantee to give you so many new machine guns, to raise your salary, and to organize a new company for you." I knew all this was a trick, for I received not one but several different letters, all unnecessarily urgent.

I was in control of the main road and the post office and the mails. I ordered investigation of all mail and military punishment for smuggling. One night we found a letter from a landlord to one of my lower officers saying that I already had the Communist "idea," and that if necessary the officers should at any opportunity try to "fix" me—that is, arrest and disarm me.

I made my plan. Most of the soldiers and officers were under my personal influence. That same night, the officer to whom the landlord's letter had been addressed disappeared before I could stop him. I estimated that within three hours the Kuomintang troops would arrive to disarm my forces. Early in the morning I gave my men the order to concentrate — without arms, because one of my detachments was not reliable and was under the influence of the gentry. At this meeting I told my men:

"We have been fighting the Reds a long time. We lead a bitter life with no salary, and now the local gentry accuse us of being Communists! To clear up this suspicion and to get our pay I want to take you back to Kian."

Just as I expected, the soldiers began arguing among themselves. Many said that they wanted to join with the Reds and not go back to the city. We then put it to a vote. Those who wanted to join with the Reds were separated from the others and were armed; and those who did not want to join the Reds received no arms. At that meeting four hundred joined the Red uprising and only ten chose to continue with the Kuomintang! Later about twenty men deserted with their arms. Altogether only thirty or so rejoined the Kuomintang. None of the remaining original participants in the uprising deserted me afterward.

We left camp and began marching to meet with the Red troops. Soon a new agitation began among my *min t'uan* and some began to waver. They sent spies back, however, and found that the Kuomintang troops had already arrived at our camp to disarm us. Then others said, "We dare not try to join the Communists because we have fought the Reds so long they will surely take revenge and kill us." I said to them that I had fought the Reds longer than anyone else—yet I knew the Communists were sincere; that they did not hate the White troops —only the gentry and the Kuomintang; and that I had complete trust in them. We sent a messenger to the Red Army with a letter.

This region was all White and far away from the Reds, but I took the men to a place where the Party had a strong secret organization. When we arrived, we gathered together, and the party delegate and I made speeches.

The men all tore off their Kuomintang insignia and said, "Let these things go to the devil! We will wear the Red Star!" Everyone was jubilant and enthusiastic.

Three days later, we marched back to our original camp at Chihhsia carrying the Red Flag high.

Kian was in chaos. The city gates were closed, and everybody suspected everybody else of planning an uprising. People said, "If even the commander of the Peace Preservation Corps is a Communist, how many others must there be?" The whole *min t'uan* of the region was reorganized directly under control of the gentry. The Kuomintang troops had fled inside the city walls already.

We called a meeting under the direction of the party delegate. Three thousand peasants came. The delegate made a speech and then I made mine. I said to the people: "Three days ago I was a commander of the anti-Red Peace Preservation Corps. Now I come back with the Red Flag. I regret with all my heart that in the past I was utilized by the Kuomintang to fight against you poor people. I am glad to declare that now I have turned to your side to fight for you instead."

The peasants who were listening were very happy and shouted: "Now you are the Red Army! Now you are our own troops! Let us forget the past!"

When I heard this, I began to cry and could not speak. I felt that I owed the people my life to pay for my past misdeeds.

Later on, two or three hundred other *min t'uan* and regular soldiers deserted the Kuomintang and joined with me. The *min t'uan* are poor mercenaries paid by the landlords, but the Red Army in general doesn't want *min t'uan* because they have lost their class consciousness in the service of the landlords, and not many of them want to join the Reds, either. If you become a *min t'uan*, a great number of people are held responsible for your actions. Not only your own family and relatives but also three other families must guarantee for you, and the landlords usually have a perfect system of investigating their *min t'uan*.

Now only a few of my *min t'uan* of the Kian uprising are still alive. Later, over twenty became regimental, company, or battalion commanders in the Red Army, and all fought very bravely on the front during the most violent engagements.

After this we fought partisan warfare for a while, and my troops soon increased to over a thousand. We had no connection with the regular Red Army then—they were far away—but we carried the Red Star and the hammer-and-sickle Red Flag. Some of the *min t'uan* wavered for a time, and a rumor went around that there were counterrevolutionary elements among us and that I had received money from the Reds and from Moscow. I made the men search my room. Finally all were convinced that I hadn't a copper and was as poor as they, and their confidence was restored.

There were two Kuomintang battalions near by but they dared not come anywhere near our region. At this time we confiscated the property of the landlords and arrested them, but few were killed and those only on demand of the local people by formal vote in a mass meeting.

In January 1930, after we had had several months of independent partisan fighting, P'êng Tê-huai and Huang Kung-liu came to meet me. One month later, Chu Tê's troops also came to the T'aiho region in Kian to unite forces. My command was then enlarged to two thousand men. After our three forces united, we had a meeting and decided to fight against the garrison brigade at Chihhsia—where I had led the uprising. In this engagement we destroyed two regiments; a third one escaped. Then we went to southwest Kiangsi and to Tingchow, Fukien.

In Tingchow we took a new Party oath and then set out for Nanchang. This was the "Li Li-san oath," which ran: "In order to co-operate with the Communist revolution all over China, we must struggle to win the support of the masses in Hunan and to capture Changsha and Nanchang and then Hankow and Wuchang, and finally carry on down the Yangtze River to Shanghai!"

I was not very clear about the political situation then, but I saw that Li Li-san was too optimistic. Li Li-san said, "The White army will collapse soon, anyway. If we fight hard this will occur all the sooner — work quickly!"

In the fighting at Nanchang I was made commander of the Twelfth Red Army. As this battle was not successful, we left Nanchang and went to Changsha, destroying one division of Hunanese White troops. We wanted to capture Changsha on August 1, to commemorate the Nanchang Uprising. I was with P'êng Tê-huai, Chu Tê, and Mao Tsê-tung (who was political commissar). In the attack on Changsha we experienced our first airplane bombing. A squadron of six airplanes came. At first the Red soldiers didn't know what the planes were and looked up with much interest when they saw something being dropped into the air. Our antiaircraft then was certainly very poor! All the soldiers innocently ran out to have a look. Fortunately the planes flew very high and did little damage.

Five gunboats fired on us in the city. We had one cannon to return their fire. We thought that all these boats were British then, as we always expect the British to fire, but maybe some of the gunboats were American—I don't know. Anyway, there were ten gunboats in all at Changsha then, as I remember.

After leaving Changsha under the command of Chu and Mao, we captured Kian, though it was strongly defended. My old *min t'uan* were active in the capture of their home base. Kian was the economic center of Kiangsi Province. Its main commercial street was over twenty *li* in length, and there were many rich merchants and capitalists there. The capture of Kian thus roused the whole province, and the mass movement developed rapidly. The Red Army gained twenty to thirty thousand new troops. This was at the end of September 1930.

Five Campaigns and the "Biped Cavalry"

Then Nanking became alarmed and sent many troops to attack the Red Army in the First Campaign. We captured Chang Hui-chang and his whole division on December 30 [1930]. Chang was the commander in chief of the "Bandit Suppression Forces" of Kiangsi. In the fight with Chang, I was on the left wing. The battle was very hard, and part of the right wing wavered. Therefore, I advanced to the rear of the Whites and defeated them. Being at their rear, I was able to capture a thousand rifles for my own troops. From Chang we also captured radios and telephones—for the first time—and began to train people to use them. In the fight against T'ang Tao-yüan, I was in command of the vanguard and P'êng Tê-huai was behind me. T'ang was division commander and had two brigades of six regiments. We destroyed two regiments and captured one. My own troops alone captured a thousand rifles from T'ang. This was the finish of the First Campaign.

This victory caused great jubilation in the whole Red Army. The determination and fighting ability of the soldiers rose tremendously. From then on until 1934 everyone thought the Red Army could never be defeated, and the high spirit of the troops never failed. We were more and more intoxicated with our successes, and I was the happiest of all. Everyone enjoyed fighting the reactionary enemy. I never counted how many battles I engaged in during those years, but sometimes there were three a day. I think I fought in at least two hundred major engagements.

During the Second Campaign, in 1931, I fought against many Kuomintang commanders, including K'ung Ping-fan, Ho Mêng-liu, Hsiang Kuan-yün, Sun Lien-chung, Liu Ho-ting, and Fu Tso-yi. The enemy line was about eight hundred *li* in length and stretched from Kian to Chienling in Fukien. We maneuvered in the enemy's rear and by two weeks of fast marching covered this entire line and broke it. The Red

Army pushed onward in a wide front and swept over the whole area without stopping. My sector captured about ten thousand rifles, and the army also captured radios, automatic rifles, machine guns, ammunition, and many good uniforms.

During the Third Campaign the important cities of the soviet districts were occupied by the enemy. Since we could not maneuver easily in the soviet areas, I was sent eastward to divert the enemy and entice them into following me in order that our main forces could leave the soviet areas and go west to attack the enemy rear. At night I led my troops eastward in several columns, carrying many torches to deceive the enemy into thinking we were a big force. Four divisions of the Kuomintang followed me, including those of Ch'eng Ch'ien and Wei Li-huang. I then surrounded and captured a village called Loan, and the enemy troops arrived near by at Nantuan. I was surrounded by four enemy divisions within a circumference of only ten *li* but, because of the mountains and forest and because we made not a sound, they didn't know exactly where my army was located. I was in greatest danger of complete annihilation, of course, as I had taken only two thousand of my men for this maneuver, the others remaining with the main Red Army. The forces against us were first-class Kuomintang divisions of about nine regiments, or fifteen thousand men, each. The enemy strength was over forty thousand troops.

In the meantime, as planned, the main Red forces left the soviet regions and marched to the rear of the enemy in the opposite direction, where they gained a big victory.

One night my troops slipped through the enemy lines, attacked their rear, and defeated one division, capturing great quantities of arms. After that we made a quick march back to the soviet districts and met the main forces after their big victory. The enemy troops, defeated in their Third Campaign, were already retreating from the soviet districts. I lost only three hundred men in this whole maneuver.

In the spring of 1933 the Fourth Campaign began. I was on our right wing. The Red Army destroyed two enemy divisions, taking one commander prisoner and killing the other. All the equipment we captured was new and modern, just bought from Germany for the campaign. Some of the automatic rifles, however, were not German but American.

Several other divisions were defeated or partially destroyed in the Fourth Campaign. I fought in all these battles, as I was on the main front then. By the end of the campaign, we had captured several tens of thousands of rifles, and for the first time the Red Army began to use machine guns and automatic rifles.

Because they often had foreign pilots, enemy airplanes were more effective during the Fourth Campaign than before. Lin Piao captured one German adviser from a blockhouse. I don't know what happened to him.

My troops are nicknamed the "Biped Cavalry" because we have specialized in swift, secret infantry movements. When the main forces are in a tight spot, I am always sent out to decoy the enemy by a fast maneuver. Liu Po-ch'êng first called us biped cavalry after a maneuver in which we attacked one brigade and captured a city in the morning and retreated that same day to another city one hundred twenty *li* away and captured it, too, the enemy being taken by surprise. They never expected my troops to attack twice in one day. My troops are famous for their ability to capture towns easily. Our method is this: If we want to capture a certain town, we make a false attack on it and then pretend to withdraw. The enemy thinks the danger is over and becomes careless for a few hours. Then we return like lightning and take the place easily by surprise. As a commander, I am always in the front line because I like to be where I can look over the terrain and judge the course of the battle correctly. I am usually no more than one hundred to two hundred meters from the enemy line. My troops are generally placed on the flank or in the rear because they are so fast. They are specially trained to make quick secret movements and to attack the enemy's rear in order to throw it into confusion. They are all selected, strong, healthy men.

In the Fifth Campaign, in 1934, I fought in the Nantuan region again. I fought against more than ten enemy divisions. Then I was ordered to escort the "Anti-Japanese Vanguards" across the Min River into Fukien. When I returned, I was sent to the Eastern Front to fight Li Yen-yen's column of six divisions of Fukien troops. Every day the planes bombed us. They came in squadrons of ten every two hours during battles. Great numbers of Whites were killed or wounded, and also many of our men. Bombing, however, killed few of our troops. Our losses came mostly from the artillery—we had good fortifications but the enemy had very heavy guns and we had none at all, so we could not defend ourselves in that way. The worst kind of shells were those that penetrated several feet into a mountain, exploding later.

At the great battle of Kwanch'ang, both the Red Army and the Kuomintang concentrated their forces. The Kuomintang had over one hundred thousand troops in this valley and the Reds almost the same number. The enemy attacked constantly, like waves over a wheat field. This battle continued two days without any decisive victory. We finally withdrew. At the beginning of the battle I was ordered to make the first attack and afterward was put in command of the right wing.

At the battle of Chienying over twenty planes in squadrons of three bombed my sector of the front alone. I was then covering the left wing. After Chienying, we went to Kaofulao, near Juikin, where P'êng Tê-huai's troops fought positional warfare for seven days. The Kuomintang troops numbered eleven divisions. The Red Army had good defenses which neither the planes nor the artillery could destroy. Our slogan then was, "We live or die in these trenches! Never retreat!" During those seven days the enemy lost seven thousand soldiers on the field of battle. They attacked us again and again, in recurrent waves. The Red soldiers stayed hidden and shot them down as they came forward. The enemy's method was that of "personal attack." The Red Army retreated, as we could not use this method ourselves. After this came the battle of Wen Hua. During this battle I destroyed Li Mei-an's brigade—he was a divisional commander under Chiang Kai-shek.

After this fighting the main Red forces concentrated in Juikin, the capital, preparing for the Long March. I was placed on the outside in order to distract an enemy column which was marching to attack Tingchow. When the enemy arrived near Tingchow, I slipped away and went to Juikin to begin the Long March with the main forces.

Rear Guard on the Long March

When we first left Kiangsi on the Long March, I was commander of the Ninth Army Corps. I was later with the First Army Corps under Lin Piao. I was always on the flank or rear for protection of the marching column. This was very difficult work, and sometimes my troops were left in the rear.

In Hunan we had to capture Yungming and Chianghua *hsien* so that the main Red Army could pass. My troops were left behind at this time and had to hurry to catch up again with the fast march.

The most dangerous position I personally was in during the Long March was at Yenshouhsü in Hunan. The road led into a very narrow pass between two mountains. I was at the rear with four regiments. The rest of the army had passed, but just as my troops came up to the pass, the Kuomintang troops caught up with us, occupied one mountain, and staged a surprise attack, cutting the road. We were in a very bad position but fought like tigers until we recaptured the mountain. Six comrades and I had to fight with our Mausers. We barely escaped capture.

During the Long March, several guard-regiments were cut off in the rear and surrounded by the enemy. Although my troops were almost constantly engaged in this dangerous duty, either in the rear or on the flank, I was always successful in these maneuvers.

After passing through Hunan, we reached Kweichow. I was with the force which blocked Wu Ch'i-wei's column of five enemy divisions when the Red Army captured Chênyüan. At Chênyüan I guarded the front for three days. The enemy had a big attacking force and the fighting was severe. I placed one battalion on two sides of a round mountain. When the enemy advanced on one side, we pretended to retreat and then swiftly attacked from both sides at once and routed them. I then occupied two *hsien*.

Some of our hardest maneuvering of the Long March was done in Kweichow. Once, at Tungtzǔ, I was in the rear. As I came to the city the enemy was already closing in from three sides. I placed two battalions in position and ordered the main forces to retreat. A few minutes after the retreat had succeeded, the enemy came up from the west and attacked the city. I fought, and one of my regiments was cut off but it escaped later. I was nearly captured and ten men in my escort company were lost before the rest of us succeeded in escaping while the enemy was eating dinner. Had it not been for skillful maneuvering at that time, my whole force would have been cut off.

The Red Army's experience in tactics and strategy was utilized to the utmost during the Long March. In Kweichow, particularly, we were in a tight spot and had to do a great deal of maneuvering. Our strategy is always to decoy and confuse the enemy. When we are surrounded on three sides, we make a frontal attack and then leave one small heroic force to hold the position while the main

body of troops retreats quickly and goes around to the enemy rear. Then when the White lines converge they have nothing in the bag except a small force and stand looking foolishly at each other. Of course, this requires the greatest spirit of sacrifice from the small Red force which has to hold the position in the meantime.

At Liupanch'ang, in Kweichow, the main Red forces planned to destroy the enemy there. I was sent with five companies to Feng-shan-pa, seventy *li* from Liupanch'ang, where three enemy divisions were marching as reinforcements. My task was to stop this enemy force. I put a company on each of two mountains, where they were clearly visible to the enemy. These companies I ordered to walk all over the mountains in circles in order to look like a big force and distract the enemy while my other three companies attacked in the rear. We held this position for two days—long enough to save our main forces elsewhere—and the foolish Kuomintang officers sent messages, which we intercepted, saying that they had "bottled up the main Red Army"! The mountain was thickly wooded. As all my men stayed in the open spaces in order to be visible, the reconnoitering airplanes thought we were a force too huge to hide under the trees to avoid their notice.

My most critical experience during the Long March was in crossing the Wu River in Kweichow, and at that time the morale of the troops was bad—just after the Fifth Campaign. At six o'clock one day I received a radiogram stating that at nine in the morning the bridge over the river would be destroyed. I was then one hundred ninety *li* from the Wu-kiang! My troops rushed to the river, but at twelve noon next day, we were still forty *li* distant. Everyone else thought we should try crossing without delay, even without a bridge, but I opposed this because I thought the enemy would concentrate on us immediately. So we retreated without trying to cross, since the Military Council had sent another radiogram saying

I could plan my strategy according to the immediate situation. The bridge had already been destroyed and the main Red forces had already crossed over. I decided that the enemy would come from a certain side where they had a blockade in two lines. I had one regiment of eight companies—fifteen hundred men—of the Ninth Red Army Corps. The Kweichow provincial troops were on two sides, the Szechuan troops on the third, and Chiang Kai-shek's troops on the other. Altogether, the enemy numbered about four or five divisions, or about fifty thousand men. My eight companies were on the bank of a small tributary of the Wu-kiang. We crossed the small river and met the enemy. Then I retreated quickly to the opposite bank again and inflicted a big loss on the enemy troops. We again crossed the river in another place, as I thought that the enemy had also crossed and was following us. The enemy had not crossed, however, and we came upon them again. Quickly, we went around a mountain for protection. One enemy division followed. I ordered my eight companies to break ranks and attack in individual guerrilla units in order to disperse the enemy. One hundred of my men were killed—and many Whites. Since we couldn't continue this desperate fighting, I led my men to another mountain. On the other side of this mountain was another enemy division, but I didn't know of it, and they didn't know we were coming, either. We made a surprise attack and got a hundred rifles. By this time, about eighty thousand enemy troops must have been concentrated near the tributary, thinking they were going to get a big prize. I maneuvered out of this difficult position, but couldn't cross the Wu River, so we went around in a circle, disarming three hundred *min t'uan* whom we met on the way. Then I set out to cross the river. Before we could make the crossing, four enemy regiments caught up with us—two from Tating and two from Pichieh. We fought one whole day, and three hundred more of my men were killed or wounded,

but the enemy lost eight hundred. Finally the remainder of my troops succeeded in crossing the river. There was no bridge, of course, but the peasants helped us to bind boards together and put them across the stones. The river was shallow, but most of the Red Army men cannot swim, as they are from inland regions.

During all this time, my regiment was like a rat trying to cross a river, scampering here and there and stealing around to have a look at the situation.

The enemy was chasing the main Red forces ahead of us, so after crossing the river we came upon the rear of the Kuomintang pursuers. They were terrified and thought they had been outmaneuvered. The enemy officers made a big campaign to capture me, and offered one hundred thousand dollars for me alive and eighty thousand dollars dead. Nevertheless, I followed along behind the enemy, which was pursuing the main Red forces.

When I began this maneuver at the Wu-kiang, I had only fifteen hundred men. Soon, however, my regiment had increased to over three thousand men from volunteers along the way—in spite of my heavy losses in fighting. These were local people. No White soldiers joined the Red Army on the Long March—the life was too hard and the situation too critical for them to stomach.

During those days at the Wu-kiang I used to make speeches to my men, telling them, "We are like a monkey playing with a cow in a narrow alley. The big stupid enemy can't move fast, and we make him look silly with our clever tricks. We are fighting a glorious war for liberty, and we cannot be stopped by a stupid cow in the path."

Morale was good during the rest of the Long March. The main Red column sang all the time. My men, however, were too busy and tired for singing, being constantly on maneuver. My political commissar at that time was Ho Ch'ang-kung, a returned student from France. His body was weak and one of his legs was crippled—but he never faltered under any of our most trying circumstances.

Nearly every day during the Long March I fought in either one or two battles, and we moved constantly—sometimes all night long. I was always sleepy and often fell asleep over my food. I rode a mule in order to get rest, sometimes, but lost the animal on the way.

Chiang Kai-shek tried every possible measure to block off and annihilate the Red Army during the Long March. It is simply nonsense to say, as you say some foreign journalists do, that he tried to divert us into certain provinces. It is true that we weakened the provincial forces and that he could get control of the provinces by following in our rear and reaping the benefits, but he was terrified of our reaching the Northwest because of the possible anti-Japanese political consequences once we arrived.

Our troops rested for a while and then passed on to Yünnan, my home province. I was sent to attack Hsishui, marched fast for two hundred seventy *li*, and arrived there within two days. The enemy arrived the next morning, but I was in the strategic positions and was able to defeat them. Then we returned to join our main forces.

After the battle of T'uch'eng, which was not very successful, I escorted the First and Third Army Corps and the Military Council across the Ch'ihshui River. I put one regiment in the first line and was myself in the second line. The officer in command of the first line made a mistake. He was told to stand guard until twelve o'clock but retreated too soon. I had to put up a terrific fight in order to save the main forces from losses.

When we arrived near Tung-chuan-fu, Yünnan, in April, I was sent out as vanguard to capture the city. As soon as we had the city under siege, I received a letter from the *hsien* magistrate and the local *min t'uan* commander. This commander had been my old friend in Yünnan long before. As soon as he learned that the troops surrounding

his city were mine, he decided to renew the acquaintance. I sent a reply to their letter, asking the *hsien* magistrate to come out and negotiate with me. He agreed to this and the result of our negotiations was that the Red Army was permitted to enter the city. Our first act was to confiscate the magistrate's official seal and use it to write a letter to the boat owners at the River of Golden Sand telling them to concentrate all boats at a certain place so that they could be guarded against the Reds, who might want to use them to cross.

The boat owners concentrated a hundred big boats as directed. In the meantime we had another trick prepared: I disguised my men in *min t'uan* uniforms and took them down to the river, pretending to be guarding against the Reds. My men got into the boats and crossed the river without any difficulties at all. Next we occupied the opposite side with four companies in order to guard it for the main Red column, and waited for them. Our comrades, however, did not know about my trick of changing uniforms, and when their scouts reported that "four companies of enemy troops are on the Szechuan side," they began crossing the river at another place. Finally, however, they discovered the correct situation and part of the troops arrived. My men guarded all of these troops across. When this was finished, we paid five thousand dollars to the boat owners and destroyed all the boats on the river, so that when the enemy Kuomintang troops arrived they had no way of crossing at all.

At Lukou, on the other side of the river, I was again given the duty of protecting the rear, and several enemy divisions caught up with me. I wanted to make a secret attack and destroy one route before the other enemy column was aware of it, but the enemy attacked first. Six of my companies immediately counterattacked these two divisions and inflicted heavy losses on them.

Then we entered the region of the Lolo tribesmen. Five or six thousand Lolos were concentrated, intending to fight, and had already captured about six or seven hundred rifles from the Red Army. However, when they saw my column battling so successfully with the Kuomintang troops near by, they dared not attack, even though we were a small force. The vanguard and the rear of my column were very compact as we passed the Lolos. Thus we had no fighting and no losses. The Lolos hated the Central government troops. After making an arrangement with the Lolos, we gave them rifles and they protected us on the march. They captured many rifles from the White troops—just as they had from us—and fought the Whites along the way. The Miao and Mantzu also attacked the White outposts.

At the time of crossing the Tatu River, Comrade Ho Ch'ang-kung had charge of guarding the rear. I was very sick with dysentery and had to be carried on a stretcher. Then, because it took too many valuable men to carry me, I tried riding a mule. There were six regiments on one side of the river and twenty regiments on the other. The enemy attacked on both sides, and our forces were in a very difficult position, one part being isolated in the mountains without food or water. I received a radiogram from Chu Tê and Chou Ên-lai telling me to divert the enemy by capturing T'iench'üan city at any sacrifice, in order to save the main column. I called my men together and told them what was expected of us. We crossed the river farther down and attacked the city as ordered. Although the enemy had three regiments of Yang Shên's troops in the city, we made a surprise attack in the rear and captured it, losing only a few tens of our number. As soon as we occupied the city, I fell unconscious for two hours. This dysentery,

however, was my only illness during the Long March.

When the main Red Army left Szechuan on the march to the Northwest, my troops were five or six days behind them. I was also four or five days' march distant from the Fourth Front Red Army. I was surrounded by the Mantzu tribesmen and had severe fighting with them. We defeated the Mantzu by climbing a mountain and going around to their rear. Being so far behind by that time, I joined the Fourth Front Army under Hsü Hsiang-ch'ien as his rear guard. Together with Chu Tê and Hsü Hsiang-ch'ien, I spent a year in this region, from October 1935 to August 1936.[1] We lived about six months in Sikang. In the meantime I was sent to escort Ho Lung's Second Front Red Army on its arrival in Szechuan, and later traveled with Ho Lung through the Great Grasslands into southern Kansu. In the Grasslands we were constantly attacked by the Mantzu cavalry. They can shoot on horseback and are crack marksmen. The Mantzu are very high-spirited and hard to fight. They fight better than the Kuomintang troops because they are expert at ambush and mountain warfare, and their morale is invincible. I had severe fighting with Wang Chün's troops in Ch'enghsien and later had difficult engagements with the cavalry troops in that region also.

Before the Sian Incident in December [1936], I was stationed at Huan-hsien and fought General Hu Tsung-nan. Afterward I went to the town of Yu Wang Pao. During the Sian Incident, my troops chased Hu Tsung-nan, and afterward my army—the Thirty-second Red Army—together with two other armies, formed the first column of the Western Expedition originally planned to go westward.

Hsiao K'ê

YOUNGEST GENERAL

Impulsive, smiling, and rhetorical: General Hsiao K'ê pauses in a Yenan street, 1937.

MISS WALES:

IN 1932, when he was only twenty-three years old, Hsiao K'ê was given command of the noted Sixth Red Army, and became the youngest of the top commanders of the Chinese Communist army. His name soon became very well known in China. After he had joined his forces with those of Ho Lung in the Hunan-Hupeh soviet area, these two men at the head of their flying columns made history move fast.

In this perpetually mobile army, Hsiao K'ê was without doubt the most mobile single unit. During my interview with him, he was constantly making short maneuvers, sliding along benches, striding about the room, pounding the table, and, on any provocation, bursting forth with lyrical slogans. He had had thirteen wounds, however, and was entitled to a certain amount of nervousness. He was a prime example of rebellion against the old, slow-mannered Confucianism.

In 1937 Hsiao K'ê was appointed to the command of the Thirty-first Red Army to aid in its reorganization. Early in the war with Japan

he was made vice-commander of Ho Lung's 120th Division in the Shansi-Suiyuan area, but later became deputy commander to Nieh Jung-chên, chief of the "Shansi-Hopei-Chahar Liberated Area." In 1949 his name did not appear on the Military Council.

I found this boy prodigy refreshing to talk with because he was bristling with exact facts and figures—unlike most Chinese, who take very little interest in mathematical details. Hsiao K'ê was in himself a complete revolution against the old Chinese humility of manner. He knew his worth and was not shy of appraising it. It was characteristic of him that he had kept a diary of all the one hundred seventy battles he had engaged in, and when I asked how many times he had been wounded, he wrote down the exact dates on a slip of paper. He did everything to a finish and never stopped at the Confucian halfway point. Like Chou Ên-lai, Hsü Hsiang-ch'ien, and Mao Tsê-tung, Hsiao K'ê is a revival of what the Chinese call the "military scholar."

131

HSIAO K'Ê:

MY father was a *hsiu-ts'ai* Confucian scholar, ranking in the lowest official class of the Ch'ing dynasty. Before 1921 he lived the life of the disintegrating *hsien* [county] gentry of China. In that year he became bankrupt. There were eight or nine persons in my home—including my two elder brothers, whose careers ran no more smoothly than my own. The eldest was executed in April 1923 after being accused of having relations with bandits. The other, Hsiao K'ê-yung, with whom I was on friendly terms, entered the Communist party in 1925 and later joined the Red Army and was killed in battle.

Our home was in Chiaho *hsien*, Hunan, in the village of Hsiao-k'ê-tien, named after my family. I was born there in August 1909. My full name is Hsiao K'ê-chün, but like most Communists I dropped the unnecessary ending.

At the age of six I went to a tutorial school and studied all the old books of Confucius and Mencius—the Four Books and the Five Classics, which I hated. After five years I went to higher primary school for three years. I then spent two and a half years in lower normal school, training to become a primary school teacher—the usual career open to sons of bankrupt scholars.

I stopped my school work when I was about seventeen, and in 1926 went to Canton to join the army. I enlisted with Chiang Kai-shek's Gendarmes as a common soldier. At that time I thought he was a revolutionary leader and he made a good impression on me. My faith in him did not entirely collapse until after he began the counterrevolution in 1927. I considered him a good follower of Sun Yat-sen and a leftist—and I had a deep respect for the *San Min Chu I*.

I wanted to go to Canton because it was the center of the revolution. While I was a student in normal school, a cousin in Canton University had mailed revolutionary books to me, including those written by Sun Yat-sen. (Incidentally, a few days ago I received a letter from this cousin asking if I was actually the K'ê-chün to whom he used to send books. I replied that I was. I recognized the handwriting as soon as I saw the envelope.) I was immediately interested in these books, especially in Sun Yat-sen's *Hsin Li Chien Shê* ["Psychological Construction"] and his *Life of a Refugee in London*. Even before this, however — in 1921—I had already been influenced toward revolution by reading the *History of Sung Chao-jen*, the famous Kuomintang leader who was assassinated by the reactionaries. Another book which influenced me was the *History of the Seventy-two Martyrs of Yellow Flower Hill* (in Canton). When I read this book I cried copiously.

My native village and family were conservative and feudal-minded. I read these books and advanced in thought by my own initiative.

I was also interested in military science, and while in normal school in 1924 I devoured the old Chinese military books such as the *Military Tactics of Sun and Wu* and *Military Tactics of the Seven Military Scholars*. I also read Tsêng Kuo-fan's *Record of the Military Training of Tsêng Kuo-fan and Hu Yün-yi*. I was very much influenced by Tsêng Kuo-fan and Hu. Even today I can read this book over, word by word, and I almost know it by heart. I remember, too, being very much interested in the record of the Battle of Verdun in the World War.

Most people think I was a Whampoa cadet in Canton. This is a mistake. However, during my four months with the Gendarmes there, I picked up a Whampoa education of my own. Although I was very young, I never forgot anything I heard. It was easy for me to absorb all the knowledge of the Whampoa officers, so that I became as well educated as they were—by keeping my ears open.

In Canton I was in Chiang Kai-shek's 65th

Supplementary Regiment of Gendarmes. At first I was a noncommissioned officer, in charge of the arsenal; then the officers noticed that I knew military affairs and made me a subordinate in order to prepare me for promotion to platoon commander. After a few months I left the Gendarmes, however, and in 1927 I joined the famous 24th Division under Yeh T'ing, the Communist. This was the best division of Chang Fa-k'uei's Fourth Army, the "Ironsides." I was a company political director.

Although I was only a political director, during the Northern Expedition I always led the soldiers at the front along with the officers. The battalion commander recognized my ability, and when the captain happened to be absent at the battle of Junan *hsien* in Honan, I was given command of the company. I played such a noticeable role during this battle that I was made acting commander for a while.

On our return to Wuhan I was still nominally only political director, but during the Nanchang Uprising on August 1, 1927, I became captain of my company in my own right.

Rebel Against the Confucian Family

I did not join the Communist party until June 1927, after the split with the Kuomintang began. As early as February a friend had talked with me and declared that Chiang Kai-shek was betraying the revolution and opposing the peasants' and workers' movement. This made me angry, and my suspicions began. Then at the end of February, I returned to Wuhan to see what was happening, and there I received a letter from my Communist brother saying that Chiang Kai-shek had betrayed and was plotting a dictatorship. I thought that if this were true we must overthrow Chiang Kai-shek or the Kuomintang revolution would fail. Then, when the whole Kuomintang itself turned reactionary, I realized that the Communists had the only solution to the problem of accomplishing the tasks of the revolution and that only

the soldiers and peasants and workers would carry on. I led my company during the Nanchang Uprising. The soldiers of Yeh T'ing's division joined the uprising to a man because the Communist organization ran from the top to the bottom. There was not one desertion.

It was natural enough for me to change from the Kuomintang to the Communist party. Although my family were gentry, they were steadily becoming declassed and bankrupt, until my father owned only six *mu* of land. When I went to school, the problem of paying the tutorial fee was a big one for my family; my clothes were ragged and poor; and the teacher often beat me, having no respect for my bankrupt family. As soon as I read of Sun Yat-sen's "Three People's Principles" I agreed with them with all my heart, especially the principle of uniting with the peasants and workers and with the Communist party and the Soviet Union. So deep was my belief in this last principle that when the bourgeoisie betrayed it, I hated the counterrevolutionaries very much and felt that the salvation of the nation depended on the overthrow of Chiang Kai-shek's dictatorship.

I cannot be considered an intellectual, but only an educated peasant. When I was a child of five to seven, I was a cowherd, and at tutorial school I worked after hours, taking care of the farm. I know how to cultivate land and crops, and I always had a deep sympathy for the peasants. In the beginning I had only a peasant consciousness. I knew nothing about the city proletariat until I saw the real Chinese working class in action in Wuhan during the Great Revolution. I had lived in a small feudal town where there were only a few workers such as carpenters and bricklayers.

From 1925 to 1927 the revolution had two primary meanings for me: the overthrow of imperialism—including not only England but all the foreign powers—in order to achieve the independence and equality of the Chinese nation; and the overthrow of the feudal gentry and landlords, including the feudal militarists.

Four or five years before the revolution, I had read about the Unequal Treaties, the Sino-Japanese War, the Boxer Rebellion, and the like. At that time I was not only a nationalist but also an imperialist—I had the narrow, egotistical hope that China would overthrow the foreign nations, including Japan, and conquer them in turn. Gradually my idea changed to wanting only the independence and liberty of China. I think that my main drive toward revolution was anti-imperialism, or nationalism.

I also hated the landlords, however. I remember that when I was fourteen or fifteen my father sent me to pay the grain-rent to the landlord. My family were gentry and could not labor with their own hands. They had to hire coolies and rent land for tilling from the landlord. It was a dry year, and my father told me to ask the landlord to decrease the payment from fourteen hundred to twelve hundred *chin*. I bargained for a long time. In the end the landlord promised to decrease the rent only twenty *chin*, and I was very angry. Then, however, I hated only that one landlord—not landlordism as a system.

Then, too, I hated the big yamen officials and the usurers. When my eldest brother was put into prison, the family borrowed five or six hundred dollars to try to secure his release, and this debt was a constant burden. The family could never pay it back. Once, when I was fourteen, I was arrested by mistake when the soldiers were fighting bandits in our neighborhood and the family had to borrow one hundred dollars from a yamen official to get my release. They could not pay this money back, and my father had to send my second brother to teach in the family of that official for a year in order to recompense him.

My eldest brother was a small merchant and had friends and customers among the bandits. He was arrested several times, and before his arrests soldiers would come to the house threatening to arrest and execute him for having relations with the bandits unless the family paid money to them. The five- or six-hundred-dollar debt was accumulated during these times. The last time my brother was arrested he was executed because we could borrow no more money to save him. I was then fifteen and he was twenty-seven.

This blackmail and the execution of my brother were caused mainly by the betrayal of a landlord of my own clan, whom I bitterly hated. It was only after I became a Communist that I learned not to be personal in my revenge and hatred, but to see the general social problems of a corrupt semifeudal society as a whole and understand that the degeneration of my own family and clan was only a part of this phenomenon.

One of the main reasons for my revolutionary tendency was my resentment against the old Chinese family system, which I experienced in its most disintegrating phase. As a child I received a bad impression of family life and I was glad to escape from it. Since I left it, I have never written a letter to my home. I suppose my parents are dead now—they were old then and would now be over seventy. When I went away, my mother thought the family could not find means to exist five years more. The house itself, she said, was in such poor repair that it must collapse within ten years.

Even as I talk I feel bitter toward my feudal family. But I loved very much my young sister and my brother who became a Communist. I never saw this brother again after the failure of the South Hunan Revolt in April 1928. He wandered around for a while after that, doing secret Party work. He was arrested in Changteh, Hunan, but escaped and joined the 85th Kuomintang Division to do further secret Party work. He was discovered and again barely escaped with his life. Then he joined the Red Army in Tahuang *hsien*, Hupeh. He first taught military training, later became chief of staff in the 3rd Independent Division, and finally was killed in battle at the beginning of 1933.

I also had two elder sisters. The husband of one was betrayed by a corrupt relative and was executed for "having relations with bandits," just as my eldest brother had been. The husband of the other sister was killed in 1927 as a member of a peasant union.

I hate intensely the feudal concept of the family. My father was very authoritarian and dominated his family. It was under an absolute dictatorship, and so was I. I obeyed my father without hesitation on every point. He ordered me not to gamble, smoke, or play chess, and I did not. At the same time, however, he tried to destroy my spirit with a conservative education. I was not a rebellious child at home, but when I was released from the family yoke for a little while, I was always carefree and daring. I remember, too, how I loved the village theater where there was noise and freedom. What a relief it was from the stern teachings of my father and his dull rules from Confucius and Mencius!

It was natural that I should want to run away from home. When I was in normal school, just before examinations I borrowed seven dollars in local currency from an old teacher, a Sun Yat-sen sympathizer, and deserted the school without letting my family know. I put on seven layers of clothing—all I had in the world—and set out. Before I left, I wrote a letter to my family and gave it to an illiterate girl-cousin to deliver after I had left. By the time they got it, I was already in Kwangtung.

I walked in the snow all the way to Shaokuan on the Kwangtung border. My only possessions were in a carryall made of my favorite sister's jacket. At the time I planned to run away, I had gone to my home and asked the family for all my clothes, saying that I needed them for a vacation trip planned by the school. My sister insisted on giving me her best jacket to wear at this festivity!

My idea then was to find adventure and to join the revolution to overthrow the imperialists and feudal militarists. I had dis-cussed this trip with my schoolmates, but of all forty-eight not one agreed with my purpose and wanted to join me. Of the four teachers in the school, only one did not ridicule me. This teacher asked what guaranty I had of success in my venture. When I replied that I had only my unconquerable ambition, but that I knew it would never fail, he smiled sympathetically and said no more. I have always had complete faith in myself and in my abilities, and unfaltering determination. This confidence developed twelve or thirteen years ago, and since then I have never been afraid. Once I believe in a thing or make a decision, I carry it out without wavering.

(You know, though I have an excellent memory, I have never even thought about these incidents since they happened years ago. For ten years I have had no time to think of "my past," as the intellectuals and petty bourgeoisie do, taking themselves so seriously.)

I remember now that on the first day of my adventure I walked eighty-five *li* and spent the night in the house of a landlord named Hsiao, who was a friend of my grandfather. The people there suspected me of running away and detained me, but because of the heavy snow they could not send any message to my family. After five days they finally permitted me to go free, convinced that my story of a cousin in Canton who had a job for me was valid. During those five days I was guarded by the two sons of the landlord, and I became very thin because I was so worried that I might fail in my plans.

After my release, I walked five days until I reached Shaokuan. Half of my seven borrowed dollars was gone by then. The railway fare to Canton was six dollars. I wandered about the town wondering how I could possibly gather this sum together. On the street I met a military officer and could tell from his dialect that his home was not far from my native place. I approached this stranger with my problem and he gave me food and a place to sleep and took me to Canton with him. In Canton I met the cousin who used to send books to me. After that, all was easy. This cousin was a graduate of Canton University. My favorite brother was also there, finishing his last semester in the Kwangtung Military School.

I was interested in military more than political matters and wanted to go to Whampoa Academy, but I was two months too late for the 1926 term and couldn't enter the Academy.

With Yeh T'ing in the Nanchang Uprising

The Nanchang Uprising of the Kuomintang troops in 1927 was the result of the Kuomintang reaction against its own revolution and a part of the course of Chinese revolutionary history. It followed logically after the 1911 Revolution, the May Fourth Movement, the Hongkong strike, and the Wuhan government of Wang Ching-wei, continuing the long revolutionary struggle. It was a warning to the Kuomintang for its betrayal of the revolution.

Along with Yeh T'ing's 24th Division, of which my company was a unit, the troops that participated in the Nanchang Uprising were: two divisions under Ho Lung and two regiments under Chou Shih-li (now chief of staff of the Second Front Red Army) from the "Ironsides" army, and one training regiment under Chu Tê.

After the failure of the Nanchang Uprising, we went to Kwangtung Province to establish a new revolutionary base. When this expedition to Kwangtung failed also, I was left in Kwangtung without money or a friend. I wandered around from Canton to Shaokuan and Swatow, living a very bitter life. Then I joined the new Thirteenth Army of Chiang Kai-shek for a while.

You ask if I was not depressed after the failures at Nanchang and Kwangtung. No, I had the iron will to fight, and I took leadership in partisan warfare afterward. In Nanchang only a few of my company were lost, but during the retreat at T'ank'eng in

Kwangtung, thirty-five men were killed. We had marched for forty-seven days from Nanchang to Chaochow in Kwangtung, fighting all the way. After our defeat at T'ank'eng we went to the Hailufeng district, and the army was dispersed, so I fled. I joined the Kuomintang army after that only in order to eat, being in terrible poverty. I was secretary to a lower officer who had no idea of my identity. Yeh T'ing left the Red Army at this time. I don't have any idea where he is now.

After one month in the White army, I returned to my native village. I was now a soldier and my father dared not bully me. When I had been at home two weeks, I heard with delight a report that Chu Tê's troops had come to south Hunan. Knowing that Chu Tê had been a leader in the Nanchang Uprising, I left my family—on December 29 of the lunar calendar, one day before the New Year—and went to the house of that same landlord who had detained me for five days when I was a boy. I wanted to get information about the new Red Army. I dared not ask directly. Pretending to be worried about having left my baggage somewhere, I asked the landlord if he thought it was "safe from bandits." He said no, emphatically, and I knew the report was true.

I returned to my home, and my mother was so happy to have me there as good luck for the New Year after my long absence that she cried. I left the next morning, however, taking two friends with me. We went to find the uprising and after three days arrived at Ichang *hsien*. Though I didn't meet Chu Tê there, I saw the peasants carrying on the insurrection in the villages.

Chu Tê's South Hunan Revolt

At the village of Ishih, I got into contact with a partisan group of three hundred peasants. They had only twenty rifles, but I taught them how to establish guards and sentries, and gave them military training, and thus became commander of this partisan detachment. Our force was small, but we fought many minor battles victoriously. My detachment became well known in Ichang *hsien*. This was a· local partisan uprising under orders of the local Communist party committee. The man in high command was Hu Hsiao-hai, who was killed in 1932.

In April the South Hunan Revolt failed and Chu Tê's main force left this region. The small partisan groups were cut off. Mine had only sixteen or seventeen rifles then. Most of the men were armed with spears, swords, and other old-style weapons. Later the partisans climbed the high mountain at Lungchüntung near Kweitung and joined with Mao Tsê-tung's troops. At that time I put my partisans under Mao and went to Chingkangshan. In the whole partisan group that left Ichang *hsien* there were four hundred men, and my own detachment numbered one hundred. Even so, it was the main group, and all these joined with Mao.

The tactics of partisan warfare in China grew out of the uprisings of the peasants against their local enemies. The peasants are enthusiastic and brave. Though they know no formal strategy, they learn by experience and create effective partisan tactics. They do not use the old books. Since they participate in a spontaneous mass struggle, their tactics have no special rules. Many old Chinese books on military tactics contain principles that can be ·applied in partisan warfare, but not as dogma. The organization and summary of the modern partisan tactics of the Red Army were done by Chu Tê and Mao Tsê-tung after Chingkangshan. Before that we had no organized system. Of course, like myself, many have read the old books and remember them.

I don't know much about the antipartisan tactics of Chiang Kai-shek, but in his book on tactics of bandit suppression he included many old quotations from Tsêng Kuo-fan, Sun, and other old authors. He quoted many useless points in this book, incidentally.

You ask me to explain the secret of the success of my partisan tactics. I am not prepared to answer this adequately, but offhand I would say that the answer is this: First of all, success is due to the fact that the partisan groups come from peasant uprisings; the fighters consequently are of good quality and naturally better disciplined than nonrevolutionary men. Second, partisans are unusually brave and determined. For instance, in one battle at Ichang over a thousand *min t'uan* surrounded one of the fortifications held by my partisan group; with only thirty rifles we went to the rear of the enemy early in the morning while they were cooking and surprised them; they were defeated in a single attack and retreated five *li* before we withdrew our small number from the chase. Third, partisans are willing and able to move secretly and quickly and without the knowledge of the enemy—the enemy may think we are a hundred *li* away when they are surprised by our thunder-attack. Fourth, the intelligence work of the partisan fighters is very good. We get news quickly and in minute detail from the masses, because they support our revolutionary movement; they tell us everything without lying. A Chinese proverb says, "If you want to destroy the enemy, you must first know all about him." Fifth, the White troops are easily defeated because they have no morale.

In the beginning the *min t'uan* and the Kuomintang armies had had no experience and it was a simple matter to defeat them. Afterward, they were much more clever and were harder to annihilate. The regular armies like positional warfare and are defeated fairly easily; the *min t'uan* use partisan tactics similar to ours and are hard to destroy.

The regular soldiers join the Red Army more readily than do the *min t'uan*. This is partly because the *min t'uan* are commanded by the landlords and their sons, and carry on the class struggle very cruelly and determinedly. They think they are fighting for their homes and property against the "Red invaders."

From Chingkangshan to Kiangsi

Chu, Mao, and others concentrated on Chingkangshan and formed a political organization on the Hunan-Kiangsi border at the mountain Lohsiaoshan, which included Chingkangshan. Because it had a large Red Army force and a large territory, and because it carried out the land policy first, this political organization became the most energetic and important of any in the Communist regions. It was a model for all the revolutionary forces in China. The enemy in Kiangsi and Hunan tried several times to suppress us but were defeated. We carried out four attacks against Yunghsing *hsien* and occupied it with success. I participated in all these battles. I was made a company commander of the Fourth Red Army at Chingkangshan.

During the autumn and winter Chu Tê fought in Suich'uan in Kiangsi with the main forces, leaving only four companies on Chingkangshan to guard it. I was with this rear guard. All day we constructed fortifications or carried rice and other supplies to the mountain. I myself climbed the mountain twice every day with thirty *chin* of rice. It was a big problem to transfer food; as there was much bamboo in the mountains, we ate small bamboo shoots so as not to have to transport too much food. I was the Communist party delegate for my regiment at that time.

In December 1928, Chu, Mao, and P'êng Tê-huai had a meeting at Chingkangshan and decided to leave P'êng to protect the rear while the other two went out to enlarge the soviets. On January 14, 1929, I left Chingkangshan with Chu and Mao, being then a regimental commander.

We marched twenty-five hundred *li* from Chingkangshan to Tungku near Kian in Kiangsi, where we met the 2nd and 4th regiments of the Red Army and took a rest for one week. We left the 2nd Regiment behind

and marched toward Tingchow in Fukien—through Paitsa, Hungt'ien, and Kuangch'ang. We captured and killed the commander of a White brigade and then occupied Tingchow.

From 1929 to the autumn of 1930 we fought all through Kiangsi, Fukien, and Kwangtung in order to organize new soviet districts and expand the Red Army. It was mostly partisan warfare. In the autumn of 1930 P'êng fought at Changsha and occupied Kian, thus establishing a victorious record for himself, though always under command of Chu and Mao.

From the end of 1930 to 1931, Chiang Kai-shek carried out three campaigns against the Red districts. During this time I was a division commander and fought with the army. However, in the Third Campaign I became sick, though I still stayed with the army—in active command, on horseback. I had a bad case of malaria and could get no sleep.

Commander of the Sixth Army

In September 1932, I was made commander of the Sixth Army (which was the Eighth Army before, originally at Chingkangshan). I left Mao and Chu at that time, and did not see Mao Tsê-tung again until two weeks ago here in Yenan. Actually, I did not see Mao nor Chu personally after parting from them on June 2, 1931, but we stayed in the same district. I never saw Chu again until we met in Sikang in the Mantzu district in 1936, five years later.

During 1933 I fought for one year against five divisions of the Hunan provincial army and also against some troops of Chiang Kai-shek. I had many victories, and defeated such Kuomintang commanders as Ch'ên Kuan-chên, Ho P'êng-fei, P'êng Wei-yin, and Wan Mo-tê—all division commanders. On January 26, 1934, I marched from the Hunan-Kiangsi district northward across the Yüanshui and Chinshui rivers and occupied the city of Shêngmi, defeating Chu Yao-hua, a Kuomintang division commander, and also a brigade of Yao Sun, another division commander. Then I went north across the Hsiu-shui River, one day's march from Liushan, the famous mountain in Szechuan. I crossed the border of Hupeh, entered the T'ungshan and T'ungch'eng districts of Hupeh, and then went southward again. On March 22 I reached the old soviet districts in Hunan and Kiangsi. Chiang Kai-shek and Ho Ch'ien sent forty-six regiments against us. As we had only six regiments, we had to retreat after many battles.

And now I will tell you an interesting thing:

In April I fought against Ho Ch'ien and defeated his eight regiments with only three regiments, capturing a battalion commander, a division commander, and the chief of staff. At that time my men were very tired and thin from long marching. One regiment had nine machine guns but only forty bullets. Another had six machine guns but only ninety rounds. Though it was a hard fight, these regiments of the Sixth Army alone defeated eight regiments of the enemy, because this was the peak of the revolutionary spirit. I was the only commander there, but others, of course, were as important to the victory as I was.

We continued to fight from April to June and had three battles. These were not such victories as the one above, but still they were great victories.

With Ho Lung in Hunan-Hupeh

On August 7, 1934, Chu and Mao sent me an order to join Ho Lung and march from the Hunan-Kiangsi border across the Hsiang River and part of Kwangsi. Again we went through southwest Hunan to reach the eastern part of Kweichow. At Nanyaochieh, a small village in Yanghohsien, I met Ho Lung. This was about October 22. It was the first time I had seen Ho Lung since the Nanchang Uprising in 1927—though he had not known me at that time. For one year we lived together in this Kweichow village,

and two years ago we married two sisters in Hunan.

Together with Ho Lung and his Second Front Army, I led my Sixth Army to the invasion of Yungshun in western Hunan. Our armies together defeated ten regiments of the enemy and then occupied Tayung, Sangchih, T'aoyüan, and T'üli, establishing the "Hunan-Hupeh-Szechuan-Kweichow Soviet District." We had about a million people in this soviet. Other leaders of our soviet were Jên Pi-shih, Kuan Shang-yin, and Wang Chêng.

Then ninety regiments, under the command of Ho Chêng-chün, were sent against us by Chiang Kai-shek and Ho Ch'ien. We fought for half a year, and at the end of August 1935, defeated Chiang's campaign. This was the most important fighting done by the Red Armies during 1935, Chu and Mao being on the Long March and comparatively out of warfare. We kept in touch with them through radio connections all the time, however.

At that time we killed the commander of the 85th Division and also about ten regimental and battalion commanders. We also captured a Kuomintang division commander named Ch'ên Ching-han, who had been teaching at the Red Academy. He was released only day before yesterday, May 10, and wanted to return to the White [Kuomintang] districts, so we let him go. Ch'ên invited us to a dinner party two days ago, and we gave him one the next night. (Now, because of the United Front against the Japanese, we don't care for revenge and hatred against the Kuomintang.)

In September 1935, we made a drive against the Kuomintang on the east and occupied Lichou, Linli, Shihmen, and Chinshih, expanding our army by about eight thousand new recruits.

The Long March of the Second Front Army

Then we began the Long March ourselves. We set out from Sangchih on November 19, 1935, and for four days fought steadily, breaking our way across two lines of the blockade of the Hunan provincial troops. We crossed the two rivers, Lishui and Yüanshui, and marched· the amazing distance of 350 *li* in those four days, fighting every step of the way. We occupied Hsinhua, Sup'u, Hsinch'i, P'ushih, and Lant'ien. These were all rich, fertile districts—but unfortunately we had no time to confiscate the landlords on the way.

Then we marched toward Kweiyang, capital of Kweichow, and passed within thirty *li* of the place, occupying the districts of Tating and Pichieh in western Kweichow. This took us three weeks. We defeated many of the enemy troops, including two full divisions. We retreated across southern Szechuan and reached eastern Yünnan, passing only thirty *li* from Yünnanfu, the Yünnan capital, as at Kweiyang. We were on our way to join the Fourth Front Red Army of Hsü Hsiang-ch'ien in Szechuan.

We marched forward to the western part of Yünnan and occupied many districts there, including Malung, Hsüntien, Fumin, Yanghsin, Ch'uhsiung, Yaoan, Mouting, Hsiangyün, Yenhsing, Pinch'uan, Hoch'ing, Lichiang, and others which I cannot remember offhand.

On April 28, 1936, we crossed the River of Golden Sand—the upper Yangtze—and reached Sikang on June 23, joining successfully with the Fourth Front Red Army of Hsü Hsiang-ch'ien and Chang Kuo-t'ao and with Chu Tê.

During those eight months from November 19, 1935, when we left Hunan, to June 23, 1936, we covered ten thousand *li* on our Long March. In those months the numbers of the enemy who chased us in the rear or attacked in the front and on the flank were, altogether, one hundred thirty regiments (one hundred thirty thousand men). We had only twenty thousand men in our armies. But the Kuomintang could not blockade us. We defeated the enemy and left them behind everywhere.

Why were we victorious? [At this point, Hsiao K'ê pounded the table and shouted emphatically:] Because of the correct political line of the Communist Party of China! Because of the bravery of the Red Army! Because of the co-operation of the rank and file and the officers! Because we were supported by the masses!

We stayed in Sikang only two weeks. On July 14, Bastille Day, we marched north under command of Chu Tê to prepare to fight the Japanese. For forty days and nights we crossed the Great Grasslands. In August we reached Hutap'u and Minchow in Kansu. We stayed in south Kansu two months; then we marched north again under command of P'êng Tê-huai, fighting against Chiang Kai-shek's main army under Kuan Lin-chên and Hu Tsung-nan. At Sanch'engp'u we had a great victory and stopped the enemy, capturing one of Hu Tsung-nan's divisions on November 21. Then the Sian revolt occurred on December 12, and the civil war was over.

Because of the peace policy of the Communist party, we made a peace at Sian and now have a peaceful, united China as the first step in the preparation for the war against Japan. This insures that China will not perish. We have five thousand years of history. We have an excellent race. We cannot be under the yoke of Japan. We must expand our glorious history and develop our culture. So I shout:

Long live the Republic of China! Long live the freedom of China!

PART FOUR

Military Academy Graduates

Chêng Tzŭ-hua

LEADER OF THE TAYEH UPRISING

MISS WALES:

CHÊNG TZŬ-HUA and General Hsü Hai-tung came to call on me together in Yenan. As the political director of Hsü's Fifteenth Army Corps, Chêng held a position in the corps second only to that of Hsü himself. Chêng himself had formerly been a division and army commander, and had been regarded as one of the most promising young military figures. This prospect changed when he received severe wounds in both hands so that he could hardly use either of them. He appeared to be well educated, noticeably so by contrast with Hsü Hai-tung.

Most of the Communists who had been to school at all seemed to have been leaders of the student body. Chêng Tzŭ-hua was one of these, stirring up a good deal of trouble for Yen Hsi-shan in the normal school at Taiyuanfu before he joined the army in 1926. He then became one of those famous cadets of the 1925–27 period at the Wuhan branch of Whampoa Academy. These cadets became a training regiment in Chang Fa-k'uei's "Ironsides" Fourth Army, the best of all the Kuomintang armies. This regiment was disarmed and rearmed again and again, but finally staged the Canton Commune in 1927. Nearly all its members were ultimately killed in Hailufeng. Such cadets of Whampoa and its Wuhan branch were usually students from the middle class and were the military elite.

Chêng Tzŭ-hua was chiefly known for having led the Tayeh uprising in 1929, when six hundred Kuomintang troops went over to P'êng Tê-huai. In 1950 he was a member of the Communist party's Central Committee.

CHÊNG TZŬ-HUA:

MY family were middle peasants and my father was a merchant. My second brother also became a merchant, but my elder brother was a doctor in the Kuomintang army. I was born in 1904 in Hai *hsien*, Shansi, and my name was originally Ssŭ, but I was given away to my mother's sister as she had no son. My adopted parents were poor, and when my foster-father died, we had only an allowance from my grandmother to depend on.

At the age of eight I was sent to a classical school and found it very dull. After two years I succeeded in changing to a modern primary school, from which I graduated at twelve. The family wanted to apprentice me to a merchant but I opposed this and entered a higher primary school. A year later, the family were unable to support me and insisted on my becoming a merchant. I hated this idea, because I did not want to be treated as a servant, which was the way apprentices were regarded in the masters' homes. Therefore, I ran away at the age of thirteen to Yünch'êng where there was a free school which provided tuition, food, clothes, and books. I graduated there in 1921, at the age of seventeen.

Borrowing money from some classmates, I went to Taiyuanfu, where I entered the Kuominshihfan, a free normal school. The master was Chao Tai-wan—he is now chairman of Shansi. One of Chao's sons was a leftist; his father put him in jail, where he died. Another was in Yenching University when the student movement began. His father warned him that he would send a squad to arrest him for being a Communist, and he left the school believing his father meant to do so. The progressive students in Chao's school were dismissed if they expressed any liberal ideas. Since most of the

143

students were very poor and afraid of dismissal, they did not act.

In my fourth year I led my class to drive away the dean. We students went in a body to see Chao Tai-wan but he was out. We talked to Yen Hsi-shan instead and told him of the dean's dishonesty in appropriating funds from the food supply intended for the school and decreasing the quality of the food. This was in 1925 when the student movement was powerful all over the country. Other staff members wanted to expel me, but Chao dismissed the dean instead, for Yen Hsi-shan had been convinced by us. Outside, the Taiyuan students' union was rising in opposition to Yen's taxes and had sent letters to our school, but Chao Tai-wan suppressed them. Indignant on learning this, the student body rose up and drove all the department heads from the school, about thirty altogether. We began by destroying furniture in the house of Yen's secretary; then, unsatisfied, we held a meeting and considered eliminating all the department heads. While this was going on, the latter climbed over the compound wall. At this time, Fêng Yü-hsiang was fighting Yen Hsi-shan and was approaching Taiyuanfu. Yen, fearing Fêng would win the students' sympathy, granted all our demands, abolished the chairmanship system in the school, and granted student government, with professors in advisory capacity only. Chao Tai-wan left and Chao Pei-lien—now chairman of the Mongolian and Tibetan Committee— became head. I was chairman of the student government. We had over one thousand students.

I had been much influenced by the May Fourth Movement and intended to join the army to fight the Japanese invaders. At this time I already felt there was no road to liberation except through revolution. I joined the Communist party in 1926 while I was still in school. I left school in the same year, and in December went to Wuhan to study there in the Military and Political Academy of the Nationalist government.

This school was a branch of Whampoa Academy. In February 1927, however, when the split between the Kuomintang and the Communists began, the school was reorganized and the cadets became a training regiment in Chang Fa-k'uei's Fourth Army.

Chang Fa-k'uei's Cadet Training Regiment

On August 4 the cadet regiment was moved to Chekiang, but the Nanchang Uprising of Chang Fa-k'uei's troops under Yeh T'ing and others had already occurred on August 1. Chang Fa-k'uei disarmed us, fearing that the regiment would join the uprising, but the cadets remained together without arms. The Communist party unit in the regiment assigned new work to the men. I returned to Wuhan and was sent to Canton and from there went to join Yeh T'ing and Ho Lung. By the time I arrived at Hongkong, Yeh T'ing was already defeated at Swatow and Chaochow and I had no party connection.

I joined Li Chi-shên's army and became a soldier in the special battalion. The company commander was a Shansi native, and he appointed me as a dispatch bearer. Later I became an army clerk in Canton. Chang Fa-k'uei now led his Fourth Army to Canton and my original cadet training regiment was there. At Chaochow they had again been disarmed—most of them were radical students. Chang Fa-k'uei moved to the West River and prepared to attack Kwangsi.

On December 11, 1927, the Canton Commune was staged by my old training regiment from Wuhan, about twelve hundred strong, together with the workers and part of the Fourth Army gendarmes, and under Communist party leadership. The regiment had just been rearmed by Chang Fa-k'uei to consolidate his rear. My battalion had been moved to Shaokuan and I escaped to join my regiment during the uprising.

Within one day the uprising had control

of Canton. Chang Fa-k'uei returned immediately and on the third day counterattacked. The Kwangsi generals meantime had begun an attack on Chang,' and ultimately he lost his base in Canton to Huang Shao-hsiung. The special regiment of cadets retreated through Kwangtung to Hailufeng, where we arrived a month later and joined the first soviet.

During the Commune the enemy's armed force was about ten thousand men. Only fifteen hundred armed men participated in the uprising, but in three days we captured ten thousand rifles. Chang Fa-k'uei and Huang Shao-hsiung were both in Canton when the uprising occurred and both fled to Shameen. The troops in the city were Chang Fa-k'uei's and the police were under the mayor, Chu Hui-erh. Hsieh Ying-po was chief of staff to Chang. The Communist Yeh Chien-ying was chief of staff of the whole Fourth Army and was much trusted. He became our chief of staff during the uprising, while Yeh T'ing was commander. The Japanese mobilized two hundred marines and landed in Canton but were driven back to Shameen. Ten or more in my company were wounded by British machine-gunning from their gunboats. The government instituted during the Canton uprising had as chairman Chang T'ai-lei, who was killed, and also included Yeh Chien-ying, P'êng Pai (then in Hailufeng), and Su Chao-chêng (the labor leader). The uprising had been planned by the Communist party of Canton.

There was no serious fighting during the uprising. Only, one divisional headquarters fought stubbornly for five hours. We did not lose many men; neither did the enemy. Most of the workers joined the uprising—all except the "Yellow"[1] unions. However, Chang Fa-k'uei's three divisions—more than ten thousand men—returned immediately and attacked the city. Meanwhile, about ten thousand workers had been armed by us, some of them joining the regiment and retreating with us. Those left behind hid their arms, or else were killed by enemy troops. On the third afternoon, one regiment of Chang's troops arrived in Canton and was defeated. The main army arrived next day, but we had retreated during the night. I do not know how many were killed. People on the streets were shot or not shot depending on how they were dressed. All who looked poorly clad were likely to be killed. Those who worked in government offices were killed because they had supported the uprising.

On the way to Hailufeng, the training regiment changed its name to the "First Division of the Chinese Workers' and Peasants' Army." We met the 2nd Division on reaching Hailufeng in January. Under leadership of the special committee there, we met to consider ways of consolidating and enlarging the soviet district. The soviet was about four hundred from li north to south, and about three hundred li wide east to west, reaching to the sea. Land was divided and a soviet was established with P'êng Pai as chairman. He was nearly thirty and had been a teacher. His family were great landlords and he was a native of Haifeng.

After two months of struggle, the enemy attacked and the army turned to Huilai, Chaoyang, and P'u-ning. In the capture of Huilai hsien town, I received a wound which crippled my left hand. Another attack, a month later, caused us to turn back to Hailufeng. During this time, I stayed with a group of ten others in a mountain forest, nursing my wound.

After a month, the Kwangtung provincial committee ordered us to return to Canton. I went to Swatow and from there to Shanghai, where I arrived with only four dollars and no Party connection. I decided to return to Shansi to make a connection there. I paid a boat servant a dollar as a bribe in place of a ticket and went to Nanking by boat, binding the three dollars to my leg to avoid detection.

P'êng Pai also later returned to Shanghai, where he was arrested in 1928 and executed.

Yeh T'ing, who like P'êng Pai was the son of a great landlord, went to Hongkong. He had been a cadet in the first class at Whampoa Academy and was married to a rich overseas woman. The rest of the Hailufeng army stayed in the district as partisans. Our army had been defeated. It fled to the seashore, where a boat was secured from the peasants, who were sympathetic. When the enemy forces occupied Hailufeng, they massacred the peasants, using the slogan: "Kill every Red even if necessary to kill ten innocent ones to get one Red."

A Battalion Deserts to the Red Army

I went in a troop train on the P'êngpu railway to Hsuchow, arriving there with one dollar. I walked along the railway to Chengchow, doing one hundred seventy *li* each day and traveling sometimes on the rods of the trains. On reaching Shansi, I found that my old schoolmates had escaped or been arrested or been killed, and that an order had been issued for my arrest. I hid in my grandmother's house. Some old clothes were sold to provide twelve dollars for me, and I escaped from Shansi. I went on to Nanyang, Honan, but on arriving there I found my relative had already moved. Fêng Yü-hsiang's troops were then fighting General Yao Wei-chên—he was later killed by the Red Army in Oyüwan—and, being broke, I joined Yo's army. Half a month later I met a schoolmate who was staff officer to the battalion and he helped me to promotion. I became a platoon commander. This schoolmate also had lost his Party connection so we organized ourselves and began work on our own.

Yao Wei-chên was a colorful character —originally a bandit leader in north Shensi, and in Tingpien, Anpien, and Yünpien, where he had organized the bandits into the Chingkuochien, or "Pacification Army," under General Hu Chin-yi. When Hu went to Honan to fight Chang Tso-lin and died there, Yo became *tupan* [provincial military governor] of Honan. He fought against Yen

Hsi-shan and Wu P'ei-fu, and was captured by Yen. Released, he went again to Shensi and organized bandits into an army. Later he joined the Kuominchün of Fêng Yü-hsiang, becoming commander in chief of the South Route Army. In the Kuominchün war with the Kuomintang he was removed by Chiang Kai-shek. At that time Yo was between forty and fifty years old.

In 1929, when General Yao moved to western Hupeh to fight Chang Fa-k'uei, three regiments were disarmed by Chang's troops while crossing the river. My regiment, however, was not disarmed. It moved to northern Hupeh. Chiang Kai-shek now sent Whampoa students to replace the old officers and thereby aroused resentment. In two regiments, the 4th and 5th, the Communists led an uprising and joined the Kiangsi-Hupeh western soviet district. I was in the 6th Regiment and had no news of the uprising. Chiang Kai-shek moved my regiment to Ichang on the Yangtze River and appointed Chao Wan-hsien division commander of the new 1st Division. On the boat we were disarmed and returned to Hankow. There we and other regiments not in the uprising were reorganized into the Fifteenth Independent Brigade. I was reappointed platoon commander in the 2nd Regiment. Few Communists were left now, but our past influence remained. Thus, in 1929, when the Red Army attacked us (the fifth column of P'êng Tê-huai's troops) near Tayeh and my regiment was sent out to fight, I led the 2nd Battalion in an uprising in the night.[2] We had a party committee in the brigade; two companies of the 1st Battalion also joined the Red Army. The others—the 2nd and 3rd battalions—were sent to chase us, but the 9th Company of the 3rd Battalion joined with us. This frightened the Kuomintang so much that all troops were withdrawn.

I was now with the fifth column of the Fifth Red Army. In March 1930, in the attack on Suichang, Kiangsi, I was again wounded—a long bullet wound in the arm. In May, P'êng Tê-huai brought the other four columns to meet with the fifth column in eastern Hupeh. There we established the Third Army Corps, and organized the Fifth and Eighth Armies.

In June I went to Shanghai to cure my wound and in January [1931] was sent to the central soviet district in Kiangsi and was there appointed regimental commander in the Thirty-fifth Red Army. After the "Third Surrounding Campaign," the army was reorganized as the Independent Third Division and I was made division commander.

In December of 1931 an uprising occurred among troops of the Kuomintang Twenty-sixth Route Army at Ningtu. The 41st Division of the Fifth Army Corps was organized from participants in the Ningtu uprising, and I was appointed political commissar to the division. Half a year later, in 1932, I was made commander of the division; then, later, I was transferred to the newly organized 14th Division.

In November 1933 I entered the Red Academy in Juikin and a month later was sent out to become commander of the 22nd Division. Later I was made chief of staff in the Kwangtung-Kiangsi military district.

In May 1934 I was sent to Oyüwan, arriving there in July. After a conference of the provincial committee I was appointed to the command of the Twenty-fifth Army, while Hsü Hai-tung was vice-commander. We moved out on the Long March to Shensi and from this time on I was with Hsü.

I had a strange wound in both hands during the Shansi campaign. As I was walking over the mountain holding my injured hand with the other, a bullet entered my wrist above the old wound, pierced the bone, then entered the palm of the other hand and came out through that wrist. Naturally, I cannot use my hands much. For two months I had no use of them whatsoever.

Hsü Hsiang-ch'ien

WHAMPOA VETERAN

In speaking of his life General Hsü Hsiang-ch'ien seemed to be unfolding a many-paneled screen. On the front were meticulous episodes from military campaigns. Perhaps on the back of the screen was his hidden personal life. He is characteristically dour in this Yenan snapshot of 1937.

MISS WALES:

Hsü Hsiang-ch'ien, known from the first as one of the most brilliant military figures among the Chinese Communists, belongs to a small group of men known among the other officers as "Whampoa Cadets," being graduates of Whampoa Military Academy in Canton. While he was there, Hsü Hsiang-ch'ien was a classmate of Hu Tsung-nan, one of Chiang Kai-shek's chief anti-Communist generals.

Hsü Hsiang-ch'ien was nervous when I talked with him, and was under the care of doctors. He was the only man I met who seemed neurotic, though this may have been a temporary condition. At the time, his army had just been decimated in the Northwest by Mohammedans; also he was being called upon to make difficult decisions in the conflict between Chang Kuo-t'ao and Mao Tsê-tung, and had taken the side of Mao. Chang had been civilian head of the soviets in Oyüwan and Szechuan while Hsü was military commander.

After 1937 Hsü was deputy commander of the 129th Division of the Eighth Route Army during the fighting against the Japanese. He then became commander and political commissar of the Eighteenth Army Group. In 1949 he was appointed one of the twenty-two members of the Military Council and chief of the General Staff. He was also one of the members of the Government Council. In 1950 he commanded the Taiyuan area in Shansi, his home province.

I found Hsü Hsiang-ch'ien aloof and reserved. He refused to give me much information about his personal life, but he did relate a long and detailed history of his military experiences, valuable now for the record. His history gives an authoritative account of several relatively unknown matters, notably the soviet in Hailufeng, and the soviets in Oyüwan and Szechuan which were the scenes of the bitterest civil warfare of the period.

148

HSÜ HSIANG-CH'IEN:

MY home is at Wut'aishan[1] in Shansi, where the governor, Yen Hsi-shan, was also born. My father was a *hsiu-ts'ai* scholar and taught school. He was also a small landlord, owning thirty or forty *mu* of land. In my family, besides me, were one younger and two older sisters, one older brother and his wife, and my parents.

I was born in 1902. As a child I studied in school at Wut'aishan for three years and went to the higher primary school for three years. After this I worked as a clerk in a bookshop before entering the Taiyuan normal school. Upon my graduation I taught in the primary school attached to the Ch'uantze Middle School in Wut'aishan—a school founded by Yen Hsi-shan. In 1924 I went to Canton to enter the Whampoa Military Academy of the Kuomintang.

Shansi Province was very backward, both socially and politically. It was difficult to get the new progressive books to read. However, I was already interested in revolution. Even in 1915, when the Japanese took occasion during the World War to present the Twenty-one Demands to China, I was the leader of a student demonstration and talked to the people on the street. The establishment of the Kuomintang had a great influence on me, and I wanted to go to Canton because it was then the revolutionary center. I joined the Kuomintang as soon as I arrived in Canton in 1924, being then twenty-two years old.

My father was very conservative and was opposed to my ideas. I ran away to Canton without his knowledge. Only my brother knew my intention of becoming a military man at Whampoa. I was already married and had a daughter. My wife died when I went to Whampoa and I have no idea what became of the child.

Whampoa and the Kuomintang

I was a graduate of the first class of Whampoa cadets in 1924. There were six detachments—about seven hundred graduates. We had received six months' training. Whampoa then had two Soviet Russian instructors, Borodin and Korloff, who made speeches to the cadets and had considerable influence on us. However, at that time I was in the middle, between the "Society of Sun Yat-senism" on the Right and the Communist Party—which many joined—on the Left.

I was made squad commander after graduation, and began the march eastward to join the campaign against Ch'ên Ch'iung-ming. We marched to Tungkiang [Hailu-feng] and to P'ingshan and Tanshui. Afterward I was appointed by Chiang Kai-shek to go to the northern provinces. I was sent to work in the Second National Army of the Kuomintang under Hu Chin-yi in Honan. I was in Kaifeng, Honan, at the time of the May Thirtieth Incident in 1925. On that day, because of the difficulty in getting news from Shanghai, we did not know the real facts but saw the students demonstrating in the streets, and I became much excited. In Hu's army I was a political worker and began organizing a *chao tao ying*, or "special training battalion," to train the young officers. I had worked at this for four months when the war against Chang Tso-lin began. At that time Fêng Yü-hsiang commanded the First National Army and Hu Chin-yi the Second. Fêng had few Whampoa cadets but there were many in the Second Army. We attacked Tehchow in Shantung. I was on the staff of one brigade which was defeated and retreated to Paoting near Peking. After resting in Mentoukou we marched to Hsuan-huafu [now Chahar] under direct command of Fêng Yü-hsiang. From there we went to fight against Yen Hsi-shan and attacked Yuchow in Shansi. This was in 1926. I was by that time vice-commander of a regiment.

In Shansi we also attacked Hungyün and P'inghsingkuan, and Fêng Yü-hsiang occupied Nankow. After that Fêng was defeated and my brigade marched to his assistance. I was sick, however, and was left behind. Wang Yun-ping—who is now head of the judicial department at Nanking, and was then chief secretary of Shansi Province—sent me to Anyang to organize a Special Training Class in a brigade of the Second Army, then under the command of Yao Wei-chên, Hu Chin-yi having died. I was soon obliged to leave Shansi and go to Peking to rest. Then the National Army occupied Wuhan and I went there in 1926. In Wuhan I was political director of the students' regiment at Nanhu; then I changed my work to become captain of the First Detachment of the Central Political and Military Academy in Wuchang; this academy was a branch of Whampoa.

It was at this time, in 1926, that I joined the Communist party. Since the party was open and legal in Wuhan, I was able to read many Marxist books and was immediately influenced by them. I was also influenced by talking with some of my Shansi provincials who had joined the party.

After the split with the Kuomintang occurred in 1927, the party [Communist] appointed me to work in Chang Fa-k'uei's army. I was on his general staff. When Chang arrived at Chôchiang in Kiangsi, he made a speech in which he asked who in his army were Communists, saying that if we confessed and gave up the party there would be no trouble for us. I escaped and went to Wuhan and Shanghai. There I was appointed by the party to work in the labor movement in Canton; I helped prepare the Canton Commune uprising.

The Canton Commune, 1927

I taught military tactics to Canton workmen. This was done very secretly. We had six hundred workmen in training, and could train only ten people in a room at a time. The men liked the training immensely and were enthusiastic for the uprisings. I could

not speak the Cantonese dialect and had to have an interpreter.

Just before the uprising the workmen divided into detachments. I was captain of the 6th Detachment; it had about six hundred workmen but not many were trained. At the beginning of the uprising the 6th Detachment had only six guns and six bombs. After the workers had occupied police headquarters, we got many guns and the men were able to use them even if they had had no training at all. The Canton Commune uprising began on December 11, 1927, and the workers fought three days before they failed. I was in the middle of the fray with my detachment. Only thirty of my men were killed in the fighting, but I have no idea how many were arrested and executed afterward. Many workmen escaped from Canton. I went to the Hailufeng soviet.

The main force in the Commune was the *chao tao t'uan* [special training regiment]. The *chao tao t'uan* was made up of students who had graduated from the Central Political and Military Academy in Wuchang, and had been under command of Chang Fa-k'uei. They had been sent to Canton from Wuchang. All were students, most were Communists, and many were Whampoa cadets. They were the backbone of the uprising. First, the *chao tao t'uan* escaped from Canton, and then I followed with other officers. We could not find the regiment at Huanghuakang, but finally, after fighting our way through some *min t'uan*, we caught up with the regiment in Huahsien and became officers in it. When we left Huahsien we went to Ts'unghua *hsien*, to Tzŭchin *hsien*, and then to Lungwo where we met the partisans of Hailufeng—happy at the sight of our friends.

The workers were still holding Canton, and few of them left when the regiment retreated from the city. It was the only armed unit that left the city. When I caught up with it, the regiment had about twelve hundred members, all armed with guns. It was soon reorganized into the 4th Division of the Red Army, with Yeh Yün [Jên] as commander, Yuan Yü as party delegate, and Wang K'an-fu as head of its political department. I was party delegate to the 10th Regiment of this division—a position the same as political commissar now.

Hailufeng, the First Chinese Soviet

From Lungwo the regiment went to the Hailufeng soviet, which had been established by P'êng Pai.[2] When we arrived, in January 1928, the peasants called a great mass meeting to welcome us. They carried the old style *t'o chung* guns used for shooting birds. None of the peasants had anything but these old relics, but some of the Red partisans had modern guns.

I was soon made chief of staff of our 4th Division, and worked closely with P'êng Pai. This amazing man had great influence over the peasantry; they worshiped him like a god. After Hailufeng failed, P'êng Pai went to Shanghai. One night after a meeting in Shanghai, a traitor betrayed P'êng Pai. The Kuomintang pounced on him with delight and arrested and executed him. This was in 1929.

We soon completely occupied Lofeng *hsien* and a part of Haifeng. I don't know exactly how many people there were in the Hailufeng soviet, but there were several hundred thousand at least. The Hailufeng soviet had another military unit, the 2nd Division, of eight hundred soldiers. These were men from the Nanchang Uprising in Kiangsi who had escaped to Hailufeng. The commander of the 2nd Division was Tung Nan, and the political director was Yang Ch'ang-yi. Altogether there were only two thousand regular soldiers in Hailufeng—the 4th and 2nd divisions.

We attacked Chiatzŭwan and Huilai *hsien*. Then the enemy counterattacked and we lost Haifeng to the Kwangtung troops under Li Chi-shên. In the fighting at Haifeng we destroyed two of Ch'ên Ming-shu's regiments and killed the regimental commanders. We captured many of the men but

at that time we had the "closed door" policy and merely released the men instead of organizing them into the Red Army.

After hard fighting we arrived again at the north side of Haifeng and planned to recapture it, but, failing in this, we escaped into the countryside and began partisan warfare. Although Haifeng city was lost to us, the surrounding areas belonged to our partisans. At that time our soviet capital was at Taanten and Jeshuit'un. Once when the enemy attacked, Yeh Yün [Jên], commander of our 4th Division, was sick and was left behind when our troops escaped to the mountain. He was captured and executed by the enemy. After his arrest, they wanted him to surrender but he refused and was killed secretly.

We had been fighting the Whites every day, and when the 4th Division returned to recapture Haifeng we had only four hundred of our twelve hundred men left. The local peasants didn't want to join the regular Red Army because they didn't understand our dialect nor we theirs. I had great difficulty with my work in Hailufeng because I still could not speak Cantonese! In the hard fighting in the mountains many of our men were sacrificed. We could not get any new recruits, and the army decreased daily. Nearly everyone in the army was sick, too, because of the heat and the hard life in the mountains. The men were not native to the region and were unaccustomed to the intense damp heat. Many died from illness. Many others were captured by the enemy. Our best revolutionary cadres were sacrificed in Hailufeng. The *chao tao t'uan* was made up of the finest Communist cadets of the Kuomintang period, and hardly any are now left even to tell the tale. The 2nd and 4th divisions were divided after the fighting at Haifeng and I never knew what happened afterward to the 2nd Division. When I left the region there were only sixty persons remaining in our 4th Division! The survivors of Hailufeng are few indeed. I have seen only one since I joined with the other armies here: Yuan Yü, of the political department of the Third Red Army Corps, now political commissar of the Military Academy at the front.

After the destruction of the Hailufeng soviet I went to Shanghai. I left Hailufeng in March 1928, escaping with the help of the secret Communist party cells.

The Oyüwan Government

In Shanghai I rested twenty days or so and then went to the region which later became the "Oyüwan" or Hupeh-Honan-Anhwei Soviet, the main district being in northeast Hupeh. On my way there I had much trouble but no serious danger. I was introduced by the party people and was led into the district by someone connected with the partisans. When I arrived, I found that the partisans in northeast Hupeh had only two hundred guns. The soviet region was not large, being only a few tens of *li* in circumference. There was no regular Red Army but only two hundred partisans, mostly native Hupeh peasants. This was called the "31st Division of the Peasants' and Workers' Army."

During the Great Revolution of 1925–27 the peasants in this district had had an uprising against the landlords in 1926. This was before the split with the Kuomintang. The peasants who armed themselves became fighters afterward and organized a Soviet area. This soviet was organized in the latter part of 1929, though I cannot remember the month. The uprising had occurred in Huangan *hsien* and Mach'êng *hsien*—these counties in northeast Hupeh became the soviet. The whole movement was organized by the Communist party; it was led by Ts'ên Wei-san, later in the Twenty-fifth Red Army; Tai Chi-yin, of the Twenty-fifth Army; and Hsü P'êng-jên, who later betrayed. All were native Hupeh Communist political leaders.

The same leaders organized the Honan movement, beginning with an uprising in Shangch'êng toward the end of 1928 and the beginning of 1929. There were only a few hundred in this uprising, but from it the

32nd Division was organized. This region became a soviet at the beginning of 1929. Later, a small part of Kwangshan *hsien* in Honan also joined the soviets. The Anhwei part of the soviet had not yet been organized. After Anhwei was added, we called the whole district the "Oyüwan Soviet." These are the three ancient names of the provinces used by the people. Hupeh was called "O" by them, Honan was called "Yü," and Anhwei was called "Wan."

The peasants had already organized and armed themselves during the 1925–27 period, and that was the reason for the formation of a soviet district in this particular area. Also, the Communist party had good organization in these districts. Although Oyüwan was very near the industrial center of Wuhan, no workers joined. During the Great Revolution the majority of the people not only had risen and killed many landlords, forcing others to escape, but also had organized the "People's Army of Self-Defense," several thousand strong. Though they possessed only ten guns, they occupied Huangan, the *hsien* city, and went on to the attack of Mach'êng. The landlords were also armed, and they led their *min t'uan* against the People's Army organized by the Communists. The "Red Spears"[3] were reactionary and were led by the landlords to fight against the People's Army, too.

It was a Communist-led movement right from the beginning, and after the split of the Kuomintang and the Communist party, the White army began to suppress the peasants. Their armed force was destroyed and many were killed or forced to flee. In the spring of 1929 Chiang Kai-shek's army began civil war with Li Tsung-jên. When the army which had occupied the Hupeh district was withdrawn, the peasants promptly rose again. The population of the district was several hundred thousand, but part of them were under the influence of the reactionaries.

When I arrived, in June 1929, I was made vice-commander of the army—that is, of the

31st Division—the commander, Wu Kuang-hao, having been killed before I arrived. Wu was a Hupeh native and a Whampoa cadet. Together with Wang Hsü-shên and Li Tzǔ-liang, he had led the present partisan army. Li was also a Whampoa cadet, while Wang was a Hupeh native born in a landlord's family and only a graduate of higher primary school. Wang is now with the Red Army on the west side of the Yellow River. The political commissar of the division was Tai Ch'uan, who later betrayed the party and joined Wang Ching-wei's group; I have no idea where he is now. Tso Wei-chên, who eventually betrayed also, was at that time commander of the 32nd Division in Honan, together with Ch'i Tê-wei, who was later sent to Shanghai by the Party.

At the time I arrived in Hupeh there was one Kuomintang brigade on the north led by Lo Ling, and this brigade attacked the Red Army. Also on the north were many bandits and Red Spears who fought against us. The Red Army moved forward on the north and destroyed many bandits. The Red Spears were then in Paishankuan. Though they were directed by the Kuomintang, they had only two hundred guns, but they had a thousand militiamen armed with the old-fashioned red spears. After a time a split occurred within their ranks. Although all had at first opposed us, after propaganda and the invitation to join our "Red" army, some of them supported us. We then fought against the "White" Red Spears and destroyed them. These Red Spears are not the same as those in Hunan province, not having very close relations with them. We next organized a new soviet district in the southwest part of Kwangsan. The enemy began a big offensive against the Shangch'êng soviet in Honan. The people were massacred, including women and children. The class struggle here was fierce because the peasants in earlier times had killed the landlords, making the gentry cruel and revengeful. When the Whites occupied Santsen, the landlords returned, and the people and the

32nd Division left the district and went to Mach'êng, Hupeh. The Red Army in Ma-ch'êng supplied guns to the division, which then returned to Shangch'êng to fight with the Whites for its native place.

At this time the main Hupeh Red Army marched to the northwest part of Mach'êng *hsien* and drove out the landlords and *min t'uan*, re-establishing the soviets.

The First Campaign, 1930

Because of the development of the soviets and the Red Army, the Whites began a "surrounding campaign," led by Hsia Tou-yin—famous for his atrocities—of the 13th Kuomintang Division and Hsü Yüan-ch'ien of the 48th Kuomintang Division. The Red Army retreated to Laochün Mountain and then attacked Hsia Tou-yin. Luckily for us, the war between Chiang Kai-shek and T'ang Shêng-chih began and most of the White troops were soon withdrawn. The units which remained changed position, moving away from the central part of our soviets.

Just before this time the Whites were in occupation of all areas except the mountains. When the Whites came, the people ran away to the mountains and any that were captured were killed. Their houses were burned by the Whites and so many were killed that I have no idea of the number. However, the peasants had previously had so much experience in learning how to escape the invaders that it was not a general massacre.

The enemy was burning houses and killing people in the south part of Huangan *hsien*, so the main forces of the 31st Red Division marched there to the defense. This was the winter of 1929. We defeated Hsia Tou-yin, and he withdrew to Huangan city. We had captured many of the enemy Red Spears, treated them well, and done good propaganda work on them, so that when they were released they always betrayed the Whites.

The Red Army marched forward to the

southwest part of Huangan *hsien* and the north part of Huangp'o *hsien,* and also into Hsiaokan *hsien,* carrying on partisan warfare in these districts. We destroyed many forces of the reactionary Red Spears and *min t'uan,* and then marched to the south part of Loshan *hsien,* named Hsüanhuatien. As soon as the Red Army passed over their districts, the masses all rose to the struggle. We distributed all the landlords' agricultural products to the people, but had not then redistributed the land. This was in January 1930.

In March of that year the First Red Army was organized by the Central Committee of the Communist Party under the direction of Hsü Chi-shên, a Whampoa cadet who later betrayed and joined Têng Yen-ta's "Third Party." Chao Ta-chün was also in command. The 1st and 2nd divisions of this army were organized in Shangch'êng, having one thousand men altogether. The 31st Division changed its name to the 1st Division and included nine detachments, having eight hundred guns, all of which had been captured from the Whites. The 2nd and 3rd divisions were organized by the armed masses themselves, and the 3rd Division had part of them been bandits.

During the time of the war between Chiang Kai-shek and the Yen Hsi-shan–Fêng Yü-hsiang coalition in 1930, the First Red Army Headquarters led the 2nd and 3rd divisions to west Anhwei and occupied Mafou, Hoshan, Yingshan, and Linch'üan, destroying two brigades of the enemy. The 1st Division marched west along the Pinghan railway and attacked Yangchiat'ing, a Pinghan station, destroying one enemy brigade, and then returned to attack Yangt'ing-k'ou, destroying one enemy regiment. We then organized two new regiments from the masses, using guns captured in these battles. From this time on we had a new policy of treating the enemy captives well; some became lower officers in the Red Army.

After the Red Army attacked Yangt'ing-k'ou, the landlords led the reactionary forces to attack the southern part of Huangan at Palich'ü. The 1st Division went back to the defense, afterward attacking Huayüan.

When we attacked Huayüan we destroyed the 5th Regiment of Chiang Kai-shek's garrison, and captured eight machine guns and four cannon. This was the first time we had had such artillery. It was about the same time as the capture of Changsha in 1930. We had then no radios or telephones. We had captured some of these, but nobody knew how to use them and we always destroyed them. At first, our soldiers didn't know how to use the machine guns and cannon and took them apart to see how they worked inside. Later they forced captured White officers to teach them. At this time, however, our economic condition was very good and we had good gray cloth uniforms like those the Red Army uses now. The Red Army always paid with money when buying goods — with money confiscated from the landlords, of course. We had no Red Star on our caps then—only a red armband with a star and two slogans reading, on the right, "Support the Third International," and, on the left, "Realize the Land Revolution."

When the 1st Division turned back to Hsiaohoch'i, we began to strengthen the Red Army with many new recruits. The 1st Division then had two regiments of nine companies each. At this time we occupied Yünmêng *hsien* on the west side of the Pinghan railway, holding it only three days and then returning to Hsiaohoch'i again and going on to Tzekuten where we joined with the 2nd and 3rd divisions led by the First Army Headquarters Staff. Here we destroyed the whole body of the 45th Kuomintang Division led by Tai Ming-ch'uan. At that time the Red Army had altogether nearly six thousand troops; there were three thousand in the 1st Division and about twenty-five hundred in the 2nd and 3rd divisions together.

Our three divisions were combined and then went to Hsiaohoch'i and defeated the

Kuomintang forces led by P'êng Chi-piao, destroying two of his three regiments.

By this time we had enlarged our areas into a big soviet district, with a very strong soviet on the east side of the Pinghan railway. In the autumn of 1930 we had sovietized ten *hsien*, but only part of each.

After occupying Hsiaohoch'i the Red Army marched against Kwangshui on the Pinghan line and attacked it, then occupied Hsinyang station on the Pinghan line in Honan, but not Hsinyang city. Because we could not occupy the city, we marched from the northeast part to Touk'ou and met the partisans of Chengyang, who were two hundred strong. The partisans then wore common clothes, having no uniforms. These partisans had survived after the failure of an uprising at Tzŭwanshan, southwest of Hsinyang. We returned to occupy Kuangshan *hsien* and destroyed two battalions of the enemy there before going on to occupy Loshan, where we destroyed one enemy battalion. As there was only a weak mass foundation in this district, we turned back to the soviet areas again, attacking Yaochiachi and Huangan city. We could not get a victory, however. The enemy there remained firm, so we went to Hsiehti and destroyed two battalions of Hsia Tou-yin's 13th Division. Later we surrounded Hsia's army in Liaop'êng and marched south and occupied Hsinchou, destroying one enemy regiment. We also occupied Lot'ien in Hupeh, and from there went to Shangch'êng in Honan, recovered Chinchiachai, and reoccupied this soviet area which had been held by the Whites, destroying most of the *min t'uan* there.

When the Red Army entered Chinchiachai the soldiers became very angry, for they found floating on the river many corpses of men, women, and children who had been killed by the Whites.

The Red Army then marched to the Honan-Anhwei border and began an attack on Luan and Hoshan in Anhwei, but did not succeed and so turned back to Mafou. This was in the winter of 1930. The army had to ford an icy river up to the breast, there being no boats. Nobody died from this exposure, however, and the men had no fear of the cold bath. At this time the Whites led by Ch'ên Tiao-yüan attacked us from three sides, with one brigade on each side. We concentrated our forces and attacked their center and right wing. We moved so fast that a Kuomintang regimental commander was captured in the middle of writing an order at his table. We captured two thousand guns—also a radio, but we still didn't know how to use it. After this campaign the 1st and 2nd divisions turned back to their original positions in northeast Hupeh. At the Erh-Tao River we met part of Fêng Yühsiang's army under Chi Hung-ch'ang, defeated him, and captured a thousand guns as well as a big mountain cannon. (This is the General Chi Hung-ch'ang who later became very sympathetic with us and was killed in Tientsin as a Communist about 1933.) The First Red Army then met the Fifteenth Red Army at Mach'êng, which was under command of Ts'ai Shên-hsi, a Whampoa cadet.

In December 1930, the Central Committee of the party ordered the number of the First Red Army changed to the Fourth Red Army, with K'uang Chi-hsün as commander and myself as chief of staff.

We attacked Mokolo and destroyed four regiments of Hsia Tou-yin. Then we occupied Hsin-chi, the base of the reactionary forces. The Fourth Red Army later attacked Hsuanhsiao-chun on the Pinghan line, fighting against the White army of Yao Wei-chün. We captured Yao and destroyed his entire 34th Division except for two companies. Yao was sent to the Soviet Military Committee of Hupeh Province and imprisoned. Though he was treated well there, he did counterrevolutionary work and was planning an uprising, so the soviets held a public mass trial for him. The people demanded that he pay retribution for the numbers of them he had killed and the many houses he had burned, and requested the authorities to kill him, which was done. No captives were executed after this, however. They were sent to the rear and put to work, many escaping on the road when not well guarded during night marches. Some died from disease and the hard life. We captured one aviator who escaped. One airplane was captured and repaired. We flew it only once to bomb the Whites. We had only one Red aviator of our own. That time we forced the captured aviator to pilot our bombing expedition under guard.

In a later period when I was in command of the Fourth Red Army, we destroyed ten airplanes—all brought down by rifle shots. We didn't use machine guns against them because our ammunition was too valuable and the planes not important enough to us.

For special bravery we gave a small red silk cloth with no writing on it. We never have medals in the Red Army. When one group wins a victory, the Military Council sends it a special Red banner.

All of the above account tells of the first stage of destroying the "First Surrounding Campaign" of the ruling class. This was now a success, and the Oyüwan soviet was firmly established.

At that time the Oyüwan soviet included more than ten *hsien*, or counties, with a population of over one million. We had expanded the Fourth Red Army to include three divisions, the 4th, the 10th, and the 11th. We also had a garrison force of three regiments.

The Second Campaign, 1931

The "Second Surrounding Campaign" of the enemy soon began, and in May 1931, the whole body of our Red Army marched eastward to the western part of Anhwei, where we destroyed two divisions under Ch'ên Tiao-yüan. Then Chi Hung-ch'ang's army from Huangan and Kuangshan attacked the central part of the soviet region. We attacked him and destroyed a small part of his forces. He retreated to Loshan. Our

Fourth Red Army then returned westward and destroyed the army of Li Pao-pin at the P'op'i River. After this the Red Army surrounded a small place called T'aohua and destroyed the 44th Division of the White army in Huangan. Thus the "Second Campaign" of the enemy was defeated.

In the meantime the troops of the Central soviets in Kiangsi had also destroyed the enemy sent against them. Chiang Kai-shek was therefore obliged to prepare for his "Third Campaign." To meet it, our Oyü-wan Red Army planned to march southward for a co-ordinated defense plan with the Red Army of the Central soviets.

The Third Campaign, 1931

The Fourth Red Army of our Oyüwan army began its march southward and occupied three *hsien*: Kuangchi, Yingshan, and Hsishui; then it destroyed one of Ch'ên Tiao-yüan's regiments, one brigade of Wang Kuan-chung, and two divisions of Hsü Yüan-ch'ien. By July 1931 the Oyüwan Red Army vanguard had reached the bank of the Yangtze River.

At this time counterrevolutionary work was discovered among the Red armies. The Fourth Red Army turned back to Mafou and began the work of liquidating the reactionaries. The leader of this reaction was Hsü Chi-shên. About this time there were many betrayals from our ranks because conditions were very bad and the White attacks severe. Also at this time the Third party of Têng Yen-ta was organized and many Whampoa cadets did not want to continue the struggle for soviets. Hsü Chi-shên was one of these Whampoa men who betrayed. Later, in Szechuan, when I was in command of the Fourth Front Red Army and Hsü Chi-shên was in command of the 12th Division under me, I discovered a letter that Chiang Kai-shek had written to Hsü asking him to betray. Because the Red Army and the soviet regions had expanded very fast, the Whites not only attacked us with military power but also used political tricks and sent many agents into the Red armies. During the development of the Red Army the life was very uncertain, sometimes bad and sometimes good. During the hard periods some elements wavered and joined the work of the reactionaries. After several leaders of the reaction had been arrested, the other members confessed their errors. The liquidation of these reactionary elements made the force of the Red Army much stronger than before.

After liquidating the counterrevolution, the Red Army turned back in order to strengthen the Oyüwan soviet. We passed through Junhochi, destroying the 4th Kuomintang Division; then through Hofungch'ao, destroying the enemy's 45th Division. Afterward our army marched south again, the main force being the Fourth Red Army.

The Fourth Front Red Army was organized at Ch'ilip'ing in the central part of the Oyüwan soviet district on November 7, 1931. It included the previous Fourth Red Army and the 73rd Division of the Twenty-fifth Red Army. I was appointed commander in chief, and Ts'ên Ch'ang was made political commissar. Ts'ên is still working somewhere near the West River.

The Fourth Front Red Army then marched southward and besieged Huangan city for twenty-seven days, capturing this White stronghold at last! We continued on through Nanyaochien, Toufutien, and Ku-szuhsien. We defeated six White divisions, the 75th and 76th, the 2nd and 12th, and the 45th and 58th Kuomintang divisions. After this victory the Red Army was able to occupy Shangch'êng hsien. This consolidated the territory of the soviets into a single whole unit — previously there had always been a White area in between the two soviets. Then the 2nd Division of the Fourth Red Army arrived at Kuang-chi and met with the 73rd Red Division. This big struggle between White and Red forces lasted over forty-eight days.

Four times the enemy sent reinforcements, and all these were defeated by us.

They sent the 7th, 12th, 55th, and 57th divisions, together with the 1st and 2nd brigades of their garrison. All were turned back by the Red Army. We also surrounded the enemy 46th Division and captured every single gun.

We then expanded the Twenty-fifth Red Army to add the 74th and 75th divisions; previously it had had only one division. We also organized an "Independent Division" in the western part of Anhwei.

The main forces of the Red Army now marched forward to the west, passing through Huangch'uan and Kuangshan, at which places we fought several battles. We defeated three White divisions: the 75th, the 76th, and the 20th. After this fighting we marched to the Pinghan railway. The Fourth Red Army and the 73rd Division turned south and besieged Mach'êng hsien, clearing away many enemies near the hsien city.

We had broken the "Third Surrounding Campaign" of the enemy. The Oyüwan soviet was at its highest period just after this defeat of the Third Campaign in 1931. There was a population of about two millions under our control at that time.

The Fourth Campaign, 1932

Chiang Kai-shek now prepared the "Fourth Surrounding Campaign." On August 11, 1932, the vanguard of the Red Army reached Huangan and fought Chiang Kai-shek's army there, destroying part of the enemy and forcing them to turn back. Then the left wing of the Whites, led by the famous commander Wei Li-huang and by Ch'ên Chi-chên, attacked Ch'ilip'ing. The main forces of the Red Army turned back to Ch'ilip'ing and fought against them for three days, destroying their 2nd Division. The battle reached a stalemate, however. The enemy decided that this front was too difficult to attack and changed their tactics to make a flanking movement on Chinchi. Our main forces turned toward Hosanchai.

At this time the White commanders

adopted a new military strategy. They attacked our weak points only, never our main forces.

In the meantime there had been heavy fighting in the western part of Anhwei against White armies led by Liang Kuanyin, Wang Chün, and Hsü T'ing-yao. Our main forces, therefore, turned to west Anhwei to help in the fighting there. Until this time the Red Army had had no chance to annihilate the White forces. Now, however, our main forces passed through Huang-p'o, Lot'ien, and Yingshan, arriving at Hok'ou in Huangan *hsien*. Here we destroyed part of the 88th, 1st, and 13th divisions of the Whites. After three more days of battle, we destroyed the whole body of their troops.

The Szechuan Soviet

At this time we decided to transfer the Fourth Front Red Army, which was composed of the Fourth Red Army and the 73rd Division. It was decided that this army should go to Szechuan and organize a new soviet, because this province was a good area for us, richer and more heavily populated. We left the Oyüwan soviet guarded by the other troops, and marched through Hupeh, Honan, and Shensi into Szechuan, arriving in December 1932. We first occupied T'ungchiang, Nanchiang, and Pachou in north Szechuan.

Before the Red Army arrived in Szechuan, the oppression of the ruling class had been very great, so that when we came the people were very excited and immediately began to struggle against their oppressors. Many were anxious to join the army, and we added a great number of new recruits. The majority, however, had the opium habit. It was only after our Red soldiers had given much advice and done educational work among them that they gave up opium. Eventually all these opium smokers voluntarily surrendered the habit and made good, strong soldiers.

We spent one month resting and supplementing our forces. Then T'ien Tsung-yao,

a Szechuan militarist, concentrated to attack the Red Army. After three months of fighting, the enemy was worn out. We concentrated our main forces and destroyed the enemy in K'unsan. T'ien had forty regiments. We annihilated half of his men; many of the remainder joined the Red Army. That was on May 11, 1933. A week later we organized the "Soviet Districts of Tung-Nan-Pa"—that is, of Tungchiang-Nanchiang-Pachou. Our vanguard reached the east side of the Chialing River, and our rear was in Pachou.

At Pachou we held our Soviet Delegates' Congress, attended by three thousand delegates who represented nearly a million population. Pachou had five hundred thousand people, Tungchiang about two hundred thousand, and Nanchiang about two hundred thousand.

After the Delegates' Congress, the Fourth Front Red Army increased tremendously. The original 10th Division was expanded into the Fourth Army, the 11th Division into the Thirtieth Army, the 12th Division making up the Ninth Army, and the 73rd Division into the Thirty-first Army.

We then fought against Yang Shên's army, occupied Yingshan *hsien* in August, and, after fighting with the army of Liu Ch'êng-hou, occupied Suiting [Ta-hsien] and Hsuanhan *hsien*. The Szechuan soviet soon included the following fourteen *hsien* [counties]: Tungchiang, Nanchiang, Pachou, Kuangyüan, Chaohua, Ts'angch'i, Nan-ch'ung, Ilung, Yünsan, Ch'ühsien, Hsüan-han, Ta-hsien, Ch'engk'ou, and Wanyüan. Some of these *hsien*, however, were only partly sovietized.

We named the soviet the "Chuan-shan [Szechuan-Shensi] Soviet District." The chairman of the government was Hsiung Kuo-pin, a Szechuan native with a strong influence on the masses; Hsiung had been a coolie worker, but had learned to read and write. I don't know where he is now—probably in the West River district. The chief of the political department of the Fourth

Front Red Army was Fu Chung. I was still in command of the army, but the highest military organization was the "Military Committee of the Northwest Revolutionary Army," of which Chang Kuo-t'ao was chairman.

We organized the new Thirty-third Red Army at this time, and our entire forces numbered about thirty-eight regiments, or sixty thousand men. Against these thirty-eight regiments the Whites mobilized about one hundred seventy regiments, including the troops of Yang Shên, Liu Hsiang, T'ien Tsung-yao, Têng Hsi-hou, Li Chia-yu, and Lo Tsai-tso. These were all native Szechuan armies—none of Chiang Kai-shek's troops were there. Liu Wen-hui did not fight against us. We estimated the total number of Szechuan White troops at that time as 250,000 men.

Because the fighting power of the Red Army was very strong, Liu Hsiang, the governor of the province, was extremely afraid of us. The Szechuan militarists prepared six routes to attack the Red Army: the first route was Liu Hsiang; the second, Yang Shên; the third, Li Chia-yu; the fourth, Lo Tsai-tso; the fifth, T'ien Tsung-yao; and the sixth, Têng Hsi-hou. We fought against this six-route campaign for ten months and defeated each one. During those ten months we killed and wounded at least one hundred thousand White soldiers. We ourselves had only ten thousand wounded in the hospitals, and I have no estimate of the number killed.

Since Liu Hsiang's was the strongest of the Szechuan armies, the Red Army used its main force in attacking this. The Red Army concentrated and closed in the soviets as a military policy for a driving attack, so that at the end we had only the small soviet district of Tungchiang and Wanyüan.

I will give you the details of our struggle against Governor Liu Hsiang in Szechuan:

After we had destroyed the armies of Yang Shên and Liu Ch'êng-hou and had expanded the soviet district to include fourteen hsien, our economic conditions improved greatly. Along with organizing the new Thirty-third Red Army, we also expanded the old Fourth, Ninth, Thirtieth, and Thirty-first Red Armies to include seven or eight regiments each. The victories of the Red Army, of course, had very much shaken the foundation of the Szechuan ruling class. Until we arrived, the militarist armies of Szechuan had quarreled and been in constant civil war. Now, however, they united to fight against a common danger—the Red Army. Therefore, the various Szechuan armies under the direction of Liu Hsiang were able to realize the united "Surrounding Campaign" in six columns, including altogether about one hundred seventy regiments.

This made our position difficult, the more so because the foundation of the new soviet had not had time to become well consolidated. Since the masses did not yet understand the meaning of revolution thoroughly, they could not struggle for the salvation of their soviets or, in the end, even for their own immediate interests. The masses were easily suppressed by the reactionary forces and subsided into passivity. The first difficulty in our position, then, was that the foundation of the soviets was weak and the masses did not know the meaning of revolution.

Our second difficulty was that, although our armed forces had expanded very much, the new recruits had had no experience in warfare and no training. Also, the line of defense was so long—about one thousand li—that the Red Army could not concentrate on the first line to annihilate the enemy. For this reason, we retreated under the enemy's attack, having no other possible way to create an opportunity to recover and use the tactics of "destroying the majority by the minority." Under these conditions we were obliged to fight for ten months. We always concentrated our main forces to attack Liu Hsiang's personal army, especially after we gave up Tungchiang city. At a place near Wanyüan we had very serious fighting with

Liu's troops. Every one of the enemy armies had severe losses, but Liu's suffered especially. At this time over one-third, and in places even two-thirds, of Liu Hsiang's men were wounded, killed, or captured by the Red Army.

Owing to the failure of the enemy's attack, we were able to choose a weak point in their line at Ch'innungkuan. We concentrated our main forces there and attacked fiercely, gaining a very good topographical position. We then pursued the White army and attacked continuously. The enemy retreated from their line on the east and we reoccupied most of the soviet region of Hsüanta. Because the enemy's right wing still had strong forces, we stopped our pursuit and moved part of our main forces westward, arriving in the southern part of Tungchiang on September 1. We concentrated our army on the front lines and from that central point destroyed Yang Shên, Li Chia-yu, and Lo Tsai-tso, and retook Pachou. We destroyed two brigades of T'ien Tsung-yao's army and also defeated Têng Hsi-hou's troops and followed him to the east bank of the Chialing River. The period from the time we concentrated our forces at the front in Ch'innungkuan to the time of our pursuit of Têng Hsi-hou was about one month.

After this warfare, both the Red and White armies were very tired and had lost much strength. It was necessary to get reinforcements, so no important fighting occurred for a while.

In order to supplement our numbers, we surrounded one regiment of Hu Tsung-nan's army. Then we went forward to Hanchung and expanded our troops there. After this we turned back to Nanch'ung and Ilung and liquidated the armies of Li Chia-yu and Lo Chê-chou.

The Long March from Szechuan

When we started the Long March in 1935, we made the very dangerous crossing over the Chialing River and defeated the forces of T'ien Tsung-yao and Têng Hsi-hou. We then occupied Nanch'ung, Chiehmêngkuan, Chienkê, Tzŭt'ung, and Hsinmin, and crossed the Peichiang River and besieged Chiangyu city.

The majority of our forces were concentrated in the Peichiang district. Many new recruits gladly flocked to join the Red Army. For instance, I remember that I had one hundred twenty men on my telephone staff. Within three days a hundred new telephone workers wanted to join this staff, and I had to send these workers to supplement the army. We had so many new recruits for the Red Army that within one month our forces had increased about two-fifths. At that time the Fourth Front Red Army had more than eighty thousand troops.

The First Front Red Army from Kiangsi had already crossed over the River of Golden Sand in Szechuan on their Long March. We sent one part of the Fourth Front Army to occupy Lifan and marched forward to Moukung [in Szechuan] to welcome the First Front Army. In June, we met the First Front Army at T'awei in Moukung *hsien*. All the campaigns of the ruling class of China to destroy the Red Armies had failed.

After meeting with the First Front Army at Moukung, one part of the armies remained there. The main forces divided into two routes and marched north. One route advanced to Paochow and Cho-chissŭ, and destroyed the enemy 49th Division. After this, in order to divide the enemy's forces, the First and Third Red Army Corps marched on northward to Shensi and Kansu. At the same time the Fourth Front Red Army and the Thirty-second Red Army, under Lo Ping-hui, turned into the T'ienlu [or Ti-chu] district and defeated the troops of Liu Hsiang and Têng Hsi-hou there, adding ten thousand new recruits to our army. In this period the situation in Chengtu, the Szechuan capital, was very bad for Liu Hsiang, and he was distracted from the anti-Red campaign. Chiang Kai-shek ordered the troops of Hsüeh Yüeh as reinforcements. These arrived at Yungyu.

In February 1936, we concentrated our forces in Sikang at such places as Taofu, Luho, Kantzǔ, Yachiang, K'angting, and several other *hsien*, and formed the "Special Independent Government of the Minorities." At that time the Second Front Red Army had begun its Long March from Hunan and crossed over the River of Golden Sand in Yünnan province. They passed through Pat'ang and at the end of June arrived in Kantzǔ and met our Fourth Front Red Army. In the beginning of July, we all began together the march to the north and for a month passed through the Great Grasslands. In the first part of August we arrived in southern Kansu in the region of Minchang, Weiyüan, Lunghsi, Wushan, and Lint'an, and destroyed many enemy troops of Liu Ta-chang, Li Yin, and T'ao Ssǔ-yeh—all these were Kuomintang division commanders.

In the beginning of October 1936 we met the First Front Red Army in the Huining district in Kansu.

Comments

Finally, let us discuss why the Red Army of China cannot be defeated and what power it has. Whether they support or oppose us, students of the political and military situation in China must recognize and admit the following points:

1. The Red Army of the people of China is led by the Communist party. It is supporting the general line of the proletarian class and acting for the liberation of the oppressed races and of the whole of mankind.

2. The Red Army comes from the masses of the peasants and workers, and a part of it has come from the revolutionary soldiers and officers of the White armies who rose against the higher command of the Whites.

3. The Red Army has strict discipline and organization.

4. The Red Army has the consciousness of its class; and its commanders and direct-

ing staff have the spirit of self-sacrifice and the spirit to struggle to the end. We have absolute faith that the final victory shall belong to us.

5. Because the Red Army represents the interests of the masses, it gets and can continue to get the support of the masses.

6. The Red Army is the most loyal force in China for the thorough salvation of the nation and of society, and it is determined to carry on this mission to the end.

7. The Red Army has the spirit of self-criticism in correcting any mistakes in the process of struggle. Therefore, from the rich collective experience of its staff of officers, each has the opportunity to express and develop his creative genius.

8. The Red Army has carried on the traditional spirit of the true Chinese Revolution and maintains the revolutionary spirit of the Whampoa Academy of the period of the Great Revolution.

We may also talk about the strategy of warfare as an evolutionary process in the struggle of the Fourth Front Red Army. The stages in this struggle were as follows:

The first stage began with the split of the Communist party and the Kuomintang in 1927. The peasants of Hupeh, Honan, and Anhwei, in order to struggle against the oppression of the ruling class, could not help having to arm themselves and to struggle. This was the basis of the partisan movement. Because there were many partisans in this district, the armies of Hsü Yüan-ch'ien and Hsia Tou-yin organized the First Surrounding Campaign against them. At this time the war was conducted by partisans, and all their tactics and strategy were of partisan nature.

Regarding such strategy and tactics, we have special books on these subjects and I need not discuss them in detail. I may point out one important point, however: Every time we made partisan warfare, it was because of the deep hatred of the masses for the ruling class. In spite of the strength of the enemy, and whether circumstances were good or bad, the masses always requested the Red Army to advance and fight for them because they hated the ruling class so intensely.

If our strategic position was good and our strength sufficient, the Red Army always responded to the demands of the masses and fought against the Whites. But sometimes the masses stood only on their own immediate interests, without regarding the Red Army's difficult circumstances or weakness, and the army was obliged to fight foolishly against White forces. If the commander of the Red Army could not handle this situation wisely, we always failed.

After every such failure in fighting many bad results were produced, such as the lowering of the morale of the fighters, the wasting of ammunition, and the lowering of the emotion of the masses themselves. In order to raise the morale of the people and the fighters and to replenish our ammunition, the only method was to search out weak enemy troops and gain a victory over them. Only after this could we again fight against the main forces of the enemy—otherwise the Red Army might fail again.

The period from the First Campaign of the ruling class in the Oyüwan area to our defeat in the Second Campaign saw a great expansion of the partisan movement. Tactics and strategy improved very much and the regular Red Army was formed. This, of course, resulted in the mobilization of the enemy against us. The strategy adopted by the Red Army was to move continually, destroy the enemy at one point, and then move on quickly to destroy the enemy at another point. I remember how at Suan-chao-chen

we surrounded the enemy and cut off their rear while the White commander, Yao Wei-chün, was still giving orders to his men, unaware of what had happened; his bodyguard even took his horse and escaped before Yü realized the situation, and by that time he was our captive. This instance indicates the usual stupidity of the White army command at that time and the wavering morale of its troops. Such things could never happen to a Red army.

During the period of the Third Campaign the enemy Whites had so many failures that they finally learned to correct their errors. Their tactics improved, more or less. They learned to stay placed in positional warfare and did not venture out one single step. Our strategy, therefore, was to surround the important points of the White army's position with many troops in order to cut off all reinforcements and sources of supplies. In short, the strategy of the Red Army was a moving, maneuvering warfare. This always achieved good results.

After we arrived in Szechuan Province, the Red Army, because of the topographical circumstances, took up position in a long line. We then used the strategy of the "night raid" and the "destruction of the central point" in breaking the enemy's position. The Red Army's strategy always improved with experience and its development followed the changes in the objective material conditions. Although we have had much experience in these ten years of warfare, still the commanders and staff of the Red Army feel that it is not enough. We must continue to learn from theory and action in order to improve our knowledge.

Lin Piao

MASTER STRATEGIST

Lin Piao, self-assured and affable—at least during this moment in Yenan, in 1937.

Miss Wales:

THE Communists consider that Lin Piao, now only in his forties, ranks with the half-dozen military geniuses of recent Chinese history. Even in 1937, when I first talked with him, he was regarded as the most expert and original tactician among all the military men; later his manuals and treatises on "maneuvering warfare" were translated and used as textbooks in Russia and some Asiatic countries. His "short attack" was regarded by the Chinese Communists as the chief tactical contribution to their successes in the Chinese civil war.

Lin Piao told me in 1937 that he was a veteran of a hundred battles and had never once been defeated when he led the First Army Corps. When I asked how he could be infallible, he smiled and raised his heavy black brows. "We never engage the enemy," he answered, "unless we are certain of victory."

He is one of the founders of the Red Army, having participated in the Nanchang Uprising in 1927, when his division of the Fourth Army,

together with Ho Lung's Twentieth Army and Yeh T'ing's Eleventh Army—all "Ironsides" soldiers of the best Kuomintang unit—went over to the Communists.

In February 1938 Lin Piao was seriously wounded during a skirmish with Kuomintang troops but recovered. His military record during the war with Japan was particularly brilliant, and he was credited with Japan's first defeat, the critical battle of Pinghsingkuan. At the end of the Japanese war, he was given the post of commander in chief in Manchuria, where in 1948 he controlled 300,000 troops and a civilian population of thirty millions. In 1949 he commanded in the taking-over of the Peking-Tientsin area and the capture of Wuhan. He then became commander of the Central China Military Headquarters, retaining command of the Fourth Field Army. In 1949 he was appointed to the Revolutionary Military Council, and was elected to the fifty-eight-man Government Council in Peking.

163

LIN PIAO:

I was born in Huangan, Hupeh, in 1908, of a lower middle-class family. My father owned a small handcraft factory which he opened at the time of the first World War. Afterward, because of the heavy taxes imposed by local militarists, he was forced to close the factory, and worked as purser on a river steamship. I have not seen my father since I joined the revolution and do not know whether he is still alive. I entered school at the age of nine, spent five years in primary school, registered in middle school in 1921, and graduated in 1924. In 1924 I entered Whampoa Academy, where I studied under General Galen and Chiang Kai-shek, graduating in 1925. I participated in the Northern Expedition with the Fourth Army, first as a lieutenant and later, in the same year, as a captain. The Fourth Army was historic for its Hunan campaign and its insurrection after the Wuhan government turned counterrevolutionary. Under Yeh T'ing, my division of the Fourth Army and one division of the Eleventh Army, together with Ho Lung's Twentieth Army, staged the uprising at Nanchang which began the Communist revolution. At that time, however, we still called ourselves the Kuomintang Army. The Nanchang Uprising was unsuccessful and Ho and Yeh next moved our troops to Swatow, where we were defeated. From there we went to southern Hunan. The remnant was then only a thousand men. Here we changed the name to the "Workers' and Peasants' Army" and for the first time adopted the Red Flag. That was in December 1927. I have fought with the Red Army since that time.

I had joined the Socialist Youth in Shanghai before entering Whampoa. In 1925, as president of Whampoa, Chiang Kai-shek ordered the students to join either the Kuomintang or the Communist party and said that they could not be members of both; those who were Communists must resign from the Kuomintang, or vice versa, making a choice. All the members of the Socialist Youth were then automatically made members of the Communist Youth League. After Chiang's order, therefore, I resigned from the Kuomintang and joined the Communist party.

I participated in the march on Chingkangshan, in March 1928, where the first soviet was formed, and there I first made a name for myself. From Chingkangshan I moved to Ningtu and Juikin, and then to Shihch'êng on the border of Fukien and Kiangsi. In 1929 I was made commander of the Fourth Red Army, with Chu Tê as commander in chief and Mao Tsê-tung as political commissar. In January 1932, at the age of twenty-five, I was made commander of the First Army Corps, with Nieh Jung-chên as political commissar. In March 1932 an Eastern Front Army was organized and began the Eastern Expedition to Amoy: this army was the First and Fifth Army Corps, and I was its commander. I have now [1937] been in more than a hundred battles.

Nieh Ho-t'ing

CHIEF OF STAFF TO LIN PIAO

Three Red Army commanders, photographed at Yenan, in 1937: Nieh Ho-t'ing (center), with Pien Chang-wu and Ho Ch'ang-kung.

MISS WALES:

FROM the time of the founding of the Red Army, Nieh Ho-t'ing was the close friend and military associate of Lin Piao, serving under him first as political director (or commissar) and later as chief of staff.

Nieh was tall, handsome, and proud of his appearance in uniform. In Yenan, where most uniforms were never ironed but simply spread out flat to dry after being washed, the care that Nieh Ho-t'ing gave his clothes was exceptional: his uniforms always looked as though they had just been pressed—as indeed they might have been. Though his spruceness could be attributed to vanity or to military training, Nieh had grounds for pride in having been one of the founders of the Red Army. Like his colleagues Lin Piao and Chêng Kên, he took pleasure in his background of specialized training and participation in the Nanchang Uprising. Like Lin and Chêng, he was of middle-class origin. His story may offer and clarify some conjectures as to why such officers as these rejected the Kuomintang and Chiang Kai-shek (commandant at Whampoa), to join the Communist forces.

During the Northern Expedition of 1926–27, the Kuomintang had ten armies. Of these, the only one to achieve distinction in the expedition was General Chang Fa-k'uei's "Ironsides." Chang's troops were the Second Army Corps, composed of Fourth, Eleventh, and Twentieth Armies; the "Ironsides" also had a cadet training regiment, the *chao tao t'uan* which staged the Canton Commune of December 1927. The Nanchang Uprising on August 1, 1927, which is remembered as the occasion of the founding of the Red Army, was staged chiefly by Ho Lung's Twentieth Army, Yeh T'ing's Eleventh Army, and Lin Piao's division of the Fourth Army. Thus, in transferring their support to the Communists at Nanchang, these "Ironsides" armies contributed the Kuomintang's best soldiers and outstanding Whampoa cadets to the Communist side and provided the nucleus for the Red Army.

Nieh Ho-t'ing was a participant in both the Nanchang Uprising and the Canton Commune.

NIEH HO-T'ING:

I WAS born in Fuyuan, Anhwei, in 1908. My family were small landlords during my grandfather's time, but when I was born my father was a middle peasant having forty *mu* of land and owed debts of seven hundred to eight hundred dollars. I entered primary school at the age of seven. At fourteen I studied at a missionary school, the Han Mei middle school of Fuyuan. A year later I en-

165

tered the Anching normal school and graduated in two years. I was student representative and a member of the student government. There were already some Communists in the school, and I was influenced by them. I read the *A.B.C. of Communism* and the *Leader*, a Left-Wing magazine. While I was in the student government we organized a movement against Tsao K'un, who was bribing the representatives in parliament. Anching students surrounded the headquarters of the *tuchun*[1] and the guards killed two students. An order was issued for my arrest. I fled to Nanchang, where I entered the military academy of Fang Wen-pen, *tuchun* of Kiangsi. A leftist schoolmate wrote a letter introducing me to the Communist circles in Shanghai and I went there, working with Kao I-han, a party leader.

After the May Thirtieth Movement in 1925, I was sent to Anching to organize students, and there became teacher in a private middle school, where I worked a year and a half. During this time I visited once in Shanghai and there joined the Communist party. This was in 1925 or 1926. There were about ten Kuomintang members and three Communists in Anching, and we co-operated in organizing the students. When I returned to Shanghai, the Northern Expedition had already begun. I was sent to Hofei, Anhwei, by the party. The encirclement of Wuhan had begun and Nanchang was already taken. Our Anhwei troops reinforced the front; the rear was empty. In Hofei I made a connection in the Sixth Middle School, together with another comrade from Shanghai. We were introduced by the middle school to the *min t'uan* in the west of Anhwei. There were about one hundred seventy or one hundred eighty of them and they had one hundred ten rifles. A landlord's son in this district was a leftist, a returned student from Japan. Through him we made a connection with the *hsien* guards in Hofei. We won over about one hundred men to our side by propaganda. In August we began an uprising and raised

the Kuomintang banner, occupying a town. But because we lacked experience, the soldiers had not been reorganized or educated and discipline was very bad. After seizing the town in Hofei *hsien* we simply raised the banner and nothing else happened. On the third day a battalion from Hofei attacked us and we were defeated. The *hsien* guards compromised, the *min t'uan* fled, the local comrades hid, and only my Shanghai comrade and I were left.

We two went together farther west in Hofei. We had only twelve coppers as our combined resources. After a day's travel we learned from the peasants that Kiukiang in Kiangsi had been captured and that the Anhwei troops were retreating. Disguising ourselves as defeated Anhwei personnel, we walked along the road back to Hofei. We first went to take a bath in a public bath and there found the guard commander who had co-operated in the uprising. Next day we hastily went on to Shanghai and made a connection with the Communist party.

Wuhan was still being surrounded by southern troops, and the party helped us to join the Northern army. En route to Wuhan, we returned to Anching and collected fourteen other students. Fearing inspection on the steamers, we disguised ourselves. When we reached Wuchang, we found it had already been captured. Kao I-han had preceded us. We now entered the Party school, but two weeks later I was called to work in the army as platoon commander in Yeh T'ing's Independent Regiment, where party organization was excellent.

When the Hsü K'ê-hsiang affair[2] occurred in 1927, we returned to defend Hankow. Yeh T'ing, with one division and one regiment, defeated Hsia Tou-yin, who had threatened Wuhan. Since Chiang Kai-shek was now openly against us and in Wuhan the Kuomintang Leftists had begun their opposition to the Communists, Yeh T'ing decided to attack Nanchang. Yeh T'ing had been commander in chief of all the revolutionary forces fighting Hsia Tou-yin, who had been responsible for the Hsü K'ê-hsiang mutiny in Changsha.

As our troops moved on the road to Kwangchow, we held a meeting outside of Nanchang and disarmed part of the troops, who, however, joined us. We now staged the Nanchang Uprising, the 24th and 25th Kuomintang divisions joining in. I was platoon commander, and later, after I was wounded, company commander.

After Hailufeng we went to south Kiangsi, where Lin Piao became commander of our reorganized 1st Detachment. I was his political director. Chu Tê was commander in chief and Yeh T'ing his vice-commander. Discipline was a problem. Chiang Kai-shek tried to induce Kuomintang men to return to Shanghai. The party sent me to Shanghai and then to Canton, where I joined the *chao tao tuan* [training regiment] cadets of Chang Fa-k'uei's army in staging the Canton Commune.[3] I was divisional staff officer in the reorganization of the Red Army following the defeat in Canton.

After a short time, I returned to Shanghai and worked there nearly three years. About 1930 I was sent to the soviet districts, where I became a regimental commander. There I was wounded in the Second Campaign and was transferred to the post of chief of staff of the 11th Division, later holding the same post in the Twelfth Army. During the fighting at Kanchow, I was an instructor in a new mobile military school which moved with the troops. After the Ningtu uprising, the East Route Army was organized, with the First and Fifth Army Corps as the basis. I participated in the attack on Changchow.

During the Fifth Campaign, I was divisional chief of staff. After the Red Army entered Kansu I was appointed vice-commander of Front Army headquarters. After the Eastern Expedition I became chief of staff to the First Front Army headquarters.

PART FIVE

Doctors

Fu Lien-chang

CHRISTIAN COMMUNIST

Fu Lien-chang, chief of the Central Medical Bureau, in Yenan, 1937. The women nurses, unusual in the Red armies, were attached to the Fourth Front Army in Szechuan and made the Long March with the troops.

MISS WALES:

THE first doctor to volunteer with the Communist-led armies was a second-generation Christian, Dr. Fu Lien-chang, who had been a victim of tuberculosis for twenty years at the time I interviewed him in 1937. He was much loved in the army, I found, and had saved countless lives. Besides being a physician and surgeon, he was an evangelist and a strong humanitarian, as you could tell immediately.

When I went with my interpreter to call at the office which he occupied as director of the Central Medical Bureau, he looked up in astonishment at seeing a foreigner. Then he jumped up and welcomed me in difficult English and gave me a long lecture on Christian ethics in relation to the attitude of Westerners toward colonial civil wars. While we were talking Chêng Kên of the First Army Corps came in—he had once been Chiang Kai-shek's aide-de-camp. He and the doctor embraced with great affection. It turned out that Dr. Fu had saved Chêng Kên's life when he was wounded, in 1927.

The combination of Christianity and Communism in Dr. Fu Lien-chang, who is truly overflowing with humanitarian impulses, makes his story unusual.

FU LIEN-CHANG:

TINGCHOW, Fukien, is my native town. I was born there in 1895. My family were Christians of the London Mission, and belonged to the poor laboring class. When I was young, the English mission doctors agreed to help me study medicine, as I was a destitute but promising Christian. My wife was also helped by missionaries as a girl and became a teacher. I am one of the earliest members of the Chinese Medical Club, or Po Yi Hui, organized by Sir William Osler of Oxford.

I was a very ardent Christian from childhood and I still believe in enlightened Christianity. I used to wonder why organized Christianity stopped short at charity and never solved any of the social problems of China, although it had a great influence before the Boxer Rebellion. It seemed to me that it made the Chinese nonresistant, and although a Christian did not cheat other people, he was easily cheated by them.

My first criticism of Christianity, however, came in 1927. At that time the troops under Yeh T'ing and Ho Lung came to Tingchow two weeks after the Nanchang Uprising and asked to send their wounded to our mission hospital during their stay of two weeks. Both the Chinese and foreign doctors, however, all ran away and refused to render any assistance. This made me very angry for two reasons: First, my colleagues were all supposedly good Christians, yet they refused to help the wounded and suffering and cared nothing for humanitarianism when the word "Red" came into their minds.

171

Second, I thought it showed a total absence of professional honor for doctors to discriminate between the wounded on a political basis. I stayed alone at the hospital and took care of three hundred patients from the Red Army, with the aid only of the teachers and students of the primary school. At that time I saved the life of Chêng Kên,[1] who had a wounded leg.

I was the first doctor to volunteer with the Red Army. As soon as I talked with the Communist leaders, I knew they had the true spirit of saving mankind and I decided to join with them. I have never regretted a minute of it, though my own daughter—at the age of twenty-one, and not a Communist —was executed because of me. Her husband also was executed. At that time my wife and my three other children were taken to Kwangtung by a friend; they are still living there, and I send letters to them. Lo Ting-yi's wife was executed. My friend T'ang I-chên, a pharmacist, was executed. Four of my medical students were executed in Tingchow—also many, many others of my acquaintance. Two of my students in Tingchow joined the Red Army with me.

Yeh T'ing and Ho Lung left Tingchow and went to Kwangtung, but I could not leave then as I had too many patients to care for and would not desert them. I secretly joined the local party. In 1928 Chu Tê and Mao Tsê-tung came to the Fukien-Kiangsi border with two thousand soldiers, and I joined the Red Army then.

One influence on my mind was a small book by Ch'ü Ch'iu-po called *Hsin Shê Hui Kuan*, or "Study of a New Society." I saw that the new society of China must be based upon these principles. Of course, my own economic background was of the poor, unpropertied class. Later the author and I became good friends. He was a great man. He was a delegate from Shanghai to the Second Soviet Congress in Juikin, early in 1934. In the same year he was captured by the Kuomintang in a village near Tingchow. A Red soldier betrayed his identity and he was executed. When the Long March began

in October 1934, Ch'ü had stayed behind with a part of the Red Army. At the same time, others were captured and executed: Liu Po-chien, a returned student from Germany—he had been the head of Fêng Yü-hsiang's political department before joining the Red Army and had helped to prepare the Ningtu uprising; Chou Yi-li, then head of the political department of the Red Army; and Ho Ch'ang, vice-chairman of the political department of the Red Army.

I was head of the medical work in the First Campaign. During that time one of the two students who had volunteered with me died. The other, Dr. Chung Fu-ch'ang, is with me now. Tingchow was then Red [territory] but not a soviet. The Red Army captured many doctors from enemy territory and several of them joined voluntarily and are still with us. At this time, I trained twenty doctors and sixty nurses at the Central Hospital and Medical School, in Kiangsi, while I was superintendent. This teaching work was later turned over to a doctor who came from Shanghai. I had organized this hospital and school when the Nineteenth Route Army attacked us in 1933.

At the time of the Second All-Soviet Congress, in 1934, I organized a special medical corps to take care of the delegates, and in April of that year I started a national hospital. Our medical work was just getting into its stride. For instance, in Juikin, on August 1, during a big meeting on the anniversary of the Nanchang Uprising, three Kuomintang planes came and bombed. More than ten were wounded, and ten were killed. In a few minutes the wounded were being taken care of in the hospital. The top authorities came to visit them to show fraternal regard.

In October [1934] we began the Long March. I worked the whole time as physician and surgeon, though I have had tuberculosis for twenty years, and I feel better now than ever. In Tingchow I used to earn two hundred dollars a month and saw only a few high-class patients. Now I never have a spare minute, but my health and spirits are better than in those days when I was young. On the Long March no high officials had chairs to carry them, but as a doctor I had to have one to conserve my strength. Once while climbing a mountain, I could not use the chair and my horse [I was riding] fell into a river. I nearly drowned, but some-one saved me.

I crossed the Grasslands three times to help the wounded, and the Great Snow Mountains seven times. I was with Chu Tê in the Grasslands and also in Sikang—we stayed there three months in the summer but snow fell even then.

It was important to give first aid and a stimulant to patients in crossing the Snow Mountains. Doctors were vitally needed there, as well as in the Grasslands. I think the worst problem was the mountain sickness in the Great Snow Mountains because of the rarefied air and the cold. Many died, though we were able to save others. A great many of our people now have heart trouble from the Long March, and others have nervous troubles from the strain, but we seldom have cases of shell shock from bombing. Just after the Long March we had numerous cases of ulceration of the feet and legs because of bad conditions, wounds, and general anemia.

Because of the blockade, I could buy only one thousand dollars' worth of medical supplies and equipment in preparation for the Long March. One of my best doctors was executed by Ch'ên Chi-t'ang in Canton in 1934—he was caught trying to buy medical supplies. The problem of getting medical supplies has always been extremely difficult. For instance, for one tin of alcohol costing seven dollars we have had to pay forty dollars to the merchants who smuggle it in. We could easily save eighty percent of the wounded if we had medical supplies. Most of our wounded die from lack of medicine and nourishing food, rather than from their wounds. All we can guarantee our wounded is loving and comradely care from our truly splendid nurses—and this means a great deal to the morale of the soldiers. Most of

the wounded in the Kuomintang armies die because they receive no good nursing. For small operations we use only a local anes-thetic but we always try to have a general anesthetic for major ones.

Here is an instance of the treatment we give: In 1936 there was the beginning of a typhoid epidemic in the Fourth Front Army in Kansu, but because of good nursing, only two of twenty patients died. The nurses are usually boys under eighteen, but the Fourth Front Army had two thousand women from Szechuan serving as nurses—all of them were married to army personnel.

There are now sixty thousand army people in Yenan and only ten trained doctors! We need trained midwives for the local people, too, and any and all kinds of doctors, of any political complexion.

In Kiangsi, Kwangtung, and Hunan, ma-laria and dysentery were scourges. In Sze-chuan, Kansu, and Shensi we have mainly dysentery, typhoid, and influenza. In Sikang our chief cases were mountain sickness, indi-gestion, typhoid, and trachoma. In Yünnan, Kweichow, and Szechuan, thyroid trouble developed because of lack of iodine; the local people often have goiters.

Plague is endemic. In north Shensi, chol-era and meningitis are prevalent, and syphi-lis has always been more prevalent there than elsewhere because of dirty conditions—under our law, all married couples are in-spected to check this. We give free treat-ment to the people. Vaccinations for other diseases are also free. So far, only ten of our soldiers have become infected with syphilis, as we are very strict on this matter. About ninety percent of our soldiers are sexually inexperienced. We have no problem of im-morality as the men are too tired and too busy, and are constantly concentrated on fighting or training. No diseased person could keep up with the life of the rank and file soldiers—they have to stay healthy or die. There is no conservatism toward foreign medicine in the army. All the men demand modern medicine if it is available. They like anything modern and scientific.

Chi P'êng-fei

AN ARMY DOCTOR

Chi P'êng-fei, chief of the Red Army Rear Medical Department, in Yenan, 1937.

MISS WALES:

THE Ningtu uprising, on December 14, 1931, was the most important revolt within the Kuomintang armies and caused Chiang Kai-shek to reorganize all his armies on a more efficient basis. Among the twenty thousand troops of Fêng Yü-hsiang's old Kuominchün "Big Swords" who were involved in the uprising, was Dr. Chi P'êng-fei, then a captain of the Medical Detachment, and four other doctors who joined the Communists.

Chi became chief of the Rear Medical Department in the Communist-led armies. He was a typical army doctor when I met him in Yenan. It is reported that he later became a general. In 1950 he was appointed Chinese ambassador to the East German Republic.

CHI P'ÊNG-FEI:

I WAS born in Yungchi, Shansi, in 1910, of a family that were then middle peasants but later became poor. I went to a middle school in Yünch'êng, Shansi, and also to one in Sian, Shensi, but did not graduate from either. I then entered the Sian Army Hospital in 1926 to study in a medical training class for army doctors.

On graduation, I joined the Second Army of the Kuominchün as a doctor. This force was commanded by Hu Chin-yi, while Fêng Yü-hsiang [general commander of the Kuominchün armies] was in personal command of the First Army—Fêng was then in Nankow, near Peking, fighting the Fengtien troops from the Northeast.

After a year, part of the Second Army was disarmed in Honan by Liu Chêng-hua, and I joined Liu's army, which was later under Wu P'ei-fu. Liu's territory was Shensi

174

and Honan. I was with him for eight months in 1927–28. During those eight months he besieged Sian, with Yang Hu-ch'êng bottled up within. Food inside the city became scarce, and the civilians were all sent out, leaving only Yang's two divisions of troops inside. Still, Liu couldn't take the walled city. Then Fêng Yü-hsiang returned by way of Paotow and Wuyuan and defeated Liu at Sian, releasing the city. On the East Gate of Sian, Fêng opened a new gate and closed the old one, but nobody ever knew why.

The majority of Liu's troops were disarmed or dispersed by Fêng, and I rejoined Fêng's army, in the 10th Division directly under Fêng. I then transferred to the Fifth Route Army, which was disarmed by Chiang Kai-shek in the fight between him and Fêng in 1929, in Honan. After this I went with a group to join the Twenty-sixth Route Army of Fêng Yü-hsiang, commanded by Sun Lien-chung. This army was reorganized by Chiang Kai-shek when he defeated Fêng, but I continued to work in it.

After a stay in Shantung, the Twenty-sixth Route Army went to Kiangsi to fight the Reds in 1931. It was now under Chiang Kai-shek. We began to fight constantly as soon as we arrived, being first at Nanchang, then at I-fang, and finally at Ningtu. We were not defeated by the Red Army—we disarmed two regiments and captured a number of guns—but our soldiers did not have much interest in fighting because of their sympathy for the ideas of revolution. Every day many of our soldiers deserted to the Red Army even before the Ningtu uprising.

The soldiers of the Twenty-sixth Route Army were natives of northern provinces, chiefly the very poor provinces of Shensi and Kansu, and their families were all poor. In 1925–27, many Communists joined this army and did propaganda, so that after the army was reorganized under Chiang Kai-shek the soldiers were discontented. They all hoped to return to the north, but Chiang ordered them to Kiangsi, wanting to destroy

this army by hurling it against the Red Army. He never trusted the Kuominchün. It was treated worse than other armies, too —we received bad food and for three months had no pay. The men hated Chiang Kai-shek very much, for one reason or another. The men liked Fêng Yü-hsiang—he treated them as his own sons and always had a good relation with the rank and file—but they felt no loyalty to Chiang Kai-shek.

We stayed in Ningtu quite a while and there was much sickness, twenty men dying every day. At the same time, the anti-Japanese emotion of the men was high as this was just after the Mukden Incident of September 18, 1931. They sent telegrams to Chiang Kai-shek asking to be sent north to fight the Japanese. Chiang refused, of course.

There were other reasons why the soldiers had neither fighting will nor power. Sun Lien-chung had left Ningtu for Nanking, saying he was sick and needed a rest and also that when in Nanking he would get Chiang Kai-shek to order the army north to fight Japan. His absence intensified internal conflicts. There were two divisions in the Twenty-eighth Army, the 25th and the 27th, totaling twenty thousand men. Sun had personally commanded the 25th. When he went to Nanking he appointed Li Tsung-k'un, one of the three brigade commanders, to his post. Li's rival, Chi Chên-t'ung, who was very active, did not like this and was insubordinate. The chief of staff of the Twenty-sixth Army was Ts'ao Pao-sun, secretly a Communist party member. He took this opportunity to get Chi Chên-t'ung to unite with the other brigade commander, Tung Chêng-t'ang, against the new chief, Li Tsung-k'un.

One day the Red Army attacked Ningtu but failed to take the city. Then Ts'ao Pao-sun called a secret meeting to prepare the uprising. Tung Chêng-t'ang showed a tendency toward joining the Communists. This whole uprising of twenty thousand troops was organized by only ten Communist party members, though the soldiers did not know they were Communists. None of the common soldiers and only ten of the officers were Communists. The most important of the Communist officers were: Li Ch'ing-yün, a company commander—he was killed in Kiangsi in 1934; Ma Liang-jui, a lieutenant —now in Kiangsi; Yüan Hsieh-tso, chief secretary to the staff—now in Kiangsi; and Liu Chên-ya, a squad commander.

The Communists had been active, always talking with the common soldiers at meals and telling them that it was wrong to fight the Red Army and that we should go north to fight the Japanese. They also said that the power of the Communists was very strong and that if we fought them we should have no future, for they were sure to win out in the end, even if we won a few battles.

Tung Chêng-t'ang now joined the Communist party and at the same time Chiang Kai-shek discovered the whole plan and the names of all the party members except Ts'ao Pao-sun. He sent a telegram on December 13 to Ts'ao Pao-sun ordering him to arrest the eight persons on the list. Ts'ao kept this telegram secret but called a secret meeting to discuss the plan for the uprising. Originally the uprising had been slated for the sixteenth, but now no time could be lost, so it broke out on December 14, the next day.

Chiang Kai-shek had appointed a military adviser named Chu, and on the eve of the uprising, Ts'ao asked Chu to invite all the lower and higher officers to have dinner with him. About forty officers came to dinner— this being the night of the thirteenth. They talked over the problem of fighting the Reds. Ts'ao and other Communists said that we couldn't fight Japan if we continued to fight the Reds. The response showed the attitude of each officer. About thirty percent wanted to stop the civil war. The soldiers had advance orders from Ts'ao and surrounded the dinner party, Ts'ao ordering them to arrest about ten officers who wanted to continue the attack on the Reds. Then the purpose of the uprising was explained to all the officers.

Meantime, headquarters had also been surrounded at nine o'clock by my regiment, but Li Tsung-k'un escaped in disguise.

One regiment of the army was stationed sixty li from Ningtu and their officer did not come to the dinner, so when the uprising began this regiment ran away and did not join the uprising, not knowing what it was all about.

On the morning of the fourteenth, the officers were set free and new officers replaced them. News was reported that the Red Army was on its way to join us. This uprising had been planned by Liu Po-chien, who was the liaison in the Red Army—thus communications were good. He was chief of the political department of the Red Army. In 1925–27 Liu had been chief of the political department of Fêng Yü-hsiang's army, and he and many officers under Sun Lien-chung had good relations. Liu was later killed—in Kiangsi in 1935.

During the night the local people did not know what was happening but next morning they were pleased and were not afraid. Many raised red flags. During the night a few soldiers took property from rich people but afterward the army gave it back to keep discipline. We did not have time to confiscate the rich because the plan was made in such a hurry and Chiang Kai-shek's army was so near. We had time only to gather up a hundred prisoners and go, and we were not sure what to do with them.

At nine o'clock that morning—December 14, 1931—the army started to march out of Ningtu to the soviet district at Ku-k'ou. Both divisions joined—all the twenty thousand men except the outpost regiment.

We took along to the soviet districts about a hundred landlords and leading merchants of Ningtu, including the mayor, all very much terrified. Chiang Kai-shek's adviser, Chu, was also taken under arrest, but was given money and set free, and he went back to report to Chiang.

At Kuk'ou, Liu Po-chien came to a big mass meeting and made a speech, explaining to the troops the meaning of the uprising and the principles of the Red Army. Then the Twenty-sixth Army was reorganized into the Fifth Army Corps of the Red Army, with two other armies, under command of Chi Chên-t'ung.

The hundred prisoners were released, after many of them had paid money. None were killed. The mayor paid ten or twenty thousand dollars to get his freedom and the others paid several hundred dollars.

We did not change uniforms the night of the uprising, waiting until we met the Red Army. We had no slogans, but the soldiers were all happy, especially after Liu's speech at Kuk'ou, and there they repeated his slogans: "Down with Chiang Kai-shek!" "Long Live the Revolution!" "Long Live the Communist Party!" "Welcome to the Whites to Join the Reds!" Liu talked about the Mukden Incident and also about the foolish policy of Fêng Yü-hsiang in making his soldiers simple-minded with feudal personal loyalty instead of giving them a real political consciousness. All twenty thousand were present at this mass meeting—including myself, of course.

At Kuk'ou we also received good food and many comforts from the Red Army, and they welcomed us with slogans. Meantime we changed to the Red Flag and the Red uniform.

The Ningtu uprising was the biggest ever held by soldiers who wanted to join the Red Army. The whole Twenty-sixth Army joined except five thousand stationed in the rear at Nanchang city and the regiment of one thousand who were at an outpost and were not informed. All the soldiers stationed in Ningtu joined and all officers but ten. However, when we marched from Kuk'ou to Tzǔch'i, many officers wanted to return home. Their wish was granted and several hundred officers left, but no soldiers deserted. The Red Army at that time sent political workers to reorganize the army. After this the army fought very well and never ran away from battle. I hear that now

only about a thousand are left. The force in this uprising became the main armed power of the Red Army at that time and was considered a good army. It was the only positional force, other units maneuvering around it. The remnant is now in the West River district with the Fifth Army.

In Ningtu I was captain of the medical department. I was informed about the uprising before it happened and was sympathetic, for my regiment was ordered to surround the headquarters and to guard the street. Because I had received political training during the 1925–27 revolution, I already had a clear concept of the Communist ideology. I joined the Red Army voluntarily, but only four other doctors stayed with me, the rest going home with the officers.

I left Tzǔch'i for Chupao, where I rested two months. Then the fighting for Changchow, Fukien, began. At this time our secret police discovered that our commander, Chi Chên-t'ung, had secret relations with the local Fukien militarists. He was an opportunist, thinking to lead the army to Kwangtung to join the Kwangtung provincial army. When Changchow was occupied, Chi was arrested and also two other persons, Huang Chung-yü and Hsiao Shih-tsui. Tung Chêngt'ang was now made commander of the Fifth Army Corps, and Ts'ao Pao-sun vice-commander. Tung Chêng-t'ang was killed in March 1937, fighting Ma Hung-p'ing and Ma Hung-k'uei. He was my friend. He had become very famous and was a good Communist.

The three plotters confessed frankly, and two of them, who repented, were sent to Juikin where they studied at the Red Academy and were given special work to do such as taking care of books. They also received ten dollars a month salary, which was higher than usual. But Hsiao Shih-tsui was executed for treason because he was the chief plotter and would not repent.

The lessons of the Ningtu uprising are these: that even a small party organization can influence a large body of troops; that economic conditions determine the subjective attitude of men in armies, as elsewhere —the Kuominchün were easily influenced by Communist propaganda because they had poor food and clothes and pay, and came of poor families; that the opportunist will always fail—as in the case of Chi Chên-t'ung; that officers cannot influence an army which has received political training; that this uprising was an important incident—causing Chiang Kai-shek to change his whole military plan and to reorganize all his armies, fearing mutiny everywhere, thus bringing about more efficient and modern organization in the Kuomintang forces; that, although the Kuomintang troops had been told that the Red Army was very cruel, the handling of the Ningtu officers proved to the outside that this was not true—the released officers went back and told the real story, and also the mayor of Ningtu and the landlords who were freed spread the story of what they knew, which was not unfavorable; and that—as my own experience and that of the other doctors proved—although the medical equipment of the Kuomintang armies was better, the medical work and the health of the Red armies were much better than theirs because of good nursing and because of organized public health work, which was never done by the Kuomintang armies in the places where they were stationed.

I stayed with my own army of the Ningtu uprising, leaving Changchow in 1933 to attack Kwangtung. We were the main force of all, then, and we destroyed many Kwangtung troops. At this time the Fifth Army Corps co-operated with the Third Army Corps in every campaign. At Huangp'o we surrounded two divisions and destroyed them, capturing the two division commanders—one died from wounds; the other is now a teacher in the Red Academy here in Yenan.

After Huangp'o we fought every day and in many noted battles. When the "Fifth Campaign" began, the Fifth Army Corps was reinforced by new troops from other armies. After that we started on the Long March, which was very difficult, especially in the Grasslands. During the Long March I was transferred to the Medical Department of the Military Committee, and in Szechuan I left with Mao Tsê-tung for north Shensi. I am now chief of this department. Every regiment has a medical officer. We now have one hundred doctors—only ten are qualified, however—and three hundred trained nurses, but we need many, many more. We do not care whether they are Communists or not.

Medical work was extremely difficult on the Long March. We were always in the rear, which is not the safest position. We had many patients, and a lack of medicine and food, but we continued to try to do ordinary work. It was hardest for the nurses, of whom he had about a thousand. Most of these were boys; only a few were women. They had to prepare meals, wash feet and clothes, rub bodies, and the like. The boys are usually from twelve or thirteen to eighteen years of age. They are the true heroes of the Long March, working hard with a good spirit and never showing fear.

PART SIX

*People of the
Theater*

Ts'ao Ping-san

ACTOR AND DIRECTOR

Ts'ao Ping-san, director of the dramatic society in Yenan, 1937, with the leading boy actor Liu Chih and two young actresses.

MISS WALES:

TS'AO PING-SAN was director of the Dramatic Society in Yenan and also the leading actor of the theater. His stellar role was Ah Q in Hsü Hsin-tzŭ's dramatization of Lu Hsün's *The True Story of Ah Q*. I saw an extremely effective production of this play in Yenan. It is a satire on the old Chinese psychology of "face." Ah Q is the village hired man constantly beaten down but always rationalizing his position as morally superior to his social superiors. Ah Q always considered it superior to run away with dignity rather than be defeated in fisticuffs.

In the Communist regions, art was a weapon cut down to its barest cutting edge. The actors had few properties and very little plot to carry the play for them. On that bare stage they had to respond to a high test of histrionic ability. The actor *was* the play, and the acting was amazingly good. The audience did not mind

the crudest kind of propaganda in the play, but when it came to judging the acting, they were critical and discriminating to a degree. This is a survival of the attitude toward the old theater in China, in which virtuosos vied in the interpretation of parts handed down for generations. Ts'ao Ping-san was the favorite actor and measured up to what was required by the local critics as well.

This is the story of a gifted actor who had never had leisure to develop his personal talents. He had been among bandits, had helped organize the Tayeh Uprising, had stayed in Kiangsi, where he was captured after the Long March, and finally had arrived in Sian in time for the capture of Chiang Kai-shek. Meantime he had gone without food and suffered so many narrow escapes, that his health was seriously injured.

TS'AO PING-SAN:

MY father was a small merchant but very poor. I was born in Yuchih *hsien* in Shansi Province in 1907. I went to the First Primary School in Taiyuan, the provincial capital. In 1927 I graduated from the Oberlin Higher Middle School in T'aiku near Taiyuan, attached to Oberlin-in-Shansi, the college founded by Dr. H. H. K'ung. This

was a Christian school of four hundred students, with many foreigners, and I felt an atmosphere of colonialism about it. The foreign teachers were all American, however, not English.

The May Thirtieth Movement in 1925 stimulated me greatly and I was leader of the student movement of all the schools in

181

T'aiku. We started a dramatic society and collected money to help the strikers in Shanghai. About two thousand students and townspeople participated in a demonstra- tion and all the schools temporarily stopped teaching. The students ousted a Chinese teacher because he opposed the demonstra- tion.

In 1926 I joined the Kuomintang, think- ing it was revolutionary, then when it turned sour I joined the Communist party in Sep- tember 1927 after the split with the Kuomin- tang. The Shansi government ordered my arrest, and I had to leave Taiyuan. At this time Governor Yen Hsi-shan was very op- pressive. He arrested at least a hundred stu- dents, one of them my friend Wang Yin, who was executed. Kuomintang members were not arrested unless they were leftists, and I was the leftist student leader. The charge against me was that I had led a group of sev- enty leftist students to beat up a teacher named Kao Shao-kao, who was a reactionary Kuomintang renegade and had tried to stop the student movement and destroy our or- ganization in 1927.

On leaving Taiyuan, I went to Wuchang. When the split occurred, I was ordered to join some bandits and organize them for revolutionary work. This was in T'ienmen, Chingshan, in northern Hupeh, about 1928. I stayed with the bandits for four months but had no success in influencing them. On the contrary, they decided to kill me and I had to make an escape. They knew I was a Com- munist.

There were sixty of these bandits under a chief named Têng Min-li. I got into the band through the guaranty of an acquaintance who knew the chief. Têng's purpose, how- ever, was only to build up a band to be incor- porated into the regular army so that he could get a post as officer. Later the band was absorbed into the government armies, as such bands often are. I could not influence them to our side because the government and army officers bribed them with money and they had no revolutionary tendencies at all.

I joined General Yao Wei-chên's army in the Hupeh-Anhwei district, first doing politi- cal work and then becoming a staff secretary. I did much fundamental work among the soldiers and helped to plan the uprising in Tayeh—the iron-mining town of Hupeh— which we carried out on December 14, 1929. The leader of this was Chêng Tzǔ-hua, my good friend and a Shansi native of Hai *hsien*, whom I had met in Honan in 1928. He was a squad commander and also a political worker, and is now Hsü Hai-tung's political commissar.

We were in the 1st Division. Six hundred men joined the uprising, there being many Communists then in the Kuomintang army. General Yao had one brigade of three thou- sand men, but in Tayeh there was only one battalion of three hundred soldiers, and in Yanghsin near by there were three hundred more. All the soldiers of these two forces joined the uprising. The commanding offi- cer was arrested but was set free later. The other officers ran away, except four who were killed by the soldiers spontaneously. The organizers of the uprising did not order anyone killed and there was no firing at all. It was very simple and easy. We sent repre- sentatives to P'êng Tê-huai and joined him in southeast Hupeh in 1930. P'êng went from P'ingkiang to Yochow and on to Chang- sha. We joined him at P'ingkiang.

P'êng led the first uprising of Kuomintang troops at P'ingkiang in 1928. The second uprising was that at Tayeh in 1929, and the one at Ningtu was the third and biggest.

At first I worked in the political depart- ment doing poster propaganda, art design, and dramatics. Then I became one of P'êng Tê-huai's five staff secretaries. I had all along in the past earned most of my money by doing finger painting and selling it to people.

I was with P'êng in the capture of Chang- sha, but in 1931 I left P'êng and went to the rear, where I became chairman of the Social Association of the Red University. I also worked for the Workers' and Peasants' Dramatic Society, of which I was one of the founders in 1932. Among the seven founders were Miss Li Po-chao, Miss Wei Kung-ch'i, Ts'ai Ch'ien, Chang Ai-p'ing—now teaching at the Red Academy, Hua Ch'ing—I don't know where he is, and Ts'ao Hsin—who seems to be lost and I suppose was killed.

This dramatics society in Juikin, Kiangsi, had two sections, each composed of forty young people. We picked the brightest and prettiest. One was the dramatics society proper; the other was its "Gorky School." The society took its plays to the front and to the villages with spectacular success. Many of the members joined the Red Army later and a few went on the Long March.

I stayed in Kiangsi as leader of the dramatics society after the army had left on the Long March. We divided into three mobile sections: the "Red Bell Players" (the name meaning "to awaken the people by ringing"), the "Fire Star Players" (meaning "the sign of the revolution"), and the "Trumpet Players" (meaning "the call to arms"). We were ordered by the party to do this work to keep up popular morale. Dramatics had an important influence in Kiangsi.

We marched with the Red troops that remained in Kiangsi. There were only a few of these, and in 1935 the army I was with was defeated by the Kuomintang. I was captured on March 8, 1935, at Hsinfêng, south Kiangsi. When the soldiers asked who I was and what I was doing, they were told that I was only an actor and civilian, so I was released three days later. Three other members of the society were arrested and two were released, but one beautiful actress was taken by an officer and forced to become his concubine. We were comparatively lucky, for the Kuomintang killed the families of all Red soldiers and the landlords came back and took revenge on the peasants.

The Kuomintang now occupied the district. I lived with a friend in the office of a newspaper, the *Hsinfêng News*, whose editors treated us very well. Nobody knew that we were Communists, and we attended the Catholic Church. I sold my paintings and my friend sold essays; in this way we were able to earn enough to live. I did a painting of Jesus for the Catholic Church for five dollars, which was given to me by two foreign missionaries who had returned. Within twenty days I had collected twenty dollars altogether, so we went away to Kanchow, Kiangsi. The missionaries gave me a letter of introduction and we stayed at the Catholic Church in Kanchow, and I earned five dollars more by my painting. Then we went to Kian, where Lo Ping-hui had held his uprising, to Kiukiang in Kiangsi, and on to Shanghai by boat.

In Shanghai nobody would buy my paintings or my friend's essays. We had no way to live. I had no possible way to find a party connection. At night we had nowhere to sleep. We went to the Social Bureau of the Shanghai municipality and asked for charity but they refused to give us anything but two steamers tickets to Tientsin.

When we arrived in Tientsin my friend was sick with a fever. We had no way to survive, so I wrote a letter home and my relatives sent sixteen dollars. They may have suspected, but never knew, what kind of work I was doing or where I was. I gave the money to my friend and returned to my home. There I found my family in terrible poverty. They had sent me all the money they could borrow, and I could not stay long. My family hid me in a panel in the wall while I was there. This was in July 1935. I was sick and weak after my long trip and my difficult experiences without enough to eat. My health has never recovered from those hard days.

In January 1936 I left home for Sianfu, my purpose being to join the local Red Army in Shensi led by Liu Tzŭ-tan. I did not know that Mao Tsê-tung was in Shensi. I should have waited at home in Shansi, for the Red

Army came to Shansi in February, one month after I left.

I found a job as servant in the Automobile Association in Sian. Then the Sian Incident occurred: the arrest of Chiang Kai-shek. One day I was absolutely astounded to meet two old friends in the street, Yeh Chien-ying and Wu Shou-chien. I had no possible way to get in touch with any Communist party connection in Sian until after the incident of December 12, 1936.

When the incident occurred, I was temporarily in Hsienyang working for the Automobile Association, but on the sixteenth I hurried to Sian and joined the National Salvation Society, organizing thirty of the automobile workers to join the society. These workers were sympathetic to the incident but uninformed. It was a great time for me and I was very happy. I immediately wrote to my friend, who had gone back to Shanghai, and he came to Sian.

On February 4, 1937, I came on to Yenan. About four hundred students came from Sian with me and several dramatics troupes.

I started my work in dramatics again and was made leader of the People's Anti-Japanese Dramatics Society. In the headquarters we have only eleven teachers, but there are many branch societies. The Red Academy has one, as does each army and each district.

We accept plays written by anyone and pay from one to twenty dollars for a good one. *Ah Q* was dramatized by Hsü Hsin-tzŭ in Shanghai. I have been in dramatics since middle-school days, and my best roles are those of old men or soldiers.

Chu Kuang

LEADER OF THE NEW THEATER MOVEMENT

MISS WALES:

CHU KUANG had been in the new theater movement in China from its beginning in the Nan Kuo Dramatic Society in Shanghai in 1929. He gave me a valuable account of it, which I had not been able to find elsewhere in my travels. When he joined the soviet movement in the interior, however, he became a director of propaganda, dramatics being the principal means of propagandizing the population. At the time I talked with him in Yenan, he was chief of propaganda for the Central "Politburo" of the Communist party, this being the bureau in control of all political activity. (Wu Liang-p'ing had this post for the government.)

Few persons of a sensitive, artistic nature can endure the hardship and danger of army life in interior China, and no important literary figures had migrated to the Communist areas by 1937 except Miss Ting Ling (the leading woman novelist of China), Ch'êng Fang-wu (who with Kuo Mo-jo had led the Creationist Literary Society), and Chu Kuang (a playwright himself). I saw several of Chu Kuang's plays performed. They were raw propaganda —but highly effective with the audiences, who apparently loved every word.

When I asked Chu Kuang about the Communist theater he said: "The open air theater such as we are reviving here has flourished for hundreds of years in China, though since the Yuan dynasty the decadent intellectuals have created little that is new and vital. Yet the people have never ceased patronizing the old plays for lack of something better. They have had no education to write plays for themselves until now, and the cultural renaissance will come and is coming from the common people. Their very first attempt is in the theater."

CHU KUANG:

I HAVE nothing to tell of my early life, as nothing happened to me until the Canton Commune. I was only seventeen at the time of the Commune, in 1927. After participating in it I went to Shanghai to study dramatic art. I entered the Shanghai Art College, where T'ien Han was a teacher—he became one of China's leading playwrights. He quarreled, however, with the principal, Chou Ch'ing-hao, and decided to start a new school of his own, called the Nan Kuo Art College. Over a hundred students went with him from the Shanghai Art College, and I was one of them. That was in 1928.

The students were all very poor and the new college was unable to continue, but the Nan Kuo Dramatic Society flourished. It had been started by T'ien Han to give the students practice and the chance to earn money by acting. Half the members were girls. The plays were romantic and sentimental, mostly French. It was before Ibsen was accepted. No Japanese influence existed, either. Oscar Wilde's *Salome*, who had John the Baptist killed, was the favorite. The favorite Chinese play was "Talking at Night in Soochow" by T'ien Han. Another of his was *Nan Kuei*, or "Turn Back to the South." Yü San was the actress of the period.

This was the first modern dramatic school in China. Until that time there had been no modern drama. The purpose was to launch a new and modern movement. There was no revolutionary political idea behind it. T'ien Han's was the whole influence, though

185

Hung Shên, who was also a teacher, later caught up with him. T'ien Han had been educated in Japan and France, and was later the translator of Ibsen. At one time he was more or less an anarchist, and in France he had been connected with the "Kuo Chia Chu I" nationalist group organized by Li Huang and Chên Ch'i. When he returned to China he was sentimental and romantic, and vaguely wanted to start a new movement. This was just after the defeat of the revolution of 1925–27, and the intellectuals all felt lost. Seeing no future in revolution, they turned to love and introspection.

As a reaction against this, a Creative Dramatic Society, part of the old Creationist literary group, began opposing the Nan Kuo. I joined this faction, which included Ch'êng Fang-wu—now teaching in Yenan, Chang Tzŭ-p'ing, Chêng Po-ch'i—now in Shanghai, Wang T'u-ching, and new members such as Fêng Nai-tsao, P'êng K'ang, Chu Ching-ho, and Li Ch'u-li. The most important member, Kuo Mo-jo, had to escape to Japan because of the danger of arrest. There were also old members, such as Chiang Kuang-ssŭ and Ch'ien Hsing-tsun.

The quarrel between the two societies rose out of the fact that the Nan Kuo wanted art for art's sake and the Creative Society wanted social literature. Then the Creative Society had a split over the nature of expression. The old members, including Kuo Mo-jo, Ch'êng Fang-wu, Chiang Kuang-ssŭ, and Ch'ien Hsing-tsun, wanted to concentrate on "revolutionary" literature, but the new members wanted "proletarian" literature.

Kuo Mo-jo and Ch'êng Fang-wu didn't quarrel much, as they soon went away, but one group splintered off and started the new "T'aiyang Society," with its own magazine, led by Chiang Kuang-ssŭ, Ch'ien Hsin-tsun, K'ung Pin-lu, Yang Ch'un-jên, and Hung Ling-fei. Fêng Nai-tsao did not join T'aiyang.

Although the Creative group and the T'aiyang fought, they agreed on attacking Nan Kuo and Lu Hsün and the Yu Ssŭ group. It was really all nonsense, a quarrel over words. After they had been arguing all during 1928 and 1929, the Communist party finally took up the question and decided that there was no difference except in degree, "revolutionary" being a large-scale concept and "proletarian" a narrower one. After that the term "proletarian" was never used. And the problem was very soon solved when both societies were closed down by the government in 1930. The T'aiyang now dropped its name and operated through the Hsiao Shan Bookshop, while the Creative group used the Chang Nan Bookshop. It was this bookshop which published *Ssŭ Hsiang*, or "Thought," edited by P'êng K'ang and Chu Ching-ho.

In 1930 the Nan Kuo was also closed by the government, as T'ien Han had by then turned to the Left. At this time repression of any kind of cultural activity became very heavy. As a result, both T'ien Han and Hung Shên changed to become progressive in the same year.

In 1930 an American movie called *Pu P'a Ssŭ*, or "Dare to Die," caused a big quarrel. It showed bandits in China. When it was played in the Ta Kuang Ming Cinema in Shanghai, Hung Shên led a demonstration in the theater and was arrested for this and was held a few hours.

When Nan Kuo was closed, the Artistic Dramatic Society was started by Li Ch'u-li, Chêng Po-ch'i, and myself. Our object was to influence the old members toward starting a new revolutionary drama opposed to the old sentimental ideas. We had fifty persons in it, including the writer Liu Chien. The well-known movie star, Miss Ch'ên Po-erh, was a member and also Miss Wang Ying, another movie star. We tried to welcome T'ien Han as the leader, as he had changed his ideas, but he did not join.

In 1930, with T'ien Han as chairman, we held a conference of the former members of Nan Kuo and the Creative Society and of the new Artistic Society. Playwrights and fiction writers were well represented. We passed a resolution to direct our efforts against imperialism and feudalism. This was preparatory to forming a new organization —the League of Left Writers.

The Artistic Society had never been able to have any public activities, and after six months the Nanking government forced it to close down. We went underground and took a new name—the Ta Tao [Highroad] dramatic society. It had the same membership as the former society—about fifty persons. The plays we put on were *Carmen*, in which Hu P'ing and An O (now a composer) took the lead; "Negro," by Yang Sao, expressing the oppressed condition of minorities; "Coal Miners," by K'ung Pin-lu; "Night Scene in a Factory," by Yüan Shu; and *All Quiet on the Western Front*. We also put on several Russian plays, one being "Forty-One," adapted from a short story, and a Japanese play called "Broken Electricity," by Lin Fang-hsiung, translated and adapted to Chinese by myself.

The Ta Tao society was also suppressed by the government. For a time we gave up and decided to do no public work, as it would only be banned. Ten of us then did plays privately for the workers in the Shanghai factory districts. These were plays such as "The Way to Live" and "Bloody Clothes," written by Liu K'uang. The purpose of the latter was to combat the error of the Li Li-san line, in which workers were being killed by too many political strikes. Several times a group was arrested, though the plays were stopped immediately whenever the police appeared, and the workers kept careful watch for them. Finally, we could not produce any plays except in the Christian schools in the factory districts.

The League of Left Writers had had a nucleus in 1930, but it was not until the early part of 1931 that it was organized, by P'an Tzǔ-nien, Hua Han, Yao P'êng-tzǔ, Miss Ting Ling, and Mao Tun. Lu Hsün, the greatest of all Chinese writers, had now come over to our side and gave us the name for the new group, though he was not very active until later. The Union published the *Great Dipper* magazine, edited by Miss Ting Ling.

Next, in the winter of 1931, we organized sister-groups, the Association of Left-Wing Dramatists and the Association of Left-Wing Artists. Over all these and in the background was the Cultural Committee of the Communist Party, which selected people to go to many different regions to do cultural work. When it was decided to strengthen the cultural work in the soviet districts, artists and writers went there to propagandize and organize, especially just before the Fifth Campaign.

The Artists' Association included Miss Liang Po-po, Lin Ssǔ, Hsiung Hsi-ling, and others—together there were sixty artists, chiefly doing woodcuts. This movement was influenced by the same activity in Japan. Artists who returned from study in Japan brought back new techniques and ideas. The Left Artists had their home base in Hsing Hua art college in Shanghai, in Chung Hua art college, and in the Eighteen Woodcuts Society. Later some of them went to the Hangchow art college and started a branch there, the Eighteen Woodcuts Society being the nucleus for this branch.

The Association of Left-Wing Dramatists was organized by T'ien Han and myself, as well as Tsen Chün-li—now a famous movie star, Chou Po-hsüan, Hsiung Hsi-ling, Chêng Po-ch'i, Hung Shên, and Miss Pai Wei. This association led the movement for dramatic work in all Shanghai, including every school. Nearly all the schools had new dramatics groups, such as those in Ta Hsia, Futan, Chiaotung, and Chung Kuo universities. In the factory districts we also organized *Lanpu*, or "Blue Denim," dramatic groups, named for the heavy blue working clothes of the factories. We had four groups, in several factories, all made up of local factory workers. First we started evening schools, and then the dramatics groups developed from these. We also had branch associations in Peking, Canton, and Sian.

The Association of Left-Wing Dramatists was the main impetus in starting the making of motion pictures, which until then had been only feebly initiated. Many of our members became prominent motion picture actors. At the end of December 1931, we started the Union of Motion Picture Workers, which led this activity.

The whole cultural movement in Shanghai, however, could not expand. This was partly because of suppression and partly because of an erroneous "closed door" policy which insisted that all members must be active revolutionary workers as well as artists. Because of this, many intellectuals did not want to join, though they were sympathetic.

When the Shanghai War occurred in February 1932 and General Ts'ai Ting-chieh began fighting the Japanese locally, the whole Association of Left-Wing Dramatists went to the front lines during the fighting to do anti-Japanese propaganda work. Some were arrested. The men also helped to destroy the Nanking-Shanghai railway, while the girls became nurses doing war work at the front. The suppression was soon intensified, however, partly because Chiang Kai-shek feared we would influence a strong anti-Japanese movement. Our leaders were arrested: P'an Tzŭ-nien, T'ien Han, Yao P'êng-tzŭ, Hua Han, and Tzŭ Ching-lo, and later Miss Ting Ling and Hung Ta—manager of the German bookstore which sold leftist books. Earlier, in 1931, after the Li Li-san period, P'êng K'ang and Li Ch'u-li had been arrested. P'êng K'ang is still in prison, but Li Ch'u-li was released in March 1937.

The highest period of the new cultural movement in China was from the Mukden Incident in 1931 to the end of 1932. The lowest period was in 1934 and 1935 during the Fifth Campaign, when a great many Left intellectuals were sacrificed. Chiang Kai-shek had then two programs, one at the military front and one in the cultural rear: the "surrounding attack" on the Communist armies and the "cultural surrounding" against intellectuals in his own areas. In 1931 the Right Kuomintang had started an ineffectual dramatic society, in Shanghai, organized by Yin Yün-wei, to combat the Left cultural influence, which was completely dominant.

In 1935, when the Communist party changed its policy to that of the United Front, the National Salvation Cultural Movement began to develop, and also the student movement. The basic work done in the past in cultural circles still showed its influence.

In 1932 I left Shanghai, where I had been a member of both the left-wing dramatists' and artists' associations, and went to the Oyüwan soviet to do cultural work. When I arrived, I was made chief secretary of the political department of the Fourth Front Army. On the Long March I was chief of propaganda of the Fourth Front Army and organized dramatics as part of this activity. I am now chief of propaganda for the Central "Politburo."

Most of the plays we put on in the Communist-led regions are brought in from the outside, not many being written here. We have been so busy fighting wars that we have not had much time to write plays. In the Fourth Front Army each unit had its own troupe, and the work was excellent.

We do not usually use the old technique of the Chinese theater in the armies but we intend to develop it, since the people in backward regions like it better. In Szechuan and in south Shensi it was necessary to use the old-style Szechuan drama. What we do is to use the old technique but change the content, and to use new words with the old songs and instruments. The people love the old songs, and some of them are very good. We adapt them in every district, and they make effective propaganda. However, we never use painted characters or symbolized costumes or any of the old tricks in place of stage properties, and we never put on the old dramas. The old drama is moribund everywhere except in Peking. In the former soviet districts, the people preferred the modern drama, but the people here, especially the peasants, still have a taste for the old. This is a job for our writers to work on. The people enjoy the old type of play with music, like opera. In adapting the old plays we do not have a realistic theater, as the West does, but use music, as in Chinese opera. The old style is more fitting in historical plays, which can be adapted with changed content. We are now writing a drama of the T'aip'ing Rebellion with this idea.

I consider that no Chinese writer has yet adequately expressed the proletarian class of city workers. In a semicolonial society like ours, the workers cannot get education enough to write, and the students have to try to interpret the life of the workers. All our writers are of the lower middle class, except possibly T'ien Chün, yet their products are sound because they are revolutionary and have allied themselves with the working people. Some good plays have been composed by the soldiers of the Red Army, but no short stories to speak of.

My old friends and colleagues of the Shanghai days have many of them been executed. Most of those killed were not well known, however, since the Kuomintang hesitated to execute famous writers and artists for fear of the repercussions. Some of my close friends who were writers and have been executed were Hu Yeh-p'ing; Hsü Po, killed in Nanking in 1931; Sao Wen-ch'iu, executed in Canton in 1928; and Sun Paoshen, killed in Soochow in 1932. Ling Poshui is still in prison. P'an Tzŭ-nien was not released. Many unknown artists, chiefly young students, were executed for their political activities. Of the dramatists, Tai Ping-wan, Mêng Tsao, Chao Ming-yi, and Liu K'uang were imprisoned.

Others betrayed. Chou Ch'uan-p'ing and Yao P'êng-tzŭ betrayed in 1930. Chou, who was head of the Mutual Aid of the Communist party, took money entrusted to him and joined the Trotskyists. Hua Han confessed and was released. Fêng Nai-tsao is now an official in Wuhan.

Wên T'ao

ARTIST, DANCER, AND MUSICIAN

Wên T'ao and a group of young actors, in Yenan, 1937. Living in a dormitory attached to the Dramatic Society School, the children practiced by day and performed in the evening.

MISS WALES:

THE clothes of Wên T'ao seemed outlandish in Yenan. With a khaki smock and leather belt, he wore black trousers very wide at the bottom, with a red stripe down the sides, and his sandals were of yarn in brilliant colors. A shock of thick black hair fell across his forehead with studied carelessness, concealing one eye.

"He's the only bohemian in the whole Northwest," someone said, pointing him out to me with a shake of the head. Wên T'ao had been in Yenan for only a few months, and people were still not sure what to make of him.

Early in life, Wên T'ao had been sold into slavery near Canton. Had he not been intelligent he could hardly have survived the hard life that was in store for him and from which he learned to be a jack-of-all-arts. He was also self-possessed, and he had the ability to face the world with complete confidence—something that few of the artistic temperament ever achieve. To have a pair of skillful hands was all he asked of life. He had worked at various times as carpenter, dentist, cobbler, and jeweler—and as a cook in the South Seas. He escaped arrest in Shanghai and got through the blockade to the Northwest as soon as possible. And at the moment he was instructor in dancing, music, and acting at the Dramatic Society School in Yenan.

When I went to call on him at the school I was greeted formally with a handshake by the two leading boy actors, Liu Chih and Wang Wên-chiang. They took my hands on either side and led me into the studio of Wên T'ao, where the three of them rushed about to make coffee for me and my interpreter.

We think of the Chinese as being slow to pick up new ideas. Wên T'ao was a complete reversal of the old Chinese type; he loved anything new, original, and different. His inventive mind created dances and skits by the dozen. When students arrived from the coast he could pick up a new song from them in half an hour and play it on his harmonica.

WÊN T'AO:

MY parents sold me as a child. I don't even know what price I brought. I never knew either of my parents, but they were poor peasants of Mei *hsien*, in Kwangtung, where I was born in 1907.

I was bought by a rich landlord, who was also a salt merchant and a government official in the Ch'ing dynasty. He was indolent, smoked opium, and was very cruel to me. He used to beat me, pull my hair, push

190

my head against the wall—and others in the family did the same to relieve their feelings. I supposed they had bought me to be a whipping boy. There were thirty persons in the big house, including the landlord's two wives, six sons, and four daughters. I fought and quarreled with the other children constantly to hold my own, for I seemed to be a rebel even then and was not content to be a slave. I was kitchen boy and had to carry the water. Nevertheless, I was sent to primary school until the age of eight. The old grandparents treated me kindly, and the second concubine of the grandfather was especially good to me and often shielded me. She was the only mother I ever knew. When she died she begged me to study diligently and become a good man. The grandfather had five concubines.

I was married when I reached fifteen. The contract had been made by the old grandmother when I was three. The girl I was to marry was brought to live with the family at the age of two to grow up as a maidservant, but later she was sent back. During festivals, the girl often came to visit. Everyone joked with me about her until I was ashamed and miserable. I was so embarrassed when I was forced to marry her that I never even spoke to her, and a few nights later I ran away. I know now that I really liked her, though she was only a country girl, but then I only felt ashamed. I never wrote to her afterward. Later I heard that she had found another husband.

That was the immediate reason why I ran away at fifteen, but the real reason was that I could bear the hard work and bad treatment no longer. I joined the Kwangtung provincial army and served for three years. I was quick and learned fast, and since I could read and write, I became a secretary. After three years I rose to be company commander.

On the Fukien border were bandits led by Ch'ên Yung-kuang—very well known in the province, though he was later killed—in 1931. My troops were sent to destroy the bandits, but we were defeated and a hundred of our men were killed. I was disarmed, and to save my life I volunteered to join the bandits. About a hundred other soldiers went over at the same time. Ch'ên also had a hundred men of his own. The band soon increased to six hundred.

The chief took a fancy to me, and I lived in his house. He had been an officer in the Kwangtung army, but his family was poor and he had many sons with no future. Their life was so hopeless that he had decided to become a bandit to rob the rich and help the poor, and he copied his ways from the old book, the *Shui Hu Chuan* ["Story of the Liangshan Bandits"]. He captured many *t'uhao* landlords for ransom. Once he ordered me to capture one, and I did so. He was a bandit chief on the border for forty years.

Ch'ên said I could become a "little chief," but I saw no future in this except being beheaded, and after two months I ran away. I wanted to go to Whampoa Military Academy, which was just opening near by, but I had no money and no connections, so I gave up this idea and went to the South Seas with a merchant.

We traveled to Singapore, to the interior of Malaya, and to Malacca. Many of our native Cantonese had migrated to Malacca, and there I found relatives of the landlord who had bought me. I stayed with the merchant as his assistant for three years. We traveled all over the South Seas. He was a middleman for other merchants and got a commission from them. He was also an itinerant carpenter, jeweler, dentist, and cobbler, and he taught me all these trades. Moreover, I had jobs as a waiter in a mahjongg place, as a cook in a restaurant, and as an accountant in a shop. I spent most of my time in Batavia, Java, and there I also taught in a primary school for a short time.

But what I loved to do was drawing. I found a friend in a bookshop who taught me to draw and paint in foreign style. After that I sold my paintings in the bookshop for ten to twenty dollars apiece, working meanwhile at odd jobs to earn my living. At the same time, I studied music and singing which I liked very much, helped by friends I had made. I learned to play the banjo and the mandolin. I also studied the violin for six months, but my fingers were too short so I gave it up. I learned most of this from music books which I bought, taking lessons only in the beginning.

I dreamed of going to Shanghai to study, and I saved my money. In 1930, at twenty-three, I entered Shanghai Art College to study music and art. Here many students and teachers were Communists and some were Trotskyists. I was sympathetic with the cause of working-class people like myself but I did not join the Communists because I did not understand Marxism. The poet and teacher Wang Tu-ching was a Trotskyist; another Trotskyist was Yü Mo-t'ao. The other teachers were Yü Ta-fu; Kuan Liang, a painting teacher who had studied in Japan; T'an Fa-mo, an artist; and Miss P'an Yü-liang, an artist who had studied in France and is now in Central University. T'an Fa-mo influenced me most. He is now in Canton.

I had scarcely any way to earn money. My life was lived down to the bare boards, though I was somehow able to borrow from friends all the time. A girl schoolmate introduced me to the Mei Hua dancing group and I studied part-time with them until the Mukden Incident. The members of this group were highly romantic, and at that time I fell into their ways. We liked foreign music and art and dancing — not the old Chinese styles, and we had no political ideas, wanting only to be expert professionals in the arts.

After the Mukden Incident I wanted to join the volunteers who were leaving Shanghai that October to fight the Japanese in the north, but I had no money to buy a uniform, which would have cost fifteen dollars. A group of my friends then raised money to buy me a ticket to Kwangtung, and when I arrived there a friend introduced me, so

I was able to get a job as teacher in a country school. This school was miserably poor and conditions were bad, but I taught music, drawing, and drama, as well as the regular lessons. I had learned about the drama chiefly from reading books and seeing plays. Nearly everything I know I have had to pick up on my own, but I have a quick mind for new ideas.

My next job was in Hongkong, teaching drawing and music in a middle school. Here I picked up a knowledge of oil painting but I had no money to buy oils—my monthly salary was only thirty-five dollars — and I had to give up oil painting and learn wood-cut technique instead. Woodcuts cost little to make—that is why most Chinese artists work with woodcuts rather than oils. I became rather good at woodcuts, and when the National Woodcut Exhibition was held in Peking in 1935 many of my woodcuts were accepted. The famous woodcut artist in Peking, Chin Tsao-yeh, wrote to me praising my work. I also wrote often to Lu Hsün[1] asking about artistic problems.

In the winter of 1935 I went to Shanghai to help edit the new magazine of woodcuts called *T'ieh Ma* ["Iron Horse"]. The revolutionary tide was rising high, and I joined the Anti-Imperialist Alliance. My life was extremely hard, for I could earn only about ten dollars a month by selling woodcuts and writing essays on art, but I now did my best work, which gave me some notice—a volume called *Chiao Hsing* ["Awake"]; however, only a hundred copies were printed. *Chiao Hsing* tells a connected story in woodcuts. It is about a girl whose parents are poor and ill. When they die, a landlord takes her as a maidservant and treats her cruelly. She grows up to be beautiful, and the landlord intends to force her to be his concubine but his wife angrily sells the girl. When the war breaks out in Chahar, the girl runs away with other working women to be a nurse to the soldiers fighting Japan and is killed by the Japanese.

I always had much sympathy for the Communist movement but I am not now a Communist party member. I came here in the winter of 1936 to do what I can. Originally I wanted to start groups to do propaganda art.

There is no way for the cultural renaissance of China to develop under the Kuomintang, and it is being held back artificially by suppression and poverty. Even an artist cannot express himself. During the Southwest Incident I wrote articles against Chiang Kai-shek. In October 1936 ten of my friends in Shanghai were arrested; they are still in prison. The police had a long list of writers and artists of the Left. My name was on the list and I had to escape. In 1934 a group of woodcut artists in Hangchow organized the Mo Lin ["Foolish"] Woodcut Society, but a Fascist named Yeh Ling-feng betrayed them to the government; about ten of these artists were arrested, and three were executed at Hangchow. Li Chün, an artist, did a well-known woodcut to describe this, called "Three of Us Sacrificed."

Lu Hsün was the person I greatly admired. His writing had more influence on me than anything else in my life. I met him in 1935 in Szechuan Road in Shanghai. We talked for a while, and later he sent me letters analyzing the problems of art in China. I also admire Mao Tun, Miss Ting Ling, and Chang T'ien-yi. T'ien Chün's writing technique is not good, but his content is. My favorite foreign writers are Gorky, Barbusse, Romain Rolland, and Tolstoy. I am interested in Shakespeare and Ibsen, but have not made a study of them. My favorite music is Beethoven and other German works, though I have little knowledge of them except by ear. The painter I most admire is Millet, who expresses the working people. Technically, however, I like the work of the French Impressionists, especially Manet and Van Gogh.

Liu Chih

A BOY ACTOR

MISS WALES:

I WAS much impressed by Liu Chih, a fifteen-year-old boy with an apparent ability to learn anything. He had joined the theater people and become a favorite actor. He was one among the hundreds of children without families in the Northwest, most of them orphans of the war. Liu Chih, however, had come to Yenan after running away from his father, a banker in Sian. Wang Wên-chiang, another boy who became an actor, had come with him.

During the summer these two boys used to call on me nearly every week. I sometimes had a borrowed phonograph, and they would listen spellbound to "Afternoon of a Faun," "Stormy Weather," and "Smoke Gets in Your Eyes." They were at the Dramatic Society School, along with nineteen other students—including seven girls—most of whom were from near-by Yench'ang. The two boys told me about a special tour of six weeks which they and a group of forty-six others had been ordered to make. They had marched on foot every day, they told me, and had played thirty-one times in seven *hsien*. The purpose of the tour was to put on open-air plays explaining the new policies of the Yenan government to the Shensi people and to encourage participation in the elections which were to begin July 15 of that year. These elections changed the old soviet system into Mao Tsê-tung's "new democracy," as it was called.

Liu Chih had had a marvelous time on the tour, and told me that the people had been very much interested in the "incredible" harmonica. The song they liked best was entitled grandiloquently "The Song for Abolishing Uneducated People," and the next best was the volunteers' marching song, "Ch'ilai." Their favorite foreign song was to the tune of "Row, Row, Row Your Boat," while others that they liked included one taken from a drama *Protect Madrid*, and two written to Russian music and entitled "This Is the Year to Recover Our Lost Territory" and "Young Vanguards." These were sung by the Army also.

Liu Chih was an accomplished mimic, and was a great favorite at the theater, especially for his street-vendor cries and old Shensi street songs. But he had sung so much that his voice was almost gone, and his doctor had ordered him to give it a rest. He could also put on a good display of fencing, or sword-boxing, as it is called. He had already become vain, wearing a black velvet red-starred beret instead of the regulation uniform cap as the mark of his high profession.

I saw Liu Chih less than three months after the Sian Incident of December 12, 1936, when Chang Hsüeh-liang and Yang Hu-ch'êng arrested Chiang Kai-shek to force him to stop the civil war. He related to me with great pride the small part he had taken in these events.

LIU CHIH:

MY father's name is Liu Pên-ch'in. He was manager of the Bank of Shensi Province six years ago. He once was rich, but now he is poor and has no job. His property was stolen by robbers several years ago. My family are natives of Shensi, and I was born in Sianfu in 1923. There are seven persons in my family besides me—my older brother, my two younger brothers, my grandfather, my parents, and my sister-in-law.

At five I started to primary school, graduating when I was eleven. I studied only two years in middle school, where I took parts in school plays. Nobody taught me dramatics but I read books about it and watched the plays carefully. My two brothers and I learned boxing from a teacher who came to us to make our bodies strong and healthy. For two years I have had no practice, and so I have made no progress. On the streets I learned the *lien hua lo*—old folk songs sung by beggars and poor travelers.

I was in the student movement of December 9, 1936, which started the Sian Incident. Many students in Sian appealed to Governor Shao Li-tze for permission to hold a memorial meeting for Lu Hsün but he forbade it and said to them, "You are all Communists." Just the same, the students decided to hold a meeting, and about ten thousand went to the Revolutionary Park early on the morning of the ninth, having no food all day and holding a meeting in the afternoon. We passed a resolution to go to Lint'ung to see Chiang Kai-shek and present demands to stop the civil war and fight Japan. We started out immediately. Not all the students from my First Middle School went—only about three hundred. At first the plan was to go by train, but the stationmaster would not let us on at the station, so we walked about eight *li*, nearly to Shihlip'u. Some student delegates were going to bring bread from Sian for us in automobiles, but they had not yet come when we saw a car drive up bringing a representative sent by Marshal Chang Hsüeh-liang[1] with a request that the students not go to Lint'ung. But the students were angry and treated the representative rudely, and he went away again in his car.

He drove so fast, and we walked so slowly, that he had time to notify Chang Hsüeh-liang. Then Chang Hsüeh-liang himself came in a hurry by car, using a short cut. He met the vanguard of our column and told them that he had come from Chiang Kai-shek's headquarters, though really he had only come from the city. He said: "I'll talk with you at Shihlip'u." The students were

glad to stop there and have negotiations with him.

"In the past," he said, "I was a 'bad egg,' but not now. Now I am good and I have a very patriotic feeling. If you go to Chiang Kai-shek, perhaps you will have no good result and he may even shoot you with guns. Let me be your representative. This is better than if you go, and you can trust me."

But the students would not consent, and then he said, "My dear students, in three days more I will reply to you by action. If I do not do this, I will commit suicide right before you."

We all clapped and cried and were happy and excited, though we did not know what he might possibly mean by "action." He then said that he was on his way to Lint'ung to carry our demands and that there would be a reply within three days. The students agreed and decided to turn back to Sian. The younger children were so slow that they strayed in the rear and were afraid in the dark, so some Tungpei people walked behind to protect them.

About nine o'clock that night we of the vanguard arrived at Sian and had a meeting at the Mingloyüan market place, but the rear did not arrive until midnight. The big city gate was closed—they struck on it with stones and it was opened up for them. They came to Mingloyüan to join the meeting but it was over by that time and they went home.

Next day we went to classes as usual. By the third day we had had no reply from Chang Hsüeh-liang and were afraid that we had been tricked. We held another meeting on the afternoon of December 11 at Revolutionary Park, but not so many came. The captain of the boy scouts led my school. We debated again about going to Lint'ung with our demands and kept our meeting going, having brought our food this time, until eleven o'clock. We stayed on afterward and at about twelve or one we heard firing, but we thought it was bandits. At one we went to our homes.

By dawn the students in the dormitory of my school were to get up and be prepared to march to Lint'ung. I was on the street leaving my house before light but on the way I heard a soldier fire and could see something was seriously wrong so I returned home. My family were still asleep and didn't know I had been out. I told them about the firing.

Then at eight o'clock an automobile rushed around the city handing out propaganda sheets and newspapers printing the "Eight Demands for National Salvation." Then we all knew that Chang Hsüeh-liang was honest. All the students loved him very much then, and loved even old Yang Hu-ch'êng—because we found that he also supported our movement.

At three o'clock the students from each different school gathered and voted to cele-brate by a five-day strike. We collected funds for the anti-Japanese work and held meetings of the different student unions and the National Salvation Association.

On the 25th of December I stopped school and joined the "Twelve-Twelve Dramatics Club," which had thirty members and was led by Ch'ên Chên-li. The club belonged to the Tungpei Army. Our first play was *Withdraw from Fengtai*, about the Twenty-ninth Army.

I also joined two other new student groups, the "Anti-Japanese Propaganda Group" and the "Political Training Group," both under the political department of the allied armies.

After the 25th, when Chang Hsüeh-liang went to Nanking by plane with Chiang Kai-shek, we had no food supplied to us. When I heard that the Red Army children-prisoners in Sian, who had been captured by Hu Tsung-nan, were going to march to the soviet district, I decided to come here with them. About twenty or thirty of the prisoners came, and altogether there were a hundred of us. We left on January 22. Most of the boys went to the front, but one is here in the Dramatics Society with me and one is in the Rear Political Department.

My family did not want me to do dramatics and refused to let me come to Yenan, so I ran away secretly and brought nothing with me. I wrote a letter to my family and told them of what I was doing here and of my success. They replied that although they had opposed me before, now they were glad I was doing well and wanted me to work hard for the revolution.

Sketch by a Communist artist commemorating the co-operation of the Tungpei Army and the Red Army following the Sian Incident. The verse runs: "Brothers don't kill brothers. We must join together to destroy the dwarf robbers and fight back to the homeland." The homeland is that of the Tungpei Army—Manchuria.

PART SEVEN

Women

Ts'ai Ting-li

EDITOR AND WRITER

MISS WALES:

I MET Ts'ai Ting-li—also called Ts'ai Tso-yin—in 1938 in Shanghai. She had been one of the Communist women leaders in the Hailufeng area of Kwangtung Province, and did not want this fact to become publicly known. Since her early political apprenticeship in Hailufeng, from which she barely escaped with her life, she had been an editor and a writer on women's problems.

Hailufeng is especially interesting for several reasons, aside from the fact that it was the first soviet area in China. In Kwangtung, as in Kwangsi, women have had more freedom than elsewhere in China and do more manual labor. Among the laboring classes, the binding of women's feet was rare. Here the influence of the primitive Hakka tribespeople was discernible. It is my impression that in Hailufeng, as in parts of Hunan, the landlords were Chinese, while the tenants were of intermixed Chinese and Hakka descent, retaining some of the aloofness and independence of the tribespeople. Before the 1925 revolution, Hailufeng was known as the most progressive agrarian district in all of China. It was here that the first women's peasant union was created, as well as one of the first general peasants' unions. I believe that P'êng Pai, the regional leader, was the first to make the experiment of distributing his own land to the peasants—a forerunner of the agrarian program.

Ts'ai Ting-li is the only person I met who could tell me of the beginnings of a local soviet, such as this one at Hailufeng, and I believe her story is unique. After a year and a half of activity there, she left early in the autumn of 1927, just before the soviet was formed. What later happened in Hailufeng was told me by a Korean participant, Kim San, and is described in my book *Song of Ariran*.

TS'AI TING-LI:

IF you go to Kwangtung you will see that none of the women under forty have bound feet. In other places girls of fifteen and sixteen can still be seen hobbling on these stumps. The women of Kwangtung were never so suppressed as in other parts of China, and have always carried on work in the fields and even as carrier coolies. They are proud and independent. Of all Kwangtung women those in the Tungkiang ["East River"] region are the most progressive. And in Tungkiang, it is in Hailufeng — where the most violent revolution took place—that women are the most spirited.[1] I was in Hailufeng during part of that time and knew P'êng Pai,[2] though I was only seventeen. Hardly anyone is alive now of the leaders of the Hailufeng soviet, which was the first in China. I left there just a little while before the soviet was formed.

Landed Humanitarians

I am a native of that region. I was born at Chinghai, near Swatow, in 1910. My family were small landlords and my mother was a Christian. In Kwangtung, and especially in the Tungkiang region, there are more Christians than elsewhere. The people are more modern-minded because so many of them have relatives overseas and receive letters from them abroad full of new ideas. In Hailufeng maybe one or two percent were Christians—more in Lufeng than Haifeng. The attitude of the Christian church was not the same then as now. My mother had a great influence on me, and had had enough education so that she could teach me. I began to study in school at thirteen, skipped classes, and entered middle school immediately. At sixteen, because of my mother's help, I graduated from normal school in Swatow.

My grandfather had been a Ch'ing dynasty official, and my father did no work—he lived on his inheritance. He died when I was three, and my mother was oppressed and mistreated by the feudal family. She was unhappy, and my earliest memory is of her reading to me many works of old fiction dealing with the suffering of people. She was humanitarian and wanted to find a way out from poverty and tragedy for mankind, so she became a Christian. All my family are emotional—my own mother, especially. She understands the suffering of others through her own personal suffering from feudal surroundings. From her I received my own understanding of the problems of people other than myself and a tendency toward Christian humanitarianism.

P'êng Pai's name was known among all the peasants in Kwantung and I was much influenced by the stories about him. At last I met him in Swatow in 1926 and determined to join in his work. He was then the leader of the Communist party in the Tungkiang region, which includes the cities of Ch'aochow, Swatow, and Huichow and the famous Hailufeng district. Tungkiang means merely "east of the river"—the river which flows through Canton. The region near Canton is divided into the East River, West River, and North River districts. Swatow is a seaport between Canton and Hailufeng, but very near Hailufeng. If an army wants to attack Swatow, it must hold Meihsien and Tapu. Yet, Tungkiang is not so important strategically as economically—it is very important in this latter respect because so many overseas Chinese come from there.

P'êng Pai was about thirty when I first saw him. He was tall, compared with the average Cantonese, and everything about him seemed big in body and spirit. His face was big and square. His mouth was big and his nose was big, and he had a peculiarity of letting his hair grow a little long. He was a healthy, strong-looking person, not at all the scholar type. His eyes were bright, intelligent, and kind. He was a kind and humanitarian person, and I consider him a very great man. He is a figure in Chinese history who must not be forgotten. In my contacts with Communists, nearly all were kind and humanitarian, but none could compare with P'êng Pai in this respect—or in any other. He was by nature emotional, affectionate, and earnest, and he loved people. In his private life he was uncommonly sentimental, but in his work he was strong and determined and showed no weakness. There was a joke that was told about him when he was a student in Japan. His wife was an old-fashioned girl, and before the Moon Festival [when it is traditional that husband and wife should be together], he wrote to her, saying that on that day she must sleep facing a certain direction and he would do the same. On the fifteenth of the Eighth Month he put her picture in the proper position, but a careless student stumbled over it and broke the glass, and the whole story became known among all the Chinese students in Japan.

His wife was killed by the Kuomintang. They took everything away from his house, even the last matchbox. P'êng and his wife had two or three sons who were sent to Moscow to study, though one may have been killed by the Kuomintang. Later, when P'êng Pai was in Swatow, he fell in love with a girl student named Hsü Yü-ch'ing and they had a daughter. She worked in the secret soviet district near Swatow after P'êng Pai was killed but I have not heard anything about her since.

P'êng Pai was born in the *hsien* city of Haifeng about 1896. Haifeng and Lufeng are neighboring *hsien*. *Feng* means "prosperity." *Hai* means "near the sea." *Lu* means "inland." Together they are called

Hailufeng. Haifeng *hsien* had about thirty or forty thousand population. Lufeng was smaller. Haifeng was much more progressive because it was poorer and more oppressed than Lufeng. Ch'ên Ch'iung-ming, the noted general, was a native of Haifeng. He thought P'êng Pai was very capable, and tried to make use of him.

P'êng was the son of a wealthy landlord and inherited at least three or four hundred *mu* of land. He was a landlord, but he was also the first leader of the present agrarian revolution. I think he learned Marxism when he was a student in Japan. He set his mind to the problem of helping the peasants in Haifeng and wanted to redistribute his own land among them. In trying to find the best method, he used to make every effort to talk with the tenants. It was the peasants' custom when they had leisure time to come together to talk and eat or drink tea. P'êng took these occasions to try to learn about their problems, and also to explain to them the cause of the injustice and suffering they had to undergo and to point out the solution. Of course, they did not trust him—he was of the landlord class—and they wondered what new devilment he was up to, to squeeze even more out of them. "You say these high-sounding words," they would say to him, "but the actions of you landlords are entirely different." He explained his Marxist theories at great length and also promised to redistribute his land as soon as he could arrange it. But the peasants were skeptical until he actually redistributed the land. This was about 1924 or 1925—before the revolt of Ch'ên Ch'iung-ming against Sun Yat-sen.

The father of P'êng Pai, of course, had died. But his mother is still alive. She was progressive, and was arrested for her political views. She went to the U.S.S.R. with the sons of P'êng Pai, her grandchildren.

Ch'ên Ch'iung-ming was the governor of the province and was reactionary and always suppressed the peasants, but he was loyal to his friends and didn't like to hurt P'êng Pai.

He asked P'êng to be head of the Bureau of Education of Kwangtung Province. Because of Ch'ên's friendship, P'êng was often able to escape when he had to flee for his life.

After redistribuing his own land, P'êng tried to help the peasants to organize. He thus built a small foundation for a mass movement among the peasants. As soon as the Kuomintang's Second Eastern Expedition took Huichow, his followers were strong enough to organize a Peasants' Self-Defense Corps, and all the landlords fled to Hongkong. This was about 1925.

Hailufeng was where the first peasant uprising of the revolutionary movement occurred. It is not surprising. The men and women of this district are all good people. In all the area around Canton and Hongkong, no woman dared to go out at night for fear of bad men or gangsters, except in Hailufeng.

Unionization

The Communists had already done educational work among the Hailufeng peasants, even before the Self-Defense Corps had been organized. Practically all the Kuomintang people in Hailufeng were Communists. Ch'ên Ch'iung-ming had established a number of private factories—for weaving, papermaking, umbrella making, and other small industries, and trade-unions had been organized among these workers. In the three weaving factories nearly all the workers were women, and their union was very strong. All the workers were devoted to their unions. At the time of the Kuomintang Eastern Expedition, Ch'ên Ch'iung-ming's factories and all his property were confiscated by the Kuomintang and were run by the workers.

P'êng Pai also founded the Hailufeng Peasant Union, which spread out to every small village. This union was unusual, being made up of both men's and women's unions. The Hailufeng Women's Peasant Union was the only one in all China, and about one-fourth of the seven thousand members of the joint union were women. This shows how strong the peasant movement was—organization had spread even to women. Nearly every peasant joined the union—if he was not a member, he had no privileges.

During the Hongkong strike against the British in 1925–26, the Peasant Union was strong and patriotic and tried to prohibit any exports from going to Hongkong. Eggs, pigs, or chickens being sent there were confiscated and distributed to union members or to those who were poor and hungry.

Both in the Peasant Union and the trade-unions there were special organizations for children. The Lao Tung T'ung-tzŭ T'uan [Workers' Children's Corps] had only about two hundred members because there was little child labor. However, in the Peasants' Union there were many children, and all received special privileges. Primary schools were started for them, and also such recreations as singing and dramatics. The children were active in all kinds of work and happier than they had ever imagined possible. They were from six to fifteen, most being from about eight to ten. Haifeng organized children before any other *hsien*.

All this organization was purely spontaneous. The workers and peasants trained themselves. So far as I know, nothing was known of similar organizations in Russia at that time. Not a person concerned with Hailufeng had been in Russia until later, when a few students returned from there and told about that country. One of the leaders was a Whampoa Communist named Wu Ching-ming, about twenty-four years old, who lived among the peasants.

The Peasants' Self-Defense Corps protected the district from the bandits, who were numerous near Hailufeng, and also against pirates on the coast who tried to make marauding expeditions. Many peasants were killed in a severe battle against the pirates. The Corps wore uniforms, not plain clothes, and all were volunteers.

There was also a General Women's Union made up of peasants, students, teachers, and industrial workers. It had over a thousand members. All were young, and they were enthusiastic because of their recent release from suppression. Some of the men hated this organization because it defended the rights of women and took care of the divorce problem. A woman would come to the union to complain against her husband's or family's treatment, and the union would investigate the case and see to it that the women either received better treatment or was given a divorce. It was teasingly called the "Bureau for Divorce and Remarriage." The concubines of rich men were prominent in the leadership—these women are often the real wives in China, yet they have no legal rights or protection whatever. The oldest in the union were not over thirty; some were girls of twelve or thirteen. This organization was active and effective. In the early period women did not do any of the fighting, but in fighting pirates and bandits they did transportation work in the rear. Many times the bandits scattered when they had been defeated, and the women and children acted as spies and caught them. The men in Hailufeng were not nearly so opposed to women's activities as men elsewhere and were not so reactionary in their views on this subject.

In women's work the industrial girls were the most progressive, but the Haifeng peasant women were more advanced than the women in other *hsien*. In the trade-unions the women usually took the leadership, but the real direction came from the Communists. Industrial girls were more determined. One reason was that they had already had experience in struggling against the exploitation of Ch'ên Ch'iung-ming.

The Peasants' Self-Defense Corps had new guns and bullets from the Kuomintang. Those who did not belong had only their old guns. The Kuomintang sent a magistrate to Hailufeng, but he was merely a puppet of the mass organizations. In all dealings he had to refer to the Peasants' Union and to settle disputes by collective bargaining. The common people settled their own troubles, though they got nominal approval from the magistrate's office.

The Defenses of a Peasant Soviet

I went to Hailufeng in 1926, one year before the Kuomintang attack, to do women's work. I was then not quite seventeen. I later became secretary to Chang San-ming and wrote his letters. Chang San-ming had visited the U.S.S.R. and had been political director of a division of Chang Fa-k'uei's Fourth Route Army commanded by Li Tzŭ-hsin. (Chou Ên-lai was then political director of the First Route Army.) Chang San-ming was very ill with tuberculosis, so he had been sent to Hailufeng—he helped us a great deal and became the head of the Hailufeng Communist party. Another important leader was a native of Hailufeng, named Ch'ên, and there were many other members. Even boys of thirteen and fourteen were active in party work.

The organization of the people's government when I was there was not soviet but transitional. The two responsible authorities were the principal of the Hailufeng middle school, who was not a Communist, and a Communist who was head of the Kuomintang *tangpu* [local or district office]. All the old officials had run away, and the leaders were all Communists or Leftists. There was not much change in the form of government when the soviet idea came in, as it was revolutionary already. The chief difference was that this government decided to defend itself by force against any Kuomintang attack.

In 1927 the Right-Wing Kuomintang decided to use force to suppress the peasant movement against the landlords. This decision was one of the chief causes of the split between the Kuomintang and the Communists, though the Communists tried to compromise on this issue and actually tried to hold down the peasant uprisings in many cases. Most of the liberal and Left-Wing Kuomintang members were in favor of the antilandlord measures and sympathetic with the Communists. In fact, many of them were also Communist party members. The Kuomintang was an entirely different organization after it had "purged" itself of all these progressive elements. The present Kuomintang is not at all like the Kuomintang of the 1925–27 period, except that a few of the leaders remain the same. The Right-Wing Kuomintang killed and suppressed far more "Kuomintang" members than straight Communists in 1927, and it turned against Sun Yat-sen's peasant program.

In Kwangtung, one month before the so-called "purge" began by armed force, the Kwangtung provincial committee found out that Chiang Kai-shek and his group were intending to betray the revolution and had made plans with the landlords to destroy the peasant movement. Hailufeng sent Wu Ching-ming to Canton to discuss what was to be done in self-defense. When Wu returned from the meeting, the Tungkiang Military Council was formed to work secretly in organizing the peasants to defend themselves. One of the men responsible in this field was Ku Ta-ch'ên—a peasant native of Meihsien, not an army man. This military council was formed in Tungkiang; there was none in Canton. Only a few knew about it. The peasants were already aware of the threat against them and the plans of the landlords to return but the attitude of the Kuomintang was not so clear to them. Therefore the Peasants' Self-Defense Corps was always vigilant. Its members now prepared to meet the offensive against them. In a few days a telegram came from Canton telling Hailufeng of the open hostility of the Kuomintang.

We called a mass meeting of all classes, though mostly peasants came. One hour later the Hailufeng People's Government was formed by decision of the meeting.

The telegram from Canton was not sent until after the "purge" had already started in Canton. It was censored, but we received the news through our connections, a little delayed. It was four or five days after the purge had started in Canton, and we called the mass meeting immediately. This was in April or May of 1927, not earlier.

One month after the purge started in Canton, the Kuomintang sent troops through Huichow to attack Hailufeng.

As I was secretary to Chang San-ming, I knew of all that was going on. As soon as we learned of the attack, all the defense forces were called out to join near Huichow to resist the invading troops. These forces were led by Wu Ching-ming, who was in constant contact with Chang San-ming. Hailufeng then had only two or three hundred members in the Self-Defense Corps, aside from spontaneous peasant volunteers. Many boys of fifteen or sixteen volunteered to fight. The Hailufeng people wanted to defend their homes and their lands, and they were strong and bitter because they had formerly suffered so much under Ch'ên Ch'iung-ming and the old landlords. They did not want any of the old regime back. Enthusiasm was high.

The Kuomintang sent two divisions altogether,[3] though maybe not all came at first. We knew there were two divisions against us.

I was in a town, not at the front. This town was Shanwei, the trade center of the whole Hailufeng district. All the peasants pass through there on the way to market. The fighting area was about fifty *li* from us. Supplies and food were transported to the front by the people. Nearly every day I saw peasants who had been hurt by their own homemade guns. The bullets flew back and wounded them. Most of them used bamboo pikes with iron tips.

In the first battle, Hailufeng had a big victory. Many Kuomintang troops were killed, but only a few peasants, so the peasants were very proud. This fighting lasted only one week because of lack of training and guns. After the retreat there were still a hundred of the Peasants' Self-Defense Corps alive. This was a difficult week, as only two thousand had received any military training whatever and our weapons were poor. Really, only enthusiasm supported the peasants. The Peasants' Self-Defense Corps had the guns and uniforms previously supplied by the Kuomintang, but these were the only good guns. Maybe two hundred peasants in the Self-Defense Corps had good new-style guns.

After the defeat, our men retreated to a district called Kungp'ing. The many ordinary volunteers went back to their homes, but the Self-Defense Corps went to Kiangsi. They were sure of protection in Kiangsi, since the Kuomintang army there was sympathetic to the Communists.

Of course, the Kuomintang troops occupied the region easily after the retreat, and everyone was miserable. The women and children cried, and many of them took their belongings and tried to run away.

I was in the city when the Kuomintang entered, but I retreated with the people. So many left that it showed clearly that all the sympathy was with the former government. The people now adopted passive resistance and mobilized secretly. The unions could only exist secretly.

Strategically, if Huichow were lost, all Hailufeng was lost, so the people in the *hsien* did not then attempt a useless resistance. The troops, therefore, did not massacre the population at that time, but upon arriving they raided all organizations and arrested many persons. They didn't get any real leaders—only a few wavering elements and rightist Kuomintang sympathizers—all the others had run away. The Communists had been prepared and were not easily caught. However, the Kuomintang made no distinction, and killed and tortured almost anybody. In the first occupation, about a hundred were executed when the troops entered. The old officials and landlords came with the army for their revenge and killed innocent people as they pleased.

About a hundred Hailufeng Corps men

joined the Kiangsi army, and later a temporary people's government was established near Kiangsi at Swatow. Kuo Mo-jo and Soong Ching-ling were elected to this government. Wu Ching-ming led his Self-Defense Corps to attack Swatow with the Kiangsi troops and was killed in battle in the winter of 1927.

The Kuomintang soldiers never dared stay in Haifeng city at night—only in the daytime. At night they went back to Huichow. They were afraid that there would be night raids and that the people would put poison in the wells and the food. There was no co-operation at all on the part of the people. This showed clearly the political line. On any suspicion, the Kuomintang executed people.

These Kuomintang soldiers were ignorant and had had no political training except that they were told many lies about the Communists—that all the Hailufeng peasants were Communists, for instance, and that none could be trusted. The distance between the troops and the people was very great, and there were no sympathizers in this army. It was impossible to make friends with these soldiers. Only by political work is the bridge between the mercenary soldiers and the people built, and when this is cut away there is no connection. The original Kuomintang armies of the Northern Expedition had many sections which had had political training and were friendly to the people. This was not one of those armies. It was impossible for the peasants to complain to the army about anything. There was complete hostility.

Haifeng being Ch'ên Ch'iung-ming's native place, the army gave back to him everything that had been taken by the peasants and workers, and the peasants and workers became indignant. Our government had given half the land to the peasants and let the landlord keep half. Now the Kuomintang gave all the land to the landlord and raised taxes, too.

Formerly our chief political work had been done in the towns; now it was done secretly in the villages. A mass basis was developed at the lower level instead of at the top. The Kuomintang troops never dared go to the villages. They were afraid of the people. They came to only a few towns and to these in the daytime. Any isolated group of soldiers might be cut off, and nobody would tell. It was easy to organize the Hailufeng peasants secretly because of their past experience and because the old Kwangtung custom of fighting among the tribes and clans had made the people used to fighting. It was a regular custom for each village to have one sentry standing duty near by and other sentries on each mountain.

After we left the cities, our first work was to reorganize the local labor and peasant unions and to check up to see how many members were still alive. Though we were safe from the Kuomintang soldiers in the villages where the people protected us, there were still many reactionary village elders of Ch'ên Ch'iung-ming's regime who could act as spies and turn us over to the troops for execution. A few of the sons of the village elders also were unreliable and had to be watched. The members of the peasant and labor unions were always vigilant and checked on all possible spies. No open leader was safe nor any open work. It was the women and children who carried on the communications system, carrying messages secretly from one place to another.

It is hard for me to remember all the incidents of those exciting days, but it was the great experience of my life. The women of Hailufeng were different from those in Swatow, which is a seaport. They worked on the farms, and it was the custom for them to carry burdens on their shoulders with bamboo poles and to take the produce from the village to market. They were not secluded but moved about freely, so they formed a good communications system. They were not timid at all, but responsible and courageous. They used to put paper messages in their bamboo hats, wrapped up in leaves, and also carried messages inside their bamboo poles.

Although these villages were traditionally suspicious of one another, at this time any stranger who came to a village was given food and shelter and was carefully hidden and guarded as soon as it was found that he was connected with the peasant unions. Here we see the revolutionary change in the old feudal character of village life. No Kuomintang sympathizer was safe in any village. If anyone came who was suspected, he might be executed by the village authority.

Life was very irregular. Communists and union leaders had to move every night to new places for safety. Most of the work could be done only at night. The whole region was one big conspiracy. Sometimes the leaders walked all night, and often they lived in stables.

I remember staying in a small room once, on a bed full of bugs, with the pigs rooting underneath, the cow inside the room, and the chickens coming and going through the door —not to speak of mosquitoes, which are bad in this region. I am what is called a "student," and this life was extremely hard for those of us who had never been accustomed to it. The peasants' life is always hard. In famine time they have nothing to eat, and ordinarily they live on rice and gruel. At this time food was scarce and we lacked money to buy it from poor families. Sometimes for several days we were without rice. We lived mostly on sweet potatoes. In Swatow sweet potatoes were considered fit only for pigs.

There were some farm production co-operatives in Hailufeng on a small scale before I went there. Most of these were for raising pigs, and there were some for raising chickens, but there were none for weaving. The pig-breeding co-operatives also killed and salted the meat and had their own shop for selling it. The Kuomintang dared not destroy these co-operatives because they were in the villages, so the co-operatives continued under the occupation.

I often stayed in a fishing boat, as it was easy to move, and sometimes I stayed in a cave in the hills because the Kuomintang people never dared follow a hill trail for fear of ambush.

This was a period of reorganization and preparation to throw off suppression by an uprising.

Warfare by Intellectuals and Peasants

Now let me tell you of the Kuomintang *wei pao*, or "surrounding attack."

After a time the towns were so quiet that the suspicions of the troops were lulled, and soldiers began spending the night in the towns. It was decided that so many troops were not needed, so only one division was kept at Huichow. We set the date of the uprising on the fifteenth or sixteenth of the seventh month [August], as I remember. All plans were decided upon by the Communist party organization. I see now that it was a mistake to try to take Hailufeng back —it could not be defended with Huichow in enemy hands, and Huichow is the key to the control of the region. It was not of much value to take the cities.

The region was divided into districts, with responsible people in each, and the Communist party had branches everywhere to serve as liaison between the peasant and the labor unions.

The signal for the uprising was to be a fire on a beautiful hill where there were lovely trees and a pavilion.

Everyone was excited and pleased to learn of the plans for the uprising. Everyone wanted revenge for his sufferings under the disruption and occupation. They were all willing to fight to re-establish their own government.

At this time, Chang San-ming and I and two or three others stayed in a village about fifty or sixty *li* from Haifeng. Chang organized the whole uprising, deciding which of the villages should take first action and how.

He was to be the leader, and when he went to the scene of action in a small boat, I asked to be taken along. The others came, too, though none of us had had any military experience.

I have never seen any place with such natural beauty as Hailufeng, though I have seen Hangchow and Soochow and Japan. The river ride from Kungp'ing to Hailufeng is unimaginably beautiful. I remember the moment we rowed into the narrowest part of the channel, which was the prettiest place of all. There we took Chang San-ming to the bank and said good-bye as he went to the city to command the uprising. We stood there with proud hearts, watching as he waved to us and disappeared in the trees.

After Chang San-ming had left us, we were unhappy in the boat because we also wanted to participate in the uprising. We hid in the trees near by, awaiting his return.

He left us at eleven o'clock and within three hours came back and told us that the city of Haifeng was ready, with the workers and peasants divided into separate forces, each waiting for the signal from the pavilion on the hill. He then left us again.

We watched. The signal appeared at the agreed time. Yet the peasants and workers did not attack.

Later we learned what had happened. Our forces inside Haifeng city did not attack in response to the signal, but those outside launched their attack as scheduled. The Kuomintang troops tried to defend themselves, and the outside forces with Chang San-ming were unable to enter the town. Our people inside the city failed to act on time because there were so many enemy troops inside that they became afraid that their forces were too small to gain a victory. There was serious fighting, but we were defeated.

This attempted uprising roused the Kuomintang to destroy our power. They had never suspected what had been going on in the villages. Now they planned to attack the villages one by one to destroy the whole people's movement.

This failure caused the party to realize that our forces were not prepared to meet the Kuomintang head on, so we took *"wei pao"* as our slogan and aimed to concentrate on training and preparation for the future. There were many hills around the villages near Hailufeng, but between Kungp'ing and Hailufeng were big mountains. The order was given that those who wanted military training should come secretly to these mountains.

In the villages there were still many of Ch'ên Ch'iung-ming's group 'of landlords. These individuals seldom went out of the villages. Some had left the villages several years before and returned now and found themselves isolated. As the uprising had failed and no open fighting was permitted by the party, the peasants became impatient and spontaneously killed some of the landlords and took their money, which was all given to the Peasants' Union—not to the Communist party, which gave no orders for this confiscation.

The killing of the landlords was not directed by responsible leaders of the union. It occurred as a natural class revenge. This proved that political education of the people of the region was not widespread. The peasants took "Left infantilist"[4] actions on their own initiative.

I remember one incident in Swatow which was like these in Hailufeng. Once some peasants captured a landlord's house and two of them guarded the gate. A man tried to come out, and the sentries asked who he was.

"I am a friend," he replied.

"No, you're not," the sentries said. "You haven't brought out anything in your hands."

So the man went back to bring out some property to prove himself.

This shows the peasant's idea that not only must the landlord be driven away or killed but also the property must be redistributed.

Some of the landlords escaped and went

to the Kuomintang army, asking the troops to take their revenge for them. When the troops came to a village, most of the peasant leaders had usually escaped. But a landlord was as anxious to torture one tenant as another. He would order the soldiers to hang peasants on trees and expose them to the sun. This was very cruel in the hot sun, and the victims often died of sunstroke. They also drove needles into the fingernails of children as well as men to force them to give information. Everyone they caught—on whom there was any evidence—was badly tortured by many methods. Others were killed, if they did not die of torture.

Nearly every peasant in the villages belonged to the Peasants' Union, which was not a Communist party organ and had been permitted under the rules of the Kuomintang. And now, here is an interesting thing: The peasants did not understand the Communist program clearly. They did not understand why the party did not want confiscation and killing of landlords but only quiet organization to prepare for retaking power later. But they understood what the Kuomintang now stood for and they hated it bitterly, as it was on the side of the landlords. The Kuomintang gave them such severe punishment that ordinary peasants who hardly knew about the Communist party used to learn the party's slogans and shout them at the Kuomintang out of hatred and spite, even though they did not know the meaning of them. They only knew that the Kuomintang hated to hear them. And as the Kuomintang hated the Communists so much, the peasants reasoned that the Communists must be their own best friends. Thus, the peasants thought it a great honor to be considered one of the terrifying "Communists," whether they were or not. They could see that the very name had a magic effect on the Kuomintang.

The peasants were always careful about having guards. There were always three— two outside the village and one inside. After the uprising they paid special attention to sentries. The outer guard would report in-

stantly, and the whole village would be roused. In an hour or two the women and children would all be gone to the hills. The Kuomintang was afraid of the hills, not knowing how large a force might be hidden there. All the villages did this when Kuomintang movements were reported. The peasants tried to estimate the size of the enemy force, and information was relayed from one village to another. If their situation was favorable, the men stayed and fought, sending the women to the hills. If they were too weak in numbers, the men went to the hills, too.

Sometimes a village received a message from the city as to when the Kuomintang might arrive and how large the force was. If the peasants were strong enough, they ambushed it on the road before it could get near the village. If too weak, they always evacuated. As soon as the Kuomintang arrived, the troops burned all the houses and then went back to the city. All the people in the hills saw the smoke and watched the troops march back to the town. I used to watch the faces of the peasants as they all cried aloud. This was not a sign of weakness but of unrepressed emotion and deep hatred. The burning of their houses deepened their hatred of the Kuomintang and made them more determined.

When a peasant's home was destroyed, he had to make a hut of bamboo or go to another village, where he would be treated with sympathy and welcomed. This village would also become indignant on learning of the attack. As more and more people became refugees, the revolt spread with them.

The Kuomintang burned about one-fourth of all the villages in Hailufeng during the three or four months of their occupation up to the time I left. Hailufeng was divided into nine ch'ü [districts] of different sizes. In the second and third districts where I went, there were fourteen or fifteen villages in each ch'ü.

Some of the villages were far apart, and when the peasants evacuated they had to walk over difficult paths that cut and bruised their feet. When they arrived, they were worn out, but they were always received well by the strange village. It was especially hard for the students and the Communist party members who had to move around constantly, as many of them were not used to hard work. There was a middle school in Hailufeng, and all the students there were revolutionary and belonged to the student union. There were also quite a few artists and writers in Hailufeng. The Hailufeng students had important leadership in the whole movement as political workers in the peasant unions, the labor unions, and the Communist party.

It is a strange thing, but true, that in revolutionary work like this the intellectuals can scarcely endure the hard life. Many must give up because of physical weakness. Yet those who stayed on in Hailufeng got strong and healthy. The hard and simple life was good for them. Chang San-ming had such bad tuberculosis that he had had to give up his Kuomintang work before coming to Hailufeng. Yet, he got well, greatly to his own surprise. He was a member of the Kwangtung provincial committee and later went to Canton to help direct the Canton Commune in December 1927. He was killed during the Commune.

A characteristic of Hailufeng peasants was that they never blamed the Communist party for bringing down the wrath of the Kuomintang upon their villages, as the peasants sometimes did elsewhere. This idea was never even mentioned. The Kuomintang always says that it burns the villages to destroy "Communists." In Swatow, some of the peasants were enthusiastic about the revolution occurring there at this same time, but others were not susceptible. Hailufeng was different. All were united. One important reason for their unity was that the seeds of revolt had been sowed by P'êng Pai, their native leader. Of course the real reason was that the peasants had experienced two kinds of life: Under Ch'ên Ch'iung-ming, life had

been hard and unsatisfactory. When they were their own masters, life was good and enjoyable even without enough food. Therefore they all agreed that revolution was best.

It was not uncommon that when old women looked down from the hills and saw their houses burning, they would lift their arms and cry out: "When will P'êng Pai come back to us? Everything will be all right again then." P'êng Pai had gone away to organize other work, as he was a leader of the whole province. He soon came back and organized the Hailufeng soviet, the first in China. He escaped to Shanghai after Hailufeng was again occupied by the Kuomintang, but he was arrested there and was executed in 1929.

Once I was in a village near a lake. I was very tired, and an old woman took me into her big house. I had slept until ten in the morning when she woke me and said that the Kuomintang had attacked and had been repelled. She told me that her son was a member of the Peasants' Union and that her grandson had been taken in the attack and that her neighbors had seen the Kuomintang soldiers hang him to a tree and torture him to death to make him give information. He was only ten years old, but he had refused to speak. He was a member of the Young Vanguards. The grandmother was proud that he had not betrayed—she told me this story with calm emotion as if she understood that her grandson belonged to the people as well as to herself. This woman was over fifty but very capable. She directed her daughters-in-law also to help the Communists, and they were all active. She warned me that a second attack would come and that I should leave immediately. Most of the Communists were not peasants and could not walk fast, so the girl Communists would go to the hills during an attack while the men stayed to fight alongside the peasants. If the whole village was defeated, the party group would then rejoin in the hills to make new plans.

This woman not only directed family affairs. She was also the leader in her village.

Her son was a member of the standing committee of the Peasants' Union, but her activity was more important than his, and it was she who directly influenced and instructed him. She told me quietly that the Kuomintang could not take her village easily because of the lake but that I must go into hiding since I was a "delicate young student."

"All the women in my family can fight, too," she informed me. "I have had them trained. Our whole village is well equipped."

Chang San-ming was hiding with me in this village. He and the old woman mapped out the strategy and arranged to ask other villages to help when the attack came. They estimated that the village could hold out three days. The woman directed people to transport food to another village so that the Kuomintang could not seize it. It was a big village full of shops, and the people were all well trained. Most of the villages had no shops.

My feet were bruised and bleeding, and I could not walk. The old woman made a chair of bamboo and two of her daughters-in-law carried me on their backs out to the hills. We had no shoes at this time. Of course, the peasants were used to going barefoot. A boy student who had returned from the U.S.S.R. went with me. He was exhausted and his feet, too, were in bad condition.

The struggle was about the same in the other villages. The party in Hailufeng did not divide the duties of the members very distinctly—all were combined. Life was extremely hard for the girls in the party, who were mostly students. A girl named Hsü Chin, a young primary school teacher, worked with me. She was pregnant, but continued to work very hard. She could not go back to her home, as it was known she was a Communist. She had to hide in a cave, where she died in childbirth. Her husband was with her in the cave, but there were no doctors. He told me how she hated so to die because she did not want to leave her work unfinished. All the women in Hailufeng worked hard. Even the wife of the head of the Department of Education went barefoot and carried water on a bamboo pole.

I left the region because I also was having a child, and my husband was afraid I would die as the other girl had. This was in the autumn of 1927.

What I have described was the preliminary struggle in Hailufeng. It was followed, when P'êng Pai returned in the autumn, by the establishment of the first soviet district in China. It was intended that the whole Tungkiang region should be made into a soviet, but the attempt failed. The Kuomintang carried out a great massacre in Hailufeng. They would have destroyed the Hailufeng population down to the last child if the soviet had not given up in 1928. The real fighting in Hailufeng began after the Canton Commune in December 1927.

K'ang K'ê-ching

A PEASANT PARTISAN

A woman wears this disguising uniform of the soldier. K'ang K'ê-ching's choice of career was Amazonian, and her physique was sturdy, but typically feminine traits were not absent. She was studying military science in Yenan when this 1937 snapshot was taken.

MISS WALES:

K'ANG K'Ê-CHING learned to read and write from slogans on mud walls while marching with the peasants of Kiangsi. She had been a slave girl and was a partisan leader, seventeen years old, when Chu Tê married her. They have been soldiering together happily ever since, though she is only half his age. She told me that she was the only woman who had ever commanded regular Red troops, with the exception of Ho Ying—the sister of Ho Lung—who was killed in battle in Hupeh. Though known as "the Girl Commander," she never commanded troops in actual warfare. She had, however, become famous for being one of the best sharpshooters in the whole army, and for having the ability to use a pistol with either hand. When I talked with her, she was studying hard at military science and had hopes of becoming a commander in her own right.

K'ang K'ê-ching was the only woman I met in the veteran Communist ranks who was in glowing health. Nearly all of the others were ill from tuberculosis or the aftereffects of preg-

nancies. During the Long March, K'ang K'ê-ching carried her own rifle and knapsack, and once or twice she carried wounded soldiers on her back. She was smoothly and roundly built, and weighed only one hundred twenty pounds, but she was said to be as strong as the average Chinese coolie. Except for her liking for soldiering, she lacked masculine characteristics and looked like a maternal peasant woman.

She was highly class-conscious. The only interest she showed in me was to ask what social class I came from. The driving force in her life seemed to be to prove, first, that the peasant is as good as a person of any other class, or better, and, second, that women are not by nature inferior to men in any field.

During the war with Japan, K'ang K'ê-ching was one of the chiefs of the political department of the Eighth Route Army headquarters; she also spent much of her time in the front lines doing first-aid work. In 1947 she organized nurseries for the children of working mothers, including the "Los Angeles Nursery"

211

in the Northwest, operated with funds from America. When the All-China Democratic Women's Federation was formed in 1949, she became chairman of its Child Welfare Department—a most responsible post in an organization of more than twenty million members.

K'ANG K'Ê-CHING:

MY mother had a girl-child every year. Six of the seven of us were given away at birth to other families because my father was a poor fisherman and could hardly provide rice enough for his three sons, much less for unwanted daughters. We were not even sold—we were given away to become servants, farmhands, and kitchen slaves.

I was born in the village of Lot'angwan in Wanan *hsien*, Kiangsi, in 1912, and one month afterward was given to a farmer's family there to grow up as a slave girl. This farmer had no children, but his parents and his three brothers lived with him. He was a poor tenant and we all worked hard to keep alive. Two of the brothers were hired laborers and the third, who had a wife, worked partly at home and partly for hire by the landlord. As soon as I could fetch and carry I tended the cows, gathered firewood, and cut wild grass for the pigs. Because the farmer and his wife both worked in the fields outside, at the age of ten I did the work of the household. I also worked in the fields and made string for sale.

The Peasant Movement, 1926–27

When I was fourteen there were several floods and a famine in the district, so we had to move away from the fields. We were desperately poor then. It was at this time that the Kuomintang started the Northern Expedition—in 1926. A Kuomintang organizer, who was also a Communist, came to our district and explained the peasant problem to the farmers. My foster father was immediately influenced and became chairman of the village Peasant Union which was formed at

that time. I helped him with this work in Lot'angwan, and I also joined the Women's Union organized by the Kuomintang in 1926.

Though I was only fifteen and could neither read nor write, in 1927 I was made Communist Youth Inspector of the work of the union in our district of ten villages. I joined the Communist Youth and was captain of the Young Pioneers. At this time the Great Revolution failed and the Kuomintang began expelling the Communist elements. In order to escape arrest, I ran away and hid in the mountains about fifty or sixty *li* from the house. The Kuomintang had a list of suspected Communists for arrest, and told the people of the village that their houses would all be burned to the ground if they did not find us. My foster father and one of his brothers were Communists, too, and had hidden in another place.

The Kuomintang told the village people that if they would guarantee certain persons not to be Communists, these would be spared, and the village sent word to both me and my foster father that if we would return we would be guaranteed, so we went back. However, in spite of this promise, many who were guaranteed were arrested as soon as they returned. The landlords took their revenge. In our district of ten villages in Wanan *hsien*, a thousand peasants were executed in February 1927. Most of this massacring was done by the 70th and 79th Kuomintang divisions, which were there then. Later, the 80th, 81st, and 91st Kuomintang divisions arrived; they also stopped to execute the farmers, but some of the farmers were able to escape because many of the soldiers sympathized with us. The soldiers of these three divisions were shocked at the atrocities and were much kinder than the first two. Farmers were arrested in the morning and executed at night. Only about a third of those killed were actually Communists. Before the split in 1927, both the Communists and the Kuomintang were open so that it was easy to get lists of members.

Some Communists were killed openly in the fields without even benefit of arrest. Some were caught and beaten in order to get them to betray the hiding places of their comrades and were afterward killed. Some were stripped naked and burned slowly at the stake. Many women and pregnant mothers were executed. The wives and children of Communists were killed with them. Many Communist Youth boys and girls were executed also. Even many revolutionary sons of landlords were executed, and the landlords were arrested.

During this terrible time of class war, the *min t'uan* hired by the landlords were the most reactionary. It was they who were responsible for finding the victims and therefore they did most of the torturing. The landlords helped track down the victims and they were helped by the poorer villagers whose lives and property were threatened if they did not.

Because of having the guaranty of my village, I had not been arrested, but during a mass meeting called by the Kuomintang someone who wanted to betray me demanded that I repent before the meeting. I refused. Then people gathered around me and defended me, saying: "She is only a child fifteen years old and knows nothing. She doesn't know what she is saying." I did not cry and still refused though I was much afraid, and my friends hurried me away and back to the house. Some Communists betrayed to the Kuomintang at this time, but I wanted to continue the revolution. The killing of my comrades made me furiously angry and more revolutionary than before. I plotted with some other comrades to revive the movement, but we had no organization left. Though the Communist chief in the district had not been killed, seven or eight leaders had run away.

Then I had a new problem. Although my foster father was a Communist, he still had a feudal mind. He had previously arranged a marriage for me with a shop clerk whom I did not even know, and the marriage was scheduled to take place. I tried to escape, and my foster father locked me in a small room. This was in 1928. On the eve of the marriage, the revolutionaries in the village received a letter from the Red Army saying that it would arrive. I saw the Red soldiers coming into the village, and my foster uncle told me he was going to join. I begged to go with him but he refused. The Red Army stayed long enough to do a little propaganda work, and the next day I escaped from the small room and joined them.

The Red Partisans

The Red Army asked all our local Communists to go out and call the mass of the farmers to support it. I participated in this agitation work among the farmers, leading the Communist Youth and making speeches. However, the Red Army did not stop but marched on, leaving only the Red partisans they had organized while there. We were afraid that after the army had gone the Kuomintang would kill us, and about one hundred from my village joined the army. I joined, together with six other girls about nineteen years old or so, some of whom were in the Communist Youth and some not Communists at all. Therefore, I joined the Red Army in 1928 at the age of sixteen. We carried the hammer-and-sickle then, but not the Red Star.

This was the Fourth Red Army under Chu Tê. We went to Suich'uan. After this the enemy also arrived there, so we all went to Chingkangshan in Linkang *hsien*, Kiangsi, in August 1928. Chingkangshan was the rear of the Red forces then.

The hundred of us who joined from Wanan *hsien* were not regularly enlisted in the Red Army but were partisan organizers. We organized partisan movements and distributed guns to them from the Red Army. Many returned to my native *hsien* to fight there. I was a partisan leader but did not carry a gun, as I did organizing and propaganda work.

Chingkangshan was a very steep mountain with a plateau on the top. The plateau could be reached only by five passes—three big and two small ones. The enemy could not attack it easily. After we had been on the mountain about four months, the Kuomintang besieged it from August to November; then the main Red Army came down from the mountain, leaving only P'êng Tê-huai's Fifth Red Army to guard the place.

There were about a hundred women altogether on Chingkangshan, but only ten or eleven were from my district.

Marriage with Chu Tê

In January 1929, Chu Tê and I were married on top of the mountain Chingkangshan. I had first met him personally in August 1928, at Suich'uan, six months before. I was then seventeen and Chu Tê was forty-three. I don't remember the day of the month. We don't make a wedding an event in the Red Army. Since then I have always been with Chu Tê except for the time when we were separated for one year after the occupation of Kian in 1930. Sometimes we don't live in the same house, of course, and we have no children because they would interfere with my work.

I didn't fall in love with Chu Tê in the romantic manner when I first met him, though I liked him very much because he lived as a common soldier and did the same work. Of course, everybody loved Chu Tê as a revolutionary leader. We have always been the best of comrades—and I must admit that, after a transition period, I probably did fall in love with him.

Chu Tê had just lost his other wife, a revolutionary girl named Wu Yü-lan, who was executed by the Kuomintang at the end of 1928. He had married her at Leiyang, Hunan, in the same year. I met her only once —at Chingkangshan.

I have never had a quarrel with Chu Tê during these eight years. Sometimes I give him a little criticism, but everything he does is usually correct. Neither of us orders the other around. Of course, when he is sick I take care of him as a comrade, but I never pay attention to his food or clothes. That is done by his bodyguards.

From Chingkangshan to the Long March

When we came down from Chingkangshan, I was one of the partisans. Sometimes I carried a gun but I did not fight in battle. I was doing propaganda work. At that time my idea was that we must fight against any odds, and I expected the "Second Great Revolution" would come. Although we were in a very difficult position, I did not mind the hardships because, of course, revolution is always hard. From Chingkangshan to Kian there were no important events in my personal life.

We left P'êng Tê-huai on Chingkangshan with a thousand troops of his own and a thousand bandits. These bandits were the followers of Wang Tso and Yen Wen-ts'ai, two leaders who were on Chingkangshan when the Red Army arrived; the bandits cooperated with the Red Army. The Fourth Red Army—under Chu Tê and Mao Tsê-tung—and the partisans wanted to go to Kanchow. At that time we still had only a hundred partisans. Three Kuomintang divisions cut the road to Kanchow, so we fought with them only a little and retreated, turning aside to T'ungku, where there was a small Red Army garrison, the 2nd and 4th regiments. About this time Lo Ping-hui, now commander of the Thirty-second Army, led an uprising of White troops to join the Red Army.

Near T'ungku we fought against two Kuomintang divisions and defeated them, so we arrived safely at T'ungku and rested for one week. Then the Kuomintang attacked. We left T'ungku and went to Tingchow in Fukien. During this fighting the Red Army killed a Kuomintang division commander. In Tingchow, where we stayed two weeks, we met Dr. Fu Lien-chang, the first doctor to join with us. The Red Army knew that he was sympathetic, and we sent our wounded to his hospital. In Tingchow we reorganized and expanded the army. At Kaoyang, a small village in Lungyen *hsien*, Fukien, the partisans had only ten guns; to help them the Fourth Red Army went there and defeated the Kuomintang. From there we went to Yungting and then back to three *hsien* in Kiangsi—Tayü, Nank'ang, and Hsinfeng. This was the time of the "Li Li-san line" of wanting to attack the cities.

The Fourth Red Army then went to Jui-kin, then again moved to the three Fukien *hsien* of Tingchow, Lungyen, and Shiang-hang, and then went on to Meihsien in north Kwangtung. The army stayed only one day at Meihsien, where we held a meeting and found the masses quite revolutionary. Next day the Kuomintang pursued us. At this time we had seven or eight thousand men but only four or five thousand guns. On Chingkangshan we had had only one thousand guns.

Ninety *li* from Meihsien is a place called called Mat'ou, and the Red Army went there but the Kuomintang did not follow so we again attacked the Kuomintang at Meihsien. The enemy stayed inside the city, and, as their equipment was better than ours, we went back to Hsünwu *hsien* in south Kiangsi and to Wup'ing *hsien* in west Fukien. Although the Red Army had previously been in Meihsien only one day and even the merchants had not run away, the Kuomintang troops killed many workers, students, and poor farmers there.

The Red Army then went to Hsingkuo, near Kanchow in Kiangsi, where the army rested and the troops were reorganized. This was in the first part of 1930. After that we attacked Kian but did not occupy it. As the Li Li-san line ordered the army to attack the cities, the Red Army also attacked Nanchang, the Kiangsi capital, but did not occupy it. We then went to Hunan Province.

P'êng Tê-huai left Chingkangshan two months after we did and fought many battles. In August 1930 he occupied Changsha, the Hunan capital, but held it only ten days. He then came out and joined with Chu Tê;

thus the Fourth and Fifth Red armies met together. They made a combined force of from ten to twenty thousand men.

After this the Fourth and Fifth Red armies went to Kiangsi and fought many battles along the Kan River on the Kiangsi-Hunan border, and attacked Kian, but the peasants themselves, thirty thousand strong, had already, occupied the city before we arrived.

Kian was captured in August 1930. At that time I became director of the Youth School for a short while. The students were all leaders from the masses or from the army. In the meantime I had learned to read and write. From the time I was on Chingkang-shan in 1929 to the latter part of 1930, I had studied so hard that I was able to read the newspapers. I had no special teacher, but learned by myself from slogans and the like. Sometimes now I write articles on the work of the Red Army. I have never read a novel in book form, but I read ordinary magazines such as *Women's Life*. I have read the *A.B.C. of Leninism*, the *Principles of Leninism*, and reports by Stalin and Dimitrov. I understand Marxism as far as I have yet studied it, and I am now working hard on theory.

After a while I was made director of the Headquarters Guard Regiment. I was the only girl in the Red Army at this time. The others all did political work. I always carried a gun and several times was ordered to prepare to fight with the Guard Regiment but I never actually engaged in battle. Nearly every day since I left Suich'uan in 1928 I had been in the middle of fighting, and had no fear of it whatever, although I had not myself participated in battle. At first most of the girls had been nervous and excitable, but by now they had lost their fear. For six months I traveled with the headquarters, mainly doing political and educational work among the soldiers.

Six months later I was transferred to the Department of Communications detachment, and after the First Campaign I was called back to headquarters and sent out as inspector to investigate the condition of communications at the front.

During the First Campaign and the first part of the Second, I was at the front all of the time. I was with Chu Tê but, of course, was in a different department.

Near the end of the Second Campaign I went to the rear. There I worked in the arms and munitions stores, where all our captured arms were concentrated. I was in the statistics department. All Red Army guns have been captured from the Kuomintang. At that time we had plenty of arms and ammunition. We had ten thousand rifles stored, fifty or sixty trench mortars, three mountain cannon, and one or two horizontal artillery pieces. We had no captured airplanes. At the beginning of the Third Campaign, we shot down one enemy plane but it fell within the enemy lines. During this period the Kuomintang was very stupid about transporting its stores and it was easy for us to capture all that we wanted during battles.

Before the beginning of the Third Campaign I returned to the front. Our troops were then moving toward west Kiangsi. I was in charge of youth work at the front headquarters. I did this work until the end of the Fourth Campaign, when I went to Juikin for the First All-Soviet Delegates Congress at the end of 1931. At this time I worked at a very important and confidential job in the radio code department of the Revolutionary Military Council. In 1931 I joined the Communist party.

In the early part of 1932 I was made detachment commander of the Women Volunteers, made up of two hundred women. This was organized in Yütu, then we marched to Juikin, the capital, to become attached to the Red Military Academy. All were peasants and most were from the local population. There were no students. After good training, intellectuals might be able to do this kind of work, but in general peasant girls have much greater endurance and are more determined and unwavering. Even

with thorough training the intellectual's social background asserts itself in actual fighting. Theoretical understanding of the revolution is not enough to overcome this background.

This detachment of Women Volunteers received six months' training in the academy and then was sent to the rural districts. During the time that I was in charge of the Volunteers, I also audited the regular classes in military science at the academy and was afterward permitted to enter the academy as a regular student. I turned out to be an excellent student and made a great advance in military as well as political knowledge. I was second in my class.

A middle-school student named Liang Ying was also permitted to join the academy. We were the first girl-cadets to study at the Red Academy. Our work was exactly the same as that of the men. The other girl, however, had had no experience in military work and made many mistakes. The school expelled her before she graduated. This was at the time when we were having trouble with the Li Li-san line; the girl was sympathetic with the counterrevolution and denied that some accused comrades were counterrevolutionary; so she was expelled. She married at that time; I don't know what became of her afterward.

Before I graduated from the academy, the soviet government ordered me to the rear to inspect hospital work, and on my return I was made instructor in a class at the Red Academy on the reconstruction of the soviets and the building up of the Red Army. After only one month, I was ordered to the front and appointed to be an instructor at Front Headquarters. Later on I returned to the rear and continued my former work until the beginning of the Long March.

Once while I was working at the rear in 1934 I led the troops in battle. This was between Wanan and Kanchow in Kiangsi. I went out to inspect the work of the Party, and by chance we met the enemy and had to grab our guns and fight. I was temporarily

Mantzu tribeswomen in the "Grasslands" of Sikong Province — a photograph preserved by K'ang K'ê-ching as a memento of the Long March. A "Special Independent Government of the Minorities" was established among the Mantzu in 1935, during the course of the march.

elected commander by the three hundred men there. I was the only woman. We fought for two hours; then the enemy retreated. I don't know whether I killed anyone or not—I couldn't see the results of my shooting—but I am a very good marksman. I must say this was a happy day for me. The enemy learned that I was in command, and I heard they were afraid of me because they said: "Chu Tê's wife has come and she is very fierce." Thus I got the nickname "the Girl Commander."

The Long March

During the Long March I was with Chu Tê all the time. We saw each other every day. However, I took no care of his food or clothes. His bodyguards did that. I was so busy that I didn't even have time to wash my own clothes, as during the Long March my work was in the organization of mass movements. Chu Tê does not like women to do housework. He cares nothing for the comforts of his personal life. Mao Tsê-tung's wife takes good personal care of him, but she has no other work to do and he does not spend his time at the front.

I had no special experience during the Long March. It was as easy for me as taking a stroll every day. Sometimes I rode a horse, but only about one-tenth of the whole time. Usually I walked with the others and carried my own belongings, sometimes helping those who were weaker. I usually car-

ried three or four rifles. I did this in order to encourage the others, because the wife of the commander in chief should always be a model for others to follow in these matters. Chu Tê always does these things too. He rode only half the time and walked the other half. Sometimes we had only straw sandals. Every night we camped together, and all the leaders would meet—Chu Tê, Mao Tsê-tung, and Chou Ên-lai. We marched in two long parallel lines and sometimes the vanguard and rearguard were two days apart.

We called mass meetings at every place along the way and spread political propaganda. We confiscated the property of the landlords, and the poor people everywhere welcomed us, especially in Szechuan, Kweichow, Hunan, and Yünnan.

I think the most difficult spot we found was in Tsok'êchi, in Szechuan, or later at Mo-erhkai, where we could get no food. We ate barley, grass, and the bark of trees. The fighting was worse at Paotso in the Mantzu tribe region. In the Grasslands the Mantzu horsemen made surprise attacks. Our men could not fight well because of the rarified air, and many of the weaker died at this time.

I crossed the Grasslands twice. The first time was when Mao Tsê-tung's army crossed the Grasslands successfully but we did not. We tried to cross in two routes, but our route was blocked by a flooded river in the middle of the Grasslands called the "Huang Ho"—this was as much our "sorrow" as the big Yellow River is "China's Sorrow." We had to go back and spend the winter in Tibet, where we lived on horse meat, yak meat, mutton, and beef. It was there that Chu Tê got his big Sikang dog which barks at anybody who does not wear a red-starred cap.

Chu Tê had separated from Mao Tsê-tung at Tsok'êchi and the two did not see each other again for a year. Mao had taken three armies and Chu Tê two armies.

In 1936 we began the march from Tibet together with Hsü Hsiang-ch'ien's five armies, making seven armies altogether, and in October we met the other Red Armies at Huining Kansu.

When I arrived in north Shensi I studied at the party school and later at the "Chinese People's Anti-Japanese Military and Political Academy," as we call the Red Academy. My ambition now is to do real military work as Ho Lung's sister did. I am hoping to become a commander in the army. Comrade Chu Tê sympathizes with my ambition and wants me to perfect my military knowledge so I can be capable of commanding an army in the future. I think I will succeed—I am very good at military science. I have learned a great deal from Chu Tê and always listen when he talks to others.

Only two women have ever been commanders in the main Red Army. One is myself and the other was Ho Lung's sister, Ho Ying, who was killed in battle. However, in Szechuan, Hsü Hsiang-ch'ien organized one regiment of women and gave the command to two women, Chang Ch'ên-ch'u and Chang Kuang-lan. Both are now in Ningshia with Hsü Hsiang-ch'ien's troops. Their regiment still has about eight hundred women, but it is now commanded by Wang Ch'üanyüan. Just before the Sian Incident on December 12, 1936, these women engaged in the bitter fighting with the Mohammedans in that region. The Fourth Front Red Army had a difficult time because the Ma generals have support from the Mohammendan masses, and also because the Red Army didn't know how to approach them properly in political work, and consequently didn't establish a good relation with the masses. Many of these Szechuan women-soldiers were captured by Ma Hung-k'uei. Some were sold, some were forced to marry the Mohammedans, some were forced to do manual labor, and some were executed by the local Mohammedan authorities.

You ask what influenced me to become a revolutionary. Of course, the objective reason for my becoming a revolutionary was the poverty I lived in. Subjectively, I was influenced by the Great Revolution and by the Communist party and by the idea of the emancipation of oppressed humankind. Then, too, Chu Tê has influenced me very much as he does everyone, but not as a personal influence.

NOTES

Introduction: COMMUNISTS OF THE CHINESE REVOLUTION

[1] Chen Pan-tsu [*sic*], "Reminiscences of the First Congress of the Communist Party of China," *The Communist International*, October 1936, p. 1363.

[2] *The Second Congress of the Communist International* (Moscow, 1920), p. 114.

[3] M. N. Roy in an interview with Robert North at Dehra Dun, India, October 15, 1950.

[4] *The 2nd Congress of the Communist International, As Reported and Interpreted by the Official Newspapers of Soviet Russia* (Washington, 1920), p. 44.

[5] *The Second Congress of the Communist International*, p. 478.

[6] *Ibid.*, pp. 570–79. Italics mine.

[7] *Protokoll des IV Kongresses der Kommunistischen Internationale* (Hamburg, 1923), p. 615.

[8] Harold R. Isaacs, *The Tragedy of the Chinese Revolution* (London, 1938; rev. ed.; Stanford, California, 1951).

[9] P. Mif, *Heroic China: Fifteen Years of the Communist Party of China* (New York, 1937), p. 53.

[10] *Manifesto of the August 7 Conference of the Chinese Communist Party* (1927).

[11] J. Stalin as reported in *Pravda*, July 28, 1927; "A Resolution in the International Situation," *International Press Correspondence*, August 18, 1927, p. 1076.

[12] *International Press Correspondence*, August 4, 1927, p. 1006.

[13] *The Communist International: Between the Fifth and Sixth World Congresses, 1924–28*.

[14] Mif, *op. cit.*, p. 54.

[15] *Ibid.*

[16] Mao Tsê-tung, *Report of an Investigation of the Peasant Movement in Hunan* (1927). Mao uses the word "democratic" in the Communist sense.

[17] Edgar Snow, *Red Star Over China* (rev. ed.; New York, 1938), p. 151.

[18] *Report on the Activity of the Communist International, March–November, 1926*, p. 118.

[19] *Hung Ch'i* ["Red Flag"], March 26, 1930.

[20] "Theses and Resolutions of the VI World Congress of the Communist International," *International Press Correspondence*, December 12, 1928, p. 1672.

[21] "A Letter to the Central Committee of the Chinese Communist Party from the Executive Committee of the Comintern" (approved by the Political Secretariat of the Comintern October 26, 1929), *Hung Ch'i*, February 15, 1930.

[22] Chou Ên-lai, *Report to the Third Plenum* (n.d.).

[23] "The Discussion of the Li Li-san Line by the Presidium of the Executive Committee of the Comintern," *Pu-êrh-sai-wei-k'o*, May 10, 1931.

[24] *Ibid.*

[25] "The Report of the Oriental Department of the Comintern in Regard to the Third Plenum of the Chinese Party and the Errors of Comrade Li Li-san," *Pu-êrh-sai-wei-k'o*, May 10, 1931.

[26] *Ibid.*

[27] *International Press Correspondence*, June 10, 1931, p. 552.

[28] Chang Kuo-t'ao, in an interview with Robert North, November 3, 1950.

[29] *Ibid.*

[30] *Ibid.*

[31] Shee Pin, "A Heroic Trek," *The Communist International*, January 1936, p. 130.

[32] O. Brière, "Les 25 Ans du Parti Communiste Chinois," *Bulletin de l'Université l'Aurore*, III, No. 3, 379.

[33] *International Press Correspondence*, January 26, 1933, p. 91.

[34] *International Press Correspondence*, December 21, 1935, p. 1728.

[35] *International Press Correspondence*, August 20, 1935, pp. 971–72.

[36] *International Press Correspondence*, November 9, 1935, p. 1489.

[37] "The Central Committee of the Chinese Communist Party to the Third Plenary Session of the Fifth Central Executive Committee of the Kuomintang, February 10, 1937," as reprinted in the *United States Relations with China (White Paper)*, Department of State Publication 3573 (Washington, 1949), p. 522.

[38] Nym Wales, *Inside Red China* (New York, 1939), p. 211.

[39] *United States Relations with China*, p. 523.

[40] The extent of Chiang's "emergency powers" and the nature of his instruments of party control can be judged from chapter iii, "Government Structure," *China Hand Book, 1937–1945* (rev. ed.; New York, 1947), and from Paul M. Linebarger, *The China of Chiang Kai-shek* (Boston, 1941), Appendixes G, 11-B, and 11-D.

[41] Ch'ên Shao-yü, "A Summary of the Conference of the Politburo in March, 1939," *K'ang-Jih min-tsu t'ung-i chan-hsien chih-nan*, Vol. III (1934).

[42] *Communist International*, July 1938, pp. 688–89.

[43] Report by Mao Tsê-tung to the Central Committee of the Communist Party of China, Peking, June 5, 1950, American Consulate General, Hongkong, Suppl. No. 3, June 28, 1950.

[44] Ch'ên Po-ta, "The October Revolution and the Chinese Revolution," transmitted by the New China News Agency via Peking radio in English Morse to North America, November 7, 1949.

[45] From a speech before the Trade Union Conference of Asian and Australasian countries, November 16, 1949, as transmitted by the New China News Agency via Peking Radio in English Morse to North America, November 23, 1949.

[46] *For a Lasting Peace, For a People's Democracy*, January 27, 1950.

Part One: TEACHERS AND STUDENTS

LIAO CH'ÊNG-CHIH

[1] Most reports give Chinese casualties as 52 killed and 117 wounded, and foreign casualties as 2 killed.

Contemporary reports state that the Chinese fired first.

[2] Leader of the Kuomintang Right Wing and deadly political enemy of Liao Chung-k'ai, leader of the Kuomintang Left.

[3] A biographical note on Chêng Kên is given in the chapter on Fu Lien-chang.

[4] On April 15, 1927, the new Rightist government was set up at Nanking, in opposition to the Kuomintang Left at Hankow (Wuhan).

[5] This name for the Hupeh-Honan-Anhwei soviet region is composed of the ancient names for these three provinces—O, Yü, and Wan. The old names are still used by the local people. Written in this form, Oyüwan usually refers to the region where the provinces adjoin or to the soviet in that region.

TUNG PI-WU

[1] Since *hsien* will appear frequently in the place names in these accounts, an explanation of its twofold usage is necessary. A *hsien* is the administrative unit of a Chinese province, each province usually having about a hundred of these units, corresponding to our counties. The *hsien* town, corresponding to a county seat, usually has the same name as the *hsien*. Whether the seat or the "county" is meant will usually be evident from context. Generally, where I have italicized *hsien*, the county is meant; where I was certain that the county seat was meant roman type is retained.

[2] Huang Hsing and Sun Yat-sen were the two most important members of the T'ung Mêng Hui. Sun was the ideologist, Huang the man of action in command of the revolutionary armies.

[3] "Betrayed" is the closest equivalent for the Chinese word used here by Tung Pi-wu—and frequently employed by the subjects of the other autobiographies, as will be seen. But the meaning is more general in Chinese than in English—it is not so strong as "deserted to" and sometimes means merely a changing-over in one's ideas. To avoid circumlocution I am retaining *betrayed* even in some instances were its use is ungrammatical, believing that the quality of the betrayal will be suggested by the context.

[4] Begun May 4, 1919, by students protesting the treatment of China at the Versailles Conference, the movement gave impetus to the earliest significant strikes and boycotts by labor organizations.

[5] *Pai hua* (plain speech) is the vernacular. Prior to the adoption of *pai hua* in the schools the only written form of Chinese acceptable in educational work was the *wên yen* of the classics.

[6] This was the "First Congress of the Chinese Communist Party" described in the Introduction to this book.

[7] Head of the Japanese puppet government at Nanking in 1944, after the death of Wang Ching-wei.

[8] H. Sneevliet, who under the name of "Maring" was the first representative of the Communist International in China.

[9] "Communist Party." The initials in English form were often used in spoken Chinese. "C.Y." (Communist Youth) and "C.E.C." (Central Executive Committee) were similarly used.

[10] A rebellion by Kuomintang troops at Nanchang, August 1, 1927. Simultaneous rebellion occurred in Hankow. These troops, some of whom were Communist-led, attempted to take Canton for the purpose of establishing a revolutionary base there. They were defeated in a series of engagements in southern China and greatly reduced in number by battle casualties. General Chu Tê led the surviving troops into Kiangsi Province, where Mao Tsê-tung joined them as political adviser. From these origins came the forces later known as the Red Army. The date of the Nanchang Uprising is celebrated as a holiday in Communist China.

[11] Tung's estimates are contradicted by other reports.

HSÜ T'Ê-LI

[1] The popular term for students who went to France during the labor shortage after the first World War and worked to support themselves and pay for their education while studying abroad.

WU LIANG-P'ING

[1] For a description see the chapter on Liao Ch'êng-chih.

[2] Then head of the Shanghai Civil Intelligence Department.

HSÜ MÊNG-CH'IU

[1] *Hsien* magistrate; administrative head of the *hsien* or county.

[2] The "Young Marshal." A biographical note concerning him is given in the chapter "Liu Chih."

[3] Recollections of Liao Chung-k'ai by his son appear in the chapter "Liao Ch'êng-chih."

[4] Hired militia maintained by local landlords to keep peace and order—particularly resented by small farmers, agricultural workers, and reformers for their part in suppressing peasant uprising.

[5] His autobiographical statements are given in the chapter "Hsü Hsiang-ch'ien."

[6] I have been unable to ascertain the real name and the later history of this person. It was said that he had been an officer of high rank in the German army. He entered the Kiangsi soviet about 1934, made the Long March, and left Yenan for Europe about 1938.

[7] In Chinese, *Kinsha Kiang*—the local name for the Yangtze in its upper reaches where it enters China proper.

[8] Independent Lololand occupied then a territory of 11,000 square miles on the Yünnan-Szechuan·border, lying in the great bend of the upper Yangtze River. The aboriginal Lolos (they call themselves *I-Chia*) fiercely tried to maintain independence and killed or captured Chinese to make slaves of them. In Yenan I talked with several of them who had joined the Red Army on the Long March and were studying Marxism. One was about six feet tall and fair, with clear blue eyes. The others had hazel-grey or light brown eyes. (They looked on me as a fellow-tribesman because of my blue eyes.) This Lolo told me he had joined the

First Army Corps at the Tatu River together with several hundred fellow tribesmen. He explained that in Lololand "there are two classes—'Blackbones' and 'Whitebones.' The 'Blackbones' are the ruling class and slave-owners, and the 'Whitebones' are slaves. Every 'Blackbone' has about fifty slaves, and can beat them or hang them as he likes. The slaves are very oppressed and unhappy, so many 'Whitebones' took the chance to escape when the Red Army came." The Lolos are said to have traces of polyandry and to worship the sky.

9 A city near the border of Szechuan and Tibet in the region of the Hsi-fan (Sifan) and Mantzu tribes.

10 Measure of weight: one *chin* (or *catty*) equals about 1⅓ lbs.

WANG SHOU-TAO

1 For an appreciation of P'êng Pai, see the chapter "Ts'ai Ting-li."

2 At Changsha, May 21, 1927. Though directed by General Hsü Kê-hsiang, the massacre was planned by General Hsia Tou-yin—perhaps the most cruel and bitterly revengeful of the anti-Communist commanders. A firsthand account is given in the chapter "Wang Chêng."

Part Two: RECRUITS FROM INDUSTRY

TS'AI SHU-FAN

1 The term applied to those unions which either had been organized by company owners or were not opposed to co-operation with the owners.

2 Meaning "too far ahead of the immediate situation," or "too radical or too leftist for the times."

WANG CHÊNG

1 *T'uhao* ["local rascals"] was applied by the peasants to oppressive, hated landlords as a term of derogation, not to landlords who were regarded favorably for their fairness or kindness.

2 The "Li Li-san period" covered the last half of 1930. During this period Li, as head of the Communist party in Shanghai, was urging the capture of cities as a means of joining the efforts of the labor movements in the cities with those of the peasant associations in the soviets.

3 Later renamed the "Sixth Red Army."

4 "Little ghost" or "little devil"—an affectionate term for the war orphans who followed the armies. In return for food the *hsiao kwei* carried water and messages; some, though only ten or twelve years old, would serve as orderlies to officers.

TÊNG FÊNG

1 Literally, "the old hundred surnames," meaning the traditional original families, but also used in some current literature in the sense of "the masses."

2 One *tan* equals 100 *chin*, or about 133⅓ lbs.

3 Refers to the archaic system of group responsibility, revived by the Kuomintang, whereby the families in a community were divided into units of ten or a hundred families each and each family could be held responsible for the acts of the others in the same "pao chia" unit. Theoretically, a unit of one hundred families could be punished if a member of one of the families in the unit joined the Communist party.

Part Three: SOLDIERS FROM THE RANKS

LO PING-HUI

1 During the winter of 1935 a part of the First Front Red Army under Chu Tê and Lo Ping-hui remained in the Mantzu region in Sikang, together with the whole Fourth Front Red Army under Hsü Hsiang-ch'ien. There they organized the first soviet "Special Independent Government of the Minorities," which included a population of about 200,000. The capital of the government was at K'angting. The Mantzu are found mainly in western Szechuan and in Sikang. While I was in Yenan I talked with four Mantzu tribesmen who had joined tne Red Army in July 1935. About a thousand other Mantzu and Tibetans from Sikang, including thirty Mantzu cavalrymen, had joined the army. These four came from the "Great Grasslands" region and were studying Marxism during their stay in Yenan. They were being trained to return home as missionaries for Marxism.

Part Four: MILITARY ACADEMY GRADUATES

CHÊNG TZŬ-HUA

1 The reference to "Yellow" unions, as in the chapter on Ts'ai Shu-fan, means those unions which were sponsored by the company owners or, if not sponsored by the owners, were not opposed to co-operation with them.

2 This refers to the Tayeh Uprising. See also p. 182.

HSÜ HSIANG-CH'IEN

1 Wut'aishan is one of the sacred mountains of China. It became the headquarters of the Eighth Route Army and the center of that army's "Shansi-Chahar-Hopei-Special Area" (also known as "Chin-chia-chi," from the ancient names of these three provinces).

2 P'êng Pai is remembered as the founder of the first Chinese soviet. The brilliant son of an important landlord family, he became sympathetic with revolution and was active in organizing peasants during 1925–27. Having previously divided his own land among his tenants, P'êng organized a soviet in his native Hailufeng district in 1927. This soviet was annihilated in 1928 and P'êng escaped to Shanghai where, in 1929, he was arrested and executed. An extended account of him is given in my book *Song of*

Ariran; see also, in the present book, comments in the chapter on Ts'ai Ting-li.

[3] The Red Spears are a secret society of long standing. In former times they carried long spears ornamented with red tassels. The word *Red*, in this connection, does not have the revolutionary or Communist significance that it does, for example, in "Red Army."

NIEH HO-T'ING

[1] Military governor of a province.

[2] The "Hsü K'ê-hsiang Massacre" of Communists, liberals, and labor leaders occurred May 21, 1927, at Changsha, capital of Hunan Province. An account is given in the chapter on Wang Chêng. Hsia Tou-yin was the superior commander to Hsü K'ê-hsiang, and ordered him to raise a mutiny against the Hankow government.

[3] This force was chiefly made up of cadets from the branch of Whampoa Academy at Wuchang (see p. 150).

Part Five: DOCTORS

FU LIEN-CHANG

[1] His friendship with Dr. Fu Lien-chang is mentioned in the introduction to this chapter. Chêng Kên was born in a landlord family of Hsianghsiang *hsien*, Hunan, in 1904. He ran away from home when twelve years old and was a soldier in Lu T'i-p'ing's army for five years; joined the Communist Youth in 1922; attended Chiang Wu T'an and Whampoa military academies; graduated in the first class of Whampoa cadets and fought against Ch'ên Ch'iung-ming as an aide to Chiang Kai-shek. He spent 1926 in Moscow as a student and on his return participated in the Nanchang Uprising. After two years of Communist party work in Shanghai he was ordered to Hsü Hsiang-ch'ien's army in the Oyüwan soviet. Wounded in the Fourth Campaign, he was sent as a delegate to Shanghai and was betrayed there to the British police by a Communist renegade and was imprisoned at Nanking. Escaped, 1933, and went to the Kiangsi soviet, serving as president of the Red Academy at Juikin for one year. Made the Long March with cadets from his academy. In the northwest, he was commander of the 1st Division, Fourth Army Corps, and served against the Japanese. In 1949 he was acting commander of the Second Field Army and led forces of 250,000 in the drive for Canton.

Part Six: PEOPLE OF THE THEATER

WÊN T'AO

[1] Novelist and critic in the literary movement of the 1920's, noted chiefly for his *True Story of Ah Q* (English translation, Shanghai, 1926) and his essays. He died in 1936. The Communist art school in Yenan was named for him.

LIU CHIH

[1] The "Young Marshal," eldest son and heir of Marshal Chang Tso-lin. He was, in 1935, commander in chief of the anti-Communist armies for the whole northwest of China. Influenced by desire to repel the Japanese invasion rather than continue the civil war, he made liaison with the Communist headquarters and in the famous "Sian Incident" of December 12, 1936, he and Yang Hu-ch'êng detained Chiang Kai-shek at Sian. The "Eight Demands," representing the terms which he and other rebels desired Chiang to agree to, were: reorganization of the Nanking government to admit all parties; cessation of civil war and adoption of stronger resistance to Japan; release of seven leaders of the patriotic movement imprisoned at Shanghai; pardon of all political prisoners; guaranty of liberty of assembly; safeguarding of popular rights of organization and political liberty; effecting of the intentions of Sun Yat-sen; and convening of a "National Salvation" conference. When the incident was settled peacefully with the release of Chiang, Chang Hsüeh-liang returned with him to Nanking to assist in reorganization of the government and was immediately imprisoned under a sentence of ten years. Communists and others demanded his release without result. Chang was, presumably, still a prisoner in 1950. He was taken to Formosa and there was an unproved report that he had been killed.

Part Seven: WOMEN

TS'AI TING-LI

[1] *Li hai* was the term used by Ts'ai Ting-li. "Spirited" does not render it precisely. Applied to a person, it means that he is of a temperament that refuses to submit to oppression.

[2] A brief biographical reference concerning P'êng Pai is given in the chapter on Hsü Hsiang-ch'ien.

[3] A Kuomintang division usually numbered about ten thousand men.

[4] The Communist party term for leftist actions of an amateurish character—rebellious actions which, through ignorance, do not follow the Communist prescription applicable to the circumstances.

Book II

AUTOBIOGRAPHICAL PROFILES AND BIOGRAPHICAL SKETCHES

PART ONE

Autobiographical Profiles

Liu Chien-hsien, Wife of Po Ku

Liu Chien-hsien (third from left); the leading proletarian woman Communist who became the director of factories and mines. The workers next to her still wear the red star, which was later dropped.

MISS WALES:

Po Ku was head of the Foreign Affairs Department in Yenan when I first met him. During the war with Japan, he and Chou En-lai and Tung Pi-wu were the chief Communist liaison officers in Chungking. Po Ku considered himself the chief expert on foreign affairs and set himself up as a theorist. He was so typically the Chinese intellectual in appearance as to be a caricature—thin, delicate, overworked, half-sick, and wearing thick-lensed glasses. His thick shock of hair made him seem top-heavy as well as brain-heavy, and Sir Archibald Clark-Kerr said he looked like a "Gollywog."

Liu Chien-hsien was exactly the opposite—a solid, healthy, apple-cheeked working-class woman, instinct with native intelligence but with her mind geared exactly to her own experience. Po Ku had attached himself to her as the mistletoe to the oak—she was his alliance with the masses and in reciprocity she benefited from his upper-class education. They had been married in Moscow in 1928, each at the age of twenty-one, when Po Ku was serving as her admiring interpreter at mass meetings. He was only a student then, and Liu Chien-hsien was a labor delegate embodying for him the experience of the 1925-1927 revolution. Rarely did a Chinese intellectual marry a working-class person. The distance between the two classes was much greater than in Western society. Even among the Communists, marriage is usually among couples with the same social origin.

Po Ku had a very indirect and complicated mind, like many Chinese intellectuals; it made me uneasy to talk with him. But Liu Chien-hsien was direct and frank and without guile, like most other simple working-class people. She and I understood each other perfectly and naturally from the start.

Liu Chien-hsien's usual job was to take charge of women workers and the

229

organization of cooperatives. When I met her, however, she had just been elected director of national mines and factories; she was only twenty-nine. Every movement was competent and quick and she was a natural leader. She had been a "delegate" so often that it had become automatic. Before the age of twenty, she had been the delegate of the Wusih silk workers, and, since then, she had been delegate to any number of labor and woman's congresses. At the age of twenty, she was one of three hundred delegates to the big National Labor Congress in Wuhan, which represented nearly 3 million labor union members in 1927. On the Long March, she was captain of the Women's Detachment. Liu Chien-hsien served as a conscious representative of the struggle for the rights of women and defender of what they had already achieved. She was the leader of the feminine front to simultaneously guard the home, the family, and the woman's right to work and have a career, too.

Liu Chien-hsien was the most emotional Chinese that I have ever known. Tears were often in her eyes as she talked with me, followed by a storm of anger at some injustice or cruelty. She was a superb orator—dramatic with earnest intensity, but without histrionics. This was one reason for her great popularity among the labor unions, for whom speech is more effective than writing. Her low voice had real appeal, and she seemed fresh and vibrant with energy and enthusiasm. She was fully aware of her platform appeal and took good care of her appearance.

Generous with her time, Liu Chien-hsien took me to visit labor unions and local industries and cooperatives, and did everything to make my stay as interesting as possible. She gave me an entirely new understanding of the working people of China, especially women. I believe it is true that working-class people show more internationalism than any other group. It was the labor union leaders in Yenan who showed the greatest friendliness to me—Liu Chien-hsien, Wang Chen, Tsai Shu-fan, Hsü Hai-tung, Ho Ch'ang-kung, Liu Hsiao-ch'i, Fang Wen-ping, and others.

The last time I saw Liu Chien-hsien we had a little adventure together, for which she was later criticized. She was with me on my return from Yenan to Sian. I was anxious to meet Liu Po-ch'eng and Jen Pi-shih whose army was stationed at Yün-yang but leaving momentarily for Shansi to fight the Japanese. When we arrived at Sanyuan, out of spontaneous generosity, as usual, Liu Chien-hsien agreed to go with me to Yün-yang. We hired a couple of rickshas and, taking along only two armed bodyguards, arrived in four hours. The army had marched away the previous night, however, and we found no welcome at local headquarters but consternation instead. It seems we had nonchalantly crossed a dangerous bandit no-man's-land, and the bandits would have considered Po Ku's wife quite a prize, not to speak of finding a foreigner wandering about. We were forthwith bundled back to Sanyuan with an escort.

I have, of course, written Liu Chien-hsien's frank, unself-conscious story exactly as she told it to me.

LIU CHIEN-HSIEN:

Because the men in my family happened to die about the time I was born, the people in our village said that I had an unlucky fate, so my family superstitiously resented having me in their household, fearing I would bring bad luck. My mother was the only one of my relatives who did not dislike me. Eighteen days after my birth, my father died, and three years later my grandfather and uncle.

We lived in a village near Wusih, Kiangsu, the most important native industrial city in China, where I was born in 1907. My grandfather made a living by collecting human excrement from people's compounds to sell as fertilizer. My father made whitewash for coating walls, so you can see that I come from the humblest sort of workmen. Before my grandfather and uncle died, we were fifteen persons living together. Then, because the three men who earned the living had died, the family was in poverty and forced to split, each part fending for itself. My mother already had one daughter of nine and a son of six when I was born. After the family divided, she was given only two *mou* of land to support us, together with half the house. She was always very sad and had a bad case of asthma. She provided food for us by cultivating silkworms and making silk thread. When I was nine, my sister and I made hair-nets for sale. All Chinese women then wore nets over their hair. We could do only fourteen a day. These we sold to a small merchant. Our earnings for the whole day were usually only seven coppers. In the spring I also went to the hills and gathered silkworms; when they became cocoons, we sold them to merchants. This was scavenger work, as silkworms were plentiful in this district and the ones we found had been thrown away.

My sister went to school for two years, the family of her fiancé paying the fee. No marriage had been arranged for me, and I could not be helped in this way. I insisted on going, however, and quarreled with my mother over this question. Finally, I was able to study for one year, paying the fee from my earnings. This was only one dollar for the year.

I was a very stubborn, willful child. My three playmates of the same age had each had her marriage arranged at the age of seven. There were many marriage go-betweens, but I cursed them and they were afraid to come to our house. I cursed them because I did not want to be given away, but wanted to stay at home. It was the custom to give girl-children to other families to be brought up as future wives, the families using them as servants in the meantime. All girls had marriages arranged in childhood.

In my village, there was a rich gentleman of high rank who had loaned money to my family at very high rates. He had a nephew for whom he was trying to find a wife, and decided upon me because I was strong and healthy and pretty and would make a good servant in his family. He had a small motorboat on the river and one day came to ask me to go for a ride in it, in order to learn more about me. I refused and ran away the whole day. I was then only ten years old, but I hated the rich because of their treatment of the poor. I was afraid of this man and his boat because all boats belonged to the officials and were used to collect rent or taxes from people. I remembered that my poor uncles had to give their farm products as rent to this man every time he came in his boat. My mother begged me to agree to the marriage because the family was rich and she was seriously ill and could not care for me, but I hated the idea and refused, though a good price was offered for me.

My brother, however, was nearly old enough to marry and would need much money for his own feast, so there was no money left for me. Out of pity for my mother's worries, I agreed to have another marriage arranged on condition that it be with a family in the city and not in the village. I asked this because I saw that people in the city ate good food and wore good clothes, while the villagers lived worse and worse every year. At the same time, I noticed that just as the villagers became poorer, the local officials appointed by the government became richer. I was puzzled by this and did not understand why, but I hated the officials for it anyway.

When I was eleven a marriage was arranged with the family of a Chinese engineer in the Standard Oil Company. He had stolen some oil and squeezed enough out of the company to start a small cotton factory, in which my cousin was an apprentice. This man had no son of his own, but had adopted one. My aunt arranged for him to buy me as a wife for this adopted son. As soon as the money was paid, my brother had his marriage feast, and I went to live in the engineer's family as a "little-wife" before the actual marriage.

In my own house I had been free even though poor. Here I was practically a prisoner, and I was very sad to leave my mother. She loved me and had only beaten me once. But here I had to kowtow every morning and night before the engineer and his wife, and speak polite words. In the morning I had to take tea and cigarettes and matches to them in bed. I could not go to bed until twelve at night, because I had to stay awake to kowtow. In my own home, I had always gone to sleep early, and staying up late made me very tired. At meals I had to be slavishly polite. I was afraid and could never eat enough. They said to me: "Don't hurry. You must eat slowly," so that I would not eat too much. I could never go out on the streets. Poor girls might go out, but, according to the Chinese custom, even the housekeepers of rich families were considered prostitutes if they appeared on the streets. In this family I did not have to cook, as there were servants for this, but had to serve opium.

The engineer often went to a brothel and the wife always quarreled with him about this and smoked much opium.

I thought my life tedious and hated the place. I had only one friend there— a young maidservant, who slept in my room. The thought of being daughter-in-law in such a family sickened me. I hated the boy I was supposed to marry so much that if I had had a gun I would have shot him. I never talked with him at all. It is the custom in China for a girl to live in the boy's family before marriage, but never to speak with him. This adopted boy knew I hated him and was afraid of me. Whenever I was near a door and he tried to get through I blocked his way. His real mother was a silk factory worker.

After a while the wife hated me and my life there was difficult. I became weak and thin, so my mother took me home, where I stayed for a year or so, making stockings in order to earn money. Then my mother died and the villagers repeated again: "This girl's fate is bad." We had to buy a coffin which cost twenty dollars. This money was borrowed from several persons and took five years to repay. We paid 2 percent interest a month, and our house deed was used as guarantee. My brother had wanted to be an apprentice but could find no work in the shops. We were miserably poor. At the New Year's Festival many creditors came to the house for payment, and my brother and his wife ran away to hide in a relative's home, leaving me to listen to their abuse. We never had enough food to eat in the house, and my brother's wife went back to her family to live. Because, at the beginning, I made the stockings badly, the merchant often returned them to me and I could hardly earn anything by this work. I cried all the time—for my mother's death, and because I was hungry.

When I was thirteen the engineer died, leaving a debt of $10,000. His creditors closed the factory, and, although the relatives tried to fight for his property, they could do nothing. The factory was sold for $3,000 and 30 percent of the debt was paid according to law. There was $500 left. The wife got $200, the boy $200, and a new concubine $100, but the boy never received his $200. Soon the engineer's wife died too. Then I had no possible place to go and my future looked bleak indeed. I wanted to live with my brother's wife's family, but she refused because my "fate was bad" and would bring bad luck to her. The villagers despised me and joked about my "unlucky fate." At this time I believed I really was born under an unlucky star—but I could not entirely accept this superstition somehow.

Then my fiancé had to take the coffins of his foster parents to be buried in a village near Taihu Lake where there was a mountain that produced yellow stone. I went along with the two coffins. I stayed in this village several months with a cousin of my fiancé, cutting wood and picking fruit every day. The wife of the cousin did not want me to leave but to stay as a servant. There was a boat going to town every morning and one morning after breakfast I ran away. I climbed the stone mountain but there was a big gulf at the top which I could not jump, so I had to go around. By that time I had just missed the boat. The second time I tried to escape, the woman captured me. She cursed me and said, "I am a well of water and you are a wooden bucket to pull water with. When you go down, you can never be free again." I had no way out and quarrelled bitterly with her. At the New Year Festival I cried and cried, though this is taboo and was thought to bring poverty and bad luck.

When I finally escaped and arrived in the village it was December 25 and the New Year was approaching. I had no place to go and no money. A relative had been keeping five dollars that I had saved from making gloves and stockings, and I hoped to return and use it, but she had run away with it. The rich despised me as a poor girl, and the poor despised me because they were superstitious about my "bad fate." I was wretched and became more convinced that I actually did have a bad fate.

I went to my sister's place, then to my sister-in-law's house, but she refused even to talk with me or to give me food. Finally, an aunt asked me to eat with her, and my grandmother of seventy looked at me and cried with pity.

Factory Life in Wusih

It was the superstition in my district that if you have a dream, good or bad, on the last day of the old year, your fate will be good. On that night I dreamed! I was so happy that I woke at dawn, opened the door, and looked at the sky and clouds at sunrise. I talked about this dream with my aunt, who said it was a good omen and that if I tried to get a job in a factory I might be successful. It was socially taboo in my district to send a girl out to work in a factory. No matter how poor the family might be, it lost face. On January 5 of the lunar calendar I went to the city and got work in a factory. I was then fourteen years old. I found a room with a couple, which was very inconvenient for me, but I paid no rent. I cooked my own food and my life was hard. Then one night when all the workers had finished at eight o'clock, I happened to meet some acquaintances from my village. This made me happy. They came and carried my luggage to their workers' dormitory.

This was the Ch'ing Hung cotton factory for weaving cloth, owned by a man named T'an, and the foreman was a native of my village. We began work at four-thirty in the morning and left at eight or nine—sixteen hours. We took lunch to eat in the factory and had no time off for this. Because the foreman was from my own village he treated me well. I was not unhappy but I was very tired. All day I had to walk around the machine and could not even stand still to rest. Payment was by the amount of work done, and I earned about twenty cents. In a month and a half I received only two dollars and seventy cents. It was the custom to work the first week without wages, and if you began working in January you had to wait until February 15 to get your money for the first two weeks in January. This was to keep the workers in arrears so they dared not leave their work. When I received this two dollars and seventy cents I was in despair and cried and cried.

Because of the low wages, I changed to a silk factory, where I was introduced by an aunt who was forewoman. My grandmother accompanied me the first time because I did not know anyone there to protect me. The first day I began work many men surrounded me and embraced me. I was very frightened and shy. Because the relations between the men and women of this factory were immoral, I left and returned to the cotton mill. When my technique improved, I was able to get more wages. Finally, after three years, I received twenty dollars a month for sixteen hours and could save money, as well as · help my poor brother and sister-in-law. The relation between me and my family was good now, because I was making money. They never discussed my bad fate any more, nor did the villagers. Soon many of my native villagers joined the factories. I still felt myself to be very pitiful, though, because I had no mother to cook and make clothes for me as other girls had.

One day I decided to see a fortune-teller. I wore an old dress the first time, and he said, "Your fate is bad." Later on, I returned to him dressed in good clothes, and he said, "Your fate is good." I was confirmed in my new idea that fate was all nonsense and only a question of economics. This cured me of my fear of fate—but still I disliked the factory.

In the beginning, regulations were quite flexible in the factory; then they became very strict. If we were ten minutes late at 4:30 A.M., the foreman cursed us. There were many children in the factory, and they were so tired and sleepy at that time that they always cried. I used to wonder why we had to begin work while the city was asleep, only to get enough to eat. We began working before dawn and returned after 8 P.M. We never saw the sky for months, and some never saw the sun for years. Every day I asked myself, "When will this hard life stop?" and prayed for the close of the day's work.

We were paid by piece work. If the machine broke and stopped, production decreased and our wages suffered, so we feared the machine and cared for it as if it were precious magic. Whenever a machine broke, the inspector punished the worker by decreasing her wages, so the workers had to pay even for the unkeep of the machinery.

Each foreman took care of sixty machines, and each was responsible for producing sixty p'i of cloth. If it was only a little less, the foreman cursed and punished the workers, and, if more than this amount, the foreman got a bonus, so he worked us very hard. He got only sixty cents a day wages and depended upon bonuses. After work every day all lunch baskets, as well as the trousers of the women workers, were searched for theft.

I hated the factory and its owner both and wondered why he was so rich.

His son had just returned from England and supervised the factory. The foreman called him "Young Lord," but if the women went to the WC for even a minute or two, they were cursed. I was very quick, and as my machine moved fast and I produced more goods than anyone else, I was valued as an expert. The foreman treated me differently from others. If a girl was beautiful, she was treated better than the old women and children, to whom the authorities were terribly cruel. Children were beaten, but not the older workers. But if a pretty girl was virtuous, she was usually treated badly, while those of bad character were treated better. I lived in one room with nine other women. Two of them were old—about thirty-six at least—and married, and they were extremely virtuous, so the foreman treated them very badly.

In the winter of 1924 a young girl fell from a high place on a big machine and was killed. Because of this, a group of workers began sabotage for three hours, and forced the authorities to give about thirty dollars to her family. We did not know the political meaning of sabotage; it was purely spontaneous. But later, all the activities were led by workers from Shanghai who had had some political training.

We hated the foreman worst of all. I used to be so angry that I would throw my cotton down on the floor, and refuse to pick it up when the foreman tried to force me to do so. For a few days I went late to my work and because of these actions I was dismissed as a bad influence in the factory.

Then I went to the Shen-hsin Cotton Mill owned by the Yung family, who are the biggest industrial capitalists in China. I worked nights for twelve hours, from 6 P.M. to 6 A.M., and the wages were poor. Food was very expensive then and cost me six dollars a month. I paid fifty cents for my room for one month.

The Revolutionary Workers of 1925–1927

When I had worked there about six months, which was during 1925, I met a Communist party member, who was a machine repairer from Shanghai. In 1926, we had a strike, and twelve workers were imprisoned with twelve-year sentences as Communists, though none actually were. We had no Communist organization in the factory then. After that, however, I kept in contact with this Communist from Shanghai, who was very good to me. I didn't understand the real meaning of communism, but I liked the way this Communist acted. He gave us books to read and said: "These are very good books. You cannot buy them anywhere, so keep them secret and don't give them to anybody else." I put them in my pocket, but didn't understand what he meant at first.

I lived in the house of a landlord who had a young son of eleven studying in primary school. When I couldn't understand the books, I asked this boy and he in turn asked his father. He was a tax-collector, and the books made him very angry. He told me they were Communist propaganda and that if they were discovered I would have my head cut off. He was polite about it but drove me away from his house. I took another room in a house owned by a policeman—and one week later everything I owned was stolen! I had no place to live and no clothes. I went to sleep in a dormitory with many other women. The Communist party held secret meetings there, and I joined the party but didn't understand its program. I had never heard of the May Thirtieth Incident then, though later on some women workers told me about it.

We had a union but it was not very good. However, many workers came from Shanghai who thoroughly understood the Communist program. At the secret meetings these workers and Communists made propaganda. They said to us: "You are not even as good as cows or horses because they at least get rest, but you work sixteen hours a day. Why is your life so hard? It is not fate, but capitalist oppression. We workers must unite and fight against the capitalists." After every secret meeting I was very excited and felt earnestly that every word they said was right.

I never missed these meetings and heard much about the victories of the Kuomintang and the national armies. I was very evangelistic and liked to tell others about the political situation and the May Thirtieth Incident in Shanghai when the wages of the workers had been increased by their struggle. Every Sunday I called as many women as I could to join the meeting, but on Sunday they had to wash their clothes or go home and had no time. Only a few would come. When I talked with them they all agreed and were happy at the idea, but they could not come to the meetings and this made me feel frustrated.

At this time many Shanghai workers who had been dismissed for the May Thirtieth movement came to Wusih, and they were very revolutionary. The foreman of this factory had treated me well at first, but now he was cruel to me, because I left my work to join the party meetings. At that time the management of the factory was terrified of the Communist party's secret actions.

The party work developed rapidly, and many workers joined the union and the party. The party was secret but we had one hundred members, which later increased. The factory had five thousand workers.

The party changed my work to the department of the women's movement. I did this work in the Ch'ing Hung factory, where I had first been employed, and was soon dismissed for this. But my work had been very successful, and many workers joined the secret meetings. When I was dismissed, I went to a silk filature. During this time, I was the delegate of the women workers to negotiate with the capitalists, and became well-known in Wusih as a leader of the labor movement.

At the end of 1926, we heard the news that the war had gone against the Kuomintang army, and that Chang Tsung-chang's army would come to Wusih. Many leaders and workers escaped, fearing execution, but I stayed with other comrades in order to give a welcome to the Kuomintang armies when they finally should arrive, as I knew the National armies would win. *There were no Kuomintang members* in any of the factories of the city. None of the workers joined the Kuomintang then; only students joined.

Up to this time I had been terrified of soldiers, but now I had a new bravery derived from my new consciousness. I had to pass the soldiers' garrison on my way between the business center of town and the industrial section, but I was no longer afraid of them.

In February 1927 a General Trade Union of all the workers in Wusih was formed secretly, and we planned a big welcome for the National Army. At the end of February, two hundred delegates from all the factories held a secret meeting in a temple twenty *li* from the city; I was one of the delegates. At this we passed a resolution that if the General Union Headquarters ordered a strike to welcome the army, all factories would respond.

Our party work and organization was really strong then. About March 12 we called this strike as soon as we heard that the National Army under Chiang Kai-shek was coming to occupy the city.

All the Wusih factories joined the strike, and 30,000 workers marched to the railway station to welcome the National Army. We arrived before the army did, and when Chang Tsung-chang's soldiers, who were defending the city, saw this unusual body of people, they thought we were the regular National Army and ran away, so the workers took the city without a blow. On our way back, the students also came out to welcome the army.

After the Kuomintang occupied Wusih, the union worked openly, and the women workers began to take a great interest in the movement. Union leaders were very busy, because all kinds of factories sent requests to headquarters for organizers to come and help their local unions. I was in charge of the organization of the women in the silk factories. At one time, the delegates of the women silk workers talked for one whole day with the capitalists and our demands were accepted. The workers got increased wages and shortened hours so that work began at 5:00 A.M. instead of 4:30 A.M., and a rest period was given for meals. The factory had been paying forty cents per month as a premium for good work, and wanted to omit this, but we also opposed this proposed change successfully.

At that time we felt that the factories belonged to the workers at last. Every factory had its union with an office building of its own. Twelve leaders who had been arrested were released and received a grand welcome from the mass of the workers. But these people had been bought by the capitalists, and later betrayed. They destroyed much of our union work by demoralizing the movement. After it was known they had betrayed, the women workers were afraid of the union, and all were very depressed.

I had met a young Communist leader named Ch'en Ch'i, who took a special interest in me. His father had been an official in the Manchu dynasty but had become bankrupt. Ch'en Ch'i had been on the staff of a flour mill which closed down, leaving him unemployed. He then became active in the labor movement. He never told his real background to anyone else, but tried to be one of the common workmen, and we all respected him. Nearly all the Communist party organizers were students, but the workers trusted them and had good relations with them, because the students did not look down on the status of the workers. We thought that the students had a good economic life and helped the labor movement on the basis of idealism.

The National Labor Congress was called for May 1927, at Wuhan, and Comrade Ch'en asked me to go as delegate, together with him. I agreed. He told me there was a country named Soviet Russia about thirty thousand *li* away, and that he would go there to study later on. He asked me if I wanted to go too. Of course, I was anxious to do this.

At this time, the split between the Communist party and the Kuomintang began and the revolutionary power was high. Once the General Union called a mass meeting and the workers went to the Kuomintang and government offices and destroyed them. The Kuomintang hated the workers and planned to murder the leaders. The Kuomintang National Army, which we had so gladly welcomed to Wusih, sent an order to the union demanding that we collect $30,000 for it, and the General Union refused, saying: "We have no $30,000 but we have 30,000 hates for you." The army asked the Labor Union and the local Peasant Union to send delegates to talk with them, and when these arrived they were arrested. Then the union called a mass meeting, which made a resolution to insist on the freeing of the delegates and sent demands to the army for this. As a result, these four delegates were released. At this particular time, the army was afraid to take action against us because they thought we were armed, as the Shanghai workers were, and knew that the union controlled the telephones and lights. There was a great body of workers in Wusih but we had altogether only three guns!

At this time Comrade Ch'en was extremely busy and so was I. We were expecting the Kuomintang reaction to begin any time in Wusih. Ch'en had his photograph taken and gave many to all his friends, as he expected to be killed. One day he came to see me, gave me twelve of his pictures and asked me to promise to keep them a long time. Then he said to me: "My situation is very serious. The Kuomintang may kill me any day. If I die, will you care?"

"Every revolutionary must expect to be sacrificed at any time," I replied.

He did not seem satisfied with this answer, for he said: "If *you* are killed, I shall be very unhappy."

About this time the Shanghai labor unions were destroyed and the workers massacred, so the Kuomintang army in Wusih prepared to do the same. They were no longer afraid because the twelve traitors had told them that the workers were totally unarmed. The Kuomintang now dared begin disorganizing the unions.

The Communist party decided not to resist the Kuomintang attack, but Ch'en disobeyed this order. He wanted to resist the Kuomintang army, and refused to leave the union headquarters, staying here to resist. Many of the workers' pickets, or "Self-Guards," defended this headquarters office. They telephoned to the factory district for more pickets to help, but this district was outside the city and the city gates were closed by the authorities, and they could not make their way into town. The headquarters was surrounded, and the workers could not even fire the three guns for some reason, but they resisted with axes for about an hour. The headquarters had a high wall around it, which the workers defended, but finally the soldiers climbed over the wall and got in.

It was dark and, when the Kuomintang soldiers entered the compound, they wore white handkerchiefs around their necks in order to distinguish each other. One Kuomintang soldier was a sympathizer and gave Ch'en a handkerchief for his neck so he might try to escape. Later a traitor indentified him with the aid of a flashlight. He was shot immediately. Before he died, he shouted: "Long live the Communist Party! You can only kill me with this bullet, you can never kill the revolutionary masses of China!"

There were about two hundred pickets defending the headquarters, and about fifty were killed. Only a few escaped arrest. They killed a few Kuomintang soldiers with their axes. Next day, before it was known that he had been killed, the Wusih newspapers offered four thousand dollars for the capture of Ch'en Ch'i as the leader of the workers.

The workers had been massacred in Shanghai on April 12, and the attack in Wusih was on April 16. I had hidden in a secret place on the night of the attack, and when I went to find the party next morning, everyone had left. Next day a party member came and ordered me to go to a silk factory to organize a strike. I went there alone to do this, but the traitors and capitalists had already lied to the workers and told them that the union planned to come with guns and kill all of them. When I arrived, the women were afraid of me and ran away.

That night I ran away to my village to escape arrest, but could not stay longer than one night in any one place. Next day I returned to Wusih and went everywhere to try to find the union or some party members, without success.

One of the capitalists with whom I had negotiated as a workers' delegate knew me and planned to give my name to the Kuomintang as a Communist for arrest, but he changed his mind again because he had only one son who was very precious. According to the Chinese superstition, if a man does a bad deed like this, his son may also die, so he did not betray me.

The next day the story of my death was published anyway and my relatives all cried and sent to Wusih for news of me. They found I was alive, and I went back to my village. Following his father's death and bankruptcy, my fiancé had begun to work in a machine factory. He had also became a Communist member. He now advised me to leave Wusih.

After the incident of the killing, many workers were arrested while others escaped. The leaders of the workers all had to run away. Many were killed secretly, though I don't know how many—fewer in Wusih than elsewhere, however. Later on, seven Communist party members were executed at one time. I think no women were killed.

In my village everyone looked upon me as dangerous to have around and made me very unwelcome, a revival of their antipathy toward me as the creature of a "bad fate." I had to leave.

After a time, I got back my connection with the party, when someone came to visit me. I gave Ch'en Ch'i's twelve photographs to him to distribute to all the factories. We had enlargements made and the workers all wore white thread on their hair in mourning for the death of their leader. Ch'en Ch'i was only twenty-seven when he was killed. I cried and cried when I learned of his death, because I liked him very much. But I had always been shy and suppressed my regard for him. Of course, he liked me too, and if he had not died we would have been engaged to each other.

The Wusih workers had wanted to resist the Kuomintang reaction but they had no arms, and the Ch'en Tu-hsiu line opposed it. Also, the failure of the Shanghai movement had a depressing influence on Wusih. When two delegates whom we had sent to Shanghai returned with the story of the April affair, the Wusih workers despaired of having any success. Had Shanghai been a victory, the workers in Wusih would also have fought through to a victory, surely.

I went to Shanghai in June 1927. Many workers were still being killed there then. Just to be cruel, Communists and workers were killed by *yao chan*, or cutting the body in two with a knife, instead of beheading. I met a party member whom I had known in Wusih and was sent to live in a secret office of the party a few days, but after a short time I went to Wuhan to join the National Labor Congress as a delegate.

I stayed in Wuhan only two months then returned to Shanghai. There, nearly all our comrades had been killed, and it was very hard to get any connection with the party. I lived in a poor hotel and had hardly enough money to keep myself, but was helped by a friend. Later I got my party connection and was ordered to go to Moscow to study. I left in October 1927.

A Chinese Factory Girl in the U.S.S.R.

In Moscow I attended Eastern University, which had only about forty work-ers, most being from the student class. For a short period we had military training in this school. I studied hard, but at first I did not know what politi-cal science was.

At the end of the year the World Labor Congress opened and I was a dele-gate. The head of the Chinese delegation was Hsiang Chung-hua, who was executed in Nanking in 1931. Wang Hsiao-hua [Wang Hsiao-hua or Wong Son-hua was the head of the Shanghai General Labor Union], the famous labor leader of the May Thirtieth Movement, was killed in 1927, so was not there. I was very excited at meeting all the international delegates at this Congress. There were about twenty Chinese delegates, and altogether about a thousand from all over the world.

Just as the congress opened the Canton Commune occurred. When the dele-gates heard this news they were much upset. The newspapers reported that about a hundred girls had been killed in the uprising, most being girl workers and some mere children. Thousands of men were killed, and we were all dis-tressed to hear this news.

I met Po Ku first during the congress, where he was acting as interpreter. He was then studying in Sun Yat-sen University. At this time, the First Five-Year Plan was just beginning and the government concentrated all attention on heavy industry, so prices were very high and the delegates had to spend ten rubles a day for food. Some of the delegates found life unsatisfactory, but Po Ku explained the meaning of this condition to me and discussed the hard problems of establishing socialism, which required that even the delegates should pass a hard life. When I heard him talking in this way, I decided that I liked him very much. He was interested in hearing me tell of the 1925-1927 Revolution, in which he had not participated, so we went around together a good deal. We were married in May 1928.

I went to the factories to see conditions and did propaganda among the Soviet workers for the Chinese revolution, asking them to help. They were all sympathetic, even the children, and shouted "Long Live the Chinese Revolu-tion" when I came to see them. Sometimes I felt so emotional at this demon-stration of solidarity that I couldn't speak, but only stood still and cried.

My first impression of the workers of the U.S.S.R. was very good because I found them so interested in the best possible methods of production. I was also surprised at their knowledge of international affairs. They always asked me many big questions about the Chinese revolution. In one primary school I was astounded to find the children discussing the important conflicts of capitalist society.

I looked around me in the U.S.S.R. and thought of the long revolutionary history behind the present stage of development there. I realized that China must go through an equally long period in order to reach the same condition. In Wusih, we workers had thought the revolution would come in three years.

I stayed in the U.S.S.R. from 1927 to 1930. I registered for the regular course at Sun Yat-sen University, which was only one year, and at the same time took private lessons in Chinese from a comrade. I had not quite finished this course when I returned to China. From 1928 to 1929 there was a serious struggle among the students of Sun Yat-sen University, which was the so-called "Trotskyists vs. the Stalinists" struggle, and because of this fight the university was disorganized in 1930. Only about 30 percent of the students were Trotskyists, but they had a big influence on the others. In 1929, there had been a purge of Trotskyists, and some of the Chinese Trotskyists confessed their errors, while others returned to China.

The Li Li-san Line

When I returned to Shanghai, I was head of the Department of Women Workers and worked in the industrial district. At first I had been appointed secretary of the National Federation of Trade Unions but refused because I felt myself incompetent, and the party criticized me.

At this time the anti-Li Li-san line was just beginning. The workers had liked Li Li-san and thought him a good leader. There was so much struggle then that we could not work well. The party was opposing both the leftist Li Li-san line and also the right wing, led by Ho Mei-yung and Lo Chiang-lung. The right wing opposed both the party and the Li Li-sanists. The Communist party work in th factories was difficult because the Yellow trade unions were strong and Li Li-san, on the other hand, also had great influence.

Following the Li Li-san line, the workers had a demonstration, which resulted in many arrests, both of workers and Communists. After these arrests, the workers were afraid, and it was hard to work among them. In the spring of 1931 we had a big strike in a silk factory, and later on many of the party organizations were discovered and a great number of arrests made. This had a bad influence on the movement. At this time many workers betrayed the party.

The Yellow trade unions had great influence then because they had a legal position and enough money to buy over the backward workers. Of course, when the workers struggled with the capitalists, the Yellow leaders always negotiated for peace and class collaboration. The workers did not like this kind of solution, but thought they had no other way.

The Chinese labor movement was high during the Pinhan Strike in 1923 and rose until 1926 and 1927. Then it was at its lowest after the failure of the Canton Commune in December 1927. In 1934, it began to rise again.

The Chief Secretary of the Shanghai Trade Unions then was Kuan Shang-yin, now political commissar to Ho Lung in the Second Front Red Army. He was arrested one day, and I was nearly caught at the same time, because I went to see him half an hour after the police arrested him.

The great achievement of my husband, Po Ku, and of Wang Ming up to this time was in breaking the influence of Li Li-san who controlled all the important party organizations.

The Workers in Soviet China

In 1933, I left for the soviet districts. I could no longer stay in Shanghai because the danger of arrest was so great that I could not even leave my house. In the soviets I took charge of the women workers' movement. At that time the All-China Trade Union Headquarters was transferred from the White areas to the soviet districts, and the head of it was Liu Hsiao-ch'i. There was a great deal of women's activity in the soviet districts and in general it was good. I was more than busy.

The revolutionary tempo in the Chinese soviets was thrilling to me. I used to become very emotional when I saw all the partisans gather on the mountains at sundown and sing revolutionary songs before they began to march out for night raids on the enemy. It was what I had longed to see—the great mass movement of the people of China marching out to fight for liberty with guns in their hands.

In the soviets the local governments were busy with economic reconstruction. We had 10,000 women workers in our trade unions and over 300,000 men. Everyone was busy from dawn to dark. The revolutionary movement among the women was excellent. Every day they took time to make shoes and clothes for the soldiers in the Red Army. More than half the women workers had husbands in the army. Among those from the cities, nearly all their husbands had joined the army, unless they were old men.

The soviet attitude toward the soldiers was entirely different from that in the rest of China. Those who went to the front to fight were highly honored and their families were happy to have them go. The peasants had got their land and they knew they must fight to protect it from the Whites.

In the soviet districts, the workers always helped the soldiers by building trenches and such. For instance, the bricklayers built first-rate fortifications for the defenses. When the men workers were busy with this kind of thing at the front, the women and children cultivated the land in the rear. In fact, in the Central soviets nearly every kind of work in the rear was done by the women and children. The women workers went to night school and nearly all the educational work was done by women. All the workers felt they were fighting for their revolution, whether it was in the rear or at the front. And the peasants, too, gladly sent their products to supply the army, keeping only enough food for themselves. When the party members went into people's houses, they were always welcomed and invited to sleep and eat there.

I had only been in the soviets one year when we had to leave on the Long March—in the middle of all our wonderful success and plans for the future.

Before the Long March began, there was a movement to expand the Red Army, and 6,000 new recruits joined. Both the men and women workers of the trade unions were mobilized up to 20 percent, including most of the women with unbound feet, and formed into an army of Red Guards. They received military training, and when the Red Army went on the Long March the men in the Red Guards went to the front to fight. Each district had one company of Red Guards. The women Red Guards worked in the rear, carrying the wounded and supplies, and nursing. All women over eighteen joined the Red Guards and those under eighteen joined the Youth Volunteers. At that time the Red Army and the Guards fought the Whites fiercely, and we were all very busy. The cotton mills carried out a competition to supply enough clothes for the soldiers on the March.

At that time I was pregnant and worried at having to begin the Long March in this condition. I had already had one boy born in Moscow and a girl born in Shanghai, which I had sent to a family to bring up one month after birth.

Airplanes were bombing our capital, Juikin, every day. One night a centipede bit me on the head while I was asleep. I could not find the centipede and was afraid it would return, so I couldn't sleep. Then I developed a high fever and was very sick. I had a miscarriage and had to rest for one month—which was just before the Long March began.

The Long March

We left Juikin about October 14, 1934. At first the marching was very difficult. Our feet were so sore we had to wash them with hot water every night. Many lagged behind and could not keep up. After a while, however, I could walk easily and work in the meantime. Only a few women joined the Red Army on the Long March because it was so difficult. There were only thirty Communist party women with us and twenty others. The party women we left behind in Kiangsi were very able, and unfortunately many were afterward killed by the enemy.

We carried many machines belonging to the government with us on the Long March. This work was organized by the Military Council, with Lo Man—who is now head of the Party School—in charge of it. There were many departments, such as hospital and transportation units, and over five thousand men were engaged in this carrying.

I was a political worker under the Military Council during the march. My duties on the way were to lecture at meetings, do educational work at times of rest, make surveys of landlords and their property, and help in the redistribution of land and goods. This political work was important because the Red Army had to be extremely careful to keep discipline during the Long March in order to make a good impression on the people as we passed. It was strictly forbidden to take the common people's goods, which must all be returned and repaired after use. In spite of our hurry, every morning the soldiers had to carefully replace doors after using them for beds and to sweep the floor before leaving any house they had slept in. Any disobedience was severely punished. Nobody was permitted to take anything personally from the landlords. Everything had to be distributed through the government organ for this. Except enough food for the army, we gave everything else to the local people on the way, which made them very happy.

The people always welcomed the Red Army along the way, and a considerable number joined us. However, we did not want many to join the march because it was too long and hard.

During the Long March the women often quarreled with the Communist party staff because they did not get enough food, and they sometimes struggled with each other at meals. Nobody wanted to carry rice but everybody wanted to eat it. We had to investigate each person to see that each carried his own rice. The women ate the same food as the men, and were not treated better than the men, except that sometimes when they could not walk they were allowed to ride horses. None of our thirty women comrades died on the way.

As we passed Kwangsi, we organized the fifty women into a special women's detachment, of which I was captain. This was segregated from the rest of the army. There was a reason for this special segregation of women. In Kwangsi the army was fighting with the Miao-tzu tribesmen and the life was very difficult. The men thought the women were getting better food and treatment, at the same time that they could not do transportation work and some did not even carry their own rice, so there was a quarrel between the sexes. We decided to put the women in one unit to look out for themselves, and had strict discipline so that nobody could lag in the rear and all must carry rice. Li Po-chao, who is now director of dramatics at the front, was in charge of the commissariat, and as I was captain we two lived and worked together. Before this the women had not been able to get enough to eat, but now we all had plenty. Li Po-chao went ahead of the detachment to arrange for food, and I did the rest of the organizing. We only had this detachment for a month, and when the army arrived in Tsunyi, Kweichow, it was disorganized, and the women were given special work in the army as nurses or in political work. After this the women had no trouble with the men, and lived the same life exactly. Of course, during the Long March the women never stayed with their husbands, but had independent work.

In Tsunyi, Kweichow, I worked in the headquarters of the political department. There were many workers there, and I helped organize them. The silk factory workers secured salary increases while we were there. When we left Tsunyi these workers were organized into three troops of partisans to defend themselves. The women also joined these partisan troops. Tsunyi was the second largest city in Kweichow and more modern than Kweilin.

There were many landlords in Tsunyi. I remember one time that Li Po-chao and I investigated the property of one such landlord. His family had run away and we stayed in his house. In this house were several hundred gourds, 2,000 *chin* of opium, a great many rich silk clothes and fox furs, and several hundred boxes of other goods. Many things were hidden in the walls, though we found no money under the floor. It took the two of us from early morning to night only to count the goods in this one house. We distributed forty boxes to the local people.

When we entered a city such as Tsunyi, we bought all necessary supplies from the people and paid for everything in soviet paper money. Then, before leaving the city, we always redeemed this money by exchanging for it products confiscated from the landlords or monopolies of the officials. The poor people liked this, and in every city several hundred joined the army. We always organized partisans in such districts before leaving.

The Red Army stayed in Tsunyi only ten days. After we left, the Kuomintang troops came. They beat and arrested the organized workers and killed a few, although, as soon as we left, many of the townspeople ran away to escape the severe White Terror. The partisans of this district were very brave and attacked the White Army, which caused many of them to be sacrificed.

After a short time, the Red Army returned to Tsunyi, but the workers' leaders had all run away and we could not find them. The people feared the new White Terror which would occur again after the Red Army had left, so ran away. We stayed only a few days and marched away again. Every day there were bombing planes in the sky, which also strafed the city with machine guns. When we had marched eighty *li* to a place called Pei-la-k'e, we again redoubled and returned to Tsunyi for only a day, leaving the next night again. In these two nights and one day we marched 240 *li!* When we arrived at Pei-la-k'e the last time, the vanguard of the Red Army was fighting far ahead of our group, and we had to cut across country to meet it.

I don't remember any particular incidents of the Long March very clearly, except for a few important places. I did not have any very narrow escapes from death myself. Once my horse fell down a mountain and was killed.

My main duty in the headquarters political department was to do mass work with the peasants and workers on the way. When we arrived at a new place, the members of this department inspected the army to see if discipline was being maintained and that no mistakes had been made. We investigated the numbers of wounded and checked up to see how many had been lost in the rear. If the soldiers disobeyed orders, they were executed by martial law. Discipline was, therefore, good. Party members were dismissed for any disobedience. Because of the good impression we tried to make, the common people all liked the Red Army and, on the whole, the Long March was a wonderful propaganda tour.

Our duties in the political department were also to investigate the landlords of the district, to find out which were good and which were bad. The bad landlords always ran away as soon as we began our survey, so it was never necessary to kill any of them. Not a single landlord was killed by the Red Army itself on the march that I knew of, because the guilty ones all escaped. The landlords with a good reputation sometimes remained in the towns and voluntarily gave up their goods, so they were not killed.

Before the Red Army arrived in a village, the landlords always began a campaign of lies and atrocity stories against us, saying that the Communists would kill everyone and confiscate their property, and tried to force the poor people to follow them when they ran away. So usually when the Red Army arrived at a new place, only a few people remained. But after three or four days of propaganda work, the mass of the people rushed back again.

In the Grasslands, it was intensely cold because of the high altitude. Our army had only light clothes, and this cold was dangerous. More of our people died here than anywhere else. It rained every day, and we had no shelter and hardly any food. You could see dead bodies lying everywhere. But the heroic spirit of the army was very good. In the most difficult circumstances, the relation between revolutionary comrades becomes closer and this provided the morale to carry through. Of course, the instinct for self-preservation caused quarrels over the distribution of food, but I never saw any of the men fight each other over this. Many children died because of the rarified air on these snow-covered mountains. And when we went through the treacherous quicksands of the boggy Grasslands, I sometimes looked up to see a strong man fall aside suddenly into the mire and disappear. Death seemed to lie in wait everywhere.

It took us five days to cross over the terrible Grasslands, and some units had to take ten. Many were sick all the time. Some had no shoes and their feet were wounded. Every face was famished and thin. The living had no strength to worry about those who were dying and passed on. But somehow our determination was strong and we kept up our revolutionary spirit.

The little boy who was my *shao kuei* on the Long March died here in the

Grasslands as we were crossing a high mountain. He was eleven years old and had come from Kiangsi as a nurse.

After passing the Grasslands, conditions were much easier. I think the happiest day of the Long March was when we reached the *Ah Si* region of the Man-tzus just after the famine in crossing the Grasslands and found good butter and cows! Everyone had all the beef he could eat for once!

When we arrived in North Shensi, we went to Wai Ya Pao. The party ordered me to take charge of the women workers and the organization of co-operatives. At the Delegates Congress of Shensi Workers held in January 1936, I was elected director of national mines and factories.

You ask me if I am now optimistic. Before the Sian Incident I was not optimistic, and our military position was very bad even if the political influence expanded. Afterward I was happy as I had my child then, too. Before I quarreled with Po Ku over my life. In Pao-an all women hated their husbands because of having babies and so much trouble. It means much to have peace here. Chiang Kai-shek is all right now, and we hope he will be the hero of the united front to save China from Japan. We will take his orders to fight Japan. I hated him before but not now if he will fight Japan. Only to stop civil war is a great victory. If there had been no peace settlement at Sian, Nanking would be under the control of the pro-Japanese clique and this would be bad.

Lily Wu (Wu Kuang-wei), shortly before she was charged with alienation of affections of Mao Tse-tung by his wife, Ho Tzu-ch'en

Lily Wu,
Who Caused
Mao Tse-tung's
Divorce

MISS WALES:

In the revised 1968 edition of *Red Star Over China,* Edgar Snow stated that in 1937 Ho Tzu-ch'en had formally charged Wu Kuang-wei with having alienated her husband's affections; that Mao Tse-tung had denied the charge and been granted a divorce by a special court set up by the Central Committee of the Communist party; that both Miss Wu and Mao's wife had been exiled from Yenan; and that the latter had gone, with her young child, to live in Russia.

I was in Yenan when this situation came about, but I was not informed of the inside story. Just the same, the self-assurance of Lily Wu, as we called her, made me think it worthwhile to write down her brief autobiography.

I first saw Lily Wu at the theater when she took the lead in Maxim Gorky's *The Mother.* She was the star actress of Yenan. She was not only talented but she carried herself with authority on the stage. She was well-bred, quiet, gracious, feminine, and charming, age twenty-six and already married but separated from her husband, at least geographically. Lily looked healthy and strong, with high color and clear, fair skin. She was quite beautiful. Her hair curled luxuriantly around her trim shoulders in the long bob of the 1930s. Other women in Yenan wore their hair cut short in a straight boyish bob, and you could hardly tell the sexes apart. Lily and I were the only two persons in Yenan who had curled hair and wore lipstick, though both very discreetly —not too red. This was contrary to the Yenan code. Lily looked frivolous on the exterior, but she had no sense of humor and she was deadly earnest. She spent her spare time studying and was a student at the university where she

250

listened to lectures by Chang Kuo-t'ao and his arch-enemy Mao Tse-tung. She had been brought up as a Christian and had been a student leader.

I do not think she and Mao had any extramarital affair because she was too clever and proud to be a "concubine." I was truly surprised to learn in 1969 that Mao's wife had taken the affair seriously. During the summer, Lily summarily rejected any hopeful admirers and told me that "love is a drug," and she had "no more time to waste on this." She was so convincing about this that it did not enter my head she might be angling for the biggest prize of all and had her line set for "the Chairman," which was the height of audacity.

Mao Tse-tung set the precedents. He could have gotten a divorce and married Lily Wu without much trouble—or at least without as much trouble as would have resulted from an affair. What happened?

Mao was the type of man (and in the prime of life, age forty-four in 1937) who especially liked women, but not ordinary women. He liked a feminine woman who could make a home for him (as Ho Tzu-ch'en did well), and he appreciated beauty, intelligence and wit, as well as loyalty to himself and his ideas. He was not afraid of independent-minded people and would not have objected to lipstick and curled hair. (From his middle school days, he had had a hair fetish and wore his hair longer than others did, a kind of Bohemianism; he also shook his mane now and then with a special flair for the dramatic.)

Lily Wu was not a Communist and she was the epitome of what was called "bourgeois" in Yenan. But Mao liked modern-minded women and admired them, and he favored raising the status of women. His brand of respect for women, however, was not based on chivalry but upon real merit, as in the case of his best friend of a lifetime, Miss Tsai Ch'ang, who was his partner in revolution.

The Lily Wu case is interesting historically because of the light it casts upon the personality of Mao Tse-tung, who set the standards for the youth of China. Mao was the King Arthur of China. He was the Chairman of the Yenan Round Table. His men were knights and the women were truly ladies, with dignity, pride, and awareness of establishing the standards for the rest of China. The Yenan mystique emanated a romantic aura made up of gallant youth, courage, and high thinking. In terms of the Confucian Chinese past, there was a certain chivalry toward women, and Mao was an open and avowed champion of women. Yet romance was frowned upon, and women had to survive by their own wits. In Europe romantic love was the invention of the French in the days of the troubadours. China was in the pretroubadour stage, emerging from the tribal clan-commune of Confucian patriarchalism. Nevertheless, the life of Mao Tse-tung does have a special romantic interest in relation to women. He had the problems typical of his time.

Mao's rigid refusal to allow anyone to take liberties was later shown by the fact that his wife Chiang Ching was not permitted to engage in any activities at all for over twenty-five years after her marriage to Mao. Nepotism was one of the Confucian hangovers which the Communists most objected to. It is all the more remarkable as Chiang Ching was shown to be a woman of the most extraordinary ability and energy.

In 1937 Mao exiled three women from Yenan—I would guess chiefly for taking liberties with him. I can see why he exiled his wife and Agnes Smedley, but the case of Lily Wu raises a question. I never heard until 1969 that she had been exiled.

Lily Wu told me she had arrived in Yenan on February 19, 1937, intending to study to become a party member. On May 31, I was invited to visit the American journalist, Agnes Smedley, in her spacious and comfortable cave on the hillside. At dusk the view was peaceful and beautiful from the hill "like a Maxfield Parrish painting, so clear and blue," I wrote in my notebook. I roasted two potatoes in a small fire outdoors and ordered my bodyguard to buy two tins of pineapple. Lily Wu cooked peppers, and eggs. Agnes Smedley ordered cabbage soup and other dishes from the restaurant.

Mao Tse-tung arrived to call just as we were talking. He was in high spirits that evening. Mao had a most attractive quality which does not show in photographs, an expressiveness and aliveness. He also had a good sense of humor and was quick to catch everything we said even though it was in English. Agnes looked up at Mao worshipfully, with her large blue eyes—which at times had a fanatical gleam. Lily Wu was also looking at Mao with hero-worship. A bit later, I was stunned to see Lily walk over and sit beside Mao on the bench, putting her hand on his knee (very timidly). Lily announced that she had had too much wine, and, as she appeared to have been affected to the point of foolishness, it seemed to be a simple fact to me then; I could have remembered that she was a professional actress. Mao also appeared startled, but he would have been something of a cad to push her away rudely, and he was obviously amused. He also announced that he had had too much wine. Lily then ventured to take hold of Mao's hand, which she repeated from time to time during the evening.

This evening in Yenan may not seem like any great shakes to an American. In Yenan it would have been all but an earthquake when it became known. The bodyguards belonged to the OGPU and reported everything they thought noteworthy. Mao's wife was not modern minded and would have jumped to conclusions only on the evidence that Lily was trying to hold her husband's hand and that he permitted it. In old China, even man and wife did not touch each other in public. Each person shook his own hand—not that of others— and it was done modestly up his own long sleeve. There was a hand fetish as well as a foot fetish in the land of foot binding. Only westernized Chinese shook hands. The Communists tried to be as westernized as possible, but they observed the taboos so they would not alienate the local villagers. I do not recall ever seeing anyone in Yenan holding hands, though a few couples dared to walk together along the ancient city wall in the daylight. This was in itself shocking to the villagers. Man and wife did not usually appear in public together.

There were only a few Communist women in Yenan among a multitude of eligible bachelors. The girl students who were arriving were highly superior or they would never have set out on such a trek, and many of them were beautiful as well. These girls could pick and choose. None of them was likely to be so foolish as to have affairs outside marriage. Even Lily Wu, who was obviously aiming to marry Mao, did not have one. Mao's wife accused her not of adultery, but of alienation of affection, according to the report. As Mao denied the charge and is said to have had Lily Wu banished from Yenan, it is most likely there had been no adultery in the case. Lily Wu may have thought that by bringing on a divorce, Mao would ask her to marry him afterward. Mao could be informal and easy, but by nature he was a man of utmost dignity when it came to loss of face. He would cut off with anyone who took the liberties, which both his wife and Lily Wu apparently took.

In 1937, Mao's wife was not in good health after the Long March and a pregnancy, but she was completely devoted to her husband, took good care of him and his household, and was considered in Yenan to be a good wife.

There was a real crisis in Yenan at the time I was there in the man–woman relationship—and it was Mao who set the precedents. If Mao's wife could retain her position in spite of the influx of beautiful and talented young students, others could too. The Yenan wives had a dictatorship over the morals of Yenan, and it could not have been more puritanical. Both Ting Ling and Agnes Smedley were anathema to the phalanx of wives because they were not in favor of marriage.

The "new marriage" was not as yet established. That was the crux of the matter. In old China, marriage was arranged by the families, but the Communists had no families. The party took the place of all other relationships, though they were trying to establish the conjugal western-style marriage of man and wife and children, directly in opposition to anything resembling the Confucian clan-family. Puritanism was the method used by the women to establish this "new marriage."

They had not as yet invented the formal marriage ceremony for the new marriage. It consisted of a verbal social contract between the two parties, but had to be announced to the Communist party officials and to be approved by them; the woman's department also handled marriage and divorce.

When I was in Yenan, I was informed that Mao Tse-tung's wife had threatened to have her bodyguards shoot Agnes Smedley and that Mao was furious with both of them. I was not told the reason why. It was assumed that Agnes Smedley had made herself so much a public nuisance that she could no longer be tolerated in Yenan. I supposed she had made trouble between Mao and his wife, but I never heard the name Lily Wu connected with this situation in Yenan nor until I read it in 1969. I never heard anything more about Lily Wu. I never heard that Mao's wife had threatened to kill Lily Wu nor that she was blaming her for alienation of affection. All this was kept secret in Yenan while I was there.

Agnes Smedley called on me to tell me she had been ordered by Mao Tse-tung to leave Yenan as soon as possible, with the first group out. In Yenan I interpreted the situation this way: for Mao's wife to threaten the life of Agnes Smedley or anyone else was a crime according to the Communist party rules and it was also taking a liberty as the wife of the chief leader. Why would Mao's wife want to kill Agnes Smedley? I now suppose she was acting as a go-between for Lily Wu and was trying to cause a divorce between Mao and his wife. Mao's wife had married him in 1930 and had suffered through every hardship and danger. For a foreigner to try to break up her marriage was unendurable.

The most important thing about this situation was that Mao was always the champion of women and youth. That was the secret of his following from the beginning. This was a test case. He finally repudiated Agnes Smedley and her antiwoman ideas, though for some time he had tolerated and even befriended her.

Mao did not marry his next wife, Chiang Ch'ing, leader of the Red Guards and the Cultural Revolution in 1966, until 1939, according to Edgar Snow, who reported that she and another actress were brought to Yenan by Yu Ch'i-wei in 1938. Yu Ch'i-wei was the leader of the Peking student movement and had sponsored my own trip to Yenan. Chiang Ch'ing had been his friend for many years and I wonder if he did not plan the whole idea of marrying her to Mao Tse-tung.

As for Lily Wu, she had been a student leader but not until the Sian Incident of 1936 did she become interested in political work. At that time, she took up the theater as a means of reaching the public, though she told me her chief concern was modern educational methods. She comes down in history now as the cause of the only divorce of Mao Tse-tung and as an example of the type of woman Mao found attractive. Her life story explains why such a westernized girl would end up in Yenan.

LILY WU:

I was born in 1911, the first year of the Republic, in Honan Province, but when I was two years old my father moved to Peking where he worked as a government official in the Salt Gabelle for the next twenty years. He was a scrupulously honest man and worked hard, seldom associating with any friends. He had a good position, neither high nor low, and his salary was enough for the family to live comfortably. In my family, there are my parents, two older sisters, one younger sister, and one younger brother. My mother also came from a good family. She has bound feet and can read but cannot write. I consider her a great woman because, though she is now fifty-two, she always received the new thinking and even quarreled with my father on political subjects almost to the point of divorce. She can talk with people of all ages and classes and everyone likes her. She is kind and always helps others without being asked. Her only backwardness is that she still believes in the Buddhist goddess Kuan Yin, though she no longer prays to her. Her marriage was arranged and was neither happy nor too unhappy. Neither of my parents had any bad habits such as smoking, drinking or playing mah jong, but my father is a very selfish man. Neither is a Christian.

My oldest sister graduated from P'ei Hua Middle School in Peking, a Christian school, and immediately married a returned student from England, a railway engineer. She was then nineteen and now has five daughters. My second sister graduated from Shih Ta University and at twenty-six married a professor at Fu Jen University, who is now dean of Tung Hu Middle School. She teaches there also and has two children. My brother is weak because he was spoiled as the only son, but the sisters are all strong and healthy. He is bright and handsome but has tuberculosis. The doctors would not even permit him to enter middle school, and he now studies French, piano, and violin in the national conservatory in Shanghai. He is twenty-four. He likes to take watches apart and put them together again, and he plays chess well and is a good photographer. My youngest sister is now studying in a commercial school in Shanghai, where she also graduated from middle school. I advised her to do this because the university is no place to learn a technique for use in earning a living. My father is not at all sympathetic to revolutionary ideas, and none of the others are either except one sister and my mother.

I studied in a Christian primary school in Peking, graduating in 1925 during the May Thirtieth period, which had great influence on me. I hated the British and Japanese so much that I changed from my school because it was English and entered Chin Shih Middle School, also a Christian school for boys and girls. The standards in this school were higher than in others, and all the students came from Christian schools. The spirit was good and teachers and students were friendly to each other. It had just recently been started by Feng Yü-hsiang, who was liberal, and the students were much more active politically than in other schools, holding regular mass meetings and joining in the May Thirtieth movement. The Christian students everywhere were active in this period and had a revolutionary tendency.

When the Japanese attacked Tsinan, a student demonstration was organized on March 18, 1926, to protest to Premier Tuan Chi-jui. About two-thirds of the older students joined but we little girls and boys stood out in the rain waiting for them to bring back the answer from Tuan Chi-jui. They came back with no result. Four or five had been wounded by the police, and one schoolmate, Li Ming-hsueh, only eighteen, had been shot by Tuan Chi-jui. We all cried when we heard that many others had been killed and wounded, and we hated Tuan Chi-jui. The graves of those killed are at Yuan Ming Yuan near Tsinghua University.

I studied hard in middle school and won the highest prizes in my classes. Then I went to Shanghai and entered the girls department of a commercial school for the purpose of studying English. The principal was from the South Seas and gave us the same lectures as he gave to the rest of the school, in English, Chinese, history, and other subjects. Commercial subjects, however, were not taught to girls but only to the boys. I liked to play volley- and basket-ball. I also was interested in the lectures given by our dean, a Cantonese with a B.A. in social science from the United States. She was fond of social work and took us to visit factories and plants in Shanghai. After this, I received high marks because I took a real interest in the subject and wanted to improve the terrible lives of the workers. At the Nanyang Tobacco Company I saw young girls and old women pale and yellow, almost too tired to pick up the dirty leaves, and, in the stocking factories, conditions were even worse. I felt very sorry for them.

The dean was popular with the students, and the principal was afraid she would seize his position. She did not receive a new contract when the old one expired and this made us angry. I led the campaign to fight the principal and was delegate of the girls' department. When we went to see him, he hid in his own room. I went in and was told he had gone by plane to the South Seas, but I knew it was a lie. I returned to the meeting and asked everyone to come with me to pull him out of his hiding place. When we found him he was frightened and denied that he had refused the dean a job. We were so young we didn't make him sign a document but thought we had been successful and were satisfied. Of course he cheated us. After a few days he still had not given the contract to the dean so I tried to organize another fight, but summer vacation had started and the students had nearly all left. He instructed his running dogs to tell the dean that he would have the police arrest her as a Communist if there was any more trouble. Of course, I had to leave the school too. This was about 1929.

I went back to the Chin Shih school, and the teachers welcomed me because I had been a good student. However, the principal was no longer Chien Yu-wen but a man named Pao Kuan-lin, a typical Christian preacher whom I disliked; he did a good deal of talking but nothing to improve the school, letting it run down day by day. Many students educated in Christian and foreign missionary schools have a great dislike for the hypocrisy they see there. In the mouths of such Christians are always words of kindness and charity, but they do nothing. Often they are even much more cruel than those who profess no humanitarian Christian principles, especially where the word Communist is concerned. Instead of a social program to help the people, they have silly prayers. Foreign Christians do a good deal of charity work, but some of them hate the Chinese who want to fight for their rights instead of being beggars!

The students were now against the principal, the dean and the teachers, for they were doing nothing to help the school progress. The dean had just got married and slept all the time. He failed to come to classes and the dust piled up on the desk in his office. We asked the principal to get rid of him but he thought some graduate student merely wanted a job in the school and refused. I was one of the student leaders, and thirty of us were expelled. The rest were so disgusted that nearly a third left the school. There were three of us girl students, and we were in a predicament because we could not graduate from any other middle school without two years attendance, and this would mean paying an extra year's costs, not to speak of wasting an extra year before being able to enter college. The brother of one of these girls was an artist so he made diplomas for us. One girl entered Yenching University and later went to the United States to study; one went to Hopei Professional Normal Academy in Tientsin; and I entered Shihta University. There were about fifty in our class and many faked diplomas because of being expelled. Some had trouble with these. Most of the class went on to Tsinghua University.

My first year at Shihta was hard because I had missed several subjects and had to catch up, but the teachers liked me as I was a good student. The first composition I wrote was a criticism, "Education in China Today," which was well received and other students read it over and agreed with me. The last three years, however, I did not study at all because I fell in love and paid no attention to my studies. Another reason was that nearly all my teachers talked only nonsense and I felt they were a waste of time. Their understanding of the problems of China and of modern society was so limited I soon became completely disgusted with the whole college curriculum. They had no new ideas and no original thinking. For example, the chairman of the education department used exactly the same material he had studied in America ten years before, which we had to copy from the blackboard. The whole system of education was weak in China, I saw, and entirely superficial, carefully ignoring all the pressing problems. Most thinking Chinese students really interested in their country are disgusted with the spirit and method of education in nearly all the schools in China. It has no aim except providing the barest superficial academic training. Any good Chinese student can get through school without studying by merely memorizing what is taught. We are actually taught not to think but only to repeat what is told to us. Professors who do their own thinking are often dismissed. We students always defend them, and that is one of the chief causes of all the trouble in school between the students and the administration. I already realized, however, that this poor education was a part of the whole backward framework of Chinese society and that the individual teachers were not to blame but were merely earning a living and saving themselves trouble. At Hung Ta University in Peking, the spirit was different, however, and classes more interesting. I was anxious to come to Yenan to see what was being done in the new methods of education. Here we have an aim and study the real problems of our country.

After four years, I was graduated from college and taught at Chung Hua Dramatics School. This is a modern school for the opera outside the south gate in Peking, and the principal was a writer named Chao Chu-yin. I taught Chinese and the natural sciences, not dramatics. All the dramatics teachers were old-style. In order to earn my own living, I also tutored a boy in a family who was attending Fu Chung Middle School, teaching him Chinese, English, and mathematics. I earned sixty dollars a month and spent twenty dollars to live. The rest I sent to my husband to help him through the Imperial University in Japan. Finally I went to Tokyo to visit him. We had been married on March 1, 1934, when I was twenty-three at Shihta and he was a student at Peita. He left for Japan in August the same year. I stayed in Japan three months, and I was greatly impressed by the much higher educational standards. Even old peasant women there read the newspapers every day, and the maidservants, too. The order and courtesy were a change from China, and I was astonished at the wide use of electricity. I liked Japan and especially the simple country people.

We are still married. My husband is progressive but inactive, like so many other Chinese. However, I feel that I cannot waste my life on ordinary family affairs. Housework is trivial, and there are important things to be done in China, requiring that women take leadership in action, as well as men. It is better for both the husband and wife in progressive circles to do their own separate work, neither hampering the other. Otherwise, it is better to live alone to be more effective.

On my return from Japan, I entered the National Dramatic Academy at Nanking started by Yu Hsiang-yuan. I had never been in dramatics before and liked it very much. My chief interest, however, is that I think it is a good medium for raising the revolutionary consciousness of the people because of illiteracy. You in America do not have this problem as everyone there can read and write.

I look upon dramatics as a form of mass education. I learned techniques at this school but soon found the training very limited. Yu Hsiang-yuan was a "pure artist" type and could not develop his art because of fascist influence in Nanking. For example, the chairman of the board of directors was Chang Tao-fan, a fascist and head of the communications department of the government. No clubs or discussion groups were permitted. This was a modern dramatics school but it had no future except to provide amusement for the rotten officials. It was entirely different from the old Peking opera and much better, but still of no consequence. The old opera in China has no thought or meaning nor is it capable of it. It is not worth cultivating except for historical tradition. It is a part of our feudal culture and must be superseded by the modern drama. In its own time, some of the operas were of value but now they are mere second-rate entertainment and have no relation to the problems of the day.

I went back to Peking and spent much of my time reading in the Peking National Library. In this way, I made up for some of the time wasted in attending school. In the summer of 1936, I took a position in Sian as clerk in the Provincial Government for sixty dollars a month. I was the only girl in the office. This was the civilian department headed by P'eng Tao-hsien, a Nanking official, and it gave orders to the *hsien* governments, also receiving orders from Nanking. At first I worked on plans for the election of a people's assembly—which, of course, was never held and if it should would be only a comic opera. We collected reports on people to be selected.

I had been in Sian only eight months when the Double Twelfth occurred— Chiang Kai-shek's arrest. I joined the work of the women's department of the Northwest National Salvation Union. I helped organize mass meetings, led the slogans and songs, and did general propaganda. We tried to organize all the Sian women to participate. I also helped write the manifestos, and we printed them in my office. My boss, P'eng, ran away, of course, and Mi Tsanchen took his place. He was not unsympathetic. It was a happy time for me; I felt I was being useful for the first time in my life. I lived with a friend who knew political affairs and she introduced me to a Communist. I was eager for revolutionary work and worried about what I could do best. I learned that it was possible to come to Yenan to study and arrived here on February 19, 1937. I hope to become a party member after I have been thoroughly trained.

The Double Twelfth influenced me to join the Communists, and especially the anti-Japanese movement. There I realized better how Nanking had suppressed the patriotic movement all over the country and what lies had been told about the Red Army. When I saw the spontaneous rise of this movement in Sian, I saw that it was suppression which was destroying the morale of China and not that the people were asleep or stupid.

Until the Sian Incident on December 12, I had had no political training and my ideas came almost entirely from my own experiences. In Peking I had read chiefly the magazines *World Knowledge* and *Translated Literature*. I liked Gorky, Dostoevsky, Mérimeé, Mark Twain, and similar writers. During my time in Nanking I was influenced by articles in a liberal magazine by Shen Chih-yuan, Chien Chün-jui and Chao T'ao-fen, the liberal who was arrested by Nanking with the seven National Salvation leaders. However, I had been interested in the Communists as early as 1932 from hearing some of my friends talk of them. I dreamed of seeing their regions and wondered about their schools. There were some Communists in the schools I attended, no doubt, but I did not know a single one. The students of China are progressive and pro-Communist without having any contact with party activities, which have been severely suppressed all during my school years. In the Chin Shih Middle School, I should say about two-thirds were leftist, and in Shihta maybe half. In the Dramatics Academy, perhaps a fifth were sympathizers, and some were Fascists. Most of the students hate Chiang Kai-shek and the whole rotten Kuomintang set-up, even though they may not be pro-Communist. After September 18, 1931, the students were isolated from the Communists and had no way to learn anything factual about their activities. We wanted information and wanted to study Marxist ideas, but we had nowhere to turn to get in touch with these things. We were still sympathetic even though we did not know whether most of the stories told against the Communists were true.

My experience in the Sian office was interesting. I wanted to break down the old idea that a girl is only an ornamental "flower jar," so I worked hard and proved my ability. The old men in the office talked of mah jong and never read the magazines. After the Sian Incident I wrote articles for the newspapers and for the magazine *Tung Wang.* One day on the streets I met an old schoolmate from the Chin Shih Middle School, Wang Chün-wen, who was writing a play *Mountains Out of Fire,* about the eve of the Double Twelfth. He made clear all the Fascist ideas and crimes of Chiang Kai-shek's Blue Shirts and guards in Sian. I had a leading part in this play, and it was the most successful drama that had ever been shown in Sian in living memory. The theater was jammed and even the streets outside. We also took it around the countryside and it had a great influence on everyone who saw it. Our purpose was to take the truth to the people.

Here in Yenan I had a part in Gorky's *Mother,* and I was Madame Chao in *Ah Q.* I also had a part in the play *Sha Ying* by the leftist writer Ch'ao T'ien Yu Chê.

At the university here, we have no printed textbooks yet, except some translations of Marxism and Leninism. We learn chiefly from lectures. Po Ku teaches Leninism, Chang Kuo-tao teaches political economy, Mao Tse-tung lectures on dialectical materialism, Ch'ang Wu-hsin teaches the history of the Chinese revolution. We have free discussions all day and all night and we are all very excited and happy. It is a thousand times more interesting than any other school I have ever been in. Here there is a rich intellectual life, and everyone is mentally alive. And there is an aim and we are able to ask why and how for every subject that comes up and to be sure of finding intelligent answers. No, I don't miss my old life. I have always hated domestic duties and now I have to wash my own clothes and help to clean, but I feel I am not wasting my time and I hardly miss not having servants. I always lived at the YWCA when I was away from home, so I am used to living alone. At first my husband objected to my coming here, but now he does not mind. Love is a drug. I wasted three or four years that way. I have no more time to waste on this. There is work to be done, and I have failed to do my part in the past. I must make up for it in the future.

Miss Ting Ling

Miss Ting Ling's School Days

MISS WALES:
I often talked with Ting Ling in Yenan. She was then thirty-one and considered the most important woman novelist China has produced. She was self-assured, a trail breaker in every field, particularly in the emancipation of women. She was one of the *li hai* Hunanese, not unlike Mao Tse-tung himself in her insistence on formulating her own ideas. This resulted in 1957 in her exile from Peking as a "rightist," though she was not put into prison. She had been a member of the Communist party.

In Yenan she was disliked by the wives, as she was known to have had rather vague ideas about marriage, taking a non-Puritan stand in such matters. In fact, Ting Ling had been an anarchist before she became a Communist, and she always retained an anarchist desire for total freedom, not only as an artist but as a woman.

Ting Ling's mother had wanted to go to France with the anarchist work-and-study students in 1920 but could not as the girl was too young. The girl wanted to go to Changsha to school but lack of money made it necessary to send her to a girls' school not requiring tuition. In the following pages Ting Ling tells of her experiences at this school and how she subsequently insisted on enrolling in a boys' school in Changsha, along with Yang K'ai-hui, who later became Mao Tse-tung's first wife. This was the first time coeducation had been considered in Changsha. She also tells of Hsiang Chin-yü, the founder of the Communist woman's movement, who was her mother's friend, and who was executed in 1927.

Following her studies at the boys' school, Ting Ling went to Shanghai to a "Common People's Girls' School." She has told at length of her experiences in my book, *Women in Modern China;* however, this fragment of her school days was not included in her life story and it is too precious not to be preserved to add to our knowledge of school days in Hunan, the nursery of the chief clique in the Communist party, led by Mao Tse-tung.

TING LING:

My mother did not have enough money to send me to school in Changsha as my young brother died about this time and the funeral was a great expense. Instead, I went to the girls' normal school in T'ao-yuan *hsien*, where there was little expense because the school was supported by the *hsien*. This school was outside the city on the banks of the Yuan River and students came to it from places along the upper river. The girls of this river district were noted for their independence and courage. At home they tilled the land and their feet were not bound. Women in the district worked just like men and they had a heavy tread, which reminded me of drumbeats. The upper Yuan valley was near the Miao tribal areas, and in western Hunan there are many Miao mixtures—this is why western Hunanese are so *li hai* and brave. In the upper Yuan valley, the scenery was strange and beautiful, and my schoolmates from that region told me many fantastic tales. In front of my bedroom were windows looking out over the river, where many boats were anchored. At dawn the boats weighed anchor, and I used to watch them and dream of the places they might be going. This was quite different from the time I had spent reading in my other garden and watching the boats broadened my imagination.

The other students were all older than I, and all were mountain dwellers from the upper valley, while I was like a city person. They were all enthusiastic, energetic, unrestrained and sincere, as mountain people usually are. Because I was the youngest, I was somewhat of a pet. Many of my schoolmates fought over my friendship, because the mountain people had strange customs and there were many pairs in the school. This was a nuisance for me and I was annoyed. Sometimes these pairs would fight and quarrel and weep so excitedly that the passengers on the riverboats would hear them. But these girls were all very simple and earnest. When we heard of the May Fourth Incident in 1919, we all went out on the streets and shouted slogans and wept.

I worked in the student government and was the leader of my class, often representing it in negotiations with other classes. I also taught mathematics in the night school for the local people. The students nicknamed me the "Young Teacher."

All my schoolmates wore the old-fashioned trousers with a skirt over them, but I wore a blue jacket and short skirt in the modern style. These girls were very simple, but as soon as anyone gave them a new idea they wanted to put it into practice. Bobbed hair first began while I was in this school, and, the minute they learned of it, the students cut theirs. The first day, eighty students cut their hair secretly, in spite of the extreme prejudice against it. I always hated to fix my long hair and cut mine too, so I have had bobbed hair ever since that day in 1919.

This school, however, was very backward. The library had only old papers and old reference and text books. The principal was a member of parliament and wrote essays in *wen li*. This principal was an old man but he liked me very much and made me a model for the school, in spite of the fact that my *wen li* was bad.

Although I loved the beautiful landscape and the boats and river and liked the simple, honest girls themselves, I hated the rottenness of the abnormal moral condition in the school and wanted to leave. This school was notorious for its custom and I dare say almost all were affected by it. It was not uncommon in schools at that time, but is better now because of coeducation and freer contact between boys and girls. The cause of it was the segregation of the sexes, and the fact that the students were thrown close together in the dormitories. These girls were lonely because their homes were hundreds of *li* away, and their naturally warm affections found outlet in this way.

After a year, I asked my mother to help me leave the school and, although it was difficult for her to arrange it, I was able to transfer to the Chou Nan Middle School in Changsha. This is the same school Tsai Ch'ang went to but I did not know her then, as she had already left for France.

The Chou Nan Middle School had already begun to teach the vernacular *pai hua* in place of *wen li*. My teacher was a schoolmate of Mao Tse-tung and taught modern literature to us, such as the works of Ping Hsin, Chou Tso-jen, Hu Shih, Ch'en Tu-Hsiu, Tsai Yuan-pei, and Wu Chih-hui, as well as translations from de Maupassant (whose *Two Fishermen* I liked) and Daudet (of whom I enjoyed reading *The Last Lesson*). The students were encouraged to write poems, essays, and sketches in *pai hua*. I then began to write both prose and poetry, and my interest in literature increased greatly.

Though I was only thirteen, I kept a diary, and wrote several volumes of original writing which were never published. My poems were published in a Changsha paper edited by one of the teachers. I can't remember what these poems were about now, but I was tremendously stimulated to see them in print and couldn't sleep at night afterward. All my stories then were very short and dealt with the problems of sentimental youth.

This middle school was entirely different from that on the banks of the Yuan River and the girls were fond of athletics—instead of each other. I took up sports energetically, such as tennis, basketball, volleyball, and dancing and dramatics work.

The girls were active politically, and, when the Hunan Provincial Council held a conference to discuss the new provincial constitution, we girls of Chou Nan demanded equality of women and the right to inherit property. The council refused the petition, so the entire school surrounded the conference hall and when they tried to escape, beat the council members with banner poles. The council was obliged to promise to grant the petition, but this was never realized.

Many well-known scholars came to Changsha to lecture, and I attended some by John Dewey, Bertrand Russell, Wu Chih-hui, and others. John Dewey and Bertrand Russell did not make much of an impression on me, but I had no criticism of them. I thought that if they were from the outside, they must be good. The students usually agreed with the opinions of the progressive teachers then.

Although I was primarily interested in literature, I followed other publications as well, such as *Awaken* and the *Republican Daily News*, which were easier to understand than the *New Youth*. The leftists opened a "cultural bookstore" in Changsha, which had a big influence. After a year, the principal of Chou Nan dismissed the progressive Chinese language teacher and two other teachers. We students opposed this action and created a great deal of disturbance over it.

After this disturbance in Chou Nan, I left the school with several other girls. We wanted a boys' school to accept us for study, because the courses in boys' schools were much better. Finally the Yu Yün Boys' Middle School accepted us. There were several other girls' schools and a missionary school in Changsha, but we didn't like these because they were either too expensive or too backward politically and culturally.

There were only five other girls who demanded to join the boys' school, and this created a scandal in town, because it was the first time coeducation had been thought of. The other five were Yang K'ai-hui, who later became Mao Tse-tung's first wife, Hsu Wen-hsuan, who was later the first girl to join the Communist party in Hunan, Chou Yu-min, who also joined the Communist party, and Hsu Ch'ien, the daughter of Hsu Teh-lieh, now commissioner of education in the soviets. I have forgotten the name of the other girl, but she did not join the Communist party.

When we first entered the boys' school, some boys were good to us and helped with our classwork, because the requirements there were stiffer than for girls' schools. Others were unkind and either jealous or angry that we were permitted to join the schools. They even wrote letters accusing us of this and that, but we adopted a very dignified, strict attitude and studied diligently, ignoring them. The boys had a fight over the question of coeducation, and one was dismissed for his attitude toward us. The majority of students and teachers, however, were sympathetic, and the experiment in coeducation was a success.

I met Mao Tse-tung only once in Changsha, when he made a speech before our school. He was very silent and wore long hair then, the same as now. He was considered a brilliant student and was already famous in Changsha. I also knew Hsia Hsi, then an active student leader and friend of Mao Tse-tung, who later became one of the best Communist leaders and was killed with the Fourth Front Red Army. Yi Li-yung, who was then in charge of the leftist "cultural bookstore," also became a Communist later, but turned reactionary. I knew about Tsai Ch'ang then, too, through my mother's friend, Hsiang Chin-yü, who married her brother, Tsai Ho-sheng. This famous girl, Hsiang Chin-yü, was tiny but a strong revolutionary. She didn't talk much, never gossiped, and was very strict. She could write well and take charge of practical affairs, too, and was very intellectual. After her death, there was never any other girl comrade to compare with her. When I learned of her execution in Wuhan later, I was infuriated because I had great respect for her and she was a good friend of my mother.

Chang Wen-ping and Chingkangshan

MISS WALES:

Chang Wen-ping was the first Red Army veteran that I met. I remember well the rainy day in 1937 when I

Two old friends from Chingkangshan, Chang Wen-ping (right) and Li Wen-t'o

arrived in Sian, planning to go to the Communist districts in Yenan in spite of the blockade. The trip had been secretly arranged, and I was hiding in the cold storeroom of a little Chinese house among sacks of millet.

The evening of my arrival, Chang Wen-ping came to call and told me to be ready to leave on a truck for Yenan early the next morning. I had brought my own sleeping bag because the Chinese family wanted to pretend they knew nothing about me, and I slept in it on the cold stone floor. Next morning never came. The Sian police arrived instead, and, from that point on, a conspiracy had to be planned. Since no more journalists were to be allowed to get through to Yenan, I escaped by climbing out of a window at night, eluding the Sian police, and driving off to Yenan.

After I escaped, I received a formal letter from Chang Wen-ping commending me on my bravery and ingenuity and apologizing for not having been able to help me. Later on, he told me he had secretly helped all he could and he said my escape was one of the bravest and most remarkable incidents he had ever known of.

Chang Wen-ping, age twenty-six, was one of the four liaison officers in charge of the Red Army headquarters in Sian, and I suppose was the intelligence officer, as he had been chief of the OGPU of the Third Red Army Corps and in Shensi of the Fifteenth Red Army Corps. Only he and Yeh Chieh-ying were in Sian during my Sian Incident, as Chou En-lai and the other man were away. Chang Wen-ping had always been a very close friend of General P'eng Teh-huai—who subsequently was removed from his post as minister of war in the Peking government and accused of being in opposition to the thought of Mao Tse-tung and in favor of rapprochement with the Russians.

CHANG WEN-PING:

I was an ardent Christian in my youth, and my first ambition was to become the Martin Luther of China. The earliest important impression I received was of the great love and humanitarianism of Jesus. At the age of five I studied at a Christian primary school in P'ingkiang *hsien*, Hunan, where I was born in 1911. I graduated at the age of eleven. My eldest brother was a clergyman, and all seven members of our family were Christians of the China Inland Mission, an English Protestant church, which we called the "Shen Tao Hui." My family were of the middle-peasant class, but we all worked diligently on the farm.

About this time I remember that my mind was full of three general ideas: Christian humanitarianism, nationalism, and the problem of how to save the farmers of China. These three ideas combined made me dream of becoming a Martin Luther. I planned to create a native renaissance of the Christian religion in China, so that it would leave the path of imperialism and colonialism, and, by realizing the original purity of the teachings of Jesus, become a great force in solving the problem of the livelihood of the peasants and of national liberation. I hated Japanese imperialism very much, influenced by the May Seventh Incident of 1915, and spent a great many school hours writing the slogan on ink-stones: "Never forget our national shame!" Once the English principal forbade these words, but this only made us the more zealous in writing our inscriptions.

My eldest brother was working in the YMCA in the provincial capital, Changsha, and I was anxious to go there to attend school but had no money. When I was graduated from primary school, my father and another older brother wanted me to stay at home to help on the farm instead. I had always helped in the fields, cared for the cows, and scattered fertilizer on the land, but had no desire to end my life in such work. I dreamed of getting an education somehow. My mother and sister were superstitious and loved having their fortunes told with the Eight Characters. Their old fortune-teller was a good man and, when I went to him secretly with my problem, he agreed to help. Whenever he told their fortunes, he would slyly put in a few words to the effect that I would have a great future if my family would give me an education. My mother believed this, so I asked her and an uncle to advise my father and elder brother to save funds to send me to school by living a poorer life themselves for a few years. My father called a family meeting at our house to discuss the suggestion. Nothing happened at this meeting, however, nor at several others. Finally, I wrote to a cousin, who also worked in the

Changsha YMCA. He replied that he would help, and that I could try my luck in Changsha without any money. This made me happy, and finally my family agreed to let me leave home, on my own responsibility. My oldest brother, who was forty, was also curious to know why a little boy of twelve was so eager to come to Changsha, and found me a place to live in the American YMCA there.

I studied by myself for half a year in Changsha. My brother had a good influence on me, as he took me around to the poor people's district and I learned to hate the injustice of our society more and more. He also sympathized with the poorer class out of Christian humanitarianism.

A Christian Convert

In 1924 I was able to go to Junior Middle School and my thinking advanced rapidly, especially along the lines of patriotism and the reconstruction of society. I was then much interested in improving the education of the poor, and when I was thirteen became head of a school for illiterate poor people. Our student committee itself organized this school. At the same time I was an active student leader doing propaganda work in the nearby villages, and joined the Kuomintang. In this work I made a contact with the Communists, because the two parties were then united, and I was able to read their manifestos and pamphlets. I soon became more and more interested in Marxism, because its program was so near my own and I could see no conflict between its aims and those of true Christianity, though I still retained my great admiration for the love and sympathy of Jesus. Before this, I had said my prayers regularly. Now I felt that Jesus was a great historical character in himself, without the need of any spiritual system. It was my greatest regret that Christianity had been perverted to the use of imperialism to dominate the weak races of the earth. I had formerly thought this merely an unlucky coincidence, but finally concluded that all churches were useless, and in 1925 I joined the Communist Youth. After that I was a most evangelical crusader for Marxism. In summer vacations I returned home, where I organized a branch of the Kuomintang and popular support for the Revolutionary Army. This was before the Kuomintang armies had reached Changsha.

I often read the articles of Mao Tse-tung, Yün Tai-yin, and Ch'en Tu-hsiu at this time. I carried on my student activities until I was sixteen, then in 1927 went to Wuhan and Hankow to enter the school for the study of the peasant movement organized by Mao Tse-tung, Yün Tai-yin, and Teng Yen-ta. I received good political and military training under these three teachers, to whom I was devoted. My determination was much strengthened, and I began to understand the role of the working class in national salvation. During this period the revolutionary tide was high and the general consciousness and feeling of the people very progressive. I considered myself a pioneer fighter for the rights of the people.

Then, in 1927, the reaction fell upon us. The Kuomintang organized the Nanking government to oppose Wuhan. The May Twenty-first Incident occurred at Changsha, and Hsia To-yin's troops turned against the people at Hsien-ming on the Hunan-Hupeh border. My schoolmates and I were depressed but full of excitement. I asked to be given an appointment as a soldier at the front in order to help carry out the unfulfilled tasks of the revolution, and the party appointed me to go to such places as P'ingkiang and Liuyang in Hunan, together with some other schoolmates, in order to organize peasants' and workers' volunteers. Our purpose in organizing volunteers was to capture Changsha. This plan failed.

I had many interesting experiences with the people at this time. Once when I was doing secret work in organizing partisans at Hsi-hsiang, in P'ingkiang *hsien*, I often had to pass the home of a poor peasant who worked hard for the revolution. The old mother of this farmer was kind and honest and sympathetic with the revolution. But she was about seventy years old and did not know how to keep a secret. We therefore often tried not to let the mother know when we visited her son. It was easy for her to find out, however, and whenever she had an idea we were coming always begged to see us. She said to her son, "If I cannot see these boys, I cannot sleep well at night. I must know if they are healthy and how their work is progressing. And I must know whether or not they are in serious danger."

Sometimes she gave her best tea—which she usually reserved for an offering to the gods—and told me that she often asked the gods to protect the revolutionaries. She begged me to drink the tea, because she said it would keep sickness away. Once I was in danger and had to hide hurriedly. She knew about this and went to pray for my safety at a temple on a mountain far away where there was an especially efficacious idol. She walked so fast that her weak old legs could not save her from falling down several times on the way. She left on this mission early in the morning and by eight o'clock at night had not yet returned. Her son and grandson had to bring her home. I felt very sorry when I learned of what she had done for me, and appreciated her kindness. When I next went to see her she told me that because of her piety in walking so far, the Buddhist gods had promised her three things: First, to protect the revolutionaries and keep them from serious danger; second, to destroy the cruel landlords; and third, to grant her a longer life so she could live to see the glorious day when the revolution would be successful.

Then she gave me some more tea. There was much dirt among the tea leaves but I had to drink anyway. I promised her that I would struggle for the revolution to the last, but tried to explain to her that it was no matter if revolutionaries were sacrificed for their work, but very much worthwhile. I did not want her to worry so much. From that day on I never saw her again.

The Kuomintang split with the Communist party, and, although we had part of the armed forces, we had to work secretly to prepare to build up our own sovereignty. We then organized the Autumn Crop Uprisings. I participated in these uprisings in my own village. At this time, the Kuomintang had become more and more reactionary and was massacring the masses. We had no method of opposing the Kuomintang except by such uprisings.

P'ingkiang—The Autumn Harvest Uprisings

Several times, a few hundred peasants tried to take P'ingkiang city but failed. Finally we organized 100,000 peasants to storm the city. I was head of the volunteers of one district and led 1,000 men during the fight, though I was only sixteen. Our first attempt was made on the Moon Festival—August 15, 1927, according to the old calendar—and our second in October. Both failed.

My 1,000 farmers had only 100 old native guns, generally used to shoot birds, and five good guns of foreign-make. The 100,000 farmers of the whole *hsien* had a total of 300 guns. The rest of the men carried bird-guns, *sou piao*, which was a kind of lance, or the *sung hsu-p'ao*. This latter was an ingenious contrivance used as a wooden gun. It had a big barrel made of strong wood. We put sulphur and old iron inside, then pounded on the rod until the thing exploded. These we called our "heavy artillery." Our enemy inside the city walls had about 2,000 foreign guns.

In our big attempt we entered the city and captured one machine gun, but it was too heavy to move in a hurry so we had to leave it behind. Had two Kuomintang companies not come from Changsha, we would have captured and held the city. It was a brave attempt, anyway. We fought from early morning until three or four in the afternoon, and lost 1,000 men.

This was one of the largest Hunan peasant movements. Many women joined the men in the fighting. After our two failures, the peasants continued to struggle in small partisan groups, thus expressing their opposition to the Kuomintang counterrevolution.

After the fight at P'ingkiang, I was arrested. Fortunately none of my ten other arrested friends betrayed, so the enemy had no political proof against me. After my family had paid a bribe of $100, I was released on the plea of being a "local boy." My old father received such a nervous shock at my near escape from execution that he died soon afterward. He was a good, honest farmer and thought the revolution was all right—but not for his own son.

During this period many people were killed in every revolutionary center, and the suppression was indeed terrible. For instance, in one small village in P'ingkiang *hsien*, with a population of only 500 people, 80 were killed. This was in Ku-chia-tung, and the killing was done by Nien Jung-ju. Twenty of these were burned alive, and others were drowned in the village pond. Neither old men, women, nor children escaped. Later on this village naturally became a center of the Hupeh-Kiangsi Soviet.

During this terrible massacre, I organized thirty partisans and left home. I was Communist party representative of this unit. Many strong revolutionaries rose to the armed struggle, the partisans of all P'ingkiang *hsien* having 600 guns altogether. Some were Communists, some were Kuomintang leftists, others were committee members of the workers' and peasants' unions. The partisans captured their guns from the landlords and their *min tuan*, usually.

My group had got our original guns for the storming of P'ingkiang from the bottom of a river. During a previous fight between Li Tsung-jen and T'ang Sheng-chih, many guns had been lost in the rivers and the partisans retrieved these. I myself was originally armed with only a paper-knife and a hand grenade! We students were unprepared for real fighting. In middle school I had not wanted to do military or political work, but was interested only in the educational side of the peasant movement. After the split between the Communists and the Kuomintang resulted in the killing of so many revolutionaries, however, we all saw that we had to learn to handle a gun. This came to me easily, and I was not afraid even during my first experience of partisan fighting.

About half my thirty men were party members and all were very young—about twenty. I was sixteen. Because I had received a better education than the others and was very decisive politically, I became the leader. Our tactics were to hide from the enemy in the daytime and to raid them at night. We could not stay in one place long but had to move constantly. At night we usually attacked the landlords, the *min tuan*, or the tax offices. The masses supported us in our activities. We confiscated our food from the worst landlords, whom the people hated, and took as much of their property as we could get to distribute to the poor people, keeping nothing for ourselves.

The partisans of three Hunan *hsien* were grouped under the name of "Liu-pi-yo Partisans," of which we were one unit. The people acted as scouts, told us when the enemy was coming and when they were vulnerable for our attack, gave us shelter, and cooked our food. Sometimes they gave us food, too, when they were not too poor. They helped us fight, though at first none of them knew how. This spontaneous fighting trained the peasants quickly, however, and many an ordinary-looking farmer who tilled his fields peacefully in the daytime was a good partisan fighter at night. The people seldom betrayed us. We could live in a house only seven or eight *li* away from the *min tuan* or White troops, and they never knew where we were.

Of my original unit of thirty, I think I am the only one alive, though one or two may still be working there in P'ingkiang.

At this time, I cried out the slogan of the land revolution, but we could not realize it immediately. We had no plan to solve the land problem. The peasants merely refused to pay taxes and rents. None of us had any experience, and we did not know how to redistribute the land.

Out of pure necessity, we tried an experiment in collectivization. The White Army constantly attacked our revolutionary district, and the farmers had to fight all the time. The Whites killed so many people, burned their houses, took their oxen and cultivating tools, and made life so hard that about 400 peasants joined together for economic and military self-defense and started a collective farm, in order that cultivation and crops could be shared. This included the two villages of Nan-k'en and Pei-k'en in P'ingkiang *hsien*. The experiment was successful for awhile, but later the land was redivided among the peasants as we found it better to let each farmer cultivate his own land. The collective spirit was good, however, and the whole 400 collective farmers fought the enemy invasions and worked together in unison. In the present stage, ours is a bourgeois–democratic revolution, which has not yet reached the socialist collective stage, so we must not experiment beyond this stage. It was better to let the farmers have privately owned land and to call on them to support the bourgeois land revolution, because the farmers are conservative and support the revolution on the basis of getting land. Our land revolution was not Communist and should be supported by all poor farmers. This particular phenomenon of experimenting with a collective farm was spontaneous. Afterward the party leaders criticized us for this. There were no other collectives then. This was the only one in our area, and I think there were never any anywhere else.

The masses always trusted the partisans, although many times the Whites came to destroy them because of their support of us. We had many dangerous crises but never gave up.

My partisans had expanded to 200 men. I was appointed party delegate for the Red Guards of the whole of P'ingkiang *hsien*, who had over 2,000 guns, though I had had only six months' study of military tactics. It was at this time that P'eng Teh-huai organized the Fifth Red Army during the P'ingkiang Uprising, which included about 3,000 men. In order to strengthen this new army, I took part of our local troops to join with P'eng, and became party delegate of the First Battalion of the Fifth Red Army. The name I used then was Liu Cheng-yi. The commander of this battalion was Li Tsan. The party delegate to P'eng's whole army then was Teng Teh-yuan, and I followed him and P'eng to Chingkangshan. We left in October 1928, passing through many Hunan *hsien*. The people were good to us, and we won victories as we marched. In two months we met Chu Teh and Mao Tse-tung in Ning-kan *hsien*, at the foot of the mountain Chingkangshan in Kiangsi.

Chingkangshan: Twenty-four Men
and a Mountain

Chingkangshan was an ideal defense position for the Red Army. The mountain with its several peaks was high and large. We could be independent there as the people of the seven *hsiens* surrounding the mountain began the land revolution and supported us. There were only five possible paths by means of which the top of Chingkangshan could be reached. My battalion guarded the path from Ning-kan village to Chingkangshan, holding a position at Wang-yang-kai, a high peak from which we could look down on the clouds below.

We had two hundred guns, enough food, and high spirits. We had carried our food up the mountain and built our own houses. But the real source of our happiness was the fact that here at Chingkangshan we were able to raise a new red flag in the sun, while all the rest of our country was under the power of darkness. Here we could continue the struggle and dream of the future from the heights of our fairyland fastnesses. But this happy life was cut short.

At the end of December [old calendar] the enemy began to attack, climbing up one side to cut the rear of the mountain.

In November, Chu Teh and Mao Tse-tung had already taken the Fourth Red Army and left Chingkangshan, before the enemy arrived to besiege us. P'eng Teh-huai's Fifth Red Army remained in defense of Chingkangshan. When the enemy attacked in force, the remaining Red Army troops were scattered. As party delegate of the First Battalion, I led twenty-four men to escape.

And now I shall tell you the story of those twenty-four men on Chingkangshan. We held our position on Wang-yang-kai peak during the enemy attack up to the third night. Many times the enemy attacked but we repulsed them. They lost several hundred men, while in our advantageous position, only two of our men were wounded. On this third night the enemy did not make a frontal attack, but fired two tremendous artillery shots. We were surprised. Our force was extremely weak then, having only a hundred men to defend the position. On our right wing was another high peak with a little valley between. This mountain seemed inaccessible and had never been climbed. We decided to try to take up a defense position there. We were afraid the enemy might come upon us through the little valley, and when we heard the echoing artillery thought it was coming from there already. This was at nine o'clock at night. Our leader, Li Tsan, then took some troops to attack, in case the enemy had arrived. I had forty men to defend our front. For an hour we heard furious firing, then there was no sound whatever. This worried us. I was momentarily expecting an attack from the front, and personally gave orders to each soldier one by one, saying that our duty was to defend the front and that we would not be afraid to stay under any circumstances. I said that no one was to be allowed to move or withdraw from the front except by my command, and that Li Tsan's battle in the rear was not ours, ours was to be at the front. We reinforced our own left and right wings in preparation.

Then we heard a noise behind us and the sound of laughing. Suddenly a flashlight stared at us. I was startled and demanded the password. No answer. We Communists had no flashlights. I knew the enemy was upon us. I ordered the four soldiers nearest me to lie down and wait until they killed the man with the flashlight. After the battle, I had only twenty-four men left. I then gave the order to withdraw quickly. The enemy had us surrounded in the front and rear, so we rolled down the left side of our mountain, and ran to the side of the opposite mountain. We planned to cut behind the enemy to meet Li Tsan, but lost direction in the darkness. It was about midnight then.

On the strange mountain we found no way to indicate directions, and a snow blizzard began. In the fierce wind, all our clothes turned to slippery ice. I gave the order to my men not to lose their guns nor rice bags and not to be afraid, no matter how these things impeded freedom of movement. Our Red soldiers always have confidence in the party delegates and my men said, "Yes, so long as we have our party delegate with us, we shall find a way out if we struggle hard and keep up our morale."

After a while, we discovered fresh footprints. Having no light, of course, we were searching for a path with our hands, and when we found the grass bent down in one direction we knew someone had walked there. I judged that this path had just been trodden by the enemy. We followed the trail, wishing to join Li Tsan somewhere according to the original plan, but could find no one. By three or four in the morning, we still could not find our comrades, and, as we were fatigued, wanted to rest until daylight, when our task should be easier. We could not find a slope to escape the bitter wind, and the steep cliffs made moving dangerous. Finally we found a clump of trees on the side of a cliff. Each of us braced our feet against a tree, to prevent falling off the precipice and we were able to rest safely.

Next morning we made the arduous climb around the mountain. Because of the clouds and snow, we could see only a few feet ahead, and had no idea of direction until we heard the sound of far-off guns and tried to make our way to the scene of the battle. We would at least be able to join our friends and die fighting with them, we hoped. However, we came to an apparently impassable forest surrounded by sheer rock precipices, so I knew it would not be possible to join our troops for some time. We examined our food supplies. We were carrying only one day's ration of rice. I ordered the men to make this last four days. No one could eat a grain of rice except by command.

I remembered that I had once heard of a man who lost direction in a mountain forest. He decided to walk in the direction in which water flows and finally got out. I ordered my men to proceed in the same direction as the water in the valley below. When we came to the top of one rock cliff, we found some hemp plants growing. These were long and strong like rope, so we tied the stems to some trees at the top and lowered ourselves down the face of the cliff by this method. Eighteen men succeeded in this before our rope broke. The six men on the top of the cliff then called to me: "Delegate, if we die here, never mind. You must go on without us." But I would not leave them thus, and called up to them to search for more hemp and make a new rope while we waited. They agreed to my command, but we had to spend about four hours before the new rope could be made. When our six companions were finally with us, it was evening, and the stormy sky was dark again.

We slept together at the foot of the cliff, and in the bitter snow many of my men had their feet frozen. Some of these brave fighters cried because of the pain. I told them stories of my life as a partisan fighter, and of how many of us had succeeded in conditions as bad as those now facing us. This took their minds off their misery, and, as all of them were strong both physically and politically, our morale was never broken for a moment.

Next morning we continued our weary march. I had already given up the idea of being able to join with Li Tsan and was only hoping somehow to reach P'eng Teh-huai, who was probably withdrawing from Chingkangshan. Our immediate purpose now was to reach a place where people lived so we could get help to carry on.

We agreed among ourselves that we must at least try to conquer every obstacle and to be killed in action rather than wait for death to come to us. We scouted around the shelf on which we were marooned, and decided which way to attempt the descent. Desperation lent new strength to our muscles and new power to our nerves, and holding on to each other like monkeys we clung to the surface of the rock and made our way down obliquely. Success! We fell into a laughing exhausted heap at the bottom of the precipice and slept like healthy children, highly pleased with each other.

On the third day we still continued to go down, stumbling up inclines, and fighting our way over new cliffs alternately. Our men with the frozen feet suffered in silence. Each cliff took long anxious hours, but on the afternoon of the third day we found a path with a bridge! We could see, however, that nobody had used this bridge in ten years because it was made of trees bound together, and the bark was so weatherworn that when we stepped on it the rottenness fell away. Nevertheless the sight made us happy.

Then we reached a place where we heard distant guns. We judged that the whole of Chingkangshan was now occupied by the enemy. Some of our fighters could no longer walk. It was necessary to wait until their frozen feet had improved before going on, though we were anxious to find some habitation where we could get food.

Fortunately we soon found a rough mountain hut made of grass, where someone had lived at one time. It was hidden behind a large rock in a forested curve of the mountain, so was invisible to any observer until he stumbled upon it, and our refuge was safe. We wanted eagerly to make a fire to thaw out our wet clothes, but had only ten matches. When we succeeded, we had only one match left, so that we would be unable to light another fire in the future. We kept one guard posted to keep the fire burning, and enjoyed our rest. The next day three of us went out to find some peasant house in order to get matches, rice, and information.

We took our three guns and walked through the tallest mountain grass we could find. We had not gone ten *li* before we discovered a house. This house had been nearly burned down, however, and nobody was there. I entered, while the messenger stood guard outside and the squad commander covered the doorway. When I saw the slogans on the walls I knew that a group of wounded Red soldiers had tried to hide there. The fire was still burning, and we were sure the enemy had surrounded and burned the place.

In a small room I found a hidden jar used to store unhulled rice. I was joyful. In trembling haste, I opened the big jar. In the bottom was a layer of good white rice! I called the squad commander to come in. He took off his trousers, and we tied the legs and waist and filled them with our precious discovery. He threw the bundle over his shoulder with a laugh, then went outside and stood guard while the messenger came in. We filled his empty trousers in the same way. I also found a wooden water vessel, and we started back to our comrades in great elation. After we had walked a *li* or two, darkness fell and we couldn't see at all. Misgiving entered our hearts. We knew that our friends would think we had been captured by the enemy. It was necessary to hurry back to reassure them so they would know they were still safe.

As we were struggling over a cliff, the squad commander lost his footing and fell. We thought he had been killed, but I instantly called down to him, "Is the rice lost?" "No," came the answer just as quickly. We often laughed at my question afterward. Fortunately, he had good presence of mind and in the middle of his fall had grabbed the branch of a tree and saved himself. He had fallen twenty feet and had not the tree saved him, would surely have been killed on the sharp rocks below. The cliff was not very steep, so we helped him climb up again. He was not hurt at all and there was no hole in the rice-bag either! "Heaven agrees that we shouldn't be killed," we declared and continued on our way thankfully.

We were stumbling along on our hands and knees, when we saw four men with fagot-torches coming in the distance. Somehow we knew it was our friends and shouted to them. We slowly made our way toward each other and returned together in triumph. They told us they had been very worried and thought we were surely captured. Some had said "We must change our place quickly." Others declared, "We must go out to find our comrades and fight the enemy to get them back." They finally decided it was impossible to go out to fight the enemy, and that they should not change hiding places until they were sure we had been cut off. So the commander in charge ordered a large unit to stand guard outside to prepare for an enemy attack, and courageously risked sending four men with torches to try to find us in the meantime. "We were determined to find our Party Delegate," these four said to me warmly, "so we risked betraying our hiding place to search for you."

When we were reunited we all sang a revolutionary song. One man whose feet were in bad condition groaned and wept tears as he sang. He took my hand and said: "Delegate, how I have cursed my sore feet that prevented me from going out myself to find you."

We hadn't eaten for two days, and when the men saw the rice they all wanted to eat it uncooked, but I sternly ordered them to lie down and sleep while I prepared food for them. The men, however, refused to permit me this grand gesture, and insisted on cooking the rice themselves, begging me to rest. But what could we cook our rice in? Among all our twenty-four men we could find only four small tin cups. If we cooked four cups of rice at a time, it would take six cookings to feed the twenty-four of us at the rate of one cup each. We began the process at two o'clock that night, but none of us had had any experience in cooking and we put the fire at the sides of the cups instead of on the bottom. Tenderly we placed twigs and grass around the four cups, thinking this would be hotter than wood because it burned more quickly. We were so hungry we lost all sense of logic. It took four hours for two cookings! Who was to eat these first eight cups? The first reaction of the men was to try to be first. Then they just as stubbornly begged everyone else to eat first. It took over half an hour of arguing to settle this problem after the rice was ready. Finally I decided that the four torch-bearers who found us, and we three who had found the rice, and the men whose feet were in the worst condition, should eat the first eight cups.

I shall never forget that moment in the dim firelight of the little mountain hut. When we eight picked up our beautiful rice to eat, the others turned over on their sides and nonchalantly pretended to sleep. One by one they stole an envious glance at us, then sheepishly turned away with a grin. The bonds of comradeship tightened at our hearts, and we all felt a great and inexpressible love for each other deeper than any brothers could feel. It is only in moments of danger and sacrifice that the splendidness of human nature reveals itself like a flame.

Next morning we decided that we needed more rice, and the squad com-

mander led four men back to the house to get the remainder in the big jar.
When they arrived, they found that the corner of the house in which the jar
was hidden had also been burned by the fire. They worked fast to uncover
the jar, and found that part of the rice at the bottom was unburned. They
took all the rice, burned and unburned, and returned about eight o'clock.
The unburned rice smelled of smoke and had a horrible odor.

We had kept our fire going as religiously as a shrine, and still had our
single match. But we had to get more rice somehow. We decided to try to
hire some farmer at a high price to go to a village to get information for us,
and some matches, salt and vegetables. We collected every cent of money in
the group, which made up a total of sixty or seventy dollars. We sent two men
out with five dollars to find some farmer for this purpose, keeping the rest
of our money for later use. When these two men had been gone only an hour,
we heard them running back, crying in fear: "The enemy is coming! The
enemy is coming! But they're still far away!"

We all prepared for a fight, except two men whose feet were so bad they
could not stand. We waited with our fingers on the trigger for two hours, but
nobody came. And there was no sound of guns. The birds on the opposite
mountain were peaceful and undisturbed, and we decided no enemy was approaching. Four men were sent out to reconnoiter.

After careful scouting, these four discovered three men on the opposite
mountain. They seemed exhausted and in fear, as they stumbled often and
seemed to be fleeing from some danger. One was bleeding from a wound. The
squad commander judged that these three were comrades and decided to call
out to them, beckoning them to join us. When the three saw our men they
tried to escape, and the more our men called out to them the faster they
scrambled away. After a time, the three finally seemed to decide that they
were being pursued only by friends, and with the help of our comrades came
to our hut. When I questioned them, I found that they were soviet people of
a neighboring village called Chin-ssu-mien. They had been driven out by the
enemy and had not eaten for three days. I had planned to find P'eng Teh-huai
at Ssu-p'ing, but they told me Ssu-p'ing was in enemy hands.

When they saw us cooking rice, the three villagers were so eager for food
that they ate it before it was cooked. We gave them double rations. They had
two boxes of matches which they gave us. Then one of them led two of our
soldiers out to forage for food. They returned with a small vessel to cook
vegetables in and a spoon to be used for stirring, together with two or three
chin of salt—and a small pig weighing eight or nine *chin!* They had bought
these from a peasant's house, who refused money when he learned who they
were.

We had been trying to cure our men with frozen feet. Among us was one
man who knew the medicinal herbs in the mountains, and we sent people

every day to get these for the cure. In spite of all we could do, however, two of them lost their toes, though the feet cured well enough. We ate boiled grass to cure our stomach troubles.

During these days I told the group stories of the partisans in the country and imparted all the scientific knowledge I knew. I also told them all about the difficulties of the soviet revolution in the U.S.S.R., which was finally victorious anyway. Another story they liked was Robinson Crusoe. It seemed very applicable to our situation. Others in the group told old Chinese stories. The men liked best the *Shui Hu Chuan,* and next the *Hsi Yo Chi,* the *Lao Ch'an Yo Chi* and the *San Kuo.* Often we sang songs. About a month passed before we realized it, our life together was so happy there.

We got together 20 *chin* of dry rice for each man and planned to march forward, as our companions' feet were almost well. We prepared to leave Chingkangshan and to go toward Ling-kan *hsien,* so we spent two days climbing to the top of the mountain. There was also a heavy snow when we reached the top and we could not see. However, we finally made our way successfully.

We discovered a small temple at the foot of the mountain. Nobody seemed to be inside. We entered and found cooked rice which had been only partly eaten, and the top was fermented and covered with mold. We thought that perhaps our troops had passed this way, and been hastily interrupted in the middle of a meal. At midday the sky cleared and the snowfall stopped. Far to our left we could see Wang-yang-k'ai. Two small villages, Hsiang-ch'iao and Hsia-ch'iao, were in view. I feared the enemy must be camped in these places but didn't see any sentries around, so decided they were safe for us to enter. We went toward the first village bravely but cautiously, and met an old farmer. As soon as he saw us, he was happy, as he was a sympathizer. He told us there was still a soviet government ten *li* away from the village and led us there. We were overjoyed to find Ho Ch'ang-kung, secretary of the *hsien* party. He and other people came to welcome us and sent us plenty of food.

The Independent Regiment
Recovers Chingkangshan

We discussed with Ho Ch'ang-kung the problem of finding the rest of our men, and after a while discovered many of them in small groups of three or five. Some had not eaten for days but had hidden in the mountains eating grass. Others had been captured by the enemy and escaped. Nearly all had lost everything but their precious guns and bullets. Finally, after twenty days, Li Tsan came back. He had been ninety *li* away, walking in the direction of this village, calling our men together as he came. He was disguised in the clothes of the farmers, and we didn't recognize him at first because the expression on his face had also changed greatly. But we all embraced happily at last.

We collected all our forces and continued our partisan fighting by forming an independent regiment, which achieved many victories. We reoccupied our lost districts and became the protectors of the people in the local soviet.

P'eng Teh-huai had gone to south Kiangsi from Chingkangshan, and the majority of the White troops had also left; however, the local landlords' *Pao-an-tui* militia were still strong, and it was these troops that we had to destroy. Not only did we retake all our former soviet districts as soon as the White army left but we also occupied new areas. Our armed force expanded to 1,000 men, and Li Tsan was made commander of this independent regiment of the Red Army, while I was party delegate—which is the same as what we later called political commissar.

At this time we received the decisions of the Sixth Congress of the Comintern, which corrected many former mistakes of our struggle, especially our "blind policy" of putschism, which was too leftist.

I think this was the happiest time of my life—being party delegate to the independent regiment and helping to recover all our lost soviets. I was very proud of this work, as I had led it personally. In my whole life I have had only two periods in which I did independent work on my own responsibility. This was the first time. The other I shall tell you about later.

In March or April of 1929, P'eng Teh-huai returned from south Kiangsi to Chingkangshan with his troops. One day we had a big victory over the enemy troops, and as we were chasing them, P'eng Teh-huai caught up in the enemy's rear and annihilated them in retreat. We were surprised! We had no idea P'eng was near at that time.

Our army was reorganized then, and I was appointed party delegate to the Fifth Battalion of the Fifth Red Army. My old Independent Regiment was reorganized into the Sixth Battalion of the Fifth Army.

After the reorganization, the Red Army went to the borders of Hunan, Kiangsi, and Kwangtung, and occupied Nan-hsiung, a *hsien* city of Kwangtung. This victory shocked the whole of south China, because Nan-hsiung was a very important place. We organized a new soviet region in Sang-yo and Ch'ung-yi in Kiangsi, but none in Kwangtung. We stayed there six months, then returned to Chingkangshan again.

We next advanced forward to Liuyang and P'ingkiang in Hunan and met with Huang Kung-liu's troops. Later on the Fifth Battalion changed to the Fourth Battalion, and I led it back to Chingkangshan. This was the second happiest period of my life. We were strong and independent and had many victories. Once my troops were only 90 *li* from the important center, Kian. The enemy was afraid of us, but the masses trusted us completely. The courage and sympathy of many of the old people always surprised us, and made us young men resolve never to give up the struggle to help them. I shall never forget one old man we met when our Red partisans reached south Kiangsi in 1929. Because of the failure of the Great Revolution many had to work very secretly under the White Terror. One responsible member of the local special committee had to hide on a mountain in Yu-tou *hsien*. He could not go out at all because of the danger of arrest and had to depend upon an old farmer about sixty years of age to take care of him. All his other friends had run away, been killed or lost their party connections. This old farmer's mother was eighty and his daughter was only ten. He had no son and owned no property. He had earned his rice by selling other people's vegetables in the market, but with the new responsibility of caring for the party member his burden was very heavy and he had no time to sell the vegetables. In the morning he had to carry food to the young man on the mountain. There he gathered one *tan* of wood to sell in the market, using this money to buy a little rice for himself, the committee member and his two other dependents. When we partisans arrived in this place and learned of this we sent the old man $40.00 for caring so well for our member, but he refused to take it. He said: "You work so hard for us poor people and the farmers, even sacrificing your lives for us, what reason could we have not to help any of you by a little extra effort? Though I am sixty and have no son, I may as well work hard before I die if it will do any good. Please keep the money for yourselves. I don't need it as much as you do. I wish the revolution would succeed soon, and that is the only payment I want."

When we heard this, we all became excited and insisted that he take the money but he stubbornly refused. Finally we secretly gave it to his old mother just before we went away, so he could not return it to us.

Campaigning on a Stretcher, with P'eng Teh-huai

At the end of the year 1929, P'eng led some troops back to this area, to such places as Jen-hsin and Sui-ch'uan. In the spring of 1930, we marched north and occupied many places, such as Sui-ch'uan, An-fu, Fen-yi, Ni-chün (Yuanchow), Lo Hsi, Hsuan-fung, Liu-k'ou, P'ingkiang, and Hsiu-shui. Later on, we attacked Yang-hsin but did not occupy it, though we occupied Ta-yeh, Huangshih-kang, Shih-hui-yao, and other places. The enemy in An-fu and Li-chün were completely destroyed, and at Lu-k'ou we destroyed one brigade. Two regiments of the enemy were destroyed at P'ingkiang (where I was wounded), and one whole division was captured at Huang-shih-kang. At Huang-shih-kang, which is near the Yangtze River, a small part of the White soldiers of the Twentieth Army were rescued by a Japanese battleship.

After these many victories, the forces of the Red Army expanded greatly and our arms improved. Our influence on the people increased commensurately. We advanced and captured Yochow. When we captured the Hunan capitol, Changsha, I was political commissar of the Third Division. Though I was wounded, I directed the political work from a stretcher in the rear.

I had been wounded twice in the same year, once at P'ingkiang, my home town, and once at Yochow. I could not walk but stayed with the troops on a stretcher all this time.

P'eng's strategy in the capture of Changsha was very good and the Red warriors were exceptionally brave. The enemy had four times as many troops, but P'eng made a fast march and a surprise attack.

Changsha under the Red Flag

While we held Changsha, I visited some of my old schoolmates and friends in the Christian church and YMCA. They were very curious about the Red Army and admired its bravery and ability to do effective propaganda. They were especially amazed at the youth of the Red Army, as most of our soldiers were under twenty-one. They felt the reaction of the Kuomintang, too, and ten of my former friends joined the Red Army then. About 20,000 new recruits joined the Red Army in Changsha. Unfortunately, the Communist party organization inside the city was weak. They had had no experience in keeping revolutionary order in public society. Many bad elements and rascals rioted and disturbed order in the city, by robbing from people and burning houses. These elements were paid by the reactionaries of Changsha to discredit the Communists. One school and a museum were burned, and the fire nearly spread to the headquarters of the Red Army. Then the reactionary elements took photographs of this destruction and said it was done by the Red Army— a total lie. The proof of who was behind this is shown by the fact that the home of the cruel warlord, Ho Ch'ien, was not burned. Had the Red Army wanted to burn anything, it would have destroyed this place first. The munitions depot was also burned by the reactionaries, to prevent us from capturing supplies. A few minor disturbances were created spontaneously by the unorganized peasants, but nearly all else was cleverly organized by the reactionaries, so the people wouldn't sympathize with the "Red menace."

After our withdrawal from Changsha, I was made commissar of the Fifth Army under Teng Ping's command. I was also chief of the Political Department. Later the Third Red Army Corps met the First Army Corps at Liuyang, Hunan, and the two forces again attacked Changsha together. But because the war between Chiang Kai-shek and Feng Yu-hsiang had stopped, the Kuomintang was able to send troops against the Red Army so the second attack failed. We returned to Kiangsi and occupied Li-lin, Ping-hsiang, Yuan-chow, Ni-fen, etc.

The First Army Corps occupied such places as Tsalin, An-fu, Kian, Chih-shui and Hsia-chiang, taking altogether twenty *hsien* or more.

In order to build up a center for the soviets and to realize the land policy thoroughly, the Red Army troops went across the Kan River and reached Yuen-fung, Hsin-kou, Lo-an, and Chih-shui. Under the direction of Mao Tse-tung, then general secretary of the Communist party, the Red Army at this time destroyed the First Surrounding Campaign of the Whites, and cleared out the anti-Bolshevik, or AB, group.

In Nungkan, Kiangsi, the Red Army captured the commander-in-chief of the White expedition, Chang Hui-chang.

Then came the Second and Third Surrounding Campaigns. In the Second Campaign, Ho Ying-ching was in command. Our material conditions were difficult, but fifteen days after the Second Campaign began, it was broken. From the banks of the Kan River, we attacked the enemy and followed him to Chien-ning *hsien* in Fukien, a distance of 800 *li*. This is an example of superb success in destroying a surrounding campaign.

The Third Campaign soon followed, led by Chiang Kai-shek personally. The Red Army troops withdrew from Fukien to Kiangsi quickly in order to prepare to fight Chiang in Kiangsi. At that time, the Whites were distributed inside the soviet region as well as outside. Only one small town, Kao-shih, remained to us as a market, as the Whites occupied every *hsien* city in Kiangsi. The Red Army retired into the countryside. But we achieved a great victory in the end because of the bravery and decisive mind of the Red warriors, because the masses of the peasants and workers supported our sovereignty so enthusiastically, because the command of the White armies could not unite and the White soldiers were tired and had no will to fight, and because the leadership of Mao Tse-tung and the party was very correct. Part of the White armies were Central Government troops and part were local, so they had no unity, and at the same time, the soldiers always feared the Red Army very much after their big defeat in the First Campaign. During the Third Campaign we disarmed the Whites of over 20,000 guns and Chiang Kai-shek had to return all our soviet regions to us.

Because my leg wound had bled a great deal at Changsha, my body became very weak. For a long time I could not walk well. By this time, however, I was much better, though our life during the Third Campaign was extremely hard. I was also hurt in a fall from horseback and coughed blood, after which I contracted tuberculosis in my weakened condition, though I was later able to cure this. My health broke down every year after all these troubles, and I had to spend two or three months of each year in the rear recuperating.

Victory in war is the best cure for any disease, and, although I was often sick, I was never sad or despairing. And my will for revolution became stronger than ever.

From the First to the Third Campaign I was too ill to do political work at the front and helped with the party work in the rear; however, after the Third Campaign, I was appointed political commissar of the Seventh Red Army under Kung Tso. I served only four months, then fell ill again, as my cure had not been complete enough. When I recovered, I was appointed chief of the OGPU of the Third Red Army Corps under command of P'eng Teh-huai. Teng Fa was then chief of the whole OGPU bureau. I then participated in the Fourth Campaign, which defeated the enemy.

During this campaign in 1933, we captured many White officers, and it was our policy to treat them well in order to let them have a true picture of conditions in the soviets and Red Army, so they would become sympathetic. We asked them to unite with the Red Army during the national crisis. Most of them were influenced by the Red Army and thanked us greatly; some joined the Red Army. I was active in this kind of political work and talked with many captive officers, such as Ch'en Tzu-yi, a well-known Kuomintang officer. These White officers sometimes sent letters of gratitude to me and to the others who helped them. One group of White military officers who were sent to the rear to talk with Mao Tse-tung issued a manifesto supporting the policy of the soviet government and Red Army to stop civil war and engage in an anti-Japanese war instead. Several tens of captive officers signed this manifesto. This was at the time that the Kuomintang press was shouting that their officers had been massacred by us!

Convalescent at Juikin

I was very anxious to be present at the Second All-China Soviet Congress in February 1934, and tried to go to Juikin, the soviet capitol, from the front then at Tsa-hsien in Fukien. I fell ill again, however, and nearly died in a Juikin hospital, so I missed this historic occasion, though I was elected one of the 200 members of the Soviet Committee anyway. I have always regretted this very much, as we have had only two great Soviet Congresses and I missed attending both of them. At the time of the First Congress in 1931, I had also been too sick to go. It was decided there to award the Red Star for good work; I received one and was very proud but embarrassed, for I felt I did not deserve it.

While I was in the hospital, the enemy was trying hard to surround us in preparation for the grand Fifth Campaign. The Second Congress was held after this campaign began, and it resolved to prepare to fight furiously. Even the villagers and children near my hospital were well prepared. The children not only begged their fathers and elder brothers to go to the front with the Red Army, but also begged their mothers, sisters, and the wives of their elder brothers to increase production in the rear to help the war. They showed amazing spirit. The children themselves fertilized the land and did light work, while keeping on with their school studies diligently. All this preparation in the rear, and the news from the front made my blood hot with impatience, but I still had to stay idle on my hospital bed in Juikin.

Gradually my illness improved, and I often went outside the city to take a short walk. I was happy to see the farmers enjoying the land they got and the new freedom they had. They worked hard to prove that they deserved this new land and freedom. One old man of sixty went every day to tend his crops near the place I took my walks, though he lived far away. He told me there were eleven people in his home. One day he said to me: "In the past, I cultivated 60 *mou* of land belonging to the landlord, and I could get only 30 *tan* of rough rice to support my family. We could not keep alive on this. I had to borrow about $40.00. Counting the interest on those loans they would now amount to about $100.00. How lucky I was that the revolution came just in time to save me, so I didn't have to return this amount! The soviets distributed 85 *mou* of land to me, and now my grandchildren have many things to eat and to wear, and have a chance to go to school. The vegetables are better now than before the revolution too. The *yü-tsai* is finer than any year I can remember." As the old man talked, he looked first at me and then at his *yü-tsai*. He laughed often in spite of the fact that he had not a single tooth, just to show me how happy he was. He knew that I was an old Red Army man, and told me proudly that two of his four sons were Red soldiers. He begged me to come to his home to eat wiht him to prove his statement that he could have four or five bowls of vegetables at every meal. In the end he asked me to come to live at his house and said he could help cure me more quickly so I could go to the front sooner to help the Red Army win the Fifth Campaign.

Talking with the farmers gave me great satisfaction. I came to have a better understanding of the work at the rear and to realize the needs of the revolutionary masses. This district was our model soviet *hsien* and we were proud of its accomplishments.

One day Yuan Kuo-p'ing, chairman of the Political Department, called to see me on his way to the front after a national meeting of the department. He said that at the front they wanted me to get well quickly and return, as every man would be needed to break the Fifth Campaign. Shortly afterward, in May, I went back to the front.

In the Fifth Campaign, our troops of the Third Red Army Corps had a good deal of experience in positional warfare; once in K'ao-fu-lao this corps destroyed six divisions of Chiang Kai-shek's army by this method. In this campaign the Red Army dug trenches for the first time. At K'ao-fu-lao we killed over 3,000 troops, although they were assisted by air bombing. We ourselves lost less than a thousand men. The Military Council caused the

Third Army Corps to become the standard army for positional warfare in the Red Army. This positional war was commanded by P'eng Teh-huai. I worked at the front with P'eng, in my capacity as chief of the OGPU of the Third Army Corps.

On the Long March with P'eng Teh-huai: Crossing the Tatu River

After the Fifth Campaign, the Red Army decided to go to another front in order to be able to fight the Japanese, so we began the Long March to a new locality. During the Long March I continued in the OGPU of P'eng's Third Army Corps. Besides these duties, I also made contact with the people and did propaganda work among them on the way. When we arrived in south Hunan, we discovered that many of the people there could sing the Internationale! Some peasants had kept the metal badges of the dramatics societies formed under the peasant unions in 1925-1927.

One morning in Kweichow I met an old man about eighty years of age on the top of a mountain. He waggled his long beard and said to me emphatically: "Now the Red sun covers the world. Of course, the Red Army will be victorious." He trusted the Red Army like a religion. Many peasants had so much faith in us that it was like a superstition. I have often seen old women praying to their ancient gods for the victory of the Red Army.

When we reached the region of the Tatu River and the River of Golden Sand, the enemy planned to annihilate us. It was here that the troops of Shih Ta-k'ai, the leader of the T'aiping Rebellion, were finally destroyed at Nan-hsün-tu. Our enemy wanted a second Shih Ta-kai defeat here, but they failed to reckon with the correct leadership of the progressive working class and its vanguard, the Communist party. We had the Red Army of nearly a decade's experience in battle.

At the banks of the Tatu, we looked down at a vast raging torrent but the deafening reverberation of the water in our ears was as stimulating as war drums in battle. Instead of weakening, our fighters became braver, and their emotion rose to high tension. Rock gorges stretched to sheer heights on either side, but our determination became fiercer at the sight of such a test. You could feel the morale of the whole army tightening up for action. Of course, we fought our way triumphantly across the Tatu bridge and marched on.

We had the support of the wide masses everywhere, and here our correct policy toward the oppressed minorities helped us. It is said that one of the important reasons for the failure of Shih Ta-k'ai was the opposition of the *Fan* (Lolo aborigine) race in this region. Our policy, on the contrary, won the support of the Lolos, and they helped us fight. We met one very old man near the Tatu who knew the story of Shih Ta-k'ai. He said to us: "The Lolos obey neither Heaven nor Earth, but only the Red Army. Your Red Army can conquer everything if you can conquer the Lolos."

We were always in difficulties during the Long March but always happy and often sang songs. Once on the march from Lo-san to Mo-kung in Szechuan we had to pass through a bamboo forest called the "Bamboo Mountain." The bamboos were so tall and thick that you could not see the sky but had to walk in darkness. The path had to be cut through with knives, and walking was difficult because of the sharp roots and stones. We had to rest often. I was with P'eng Teh-huai and Yang Shan-kun, political commissar of the Third Army Corps, as we passed through this strange twilight place. When our feet ached bitterly, the Red fighters began to sing to ease the pain. P'eng Teh-huai cannot sing. He is a very serious man, superlatively brave in battle but kind to his companions. I was never sad during the Long March. The greater the difficulties, the greater the spirit of comradeship and the stronger the will to conquer, we always say in the Red Army.

In the Grasslands I fell sick again, and my tuberculosis was bad. I had to spend much of my time on a stretcher. But because the doctors and nurses were so attentive to me, I did not have much trouble and passed through the Grassland swamps quite easily. In my sickness, I felt that the love of comrades was much finer than that of parents or brothers could ever be.

Although we suffered much during the Long March, it is my belief that this ordeal not only tested and trained our whole body of troops, both militarily and politically, and gave us a new confidence and power to conquer any future obstacles, but the experience had a great revolutionizing effect on every individual. I feel that every veteran of the Long March is so loyal in his revolutionary faith that he now has confidence in his ability to conquer anything. Not only that, but after recovering from the temporary exhaustion of the Long March, these veterans found themselves far tougher in body than before, and it improved the health of many weaker persons. For instance, in the last days of Kiangsi I looked thirty. Now I feel like a boy again.

With Hsü Hai-tung on the Shansi Expedition

On our arrival in North Shensi I was appointed to work in the OGPU of the Fifteenth Red Army Corps, commanded by Hsü Hai-tung. After defeating the Tungpei Army at Chih-lo-chen, near Lochuan, I then went with the troops across the Yellow River on the Shansi expedition in 1936. We went to Shih-lo *hsien* and to Fenyang, Chieh-hsu, Wen-shui, Chin-lo, Lan-hsien, Lin-hsin, etc., and to Chiao-ch'un, which is only 100 *li* from the Shansi capitol, Taiyuanfu. The troops of this corps can march rapidly and fight well. One day we marched 110 *li*, and had a victorious battle the same day. Hsü Hai-tung is a valiant fighter. He took many guns, and even captured one of the regimental commanders of the two regiments defeated that day. I talked with the *hsien* magistrate of that district, and with the captain of the local district forces, to explain the new anti-Japanese policy of the Communist party to them. We visited many Kuomintang officials and discussed this question with them. They all agreed with our anti-Japanese policy, and the people in Shansi, both poor and rich, showed great trust in the Red Army. I saw several old men taking their grandsons to enlist in the Red Army. Once at Lin-hsin I talked with an old man of eighty, who had been a soldier for thirty years under the Manchu dynasty. He had two sons, one a soldier under Yen Hsi-shan and the other only sixteen. This old warrior said to me: "I have never seen such an army as this in eighty years, and I know the Red Army can solve the people's problems. My oldest son is hopeless, because he has been a White soldier too long. But my young son of sixteen years I now give to you. I hope you will give him a good education, and I am sure his future will turn out well." There were many such incidents, though the Kiangsi people were much better than those in the north.

When we returned from the Shansi expedition I was appointed to do United Front liaison work in Sian. After the Sian Incident on December 12, 1936, I worked with Chou En-lai in his mission of helping to realize unification, peace, and an anti-Japanese front of the whole nation.

After Ten Years

For ten years I had no contact with my family, until I received a letter from my clergyman brother in Hunan a few weeks ago. This letter said, "It is our duty to realize unification and peace in order to fight against Japan. I know your body and mind are stronger and wiser after the difficult life you have led. No doubt the future of your task will see success. I want you to carry on cheerfully and continue to advance. Every day I pray to God for you."

This brother had been imprisoned for one year and accused of being a Communist, but he never was, of course. My younger brothers had to run away to escape arrest, and my two sisters were arrested because of my revolutionary activities.

I was once engaged to a revolutionary girl, named Huang Hsi-feng. I was very much in love with her and chose her myself. She was executed in P'ing-kiang in 1929 partly because of her own revolutionary activities, and partly because it was known that she was my fiancée. She died bravely and shouted slogans when they took her to be executed. I did not grieve so much for her death, because I realized that it was splendid and heroic. But I resolved to carry on the revolution for both of us, and I have been faithful to her and never married since.

After this long ten years of struggle, I am now happy and enthusiastic, because I feel myself lucky to have the correct leadership of the Communist party. Had it not been for the Communist party, I might still be merely a Christian reformist. However, I now have a decisive revolutionary will of my own to carry on the struggle for the Chinese Revolution, for the liberation of my race, and for the international emancipation of mankind.

But I am ashamed of the little I have done, when I look at those venerable old men with white beards, who have given a lifetime to revolution, and when I remember those who have struggled at my side and sacrificed themselves bravely up to the last drop of blood. But I am proud of youth, when I see others younger than I now courageously entering the work. Some of them I have seen join the Red Army when they were little boys and watched them grow up in it. Especially I am proud of those young sons of the poor farmers and workers whose cultural level and opportunities were so limited to begin with, and yet who have educated themselves so well because of their strong will and passion for the cause. It is they who are the creative power of our revolution and who will be able to carry on its important work. In their determination to progress lies the future success of our movement.

I must now devote myself to further progress. Under the direction of our party and its correct political program, I will never hesitate to give up my last drop of blood and sweat for the liberation of my race and for the future happiness of all humankind.

Ho Lung (right) and Hsiao K'eh, commanders of the famous Second Front Red Army

Ho Lung, China's Red Robin Hood

MISS WALES:

Ho Lung was the most glamorous figure of all the Chinese Red leaders, as well as the most elusive. Or perhaps distance has lent enchantment to the view, for at the head of his flying columns of Hunanese, he was usually here, there, and nowhere like a whirlwind, gathering legend as he went. Everybody I met had different stories to tell about him, none of which quite coincided. But on one point all agreed: Ho Lung had had the most exciting personal life of any of them. He even had a glamorous sister, Ho Ying (the idol of Chu Teh's wife, K'ang K'e-ching), who was an army commander killed in battle in 1933. He was indirectly responsible for my being marooned in the interior for two months, as I was so anxious to get the personal story of this hero on my way back that I missed the last truck before the flood season made the roads impassable.

Unlike the majority of the Red leaders, who made a great point of self-effacement, Ho Lung did not object to cutting a dashing heroic figure. He was generally considered the handsomest commander in the Red Army, wore a well-cut uniform with a jaunty air of distinction, always rode a spirited horse, and led his men into battle in the tradition of antiquity. He was also gay and witty and loved to tell stories around the camp fires at night. He was the only Red commander to indulge in that bit of vanity, a mustache, and admired beautiful women as well as beautiful horses. He and Hsiao K'eh were considered to have the only strikingly beautiful wives in the whole of the army— and they were sisters. Ho Lung's life and personality have become a kind of romantic leitmotif in the saga, and remind one of Robin Hood and his men. Even the setting was similar, for Ho Lung's men sallied forth out of the wild green-covered mountains of that untamed province Hunan, where tribesmen still lurked in the hills and dales.

291

Hunan is the one province in China distinguished for the high quality of its soldiers and an unconquerable fighting spirit. Most of the early Red leaders came from that province, and, of them all, Ho Lung seems to typify the fighting Hunanese. He was a natural leader and had a magnetic personal quality that seemed to make all his followers proud even to be associated with him. Just as Chu Teh embodied a kind of quiet elemental strength and goodness inherent in the heart of interior China, so Ho Lung seemed to embody the fire and spirit of the rebellious Chinese peasantry.

Ho Lung had a long revolutionary record, and his story is of particular interest because it tells of the most militant peasant movement in China—in western Hunan—which began under the leadership of the T'ung Meng Hui in 1916 against Yuan Shih-k'ai, erupted again as an agrarian revolution during the Kuomintang period, and finally formed the base of one of the most important soviets. During 1925–1927, Ho Lung was commander of one of the finest Kuomintang armies, the Twentieth Army of the "Ironsides" troops under Chang Fa-kuei, which he led in the Communist Nanchang Uprising in 1927, together with the troops of Yeh T'ing and Chu Teh, though he was not then himself a Communist. This Twentieth Army was destroyed and Ho Lung returned to western Hunan and organized an entirely new movement, beginning with "ten guns," which soon became the "Hunan-Hupeh Soviet." He was commander of one of the three main Red armies, the Second Front Red Army, famed for its spectacular victories and "Hunanese fighting spirit."

Though I did not see Ho Lung in person, fortunately I was able to meet his political commissar, Kuan Shang-yin, who had been with Ho Lung since 1932, and who agreed to tell me the correct story. Although Kuan Shang-yin's account has no romantic flourishes and spares all details, it is perhaps relatively more accurate than more florid narratives. Commissar Kuan was himself an interesting person. Small, dark, and extremely solemn, he puffed on a big cigar as he talked. He was a Manchu, and had been a leader of the Shanghai workers in their insurrectionary days. In 1930, he was head of the Shanghai Trade Unions, just before casting his lot with the Red Army.

At the end of 1937, Ho Lung's troops were reorganized into the 120th Division of the Eighth Route Army. In 1940, the Shansi-Suiyuan Liberated Area was organized and Ho Lung was commander of the army, with Hsu Fan-ting as deputy, the latter being chairman of the government. He fought all during the war with Japan and the renewed civil war.

Here is Kuan Shang-yin's story of Ho Lung told to me in 1937.

HO LUNG:

Ho Lung was born in Shang Chih, Hunan. He is, in 1937, forty years old. His father was a tailor and the family was very poor. Ho Lung inherited from his father the special characteristics of western Hunan, the rebel center of China: fearlessness, quick intelligence, and self-confidence. The father loved his son very much and had a great influence on his future political career. Ho Lung's father had never attended school, but had acquired some education by his own efforts and, when his son began doing political work for the Kuomintang, did not oppose him. It was a small family and now all are dead but Ho Lung. His two sisters and father were killed in the revolution.

When Ho Lung was nineteen, in 1916, there was a peasant uprising in western Hunan, of which he became leader as a member of the T'ung Meng Hui, which had much influence there. At that time, Yuan Shih-k'ai was trying to make himself emperor, and there were many soldiers from the north in Hunan, who oppressed the people cruelly, and this was the cause of the uprising. The uprising destroyed about one division of these northern soldiers. Tsai Ao in Yün-nan had led in this anti-Yuan Shih-k'ai movement before it spread to Hunan.

There was no further activity among the peasants, and Ho Lung felt that the social and political outlook was very dark, so he began a wandering life. Before this he had been a farmer on his own land, but was not married. In Changsha he planned to assassinate T'an Yen-k'ai, the ruler of Hunan, but failed and was arrested. He was freed after awhile, but as he told me, "This incident taught me a lesson. It taught me that assassination is useless and that without military power little can be accomplished in China. I felt that I must begin to create a revolutionary army."

Ho Lung then went back to his village, gathered together some friends, and began to organize this army from participants in the western Hunan uprising. He was commander of this battalion and captured the military power in that district from the magistrate. It has often been said that Ho Lung was a bandit at this time. This is not true; he was never a robber at any time in his life. He was leader of Sun Yat-sen's revolutionary party, the T'ung Meng Hui, from the age of nineteen, and it was part of their program to usurp military power whenever possible, as he did in taking it away from the magistrate.

Ho Lung's army began with only a few persons, but later expanded until he became commander of a brigade. This he took twice to Szechuan to fight. At that time, his brigade carried the flag of the present Kuomintang, and his political advisor was Shih Ch'ing-yang, a famous member of the T'ung Meng Hui who later became a high official at Nanking. Ho Lung's superior officer then was Hsiung K'e-wu, a Kuomintang commander of the Szechuan Frontier Army. Ho Lung was made commander of the local garrison.

During 1925-1927, the Great Revolution caused a change in the social and political situation in China, and this revolutionary tide influenced Ho Lung very much. He left Szechuan and went back to Li Chou in Hunan. The Kuomintang Government in Canton then sent a propaganda group to Li Chou to influence his army. The members of this group were Communists and the captain was Chou Yi-ch'ün, a Whampoa student who was later killed at Hung-hu Lake in Hupeh in 1931.

Ho Lung had faith in the Communists already and trusted Chou Yi-ch'ün, so he not only welcomed the propaganda group but collected many students from other places to come and give his army political training, and to reorganize and rebuild it along the new lines. Ho Lung and his entire brigade of some 10,000 men were very much influenced by these Communist propagandists for the Great Revolution.

When the Kuomintang Army occupied Wuhan, Ho Lung also arrived there, and his army, which had until then been independent but closely related with Kwangtung, was reorganized into a national division.

In 1927, Ho Lung's troops were sent to fight against Chang Tso-lin's Fengtien army in Honan and played an important role in defeating them. Then the split between the Communist party and the Kuomintang occurred. At that time Ho Lung was commander of the Twentieth Army of Chang Fa-kuei's "Ironsides." He was not a Communist party member, but his political idea was in agreement. He told me that he had asked to join the party previously and been refused. Why he was refused he did not know, unless it was that the party then wanted to be very careful and preferred him to remain a left Kuomintang member instead of being inside the party. He did not join the Communist party until just after the Nanchang Uprising.

Ho Lung left Honan and went to Hankow, then joined the Nanchang Uprising on August 1, 1927, which was led by the Communist party, under Yeh T'ing, Chu Teh, Chou En-lai, and Chang Kuo-t'ao. Ho Lung led his Twentieth Army in this uprising, and afterward all the insurrectionary armies marched to Kwangtung to build a revolutionary base there. They were defeated in Kwangtung and Ho Lung went alone to Shanghai afterward. There he lived for awhile, then was ordered by the party to return to his native village in Hunan.

The Hunan–Hupeh Soviet

In Hung-hu, on the Hupeh–Hunan border, Ho Lung began to organize a new army from the farmers of the two provinces. His Twentieth Army had been destroyed in Kwangtung, but a few officers escaped and joined him in Hunan. During the Great Revolution, the peasants of this area in Hupeh and Hunan had struggled very hard, and the land revolution had already begun. These peasants were land hungry and, because of their previous experience of struggle and high emotion, gladly joined the new revolution. The organization of the Communist party in these districts was also very strong, and, because of these factors, the Red Army expanded rapidly.

At first there were two movements in this Hunan–Hupeh soviet region. Ho Lung led the Sixth Army in the Hung-hu Lake district, which included the *hsiens* of Chien-li, Mien-yang, Chiang-ling, Ch'ien-chiang, Shih-shou, Hwa-yung, Kung-an, and Shih-men. The leader of the other movement in the *hsiens* of Ho-hung, Wu-hung, and Hsiang-chih was Chou Yi-ch'ün, commanding the Second Red Army. Afterward these two armies united in Hung-hu.

The organization of the Red Army here began in 1928 and after one year had 20,000 soldiers. In the beginning, the army of Ho Lung had had only 10 guns and 10 followers, which quickly expanded to 100. All were peasant partisans; there were no Kuomintang troops among them at first. After Ho Lung and Chou Yi-ch'ün united their armies, the whole force went to Huang *hsien* in Hupeh to build a new soviet, keeping the older Hunan soviets too. This united army was called the Second Front Red Army, and Ho Lung was made commander. The Communist party appointed an important member as political commissar to direct the party work there. This was Teng Chung-hsia, a student, who was later executed by Nanking in 1933. At that time, the party leader in the whole district was Hsia Hsi, a student and schoolmate of Mao Tse-tung, who was later killed in Kweichow during the Long March.

In the meantime a new Sixth Red Army of about 10,000 men had been created in Hung-hu, and the other army returned to Hung-hu from Huang *hsien* to join with it.

During 1931 and 1932, there was a flood in the Hung-hu district. Many houses were destroyed and the peasants had to leave. This was bad for the partisan movement. At this time all the armies were reorganized into the Third Red Army, which then had about 20,000 men.

From its beginning in 1928, the Red Army in this area had fought fiercely every day and defeated three campaigns against it. Ho Lung fought against the Kuomintang generals, Ho Ch'ien, Liu Hsiang, and Hsu Yuan-chien, as well as the Shensi armies under Li Yün-nung.

In 1931 and 1932, when the Fourth Blockade began, the material conditions of the district were very bad. Nevertheless, in this fighting one regiment of Hsu Yuan-chien was destroyed, and one Szechuan division of Fan Tsao-cheng was completely annihilated. When the White troops were defeated, the majority of the soldiers joined the Red Army. In the meantime the partisans fought fiercely with the *min tuan*.

I [Kuan Shang-yin] joined Ho Lung as his political commissar in January 1932.

In July 1932, Ho Lung's army withdrew from the Hung-hu district and marched into Honan, southern Shensi, Szechuan, and back into Hunan. This was Ho Lung's first "Long March." It was undertaken because the army could not maintain itself in Hunan after the flood, and had to seek new places for food. The purpose in returning was to meet Hsiao K'eh. When we returned to

Hunan, we rebuilt the soviet districts in the same places as before, but also in Pa-tung and Hsuan-an *hsiens*. This was the "Hunan–Hupeh Frontier Soviet" district.

In 1934, Ho Lung's Third Red Army met with the Sixth Red Army under Hsiao K'eh, in the Kiangsi-Hunan soviet district, and began developing new soviet areas, such as in Hsiang-chih, Yün-hsün, Ta-yung, Lung-shan and Tze-li *hsiens*.

We occupied T'ao-yuan *hsien* of Hunan and then Chen-tzu, Li-chou, Shihmen and Lin-li *hsiens* in Hunan. This was very hard fighting, and we destroyed the Kuomintang army of Ch'en Yao-han and also one division belonging to Chang Chen-han. We then destroyed one Kuomintang division under Hsieh Ping and killed Hsieh in battle, and afterward three brigades of Hunan troops under Ch'en Yun-mo were destroyed. The chief of our Political Department had been Hsia Hsi, but was now changed to Jen Pi-shih.

After this we began our Long March in November 1935. We went through the provinces of Hunan, Kweichow, Yün-nan, and then to Sikong. We met with the other Red armies in October 1936 in Kansu.

After the fight with Hu Chung-nan's army in Kansu in November, the Sian Incident occurred and the civil war stopped. This first occurred in San Cheng Pao when 13 companies (about 1,000 men) of the First Front Red Army under P'eng Teh-huai, Nieh Jung-chen, and Cheng Ken ambushed, attacked, and defeated Hu Chung-nan's famous First Division of about 15,000 men.

The Second Front Red Army is now composed of three armies—the Second, Sixth, and Thirty-second Red armies—and is resting at Fuping.

Ho Lung's two sisters were well-known revolutionaries. His younger sister was active in the mass movement and a leader of the Peasant Union. She was arrested and executed in 1928. His elder sister, Ho Ying, whom I knew, was a commander and led the troops in battle. She was shot in battle in 1933 in Hofeng, Hupeh. Ho Lung's first wife was arrested in the French Concession in Shanghai and is still in prison there. Then he married again.

You ask my impressions of Ho Lung's personality. He is unusually frank, brave, and heroic, and has a special style as a soldier. He makes quick, sharp decisions and has great self-confidence. He is a natural leader, and I think may be said to be a military genius, with much experience. When he fights, he makes very careful plans and all his decisions are sure. In battle, he is cool and calculating and never loses his temper. He is careful in his treatment of all his men, but gives them strict discipline for errors. His political understanding is good, and he is honest and obedient to the Communist party, always following the line carefully. Personally, Ho Lung is kind and naive and almost childishly frank. He is very healthy and strong, and loves to ride a beautiful horse. He smokes cigarettes—but has no other bad habits at all.

PART TWO

Biographical Sketches

Prefatory Note and Abbreviations

These notes were originally written before the Communists took power in 1949, and the information was obtained from the Chinese Communists themselves. As such, these personal data have a special interest. In most cases, I have left the notes as they were first written. In some cases, I have added information gleaned from later sources, which include Edgar Snow's 1968 edition of *Red Star Over China*, the Union Research Institute's *Who's Who in Communist China* (1966, 1969, 1970), and various publications from China.

I have used the common English spelling of the 1930s, which has since been changed, in some cases, in an attempt to standardize it. No diacritical marks are necessary in English, and few are now commonly used except the apostrophe, which indicates sound.

In these informal notes, I have taken the opportunity to record some personal impressions.

A list of abbreviations used in this section follows.

AASCC	Afro-Asian Solidarity Committee of China
ACDWF	All-China Democratic Women's Federation
ACFDY	All-China Federation of Democratic Youth
ACFTU	All-China Federation of Trade Unions
adv.	adviser
amb.	ambassador
apptd.	appointed
assn.	association
asst.	assistant
b.	born
CC	Central Committee
CCP	Chinese Communist party (national)

CEC	Central Executive Committee
Cmte.	Committee
comdr.	commander
conf.	conference
Cong.	Congress
CP	Communist party
CPACRFA	Chinese People's Association for Cultural Relations with Foreign Countries
CPCWP	Chinese People's Committee for World Peace
CPPC	Chinese People's Political Council
CPR	Chinese People's Republic
CY	Communist Youth
d.	died
del.	delegate
Dept.	Department
dir.	director
div.	division
ed.	educated
el.	elected
Exec. Cmte.	Executive Committee
Fed.	Federation
GAC	Government Administration Council
govt.	government
GPCR	Great Proletarian Cultural Revolution
grad.	graduated
Inst.	Institute
KMT	Kuomintang
m.	married
mem.	member
MFA	Ministry of Foreign Affairs
Min.	minister or Ministry
Natl.	National
NPC	National Political Council
PCSC	Physical Culture and Sports Commission
PLA	People's Liberation Army (mainland army)
pol. com.	political commissar
Pol. Dept.	Political Department
Prep. Cmte.	Preparatory Committee
PRMC	People's Revolutionary Military Council
rep.	representative
retd.	returned
RMC	Revolutionary Military Council

SC	State Council
secy.	secretary
secy.-gen.	secretary-general
UN	United Nations
Univ.	University
WWCC	*Who's Who in Communist China*

Political Leaders

CHANG CHAO-LIN—native of Mukden, in Manchuria; b. about 1914. In 1935, he was a journalism student at Yenching University near Peking and president of the student government. He was the original leader of the December 9th Student Movement, together with his friends, a fellow-refugee from Manchuria, Ch'en Han-p'o, also a journalism student, and Wang Ju-mei (later known as Huang Hua and Peking's first ambassador to Canada, 1971). Chang Chao-lin took the leadership in Yenching and the entire body of officers of the student government completely supported him. On November 1, 1935, a Yenching student named Kao Ming-k'ai wrote a petition for them. It demanded "the rights of free speech, press, assembly, and association," and attacked the Nanking government's repression. It was signed by "The Students' Self-Government Associations" of Yenching, Tsinghua, National Normal Universities, the College of Law and Commerce of Hopei Province, the Girls' Teachers College of Hopei and six middle schools—eleven in all. He later worked under Kuo Mo-jo at Wuchang.

CHANG CH'IN-CH'IU (CHANG CHING-CHIU)—b. Chekiang; grad. from Sun Yat-sen Univ. in Moscow; a Communist of long standing, who was in the labor movement in the Japanese-owned Shanghai Cotton Mill, Shanghai, 1925; pol. com., 4th Front Army, 1932–1933 and was pol. com., Women's Corps, 4th Front Army during Long March; dean of studies at Yenan Women's Univ., 1940; secy.-gen., All-China Democratic Women's Fed. Preparatory Committee, 1949, and on its Standing Cmte.; vice-minister of textile industry, 1949; del. to Bucharest, to the U.S.S.R., 1953; deputy for Chekiang to NPC, 1954–1964; was del. of ACDWF to 2d Natl. Congress of Sino-Soviet Friendship Assn., 1954; el. to Ex. Cmte., ACWF, 1957, and had previously been on this Ex. Cmte. since its founding in 1949; formerly the wife of Ch'en Ch'ang-hao, pol. com., 4th Red Army, who went west with Chang Kuo-t'ao during Long March in 1936 and since has not held any important post; widow of Su Ching-kuan, the first medical doctor to work for the Red Army.

CHANG HAN-FU—according to WWCC, b. 1906 a native of Changchou, Kiangsu, of a well-to-do family; studied at Tsinghua and in California; during Sino-Japanese war was editor-in-chief of the Communist *New China Daily* in Chungking and secy. to Chou En-lai, 1937–1945; fled to Hong Kong, 1945–1948; m. K'ung P'-u-sheng, former national student secy. of the YWCA, 1948; vice-min. of Foreign Affairs since October 1949; visited India 1955, 1959, and Egypt and Iraq, 1959; accompanied Chou En-lai to Burma, India, and Nepal, 1960; at Geneva Conf., 1961–1962, for large part of which he was acting head of Chinese delegation; decorated by Burma and Cambodia; accompanied Chou En-lai in 1965 on tour of Rumania, Albania, Algeria, Egypt, Pakistan, and Burma, 1965; to Indonesia, 1965, to Tanzania, 1965; accompanied Liu Shao-ch'i to Afghanistan, Pakistan, Burma, 1966; president, China-Cambodia Friendship Assn., 1966; el. alternate, CCP 8th CC, 1956, but was not on the 1969 list.

CH'ENG CH'ANG-HAO (CHANG-HAO)—b. in Hupeh about 1906 of a peasant family; studied in Suhan; he and Lin Piao belonged to Yün Tai-yin's group of student leaders, very early joining the Socialist Youth and the Communists; studied in U.S.S.R. several years; entered Ouyüwan Soviet and became pol. com. to the 4th Front Army under Hsü Hsiang-ch'ien; when this was reorganized as the 129th Div. of the 8th Route Army, he retained this post under Liu Po-ch'eng; WWCC says he went west with Chang Kuo-t'ao during the Long March, 1936, instead of going to Shensi, and has not held any important post since that time; m. famous leader, Chang Ch'in-ch'iu.

CH'EN CHIA-KANG—The following was told to me when I met him in San Francisco during the United Nations Conference in 1945 where he was secretary to Tung Pi-wu: "I came out of the student movement of 1925. I was only thirteen then but I was in the May 30th Movement in Hankow where we had a demonstration. No foreigners were sympathetic with us then except some Indians; the Sikhs were hated by the Chinese, yet they made speeches in sympathy. I was in the student movement constantly while I was in school. In 1929 I went to Wuhan University and left in 1933. In 1934 I became a member of a left-wing sociology society, which existed under the national Cultural League of artists, writers, playwrights, and newspapermen. The sociology society was the biggest unit of this league.

"In 1935 I joined the Communist party at the age of twenty-three as I was by then qualified. At that time qualifications were very strict. I was in Shanghai then working, and in the student movement. I was in charge of all the

Shanghai youth movement. In 1936, I was put in charge of workers' education. Before the war, we had the railway workers union, the seamen's union, and the postal workers' union. The Red unions were weak and were dissolved. In the spring of 1936, we organized the Workers' National Salvation Association, which had a secret connection with the Communist party's workers' movement. In May, I went to a meeting in Yenan but there I kept secret and practically nobody in Yenan knew of me or my work. After the outbreak of the war, I became a member of the Kiangsu Military Committee and helped organize guerrillas to fight the Japanese. In the winter (December 1937), I went to Hankow to make a report. The party in Hankow asked me to stay to do educational work for the workers, and I organized a cadres training class for the trade union movement. While I was in charge of this, I was appointed secretary to Chou En-lai in 1938 and held this job during the following years."

Later sources say Ch'en Chia-k'ang joined the CCP after leaving Wuhan Univ., and promoted youth work in Communist areas during the war with Japan; became secy. of Chou En-lai, Yenan, June 1944; was secy. to Tung Pi-wu at UN Conf., 1945; del. of Youth Fed. of Liberated Areas in China at London Cong. of World Fed. of Democratic Youth and el. mem. of its Ex. Cmte., Nov. 1945; spokesman in Shanghai of CCP at Political Consultative Conf. to negotiate rapprochement with CCP, 1946; mem., CPR del. to Cong. of Peoples for Peace, Prague, Mar.–Apr. 1949; el. to CC New Democratic Youth League of China and deputy dir., Liaison Dept., Apr. 1949–June 1953; mem., Standing Cmte., Natl. Cmte., ACFDY, May 1949–June 1953; secy.-gen., CPR del. to 2d General Assembly of World Fed. of Democratic Youth, Budapest, July 1949; ex. secy., Sino-Soviet Friendship Assn., Oct. 1949–Dec. 1954 and on its council; mem., China Cmte. for World Peace, Oct. 1949–Oct. 1950; mem., CPR del. to Sofia for funeral of Premier Gheorghi Dimitrov, Oct. 1949; deputy secy.-gen., Natl. Cmte., ACFDY, 1950–June 1953; deputy dir., Dept. of Asian Affairs, min. of Foreign Affairs, May 1950–July 1952; council mem., Chinese People's Institute of Foreign Affairs, May 1950—; acting dir., Dept. of Asian Affairs, MFA, Jan. 1951; dir., Dept. of Asian Affairs, MFA, July 1952–May 1955; adviser, CPR govt. del. to Moscow for transfer of Changchun Railway to China and to extend term of Soviet use of Port-Arthur-Dairen, Aug.–Sept. 1952; adviser, CPR del. to Geneva Conf., Apr. 1954; adviser to Chou En-lai at Bandung Conf., Apr. 1955; asst. min. of Foreign Affairs, Oct. 1954–June 1956; dir., 1st Dept. of Asian Affairs, MFA, May 1955–June 1956; first CPR ambassador to Egypt, July 1956–Feb. 1958; amb. to United Arab Republic, Feb. 1958—; concurrently minister (amb. after Feb. 1963—) to Yemen, Apr. 1958–Feb. 1963; made official visit to

Sudan, Dec. 1958; observer, African Foreign Ministers' Conf., Leopoldville, Aug. 1960; chief of CPR del. to Yemen for opening of Sana-Hodeida Highway built with Chinese aid, Jan. 1962; council mem., Asia-Africa Society of China, Apr. 1962—; attended talks in Peking between Chou En-lai and Aly Sabry of United Arab Republic, Apr. 1963; attended talks between Chou En-lai and Nasser in Cairo, Dec. 1963; attended talks between Chou En-lai and King Haile Selassie I in Asmara, Ethiopia, Jan. 1964; vice-min. of Foreign Affairs, Jan. 1966—; m. Hsü K'el-li; 1967 Canton tabloids reported him among those to be criticized, repudiated, and no longer in power.

CH'ENG FANG-WU—The following was told to Nym Wales in Yenan, 1937: "I was born in Hunan, in Hsing Hua *hsien* in 1896, of a large landlord family, my grandfather being a high official, though he had not much money and later became bankrupt when I was young. He was a *chin-tzu*, which is higher than a *hsiu-tsai* scholar, and he loved to read and study. My father did no work and smoked opium.

"At the end of the Manchu dynasty, the government sent many students abroad and my brother was sent to Japan. Rich families did not want their sons to go abroad, but the poor intelligentsia did. The rich clung to the old traditions and didn't want to change. They had a prejudice against foreigners and said they 'walked with straight legs,' meaning their trousers were too stiff to bend. My brother took me to Japan with him. I was then thirteen, and it was 1910.

"In 1911 the Revolution broke out and my brother returned, so I was left alone in Japan where I stayed eleven years. I studied in the Imperial University in Tokyo, specializing in the technology of arms. In 1915, the 21 Demands were made, and many Chinese students in Japan returned home. I went to Shanghai and planned to organize a school to build up a new study group, but this idea failed. Then I returned to Japan again, where I studied philosophy by myself, though I continued the study of the technology of arms.

"It was at this time, about 1916, that I began my literary work with Kuo Mo-jo, Yü Ta-ru, Chang Tzu-p'ing, T'ien Han, and Chen Po-ch'i—there were six of us, mostly students at the Imperial University. From this time I adopted a literary career and lost interest in arms and armies.

"In 1921 I returned to Shanghai with Kuo Mo-jo, and we established the *Creationist* magazine, first as a quarterly, then as a monthly. In 1925 it was very popular with the Kuomintang armies. In 1924 I taught in Canton University—physics and dynamics. This was during the time of the reorganization of the Kuomintang. Next year I left Kwangtung for Hunan, but in 1926 I returned to Kwangtung again. In 1927 the purgation of the Communists occurred, and many revolutionaries left Kwangtung when the counterrevolution came—I was one of them. That same year the Creationist Society in Shanghai was suppressed by Chang Tso-lin, whose army was there, and later by the Kuomintang, also. There was no freedom in Shanghai, so I went to Japan for a short time; then later I went to France.

"I had joined the left wing in 1925 and was one of the founders of the group, but I had no interest in Marxism until 1927. The purgation made me very angry and turned me sharply toward the Communists, causing me to study, and, in the latter part of 1927, I began to translate Marxist books.

"I stayed in France a year and went on to Germany, where I studied social sciences in Berlin. After leaving Shanghai I had not much relation with Chinese literary circles, and, upon my return in September 1931, we organized the Union of Social Scientists in Shanghai and I took care of the newspaper, which we had to publish secretly. At the end of the year, I was ordered to go to the Hupeh-Honan-Anhui soviet district."

In the Ouyüwan district, Ch'eng Fang-wu was com. of education. After the Long March, became dean of the Communist party school, the fountainhead of theory; later sources say that he was mem., 2d Ex. Cmte., Central Kiangsi Soviet Govt., 1934; alternate on the Natl. Cmte., All-China Fed. of Literary and Art Circles, July 1949–1953; mem., Standing Council, Assn. for Reforming Chinese Written Language, 1949–1952; vice-pres., Chinese People's Univ., 1950–1952; mem., Kirin PPC, 1955; mem. del. to 1st World Conf. against A and H Bombs, Hiroshima, 1955; deputy for Kwangsi to 2d NPC, 1959; mem., Standing Council, Chinese-African People's Friendship Assn., 1960—; pres., Shantung branch, Sino-Soviet Friendship Assn., 1960—; mem., All-China Fed. of Literary and Art Circles, 1960—; pres., Shantung Univ., Tsingtao, 1961—; deputy for Shantung to 3d NPC, 1964; mem., Presidium 1st session, 3d NPC, 1964.

CH'EN HAN-P'O—native of Manchuria; journalism student and ed. of Yenching Univ. school paper, 1935, at which time he and Chang Chao-lin and Huang Hua initiated the December 9th Student Movement; vice-pres., Peking Information School, 1946–1966(?); council mem., China Information Service, Dec. 1952—; council mem., China Afro-Asian Society, Apr. 1962—; mem., Chinese scientists' del. led by Chou P'ei-yuan to attend 1964 Peking Science Symposium, Aug. 1964; del. of news and publication circles to 4th CPPCC, el. mem., Natl. Cmte. and convener, Motions Examination Cmte., 1st session, 4th CPPCC, Dec. 1964; criticized by *People's Daily* for his historical and academic viewpoints, March 1963; chief ed., *Commercial Press*, and concurrently deputy secy.-gen., China Afro-Asian Society; branded an antiparty element, 1966.

CH'EN HUI-CH'ING, Miss—b. in Hongkong in 1910 and raised in Canton, her father being a machinist who ran away and left his wife to support two daughters; worked in a stocking factory at fourteen and in 1925 participated in the Hongkong Strike, joined the CP, went to Canton, and worked there three years as mem. of the Kuomintang Propaganda Department; helped organize the Canton Commune, but escaped; entered the Kiangsi soviets and was one of the thirty women on the Long March with Mao Tse-tung; m. Teng Fa early, both being active in the Hongkong Strike; a leading woman CP member, active in political work and labor activities.

CH'EN PO-TA—I have no personal information about him. Other sources report the following which may not be correct: b. 1904, native of Huaian *hsien*, Fukien; ed. at Chimei Middle School, Amoy, Labor Univ., Shanghai, and Sun Yat-sen Univ., Moscow; served as clerk under General Chang Chen and about 1925 secretly joined the CCP; arrested and imprisoned for several years in Nanking; upon his release, went to Moscow to school in 1926 and one source says he joined the "branch faction" of the CCP, 1927, and was reprimanded for "factionalism" in a purge; returned to China and began a study of Communist theories in Peking, 1931; taught under a false name (Ch'en Chih-mei) at China College in Peking, 1933; carried on underground work in Tientsin, and went to Yenan on the outbreak of the war with Japan in 1937; later became pol. secy. of Mao Tse-tung; went to Chungking as an editor of *Hsin-hua Jih-Pao*, 1942, but in 1943 was in Yenan in the propaganda department; was consulted during Mao's writing of *Resolutions on Some Questions in the History of Our Party*, and was el. as alternate to the CC at the CCP 7th Congress, April 1945; was elevated to full membership of the CCP CC following the death of Wang Jo-fei, 1946; became deputy dir., Propaganda Dept., CCP CC, Oct. 1949–July 1955 under Lu Ting-yi and was instrumental in removing Lu, whom he replaced in 1966, after the fall of T'ao-chu; held many posts in political science groups and was vice-pres., Marxism-Leninism Institute, Peking, 1949; vice-pres., the Chinese Academy of Sciences, Oct. 1949; council mem., Assn. for Reforming the Chinese Written Language, Oct. 1949–Feb. 1952; council mem., Sino-Soviet Friendship Assn., Oct. 1949–Dec. 1954; mem., Cmte. of Chinese Cong. of Defenders of World Peace, Oct. 1949–Oct. 1950; accompanied Mao Tse-tung on first visit to Moscow, Dec. 1949–Feb. 1950, to negotiate Sino-Soviet Treaty of Friendship, and may have served as Mao's interpreter during his talks with Stalin; eulogized Stalin's contribution to the Chinese Revolution, 1949–1952; a prolific writer on political subjects, history, and philosophy; a "deifier" of Mao, building his public image; published *Theory of the Chinese Revolution Is the Combination of Marxism-Leninism with the Chinese Revolution* and

Mao Tse-tung on the Chinese Revolution, 1951; edited *The Thought of Mao Tse-tung* and *Quotations from Chairman Mao Tse-tung;* deputy dir., Rural Work Cmte., CCP Central Cmte., 1955–1957; editor in chief, *Hung Ch'i,* 1958—; vice-chairman, State Planning Commission, Oct. 1962; el. to the Standing Cmte., Natl. Cmte., 4th CPPCC, Jan. 1965; published a series of articles on "The Great Proletarian Cultural Revolution," 1966–1967, circulated throughout the world; el. to Standing Cmte. 9th Cong., CCP, 1969, marking the final success of the Cultural Revolution in breaking the Liu Shao-ch'i bureaucracy and reviving the prestige of Mao Tse-tung and the Old Guard; head of the group that directed the Cultural Revolution; probably informed teen-age Red Guards of facts to use in wall-poster attacks on the bureaucracy and probably largely instrumental in bringing down his former superiors, such as Liu Shao-ch'i, Lu Ting-yi, and Teng Hsiao-p'ing; in 1971, he and his group seem to have taken a back seat.

CHEN SHAO-MING (CHEN SHAO-MIN), Miss—b. 1905 of a poor family native to Tsinan, Shantung, and received no formal education; joined CCP, 1929; went to Kiangsi soviet area; was cadre of Women's Army Corps on the Long March, 1934–1935; grad. from Party School of CCP in northern Shensi and went with Tseng Shan to Kiangsi to become dir., Women's Dept., CCP SE Bureau, 1937; mem., CCP Central China Bureau; cmdr., Guard Regt. 5th Div., and pol. com., 5th Div., 4th Army of New 4th Army, 1941; deputy, CCP Central Plain Sub-bureau and cmdr., 15th Brigade, 2d Column, at end of war in 1945; mem., Exec. Cmte., All-China Women's Fed., 1949–1959; del. rep., All-China Fed. of Labor to 1st CPPCC and el. to its Natl. Cmte., 1949–1954; mem., People's Procurator General's Office, 1949–1954; Natl. Cmte., Textile Workers' Trade Union of China, 1950–1957; el. Exec. Cmte., ACFTU, 1953–1957; alternate mem., Exec. Cmte., World Fed. of Trade Unions, 1954–1957; vice-chmn., Textile and Garment Workers' Trade Union Intl., 1954; el. deputy for Shangtung to 1st NPC, 1954, and mem., Presidium; el. 7th CC as alternate, 1945, No. 8; full mem., CCP 8th CC, 1956; full mem., Control Committee of the 8th CC, 1963; vice-chmn., ACFTU, 1957; del. rep., ACFTU to 3d CPPCC and el. mem. Natl. Cmte., 1959; vice-chmn., Cmte. March 8 Intl. Women's Day, Feb. 1960; mem., Standing Cmte., 3d NPC, Jan. 1965.

CH'EN YUN (original name LIAO CH'ENG-YUN)—b. about 1900, native of Chingpu *hsien,* Kiangsu; worked for Commercial Press, Shanghai, after six years of primary school; helped Liu Shao-ch'i organize workers in May 30th Movement, Shanghai, 1925; joined CCP 1924 or 1925; participated in meeting of Shanghai Fed. Trade Unions on eve of 2d armed uprising, Feb. 1927; as pres., Commercial Press Trade Union led in 3d armed uprising, March

1927; returned to Chingpu to organize peasant uprising, 1927; went to U.S.S.R., then to Kiangsi soviet, 1929; mem., 6th CCP CC, 1931; pres., All-Soviet Trade Union, 1931; mem., Politburo, 1934; participated in Long March, 1934; mem., RMC, Jan. 1935; supported Mao Tse-tung at Tsunyi; went to U.S.S.R., May 1935, for 7th Cong. Comintern, July–Aug. 1935; ret. to China after outbreak of Sino-Japanese war, 1937; deputy dir., org. Dept. CCP CC, 1937; sent to Urumchi to take charge of remnants of Red 4th Front Army, which had been all but annihilated in march to Sinkiang, 1937; dir., Peasants Dept. CCP CC, 1939; No. 8 on the CCP CC, 1945, 1956; No. 5 on the Politburo, 1945, 1956; No. 11 on the Politburo, 1966; went to Manchuria with Lin Piao and Kao Kang, Sept. 1945; secy., NE Bureau CCP CC, Jan. 1946; chmn., Mukden Military Control Cmte., 1948; vice-premier, Govt. Administration Council, 1949–1954; min. of Heavy Industry, 1949–1950; acting premier in absence of Chou En-lai, 1956–1957; was attacked in Peking tabloids as a top capitalist-roader, 1967.

CHIANG CH'ING (LAN PING)—third wife of Mao Tse-tung; sources say she was b. 1912 in Taian, Shantung, in Chucheng county; ed. primary school in Tsinan where she and her mother lived with the maternal grandfather, Li Tzu-ming, superintendent of a middle school; enrolled at the new Provincial Experimental Drama Academy in Tsinan under Chao T'ai-mo, husband of Yu San; influenced by Yu San's brother, Yu Ch'i-wei (Huang Ching), secretly joined CP, 1933; some sources say Chiang Ch'ing married Huang Ching; went to Shanghai as an actress in the Tien Tung Motion Picture Company, promoted by the Alliance of Chinese Leftist Writers; m. T'ang Na, a talented director, about 1934, and both worked in the infant film industry; was divorced in 1937; some sources say she was escorted to Yenan in 1938 by Huang Ching; there entered the Lu Hsun Art Institute and met and married Mao Tse-tung by 1939; two daughters by Mao, Li Na, who led a work team to Peking Univ. during the Cultural Revolution, and Mao Mao, both said to be married; stayed in background until the Cultural Revolution of 1966 when she was "first deputy leader" under Ch'en Po-ta; cultural adviser to the armed forces and the chief authority on drama, films and music in the art world, as spokesman for Mao; at the 9th Congress of the CP, 1969, she mounted the rostrum and was on the presidium with Mao, Lin Piao, Chou En-lai, Ch'en Po-ta, K'ang Sheng, Tung Pi-wu, Liu Po-ch'eng, Chu Teh, Chen Yun, Chang Chun-chiao and Yao Wen-yuan; el. to the Politburo of 21 members but not to the Standing Committee of five, on which were her close associates, K'ang Sheng, Ch'en Po-ta and Mao Tse-tung, along with Chou En-lai and Lin Piao; appeared at army celebrations in 1971 and welcomed the party of Joris Ivens, famous film-maker, 1971.

Chou En-lai

CHOU EN-LAI—b. 1898 in Huai An, Kiangsu Province, of the "bankrupt mandarin" class; at thirteen moved to Fengtien in Manchuria; at fifteen cut off his queue and went to Tientsin to school at Nankai Middle School, graduating after four years; was an active student leader and interested in revolutionary movements; in 1917 went to Japan as an "auditor" student at Waseda and Japan universities for a year and a half; then returned and went to Nankai Univ. and was editor of the student newspaper; at the end of 1919 was arrested for leading a student demonstration and imprisoned; after his release joined radical society called "Awaken," of which his future wife, Teng Ying-ch'ao, was also a member; went to France in 1920, spending two years and later one year in Germany; became member of the CY, which was admitted to affiliation with the CP in 1922; returned from France in 1924 and went to Canton, joining CP as secy. of the Provincial Committee; became chief of the Pol. Dept. of Whampoa Academy under Chiang Kai-shek; his first battle was in the fight against Chen Chiung-ming; worked at Whampoa from 1925–1926; during Chiang Kai-shek's first coup in Canton, was arrested in Swatow (where he commanded three divisions under Ho Ying-ching), however Chiang retained Chou as "advisor" because of his great influence with the cadets; Chou was then appointed by CP as head of the party work in the Kuomintang armies; in the meanwhile studied military tactics and strategy under General Bluecher and other Soviet teachers at Whampoa; at beginning of 1927 Chou went to Shanghai and was put in charge of the workers' uprisings there; the first uprising (November 1926) was a failure; Chou led the second and third (on February 25 and 26 and March 21 and 22, respectively), and the third was a famous success, the purpose being to welcome the Nationalist armies; he had 5,000 armed workers in Shanghai and 80,000 pickets; Chou was arrested in 1927 and nearly executed but was saved because, though Pai Chung-hsi had ordered his execution, a division commander released him, as his brother had been Chou's student (this Kuomintang commander was later captured by the Reds and became a teacher in the soviets); after the Shanghai affair,

Chou went to Wuhan, working in the party's military committee, then to Nanchang where he was secy. of the Front Committee of the Nanchang Uprising on August 1, 1927, and went with the first Red Army to Swatow; then did political work, went to Moscow twice, first as delegate to the 6th Cong. of the Comintern and then in 1930 as Red Army delegate; in 1931 went to Kiangsi soviets; first became secy. of the Central Political Bureau, then after six months became pol. com. under Chu Teh; after 4th campaign returned to Juikin as vice-chairman of the Military Council; went on Long March during 1934–1935; became vice-chairman of the Eighth Route Army's Military Council second to Mao Tse-tung, chairman, and after 1936 acted as chief liaison officer between the Communists and the Kuomintang; in 1948 was one of the seven members of the CP Political Bureau; in 1949 el. vice-chairman of the People's Revolutionary Military Council and minister of Foreign Affairs, and concurrently premier of the State Administration Council; remained premier in 1969 after the Cultural Revolution, in which he was one of the leaders; in 1969 el. to five-man Standing Comte. of the Politburo of twenty-one members; in 1971, engineered attempt at rapprochement with West; acts as balance wheel for all factions in the Chinese Communist movement and as liaison for non-Communist elements in China; liaison between the army and the civil power, as Mao Tse-tung was, and the liaison with foreign powers; represents the youth of the bankrupt patrician mandarin families in China (his father was said to be a scholar Chou Yün-liang), in revolt against Confucianism and in alliance with the peasantry (Mao Tse-tung represents the peasant movement as such).

CHOU HSING—b. in 1908 in Yuanfeng, Kiangsi, his parents both handicraft workers; studied in primary school three years, then higher primary school three years; next was apprenticed in a shop and in 1925, a student talked to the young apprentice and induced him to enter the CY; during the 1925–1927 Revolution, became a functionary in the local peasant union; in 1927 was ordered to Nanchang to study in Chu Teh's military academy but did not go because of illness; later returned to work in the peasant union with Fang Chih-min and participated in the T'ungku Uprising of peasants led by Mao Tse-tung; until 1930 led a partisan detachment and became chief of partisan guards; in 1930 joined the Cmte. to Repress Counter-Revolutionaries, which later became the Pao Wei Chü, or Political Defense Bureau, of which he was assistant chief, then chief after 1936 (this was the only police force known in the Communist regions, and it provided bodyguards for all important figures); vice-chief, CCP Political Defense Bureau under Teng Fa, summer of 1937; del. of East China to 1st CPPCC, Sept. 1949–1954; vice-min. of Public Security, Sept. 1954–Feb. 1958; deputy procurator, 1958–1962; mem. del. led by Wu Hsiu-ch'uan to 8th Cong., Hungarian Workers' Party, 1962;

att. 12 Cong., Czech CP, 1962; gov. of Yunnan and secy. Secretariat, CCP Yunnan Prov. Cmte., 1965; vice-chmn., Yunnan Prov. Rev. Cmte., Aug. 1968; el. to the Central Committee of the CCP, 1969; m. Yang Yü-ying.

FANG WEN-PING (FENG WEN-PIN?)—b. 1911 in Chu Chi *hsien*, Chekiang; in 1920 went to Shanghai to work in match factory with father and sister; studied one year in primary school and attended night schools; joined Kuomintang in 1926, the CY in 1927, and the CP in 1928; in 1927 became apprentice in coal company and joined trade union activities; worked in Trade Union Council in Shanghai until its suppression in September 1930; fled to escape arrest, and in November 1930 entered West Fukien Soviet and joined 4th Red Army, doing the work of the local CP Cmte.; became pol. com. successively to the Radio Brigade, Communications Brigade, and Special Police; went to Kiangsi in 1932 on an inspection tour, and in 1933 apptd. secy. of Fukien Provincial CP; when CY division was established in August 1933 was made pol. com. and remained this throughout Long March; in 1935 was apptd. natl. secy. of CY; later secy. of the Central Cmte. of the China New Democratic Youth League; in 1949 was made one of the fourteen members of the Supreme People's Court; mem., youth del. at World Peace Conf. of Youths and Students, 1951; dir., Dept. of Industry, CCP Tientsin Municipal Cmte., 1952; mem., Financial and Economic Cmte., Tientsin PPG, May 1953.

FU CHIN-KUEI—"My home is in a *hsien* in southern Kiangsi where rice is so plentiful even the poorest man could eat it. You could buy several *tou* for a dollar. Still my home was very poor and always in debt and even rice as a diet becomes tiresome. I heard of a place in central Kiangsi called Chingnan, only two days away by steam launch on the river nearby. I went to the wharf often and asked the boatman about Chingan. There were factories, electricity and a hot bath house, he told me. For five *tiao* of cash you could get there. So when I had five *tiao* I went and on arriving found a job in a weaving mill. I liked this as I received more money than I had ever seen, though I had to spend it all in order to live. Still, I had a bath occasionally in the hot bath house and saw the electric lights. I learned a few characters meantime. When the revolution came I was popular among the younger workers and influenced them to join the CY. They understood that the revolution was against the landlords and the rich; that was enough. I participated in strikes and other labor activity and became known as a leader. After the counterrevolution, scores of young people in Chingan were killed by the Kuomintang under Chiang Kai-shek. I was arrested and put in prison. Over five hundred of my fellow workers signed a petition asking for my release and guaranteeing me not to be a Kungchangtang member. This was published in the local paper and eventually I was freed.

"In 1930 the Red Army came to Chingan and captured it, and over 6,000 workers joined. For a month, the factories were under the control of the Red Army; salaries were quadrupled, every worker was given a bonus (I got $30); and for days the Red Army provided feasts of pork, mutton, and beef seized from the landlords. There were plays every night, singing until everyone was hoarse, to celebrate our new system. It was a wonderful experience except for the landlords. Several tens were captured when the *hsien* was taken, along with some White officers. This was in 1930 when the Li Li-san line was dominant and the Trotskyists, who urged a ruthless and indiscriminate war on the landlords and capitalists. Shortly afterward Li was deposed and the party line altered to its present policy of moderation. I joined the Red Army at this time and have been with it ever since. I am entirely self-taught and have studied hard."

Fu Chin-kuei was an official in the Foreign Office of the Shensi-Kansu-Ninghsia Govt., taking charge of foreign visitors.

Fu CHUNG—b. Szechuan, about 1888; said to be of working-class origin; went with Work-and-Study Students to France from 1919 to about 1922, and helped found Paris branch of CP; attended a univ. in Moscow three years; entered soviet and was chairman of pol. Dept. of Fourth Front Army in Szechuan; in 1937, was instructor in Red Academy and later chairman of the Pol. Dept. of 129th Division, 8th Route Army; in 1928 was made vice-chief of the Pol. Dept. of entire 8th Route Army under the chief, Jen Pi-shih; dir., Org. Dept., PLA, General Political Dept., 1954–1958; made full general, 1955; mem., Natl. Defense Council, 1959—; was at May Day celeb. in Peking, 1967.

Ho CH'ANG-KUNG—b. Hunan, about 1902; after World War I went to France with Tsai Ho-sheng in 1919 and the Work-and-Study group of 1,200 and labor battalion and worked in factories to earn his way through school in Paris and at the Labor Univ. in Belgium; joined CP in France in 1921; on return to China in 1924 was active in revolutionary work and joined the Soviet movement at an early period; was veteran of Chingkangshan and in 1928 CP secy. of the *hsien* at the foot of Chingkangshan; commander of the 8th Army and later pol. com. to Lo P'ing-hui, commanding the rearguard during the Long March; in 1937 was one of the directors and instructors of the Military and Political Academy; in 1938 was made comdr. of the Yellow River Defense Force in Shansi and Honan, of 8th Route Army; mem., NE People's Govt., 1949; vice-min. of Heavy Industry, 1949–1952; dir., Aviation Industry Bureau, 1951; leader of "three-anti's" movement in Heavy Industry, 1951; vice-chmn., All-China Cmte. on Territorial Stratification, 1959; led min. of geology del. to Hungary, Sept. 1960; mem., Standing Cmte., 4th

CPPCC, 1965; pres., Peking Geology College, 1966; "publicly humiliated by Red Guards and stripped of all authority, Oct. 1966" (WWCC).

Ho Tzu-ch'un, Miss—b. Hunan, about 1907; grad. Hunan Normal College; entered CP in 1927, joined Mao Tse-tung's first army as propagandist, and, when his first wife died, married him in 1930 in Kiangsi; received wounds during Long March; formerly active in CP women's work; mother of three of Mao Tse-tung's first five children as of 1937; divorced by Mao in 1937 and is said to have visited Russia afterward.

Hsieh Fu-chih—b. 1899 in Hunan; joined the partisans in the Ouyüwan soviet in the 1930s and was said to have been ed. in the army; deputy brigade comdr. in 1938 under Ch'eng Ken; took part in the 1940 "100 Regiments Battle"; held leading positions from 1949 in the Southwest Military Region and was secy. of the Yunnan Provincial party when Ch'eng Ken was military comdr., 1950–1953; min. of interior, 1949; succeeded Lo Jui-ch'ing as min. of Public Security and was a leader in the purges of those "leading the cultural revolution under the CC"; el. to the CCP CC, 1956 (No. 86); el. to the Politburo as alternate, 1966; in 1969, was on the Politburo as a regular full member.

Huang Hua (real name Wang Ju-mei)—b. 1913; said to be a native of Kiangsu, though in 1936 he told me his mother and her other children were living in Peking at the time of his imprisonment; a senior at the American Yenching Univ., Peking, in 1935–1936; with two other student leaders, Chang Chao-lin and Ch'en Han-p'o, initiated what is called the December 9th student movement in the late fall of 1935 and as one of seven Yenching student government officers (the others included Cheng Chieh, K'ung P'u-sheng, Chang Hsu-yi, and Li Min), planned the famous demonstration on December 9th, which spread all over China, checking the Japanese occupation until 1937 and influencing the Sian Incident of 1936 when Chiang Kai-shek was arrested. Li Min told me: "We called a mass meeting of the students and Chang Chao-lin and Wang Ju-mei made good speeches. The student body agreed on a demonstration." It has been stated that the Communist party "led" the December 9th movement though I have not seen a statement claiming that it started the movement, which it did not. When he learned of the Yenching movement, the Communist ex-student Huang Ching (Yu Ch'i-wei) got in touch with the Yenching initiators and Huang Hua was his liaison (during 1935–1936), after which Huang Ching did "lead" the student movement; he influenced Huang Hua to join the Young Communist group (Vanguards) and about 1936 the CCP, both changing their real names to Huang.

Ch'en Han-p'o (right) and Wang Ju-mei (Huang Hua), during the 1935 Student Movement

Huang Hua (with chopsticks), Constance Chang (left of Huang), and Ch'en Han-p'o (with helmet) on a propaganda tour to villages near Peking in 1936. Huang, the first Peking ambassador to North America, now heads the Chinese delegation to the United Nations.

Early in 1936, Huang Hua and Ch'en Han-p'o were among the chief organizers of a propaganda tour to the villages near Peking to arouse the peasants.

Huang Hua was imprisoned in Peking from March 31 to April 13, 1936. A few weeks later I telephoned him at his Yenching dormitory, asking him to join Edgar Snow in Sian as interpreter on his trip to the Communist regions; this he agreed to do and became the "1st volunteer to go into Chinese Soviet Area, 1936" (as WWCC states). As such, he became a celebrity in his own right and as Edgar Snow's interpreter met the top CP leaders. When I saw him in Yenan, 1937, he was the person "responsible" (as the Chinese say) for the many new student volunteers as they arrived, which included his old Yenching friend Ch'en Han-p'o.

He was the founder of the December 9th dynasty in the MFA, under the protection of Chou En-lai. This began in 1938 in Hankow, when he was in charge of the Chinese People's Volunteers; among these he recruited the sisters K'ung P'eng and some years later his old Yenching friend, K'ung P'u-sheng. (though her fiancé Chang Chao-lin worked with Kuo Mo-jo). Some of these December 9th people survived the Cultural Revolution and provided personnel for the rapprochement with the West, in which Huang Hua was the pioneer in North America, 1971. However, at one time the ministry was controlled by an ultra-leftist group which even attacked Chou En-lai himself.

Huang Hua became well-known to foreigners as chief, Information Dept., CCP Section, Military Mediation Cmte., 1946–1947, and dir. of external affairs in Nanking in 1949, at which time he negotiated with the American ambassador, J. Leighton Stuart, former president of Yenching Univ.

In 1952–1953 became Councillor, MFA, and conducted the bitter, vituperative terminal truce talks with Americans in Korea; in 1954, was spokesman at the Geneva Conference; dir., West Europe and Africa Dept., MFA, 1954–1956, and of West Europe Dept., 1959; as first mainland ambassador to Ghana, 1960–1965, opened up Africa to Chinese influence; mem., China-Cuba Friendship Assn., 1962; appointed ambassador to the United Arab Republic, January 1966, remaining at this difficult post until after 1968, when he was the only Peking ambassador not recalled, during the Cultural Revolution, west of Cambodia and Vietnam; was one of four to welcome Henry Kissinger to Peking, 1971, and participated in the talks with Chou En-lai; arrived in Ottawa as Peking's first ambassador in North America, 1971.

As a student, Huang Hua was quiet, self-possessed, discreet, responsible, proud and moody, a natural leader. He was emotional, flushed easily and stood on his dignity. It took special courage in 1935–1936 to even associate with any Communist, and he risked capital punishment for it.

K'ANG SHENG (original name CHAO JUNG)—b. about 1903 in Shantung Province, said to be a native of Chucheng county, of the big landlord gentry;

attended No. 1 Middle School in Shantung and Shanghai Univ., where he joined the CYL and CCP, 1924 and 1925; was a leader in the insurrections led by Chou En-lai, 1926–1927; hid in Shanghai four years, continuing to organize workers' uprisings and was arrested but released in 1930; ex. secy., CCP Central Org. Dept., 1930; studied in the U.S.S.R., 1930, where he was secy., Manchuria Bureau, 1932, and returned to Shanghai, March 1933; el. to CC secretariat, 1938, but criticized during the 1942 "rectification"; after self-reform, replaced Li Wei-han as dir. of the party school; worked closely with Lin Piao, dir. of K'ang Ta, and dissociated himself from Wang Ming (who personified the Comintern line); secy. of Secretariat, Politburo, and dir., Central Intelligence Dept., chmn., Editorial Cmte., 1938; on the CCP CC of 1945 (No. 18) and 1956 (No. 49); el. to its Secretariat, Sept. 1962, with Lu Ting-yi and Lo Jui-ch'ing; el. to the Politburo as No. 7 in 1945, was an alternate in 1956; in 1945 was dir., Org. Dept., CCP CC; secy., CCP Shantung Bureau, March 1949–Oct. 1954; mem., Central People's Govt. Council, 1949–1954; mem., board of directors, Sino-Soviet Friendship Assn., Oct. 1949–Dec. 1954; vice-chr., Cmte. for Popularizing Common Spoken Language, Feb. 1956; chief del. to East German United Socialist party, March 1956; went to Moscow to sign Sino-Soviet Economic Cooperation Agreement, Sept. 1959; observer, Conf. Warsaw Treaty Nations, Feb. 1960; mem. del. to Rumanian Workers party, 1960; mem. del. to U.S.S.R., Nov. 1960; mem. del. to Korea to Korea Workers' party, Sept. 1961; participated in Treaty of Friendship with N. Korea, Sept. 1961; mem. del., CPSU, Oct. 1961; participated in talks between Liu Shao-ch'i and secy. British CP, Feb. 1963; mem. del. led by Teng Hsiao-p'ing to Moscow, July 1963; mem. del. led by Liu Shao-ch'i in talks with Japanese CP, March 1964; participated in talks with Belgian CP, 1964; mem. del. to 47th Anniversary Moscow, 1964; with Teng Hsiao-ping in talks with Morocco CP in Peking, Feb. 1965; vice-chr., Natl. Cmte. of 3d CPPCC, 1959–1964; at 10th Plenary Session, 8th CCP Cong., el. secy. of Secretariat of CCP CC, Sept. 1962—; vice-chr., Standing Cmte., NPC, Jan. 1965—; adviser of Cultural Revolution Group, CCP CC, 1967; attacked Liu Shao-ch'i and Teng Hsiao-p'ing as "revisionists," 1967; at the opening of the 9th Congress CCP, mounted the rostrum with Mao Tse-tung, Lin Piao and others, and was el. to the five-man Standing Committee of the Politburo; during the Cultural Revolution, worked with Chiang Ch'ing (his fellow-Shantungese) and was one of the half-dozen leaders.

K'UNG P'U-SHENG, Miss—b. 1917, native of Hofei, Anhui, daughter of a well-known general on the general staff before 1922; vice-pres. of the American Yenching Univ. student body in 1935, when its officers started the Dec. 9th Student Movement; Natl. Student secretary, YWCA, Shanghai, 1938; connected with the United Nations Commission on the Status of Women in the

1940s, New York; vice-dir., Intl. Affairs Dept., MFA, Central People's govt., Oct. 1949; mem., Standing Council of China Red Cross Soc., Aug. 1950; del. to the Security Council of the UN in New York to discuss the Taiwan problem, on group headed by Wu Hsiu-ch'uän, 1950; council mem., China-India Friendship Assn., May 1952; mem., 2d Ex. Cmte., Democratic Women's Fed. of China, Apr. 1953; deputy sec.-gen., Ex. Cmte., NPC del. to Inter-Parliament Union (but did not go), Aug. 1955; mem., Chinese Women's del. to World Women's Conf., Apr. 1960; advisor, Chinese govt. del. to Geneva Conf., May 1961; dir., Intl. Affairs Dept., MFA, State Council, Apr. 1965—; accompanied Chou En-lai to Djakarta for celebrating 10th anniv. of Bantung Conf., Apr. 1964.

LI LI-SAN—b. about 1896, a native of Liling *hsien*, Hunan, the son of a rural schoolteacher; studied in the Hunan grade schools seven years; then was one of the Work-and-Study students who went to France during 1919 and 1920 at the same time as Chou En-lai, Lo Man, and others; for a time was sympathetic with anarchist ideas, but joined CP before 1922; in 1922 went to the Hanyehp'ing mines, using the name Li Lung-tzu, where he started a Supplementary School for Workers; from this school an Anyang Workers' Club developed, which organized the large successful strike of 1922 led by Li Li-san; in Feb. 1925, helped organize a strike movement of 100,000 workers; del. to the Pan-Pacific Trade Union Conference in Hankow and made the official "Report on the Labor Movement in China" in 1927; after the Canton Commune was ordered by the CC CP to go to Kwangtung to remedy their right opportunist errors and from that time on led the left-wing policies of encouraging labor uprisings though these were not put into effect until 1930; from 1929 was in control of the Political Bureau of the Kungchangtang in Shanghai and ordered an insurrectionary policy in Kuomintang areas and seizure of cities in soviet areas; went to Wuhan to organize a workers' insurrection and general strike in connection with the Changsha campaign of the Red Army in July, but failed; at the same time was el. chairman, Hunan Provincial soviet, but never arrived there; was expelled from the Political Bureau, going to Moscow in 1931 and remained abroad until 1945 when he returned to Manchuria and became an important political figure under Lin Piao; later sources state he was given a "trial" in Moscow by the Comintern, November 1930, and removed from the Politburo; stayed in Moscow (probably involuntarily, Edgar Snow says) as translator in the Foreign Languages Press and in 1936 was arrested as a Trotskyist but released in 1938; readmitted to the CCP with support of Mao Tse-tung (at Stalin's suggestion) and el. to the CC in 1945 as No. 16; joined Lin Piao in Manchuria as adviser, 1945; el. to presidium of the 6th All-China Congress of Labor and delivered the opening address in Harbin, 1948; confessed to "leftist opportunist mistakes" and was reel. to the CC as No. 89, 1956; secy., CC North China Bureau, 1962; was considered an example of Mao's political generosity and "forgivingness"; was not attacked in the Cultural Revolution and was still in the CC when it started, Aug. 1966 (Edgar Snow); his name was not on the 1969 CC.

Li Po-chao, Miss—b. Chungking, Szechuan, 1911; father the *hsien* magistrate; joined CY in 1925 while attending the Girls' Normal School; fled to Shanghai in 1926 to escape arrest, but was imprisoned there briefly; studied at Sun Yat-sen Univ., Moscow, 1927–1930; entered Fukien soviet in 1930 and worked in Polit. Dept. until 1932, then went to Juikin, Kiangsi, and became editor of *Red China* newspaper; helped organize Gorky Dramatics School in May 1934; participated in Long March and stayed in Tibet in winter of 1935; was dir. of Front Theatre after 1937; secy., N. China Bureau, CCP CC, in final stage of Sino-Japanese war; led a Chinese youth del. to World Students and Youth Friendship Gathering and 2d World Democratic Youth Cong., Budapest, Oct. 1949; deputy secy., Cultural Work Cmte., CCP Peking Municipal Cmte., Dec. 1949; mem., Ex. Cmte., ACDWF, 1953, 1957; deputy for Szechuan 1960–1964 at NPC; vice-pres., Central Academy of Stage Art, 1961, and also secy., CCP Cmte. there, 1964; led del. of stage artists to Albania, 1964; council mem., China–Rumania Friendship Assn., 1965; branded a counterrevolutionary revisionist, Feb. 1967; was placed under struggle with T'ien Han, May 1967.

Liu Chien-hsien (or Liu Ch'un-hsien), Miss—b. 1907 in Wusih, Kiangsu, her father being a whitewasher; in 1924 began working in a cotton-weaving factory; joined CP in 1926 and was leader of women's labor movement during 1925–1927 Revolution; went to Wuhan as delegate to National Labor Congress, 1927, then to Moscow for study, 1927–1930, and married Po Ku; returned to China, 1930, and worked in Shanghai as head of Dept. of Women Workers; entered soviet in Kiangsi in 1933 as head of the Dept. of Women Workers; after Long March was el. director of National Mines and Factories and was in charge of women workers' movement and the organization of co-operatives, and head of Organization Dept. of Labor Unions; divorced by Po Ku before his death in 1946.

Liu Shao-ch'i—was the chief Communist expert on labor; one of the earliest labor leaders; joined the Socialist Youth League in 1920, and 1920–1921, was one of the founders of the Secretariat of the China Labor Organization, which directed the strike movement of 1922–1923 that heralded the first stage of the labor movement; in the autumn of 1923, organized the Anyuan Trade Union at the Pinghsiang Mines and was el. its head; el. vice-chairman, All-China

Federation of Labor, when it was created in Canton, May 1, 1925; returned to Shanghai the same year, working in the Shanghai Trades Union Council, and returned to Canton in the winter with the Federation. Not until 1957 did I learn that he had been deep underground in north China during the student movement, but it is not known just when he arrived in the north to revive the shattered Communist apparatus, whether it was 1935 or 1936.

Li Ch'ang in "Recollections of the National Liberation Vanguard of China," (*Chung-kuo Ch'ing-nien*, Nov. 16, 1961) stated that he, Huang Ching, and two other students were in Yenan as delegates in 1937 to the May Congress of the CP; that Chairman Mao Tse-tung and Liu Shao-ch'i came to see them and "we all sat on the floor and the Chairman acquainted us with Comrade Liu Shao-ch'i as the person in charge of the work of the Party center in the white zone. After they had left, we young party members realized that the beloved 'K.V.' who published articles which combined theory with practice . . . in the mimeographed magazine *Huo Hsien* published in secret by the North Bureau of the Party was in fact Comrade Liu Shao-ch'i" (indicating that the top Communist student leaders also were unaware of the secret identity of Liu Shao-ch'i until introduced to him in Yenan, 1937).

Later sources state of Liu Shao-ch'i: b. 1898, native of Huaminglou, Ninghsiang, Hunan; labor commissioner, Kiangsi Soviet Area, 1932; mem., Politburo, CCPCC, 1932–1968; secy., Central Plains Bureau, CCPCC and was in Tientsin, April 1936; vice-chmn., PRMC, 1943, also of CCP, 7th CC, 1945–1956; pres., Sino-Soviet Friendship Assn., Oct. 1949–1954; chmn. of CPR, April 1959–Oct. 1968 (replacing Mao Tse-tung as chief of state); formally expelled from CCP and dismissed from all posts by Plenary Session of CCP, 8th CC, Oct. 13–31, 1968; reported under house arrest, 1971. The Red Guards branded him as "the No. 1 Party person in authority taking the capitalist road."

LIU NING-YI—b. 1905, native of Mancheng, Hopei; imprisoned 1932–1937; was underground in labor movement, Shanghai, 1937–1943; returned to Yenan, 1943; helped Teng Fa, 1943–1946; el. council mem., 1946 at World Fed. of Trade Unions, Moscow; vice-chmn., ACFTU, 1948–1957; No. 52 on CCP CC, 1956; denounced, July 1968.

LIU SHAO-WEN—b. Honan, 1903, of landowning family; ed. Honan middle schools and two years at a univ. in Moscow; entered soviets and became pol. com. to Hsiao K'eh and chief of Propaganda Dept. of 2d Front Army. In 1938 in Shanghai, Liu told me he had been with Chi Hung-chang. He told me about Chang Kuo-t'ao at the time of the Long March when Chang stayed in Sikong four months: "When the Second Front Army went, he decided he must go to Kansu. The Second Front Army got new recruits—we had 20,000 men. Many died in Sikong, but our Long March was the best of all, except for the Snow Mountains where many died suddenly. At Day Ge we fought the Thibetans and captured Chief Tei-ke. We made friends with him; he was wounded. I was his friend. We established a republic and put him on the executive committee. The name was Hsiao K'e-To-Teh. We had also one big lama. The Communist party wanted to lead the revolution; we could not stay quiet in Szechuan. We met the 4th Front Army 90 *li* from Mo Kung *hsien* at Ta Wei. Chang Kuo-t'ao wanted a base in Szechuan; the Communist party thought this was under British influence and wanted to leave. There was a conference at Mau-kung. The Politburo had already settled this point and gone on to Shensi before they met Chang Kuo-t'ao. Chang was the only one who did not want to leave. They went north in two columns—Mao Tse-tung on the right and there was a left (west). Then they wanted the general staff to go on the left route, so Chu Teh went with Chang Kuo-t'ao on the left or west. They met on the river in the west at Pao-tso. There was good food for them to stay, but they couldn't cross the river—it was too wide and in flood. At Aba they turned back.

"Then Chang Kuo-t'ao raised the question again after the 1st Front Army left (the river was the Kuo Chu Ho). It was too late to take the first route. Chu Teh had two corps, the 5th and 9th Corps, and could not go on alone; he was too small and did not want to be separated. Chang then organized a new Politburo and tried to overthrow Chu Teh and made great trouble." Appt. lt. gen., 1958; deputy pol. com., PLA Peking Garrison Dist., Jan. 1963–1965; 3d Pol. Com., PLA Peking Municipal Revolutionary Cmte., Apr. 1967; appeared at public celebrations, 1971.

LIU TING—(all according to WWCC) joined the CCP, 1924; was arrested in Germany, 1925; imprisoned in Shanghai, then in Nanking, Oct. 1931; soon released "and worked for Assn. for Students [who] studied in Russia," an organ under the KMT Blue Shirt Society; when serving as dir. of a factory in soviet area, captured by KMT again but managed to escape, 1935; was vice-min. of Heavy Industry, 1949–1952; mem., Standing Cmte., Natl. Cmte., All-China Fed. of Scientific Societies, 1950; dir., General Arsenal Bureau, 1951–1952; vice-min., 2d Min. of Machine-Building, 1952–1958; vice-min., 1st Min. of Machine Building, 1958; vice-min., 3d Min., 1960; pres., China Mechanical Engineering Soc., 1960; deputy dir., General Bureau for Economic Relations with Foreign Countries, SC, 1961–1964.

LIU TZE-CH'I—b. in eastern Hunan in 1907 of a very poor peasant family; seven months in school at the age of nine was the only education afforded him; apprenticed to a shoemaker in the village at age twelve and three years later became a journeyman shoemaker; in 1926 joined the revolutionary movement and was a labor union inspector; in 1927 escaped to Canton, where he carried on political work among the unions and was an organizer of the Canton Commune; when this was defeated, he went back to Hunan, hiding from the local landlords, and joined the partisan group that later became the Independent Regiment and the 359th Brigade; received some military training and was ordered back to his home to organize more partisans; formed a group that continued active for two years, their weapons being chiefly homemade guns and bombs; the Kuomintang five times ordered Liu's arrest and offered a high reward; later had a command of ninety rifles in the Red Defense Corps, then became commander first of a company, then of a regiment and finally was chief-of-staff of one of P'eng Teh-huai's divisions; on the Long March commanded a regiment under Chu Teh, and his men lived once for fifteen days on grass; arrived in the northwest and took a year's course in the Military Academy, but had to cut it short at eight months and hurry to the front; during war with Japan, was Wang Chen's chief-of-staff of the famous 359th Brigade.

Lo Fu (Chang Wen-t'ien)—b. 1900 on the outskirts of Shanghai, in Nanhui *hsien,* Kiangsu; father, Chang Tao-yuan, was a scholar under the Manchu regime in Honan, and established a business in Shanghai and prospered under the Republic; graduated from Nanking Hohai Engineering School; went to the U.S. to study science at the Univ. of California, 1921; returned in 1923 and taught school in Szechuan; joined the CCP on recommendation of Ch'en Yün, 1925; was picked by the Comintern to study at Moscow's Sun Yat-sen Univ., 1926, under Pavel Mif, who returned in May 1930 to China with his group called the "28 Bolsheviks," including Lo Fu; became CCP CC dir., Peasants Dept. and editor-in-chief of *Red Flag;* went to Kiangsi, winter 1931, and edited *Tou Cheng;* during Long March replaced Po Ku as general secy. of CCP CC in January 1935 and held this post until 1945 when it was temporarily abolished; was first ambassador to the U.S.S.R., 1949–1955; vice-min., Foreign Affairs, 1954–1959; mem., Standing Cmte., 1st NPC, 1954–1959, and 2d NPC, 1959–1964; demoted from mem. to alternate mem. of Politburo, 1956; served as acting min. of foreign affairs during Premier Chou En-lai's visits abroad, 1956–1957; was dropped from the Politburo in 1966 and attacked in 1967 as an ally of P'eng Teh-huai and Liu Shao-ch'i; in May 1967, was called a party capitalist-roader.

Lo Man—b. Hunan, of peasant family, about 1897; active student leader and member with Mao Tse-tung of the Hsin Min Hsüeh Hui, 1917; went to France with Chou En-lai in first group of Work-and-Study students, 1919, and worked in a factory to earn his way through college; was one of the founders of the Paris branch of CCP, 1922; returned after few years and became active in revolutionary work; entered soviets and was active in CP work, being head of Org. Dept., 1936, and afterward principal of the Communist Party School; from 1944 was general secy., Shensi-Kansu-Ninghsia government; married to Miss Ah Ch'ing.

LU TING-YI (LO TING-YI)—b. 1907 (WWCC says 1904) in Kiangsu of official class; grad. Nanking Univ.; attended Sun Yat-sen Univ., Moscow; joined CP, 1924; in 1937 was chief of Propaganda Dept., 1st Front Army, later of 120th Div.; was on Long March; dir., Propaganda Dept., CCP CC, 1949–1966; council mem., Sino-Soviet Friendship Assn., 1949–1966; vice-premier, State Council, 1959–1966; min. of culture, Jan. 1965; accused as collaborator with P'eng Chen in 1962 in forcing Mao Tse-tung to retire and dropped from CCP CC and all posts, 1966; branded a counterrevolutionary revisionist, Dec. 1966; placed under public trial, Peking, Jan. 1967.

MAO TSE-TUNG—b. Shao Shan village, Hsiang T'an *hsien,* Hunan, in 1886, of peasant family; studied classics in local school; graduated from Hunan Provincial First Normal School in Changsha; in 1917 founded New People's Study Society in Changsha; in 1918 went to Peking, working as assistant librarian to Li Ta-chao at Peking National Univ. and attending classes there; edited several student magazines and organized various groups after this; in May 1921 went to Shanghai to found CCP, together with Ch'en Tu-hsiu and Li Ta-chao; in 1924 was concurrently a mem. of Central Committee of CP and of the Exec. Bureau of the Kuomintang in Shanghai; in 1925 went to Canton as editor of Kuomintang paper, *Political Weekly,* and head of Kuomintang Propaganda Department, then did peasant organizing work in Hunan; as pres. of All-China Peasants' Union, overthrew Ch'en Tu-hsiu as leader of CP in 1927, and organized Hunan Autumn Crop Uprisings in Sept., beginning Red Army movement; was chairman of Party Front Committee of "1st Division of Peasants' and Workers' First Army" in 1927, and in 1928 made pol. com. of 4th Red Army (Chu Teh being commander), then in 1929 of "First Red Army Corps" of 10,000 men, and in 1930 of "First Front Red Army"; in 1931 el. first chairman of Central Soviet government in Kiangsi, and reel. until soviet system was abolished in 1937; member of Political Bureau and chairman of Military Council of 8th Route Army with headquarters until 1947 at Yenan, North Shensi; m. first to Yang K'ai-hui, daughter of a Peita professor, 1920; after she was killed in Hunan in 1930, m. Miss Ho Tzu-ch'un, school teacher, by whom he had two children; in 1938 or 1939 m. Miss Chiang Ch'ing (Lan Ping), CP mem. since 1933 and actress from Shanghai where she helped organize the modern dramatics movement.

Over the years Mao's post was as chairman of the CP and mem. of its Politburo; el. chairman of the People's Republic of China and also chairman of the People's Revolutionary Military Council, 1949; visited Moscow, his first time outside China, 1949; the Mao group sponsored the Great Leap Forward and the communes, 1958, which were ridiculed by Khrushchev and reported opposed by P'eng Teh-huai; retired as chairman of PRC at end of 1959, when Liu Shao-ch'i took over the chairmanship; in the Cultural Revolution, P'eng Chen, Lu Ting-yi, Lo Jui-ch'ing, and other "anti-Maoists" were accused of trying to force Mao's effective retirement in 1962 and the group was dismissed from all offices 1966–1967. In the Cultural Revolution Mao's chief aides were his wife, Chiang Ch'ing, and his secretary, Ch'en Po-ta, as the Yenan Old Guard made a last stand. Mao was el. chairman of the Politburo at the 9th Congress, 1969, with Lin Piao as deputy chairman and designated heir, and remained active as of 1971.

By way of his various writings, *The Thought of Mao Tse-tung* has been studied widely in translations and his little red book has become the totem of the Chinese Communists.

P'ENG CHEN—b. in Shansi, 1899, in an impoverished gentry family; at normal school was influenced by the May Fourth Movement; studied Marxism in the CYL in 1922, organized railway workers and was jailed briefly in Peking; in 1937 visited Yenan and was assigned to work in Shansi and Hopei; from 1939–1942 he taught at the party school in Yenan and was deputy director under Lin Piao in the "rectification"; el. to the CC, 1945; went to Manchuria with Lin Piao (1946–1949) as party deputy under Ch'en Yun; became party secy. of Peking, 1949–1966, and mayor of Peking, 1951–1966; in 1945 was No. 12 on the Politburo and in 1956 No. 10; said to have had a close relationship with Liu Shao-ch'i from 1935 to his eclipse in 1966, at which time he was first deputy to Teng Hsiao-p'ing; Red Guards applied worse epithets to P'eng Ch'en than to anyone else accused of "taking the capitalist road"; was accused of planning a coup against Mao in February 1966. P'eng never "confessed" so far as known now.

Po I-Po (real name Po SHU-TS'UN)—b. in 1907 in Tingshang, Shansi, of gentry family; joined the CCP in 1926; was imprisoned in Peking in 1933 and released in 1936; was pol. com. in North China guerrilla areas during World War II and the Second Civil War; specialized in economic affairs and state planning from 1951 and held important posts over major industrial ministries to 1967; was on the CC in 1945, and reached the Politburo by 1956, and was reel., August 1966, but was not on the CC in 1969.

TENG HSIAO-P'ING—b. 1904 in Chiating, Szechuan; was with the Work-and-Study students in France, 1920, and became a member of the French CP; after the 1927 split worked in the party underground in Shanghai until 1929, then formed the 7th Red Army at Lungchow, Kwangsi; went to Chingkang-shan with remnants of the 7th Army, where they were reorganized into the 8th Army and took part in capturing Changsha, 1930; from 1932–1934 was editor of *Hung Hsing* and supported Mao Tse-tung's guerrilla policies in opposition to the Politburo line; at Tsunyi voted for Mao to head the Polit-buro, backed Mao against Chang Kuo-t'ao at Maoerhkai, and went with Mao on the Long March; at the 7th Congress, 1945, became No. 28 on the CC, but jumped to No. 4 in 1956 and became general secy.; from 1952–1954 was minister of finance and on the State Planning Commission; in 1954, became deputy premier and deputy chairman of the National Defense Council; was acting premier during the absences of Chou En-lai, 1963–1965; during the Cultural Revolution was attacked as the No. 2 capitalist roader.

Tsai Ch'ang, Miss—b. Hsiang-hsiang *hsien*, Hunan, 1900, of bankrupt scholar class; studied in France 1919–1924; joined Paris branch of CP at time of formation and married Li Fu-chün; partic. 1925–1927 revolution at Wuhan; del., 6th Congress of Comintern, 1928, then studied in Russia; entered Kiangsi soviet, 1932; after partic. in Long March was head of organization work in non-Communist areas stationed in Kansu; made chief of Women's Work of Shensi-Kansu-Ninghsia Border govt.; in 1946 was chairman of the Organizing Committee of Women's Organizations in the Chinese Liberated Areas, an overall group connected with the CC CP; for many years was the only full woman member of the CCP Central Committee; in 1947 organized women in south Hopei and went to Manchuria to join her husband in charge of a branch of party work there; was, until 1966, when Chiang Ch'ing usurped this position, the leading Chinese woman Communist and a close friend of Mao Tse-tung; el. chairman of the All-China Women's Federation, 1949; attended Peace Congress at Prague, 1949; was the only woman on the committee which prepared the Consultative Conference in Peking in 1949, and was elected to the fifty-eight-member Government Council; presided at the Asian Women's Conference in Peking, December 1949; from 1962 re-mained pres., Natl. Women's Fed. of the People's Republic of China; on the 7th CC CCP of forty-four members was No. 27, 1945; in the 8th CC, was No. 12, 1956; not prominent in the Cultural Revolution; el. to the Central Cmte., CCP, 1969; was one of the two chief woman Communists from 1927 to the rise of Chiang Ch'ing, wife of Mao Tse-tung, 1966–1969; made her marriage the prime example of modern marriage among the Chinese Com-munists.

Tsai Ch'ien—"I was born in 1906 in Taichueng, Chunghua, on the island of Formosa. My father was descended from the three hundred Fukien 'first families' who went to settle Formosa under Koxinga, in rebellion against the

Manchus. He was an accountant in a rice shop. At the age of six, I started the Chunghua primary school, studying Japanese and using Japanese textbooks, for eight years. I then taught in this same school for a year.

"In 1924 I went to Shanghai to attend Shanghai University, half supported by my father and half by the Chinese Cultural Association of Formosa, an organ for liberating Formosa. Yu Yu-jen was then president and I majored in sociology and became interested in Marxism.

"In December 1926, I returned to Formosa to do propaganda work for the Chinese revolution, being then eighteen. I made speeches about the Kuomintang, but I had joined the Shanghai Communist Youth in 1925. The local Cultural Association was reorganized by Leftist elements who took power and adopted a radical program. The Japanese learned of this and arrested the leaders, ten altogether, all Chinese-returned students, and twenty Formosans. I was arrested in January 1927 at Taihoku and charged with being an agent of the Chinese Communist party on the basis of radical literature found in my luggage. I was sentenced to a year in prison and was paroled in November 1927. Others were tortured in prison but I was not. There was only one man to a cell—not so bad as in China. The Cultural Association was allowed to send me food.

"After my release, I worked on the *Ta Tsun Shih Pao*, a leftist paper, as a reporter. In April 1928, the Communist party of Formosa was organized, first in Shanghai by Formosan and Japanese students. This was destroyed by Japanese police in Taihoku (Taipeh) and the leaders arrested, but it was later reorganized.

"In February 1929, I left Amoy for Changchow, Fukien, and became a teacher in the Shih Ma Middle School; then in 1932 I left Changchow to enter the soviet districts when the Red Army captured the city. I was then in the Changchow party.

"I reached Juikin in May and taught in the Lenin Normal School—sociology, land problems, and other subjects. After six months I was made chairman of the Anti-Imperialist Alliance, later changed into the Anti-Imperialist Alliance to Support the Soviet Union. During the Long March, I served as a political commissar in the Political Department. In Shensi I became chairman of the Association Against Japanese Imperialism. Then in April 1936 I was made Commissioner of the Interior of the soviet government. My wife was a Formosan who stayed in Kiangsi. I studied Marxism under Ch'ü Ch'ü-pai and Ch'en Tu-hsiu in Shanghai." In 1937 Tsai Ch'ien left the soviet districts to work outside.

TSENG HSIEN-CHIH—wife of Marshal Yeh Chien-ying by 1962; native of Hsianghsiang *hsien*, Hunan; raised in Changsia; studied in Japan in her early years; secy.-gen., Prep. Committee for ACDWF, 1948; secy.-gen., 1st Natl.

Women's Cong., Peking, March 1949; alternate on its Ex. Cmte., deputy secy.-gen. of Standing Cmte., and dir. of Secretariat, Apr. 1949; mem., Prov. Board of Supervisors of All-China Fed. of Cooperatives, July 1950–1952; dir., Adm. Dept., ACDWF, 1952; mem., Presidium, 2d Natl. Women's Cong. and later el. mem. Ex. Cmte. and Standing Cmte. and secy., Secretariat, ACDWF, March 1953; el. deputy for Hunan to 1st NPC, 1954; mem. of Presidium, deputy secy.-gen., and vice-chr., Election Cmte. of 3d Natl. Women's Cong.; subsequently el. to Ex. Cmte. and new Presidium, as well as secy. of Secretariat of National Women's Fed. of China (renamed from ACDWF), Sept. 1957; del. of NWF to 3d CPPCC and el. mem. of its Natl. Cmte., 1959; del. of CCP to 4th CPPCC and el. mem. of presidium, Dec. 1964 and Standing Cmte., Jan. 1965; chief of Chinese women's del. to visit Rumania, Sept. 1965.

WANG CHIA-HSIANG—b. Wuhu, Anhui, about 1903 of peasant class; studied in Christian mission middle school; graduated from Shanghai Univ.; studied four years at the univ. in Moscow; in 1930 was leader of Li Li-san opposition in Shanghai, together with Wang Ming and Po Ko; entered soviets and was one of the seven members of Politburo at time of formation of Soviet Republic; chief of Pol. Dept. of Red Army and vice-chairman of Central Govt. and also of Military Council; dir., Pol. Dept., 18th Group Army, 1939–1940; mem., presidium for mass rally in Yenan to denounce Wang Ching-wei and to support Chiang Kai-shek, 1940; CCP del. to 1st CPPCC and el. to Natl. Cmte., 1949; amb. to U.S.S.R., Oct. 1949–Apr. 1951; CCP rep. to Cong. of East Socialist Unity party, July 1950; vice-min., Foreign Affairs, 1949–1959; CCP del. to Poland, 1959, to Cong. of British CP, 1959; del. rep., CCP to 4th CPPCC, Dec. 1964; alternate No. 2 of the CCP CC, 1945; full mem. CCP CC, March 1949 as No. 48 (his name is not on the 1969 list) ; was accused of capitulationism and outrageous activities of treason at the 1962 Moscow Disarmament Conference, Nov. 1967.

WANG KUAN-LAN—b. in Linghai *hsien*, Chekiang, 1908, of a poor, urban family, his father being a handicraft carver; attended the Provincial Normal School at Linghai; joined the CY in 1925 and the CP in 1926; did party work in Chekiang and Shanghai, 1925–1927; at end of 1927 went to Soviet Russia and studied three years at the Eastern Univ. and the Chinese Labor Univ. (formerly Sun Yat-sen Univ.) ; returned to China, 1930, and went to the Kiangsi soviet to be placed in charge of the Propaganda Dept. of the CC, responsible for the *hsien* CP committee work and the political departments of the local militia; editor of *Red China*, the Central Soviet government paper, 1932; apptd. vice-chairman of the Land Dept. of the Central govt., 1933; in 1934 during Long March was placed in the Pol. Dept. of the Central govt. and of the 1st Army Corps; he was commissioner of Lands of the Northwest

Central govt., 1935–1937, and continued in same post after the change of government; vice-min. of agriculture, 1952–1954; del. of "peasants" to the 2nd Natl. Cong. and deputy dir., Rural Work Dept., CCP CC, 1958–1967; and deputy dir., Office of Agriculture and Forestry, 1962–1967; del. of the CCP to the 4th CPPCC, 1964, and secy., CCP Cmte., Peking Agricultural Univ. to 1967; in March 1967 was branded a counterrevolutionary revisionist.

WANG MING (real name CHEN SHAO-YU)—The following information was provided by Po Ku: b. about 1906, the son of a rich peasant in Anhui; graduated from a provincial middle school in Anhui; joined the CP about 1925; until 1927 attended Sun Yat-sen Univ. in Moscow; in the Wuhan period returned to China and worked in Wuhan; returned to Moscow, staying until the second half of 1929; then worked in the Propaganda Dept. of the CC in Shanghai and later in the All China-Labor Federation as propaganda dir.; after leading opposition to Li Li-sanism, worked in the Propaganda Dept. of the Shanghai party committee, not as chief but as a member; at the 4th plenary session of the CC in July 1931 became mem. of the CC and the Politbureau; in June 1931 went to Moscow as del. to the Comintern of CCP; returned to China from Moscow in 1938; became one of the leading figures in liaison work with Chiang Kai-shek's government during the war with Japan; proposed a complete merger of Red troops with KMT, in opposition to Mao's united front concept requiring separate CCP command of armed forces and bases; republished *The Two Lines*, 1940, attacking Mao and calling for proletarianization of the CCP; party repudiated Wang Ming, 1945, adopting Mao's "Resolution on Some Questions of the History of Our Party"; chairman, Commission of Legislative Affairs, GAC, 1949–1954; mem., Supreme People's Court, 1949–1954; mem., Sino-Soviet Friendship Assn., 1949–1954; mem., CCP 7th CC, 1956; accused of "rightist opportunism and surrenderism," August 1966; reported to have escaped to Moscow.

WANG PING-NAN—b. 1906, native of Sanyuan, Shensi, a few miles from Sian, son of a rich landlord; sent to Germany to study; returned to Sian in 1936, becoming secy. of Gen. Yang Hu-ch'eng and underground liaison with the CP; was involved in the Sian Incident, December 1936; secy. to Chou En-lai in Chungking, 1938–1945; involved in the peace talks with the Kuomintang, 1946; after the death of Po Ku, became one of the leading Communist spokesmen in Kuomintang areas; dir. of the General Office, MFA, 1949–1955; secy.-gen. to the Geneva Conf., April 1954; amb. to Poland 1955–1964, and was considered the senior diplomat in Europe and the chief representative to the U.S.-China ambassadorial talks in Warsaw, 1955–1964; vice-min. of Foreign Affairs, 1964–1967, under Ch'en Yi; China's chief expert on Polish and German affairs; "accused of being a traitor, Feb. 1967" (WWCC).

WU MAN-YU—known as the famous "Labor Hero" of the Shensi-Kansu-Ning-hsia border; came to Yenan as a destitute famine refugee before the Communist armies arrived. He had to sell his three-year-old daughter for six pounds of corn to feed his family until he could cut wood in the hills to pay for more food and tools to till an acre of land he had rented. His landlord threw him into jail for failing to pay rent, while his wife starved to death. The Communists came shortly after this in 1935 and he received "one hill" when the landlord's estate was divided among the tillers, where he lived in a cave. Within eight years, being then in his fifties, he built up a farm of sixty-five acres, all reclaimed hill wasteland, had forty sheep and goats, a horse, four oxen, four beehives, and chickens, and had invested his surplus in a farmers' cooperative, also voluntarily contributing to the armies. The beehives General Wang Chen had given him in exchange for teaching his soldiers how to do better farming. When the Production Movement for self-sufficiency started, he was picked because of his record as the "Labor Hero" of the border, and in 1943 he and his labor-exchange group reclaimed 447 *mou* of wasteland, which was 250 percent better than their plan called for, stimulating much emulation. His model form became known as "Wu's Date Orchard."

YANG SHAN-KUN—b. Szechuan about 1905, of land-owning family; ed. Szechuan schools; spent three years in Sun Yat-sen Univ., Moscow; chairman of Pol. Dept., Lin Piao's First Front Army; during Japanese war held same post in 115th Division under Lin Piao; secy. of CC in Shansi, 1937–1943; in charge of united front dept., then dir. of the CC office, 1943–1959; in 1956 was listed No. 42 of full members of the CCP CC and alt. secy. with Hu Ch'iao-mu and Liu Lan-t'ao; in this post he attended meetings with Soviet and other foreign Communists, especially after the Sino-Soviet split; in 1966 was accused of using this chance to conspire against Mao Tse-tung and was dismissed from all posts. Red Guard posters said he had tried to wiretap Mao's conversations and, in Apr. 1967, it was reported that "revolutionary cadres" were demanding his execution along with that of Liu Shao-ch'i, Lo Jui-ch'ing, P'eng Chen and others. *People's Daily*, May 1968, branded Yang a renegade, traitor, and counterrevolutionary revisionist.

YAO YI-LIN—b. Anhui in 1916, son of "bankrupt bourgeois family which lived" by periodically "selling some article"; received secondary education in Shanghai and Peking and was enrolled in Tsinghua Univ. in Peking, but left in his second year (1935) to spend full time on revolutionary work; "worked for CCP Peking Municipal Cmte., Feb. 1936; during Sino-Japanese War, secy.-gen., CCP North China Bureau, 1937" (WWCC); mem., Financial and Economic Cmte., and dir., Dept. of Industry and Commerce, North China People's Govt., 1948–1949; mem., Standing Cmte., China Democratic Construction Assn., Sept. 1949–July 1952; vice-min. of Trade, Oct. 1949–1952; mem., provisional board of directors, All-China Fed. of Cooperatives, July 1950; principal, Central School of Cadres for Trade, Oct. 1950; mem., CC to Check Austerity Program, Dec. 1951; vice-min. of Commerce, 1952–1958, and full min., Feb. 1960–1967; el. deputy for Kiangsi NPC, 1954–1959; deputy-dir., Finance and Trade Adm. Office, State Council, Sept. 1959—; leader of commercial and friendship del. to North Vietnam, March 1964; party career: joined Young Vanguards, 1935–1936; No. 96 alternate of the CCP CC, 1956; CCP del. to Natl. Cmte., 3d CPPCC, 1959; Standing Cmte., 3d CPPCC, 1959; CCP del. to Natl. Cmte., 4th CPPCC, Dec. 1964; "accused of being a counterrevolutionary revisionist, April 1967" (WWCC).

YAO WEN-YUAN—mem. of the Council in Shanghai of the Union of Chinese Writers and correspondent for *Literary Gazette*, 1951; in 1955, attended symposium denouncing Hu Feng; el. to Natl. Cmte., All-China Federation of Youth, 1958, 1962; a leader of the Cultural Revolution Group of the CCP Central Cmte., 1966—; chief ed., *People's Daily*, 1967—; led a Red Guard del. to Cong. of Albanian Federation of Youth, 1967; el. to Politburo, 1969; considered a chief youth leader of the Cultural Revolution.

CHANG CHU-YUAN—celebrated "militia hero" of the Shansi-Suiyuan Liberated Area; in his local Ning-wu region developed methods consisting of mutual aid groups enabling the peasants to protect themselves militarily and against seizure of crops and animals, though using only old-fashioned weapons for the most part; is often cited in literature dealing with these areas such as in the pamphlet *The Liberated Regions of China Behind the Enemy Lines, 1945*: "In January, 1943, Chang Chu-yuan, who was then secretary of the peasant association and squad-leader of the people's militia, put the already organized people's militia on a working basis to protect spring cultivation. . . . [He] flexibly adapted himself to the needs and environment of the base behind the enemy lines and of the militia movement and created the method of combining labor power with armed force on the basis of the people's militia and the mass movement."

CH'EN KUANG, General—b. Hunan about 1907; commander of the famed 2d Division of the 1st Red Army Corps, when Lin Piao was overall commander; when the 1st Front Army became the 115th Division in 1937, Ch'en Kuang continued to command his former unit; was a noted commander and his division rivaled that of Ch'eng Ken's famous 1st Division.

CH'EN PO-CHUN, General—b. Szechuan, 1910; grad. Wuchang Military and Political Academy (branch of Whampoa at Wuhan), 1926–1927; Chingkang-shan veteran; in 1937 apptd. comdr. of famous 6th Red Army (formerly under Hsiao K'eh); during Japanese war this was under the 120th Division of the 8th Route Army; deputy comdr., Hunan Military District, PLA, Jan. 1950; mem., Council Hunan Provincial People's Govt., Jan. 1950; became full general, with military honors, 1955; cmdr., PLA in Nanking, July 1957; superintendent of a military school in Nanking, Aug. 1957; el. deputy for PLA units in Mukden to 2d NPC, July 1958; in Peking welcomed last of officers and men of General HQ, Chinese People's Volunteers, from N. Korea, Oct. 1958; mem., Chinese military goodwill mission to Poland, Czechoslovakia, Hungary, Rumania, Bulgaria, Albania, E. Germany, and Outer Mongolia, Apr.–June 1959; Natl. Defense Council, Apr. 1959—; received Albania's Order of Skanderbeg, 2d Class, June 1959; vice-pres., Higher Military Academy, June 1959.

CH'EN YI, General—b. about 1898 in Szechuan near Chengtu of wealthy landlord family; studied chemistry in middle school; studied in Paris and Lyons, France, three years after World War I, but was deported for student activities against the French government's negotiations to monopolize railway building in southwest China; returned to Szechuan in 1921 and started a newspaper, *Hsin Hsu Pao*, which failed to have any influence; went to Peking where he joined the Kuomintang and also the CP; soon after went to Canton to join the Northern Expedition; when this reached Wuhan he was instructor in the Military Academy there; was sent to Chungking and Chengtu to influence Szechuan warlords to support the Kuomintang; upon his return went to Nanchang in 1927 with some of his cadets, and joined the Red Army; after the Long March was ordered to remain behind to keep the partisan movement alive, together with Han Ying and Fang Chih-min, in the Kiangsi-Fukien area; Fang Chih-min was soon captured and killed and Han Ying and Ch'en Yi combined and spent two and a half years of great hardship with a guerrilla base in the Wu Ling mountains; in May 1937, an enemy battalion nearly captured both the leaders at the foot of a hill, but they escaped; in January 1938, the new 4th Army of 12,000 men was organized, with Yeh T'ing as nominal comdr., Han Ying as vice-comdr. and Ch'en Yi as No. 3; made comdr.-in-chief of the New 4th Army and in 1947 was in command of one of the eight Liberated Areas, the Shantung Area, while General Su Yu was in command of the Central China Areas where the New 4th started out; vice-premier of the CPR State Council and vice-chairman of the Natl. Defense Council, 1954; el. to the CC CCP at the 7th Congress and in 1956 to the Politburo; apptd. min. of foreign affairs, 1958, when Chou En-lai relinquished this post; during Cultural Revolution, his ministry was attacked and his diplomats abroad were accused of taking on decadent bourgeois habits; at the 9th Congress in 1969, Ch'en Yi remained on the CC, was a mem. of the presidium and seated prominently at the sessions, but was not on the Politburo; his old associate Su Yu was on the 9th CC, Sept. 1969, and it was reported that Li Hsien-nien was taking his place as foreign minister.

CHU TEH (CHU TE), General—b. 1886, Ma-an Ch'ang village, Yi Lung *hsien*, Szechuan, and adopted and ed. by a well-to-do uncle; grad. Yünnan Military

Academy; promoted to brigade comdr., 1915, in Yünnan Army of Ts'ao Ao; studied in Berlin and Göettingen, 1922–1925; had joined Tung Meng Hui, 1909, and CP, 1922, and on return to China was chief of police of Nanchang, where helped organize Nanchang Uprising August 1, 1927, which founded the Red Army; comdr., 4th Red Army until 1931; el. mem. of Politburo and made cmdr.-in-chief of whole Red Army and in 1937 of Eighth Route Army, with P'eng Teh-huai as his field deputy; reappt. comdr.-in-chief, PLA, and vice-chairman, Revolutionary Military Council, 1949; el. one of six vice-chairmen, People's Govt., a post held until 1956 when he became chairman, NPC; was No. 4 on the Politburo, 1945 and 1956, but was dropped in 1966; re-el. to the Politburo, 1969; mounted the rostrum with Mao, Lin Piao, and nine others at the opening of the 9th Cong.; instituted new concept of "face" by superiority in Spartan living, physical culture, and personal identification with the rank and file; known as "the dean" of the Szechuan clique and the liaison between the army and Mao Tse-tung over the years.

Ho WEI, General—b. Kwangtung, about 1898, of working-class origin; comdr., Pickets Corps during the Hongkong Strike in 1925–1926; participated in the Canton Commune, 1927, then went to Kwangsi with the 7th Red Army; comdr., 9th Army of the 4th Front Army, 1936, later incorporated in the 129th Division of the 8th Route Army.

HSIAO CHING-KUANG—b. Hunan, 1904; ed. in local Hunan schools; studied in Moscow, 1920–1924; returned to China, studying at Whampoa Academy, then in Moscow again, 1927–1931; returned to China in 1931 and entered Kiangsi soviet area as comdr. of 7th Red Army Corps; helped organize 29th Army during Shansi Expedition of 1936 and was made comdr.; when war with Japan began in 1937 was apptd. chief-of-staff; was a deputy comdr. under Lin Piao, World War II and the Second Civil War; apptd. marshal, 1955; mem., CCP CC, 1945–1969, but was not on the 1969 Politburo.

HSU HAI-TUNG, General—b. Huangp'i *hsien*, Hupeh, in small village in 1900, of a second generation of potters; attended primary school three and a half years; became apprentice at pottery works at age of eleven; married at eighteen, but soon ran away from his wife and wandered to Hankow, Kiukiang, and Nanchang; worked at a kiln at Huang-tou-pu near Nanchang; at twenty-three joined Kiangsi army and in 1925 was promoted to squad comdr.; later joined Chang Fa-kuei's 4th Army; in 1927 returned to his native village in Huangp'i, joined CP, and began leading labor movement there, being then comdr. of the local Peasants' Guards; escaped execution in 1927 by hiding on a mountain, and in 1928 organized a partisan group; from this nucleus quickly organized a local Red army, which became an important force in the

Ouyüwan soviet; when 4th Front Red Army left Ouyüwan soviet for Szechuan, he remained, in command of the 25th Army, then left on the Long March in 1934; on arrival in Northwest was given command of 15th Army Corps; during the war with Japan this corps was under Liu Po-ch'eng's 129th Division, and Hsu commanded chiefly along the Yellow River in the Tapieh mountain region and later in north Kiangsu and Shantung; commanded the 344th Brigade of the 115th Division, 8th Route Army; vice-comdr., headquarters north of the Yangtze River; mem., Central Military Council; mem., CCP Shantung Bureau, 1939; comdr., Shantung-Kiangsu-Honan Military Region, 1944; vice-comdr., 115th Division, 1945; deputy chief, Military Liaison Del. to stay in Outer Mongolia, winter 1946; mem., RMC, June 1954; mem., Natl. Defense Council, Sept. 1954; apptd. general, PLA, Sept. 1955; participated in 30th anniversary of Army Day, Aug. 1957; mem., Presidium for celebrating 10th anniversary of CPR, Sept. 1959; attended in Peking a celebration of Gen. Political Dept., PLA, Oct. 1964; appeared at Natl. Day celebrations, Oct. 1966; el. to CCCP, 1956 (No. 79), and 1969.

HSIAO HUA—b. 1914 in Hsingkuo *hsien*, Kiangsi, of poor peasants (according to WWCC, b. 1915); joined Youth Training Class organized by Mao Tse-tung in Hsingkuo, 1929; in charge of work for youth in the army, 1929; dir., Young People's Sect., CCP Gen. Pol. Dept., 1932; led political work for vanguards led by Liu Po-ch'eng and Nieh Jung-chen, spring 1935; dir., Org. Sect. Pol. Dept., 1st Army Corps, 1935, then of 115th Div., 1937; fought in war with Japan throughout; comdr., Shantung-Hopei-Honan Military Region, 1942; mem., Central Cmte., New Democratic Youth League, and on Natl. Cmte., ACFDY, 1949–1953, and led its del. to Hungary, 1949; went to Bulgaria, Hungary, Czechoslovakia, Poland, U.S.S.R., Nov. 1949; vice-dir., Gen. Pol. Dept., PRMC, 1949; vice-chmn., Cmte. for Implementing the Marriage Law, 1953; apptd. general, 1955; dir., PLA Gen. Cadres Dept., 1956; mem., military del. to seven East European countries and Mongolia, 1959; deputy secy.-gen., Military Commission, 1961; dir., PLA Gen. Pol. Dept., Sept. 1964–Jan. 1968; vice-chm., Standing Cmte., All-China Cultural Revolution Group, May 1967; vice-head, Support-the-Left Group, Military Commission, CCP CC, Aug. 1967; party career: No. 80 on the 1956 CCP CC and on its Control Committee, on which he became deputy-secy., 1956–Jan. 1968; not listed in 1969 CC.

HUANG YUNG-SHENG—b. 1906, native of Yungfeng *hsien*, Kiangsi; comdr., Guard Regiment, Red Army HQ, Kiangsi, 1931; accompanied the famous 1st Division 1st Red Army Corps, 1932; after the Long March, studied in the 1st class at the Red Academy, North Shensi, 1935; held commands in the 115th Division, 1937–1946; advanced steadily in the army; mem., Natl. Defense Council, 1954—; visited N. Vietnam, 1961; set up the Cultural Revolution Kwangtung Revolutionary Cmte., 1966–1967, of which he was chairman, 1968; chief of general staff, PLA, 1968, and headed del. to Tirana to celebrate liberation of Albania; as chief of General Staff was at the head of the diplomatic rapprochements beside Chou En-lai, Li Hsien-nien, Yao Wen-yuan, etc., 1971; in 1956, was an alternate on the CP Central Committee and in 1969 was el. to the Politburo.

LI HSIEN-NIEN—b. 1905 in Huangan County, Hupeh, was the son of a worker and himself a carpenter's apprentice; joined the Northern Expedition when it reached Hankow and in 1927 joined the CCP; was a Red Guard guerrilla leader in Hupeh peasant uprisings but was given a regular command under Hsu Hsiang-ch'ien; went westward with Hsu and Chang Kuo-t'ao and stayed with Chang during his dispute with Mao Tse-tung, whom he first met at Maoerhkai in 1935; Li Hsien-nien's 30th Army, called the West Route Army, tried to get to Sinkiang but suffered heavy casualties; Li arrived in Yenan 1937 and entered K'ang Ta Univ. for a year; went behind Japanese lines in Hupeh to organize guerrilla war, 1938, and built an army of 60,000 by 1941; became a field comdr. during the civil war; became the chief political and military person in Hupeh; in 1949 he was on the Revolutionary Military Council as both comdr. and pol. com. of the Hupeh Military HQ; in 1945 was No. 39 on the CCP CC but rose to No. 24 by 1956, when he was No. 17 on the Politburo; in August 1966, was confirmed in the Politburo and in 1969 was el. to the Politburo; took a leading part in talks and agreements with Albania, Mali, Tanzania, Guinea, N. Korea, N. Vietnam, and other countries; traveled in Asia and Eastern Europe; el. vice-premier under Chou En-lai, 1962; led the second del. to Hanoi at the time of the death of Ho Chi Minh, with Hsieh Fu-chih, 1969; accompanied Premier Chou En-lai at his talk with Kosygin in Peking, Sept. 1969. The *Christian Science Monitor*, Sept. 13, 1969 reported: "Since the disgrace of Foreign Minister Chen Yi, Mr. Li has been acting virtually as China's Foreign Minister. Mr. Hsieh is China's tough Public Security Minister."

LIU PEI-CH'ENG (LIU PO-CH'ENG), General—b. Szechuan, 1892; was an officer in the Szechuan armies; joined CP before 1926; in November 1926, was Kuomintang party del. to the 20th Natl. Revolutionary Army commanded by Gen. Yang Sen; helped lay the groundwork for the revolutionary movement in west Hupeh, in the districts of Anyuan, Ichang, Tzu-kuei, Patung, and Paokang; was chief-of-staff of military cmte., which organized the Nanchang Uprising on August 1, 1927, while Chou En-lai was vice chief-of-staff; when this uprising failed, went to Moscow to study at the Red Army Academy and remained there three years; on return was made a member of the general staff of the Central Revolutionary Military Council (located in Shanghai), in which capacity he moved between the Central soviets and the other 2d and 4th Front armies in the Hunan-Hupeh and Ouyüwan soviets, respectively; in 1931 was ordered to enter the Central soviets to train recruits for the Red Army and became also chief of General Staff of the Workers' and Peasants' Red Army; during Long March often commanded the vanguard, negotiated the treaty with the Lolo tribesmen, led the advance at the Ta-t'u River, and otherwise distinguished himself; in 1937 was given command of the 129th Division of the 8th Route Army (formerly the 4th Front Army); during the Japanese war his troops were based chiefly in the Tapieh mountains of northeast Hupeh and southeast Anhui, where he controlled river traffic; in 1947 took his troops to their old soviet region to recapture it, the Ouyuwan, or Hupeh-Anhui-Honan area, having then about 40,000 soldiers; has translated many books on military science from Soviet Russian manuals; April 25, 1949, Nanking was taken and Liu became mayor on May 11, being comdr. of the 2d Field Army; was one of the Govt. Council and apptd. to the Revolutionary Military Council, 1949; No. 24 on the CPP CC, 1945, and No. 20, 1956; No. 15 on the Politburo, 1956, and el. to it, 1969; took no noticeable responsibility during the party struggles of the Cultural Revolution (according to Edgar Snow); appeared with other marshals at public celebrations, 1971.

LI YUEN-CHANG (LI YUN-CH'ANG?), General—One of the eight area commanders of the Liberated Areas, in charge of the Chahar-Jehol-Liaotung area, of whom I have no information except the following, taken from the pamphlet *The Liberated Regions of China Behind the Enemy Lines, 1945:* in the province of Hopei, "in June, 1938, anti-Japanese uprisings took place in seven *hsien* under the leadership of Comrade Li Yuen-chang, and so, large-scale guerrilla warfare extended over 17 *hsien*. After October they suffered some losses. In the spring of 1939, Comrade Hsiao k'e went to the area west of Peiping to Organize the Advance Detachment. . . ."

LU CHENG-TS'AO, General—comdr. of the Central Hopei Military District, of whom little information is available; was a well-educated native of Manchuria and formerly a Tungpei officer. The pamphlet *The Liberated Regions of China Behind the Enemy Lines, 1945,* reports: "In Central Hopei, when the main forces of the Government were retreating southward, Comrade Lu Cheng-ts'ao led two battalions to penetrate into the enemy's rear, smashed the puppet governments of Shengtse, Ankuo, Jenchiu, Hochien, Hsien-hsien, Anhsin and Kaoyang. On April 1, 1938, the Bureau of Political Affairs of Central Hopei was established." Lu Cheng-ts'ao commanded the forces on the big Hopei plain centralized as the 3d column, assisted by the 120th Division under Ho Lung, which came and went in the region.

According to WWCC, 1969, Lu was b. 1903, native of Haicheng *hsien*, Liaoning, apprentice of an oil store there, 1920; joined army as a regular soldier, 1921; entered NE Military Academy, Dec. 1922; apptd. chief of staff, 16th Brigade, NE Army, 1930; fought the Japanese at Great Wall, March 1933; joined the KMT Li-chih-she, 1934; comdr., 116th Div., 53d Army under Wan Fu-lin, 1937; after Marco Polo Bridge Incident, lost contact with Div. HQ and joined CCP, July 1937; joined forces with Nieh Jung-chen; acting comdr., 120th Div., 1939; alt. mem., CCP, 1945, No. 25, and regular mem., No. 93, 1956; deputy comdr.-in-chief, NE Democratic Allied Army under Lin Piao, 1946; deputy dir., Railway Dept., PRMC, 1948; vice-min. of Railways, 1949–1961; comdr., PLA Navy, 1949; mem., Natl. Defense Council, 1954; chief del. to negotiate with N. Vietnam on communications, 1954; given 1st class Orders of Independence and Freedom and Liberation, 1955, and made full general, 1964; deputy for Liaoning to 2d NPC, 1958–1964; led del. to Budapest, 1961, to Warsaw, 1963, to Moscow, 1964, to N. Korea, 1964; min. of railways, 1965–Dec. 1966; branded by Chiang Ch'ing as counter-revolutionary revisionist, Dec. 1966 and reportedly paraded before the public in Tienanmen Square, Jan. 25, 1967. His name is not on the 1969 list of CCP CC.

NIEH JUNG-CHEN, General (also spelled NIEH YUNG-CHIEN)—b. near Chung-king, Szechuan, 1899, of small farmers; participated in May Fourth Movement in Chungking Middle School and was influenced by Ch'en Tu-hsiu and *New Youth* magazine; left for France in 1920 as Work-and-Study student; joined CY in 1921 and studied natural sciences in Paris Univ. one year, then studied electrical engineering in Belgium 2 years at Charles Rowe's Workers' Univ.; retd. to Paris, 1923, and worked as engineer, carrying on party work among students and Chinese workmen; went to Berlin where impressed by internationalism, 1923; studied 6 months at Eastern Labor Univ. then entered Red Army Academy, Moscow, 1924; returned to China, 1925, and apptd. secy. of Pol. Dept. of Whampoa Academy until March 21, 1926; then did CP work among KMT armies in Hunan and Hupeh, and organized workers in Shanghai, 1927; participated in Nanchang Uprising, 1927, as pol. com. of one of Yeh T'ing's divisions; after defeat in Kwangtung, participated in Canton Commune; fled to Hongkong and stayed until 1930; during 1930 did CP work in Hopei Military Cmte. in Peking, Tientsin, and at Tangshan Mines; in 1931 entered Kiangsi soviets as vice-chairman of Pol. Dept. of Red Army, then became pol. com. of First Army Corps until 1937; then apptd. head of the first liberated area, the Shansi-Hopei-Chahar Border govt. under

Communist control after the war with Japan; was one of the eight Liberated Areas army commanders of the 8th Route Army; dir., Military Dept. of the CCP North Bureau, 1937; inflicted heavy casualties on the enemy, Nov. 1939, in several battles; comdr., Red Shansi-Suiyuan Army, Oct. 1943; comdr., Shansi-Chahar-Hopei Field Army, 1947, and of North China Military Region, 1948, 1949; CCP rep. to negotiate with KMT, Apr. 1949; comdr., Peking-Tientsin Garrison, 1949; army del. to 1st CPPCC, Sept. 1949; mem., Central People's Govt. Council, 1949–1954; apptd. marshal, 1955; No. 32 on the CCP CC, 1945, and No. 26, 1956; el. to the CC, 1969 but not to the Politburo though in 1966 he was a full mem. of the Politburo, still responsible for the nuclear installation presumably.

Foreign assignments: deputy chief, del. to comfort Soviet Army in Port Arthur, Feb. 1955; del. to Rumanian Workers party, Dec. 1955; del. to E. Germany, 80th birthday of president, Dec. 1955; del. to Hungary, Czechoslovakia, Poland, Rumania, Jan. 1956; attended Political Consultative Cmte., Warsaw Treaty Countries, Prague, Jan. 1956; participated in signing ceremony of its manifesto Jan. 27, 1956; visited U.S.S.R. and Mongolia, March 1958; led del. to N. Korea, Workers' Party Conf., Apr. 1956; special envoy at Ghana's Independence Day, March 1957; attended signing of China-Czechoslovakia Treaty, March 1957; chief del. to E. Germany for 10th anniversary of GDR, Oct. 1959; participated in talks between Liu Shao-ch'i and Nkrumah, pres. of Ghana, and signing of treaty, Aug. 1961; participated in Peking talks between Chou En-lai and chmn. Council of Ministers of U.A.R., Apr. 1963; attended signing of China-Albania Public Health Cooperative Agreement, Peking, Jan. 1964; received Tirana Univ. del. at Shanghai, March 1964; appeared at public celebrations, 1971.

P'ENG TEH-HUAI (P'ENG TE-HUAI), General—b. Hsiang T'an *hsien*, Hunan, in 1900, of rich peasant family; attended local school until age nine, then ran away to become an apprentice; joined army, becoming platoon comdr. at eighteen; studied in Hunan Military School, and, after graduating, apptd. battalion comdr. in 2d Hunan Division under Lu Ti-p'ing; joined CP, 1927; led KMT troops in revolt at P'ingkiang, Hunan, and joined Red Army, being given command of the 5th Red Army in Kiangsi, 1928; captured Changsha for awhile, then was put in command of Third Army Corps, composed of 5th and 8th Armies, 1930; fought in command of these troops until he reached Northwest after Long March, 1935, then put in direct command of 1st Front Army and made comdr.-in-chief of all Northwest armies before arrival of Chu Teh in late 1936; in August 1937, was apptd. by Chiang Kai-shek as field comdr.-in-chief of 8th Route Army in Shansi, as deputy under Chu Teh; in active command during Japanese war; author of many treatises on military strategy and tactics, and expert in manuevering warfare; commanded in the Northwest area during the renewed civil war and took Sian May 20, 1949; mem., Government Council, and vice-chairman, Military Council, 1949.

Later sources state of P'eng Teh-huai: that he suppressed the Futi'en coup in 1930 and supported Mao Tse-tung at Tsunyi and Maoerhkai on the Long March; that he was vice-chairman, NW Military and Adm. Cmte., Feb. 1936; after Japan attacked, July 1937, he went secretly with Chou En-lai to Taiyuan and Shihchiachuang to plan resistance; 8th Routh Army Front Line HQ were in the Taihang Mountains with P'eng as comdr.-in-chief; when CCP established communications control on Tientsin-Pukow Railway, he was in charge of that office, 1946; when KMT attacked Yenan and CCP CC evacuated, P'eng remained behind to direct warfare, March 1947; went to Hsiaoho for military conf. convened by Mao Tse-tung, June 1947; comdr., NW Military Region, 1948, and also of 1st Field Army, and its pol. com., 1948; mem. Natl. Cmte., 1st CPPCC, 1949–1954; vice-chr., PRMC, 1949–1954; chmn., NW Milit. and Adm. Cmte., 1949–1953; comdr. and pol. com., Sinkiang Milit. Region, Dec. 1949; comdr., Chinese People's Volunteers, Oct. 1950–Sept. 1954; awarded Hero of N. Korean People's Republic and 1st class Order of Korea Natl. Flag, July 1953; deputy for PLA to 1st NPC, 1954, and to NPC, 1959 and 1964; vice-premier, State Council, 1954–1959, and at same time min. of national defense, 1954–1959; vice-chairman, Natl. Defense Council, 1954–1959; led del. to comfort Soviet Army at Port Arthur, Feb. 1955.

Party career: joined CP, 1927, but was not on the Politburo in 1937; No. 33 on the CCP CC, 1945, and No. 22, 1956; on the Politburo, he was No. 11, 1945, and No. 14, 1956; first secy., CCP NW Bureau, Nov. 1949; was purged and disappeared from public view by July 1959, but not removed as min. of Defense until Sept. 1959, when Lin Piao took his post, as the result of a meeting of the CP with the defense chiefs. It was his dismissal, apparently insisted upon by Mao Tse-tung, which was the signal for the later Cultural Revolution when "Hai Jui Dismissed from Office" appeared as an indirect criticism of Mao in dismissing P'eng. Personal antagonism was reported to have existed between Lin Piao and P'eng.

Foreign affairs: held command in North Korea, 1950; led the del. to E. Germany for the 10th Anniversary, May 1955; attended Warsaw Conf. as observer and visited U.S.S.R., Sept. 1955; mem. del. to U.S.S.R. for October Revolution celebration, 1957; chief, Military Del. to U.S.S.R., Nov. 1957; led del. to Soviet Union, Eastern European countries and Mongolia, Apr. 1959; decorated 1st-class Order by Albania, June 1959; as min. of defense from 1954, he was until 1959 the chief liaison of the PLA with the Soviet military advisers during the modernization of the armed forces and basic construction of modern military industries; charged as a counterrevolutionary who in 1959 conspired with Liu Shao-ch'i against Mao in 1967.

PIEN CHANG-WU—b. Hopei, about 1905; grad. Paotingfu Military Academy, 1923; joined Feng Yü-hsiang's Kuominchün, and when this was reorganized after Feng's defeat in 1929, was an officer in Sun Lien-chang's 26th Route Army (former Kuominchün) sent to Kiangsi to engage in the anti-Red campaign; participated in the Ningtu Uprising, 1931, when the 26th Route Army deserted to the Red Army; was kept in command in 5th Army Corps created from the 26th and in 1937 was one of the dir. and instructors of the Anti-Japanese Military and Political Academy; when war began with Japan apptd. head of the Northwest Military Affairs Council; was military attaché in Moscow, 1950.

SU YU, General—b. in 1909 in Fukien; attended the 2d Hunan Normal School; joined CYL established by Mao Tse-tung, 1926; enlisted in Yeh T'ing's army, 1927; participated in the Nanchang Uprising; two years later led a division of the 4th Red Army; by 1932 was chief-of-staff of the 10th Army; when the Red Army evacuated Kiangsi and left on the Long March, stayed to command the defeat, creating a rearguard action to safeguard the evacuation; was chief-of-staff to Fang Chih-min and after Fang's capture and execution took command; later merged with Ch'en Yi's army, which, in 1937, became part of the New 4th Army, with Su Yu as vice-comdr.; was with Ch'en Yi until 1949, being vice-comdr. of the 3d Field Army, when he became a mem. of the Revolutionary Military Council; one of eight area comdrs. in the Communist-led districts of all China, commanding in the Central China Liberated Area; chief-of-staff, PLA General Staff, 1954–1958; mem., Standing Cmte., 3d NPC 1965—; on the CCP CC as alternate No. 13, 1945, and No. 36, 1956; was on the 1969 CCP CC with Ch'en Yi, Teng Tzu-hui and others; vice-min. of natl. defense, 1959—; mem., Standing Cmte., Military Commission, CCP Central Cmte., from Sept. 1967.

TAN TEH-CH'ANG—b. Hunan; comdr. of Ho Lung's best division, the old 9th Division of the original 6th Army, made up of the famous Liuyang-P'ingkiang partisans; deputy co. comdr., 1st Company, Special Service, Battalion under Ho Lung's 20th Army, 1927; rep. of CCP at 2d Co., 28th Regiment, 4th Red Army under Lin Piao at Kiangsi, 1928; was on Long March; pol. dir., Wuhan Garrison HQ under Hsiao Ching-kuang, 1949; pol. com., Air Defense Force, 1953; deputy-dir., General Rear Services Dept., PLA, 1954–1963; apptd. lt. gen. and Orders of Aug. 1st and Liberation 1st class, 1955; CCP del. to Natl. Cmte., 4th CPPCC, 1954; mem. Standing Cmte., 4th CPPCC, 1965.

WANG SHIH-TAI—comdr., armed forces of the Shensi-Kansu-Ninghsia border area.

WANG TSO-YAO—leader of the guerrilla forces in the Tungkiang area in Kwangtung, and on the Canton-Kowloon railway; comdr., Kwangtung People's Guerrillas; helped save many American flyers during the war and also assisted foreign refugees to escape.

WAN YI—b. 1902 or 1904, native of Haich'eng *hsien*, Liaoning; grad. from NE Milit. Institute; comdr., 33d Regt., 111th Div. of Chang Hsueh-liang's NE Army; joined CCP, 1933; during early period of Sino-Japanese war, comdr. of a brigade in KMT 111th Div. under Ch'ang En-to and operated in Shantung-Kiangsu border region, 1937; led troops in S. Shantung to force Ch'ang En-to to surrender to the Communists, Aug. 1939; deputy comdr. of Artillery PLA, 1950–1952; vice-min., 2d Min. of Machine Building, 1952–1954; mem., Natl. Defense Council, 1954–1965; adviser to Chinese Observer Del. to Cong. of European States for Defense of Peace and Security in Europe (Warsaw Pact), Warsaw, May 1955; apptd. lt. gen. and Orders of Independence and Freedom and Liberation 1st class, 1955; mem., Planning and Scientific Commission, SC, 1957–1958; dir., Dept. of Milit. Equipment, General Pol. Dept., PLA, May 1958; vice-chmn., China Assn.. of Science and Technology, Sept. 1958—; was No. 20 alternate on the CCP CC, 1945, and No. 17, in 1956; not on the 1969 CC list; accused "of being a trusted man of P'eng Teh-huai, Nov. 1967" (WWCC).

WU HSIU-CHUAN—b. 1908. The *New York Herald-Tribune*, Nov. 26, 1950, reports: "now forty-two years old, he joined the Communist party in China some twenty years ago. . . . he spent six years in Russia studying military tactics in Moscow's Sun Yat-sen University. . . . most of his career has been in China's Red Army, in which he is a general. . . . in the post-war Communist offensive against Generalissimo Chiang Kai-shek, he served under Red China's top field commander, Gen. Lin Piao. . . . was left behind in Manchuria as one of the governors of Mukden. . . . he went into the Foreign Ministry at Peking late in 1949 and now is director of the Russian and Eastern European Division. . . . early this year he accompanied Mao Tse-tung to Moscow for the extended negotiations that resulted in a treaty linking the two countries"; chief of the Peking del. to the UN, November 1950; No. 62 on the 1956 CCP CC; was with CCP del. led by Teng Hsiao-p'ing to Moscow, 1963, and to Canton to welcome secy.-gen., Japanese CP, 1964; participated in talks of CCP del. and Rumania Workers' party, Peking, 1964; del. to Moscow and Albania, 1964; mem., Standing Cmte., 4th CPPCC, 1964–1965—; del. to Tirana to celebrate anniversary of Albanian Labor party, 1966; "accused of being a big renegade, April, 1967" (WWCC).

YEH CHIENG-YING, General—b. Canton, 1903, of merchant family; studied in the Cantonese primary schools and from there went to Yünnanfu, then a revolutionary center, T'ang Chi-yao being governor; participated in the overthrow of Yuan Shih-k'ai and was in the 12th class of the Military Academy; went to Fukien and joined the army of Chen Chiung-mei, under whom Chiang Kai-shek also served; shifted to Canton, he worked for awhile with Sun Yat-sen and the Kuomintang, later becoming a CP mem.; after the Sun-Joffe agreement, became an instructor at Whampoa Academy under Galen; served in Whampoa until 1927, and commanded the 21st Division, one of the three divisions under Chiang Kai-shek's personal command, during the North-

Yeh Chien-ying

ern Expedition; chief-of-staff during the Canton Commune and el. to the govt.; escaped to Hong Kong and later to Shanghai; in 1929 went to Moscow to study for two years, returning in 1931 to Shanghai but leaving almost immediately for Kiangsi; became chief of the general staff and a mem. of the Military Council; del. during Sian Incident, 1936; during the war with Japan was one of the chief liaison officers with the Kuomintang; mem., Govt. Council and Military Council, 1949; mem., Commission of Overseas Chinese Affairs of the Govt., 1949; secy. of the Secretariat, CCP CC, 1966, and helped start the Cultural Revolution; apptd. vice-chairman, Military Commission, CCP CC, 1966–1971; accompanied Chou En-lai to Hanoi to mourn death of Ho Chi Minh, Sept., 1969; el. to the Politburo, 1969; welcomed Henry Kissinger to Peking airport, 1971.

CHANG KUO-T'AO—b. in Pinghsiang, Kiangsi about 1897; ed. Peking National Univ. and became known as a leader of the student movement and literary renaissance during the May Fourth period, 1919; was one of the twelve founders of the CP, 1921, being one of the two delegates from Peking; at first CP Conference, July 1921, was chairman, and el. to its CC; was in charge of the Pinhan Railway Strike, 1923; helped plan the Nanchang Uprising, August 1927; during the soviet period was political head of the Ouyüwan and Szechuan soviet governments, being secy. of the local CP and chairman of the Military Cmte., after about 1930; moved 4th Front Red Army out of Ouyüwan to start new soviet in Szechuan, arriving with Hsü Hsiang-ch'ien in December 1932 and by 1933 had organized a soviet of a million population; the 4th Front Army began the Long March to the Northwest in 1935, meeting Chu Teh's 1st Front Army in June 1935 at Mokung *hsien*, at T'a-wei; here the forces were divided, the 1st and 3d Army Corps marched on to Shensi and Kansu, while the 4th Front Army and Lo P'ing-hui's 32d Army concentrated in Sikong in February 1936 and formed a government; in June 1936 the 2d Front Red Army arrived from the Hunan-Hupeh soviet, and the 4th Front Army marched on with them to the northwest, arriving in southern Kansu in August; here the 4th Front Army suffered severe losses at the hands of the Mohammedans under the two Ma's; Chang Kuo-t'ao was in Yenan in 1937–1938, being then vice-chairman of the Military Council and a member of the Political Bureau; in 1938 was expelled from the CP as the result of a long and complicated disagreement with the majority of the Political Bureau beginning about 1935. It is said to have started when Chang favored remaining in Szechuan and wanted to restore influence in the south, while the other side wanted to build its base in the Northwest against the Japanese.

342

CHANG T'AI-LEI—a well-educated student and one of the earliest mem. of the Socialist Youth, founded in 1918, and one of eight founders of the Chinese CY, May 1920, which joined the CY International, but name was not changed to CY until 1925; second person to become natl. secy. of this CY; one of chief organizers of the Canton Commune on Dec. 11, 1927, and killed in the fighting Dec. 17, having remained to lead the last defensive effort.

CHANG WEN-PING (also known in early period as LIU CHENG-YI)—b. P'ing-kiang *hsien*, Hunan, in 1911, of middle peasants; his brother was a Protestant clergyman and he an ardent Christian; after attending a Christian primary school, went to Changsha to live at YMCA and attended middle school; was active student leader and joined CY, 1925; in 1927 went to Wuhan and attended a class in organizing the peasant movement organized by Mao Tse-tung and Teng Yen-ta; party sent him to P'ingkiang and Liuyang *hsien*, Hunan, to organize peasant partisans and he led 1,000 peasants to capture P'ingkiang city in 1927; was arrested in 1928, after participating in the later P'ingk'iang Uprising led by P'eng Teh-huai; apptd. party del. to Red Guards of the whole of P'ingkiang *hsien* (at age of seventeen); joined 5th Red Army as del. and spent year at Chingkangshan; in 1932 apptd. chief of Gaypayoo of Third Red Army Corps, which position held during Long March; in Shensi apptd. Gaypayoo chief in 15th Red Army Corps, and after the Sian Incident, 1937, was one of the four Communist delegates in Sian with Chou En-lai; ordered to the south on liaison work with the Kuomintang, he was arrested and secretly executed about 1943 by Chiang Kai-shek's police in Kwangtung.

CHAO PAO-SHEN—b. North China; student; joined Feng Yü-hsiang's Kuomin-chün and became Communist secretly; as chief-of-staff of 26th Route Army under Sun Lien-chung (reorganized Kuominchün), was main organizer of Ningtu Uprising of 20,000 men of this army in Kiangsi on December 14, 1931, which joined Red Army and became Fifth Army Corps (the only army engaging in positional warfare); killed in battle when pol. com. of this corps, and was succeeded by Teng Chen-tang, also killed in 1937.

CHAO SHIH-YEN—b. Szechuan about 1900; studied in local schools; was an active student leader during the May Fourth Movement, 1919; went to France with the Work-and-Study students about 1920; led the working students in the February 8, 1922, demonstration against the Chinese Consulate, with Chou En-lai, Tsai Ho-shëng, and Chen Yen-nien; one of the founders of the CP branch in France in December 1922, with Chou En-lai and Chen Yen-nien, son of Ch'en Tu-hsiu; on his return to China was el. mem. of the CC CP and of the Kiangsu Provincial Cmte.; during the taking over of Shanghai on

March 21, 1927, was one of the five chief leaders, together with his friends, Chou En-lai and Ch'en Yen-nien; was executed by the Kuomintang about 1927, around the same time as his old French-returned friends, Tsai and Chen.

CH'ENG KEN, General (also spelled CH'EN KENG or TSENG KEN)—b. Hsiang-hsiang *hsien*, Hunan (home of Tseng Kuo-fan), of landlord family, in 1904; ed. in old Chinese classics until twelve years old; then ran away and joined Lu T'i-p'ing's army for five years as 2d class soldier; joined CY about 1922; entered Chiang Wu T'an Military Academy in Canton (under Ch'en Chien), then grad. in First Class of Whampoa Cadets; was lieutenant in Whampoa troops and fought against Chen Chiung-ming as aide to Chiang Kai-shek; sent to Moscow in 1926 for one year of study; returned and participated in Nanchang Uprising; after defeat of the troops in Kwangtung was badly wounded but saved from arrest by a nurse and escaped to Shanghai; did party work in Shanghai two years, then was ordered to join Hsü Hsiang-ch'ien's army in Ouyüwan soviet; wounded in 4th Campaign and sent as del. to Shanghai; was recognized by CP renegade and betrayed to British police; transferred to Nanking prison where Chiang Kai-shek tried to influence him to return to Kuomintang; he refused and escaped from prison, 1933; went to Kiangsi soviet as president of Red Academy in Juikin one year; on Long March led his Academy Cadets; in Northwest made comdr., 1st Div. First Army Corps; during war with Japan led this under Lin Piao's 115th Division of the 8th Route Army with great distinction, and took command when Lin Piao went to Manchuria; in 1947 had about 50,000 troops below the Lunghai railway in west Honan, one of main armies in Central China; acting comdr., 2d Field Army, 1949; became full general, 1955; was deputy defense min. at time of his death, March 16, 1961.

CH'EN TU-HSIU—b. Huaining, Anhui, 1879; a brilliant scholar and essayist; ed. Japan and France; was dean of dept. of literature at Peking National Univ. and with Hu Shih led the *pai hua* literary renaissance of 1917; founded and edited *New Youth* magazine, the most important magazine and political influence of the period; was the leading spirit in founding CCP, 1921, and became its first secy., holding position until 1927; then was expelled as a "right opportunist" and later accused of Trotskyism; joined KMT in 1924, and was mem., CEC of KMT, 1925–1927, but was expelled in 1928; domi-nated Chinese CP until mid-1927; was arrested by Kuomintang in Shanghai, 1932 and sentenced to 15 years' imprisonment; released in 1938; d. in 1942, at which time it is said he was a writer of literary works in the ancient Chi-nese langauge.

CH'U CH'IU-PAI (or CH'U CH'U-PAI)—b. Ch'angchow, Kiangsu, in 1892, of bankrupt mandarin family and known as a brilliant student; became a journalist and was sent to Russia by the *Shanghai Times* as correspondent; stayed there and studied at Eastern Univ., becoming the most important early Chinese Marxist theorist, his many books having great influence in China; founded the branch of CCP in Moscow about 1921, and on his return was the principal founder of Shanghai Univ. about 1923, where his lectures educated many present Communists; mem., CP Political Bureau, and was one of those who deposed Ch'en Tu-hsiu, August 7, 1927, after which he succeeded him as secy. of the CP, 1927–1928; was sent to the Kiangsi region as the Shanghai delegate to the 2d Cong. of the Soviet Republic early in 1934, and remained in Juikin as commissioner of education, assisted by Hsu Teh-li; did not leave on the Long March and was trying to return to Shanghai, as he was ill with tuberculosis, but he was captured and executed in a village near Tingchow, Fukien, late in 1934 or early 1935.

FANG CHIH-MIN—b. Kiangsi, about 1905; a student; one of the most important organizers of the early partisan and Red Army movement; comdr. of the Tenth and Seventh Army Corps; stayed behind after Long March with Han Ying and Chen Yi, having his base at Yi-yang, northeast Kiangsi, where was captured and executed in 1935, when these corps were entirely annihilated by Kuomintang troops.

HAN YING (or HSIANG YIN)—b. Huangpo *hsien*, Hupeh, about 1897; father died when the son was small and mother supported family as seamstress, while the son and daughter collected dried grass and faggots from the hills to sell as fuel; became apprentice in pawnshop at age of fourteen, and this contact with usury caused him to join the CP during the 1923 Pinhan Railway Strike; in 1926 was secy. of Hupeh General Labor Union, and later of the Shanghai General Labor Union; was a close co-worker with Li Li-san; entered soviets before 1931, and was el. mem. of the Politburo at time of formation of Soviet Republic; when the main Red Army left the south on the Long March to the north, remained behind with the 24th Independent Division from Fukien, and directed the general Red guerrilla warfare in the southern provinces, 1934–1937, with a base in the Fukien-Kwangtung-Kiangsi area, and a remnant army of a few thousand called the 20th Red Army Corps; in January 1938, these troops were reorganized as the New 4th Army, in memory of Yeh T'ing's old Ironsides, and Yeh T'ing was brought out of retirement and made overall comdr., with Han Ying as vice comdr.; in January 1941 Kuomintang troops ambushed Han Ying's column of the New 4th, killed many thousands, including Han, and imprisoning Yeh T'ing. Chen Yi took over the command.

HSIA HSI—b. in Hunan about 1886 of peasant origin and became an intimate friend and classmate of Mao Tse-tung and a mem. of his Changsha Hsin Min Hsüeh Hui; later studied two years in Sun Yat-sen Univ. in Moscow; became secy. of Hunan provincial CP and during the soviet period was CP leader during formation of the Hunan-Hupeh soviet; became chairman of Pol. Dept. of Ho Lung's 2d Front Red Army and was killed during the Long March in Kweichow in 1936, succeeded by Jen Pi-shih in his political control.

HSIANG CHIN-YU, Miss—b. Hsi-p'u *hsien*, west Hunan, 1897, of wealthiest merchant family in the *hsien*; grad. Changsha Girls' Normal School and was always leader of all activities she engaged in; founded a Girls' Primary School in her native *hsien* and led May Fourth Movement activities there, 1919; together with Miss Tsai Ch'ang, organized the Hunan group of Work-and-Study students, and went to France with them to attend college, 1919; in Montaigne, France, 1922, married Tsai Ho-sheng; was one of earliest members of CP, and first chief of women's dept. of CP, in which capacity organized first women's labor movement, 1923–1925; attended Eastern Univ. in Moscow, 1925–1927; on return worked in Hankow as secret CP organizer, and was arrested and executed, May 1, 1928; famous women's leader, writer, and public speaker; still considered greatest Chinese woman Communist leader and is known as the "Grandmother of the Revolution."

HSIANG CHUNG-HUA (HSIANG CHUNG-FA)—important early Communist labor leader, succeeding Wang Son-hua in Shanghai; head of the Chinese del. to the World Labor Congress in Moscow, 1928; became third natl. secy. of CP, 1928–1931; after Li Li-san was deposed from control, Hsiang Chung-hua, Wang Ming, and Po Ku were the chief figures in the CC in Shanghai; in 1931 he was arrested and executed.

HUANG KUNG-LIU—b. Hunan, 1895; principal of the Military school at P'ingkiang and led one brigade to join the Red Army in the P'ingkiang Uprising, which he and P'eng Teh-huai organized; founded first permanent soviet in Hunan in Liuyang *hsien*, 1928, and led partisan warfare in that region; made comdr., 3d Red Army, 1930, ranking with Chu Teh, Mao Tse-tung, and P'eng Teh-huai; with P'eng Teh-huai captured Changsha, 1930; killed in battle by an air bomb in T'ungku, Kiangsi, 1932; Communists erected several monuments to his name, and named their military school and "Kung-liu" *hsien* in Central Soviets for him; a scholar, military leader, and popular leader.

JEN PI-SHIH—b. Hsiangyin County, Hunan, about 1904; studied in Hunan schools (where about 1917 was in Mao Tse-tung's Hsin-min Hsueh-hui) and later in Eastern Univ., Moscow, returning with Ch'ü Ch'ü-pai; one of earliest

CY mem. and was 3d person to become national secy. of the CY after Chang T'ai-lei was killed in 1927; entered soviets after CC moved there from Shanghai, and was el. Political Bureau, 1931; did political work in the 6th Army, which he helped lead to west Hunan-Kiangsi and join Ho Lung as political dir. in Hunan-Hupeh soviet; after death of Hsia Hsi in 1935 became political head of the region, as well as army; when Eighth Route Army was organized in 1937, was made chairman of the Pol. Dept. of the whole army, his headquarters usually with General Liu Pei-ch'eng; in 1948 was secy. of the CP and mem. of its Political Bureau; d. 1950.

K'AI FENG—b. Hunan, about 1907; a student in Chinese schools, then studied in Moscow; was 10th natl. secy. of the CY, 1933–1936; in 1937 was made chief of Army Propaganda Dept.

KAN SHIH-CH'I (KAN SZU-CH'I)—b. of peasant stock, Hunan, about 1907, and ed. in a Hunan middle school, with two years in Moscow; vice-chairman, Pol. Dept. of the 2d Front Army under Ho Lung; during the war with Japan was chairman, Pol. Dept. of 120th Division; held many offices after 1949; dir., Pol. Dept., Chinese People's Volunteers, 1951; deputy pol. com., CPV, 1952; awarded Korean 1st Class Order of Natl. Flag, 1953; deputy dir., General Pol. Dept., PRMC, 1953–1964; made col.-gen., 1955; No. 8 on the alternate cmte. of the CCP CC, 1956; deputy-chief, N. Korea Friendship Month celebrations, 1958; d. in Peking, Feb. 1964.

KAO KANG (KAO CHUNG-YU)—an early founder of the CCP in Shensi; b. Hengshan, Shensi, in 1891, son of a landlord; he and Liu Chih-tan (Liu Tze-tan) built the party there, which later became the sanctuary for the Mao Tse-tung group at the end of the Long March, 1935; No. 13 on the 1945 CCP CC list; chairman of the CP Northeast Bureau before 1948; el. vice-chairman of the Central Govt. at Peking and mem. of the Revolutionary Military Council, 1949; pol. com. for PLA, Manchuria, 1949; chairman of the People's Govt. for the Northeast in Manchuria, 1949; secy., party Northeast Bureau, and military comdr., 1950; chairman, State Planning Commission, 1953; removed from office as being "anti-Party," 1954; reported to have committed suicide.

KUAN SHANG-YIN—b. in 1905 in Manchuria, of Manchu family; became a worker in textile factories and also on the railway; was 4th natl. secy. of CY, about 1928–1929, following Jen Pi-shih; in 1930–1931 was chief secy. of the Shanghai General Labor Union; entered soviets and went to Hunan-Hupeh soviet; became political dir. of Ho Lung's 2d Front Army, keeping this post when it was reorganized into the 120th Division during the Japanese war and becoming mem. of the Political Bureau of the CP; remained with Ho Lung as political dir. of the Shansi-Suiyuan Liberated Area; el. to CC of CP in 1945; d. about 1945.

K'UNG P'ENG—b. Anhui 1920, in Hofei, younger sister of K'ung P'u-sheng; a leader in the December 9th Student Movement, 1935; achieved the highest post of the "Yenching dynasty" in the Peking govt. as asst. min. of foreign affairs, Apr. 1964–1969; grad. from Foreign Languages Dept., Yenching Univ., Peking, and became secy. of Chou En-lai, about 1938–1939; went to Chungking as a newspaper reporter and was later secy. of 8th Route Army office there; was also later editor-in-chief of English-language *China Digest* in Hong Kong; el. alternate mem., 1st CC ACFDY May 1949–June 1953, and was its del. to 1st CPPCC and mem. Natl. Cmte., Sept. 1949–Dec. 1954; mem., Natl. Cmte., CPCWP, Oct. 1949–July 1958; dir., Dept. of Intelligence, Ministry of Foreign Affairs, Dec. 1949–July 1955, and to successor Dept. of Information, MFA, Aug. 1955–April 1964; adviser to del. headed by Chou En-lai at Geneva Conf., Apr. 1954; with Chou En-lai on visit to Southeast Asia, Nov.–Dec. 1956; adviser and spokesman, del. at Geneva Conf., May–July 1961; accompanied Chen Yi to receive reporters from Sweden in Shanghai, Feb. 1963; participated in Peking talks between foreign min. and Pakistan foreign min., March 1963; participated in ceremony signing China-Pakistan Border Agreement, Mar. 1963; mem. del. led by Liu Shao-ch'i to visit Indonesia, Burma, Cambodia, N. Vietnam, Apr.–May 1963; sent by Chou En-lai to visit Asia-Africa countries, Dec. 1963–Feb. 1964; el. deputy for Anhui to 3d NPC, Sept. 1964; mem. del. to 2d Afro-Asian Conf. and to visit Algeria and UAR, June 1965. Her death was reported in the press, 1970.

KU TSO-LIN—b. Hunan in 1906; a student; studied at univ. in Moscow; was secy. Kiangsu provincial CY, then went to Kiangsi as head of CY Organization Dept.; became 9th natl. secy. of CY, following Jen Pi-shih and Kuan Shang-yin; in 1931 at time of formation of Soviet Republic was el. mem. of the Political Bureau; in the Fifth Campaign was acting chief of the Pol. Dept., and during the difficult Kwanch'ang battle he worked day and night and became ill from strain but continued to overwork; died of exhaustion in 1934; is stated to have had very great influence upon youth during his career.

LI CHUN-CHEN, Miss—b. 1907 Hung Hsun *hsien*, in the Tungkiang region, Kwangtung, in brick-carrier's family, and was adopted at birth by merchant-peasant family, and married one of the sons at age of seventeen; joined CP in 1927 with husband; participated in Tungkiang peasant revolt, 1927, and joined Ku T'ai-chen's 11th Red Army as propagandist for one year; later worked as organizer in various Kwangtung districts; in 1930 went to Fukien soviet and worked in local soviet government until 1933; then went to Juikin, Kiangsi; married to Teng Chün-hsiung; participated in Long March and was afterward chief of the Women's Dept. of govt. in Yenan.

LI K'E-NUNG—b. Anhui, about 1907; worker and student; entered soviets and became chief of communications dept. after 1936; became head of Dept. of Social Work of the CC of the CP and in 1949 vice-min. of foreign affairs.

According to WWCC he was a native of Ts'ao *hsien*, Anhui, and died Feb. 9, 1962; went to France on the work and study plan; joined the CCP in Shanghai, 1926; after arrest of Ku Hsun-chang he surrendered to the KMT at Wuhan and gave information to enable arrest of Hsiang Chung-fa, spring of 1931; went to Kiangsi and as spy on Nationalist military organizations, 1932; chief, Investigation Dept., Political Security Bureau, CCP, 1st Front Army, 1932–1933; took part in Long March; dir., Communications Dept., CCP Foreign Affairs Office, Paoan, 1936; participated in negotiations that led to release of Chiang Kai-shek and a united front against the Japanese, Dec. 1936; participated in negotiations of KMT-CCP military alliance, 1937; deputy dir., CCP Central Intelligence Dept., 1938; dir., CCP Social Affairs Dept., 1949; vice-min. of foreign affairs, Oct. 1949–1954; accompanied Chou En-lai to Geneva Conf., 1954; deputy chief of staff, PLA, 1955 to time of his death; made full general with orders, 1955; on the 1956 CCP CC, was No. 41; was on Standing Cmte., 3d CPPCC, 1959; participated in Militia Cong., Apr. 1960.

LIN TSU-HAN (also known as LIN PEI-CH'U and LIN PAI-CH'U and also spelled LIN SHU-HAN and LIN HSU-HAN)—b. Lin-li *hsien*, west Hunan, in 1882, of one of the leading Hunan families; father a schoolteacher; studied classics; at eighteen entered New Normal School in Changtehfu; entered normal school in Tokyo in 1904 on govt. scholarship; mem., Hua Sheng Hui, forerunner of Tung Meng Hui and of the latter, which sent him to Manchuria to work; there taught school in Kirin two years; returned to Hunan in 1909 doing secret KMT work; fled to Japan; returned in 1915 again as agitator in Hunan; in 1916–1918 was chief-of-staff to Cheng Chien (later Chiang Kai-shek's chief-of-staff); resigned from army, went to Shanghai, met Ch'en Tu-hsiu and joined CP in 1921 at time of founding; between 1921–1925 spent entire time with Sun Yat-sen as chairman of General Affairs Dept. and was chairman of KMT Party Affairs Dept., 1922–1923; when Sun died in 1925 became chairman of Peasant Ministry of Canton govt.; in 1926 organized 6th Army with Cheng Chien and marched with it on Northern Expedition as KMT party delegate; el. mem., CEC of KMT, 1926; went to Wuhan as chief secy. of Revolutionary Military Council of KMT; after 1927 split joined Ho Lung's troops as chairman of finance cmte. after Nanchang Uprising, then went to Hongkong and in Nov. 1927 went to Moscow to study; in 1929–1931 went to Harbarovsk to organize school for Chinese workmen; returned to China at end of 1931 and entered Kiangsi soviets in 1932; became commissioner of finance, holding this post until 1938 when became chairman of the Shensi-Kansu-Ninghsia border government temporarily and again, 1943–1948; during negotiations with Chiang Kai-shek and the Kuomintang, was often a liaison agent with Chou En-lai, Yeh Chien-ying and others; apptd. secy.-gen. of Govt. Council, 1949; vice-pres., Sino-Soviet Friendship Assn., 1954–1959; vice-chairman, Standing Cmte., 1st NPC, 1954–1959; head of del. to Mongolia, Aug. 1959; d. May 29, 1960.

LIU TZU-TAN (LIU CHIH-TAN)—(founder of North Shensi Soviet) b. Pao-an, North Shensi, of peasant family who lived in a cave; ed. Yulin Middle School; grad. from Whampoa Academy, 1926, where joined CP; participated in Revolution of 1925–1927, then returned to native district and led several peasant uprisings in Shensi after 1929; in 1930 organized the *min tuan* of Pao-an and the Ke Lao hui (secret society) and by August had a force of 300 men; after several reverses finally organized the "Anti-imperialist Army" carrying the red flag and numbering about 500 men; in April 1932, reorganized this into the "Shensi-Kansu Partisan Brigade," of about 1,000; after further reverses in local fighting, in June 1933, reorganized the 26th Red Army, of 500 men, with connections with the Red Army in the south; organized and became chairman of North Shensi Soviet govt. in summer of 1934, which finally had 20 *hsien* under its control; after the First Front Army arrived, completing the Long March from the south, Liu was one of the comdrs. of the expedition into Shansi in the spring of 1936; was killed in battle near the Yellow River.

LI TA-CHAO—b. Hopei, a brilliant scholar and leader of the May Fourth Movement in 1919 at which time was librarian of Peking National Univ.; played leading role in Ch'en Tu-hsiu in organizing CCP, May 1921; was executed in Peking in 1928; had tremendous personal influence on youth of China, including Mao Tse-tung and Mrs. Chou En-lai.

MAO TSE-MIN—brother of Mao Tse-tung; b. Hsiang T'an *hsien*, Hunan, about 1895, of peasant family; a student; after 1937 was commissioner of People's Economy of Shensi-Kansu-Ninghsia govt.; about 1947 was reported murdered by the Kuomintang in the northwest, for which the Communists demanded punishment.

P'ENG P'AI—b. in Hailofeng district, Kwangtung, of important landlord family; a brilliant student; became sympathetic with revolution; joined CP and was active in organizing peasants, 1925–1927; in October 1937 organized and was chairman of the first soviet in China in his native district, Hailofeng, where he had divided his own land among his tenants, this Hailofeng soviet being annihilated by March 1928; escaped from Hailofeng to Shanghai; there was arrested and executed in 1929; was one of the earliest agrarian leaders.

Po Ku (Ching Pang-hsien)—b. in Ningpo *hsien*, Chekiang, 1907, son of a *hsien* magistrate; ed. in the Wusih primary schools and the Soochow 2nd Provincial Technical School, 1922–1925, where he was el. president of the Student Union of Soochow and participated in the 1925 student movement; also active in the Kuomintang; went to Shanghai, summer of 1925, and entered Shanghai Univ. in September, joining the CP in October 1925; participated in the 2d Shanghai Uprising, but left shortly after for Moscow, arriving in November 1926; studied at Sun Yat-sen Univ. until 1930; after graduation spent one year in the Institute for Chinese Studies, returning to Shanghai, May 1930; there worked in the All-China Labor Federation and joined the opposition to Li Li-san, which succeeded in eliminating his influence; organized workers in the Shanghai trade union organizations; worked with Hu Yeh-p'ing while he was editor of the *Shanghai Worker*; after 1931, worked in the Chinese CY, organizing young people; worked in the party CC in Shanghai, 1931–1932, participating in talks on Mukden Incident, which adopted slogan "Arm the masses for revolutionary warfare against Japanese imperialism"; secy. of the CC, then commissar for Foreign Affairs in the Yenan govt.; during the war with Japan, was one of the liaison figures with the Kuomintang, and was killed in a plane accident in 1946, together with Yeh T'ing and others.

Su Chao-jen (also spelled Hsu Chao-cheng)—the first nationally known labor leader in China; b. 1888 in Hsiangshan, Kwangtung, near Sun Yat-sen's birthplace, of poor peasant family; went to sea as a boy and was seaman twenty years; became mem. of Sun's T'ung Meng Hui before 1911, and was one of the messengers carrying Sun Yat-sen's secret party communications; mem. of the Seamen's Mutual Benefit Society, nucleus for the later union, and was imprisoned in Hong Kong a year for his labor activities; during 1920, with Lin Wei-ming, laid the groundwork for the Chinese Seamen's Union, one of the earliest in China, inaugurated February 28, 1921; on January 12, 1922, began the Hongkong Seamen's Strike, first big labor action in China, and Su was chairman of the strike cmte.; Hongkong was paralyzed two months and the strike was victorious; in June 1924 helped organize Pacific Transport Workers' Conference in Canton, first international labor activity in Far East; joined CP, 1925, and was Kuomintang del. in Peking at time of Sun Yat-sen's death; el. to cmte. of All-China Labor Federation, 1925, and el. chairman, 1927–1929; d. 1929.

T'AN PING-SHAN—b. Canton; a student leader of Peking National Univ.; one of earliest Communist mem. and held high rank in KMT, 1925–1927; in 1925 was chief of Labor Dept. of KMT and mem. of CEC; about 1928 was excluded from CP and with Teng Yen-ta organized the "Third Party."

TENG CHEN-T'ANG—b. about 1900 in North China (probably Hopei); joined Feng Yü-hsiang's Kuominchün and as brigade comdr. of 26th Route Army (reorganized Kuominchün) became Communist and led Ningtu Uprising on December 14, 1931, together with Chao Pao-shen, and joined Red Army; was comdr. of the Fifth Army Corps, 1933–1937; killed in battle in Kansu, February 1937, when most of his old veterans were destroyed.

TENG FA—b. Kwangtung about 1905, of working-class family; was a cook on a Canton-Hongkong steamer; in 1925–1926 was a leader of the Hongkong Strike; joined CP; grad. Whampoa Academy and participated in 1925–1927 Revolution; afterward carried on party work in Hongkong for a time before entering soviets; in 1931 one of the seven members of the Politburo at the time of the formation of the Soviet Republic; was chief of the Pao Wei Chü (Gaypayoo) until 1937 when his assistant, Chou Hsing, took over; in 1936 just before the Sian Incident was in charge of secret party work in Sian and lived in Marshal Chang Hsueh-liang's house; during the war with Japan was head of the Mass Movement Cmte. of the CP and in 1946 was chairman of the Labor Fed. of the Chinese Liberated Areas, which organization sent him as del. to the first conference of the World Federation of Trades Unions in Paris, February 1946; visited Great Britain and the Philippines during this trip; on his way back to Yenan by plane in 1946 was killed in accident with Yeh T'ing, Po Ku, and others.

TSAI HO-SHENG—b. Hsiang-hsiang *hsien*, Hunan, about 1898, of bankrupt gentry; brother of Tsai Ch'ang; intimate friend and classmate of Mao Tse-tung in Changsha, and with Mao organized the "New People's Study Society" and the "Work-and-Study in France" group; went to France to study in 1919, married Miss Hsiang Chin-yü, and was organizer of Socialist and later of Communist movement; on return to China in 1922 was chief of CP Propaganda Dept. and in 1925 was Chinese del. to Comintern; returned to China in 1927 and worked as secy. of Kwangtung-Kwangsi Provincial Cmte.; arrested and executed by Chen Ch'i-t'ang in Canton in 1931.

Tso Ch'uan—b. Hunan, 1906, of farmers; grad. of first class at Whampoa Academy; joined KMT, 1923, and CP, 1925; battalion comdr. during 1925–1927 Revolution; in 1927 went to Moscow and studied at Red Army Academy four years; grad. with highest honors; returned and went to Kiangsi soviet, 1930; comdr. of First Army Corps, succeeding Lin Piao, which was reorganized in 1937 under Lin Piao's 115th Division; kept his command and was asst. chief-of-staff of the 8th Route Army; when his troops were driven out of Central Hopei general headquarters they were surrounded in the mountains of southeast Shansi and Tso Ch'uan was killed. He was one of the most promising young comdrs., together with Lin Piao and Cheng Ken, and his death was considered a major loss in the staff.

Wei Kung-ch'i, Miss—b. in Honan, 1908; ed. in the primary and middle schools of Kaifeng and during the 1925–1927 Revolution joined the Women's Propaganda Dept. of the Kuominchün, arriving finally in Wuhan; there joined the CP and was sent to Kwangtung after 1927, returning to Honan in 1928, doing secret party work; went to Paris and to Russia for a year's study at Sun Yat-sen Univ. and the Eastern Labor Univ., 1929; returned to China in 1930 and went to Kiangsi; in 1932 helped organize the dramatics groups and continued in this work, though she had had no previous training, becoming dir. of the People's Dramatics Society; in 1936 m. Yeh Chien-ying, chief-of-staff, and assisted him in his liaison mission.

Yeh T'ing—b. Kwangtung; was one of best Kuomintang comdrs. during 1926–1927 Northern Expedition; joined CP before 1926; was in command of 24th Division of 11th Army of Chang Fa-kuei's "Ironsides," this Fourth Route Army being made up of the 11th, 20th (commanded by Ho Lung), and 4th armies (commanded directly by Chang Fa-kuei); during the Nanchang Uprising of August 1, 1927, led his division of the 11th Army in the uprising, joined by Ho Lung's 20th Army, and part of the 4th Army; fought across several provinces with his insurgent troops but was disastrously defeated; was then one of the leaders in the Canton Commune; after the failure of the commune resigned from the CP and retired in Hongkong; in 1938 was given high command of the New 4th Army, which was under field command of Han Ying, and under superior direction of the original Kuomintang Ironsides comdr., Chang Fa-kuei; in January 1941, the New 4th Army was attacked by Kuomintang troops and Han Ying killed, while Yeh T'ing was imprisoned until 1945; in 1946 as he was proceeding by plane to Yenan, he was killed in the same accident with Po Ku, Teng Fa, and several other important Communists.

YUN T'AI-YIN—one of the earliest national youth leaders of China and a brilliant student; leader of the "New Village" movement, a non-Marxist, semianarchist utopian tendency along Tolstoyan lines that appeared briefly in China from 1920 to 1923. This centered in Chung Hua College in Wuhan, Hupeh, where Yun studied, and his group organized the Li Chün Book Company to publicize their ideas; joined the CP in Szechuan; became nationally known in the Kuomintang during the 1925–1927 period and in 1926 was one of the five Communists elected to the Kuomintang CC; in 1925 he taught in a Girls' Normal School in Szechuan, where he had great influence on such future Communists as Miss Li Po-chao, daughter of the Chungking *hsien* magistrate, during the May 30th Movement; was executed by the Kuomintang, 1932.

The Kuomintang Side
in the Civil War

CHANG HSUEH-LIANG, Marshal—b. Liaoning, 1898, eldest son and heir of Marshal Chang Tso-lin, governor of Manchuria; grad. from the Military Academy in Manchuria and joined the army at age nineteen, commanding his father's bodyguard; fought in the Anfu-Chihli War, then went to Japan in 1921 to study military science; on his return, became principal of the Military Academy and comdr. of the 1st Fengtien Army during the Chihli-Fengtien War, 1924, and was in charge of military affairs in the lower Yangtze Valley. His father had formerly fought against the Kuomintang forces, but, at his death, his son joined the Kuomintang and threw his weight into the support of Chiang Kai-shek and saved his power, with the object chiefly of unifying China to resist Japanese encroachments; succeeded his father as governor of Manchuria and comdr.-in-chief of all armed forces there and was chancellor of Tungpei Univ.; in 1929 fought in skirmishes with the Russians on their common frontier; his intervention on the side of Chiang broke Feng Yü-hsiang's Northern Coalition in 1930, in recognition of which he was in 1930 made vice comdr.-in-chief of all China's armed forces, second to Chiang Kai-shek, spending some time in Nanking planning with Chiang Kai-shek; was military head in Peking, 1931–1935, and while he and nearly all his troops were south of the Great Wall (defending the interests of Chiang), the Japanese invaded Manchuria on September 18, 1931; in March 1933, sailed for Europe, visiting ten countries for the study of conditions there, returning in January 1934 to become deputy comdr.-in-chief of the anti-Communist armies in Honan-Hupeh-Anhui (Ouyüwan), which post was abolished in February 1935, and he was made dir. of Chiang's headquarters in Wuhan; he was next sent to Sian with his army to fight the Communists, who had arrived in the Northwest in October 1935 and became comdr.-in-chief of the anti-Communist forces of the whole Northwest. His troops were severely defeated and they did not want to fight civil war but to fight the Japanese in

355

their occupied homeland, Manchuria; Chang went secretly to talk with Chou En-lai at Communist headquarters; they made a secret truce and agreement to fight Japan, and the Communists in Sian lived in the Young Marshal's own home for protection. On December 9, 1935, the student movement broke out, initiated and led chiefly by Tungpei natives in Peking universities, who influenced Chang and his young officers. As Chiang Kai-shek refused to stop the civil war or to prepare to fight Japan, Chang Hsueh-liang and Yang Hu-cheng "detained" him during the famous Sian Incident of 1936. When it was decided to settle the incident "peacefully," and not to kill Chiang Kai-shek or turn his fate over to a people's mass meeting, Chang Hsueh-liang readied his own plane to take Chiang Kai-shek back to Nanking safely, and went with him, hoping to reorganize the reactionary element in Nanking and not expecting Chiang Kai-shek to betray him. Chang Hsueh-liang had received assurances from Chiang Kai-shek and all the persons involved in the release of Chiang of his own personal safety and their assistance in "reorganizing" the government. Instead, Chiang Kai-shek had him imprisoned immediately on a ten-year term, in 1937. The Communists and others demanded his release periodically with no result, and the treatment of Chang Hsueh-liang did much to prevent the unification of all north China and Manchuria in time to fight effectively the Japanese, for he would have been the leader in this liaison of all armed forces. Chang Hsueh-liang remained a prisoner and in the 1940s declared that whenever he was free he would lead a revolution. Chiang Kai-shek took Chang Hsueh-liang with him as a personal prisoner to Taiwan when he fled there in 1949, and he was still a prisoner, 1968. It was reported that he had become a research scholar on the Ming dynasty.

CHEN CHENG, General—b. 1900 at Chingtien, Chekiang, the native province of Chiang Kai-shek; graduated from Paoting Military Academy; apptd. instructor at Whampoa and comdr. of the Kuomintang Artillery Corps; was part of the Canton Military govt.; in 1930 was given command of the 18th Army with headquarters at Nanchang, Kiangsi, where he fought the Communists and became in 1934 field comdr. of the Communist Suppression Forces for Kiangsi, Kwangtung, Fukien, Hunan, and Hupeh; later stationed in Wuhan; in 1932 m. the daughter of Tan Yen-kai, Miss Tan Chang; fought actively in the field during the Northern Expedition and during most of the war against the Communists; commanded against the Communists in the south and was for some time stationed in Wuhan; in 1937 was made vicemin. of war and commander-in-chief of the 9th War Area, with Wuhan headquarters; from 1938 to 1940 was secy.-gen. of the Kuomintang Youth Corps and was governor of Hupeh Province after 1937, and subsequently comdr. over the 6th War Area; in 1948 was field comdr. of the nine Nanking armies in Manchuria, estimated at about 400,000 men opposing Lin Piao, reported to have forces numbering 320,000. One of the top Communists described Chen Cheng as a "steady plugger, nothing brilliant. He never takes the offensive in open battle but uses defensive factors. He hunts around for our troops and when he finds them, stops and builds forts and consolidates his position, and only ventures an advance when he has a deep line of forts behind him. He has no spirit to attack or will to fight. He is one of the ablest commanders under Chiang."

CHENG CHIEN, General—b. at Liling, Hunan, 1881, a former friend of Lin Tsu-han; attended Hunan Military Academy and the Japanese Military Academy; upon return apptd. comdr. of National Defense Army fighting against Yuan Shih-k'ai, 1916; organized with Lin Tsu-han the 6th Kuomintang Army in 1926, Lin being his political dir. and he comdr.; his 6th Army first captured Nanking in 1927 but had to retreat when part was disarmed by Chiang Kai-shek who marched up almost immediately; after the collapse of the Wuhan govt., did nothing of consequence but was at one time chairman of the Hunan provincial govt.; was imprisoned for a time in 1928, suspected of trying to overthrow Nanking, but released, and in December 1935, accepted a post as chief-of-staff in Nanking until 1937; was governor of Honan in 1939 and dir. of Chiang Kai-shek's Northwest Headquarters, 1939–1940; after 1940 he was deputy chief-of-staff.

CHIANG KAI-SHEK, Marshal—b. 1888 in Fenghua, Chekiang, where his forebears on one side had controlled the salt monopoly and were small merchants; his father died when he was eight and his mother gave him a disciplined training; in 1906 he and forty other Chekiang students enrolled at Paoting Military Academy; from 1907–1911 he spent four years at the Tokyo Academy, so that he was able to claim loyalty from classmates of both these cliques as well as the Whampoa P'ai (clique), Ho Ying-ch'ing being a friend in Tokyo; had a command in the 83d Brigade during the capture of Shanghai in 1911 and in 1913 joined Sun Yat-sen's party; seeing no future in military matters at the moment, he in 1920 became an exchange broker in Shanghai; in 1923 he went to Canton and was made principal of the new Whampoa Academy founded in May 1924, with Ho Ying-ch'ing as dean, and won his first military honors by defeating the Canton Volunteers (a merchants' uprising) and Chen Chiung-ming and by other fighting in the Tungkiang area; in 1924 was sent by Sun Yat-sen to Moscow to study the Soviet military organization; in March 1926, he tried his first *coup* which failed; in July 1926, he was made comdr.-in-chief of the Northern Expedition which started that month, having under his personal command only Ho Ying-ch'ing's 1st Army, out of eight field armies. The high command was in the Kuomintang Military Cmte., but when Nanchang was captured in October 1926 by Cheng Ch'ien's

6th Army, Chiang began to refuse to carry out their orders and to plot against the left control; wanted the new capital to be Nanchang but the Kuomintang insisted on Wuhan, where it was moved from Canton; remained in Nanchang angrily refusing to cooperate and also quarreled with the chief Russian advisor, Borodin; wanted to capture Nanking but the Military Cmte. ordered Cheng Ch'ien, who was more loyal, to take the city, which he did, Chiang's troops making a forced march but arriving just a little too late. The Nanking Incident occurred, in which six foreigners were killed; two Britons, two Americans, and several Japanese were wounded, and there was much looting of consular and private property. Chiang used the incident as an excuse to get together with the foreign powers to break the left Kuomintang govt. at Wuhan, which had just taken back the British concession there; the other foreign powers were afraid of losing more of their concessions, so they picked Chiang Kai-shek as the instrument of splitting and opposing such nationalistic successes against foreign control, and immediately recognized the govt. he set up in Nanking opposed to the Wuhan govt., which collapsed in July 1927. After gaining hold of Nanking, Chiang Kai-shek took control of Shanghai—which the Military Cmte. had been opposed to attacking—through the April 12th Incident in which the labor unions were broken. In 1927 Feng Yü-hsiang went over to Chiang Kai-shek against the Wuhan govt. Peking was occupied in 1928 and Chiang smoothed over the Tsinan Incident when a clash had occurred between the Japanese and Chinese. In October 1928, the Nanking govt. was formally organized, and Chiang held the post of chairman and comdr.-in-chief. Soon all of the original Northern Expedition armies rebelled and fought against Chiang, except Ho Ying-ch'ing's loyal 1st Army and the garrison force at Canton. By the time these had subsided somewhat, the Communist agrarian movement had reared its head in a formidable way, and, after 1930, Chiang spent most of his time fighting the Red armies, being defeated in his first four campaigns, until he was arrested in Sian on December 12, 1936, by Chang Hsueh-liang. Six months later, Japan attacked at Liukouch'iao Bridge and Chiang was accepted as comdr.-in-chief of the national forces by all parties and groups. After V-J Day, the civil war flared up anew and despite efforts to arbitrate the differences, the armed struggle continued.

In December 1927, Chiang Kai-shek married Miss Soong Mayling, younger sister of Madame Sun Yat-sen and of T. V. Soong and Madame H. H. K'ung. She served as a useful liaison with the foreign press and in contacts with foreign elements, especially missionaries. Chiang Kai-shek had one son by his first wife in Chekiang, Chiang Chiang-kuo, who was a student in Moscow for many years and a Communist, but returned to assist his father when the war with Japan began. Chiang Wei-kuo is an adopted younger son.

Chiang Kai-shek was, for a time, the pivotal force around which all the contradictory elements in Chinese society gravitated and balanced themselves over the years, thereby maintaining power, and served as a balancing wheel for the foreign interests. His policy was based on the old Roman "divide and rule" and was successful in keeping his rivals at loggerheads, and in playing the foreign powers off against each other. Chiang Kai-shek is a plebian soldier and a skillful statesman, but not in the tradition of the scholar though he is a great defender of Confucianism. He has not what could be called a "modern mind," but he is well adjusted to the mixture of Chinese society, which is half-"feudal" and half-modern, most of the modernization being in the military field. He was an effective liaison between the old landlord system of China and the new city middle-class and armies, which had contradictory interests and a common cause only in fighting the Communists. When the mainland was taken over, Chiang Kai-shek fled to Taiwan, where he set up his government in 1949.

FU TSO-YI, General—b. in Shansi, 1885, and grad. from Paoting Academy, after which he rose from the lower officers' ranks; in 1927 joined the Kuomintang forces and captured Chochow in Hopei; apptd. comdr.-in-chief of the 5th Army under Yen Hsi-shan's 3d Group Army, and garrison comdr. of Tientsin, 1928–1930; became governor of Sinkiang Province in 1933; during 1933 was concurrently comdr. of the 7th Army of the Northern Armies to resist the Japanese, and the next year campaigned against Sun Tien-ying. When Chiang Kai-shek was arrested in Sian, 1936, it was expected Fu Tso-yi would join Chang Hsueh-liang, but Chiang was released before he made a decision. He has received many medals from the Nanking govt., perhaps partly to encourage loyalty. In addition to being governor of Suiyuan, 1937–1938, was comdr.-in-chief of the North Route Army against Japan and vice-comdr. of the 8th War Area; in 1948 was comdr. of the North China Area; after Japanese surrender led three armies back to Suiyuan, 1945; when KMT-CCP peace talks broke off, routed CP army at Kalgan, 1946; was comdr. of the North China Bandit-Suppression headquarters in Peking, 1947; was defeated by Communists at Battle of Peking-Tientsin-Kalgan, 1948; defected to Communists in Peking, Jan. 1949; del. to 1st CPPCC, 1949; mem., Natl. Defense Research Group, 1949; comdr. of Suiyuan Military Region, 1949–1950; min. of water conservancy, 1949–1954; held many posts and participated in signing treaties with North Korea, Nepal, etc.; del. to 4th CPPCC, 1964; present at reception in Peking given by min. of natl. defense for 41st anniversary of PLA, Aug. 1968.

Ho CHIEN, General—b. in 1887 at Liling, Hunan, one of the three *hsien* first sovietized, so he had, like Hsia To-yin, a special hatred and revenge to take out on the Communists; a Paoting graduate; comdr. of the 2d Division in the 8th Army, 1926, and of the 35th Army, 1927, when he was given responsibility for obliterating the peasant movement in western Hunan; governor of Hunan stationed in Changsha from 1928 and head of many commissions for "Communist-suppression" and "Pursuit Forces of the Communists"; mem., CEC of the Kuomintang; author of *The Five Human Relationships and the Eight Virtues.*

Ho YING-CH'ING, General—b. 1889 at Hsingi, Kweichow; grad. from Tokyo Military Academy, 1909, where he joined the T'ung Meng Hui; became chief-of-staff of the Kweichow Army and chief of Kweiyang Police Dept.; in 1924 was an instructor and dean of Whampoa and comdr. of the 1st Brigade in Kwangtung, 1925; put down the Canton merchants' insurrection and that of Yang Hsi-min and Liu Ch'en-huan; was in Weichow, Mienhu, and Pelo expeditions and became division comdr., 1926; was head of police forces in Tungkiang region (Chaochow and Meihsien), Kwangtung during first part of the Northern Expedition, 1926; then given command of the East Route Army with Pai Chung-hsi as field comdr., and marched into Fukien where became chairman of the govt., then to Chekiang; pretended to an attack on Shanghai where he sent General Pai Chung-hsi to take over (Wuhan had opposed an attack on Shanghai), but instead marched secretly to Nanking, under Chiang Kai-shek's orders, to carry out a coup d'etat and to prevent the Wuhan Kuomintang forces from controlling the city, where he disarmed Cheng Ch'ien's troops loyal to Wuhan (which had arrived first) and held the city. Cheng Ch'ien's troops retreated to Wuhan and Chiang Kai-shek's revolt against Wuhan succeeded, Ho Ying-ch'ing being his one dependable lieutenant then and during subsequent years; mem., CEC of the KMT and Chiang's chief-of-staff, holding this position through the years and also as dir. of Field Headquarters fighting the Communists; negotiated for Chiang Kai-shek the pro-Japanese Ho-Umetsu Agreement 1933–1934 and brought on himself the charge of leading the anti-Communist, pro-Japanese clique in Chiang's government; given responsibility for the negotiations with the Kungchangtang New 4th Army and ordered the attack on them in January 1941; was in 1941 military attaché in Washington, D.C.

HSIA TO-YIN, General—b. Nov. 10, 1885, at Machen (also spelled Matsen) in Hupeh, the *hsien*, which was early sovietized; trained at the Hupeh Military Academy; was field comdr. of the Kuomintang 21st Army and garrison comdr. of Wuhan in 1930; became in 1932 governor of Hupeh Province, but later was replaced. He was perhaps the most bitterly revengeful and cruel of the anti-Communist commanders, engineering the Hsu K'e-hsiang Massacre and fighting especially against the Ouyüwan Communists. He was an oldtime militarist who disregarded human life in the old warlord way.

Hsu K'e-hsiang, General—b. 1879 in Hsiang-hsiang *hsien*, Hunan, also the home of General Cheng Ken, Miss Tsai Ch'ang, Tseng Kuo-fan of the T'aiping Rebellion, and others; belonged to the old Imperial school of militarist; served in the Hunan army; in 1921 went to Kiangsi and fought the North; in 1924 was made brigadier and sent to the Szechuan border during the war with Wu Pei-fu; carried out on May 21 the Changsha "Massacre"; then continued to fight the Communist armies.

Hu Tsung-nan, General—b. Chekiang, 1902; grad. in the first class at Whampoa; after 1931 was considered the leader of the Whampoa P'ai, or clique, and became interested in fascist theories while fighting civil war; during the war with Japan was comdr. of the 34th Group Army and dir. of Chiang Kai-shek's headquarters in Sian, Shensi, where he had half a million troops blockading the Communist regions during the war; headquarters remained at Sian during the renewed civil war. One of the important Communist military experts said of him: "He is Chiang's only brilliant commander and he was trained by Borodin. His fighting against our troops was probably the most effective."

Ku Chu-tung, General—b. Kiangsu; grad. from Paoting Academy; became an instructor at Whampoa and commanded the 1st Division of the 1st Army of the Kuomintang, under Ho Ying-ch'ing, the division loyal to Chiang Kai-shek, and afterward the 16th Route Army; from 1931–1933 was governor of Kiangsu Province and had formerly been a mem. of the provincial govt. after 1927; during 1933–1934 was comdr.-in-chief of the Northern Route Communist-suppression forces; in 1934–1935 was pacification (anti-Communist) commissioner of Kiangsi after the Communists had evacuated the place, then of Szechuan in 1936; in 1936–1937 was dir. of Chiang Kai-shek's headquarters in Sian, following the Sian Incident; in 1937 was again made Kiangsu governor and comdr. of the 3d War Area during the Japanese war; in 1948 was comdr. of Nanking's ground forces of the Yellow River Valley area against the Communists, with about 280,000 men, defending the Lunghai railway from Kaifeng to Suchow, and also in Shantung.

Li Chi-sen (also spelled Li Chai-sum), General—b. Kwangsi, 1886; grad. from Peking Military College; participated in 1911 Revolution as chief-of-staff to 22d Division, holding same post in Kwangtung Army, 1921; assisted Sun Yat-sen against Chen Chiung-ming's rebellion, 1924; was comdr. of the 4th Army of the Kuomintang, the famous Ironsides; suppressed the famous Hailofeng soviet in Tungkiang, Kwangtung, in 1927; was comdr. of 8th Route Army and chief of the general staff of the Nationalist Forces Headquarters and also chairman, Canton Political Council, 1928, as well as state councilor; relieved of all posts due to participating in the Kwangsi faction's revolt in Wuhan, 1928–1929, against Chiang Kai-shek, and was imprisoned in Nanking in 1928–1929; pardoned in 1931; apptd. inspector-general of military training, 1932–1933; was one of the chief figures in the Fukien Revolt of 1933–1934, being elected chairman of the "People's Government" established in Foochow, which wanted to cooperate with the Communists, but they failed to make the connection before it was suppressed; was again relieved of all posts and expelled from the Kuomintang, living in retirement; in 1936 was apptd. a mem. of the Natl. Military Council to fight Japan, and dir. of Chiang Kai-shek's headquarters at Kweilin, Kwangsi, after 1941; became disenchanted again with Chiang Kai-shek's implacable civil war and refusal to institute democratic methods; was considered sympathetic with the progressives in China against Chiang, and openly attacked the Kuomintang; in 1947 in Hong Kong held 1st Conference of Democratic Representatives of the KMT with other disgruntled KMT members; chairman, Revolutionary Cmte. of the KMT, Jan. 1948; vice-chairman, Standing Cmte., Prep. Cmte., 1st CPPCC, June 1949; vice-chairman, Central People's Govt., 1949; held many posts in the new Peking government; d. Oct. 10, 1959. His life is most important in understanding the real forces at work in Chinese politics and society.

PAI CHUNG-HSI, General—b. Kweilin, Kwangsi, 1893; grad. Paoting Academy in Hopei; participated in 1911 Wuchang Incident; in Northern Expedition was comdr. 13th Army and acting chief-of-staff of Nationalist forces; served under Chiang Kai-shek and Ho Ying-ch'ing and was ordered by them to occupy Shanghai at the time the April 12th Incident occurred (massacre of the labor unions); in 1927 commanded 2d Route Army Corps in occupation of Hsuchow and fought with his Kweilin fellow-officer, Li Tsung-jen, and Cheng Chien in the Nanking Punitive Expedition against Tang Sheng-chih; was then made vice comdr.-in-chief of the 4th Group Army under Li Tsung-jen, controlling Hunan and Hupeh, 1928; became deputy comdr. of the Kwangsi Provincial Army under Li, and they revolted against Chiang Kai-shek again in 1934; united with Chiang Kai-shek during war with Japan; became deputy chief-of-staff and, in 1948, was min. of defense with headquarters in Hankow, in charge of the Yangtze Valley operations against the Communists; was considered by some to have the greatest military mind in the Kuomintang forces.

T'ANG EN-P'O, General—b. Chekiang; grad. Paoting Academy; from 1925–1926 was instructor at Whampoa Academy; comdr. of the 13th Army and later of the 31st Group Army; was a close follower of Chiang Kai-shek, and one of the most irreconcilable and ruthless enemies of the Communists, being responsible for many grave atrocities against the civilians in their areas, especially in Ouyüwan; distinguished himself in the war against Japan, both at Nankow Pass and Taierchuang, and was active in the Civil War. Some Communist military experts considered him the most effective opponent they had, and a brilliant commander.

Appendixes

Index

Appendix A: Glossary

Chin (or catty)—a measure of weight corresponding to the pound, but equivalent to sixteen ounces.

Chinchiachi—the Communist-led border government of the liberated areas of Shansi-Hopei-Chahar, respectively, being the ancient Chinese names of these provinces.

Chinsui—the Communist-led border government of the liberated areas of Shansi-Suiyuan.

Chuan—"Cash," this is the usual translation of the money term referring to small denominations in metal; copper is a term used for copper cash.

CP and CY—English initials for Communist party and Communist Youth, commonly spoken in English among the Chinese.

Hsiao kuei—literally, "little devil," a term of affection given to the boy war orphans who follow the army as orderlies, water carriers, etc.

Hsiao mi—millet, the staple food of northern Chinese.

Hsien—administrative unit of a Chinese province, similar to a county, each province containing about 100 *hsien*. The county seat, or *hsien* town, usually has the same name as the *hsien*, and it is sometimes difficult to judge whether the town or county is referred to.

Hsienchang—*hsien* magistrate or head of the *hsien* government.

Hsiu-ts'ai—a scholastic degree conferred by examinations under the Ch'ing dynasty, second to Hanlin, which is the highest.

K'ang—a bed made of bricks or mud in the form of a raised platform across one end of a room.

K'e-ch'i—courtesy, Confucian rules of manners.

Kungchangtang—the Chinese term for Communist party, meaning share-production party, somewhat different from the English connotation.

Kuomintang—National People's party, formed in 1924 by Sun Yat-sen by reorganizing his former party, which was joined by the Communists until 1927.

Lao Pai Hsing—literally the "Old Hundred Names," the term used for "the people" or "the masses." It means the common people descended from the original "hundred surnames" of China, though, of course, there are far more than a hundred surnames now. In one context it means that everybody is interrelated with everybody else in China so none can claim aristocracy.

Li—the unit for distance, approximately one-third of an English mile.

Li-hai—an expression often used of rebels, meaning spirited or of courageous disposition.

Min tuan—militia organized and hired by local landlords to keep peace and order and suppress the peasants.

Mou (mu)—the land measure equivalent to about one-sixth of an English acre.

Ouyüwan—name of the Hupeh-Anhui-Honan soviet region, taken from the ancient names of these three provinces, respectively, Ou, Yü, and Wan. Written in this form, the expression implies a border region, the old names still being used by the local people.

Pao chia—an old system of controlling the village population to maintain peace and order, revived by Chiang Kai-shek, by means of which families are divided into tens and hundreds, each held responsible for the whole and for the individual by "guarantees." Under this system, whole families are killed for the act of one member.

Red Spears—an old Chinese secret society, whose members carried pikes with red tassels.

San Min Chu I—Sun Yat-sen's book, *The Three People's Principles.*

Shan—mountain, often used at the end of the name of a mountain region.

Shenkanning—the Communist-led border government of Shensi-Kansu-Ninghsia, respectively.

Sheng—province, of which China proper has eighteen.

Ta Ke Ming—the "Great Revolution," used by the Communists in referring to the 1925–1927 revolution.

T'an (or picul)—a measure of weight equal to 100 *chin*, or about 133.33 English pounds.

T'u-hao—literally "local rascal," a term of opprobrium used by Chinese peasants in referring to landlords whom they hate and find oppressive.

T'uchun—governor of a province, usually a warlord.

Appendix B: Chronology

1900 The Boxer Rebellion against foreigners in China.

1911, March 29. Martyrs' Day, when the seventy-two martyrs fell storming the government at Canton. (This became under the Republic one of the five national holidays, the others being Confucius' birthday on August 27, called "Teacher's Day"; Sun Yat-sen's birthday on November 12; National Day on October 10, 1911; and January 1, 1912, the date of the founding of the Republic of China, from which the new calendar begins.)

October 10. The Double Tenth or the Wuchang Incident, a mutiny of troops in the city of Wuchang, which marks the founding of the Chinese Republic informally. Tung Pi-wu was in Wuchang as a member of Sun Yat-sen's T'ung Meng Hui at that time.

1915, December 25. The Yünnan Revolt, when Yuan Shih-k'ai attempted to make himself emperor and Tsai Ao and the Yünnanese troops raised armed force against him. Lo P'ing-hui tells of the Yünnan armies in this period and Chu Teh fought with Tsai Ao.

1917, January 18. First contingent of the Chinese Labor Corps sent to France to aid in World War I, resulting in knowledge of labor organization. Ho Ch'ang-kung, later political director for Lo P'ing-hui, was in France with this group.

The literary renaissance began, which led to the adoption of the *pai hua* vernacular and to modern education, as well as to modern literary writing. One of the leaders was Hu Shih; another was Ch'en Tu-hsiu, editor of the *New Youth* magazine, an organ of widespread influence on the lives of young Chinese.

1918 Socialist Youth organized in China by some students.

1919, May 4. The May Fourth Incident, or Movement, originally a student movement beginning as a protest against the treatment of China at the Versailles Conference. The May Fourth Movement resulted in the first significant strikes and boycotts among labor.

"Work-and-Study" students arrived in France, soon 3,000 strong, where they were influenced by socialism, anarchism and social-democracy, and learned trade union organization. Among these were: Miss Tsai Ch'ang, Li Li-san, Chou En-lai, Li Fu-chün, Fu Chung, Nieh Jung-chen, Lo Man, Hsü Teh-li, and others, all of whom became Communist leaders later.

369

1920, July. Nucleus of the Chinese Communist party formed by Ch'en Tu-hsiu and Li Ta-chao, publishing the first newspaper for workers in China. Tung Pi-wu founded the Hupeh branch.

1921, May 5. Establishment of Sun Yat-sen's revolutionary government at Canton, though it was later temporarily driven out.

July 1. (?) First Congress of the Chinese Communist party in Shanghai, with thirteen delegates representing fifty-odd members in Peking, Tientsin, Shanghai, Hunan, Hupeh, Kwangtung, and Shantung. A manifesto and constitution were agreed upon.

Labor Secretariat created in Shanghai by the Communists, which organized the first systematic drive for unions in China.

1922, January 13–March 5. Hong Kong Seamen's Strike, of about 50,000 workers, marked the first stage of an organized national labor movement.

July. Second Congress of the Communist party at Hangchow with twenty delegates representing about one hundred members.

1923, February 7. The Pinhan Incident. General Wu Pei-fu broke the strike of Peking-Hankow railway workers by armed force.

1923–1926. The Canton government established by Sun Yat-sen in opposition to Peking.

1923, June. Third Congress of the Communist party in Canton, with twenty delegates, representing three hundred members. United front with Kuomintang is agreed upon.

1924, January 20. First National Congress of the Kuomintang in Canton. Sun Yat-sen reorganized his former revolutionary party into the new Kuomintang, admitting Communists to membership and establishing a new policy of stirring up a mass movement of both labor and peasants.

May. Founding of Whampoa Military Academy in Canton under Russian direction, providing a nucleus of trained officers for the civil war.

1925, January 22. Fourth Congress of the Communist party in Shanghai representing about 1,000 members. The constitution was revised.

March 12. Death of Sun Yat-sen in Peking.

May 1–7. Founding of the All-China Labor Federation at the Second National Labor Congress held in Canton, which joined the Red Trade Union International.

Partial closing of the Hanyehp'ing Iron Works near Wuhan sent workers into the "Ironsides" Army under Yeh T'ing; later they formed units in the first Red troops in 1927. The Hanyehp'ing Union of 7,000 members was second largest in China. Tsai Shu-fan was a leader.

May 30. The May Thirtieth Incident, touched off by the British police firing on a demonstration of students and workers.

June 23. Shakee Road Massacre in Canton. British and French troops fired on a Chinese street demonstration.

June to October 1926. The great Hong Kong Strike and boycott of the British, involving from 160,000 to 250,000 strikers.

August 20. Assassination of Liao Chung-k'ai in Canton by Kuomintang rightists, he being then in control of the Canton government and logical successor to Sun Yat-sen.

1926, July 9. The Northern Expedition started from the south to conquer China for the Kuomintang government, reaching the Yangtze valley in six months. Participating in this were Ho Lung, Hsü Hsiang-ch'ien, Hsiao K'eh, Yeh T'ing, Lo P'ing-hui, Hsü Meng-ch'iu, and many others.

November 10–July 15, 1927. The period of the famous "Wuhan Government," which moved from Canton to Wuhan; on July 15 the left Kuomintang split with the Communists, and the government dissolved.

1927, March 12. Chinese labor unions took over Shanghai for the Kuomintang, after an uprising of 600,000 workers. Chou En-lai was a leader in this.

March 23. The Nanking Incident, in which Kuomintang troops fired on foreigners in Nanking and on the Standard Oil plant, causing several deaths. During the civil war, 400 British troops had landed in Shanghai January 27, 1,200 American marines March 5; and Japan, France, Spain, Portugal, and Holland put over 15,000 troops ashore.

April 12. The April 12th Incident, Chiang Kai-shek's coup d'etat in Shanghai in which several thousand workers were killed in three days' fighting. This marked the split between Chiang Kai-shek and the Communists, resulting in ten years of civil war.

April 15. Chiang Kai-shek set up a government in Nanking in opposition to the leftist Kuomintang government in Hankow.

May. Fifth Congress of the Communist party, representing 58,000 members held in Hankow. Ch'en Tu-hsiu was criticized and new agrarian principles were formulated.

May 20. First Pan-Pacific Trade Union Congress held in Hankow and creation of a Secretariat.

May 21. The Hsü K'e-hsiang Incident in Changsha. The militarist, Hsü K'e-hsiang, caused a bloody massacre of liberals, Communists, and labor union people.

June 23. Fourth National Labor Congress held in Hankow with 300 delegates, said to represent 2.8 million union members.

July 1. Establishment of the National government at Nanking by Chiang Kai-shek.

July 15. Split between the left Kuomintang and the Communists in Hankow and dissolution of the government.

August 1. The Nanchang Uprising of Kuomintang troops marking the founding of the Red Army. It was led by Ho Lung, Yeh T'ing, Chu Teh, Hsiao K'eh and others.

August 7. Chinese Communist party Emergency Congress voted to change opportunist policy of Ch'en Tu-hsiu and to use armed resistance. Li Lisan and later Mao Tse-tung became the political leaders; Ch'en was expelled from the Communist party and imprisoned by Chiang Kai-shek for many years.

August 17. First soviets set up in Hailofeng, the Tungkiang region near Canton.

September. Autumn Harvest Uprisings organized in Hunan province by Mao Tse-tung, taking place among peasant unions in P'ingkiang, Liuyang, Liling, and two other *hsien*. From these uprisings, the Red Army was formed, together with Hanyehp'ing workers and soldiers who revolted.

November. Mao Tse-tung set up the first permanent soviet (after Hailofeng which was destroyed within a few weeks) at Tsalin (Ch'alin) on the Hunan border.

December 11. The Canton Commune. Armed workers and cadets held the city three days but were defeated.

Winter. Chingkangshan. To this mountain stronghold, Mao Tse-tung led his thousand remaining followers for a winter. Chingkangshan was held as a base until 1929, Chu Teh arriving with his troops in May 1928, and P'eng Teh-huai later.

1928, January 1. The South Hunan Revolt, led by Chu Teh among the peasantry.

May. Chu Teh goes to Chingkangshan to meet Mao Tse-tung; they joined forces by reorganizing as the Fourth Red Army.

July–August. Sixth Congress of the Comintern reviewed the Chinese situation and sanctioned Mao Tse-tung's line of establishing soviets and stressing the agrarian movement.

Ho Lung began the formation of a Red Army in Hunan resulting in building the Hunan-Hupeh soviet of 1 million population by 1934, when Hsiao K'eh arrived October 22 with his Sixth Army, and both armies retreated together on the Long March.

July 22. The P'ingkiang Uprising in Hunan, of 3,000 soldiers, led by P'eng Teh-huai, regimental commander in Ho Ch'ien's 35th Army, and Huang Kung-liu, principal of a military school. On December 11, 1928, P'eng Teh-huai at Chingkangshan met with Chu and Mao, and P'eng was made commander of the Fifth Red Army. P'eng was left at Chingkangshan while Chu and Mao led their troops to Fukien where they captured Tingchow.

1929, April. P'eng Teh-huai captured Juikin, Kiangsi, later selected as the capitol of the Central Soviet government. Chu and Mao joined him there from Tingchow.

The Kian Uprising in Kiangsi, led by Lo P'ing-hui, commander of *min tuan* in Kiangsi. He joined the Red Army, commanding the Twelfth Red Army. Kian soon became the heart of the soviet strength.

Formation of soviets in the Ouyüwan region, which by 1931 had a population of 2 million. On November 7, 1931, the Fourth Front Army was created there under Hsü Hsiang-ch'ien, who took a part of it to Szechuan in 1932.

December. P'eng Teh-huai and Huang Kung-liu captured Chi-an, Hunan, and the Third Red Army was formed under Huang Kung-liu. From this point on, success was rapid in capturing *hsien* towns and sovietization.

Mao Tse-tung, at the Kutien Conference, lay down permanent principles for the organization of the Red Army.

1930, from the middle of the year to the end is the Li Li-san period, when Li Li-san, as head of the Communist party in Shanghai, ordered the capture of cities with a view to joining the labor movement with the peasant soviets, etc.

June. P'eng Teh-huai captured Tayeh, site of the Hanyehp'ing iron works, and fought the Japanese, principal stockholders in the works. The Eighth Red Army and the Eighteenth Army were created.

July 22. P'eng Teh-huai captured Changsha, capital of Hunan. After three days he retreated, with 10,000 new volunteers from Changsha.

Winter. Organization of Hunanese partisans into the Independent First Division, commanded by Liu Po-ch'eng, Wang Chen being political director. In 1932, this was put under the Eighth Red Army commanded by Li

T'ien-chu, but, in the autumn, Hsiao K'e was sent to take command and it was reorganized into the Sixth Red Army. In August 1934, Hsiao K'e started his sector of the Long March, joining with Ho Lung and his Second Front Red Army on October 22, 1934.

The overall command was consolidated and the First Front Army created of the First Army Corps and the Third Army Corps, commander-in-chief being Chu Teh, and political director, Mao Tse-tung. The First Army Corps of 10,000 men, with Chu and Mao at the head, consisted of the Third Army under Huang Kung-liu (killed in battle), the Fourth Army under Lin Piao, and the Twelfth Army under Lo P'ing-hui. The Third Army Corps, commanded by P'eng Teh-huai, included his army, the Fifth, Eighth, Fifteenth, and Sixteenth armies.

December–January 1931. The First Surrounding Campaign of 100,000 Kuomintang troops against the Red Army of some 40,000 men was defeated.

1931, May 19. The Second Surrounding Campaign began with 200,000 troops under Ho Ying-ching; they were ignominiously defeated by the Red Army within a month.

July–October. The Third Surrounding Campaign of 300,000 troops commanded by Chiang Kai-shek, with Ho Ying-ch'ing, Ch'en Ming-shu, and Chu Shao-liang, was defeated.

September 18. The Mukden Incident, when Japan began the occupation of Manchuria.

November 7 (?). First All-China Soviet Congress called in Kiangsi but date of convening is uncertain.

December 11. The Central Soviet government was created at Juikin, Kiangsi, with Mao Tse-tung elected chairman, and Chu Teh commander-in-chief of all the Red armies.

December 14. The Ningtu Uprising in Kiangsi, led by Teng Tseng-t'ang and Tsao Pas-sun (later killed in battle), of 20,000 troops of the Twenty-Sixth Route Army of the Kuomintang. These joined the Red Armies and were organized into a new Fifth Army Corps.

1932. Capture of Changchow in Fukien, a major battle.

January 28. The Shanghai Incident, or the Shanghai War. Fighting between General Tsai T'ing-k'ai and the Japanese for several weeks.

February. The Soviet Government offered a united front to all other armed forces against the Japanese, but no attention was paid to it, except by General Tsai T'ing-k'ai.

1933, April–October. The Fourth Surrounding Campaign, of 250,000 Kuomintang troops, was defeated; Chiang Kai-shek called it "the greatest humiliation" of his life. 13,000 of Chiang's troops were captured in one battle in Lo An *hsien.* Chiang secured German advisors.

May. Formation of the Szechuan-Shensi Soviet by Hsü Hsiang-ch'ien of 1 million population.

The Fukien Rebellion led by General Ts'ai T'ing-k'ai, hero of the Shanghai Incident of 1932, in Fukien against Chiang Kai-shek. First of mutinous threats against Chiang's policy of fighting civil war and refusing to prepare against the Japanese, culminating in the Sian Incident, 1936.

October, to October 1934. The Fifth Surrounding Campaign using blockhouse tactics and blockade of the entire areas, causes the Red Army to retreat on the Long March to the northwest. About 400,000 troops were used against the Kiangsi area and over 900,000 against the whole three main soviet regions.

1934, January. Second All-China Soviet Congress convened in Juikin, Kiangsi.

October 15, 1934–October 20, 1935. The Long March of 6,000 miles from Kiangsi to north Shensi. The First Front Army broke through the Kuomintang blockade and arrived at Tsunyi, Kweichow, by January 1935.

1935, January 4. Mao Tse-tung called a conference at Tsunyi, Kweichow, which corrected errors in strategy on the Long March.

May. Crossing the Tatu River, a famous incident of thirty heroes who were decorated for saving the army at the Liu Ting Chiao Bridge.

August 1. Communist party declaration proposed a united front against Japan.

December. Communist government moderated its policies and proclaimed a ten-point anti-Japanese program.

December 9. The December 9th Student Movement, beginning in Peking and spreading over the country. This had a direct influence on officers of Chang Hsueh-liang who mutinied during the Sian Incident, some of whom were propagandized by student leaders from Manchuria.

1936, July 14. Ho Lung's Second Front Army, Hsu Hsiang-ch'ien's Fourth Front Army, and the troops of Lo P'ing-hui and Chu Teh began the march to the Northwest from Sikong, where they had spent the winter after forming the Special Independent Government of the Minorities, in February 1936, of about two hundred thousand population in Sikong.

October. All the Red armies met together at Hui-ning, Kansu, for the first time, as the Second and Fourth Front armies completed the Long March, meeting the First Front Army in Hui-ning.

December 12. The Sian Incident. Chiang Kai-shek was arrested by Chang Hsueh-liang and Yang Hu-cheng in Sian but released. Chang Hsueh-liang returned with him in the plane and was imprisoned.

1937, February. Last battle of this decade of civil war, between the Mohammedans in Kansu and Hsü Hsiang-ch'ien's Fourth Front Army, which suffered severe losses.

February. Communist party wired Kuomintang promising to cease armed civil struggle and cooperate against Japan.

July 7. The Liuk'ouch'iao Incident. The Japanese attack on Marco Polo Bridge near Peking, marking the beginning of the war with Japan.

July 15–October 15. Elections by universal suffrage in the former soviet region inaugurated a new Shensi-Kansu-Ninghsia Border government, and the former Soviet Republic abdicated.

August. The Communist-led Eighth Route Army moved into Shansi to fight the Japanese.

September 22. United Front manifesto issued by the Communist party announcing the change of soviets into universal suffrage and change of the Red armies into three divisions of the Eighth Route Army, the First Front Army into the 115th Division, under Lin Piao; the Second Army into the 120th Division under Ho Lung; the Fourth Front Army into the 129th Division under Liu Po-ch'eng.

September 24. The Battle of Pinghsingkuan won by the Eighth Route Army against the Japanese, first Chinese victory of the war, which encouraged all north China to resist.

December. Formation of the new Communist-led Shansi-Hopei-Chahar Frontier Government, or "Chin-chia-chi," headed by Nieh Jung-chen.

1938, February. Former Red guerrillas in central China organized into the New Fourth Army operating along the banks of the Yangtze River.

April 2. The Emergency National Congress of the Kuomintang agreed to permit a People's Political Council to be formed. Among the delegates were Tung Pi-wu, Chou En-lai, and Miss Teng Ying-ch'ao, while Mao Tse-tung was also elected.

July. Publication of Mao Tse-tung's *On Protracted War*, with its sequel, *The New Stage*, with wide influence outside Communist ranks.

August. Chinese Industrial Cooperative movement inaugurated in Hankow by Rewi Alley, which created a network of small industries group-owned and managed by the workers themselves. This spread to the Communist-led regions.

1939. A year of stalemate in the war with the Japanese.

December 15. Publication of Mao Tse-tung's *The Chinese Revolution and the Communist Party of China*.

1940. January 19. Publication of Mao Tse-tung's master thesis *New Democracy*, which quickly became the handbook of the whole progressive movement in China.

July 7. The Communist party issued a statement urging a more active war against Japan, indirectly criticizing Chiang Kai-shek's vacillation.

August 20–December 5. The Battle of a Hundred Regiments, an offensive launched by the Eighth Route Army along the Japanese front from Shansi to Shantung, planned by Chu Teh and P'eng Teh-huai.

Autumn. Formation of the Shansi-Honan-Hopei Liberated Area under Liu Pei-ch'eng as military head, later under Li Hsien-nien.

1941, January 7. The Anhui Incident, a Kuomintang attack on the Communist New Fourth Army ordered by General Ho Ying-ch'ing, resulting in the death of Han Ying, its commander. After this, relations between the two sides became uneasy, and the Communist party went completely underground in Kuomintang areas except for a newspaper and liaison office in Chungking.

February. Publication of Mao Tse-tung's *Strategic Problems of China's Revolutionary War*, a standard historical outline, which had much influence.

December 7. Pearl Harbor attacked by the Japanese; the foreign powers enter the war.

1942, October 10. Relinquishment of extraterritoriality rights in China by the United States and Great Britain, under which foreign laws were applied to their nationals in China.

1943. North China Federation of Trade Unions was organized in guerrilla areas, claiming to represent nearly a million union members. Teng Fa was chosen as their delegate to the World Federation of Trade Unions in 1945.

1945, March. Federation of Trade Unions of the Liberated Areas was formed at a conference in Yenan, claiming to represent 925,640 organized workers. The chairman elected was Tien Tsui-fu, and Liu Ning-I was sent as delegate to the World Federation of Trade Unions.

April. Seventh Congress of the Chinese Communist party, announcing membership at 1.2 million. Mao Tse-tung was elected chairman and his sequel to *New Democracy* was timed for simultaneous publication under the title *On Coalition Government.* Following these he published *Problems of Economy and Finance and Remaking of Ideology.*

August 14. V-J Day, end of World War II and the signing of the Sino-Soviet Treaty of Friendship and Alliance.

1946, January 13. "Cease Fire" truce under auspices of the Marshall Mission to halt the civil war. The Communists report a population of 140 million in their areas and 835,000 square miles.

July. Renewal of civil war between the Communists and Kuomintang.

1947. During the first part of this year, the Marshall Mission was shown to be useless effort.

October 27. Outlawing of the China Democratic League by the Kuomintang government, causing intellectuals and middle-elements to swing to the left.

December 25. The Constituion adopted previously on December 25, 1946, by the National Assembly of the Kuomintang was slated to become effective.

1948, May. North China Liberated Area formed by the Communists of the former Shansi-Chahar-Hopei Border Region with Tung Pi-wu as chairman.

June. The Communists claim 158 million population in their Liberated Areas. The members of the Politburo announced at this date were: Mao Tse-tung, chairman, Jen Pi-shih, secretary; Chu Teh, Chou En-lai, Tung Pi-wu, Liu Shao Ch'i, P'eng Chen.

August 1–22. Sixth All-China Labor Congress held in Harbin with 500 delegates, resolving to revive the All-China Federation of Labor created in 1925. This was the only national Congress held since 1929, a lapse of nineteen years. President elected was Chen Yun, and vice-presidents Li Li-san, Chu Hsueh-fan, and Liu Ning-I. This had an executive committee of fifty-three members and twenty alternates and claimed to represent 2.83 million members as of August 1948. Later Liu Shao-ch'i was elected honorary president.

September 24. People's Liberation Army took Tsinan, marking control of Shantung.

October 19. Lin Piao's troops took Changchun, marking control of Manchuria.

November 21–23. First election held in Kuomintang areas.

1949, January 16. Lin Piao took Tientsin, followed by surrender of Peking.

January 21. Chiang Kai-shek retired as active commander-in-chief and president, Li Tsung-jen taking over these offices. Chiang later moved his headquarters to Formosa.

March 24–April 3. First National Congress of Chinese Women held in Peking, called by the Women's Union of the Chinese Liberated Areas, the chairman being Tsai Ch'ang. She was elected chairman of the new All-China Women's Federation created at the Congress, claiming a membership of over 20 million, nearly all in the Communist areas. Teng Ying-ch'ao was elected vice-chairman, and the executive committee of fifty-one included Madame Liao Chung-k'ai, Madame Feng Yü-hsiang, K'ang K'e-ching.

April 10. First All-China Youth Congress held in Peking, and formed the New Democratic Youth League, with Feng Wen-pin (Fang Wen-ping) as secretary-general. This claimed 190,000 membership at its founding and by the end of 1949 1,217,075. It put out over fifty periodicals for youth in Marxist studies. This, later formed into the All-China Democratic Youth Federation, affiliated with the World Federation of Democratic Youth and sent Hsiao Hua to Budapest to that Congress in August 1949. Liao Ch'eng-chih became chairman of the Youth Federation.

April 13. Formal peace negotiations between the Kuomintang and Communists began, the Communist party having on March 26, 1949, appointed as delegates Chou En-lai, Lin Tsu-han, Lin Piao, Yeh Chien-ying and Li Wei-han. Chang Chih-chung headed the Kuomintang delegation, Ho Ying-ching then being premier.

April 19. The Kuomintang rejected the Communist proposals.

April 20. The All-China Women's Federation sent delegates to the Peace Congress at Prague, including Tsai Ch'ang, Ho Hsiang-nin, Madame Feng Yü-hsiang, Madame Lu Hsun (Hsu Kuang-ping), and Ting Ling, the novelist. Youth delegates included Liu Tsui, China delegate to the Women's International Democratic Federation; K'ung P'u-sheng, former student secretary of the YWCA and on the United Nations staff; Tai Ai-lien, dancer. This was the first time a group of Chinese women appeared abroad at international gatherings as representatives of women's mass organizations. The men delegates included: Kuo Mo-jo, Liu Ning-I, Dr. Ma Ying-chu, Dr. W. C. Pei, Hsu Pei-hung (Ju Peon), the artist; Ma Sitson; Chao Shu-li, Chang Tien-yi, Hsiao Shan (Emi Siao); Ch'en Chia-kang, Alexander Hu; Chien Chun-jui, Ko Pao-chuan, Tsao Yu, T'ien Han, Ouyang Yu-chien, Chang Yen-chiu, Y. T. Wu, YWCA secretary.

April 21. Chu Teh and Mao Tse-tung sent out the "Order to Liberate All China" addressed to: "Comrades, P'eng Teh-huai, Chang Tsung-hsun and Chao Shou-shan of the 1st Field Army of the People's Liberation Army; Liu Po-ch'eng, Teng Hsiao-ping, Chang Chi-chun of the 2d Field Army; Chen Yi, Jao Shu-shih, Su Yu and Tan Chen-lin of the 3d Field Army; Lin Piao, Lo Jung-huan, of the 4th Field Army; Hsü Hsiang-ch'ien, Chou Shih-te and Lo Jui-ching of the People's Liberation Army at the Taiyuan front."

April 24. Nanking taken and on May 11, Liu Pei-ch'eng (Liu Po-cheng) became mayor.

May 16. Wuhan was taken by Lin Piao's Fourth Field Army.

May 20. Sian, capital of Shensi, taken by P'eng Teh-huai. This is the Northwest city where Chiang Kai-shek was held prisoner in 1936.

May 25. Chen Yi's Third Field Army took Shanghai, and, on May 28, Chen was appointed mayor and director of the Military Control Committee, together with Pan Yen-nien, Tseng Shan and Wei Chueh as vice-mayors.

May 30. The All-China Federation of Labor appointed twenty-six delegates to take part in the Second World Trade Union Conference, led by Liu Ning-I. Liu Hsiao-ch'i was elected honorary president of the federation.

June 15. Political Consultative Conference held in Peking to prepare the framework of a new national government, with Mao Tse-tung as chairman of the Preparatory Committee. He stated that since July 1946, "the People's Liberation Army has wiped out 5,590,000 reactionary Kuomintang troops."

July 1. Chinese Communist party celebrated its 28th anniversary, claiming 3 million members. It is stated that "the Communist Party of China was first initiated in 1920 by a handful of Chinese Marxists and was formally founded in July, 1921." A statement comments that from 1921 to 1925 the party recruited 15,000 members and by 1927 50,000, but the 1927 repression reduced it to 10,000 members. At the height of the Soviet Republic it rose to 300,000 members and after the Long March was reduced to 40,000. The figure for 1945 was 1.2 million, for 1947, 2.2 million.

July 2. All-China Conference of Writers and Artists held, among the delegates being Mei Lan-fang, Tai Ai-lien, Pai Yang, and Ch'i Pai-shih (Ju Peon).

August 2. The Amethyst incident of the British naval vessel.

August 26. Taking of Lanchow, capital of Kansu.

August 27. A Housewives Union is organized in Shanghai to mediate family and marital disputes, with a Women's Service Department—women taking matters into their own hands apparently. Formerly the Chinese Women's Association handled such matters, Madame Lu Hsün being chairman.

August 28. Northeast People's government in Manchuria established with forty-one members, headed by Kao Kang.

September 19. Suiyuan came over to the new government "peacefully." On this day General Yang Chieh was assassinated in Hong Kong by Kuomintang agents.

September 20. Fifty-three members of the Kuomintang Legislative Yuan announced severance from the Kuomintang.

September 21. Mao Tse-tung announced the People's Republic of China at a People's Consultative Conference in Peking, with over 600 delegates present. The flag was changed to a red ground with one large yellow star and four smaller ones symbolizing four classes—workers, farmers, petty-bourgeoisie, and national capitalists. *The March of the Volunteers* was voted the anthem.

September 25. Sinkiang province came over.

September 29. The "Common Program" passed by the Peking Conference.

September 30. Mao Tse-tung unanimously elected chairman of the People's Government of the People's Republic of China. A Council of fifty-eight members was also elected.

October 1. The Peking government took office, and personnel announcements were made.

October 2. Diplomatic relations established with the U.S.S.R., followed by Poland, Czechoslovakia, Bulgaria, Rumania, and Yugoslavia. Wang Chia-hsiang became ambassador to the U.S.S.R., and Pien Chang-wu military attaché.

October 5. Sino-Soviet Friendship Association formed with Liu Shao-ch'i as chairman and P'eng Chen chairman of the Peking branch.

October 14. The taking of Canton. General Yeh Chien-ying was chief in south China, having been appointed secretary of the South China Bureau of the Communist party on September 8. Yen Hsi-shan and Li Tsung-jen escaped.

October 24. The Youth League voted to form the Young Pioneers of children from nine to fifteen, which by January 1950, reported 100,750 members.

October 26. Miss Ting Ling headed a delegation to Moscow for the 32d October anniversary.

November 15. Foreign Minister Chou En-lai sent message to the United Nations repudiating the Chinese delegation there. Kweiyang, capital of Kweichow, was taken.

November 16. Trade Union Conference of Asian and Australasian countries opened in Peking.

November 21. Angus Ward, U.S. consul in Mukden, sentenced by the local court for assault on a Chinese, eliciting strong Washington protest.
Peking All-Circles Representatives Conference held.

November 22. Kweilin, capital of Kwangsi and headquarters of Li Tsung-jen, taken.

November 23. The U.S.S.R. declared it no longer recognized the right of the Kuomintang government to be represented on the United Nations and on January 10, 1950, began a series of walk-outs to force the issue.

November 27. General Yang Hu-cheng and his son were reported killed among 300 executed in Chungking SACO secret police camp. He and Chang Hsueh-liang arrested Chiang Kai-shek at Sian in 1936.

November 30. The taking of Chungking, former national capital.

December 5. Acting President Li Tsung-jen leaves for the U.S. Formosa declared capital.

December 8. First National Agricultural Production Conference held, stressing cotton production.

December 9. Yünnan, Sikong, and Szechuan provinces came over, as the governors capitulated.

December 10. The Asian Women's Conference held in Peking, first of its kind. Tsai Ch'ang presided, with Liu Tsui as secretary-general, and Teng Ying-ch'ao as vice-chairman of the Chinese Federation as delegate. The 165 delegates claimed to represent 5 hundred million women of 14 Asiatic countries, while 33 "sororal" delegates came from other countries, including Mrs. Paul Robeson, delegate from the U.S.

December 16. Mao Tse-tung went to Moscow to negotiate treaty—his first step outside Chinese territory.

December 17. Burma recognized the Peking government.

December 27. Chengtu, capital of Szechuan, taken, defended by Hu Tsung-nan, marking Communist control of the continental area of China.

December 30. India recognized the Peking government.

1950, January 2. Senator Robert A. Taft and Herbert Hoover called on the U.S. to "protect Formosa" by naval force if necessary.

January 6. Great Britain recognized the Peking government, followed by Norway, Denmark, and Ceylon.

January 8. Foreign Minister Chou En-lai demanded expulsion of Kuomintang representative from the United Nations Security Council.

January 10. Madame Chiang Kai-shek traveled to Formosa after fourteen months in the U.S. to encourage continued fighting against the Communists.

February 5. A communique from the People's Liberation Army headquarters stated that "the Kuomintang lost 1,754,220 men, or 259 entire divisions . . . (from July 1, to December 31, 1949). This brings the total losses of

Kuomintang troops during the past three and a half years to 7,445,620 men." It is further stated that "during this six-month period (ending December 31, 1949), a population of 181,256,000 was liberated."

February 14. China and the U.S.S.R. signed a thirty-year "Treaty of Friendship, Alliance and Mutual Aid," with two subsidiary treaties giving loans to China and sole control of the Changchun railway and the ports of Dairen and Port Arthur when a Japanese peace treaty was signed.

February 17. Mao Tse-tung left Moscow, accompanied by Chou En-lai and his staff.

February 28. After thirteen months of "retirement," Chiang Kai-shek took back his posts as president and commander-in-chief with capital in Formosa, causing Li Tsung-jen to denounce him from New York where he had been for three months. General Chen Cheng made premier in place of Yen Hsi-shan.

April 13. The "New Marriage Law" passed in Peking, providing for marriage and divorce by mutual consent, and abolishing polygamy, child betrothal, and child marriage, the age set for men to marry as twenty and women eighteen years. Miss Shih Liang, minister of justice, commented: "Women need special support if they are to attain real equality. After land reform, women who had been victims of unreasonable marriage arrangements in the past now have land in their own right."

April 17. The Fourth Army landed on Hainan Island, and on April 23 Lin Piao's troops took the capital, Hoihow, from General Hsueh Yueh.

May 1. At a celebration of Labor Day, Liu Ning-I, vice-president of the All-China Labor Federation reported a membership of 4 million as of March 1950, compared with 2.83 million in August 1948.

May 4. The Celebration of the May Fourth Movement continued as Youth Day, with 80,000 youth parading in front of T'ien An Men, the public square in Peking.

May 5. The Chinese People's Relief Association formed in Peking, with Madame Sun Yat-sen as chairman, Tung Pi-wu as vice-chairman. On the executive committee of forty-five were Wu Yao-tsung of the YMCA, Hsieh Chueh-tsai, minister of the interior, Madame Feng Yü-hsiang, minister of health, Teng Yu-chih (Cora Deng) of the YWCA, and Tan Kah-kee, overseas leader.

June 9. It is reported that T. V. Soong resigned from the Kuomintang.

June 25. Outbreak of the Korean conflict on the 38th parallel.

June 27. President Truman enunciated a policy of neutralizing Formosa and ordered the Seventh Fleet "to prevent any attack on Formosa," calling on the Chinese government in Formosa "to cease all air and sea operations against the mainland." The Peking government denounced this action and threatened to take Formosa.

June 28. Trade Union Law adopted by the Central People's Government Council, with voluntary union membership.

July 22. The Shanghai General Labor Union of 1 million members held a rally "against American aggression in Korea and Taiwan (Formosa)." Twenty thousand workers in Canton were reported organized in unions. Liu Shao-ch'i, a member of the Secretariat of the Central Committee of the Communist party, reported in "Analysis of The Agrarian Reform Law": "At present, agrarian reform in China has been completed in an area with a rural population of about 145 million (total population of the area is about 160 million). There is still an area with a rural population of about 264 millions . . . where agrarian reform has not been carried out."

August 5. Issue of *China Weekly Review* stated in "Liberation War Statistics": "A recent communique from the PLA (People's Liberation Army) headquarters, which summed up the past four years of the liberation war, revealed that the KMT (Kuomintang) lost more than 8,000,000 troops . . . the PLA lost slightly more than a million and a half troops. The ratio . . . was 5.3 to 1. . . . War materials captured by the PLA included 54,430 artillery pieces, nearly 320,000 machine guns, 3,161,912 small arms. . . . During 1949 alone, the KMT lost 2,379,950 men, of whom 1,122,740 were taken prisoners. . . . The ratio . . . was more than 26 to 1."

August 26. Chou En-lai made his sixth move to have his government accredited to the United Nations and announced the appointment of five representatives: Chang Wen-t'ien (also known as Lo Fu), Li Yi-mang, Chou Shih-ti, Chao Ting-chi, and Meng Yung-chien (formerly with the Chinese Industrial Cooperatives).

September 19. The United Nations Assembly barred the admission of the Peking government by a vote of 33 to 16, with 10 abstentions.

September 29. The United Nations Security Council voted to permit the Chinese government in Peking to testify before it in an investigation of charges that an act of aggression had been committed in Formosa by the U.S.

October 1. As the United Nations troops reached the 38th parallel in Korea, Chou En-lai warned that China "will not stand aside" when a neighbor is invaded.

October 4. The United Nations voted "indirect but clear" authorization for General Douglas MacArthur to move across the 38th parallel. North Korean losses reported at 200,000.

October 7. A *New York Times* article stated: "An expanding network of cooperatives is being established in Communist China to provide a link between the state companies and organized groups of small private farmers and handicraftsmen. . . . More than 20,000,000 persons already have been organized into 34,000 rural and 3,000 urban cooperatives. . . . Kao Kang, chairman of the Northeast Regional Government, declared . . . that 24 percent of Manchuria's total population belonged to state-supervised cooperatives.

October 12. General Chi P'eng-fei, ambassador to the East German Republic, called on President Wilhelm Pieck.

October 15. Li Teh-chuan (Madame Feng Yü-hsiang), minister of health, traveled to Monte Carlo, Monaco, for the World Red Cross Conference.

October 18. Chinese Communists turned down the United Nations Security Council invitation to take part in the discussion on Formosa (later changing their minds).

October 19. The United Nations forces took Pyongyang in Korea, and Premier Kim Il Sung moved north.

October 24. Chou En-lai announced that Peking delegates would be present at the United Nations discussion on Formosa.

October 27. India officially expressed disapproval to Peking of Chinese action in Tibet.

October 28. Chinese soldiers reported sixty miles within the Korean boundary.

October 29. Peking radio said the "United Nations advance into Northern Korea was a threat to Manchuria" and asked the people to "be on the same front as the Korean people."

October 31. The *New York Times* reported: "soldiers of the Chinese Red Army launched today a strong counter-attack against the South Korean Republican divisions on the east coast."

India received an uncompromising note on the Tibetan question saying that Peking "would not tolerate" outside intervention in the Tibetan affair. The ambassador to India was General Yuan Chung-hsien. Fifty thousand Chinese troops reported 200 miles northeast of Lhasa moving without opposition.

November 1. United Nations columns reached the Manchurian border.

November 2. "United States casualties in the Korean fighting stood today at 27,610, including 4,403 dead," according to the *New York Times*.

India sent a sharp note to Peking on the move into Tibet saying it damaged friendly relations between China and India and "the interest of peace all over the world."

November 3. *New York Times* reported, "there appeared little question that United States and Chinese Communist troops were now in contact."

November 5. According to the *New York Times*, the New China News Agency reported that all parties participating in the Communist-dominated Peiping coalition had issued a formal joint declaration pledging full support to those Chinese who "voluntarily undertake the sacred task of resisting America, aiding Korea, protecting their homes and defending their country."

November 6. Tito stated he would back United Nations decision in event of conflict with China and that he was still unable to exchange envoys with Peking.

MacArthur "identified the Chinese Communists as the 'alien' forces who were aiding the North Koreans and the United States laid the question of this intervention before the Security Council," according to the *New York Times*. MacArthur sent a report of this, charging it as "one of the most offensive acts of international lawlessness of historic record." A Hong Kong report in the *New York Times* said the Chinese opened "nationwide recruiting drive to enlist 'volunteers' to fight alongside the North Koreans."

Peking demanded that India withdraw the troops stationed in Tibet.

November 8. The Security Council of the United Nations called an emergency session to decide on MacArthur's charges that Chinese Communists were fighting with the North Koreans. By a vote of 8 to 2, the council invited Communist China to take part in the discussion of the charge of intervention, but it again rejected a Soviet proposal that China take part in all discussions of the Korean question.

A New Delhi report said "Chinese Communist and allied Tibetan forces were reported within forty miles of Lhasa."

November 9. Deputy Prime Minister Sardar V. Patel stated that "Communist China's invasion of Tibet might be sufficient, in view of international tension, to start a new world war."

The *New York Times* reported that Chen Yi's Third Field Army of east China was moving into Shantung, with 400,000 men, and that Lin Piao's Fourth Field Army was heading back into Manchuria from central and south China.

November 10. MacArthur estimated there were 60,000 Chinese Communists in the North Korean forces.

November 11. United Nations Security Council resolution assured China that the border between Korea and Manchuria would be respected; that United Nations forces would be withdrawn from Korea as soon as possible; and demanded that Chinese troops be withdrawn with the threat that the Allies would take all-out military measures against them if they did not.

November 13. It was reported that the Tibetan National Assembly was sending a peace delegation to meet the Chinese forces marching on Lhasa.

November 17. President Truman stated "we will take every honorable step to prevent any extension of the hostilities in the Far East" and that the U.S. forces would not cross to the Chinese border.

November 21. United States troops reached the frontier of Manchuria in the northeast.

November 23. Communist China charged officially that French ground and air forces in Indo-China had carried out "provocative invasions" of Chinese territory.

November 25. The Peking delegates to the United Nations arrived in New York, seven men and two women, the two women being K'ung P'u-sheng, former National Student Secretary of the YWCA and also on the staff of the U.N. until 1948; and Chao Yen. The delegation was headed by Wu Hsiu-chuan, supported by Chiao Kuan-hua, Pu Shen (as interpreter), formerly in the United States; the two T'u brothers.

November 27. In the U.N. Vishinsky charged that the U.S. had "invaded" Formosa.

November 28. MacArthur said the U.N. faced an "entirely new war" in Korea.

November 29. At the U.N. the United States accused China of "open aggression" in Korea. Wu Hsiu-chuan made his maiden speech asking the U.N. Council to "condemn, and take concrete steps to apply severe sanctions against the United States for its 'criminal act of armed aggression against the territory of China, Taiwan (Formosa), and armed intervention in Korea." He demanded "effective measures" for withdrawal of the forces of all countries from Korea to "leave the people of North and South Korea to settle the domestic affairs of Korea themselves."

November 30. Allied forces continued retreat and the Chinese were within thirty-five miles of Pyongyang. The U.S. delegate demanded a vote on a resolution for the withdrawal of the Chinese from Korea. Secretary of State Acheson stated by radio that the Korean situation was one "of unparalleled danger," and "no one can guarantee that war will not come."

A *New York Times* report stated that in Korea were "about two-thirds of Gen. Lin Piao's Fourth Field Army . . . in addition to one army group, of three armies of three divisions each from the Third Field Army of Gen. Chen Yi and two armies each from the forces of Gen. Nieh Jung-chen and Gen. Peng Teh-huai."

December 11. Thirteen Asian and Arab nations proposed a cease-fire which was rejected by the Chinese.

December 24. The Communists closed in on the 38th parallel in Korea.

1951, January 4. Seoul abandoned to the Red armies, and the city fired. The "scorched earth" policy was put into effect, in the villages by the United Nations.

January 7. Wu Hsiu-chuan promoted to vice-minister of Foreign Affairs in Peking.

January 8. Lin Piao appointed chairman of Central South China's Financial and Economic Commission, with headquarters said to be at Nanning in Kwangsi, controlling relations with Indochina.

January 14. United Nations, 50 to 7, voted peace plan, opposed by Soviet bloc.

January 17. United Nations pushed within twenty miles of Seoul in counter-attack.

January 18. Chou En-lai rejected the United Nations peace plan, based on an agreement for a cease-fire in Korea, as merely providing a "breathing spell" for United Nations troops, and presented China's demands.

January 19. Tibet's Chamdo fortress fell to the Chinese, the last bastion.

January 24. United States casualties in Korea given as 46,201, with 7,499 dead.

January 29. Mao Tse-tung informed India that peace would be barred if the United Nations voted China the aggressor.

January 30. The Political and Security Committee of the United Nations General Assembly voted to name Communist China an aggressor in Korea by a vote of 44 to 7, with 7 abstentions. It also voted for a study of collective measures against Peking and formation of a committee to seek a peaceful settlement. Earlier the committee had rejected an Arab-Asian bloc proposal for a seven-power conference, which had been accepted by Peking.

February 2. The United Nations General Assembly adopted its committee's resolution voted January 30 to name China an aggressor, the vote being 44 in favor, 7 against, with 9 abstentions.

February 11. United Nations artillery pounded Seoul as tanks seized air-field and port.

February 13. United Nations rejected Soviet charges that the United States had committed aggression by its cordon around Formosa and bombings of Manchuria.

March 9. "A simple promise by the Mao Tse-tung government to the Dalai Lama of internal autonomy in Tibet—while the Chinese Communists take over the frontier patrol of the Himalayan state—apparently has ended the four-and-a-half-month-old war in the realm of the living Buddha with victory for Communist China without a single real battle." *New York Times.*

March 15. Seoul recaptured as the Chinese withdrew without defending it.

March 27. The village of Kaunpo north of the 38th parallel captured by

South Korean forces. The Joint Chiefs-of-Staff in Washington told General MacArthur to clear future statements with them.

March 31. "The British have told Washington officially that they believe the United Nations forces should halt for the present on the Thirty-eighth Parallel." *New York Times.* United States casualties in Korea totaled 57,120, including 8,511 killed.

April 3. MacArthur reported that the enemy in Korea had about 440,000 troops. In London Foreign Secretary Herbert Morrison said "this is a psychological moment" for all parties to the warfare to end it. Lester B. Pearson of Canada also warned that the United Nations should not over-extend.

April 4. "U.S. troops in force cross parallel on ten-mile front," *New York Times.*

April 5. "MacArthur favors a Nationalist second front on China's mainland and is convinced that the fate of Europe will be decided in the war against communism in Asia" in letter to Representative Joseph W. Martin Jr. *New York Times.*

April 11. "Britain asks that Red China have role in Japanese Pact . . . wants Formosa handed to the Communists eventually." *New York Times.*

April 12. "Truman says he fired M'Arthur to avoid risk of New World War; offers 3-point peace plan cessation of hostilities, taking of concrete steps to insure that fighting would not break out again, adoption of measures to put an end to aggression." *New York Times.* General Matthew Ridgeway took over the MacArthur duties.

1953 Korean armistice signed. Soviet granted support for 156 large-scale Chinese projects. Moscow withdrew all troops from China. Chinese attended Stalin's funeral.

1954 Geneva Accords recognized the independence of Vietnam, Laos, and Cambodia. Chou En-lai headed CPR delegation to Geneva. He visited India, Burma, North Vietnam, later East Berlin, Warsaw, Moscow, and Ulan Bator, as Minister of Foreign Affairs and Premier.

Mao Tse-tung elected chairman, People's Republic of China, September; 1st National People's Congress.

1955 Chou En-lai headed CPR delegation to Afro-Asian Conference, Bandung in April, signed Sino-Indonesian Treaty on Dual Nationality, Djakarta, April.

1957 Mao Tse-tung in Moscow signed Manifesto of Communist and Workers' Parties of twelve countries, and peace manifesto of sixty-four countries. His East Wind-West Wind speech frightened Khrushchev, and the breakup with China began.

1958 Chou En-lai made public offer to resume Sino-American ambassadorial talks "to safeguard the peace."

Year of the Great Leap Forward and the People's Communes.

December. CCP accepted Mao Tse-tung's relinquishment of candidacy for chairman. Liu Shao-ch'i took this post.

1959 Khrushchev visited Peking and declared "imperialist war is not inevitable," advocating peaceful coexistence with the U.S., which the Chinese rejected. He refused to give China the sample atomic bomb promised earlier. He ridiculed the communes. During China's disputes with India and Indonesia, he offered to aid the latter. Castro took power in Cuba. Lin Piao took P'eng Teh-huai's post as minister of defense, at Lushan Conference of the CCP August.

1960, July. Moscow recalled Soviet advisers from China and canceled over 300 contracts, also withdrawing technicians. Russians accused Mao of seeking a "world holocaust," and the Chinese called Khrushchev's group "revisionists."

1961 Chou En-lai walked out when Khrushchev banned the Albanian Party at the Soviet Party Congress in Moscow. The Chinese replaced the Russian advisers in Albania.

1963 Moscow signed nuclear test-ban treaty with the U.S., which China opposed. Peking tries for ideological leadership among the "third world" nations in Asia, Africa, Latin America.

1964 China attacked on two fronts—against Soviet revisionism and American imperialism. China turned to Europe and Japan for economic ties.
In 1969 China accused the U.S.S.R. of provoking 4,189 border incidents from October 15, 1964, to March 15, 1969.
China exploded its first nuclear device.
Third National People's Congress. The wives of Mao Tse-tung and Liu Shao-ch'i were deputies.

1965, July. Lin Piao published "Long Live the Victory of the People's War," advancing the theory that the world can be looked at as China was by the Mao thesis—the industrial powers are the "cities" which can be surrounded and strangled by the nonindustrial nations, just as the peasants of China took the cities by maneuvering around them, not by confrontation.
The United Nations vote on seating China ended in a 47-47 tie with Great Britain voting in favor of seating Peking for the first time.

1966, February 2. Forum on the Work in Literature and Art in the Armed Forces was convened and directed by Chiang Ch'ing in Shanghai.
March 23. Lin Piao directed the army delegates to send their documents to her, and endorsed the minutes of the above forum.
May 16. Central Committee circular abolished the old Cultural Revolution Group and declared a new one under the Politburo, with Ch'en Po-ta as chief and Miss Chiang Ch'ing as deputy. May 16th Circular by Mao laid down the line for action.
May 25. A woman teacher, Nieh Yuan-tzu, put up the first *ta tze pao* poster at Peking University and Mao Tse-tung on June 1, 1966, ordered the text published everywhere calling it "the first Marxist-Leninist big-character poster in the entire country." This was the official signal for the beginning of the Great Proletarian Cultural Revolution. Nieh Yuan-tzu was elected alternate on the Central Committee of the CP in 1969. The birth of the Red Guards was said to be June 24, at Tsinghua Middle School, though the name was not officially used until August 18, 1966.
July 22. Liu Shao-ch'i made his last official statement before being purged.
August. Eleventh Plenary session of the 8th Congress (elected in 1956) of the Chinese Communist party. Mao Tse-tung presided after a long absence from public appearances, during which he presumably planned the Great Proletarian Cultural Revolution.

1967 China detonated its first hydrogen bomb.

November. 50th aniversary of the October Revolution rally in Peking.

1968, Oct. 13–31. Enlarged 12th Plenary Session of CCP 8th CC. Liu Shao-ch'i formally expelled and dismissed from all posts.

1969, February. Opening of Canadian talks in Stockholm to recognize China.

March 2. Frontier confrontation at Chenpao Island.

March 13. The Chinese ministry of foreign affairs protested to the Soviet embassy against armed conflict beginning March 2 and specifically on March 3 when the Soviets were accused of entering the territory.

April 1. Ninth Congress of the Chinese Communist Party held in Peking, electing Mao Tse-tung chairman and Lin Piao deputy and successor. Many are purged.

April 3. The *Kommunist* in the U.S.S.R. accused China of opening a second front; it stated that since 1966 Mao had broken all contacts between the Chinese and Soviet parties and, in 1967, broke all cultural ties, as well as contacts between friendship societies and exchanges of tourists. Wang Ming was resurrected to attack Mao and his article was carried by Pravda, Izvestia, and Tass News.

May 17. Redeployment of ambassadors begun.

July. Last of Peking's forty-five ambassadors recalled, the other forty being recalled in early 1967 at height of the Cultural Revolution.

September. Li Hsien-nien, acting as foreign minister, and Hsieh Fu-chih, security chief, went to Hanoi at death of Ho Chi Minh. On his return, Kosygin paid surprise visit to Peking, the first official contact in several years. Wreaths presented before the D.R.V.N. Embassy in Peking show names of government officials as follows from *Hsinhua*: Soong Ching-ling, vice-chairman of the People's Republic of China; she called at the embassy, as did Chou En-lai, Chen Po-ta, Kang Sheng, Yao Wen-yuan, etc. Others who called are listed by title: Chen Yi, Hsu Hsiang-chien, Nieh Jung-chen, vice-chairman of the Military Commission of the Chinese Communist Party Central Committee; Kuo Mo-jo, vice-chairman of the Standing Committee of the National People's Congress; Li Fu-chun, vice-premier; Teng Tzu-hui, Li Ssu-kuang, Teng Tai-yuan, Shen Yen-ping, Hsu Teh-heng, vice-chairman of the National Committee of the Chinese People's Political Consultative Conference; Fu Tso-yi, vice-chairman of the National Defense Council.

September 17. Victor Louis wrote that "Soviet nuclear rockets are pointed at Chinese nuclear installations." It was reported that China was moving its nuclear installation to Tibet. At the end of August, the Soviet Central Committee was reported to have sent a circular raising the question of a preemptive strike against China's nuclear installation, which had been in Sinkiang.

September 20. *Peking Review* attacked the Stanislavsky "method" in the theater and recommended the thought of Chiang Ch'ing on this subject.

October 1. Celebration of founding of the republic in 1949. News reports indicated appearance of Mao Tse-tung.

October 4. Release of British newsman Anthony Grey of Reuter's who had been imprisoned since July 1967. AP in Hong Kong reported other foreigners remained detained in Communist China, including nine Americans, twelve Britons, eight West Germans, fourteen Japanese, and one Belgian.

October 7. Peking announced an agreement to negotiate with the Soviet Union on border disputes.

1970, October 13. Establishment of diplomatic relations between the People's Republic of China and Canada, with Ralph Edgar Collins as Canadian ambassador.

1971, June 28–July 4. The first Canadian government delegation visited the People's Republic, received by Premier Chou En-lai and Vice-Premier Li Hsien-nien.

July 1. The 50th anniversary of the founding of the Chinese Communist Party celebrated.

July 9. Henry A. Kissinger visited Peking, discussing the plan for a visit to Peking by President Richard Nixon.

July. Huang Hua (Wang Ju-mei) arrived in Ottawa as the first ambassador from the People's Republic of China, having been delayed because of his role in the discussions with Kissinger. He was one of the student leaders of the famous December 9th student movement in Peking, 1935, when studying at the American Yenching University.

August 1. Madame Mao Tse-tung gave a banquet for Joris Ivens and Marceline Loridan, famous film-makers, indicating a softening of her hard line against foreign drama. Later her two Cultural Revolution aides and Red Guard leaders, Yao Wen-yuan and Chang Chun-chiao accompanied the foreigners to a dance drama.

September 21. Session of the United Nations at which United States sponsored seating Peking in the Security Council and General Assembly, but opposed the expulsion of the Taiwan government.

October 25. People's Republic of China admitted to the United Nations. Taiwan government expelled.

November 11. Peking delegation to the United Nations arrived in New York.

Index

About the Author

HELEN FOSTER SNOW [NYM WALES], former wife of Edgar Snow, has written many books on the Orient. Among them are: *Women in Modern China, Inside Red China, China Builds for Democracy, The Chinese Labor Movement,* and *Song of Ariran.* Mrs. Snow was included as one of the six American authors in the Pacific field by Sterling North in his *Literary Map of the American Renaissance.* She has been elected to membership in the Society of Women Geographers, the International Institute of Arts and Letters, the Intercontinental Biographical Association, and the Marquis Biographical Library Society, among others.

The Chinese Communists was composed in
Bodoni typefaces, and the new material for
this edition was set by Pyramid Composition
Company, Inc., New York, New York. The entire
book was printed by offset lithography by
Litho Crafters, Inc., Ann Arbor,
Michigan.